BILL MOYERS
A WORLD OF IDEAS

BILL MOYERS
A WORLD OF IDEAS

Conversations
with Thoughtful Men and Women
About American Life Today
and the Ideas Shaping Our Future

BETTY SUE FLOWERS, Editor

DOUBLEDAY
NEW YORK   LONDON   TORONTO   SYDNEY   AUCKLAND

Published by Doubleday, a division of Bantam Doubleday Dell Publishing Group, Inc., 666 Fifth Avenue, New York New York 10103

Doubleday and the portrayal of an anchor with a dolphin are trademarks of Doubleday, a division of Bantam Doubleday Dell Publishing Group, Inc.

Library of Congress Cataloging-in-Publication Data

Moyers, Bill D.
  A world of ideas.

    1. United States—Civilization—1970–   . 2. United
States—Politics and government—1981–1989. 3. United
States—Politics and government—1989–   .
4. Interviews—United States. I. Title.
E169.12.M69 1989   973.92   89-1109

ISBN 0-385-26346-5 (pbk.)

DESIGN: Stanley S. Drate/Folio Graphics Company, Inc.

BOMC offers recordings and compact discs, cassettes
and records. For information and catalog write to
BOMR, Camp Hill, PA 17012.

For my parents,
Ruby and Henry Moyers,
and their friends
in Marshall, Texas

Introduction

As I traveled the country to tape "A World of Ideas" for public television, I thought occasionally of a letter I received several years ago from an inmate at the federal prison in Marion, Ohio. He had been a faithful viewer of my series of PBS programs on "Six Great Ideas." Now he wanted to tell all the participants in the series of his "heartfelt gratitude that you shared your time and thoughts in so open a medium. You can understand what a truly joyous opportunity that program was for an institutionalized intellectual. After several months in a cell, with nothing but a TV, it was salvation."

For me, talking to the men and women who appear in this book was also a truly joyous opportunity. Sometimes during the 1988 election season, it had seemed to me that we were all "institutionalized" in one form or another, locked away in our separate realities, our parochial loyalties, our fixed ways of seeing ourselves and strangers. Sometimes it had seemed that depending on a TV to connect us to the outside world could only fortify our walls and wither our intellects.

But working on this series reminded me again that ideas can open our cells. They can liberate us from prisons we have ourselves built. In the laboratory of the scientist, the vision of the poet, the memory of the historian, the discipline of the scholar, the imagination of the writer, and the passion of the teacher, I went looking for what the veteran broadcast journalist Eric Sevareid has called "the news of the mind." I found a kingdom of thought, rich in insights into our times.

Most of all, I found a love of sharing, a passion for connecting. In their own way, all of the men and women with whom I talked are teachers. Sharing is the essence of teaching. It is, I have come to believe, the essence of civilization. The impulse to share turns politics from the mere pursuit of power and makes of journalism a public service. It inspires art, builds cities, and spreads knowledge. Without it, the imagination is but the echo of the self, trapped in a soundproof chamber, reverberating upon itself until it is spent in exhaustion or futility. For this reason democracy, with all its risks, must be a public affair. Ideas cry out for an open hearing, and the true conversation of democracy occurs not between politicians or pundits but across the entire spectrum of American life where people take seriously the intellectual obligations of citizenship and the spiritual opportunities of freedom.

The men and women who shared their ideas in the series are public thinkers. Their ivory tower is just a mailing address; they are at home in the world. They have in common a deep caring for this country, and each in a different way tries to serve it. If we could gather them in one room, we would not get much argument about the condition of things. Running through all the conversations is the notion that change is happening so rapidly and globally that our institutions are not keeping up. No grand solution for confronting this predicament appears anywhere in these pages. What emerges is a consensus that we can best negotiate the future through a multitude of shared acts in science, education, government, politics, and our local civic life.

It is a consensus these men and women already act upon in their own lives. Tom Wolfe, for example, takes seriously the presidency of his block association on the East Side of Manhattan. Joseph Heller, who registers his protest by not voting, nonetheless gives money to favored political causes because at heart he is not a cynic and still wants to save the Yossarian in each of us. In his research as a scholar, Robert Bellah reaches broad conclusions about religious values, but he takes concrete steps to put his own faith to work in his local community and church.

None have given up on America. Even the foreigners who appear—Chinua Achebe, Carlos Fuentes, Northrop Frye, David Puttnam—see America critically but affectionately, and they talk hopefully about the moral leadership this country could yet exert if we began to see the world in all its intricate design. I am struck by the extent to which each person in this book believes that the life of the mind and the life of this republic are inseparable. And I am encouraged by the realization that for every one with whom I talked, there are scores more out there, waiting to be heard. America is rich in many things, but it is especially rich in thinking men and women.

The value of listening to such people has seemed obvious to me ever since I sat at the feet of caring teachers—Inez Hughes in the tenth grade, Selma Brotze in the eleventh, Mary Tom Osborne in freshman English, Eva Joy McGuffin in sophomore lit, Frederick Ginascol in junior philosophy, DeWitt Reddick in senior journalism, T. B. Maston in graduate ethics, and James Stewart in postgraduate rhetoric. Because of them, my work has been for me a continuing course in adult education; this series was the latest course.

The chief reward of it is the joy of learning, of coming away from each person with a wider angle of vision on the times I live in, on the issues I am expected to act upon and the choices I can make as father, husband, journalist, and citizen. The main reason I seek the ideas of others is for help—the diagnosis and treatment of my own isolation and the enlargement of my understanding. If you have ever hiked in the Rockies and seen the vista change as you move from one plateau to another—revealing peaks, contours, crests, clouds, colors, and vegetation previously hidden—you know what I am trying to say. I have had a career of discovery and feel compelled to share it.

Like the author of that letter which I quoted earlier, I too feel heartfelt gratitude—for the men and women who shared their time and thoughts in "A World of Ideas"; for the support of the trustees of the John D. and Catherine T. MacArthur Foundation, who were willing to promote the conversation of democracy in this open medium; for Jacqueline Kennedy Onassis and Judy Sandman of Doubleday, who twice now have seen something permanent in the fleeting images of television; for Betty Sue Flowers of the University of Texas, who, as with *Joseph Campbell and the Power of Myth*, edited the full transcripts of these interviews to capture on the printed page the vitality which had been revealed on the screen; to Judith Davidson Moyers, for adding savor to the series with many of her own ideas; and for my colleagues at PAT and PBS who, in this video age of sound bites, fast fades, and flashing graphics, still cling to faith in talking heads and thinking minds.

—BILL MOYERS
January 1989

Editor's Note

During the election year of 1988, Bill Moyers interviewed a number of remarkable men and women for a PBS series called "A World of Ideas." Editing these forty-one conversations was like participating, sentence-by-sentence, in a seminar on our changing American values and how these values affect our lives in an increasingly global culture. The articulation of these ideas by thoughtful people is significant in itself. But even more significant is that the reader comes away from the conversations with a sense of hope, inspired by the wisdom and energy of those who see other and better possible futures for the world. I'm grateful for the willingness of these men and women to talk about their ideas and to allow their talk to be translated into written form.

I'm grateful, too, for the encouragement of Jacqueline Kennedy Onassis, the Doubleday editor, who allowed us to use the full transcripts of the original conversations as the basis for this book. Thanks to John Flowers for many fine editing suggestions, and to Winona Schroeder, Alice Fisher, Karen Bordelon, Ellen McDonald, and Lynn Cohea, who enabled me to do this book by helping me out with other projects. Alex Banker co-ordinated the project in New York, as well as joining Andie Tucher to write the biographical sketches. I owe special thanks to him, to Judy Doctoroff, and to Judy Sandman at Doubleday. And thanks to the typists—Lynn Cohea, Pat Ellison, Cathy Mackin, Peggy Detlefsen, and, above all, Maggie Keeshen, whose dedication and good humor in handling thousands of pages of material in so brief a time meant as much to me as her excellent typing.

If it were the custom for editors to dedicate books, I would dedicate this one to Bill Moyers, whose work bears witness to his faith in the power of ideas and in our willingness to be challenged by them.

—BETTY SUE FLOWERS
University of Texas at Austin
January 1989

Contents

OUR CHANGING AMERICAN VALUES

Barbara Tuchman

HISTORIAN

Barbara Tuchman was one of America's best-known historians. An advocate of the notion that it's worth knowing where we've been, she looked at the changes in America since the days of Washington, Adams, and Jefferson. At the root of our contemporary predicament, she concluded, was the absence of a sense of honor. Tuchman twice won the Pulitzer Prize. Her last book, The First Salute, *explores the American Revolution.*

MOYERS: Why have you gone back to the American Revolution for your latest book?

TUCHMAN: It was really mostly by accident. I was speaking at a ceremony commemorating the liberation of Holland from the Nazis, and I was looking for something a little bit fresh to say. I came across an intriguing incident concerning the first salute to the American flag by a foreign official. Starting there, I became interested in episodes of the American Revolution, especially when I learned about the march Washington led from New York to Virginia to trap Cornwallis. It was such an extraordinary adventure, such a courageous thing to do, to invest his army, such as it was, into this walk all the way down to Virginia. I knew nothing about it, and it seemed to me that almost no one else knew anything about it.

MOYERS: What feature of the period most fascinated you?

TUCHMAN: Perhaps it was the degree of belligerence that was exercised by all the nations against each other all the time. Nobody was doing anything but fighting. They had a wonderful concept called the sociability of nations, which was just the opposite, of course, of all this antagonism.

Another feature that fascinated me was the degree to which the American Revolution was made possible by the help of foreign nations. The British interference with trade at sea and their attempted domination of Europe made such enemies that nations sided with the Colonies just because of their antagonism to Britain. We never would have succeeded without French help.

MOYERS: I know that you are wary of drawing lessons from history, but can we learn anything from that period that might help us come to grips with American life today?

TUCHMAN: I think so. Somehow, now, we have a lapse in initiative and the exercise of activity toward a goal. When people don't have an objective, there's much less dynamic effort, and that makes life a lot less interesting.

MOYERS: But of course the revolutionaries had the rare goal of being able to fight for their independence and to establish a new republic.

TUCHMAN: I don't think they thought at the beginning of establishing a new kind of government, but very soon they realized that that was what they were doing—and that was very exhilarating, the idea that they had the opportunity to create a new political system that eradicated tyranny and oppression by autocratic government, as it had existed for centuries. This vision of being able to free themselves from tyranny was really very exhilarating. This is what is lacking for us. We have nothing that's exhilarating, nothing that's drawing us forward. A negative vision, like stopping or containing the Russians, doesn't get anybody very excited.

MOYERS: Although, as Benjamin Franklin said, keeping the republic should be as exhilarating and exacting as winning it in the first place.

TUCHMAN: Yes, but the exploration of our great continent, the extraordinary place that we have, with all its resources and reaching from ocean to ocean—that, too, was an exhilarating task.

MOYERS: What about leadership? This was an extraordinary period of political fertility and leadership.

TUCHMAN: There was an amazing burst of talented political men, all of whom emerged at the same time—Jefferson, Washington, Franklin, Jay, Madison, Hamilton. Today, the main activity that draws men of talent is business; but then, nobody thought in terms of making a life or great success of business. Of course, business was not an activity that was particularly fruitful.

MOYERS: The public business commanded their allegiance and their time.

TUCHMAN: And this extraordinary opportunity to create a new political system was what seemed to them truly significant and truly adventurous.

MOYERS: But there is the paradox that these formidable men with extraordinary qualities of leadership were not able to solve the overriding moral dilemmas of their day—slavery, for one. And you as a female were excluded from the Constitution. If you were living in those times, would you have made the same judgment about these men?

TUCHMAN: Certainly women did feel relegated to the other room when men were discussing public affairs. Women were never invited to join in discussion because it was not thought that women had opinions that were important or that could affect the decisions that were being taken. But I don't know that anyone would have thought at the time, well, these men are stupid or shortsighted.

MOYERS: I have an essay you wrote in 1976, the bicentennial year, in which you talked about America as an idea. How would you sum up the original idea of America?

TUCHMAN: A liberation from tyranny which had existed for centuries, in which government was in the hands of rulers with no particular right other than dynastic, of nobles who had nothing but property to justify their exercise of rule, and of monarchs who had only heredity to justify theirs. The interesting thing was that I found that the Dutch had voiced the same thing when they abjured the rule of Spain. The Oath of Abjuration written almost two hundred years before our Declaration of Independence contains almost the same words.

MOYERS: That might get one disqualified from running for office today, but in those days men borrowed freely the great ideas of others and applied them to this new experiment. In 1976 you said it was still an open question whether or not we can reconcile democracy with the idea of social order and individuality. What do you think about that today?

TUCHMAN: On the whole, the ruling groups don't truly govern in the interests of the underprivileged classes. We see that now every day, for example, in this question of the homeless, which is not adequately addressed by our government. The problem of the homeless is much more important than AIDS, which is an acquired condition, which is self-inflicted through drugs or through behavior. But the condition of the homeless, the necessity of living on an adequate basis, is something which government must concern itself with. Otherwise, we're going to feel the effects, just as the French did when the French Revolution occurred, through the same ignoring of the misery of the poor classes, and through the same financial irresponsibility. What really started the French Revolution was the condition of the deficit, which was owed because of their help to us—which is again another irony.

MOYERS: You once asked the question, what's happened to the America of Washington, Adams, and Jefferson? In writing *The First Salute*, have you found the answer?

TUCHMAN: What's happened is the disappearance of a positive goal. The public as a whole is not concerned with solving the problems of the poor, of the homeless, though they should be, because these ultimately can be dangerous to everyone's ordinary life.

> *The public as a whole is not concerned with solving the problems of the poor, of the homeless, though they should be, because these ultimately can be dangerous to everyone's ordinary life.*

But something more seems to me to have happened, and that is the loss of a moral sense, of knowing the difference between right and wrong, and of being governed by it. We see it all the time. We open any morning paper and some official has been indicted for embezzlement or corruption. People go around shooting their colleagues or killing people. How is killing so easy nowadays? People say that hypnotism, for example, cannot cause a person to do something he wouldn't normally want to do. Well, I ask myself, can drugs cause people to do things for which there is no inherent impulse? I don't suppose they can. There would have to be the impulse to kill. People always say to me, oh, wasn't there a lot of violence in the old days too? Well, of course there was, but there wasn't the same kind of meaningless violence, and it was contained, when there was an impulse, by the fear of hell, which was felt very seriously because of religious training. I ask myself, have nations ever declined from a loss of moral sense rather than from physical reasons or the pressure of barbarians? I think that they have. I think Germany has declined as a result of the loss of a moral sense, which was made evident under the Nazi regime—and they are certainly not the leaders of civilization, as they thought themselves in 1914. The loss of Germany in behavior and conduct and policy was immensely serious and destructive—more so than anybody will admit now. It happened, for example, to the Turks in the Ottoman Empire. The disappearance of a moral sense, of a moral rule, led to fierce, barbarous oppression and massacres and to the decline of power in the end—just as it did in Germany.

MOYERS: What do you mean by moral sense?

TUCHMAN: The sense of what is inherently right and wrong, and of following your belief in what is right. For example, it's not only true in white collar crime, as we read about every day, but in criticism, where critics of art and drama and—I hesitate to say—

MOYERS: You may include journalists too, if you wish.

TUCHMAN: All right—they will accept as great almost any damned thing that they think is funny or that they think will sell or will tickle the art dealers or that's got some attraction that appeals to the mass public, even if it is basically trashy. The acceptance of that kind of thing is an absence of moral sense.

MOYERS: You recently wrote that false dealing is now the prevailing element of American life.

TUCHMAN: It certainly seems to be. We keep reading about congressmen and municipal officials who are being indicted for one kind of misbehavior or another. What's happened to them? Are they not afraid of some kind of punishment, whether social or legal or in conscience? Don't their consciences somehow affect them?

MOYERS: If taste or moral standards have declined, people have less fear of the public judgment that once upon a time would have said, "Let's throw the rascals out."

TUCHMAN: That's absolutely true. We're being fed on—well, all I can say is trash, through, I regret to say, the organ of television. Television is moved by the desire to make profits, by appealing not to the audience of quality, but to the largest number—I suppose what used to be called the lowest common denominator. This is not the way to increase the thinking of the public on truth or serious matters, or to help it recognize the values in life that are creative.

MOYERS: You asked a rousing series of questions not long ago: Where's the anger that ought to have met the deaths of two hundred and forty-one U.S. Marines through the incompetence of their superiors? Where's the anger over the thirty-seven deaths on the U.S.S. *Stark* through official negligence? Where's the outrage over disclosures of misconduct and incompetence revealed in the Iran-Contra scandal? And I could add to that list—where's the outrage over the swindling by the defense industry? What's happened to the outrage?

TUCHMAN: Mr. Moyers, I don't know what's happened to it, except that somehow people don't take wrongdoing seriously. Perhaps there's just too much of it. We're not surprised any more. We're just used to it.

MOYERS: But how different is that from any period of history? Take the Revolutionary period that you write about. Some of the movers and shakers of this country were guilty of the very conduct that you find so alarming today. John Hancock profited from the privateer navy that looted during the Revolutionary War. Robert Morris, one of the signers of the Declaration, charged such high prices for food in those days that the people revolted against him. And couldn't it be that what you characterize as the evils of the modern age are just endemic in every age?

TUCHMAN: I think they are. But when they become prevailing, that makes the difference. And where is the outrage? It's absent because the exercise of this kind of crime is prevailing. We get so used to it that we don't seem to get excited about it or resentful, nor do we realize its ultimate dangerous effects on public opinion and public activity. We have lost a sense of respect for serious, honest conduct. If we are moved merely by greed, and there's no longer any respect for decent or honest government, then we will suffer the results. We've been suffering from them ever since Watergate—and now again with the Iran-Contra business.

MOYERS: You and I first held a conversation on television like this during the height of the Watergate scandals. I would not have thought that fifteen years later, we'd be discussing a similar manifestation of the extreme behavior of a government run amok. I would have thought we might have learned the lesson of history.

TUCHMAN: Well, history's lessons move very slowly. People don't put them into operation right away, when they've become visible, but only when they rise to the surface, and begin to flood the bottoms of your cellars, only when they affect your own living conditions. In the Middle Ages, the sewage wasn't properly disposed of, but people didn't pay attention to it until the waters of the rivers and the filth rose over the doorsteps. Then they had to. That's what is beginning to happen, it is beginning to rise over the doorsteps. It is already, isn't it?

MOYERS: One could certainly say that the sewage is rising. Just in our time we've had the folly and deception of Vietnam. We had the White House crimes known as Watergate and the resignation of a Vice President and a President because they were corrupt. A few years ago we had the Iran-Contra scandals. Now we have the Pentagon scandals, perhaps the biggest military swindle in American life. What does it say when we don't grow angry over this banality and stupidity in high office?

TUCHMAN: It says that we're becoming accustomed to and almost satisfied with people in government who are either venal or stupid. And with the emphasis on fund-raising for all elections, which is ruining the electoral system, we will be accepting entertainers as our candidates, not those who have learned the processes and practices of government. You can't govern without having the training in it. Even Plato said that a long time ago. You need to be trained in government, to exercise it, to practice it. But the American public is now satisfying itself with entertainers.

I was at a seminar a few weeks ago, down at the Smithsonian. They held a conference on the subject of the hero, because it was the fiftieth anniversary of the birth of Superman. I guess I should have realized, given the occasion for the conference, that what we would discuss would not be exactly my idea of a hero. And it certainly was not. It was quite weird, what they considered a hero. The real hero of the discussion was the little girl who'd fallen down a well. She didn't do anything to make herself a hero, she was just in the news. Other heroes discussed were Elvis Presley and somebody whom I had never heard of, the Mayflower Madam. Who was that?

MOYERS: She was a woman who ran a brothel near my apartment in New York City.

TUCHMAN: Why was she a hero? Anyway, finally, I got totally fed up, and stood and said that they were confusing celebrity and notoriety with the word "hero," and that this was not the definition of the word. Well, they said, these are pop culture heroes, what public opinion takes as heroes. But, I said, why should we accept what pop culture says about the definition of hero any more than we accept what pop culture says about grammar? We don't say "it is me" simply because that is accepted as a phrase in pop culture. We say, "it is I." We don't change our definitions for the sake of what is the lowest common denominator.

Their definition of hero was really scary. Fortunately, I had taken the precaution of looking up the word "hero" in the dictionary before I went down there. According to the dictionary, one of the attributes of a hero, apart from being originally half-mortal and half-divine and performing deeds of valor, is nobility of purpose. I was very glad the dictionary had said that, because that, of course, is essential. The hero must have some form of higher purpose in life. "Nobility of purpose" was a very good phrase, I thought, so I quoted it in this seminar, which everybody thought was rather extraneous to the whole problem of Superman, etc.

MOYERS: Does history tell us anything about the fate of societies that cease to make distinctions between right and wrong, between heroes and celebrities? I remember your descriptions of the Bourbons in France. You said the common people were so taken with the mystique of the court that they overlooked the decadence of the court until the French Revolution was made inevitable.

TUCHMAN: But they did not overlook the oppression and their own misery. I was just reading something the other day about the brink of the French Revolution and the outbreak in Lyons by the weavers, who spent their lives creating gorgeous fabrics, silks and brocades, and were paid one sou a day and simply could not live on it. But that was the way the employers made their profit, by the gap between what they paid the workers and what they sold the fabrics for. The merchants just refused to make a change, and there was an uprising. The leader was hanged, but this was the real beginning of the French Revolution. We haven't learned anything from this. We haven't learned that ignoring the evils of our society, the homeless and the deficit and such things, will hurt us.

MOYERS: But weren't the subjects of the monarchy so overcome by the mystique of it that they allowed the Bourbons to reign in decadence until the Revolution became inevitable?

TUCHMAN: Yes, the King had such mystique, such a halo of righteous exercise of rule, that people didn't seriously consider attempting to do anything except occasional assassinations.

MOYERS: We don't have monarchy, although it seems symbolic to me that the President is himself untouched by the Iran-Contra scandal, by the Pentagon scandal, by the sleaze of so many Administration officials who have to resign under fire, by the minimum ethics of his Attorney General. The sewage doesn't seem to rise to the steps of the White House, although it comes from the basement.

TUCHMAN: No, it doesn't. And I wonder, is it the person or is it the nature of the office? I suppose it's both. Reagan does seem to be a person remarkably impervious to trouble. But I think all these developments must certainly affect, if not the person in government, at least the office. And it would be too bad if we lost respect for the office.

I think that's the point I was trying to make in the chapter on popes in *The March of Folly*. The activity of the popes themselves cost the papacy so much respect and so much prestige that it made the Reformation possible. It didn't cause the Reformation, but it made the idea of overthrowing the Roman Church possible.

MOYERS: That brings to mind something you wrote during the Watergate crisis. You said that the American presidency has become a greater risk than it is worth. You said, "It's no longer my country, right or wrong, but it's my president, right or wrong, so that the loyalty has been transferred from the country to the man, from the institution to the incumbent."

TUCHMAN: And no man can support that now. The only person who ever did was George Washington, who's my example of the true hero. Washington was a remarkable man in every aspect of his character, in his courage, in his persistence, and in his amazing belief that he was right and that he would prevail in spite of enormous frustrations and difficulties. I related him to this earlier revolutionary hero,

William the Silent of the Netherlands, who is supposed to have said at one time, it is not necessary to hope in order to persevere. That is a wonderful sentiment, it seems to me. William the Silent succeeded, too, although that revolt took eighty years. This little swamp-bound people on the edge of Europe who had really nothing but the land they had created themselves, lifting it out of the bogs—this group maintained the revolt for eighty years against the most powerful empire of Europe at that period. Extraordinary story, really, the history of the Dutch.

MOYERS: But I wonder if William the Silent would have had to become William the Garrulous to survive in our television age, and if George Washington would have had a difficult time maintaining that dignity if he had been constantly exposed to the talk shows and the interrogations of the Sunday weekend political broadcasts.

TUCHMAN: Well, he was not a very vocal person. But he was so above it that I don't think he would have succumbed. He exerted an extraordinary quality of nobility that people felt just by being introduced to him, by seeing him, in spite of the terrible frustrations and difficulties that he faced when all the generals were pouring letters onto his desk telling him of their shortages—you know, no shoes, no money, no wagons to transport their food, and no food. In one area there were plenty of thin, starving steers that were ready to be slaughtered for meat, but they couldn't slaughter the steers because they couldn't pay butchers to salt them because they didn't have any ready cash, and the butchers wouldn't do it without cash. Everything that Washington had to handle—and it was every aspect of running a large war—every aspect was a frustration, not only in actual shortages but also in the failures of his assistants and of his colonels and generals.

And when it was over, and he gave up his commission at the famous scene where he said good-bye, he took out a pair of glasses, which nobody had ever seen him wear before, and put them on and said, "I have grown gray in your service and my eyes have—" I forget the exact words. All the soldiers wept because they loved him. It makes me cry, too. And I didn't use this very affecting scene in my book because I didn't want to try to rewrite what so many other people had done already. Just this gesture, putting on glasses for the first time in public, I find very moving.

When my daughter was helping me with the problems of filling out the notes and the annotations and all this awful business of first names that the publishers want for their index, I discovered I had been rather careless in my research because my eyes were already going bad, and we just didn't have the first names. We had to reproduce them, and we were having a terrible time, and I was carrying on with my agonies over loss of eyesight, and our slogan became, "Think of George." We always wanted to call the book that.

MOYERS: "Think of George."

TUCHMAN: "Think of George." Because he overrode all these difficulties in the most extraordinary way.

MOYERS: Is it romantic to believe that in this era of politics by television that politicians can think of George Washington when they get to the White House, or are they subjecting themselves to an impossible imperative?

TUCHMAN: Yes, who's going to be able to handle it? Maybe the person could think of George and find the stamina and the faith. The real thing Washington had was faith. He had such faith in Providence, as he called it. *Providence will prevail.* No matter what we've suffered and what is going wrong, he said, Providence will bring it right, as it has so often before.

MOYERS: Every President of late—Ronald Reagan, Jimmy Carter, Gerald Ford, Richard Nixon, Lyndon Johnson—appealed to God.

TUCHMAN: They appealed to God, but that's phrase-making. The question is whether they had the confidence, whether they had the faith that they were doing the right thing. Washington had total faith in what he was doing. Think of the decision to march his army all the way from New York to Washington—on foot—because he had made this arrangement to meet the French at the bottom of the Chesapeake to envelope Cornwallis. This was arranged across an ocean by letter. No telephone, no telegraphs, no satellites, no nothing, but letters. To think that he was able to do it on foot, and the French were able to come across an ocean and that Washington and the French met just as they had planned. In many ways, it was a miracle. Here Washington invested his reputation, the army, the fate of the Revolution, in this one adventure of marching down to Virginia from New York. It was a tremendous dare, which no one else would have ever been able to take, because no one else had the self-confidence that Washington had.

MOYERS: In terms of our public morals today you've described a pretty desperate situation. Would we think of a Washington almost as an oddity?

TUCHMAN: The trouble is that our public men are really artificial. They're created by the most devastating tool that technology has invented, which is the teleprompter. They don't speak spontaneously. You don't hear them meet a situation out of their own minds. They read this thing that's going around there in front of them, these words that have been created for them by PR men. This is not the real man that we see. It allows an inadequate, minor individual to appear to be a statesman because he's got very good speech writers, and to read the stuff off because he's a trained actor.

> *The trouble is that our public men are really artificial.*

MOYERS: And yet George Washington had Alexander Hamilton as a speech writer. Is there a correlation?

TUCHMAN: No, because the teleprompter shows the person in a situation that is not real. We're a public that is brought up on deception, through advertising. From the moment we are children, we learn that some kind of cereal is going to make us strong, and the next thing you know, if you use a particular kind of toothpaste, you're going to marry Gary Cooper, or at least have a glamorous romance somewhere, or if you use a particular kind of shampoo, you'll be running down the beach with all this beautiful hair flowing in the wind. All that is deception. But we're accustomed to being deceived. We allow ourselves to be deceived. Advertising is really responsible for a lot in the deterioration of American public perceptions.

MOYERS: Would you ban the use of the political commercial, the thirty-second and sixty-second spot?

TUCHMAN: Oh, absolutely. I think we should require political appearances to be live.

MOYERS: So that you can see the men think aloud, on their feet.

TUCHMAN: Yes. It should be live, and it should be more than thirty seconds.

MOYERS: You're asking for a chance to test the merits of the individual as he stands on his own two feet. Certainly everyone knew George Washington had genuine accomplishments behind him. Everyone knew this was a real man.

TUCHMAN: Even though they often disapproved or tried to insult him and dispose of him. That was not because he was a phony, but because he was too effective.

MOYERS: You've said on other occasions that the media age has caused us to put into the presidency a person who is likable and avuncular, but who is ill-equipped for the office. But we've had likable and avuncular presidents who were ill-equipped for the office prior to the age of television—Warren Harding, for example.

TUCHMAN: Yes, but we didn't have circumstances that were so demanding.

MOYERS: What do you mean?

TUCHMAN: Well, I mean that now the circumstances that surround us are very dangerous in many ways, they're very high-pressured and difficult to deal with, whereas Harding and Coolidge were leading a society under less dire circumstances.

MOYERS: Much smaller armies, much smaller budgets, less power over the lives of other individuals.

TUCHMAN: For example, look at our CIA activities. In the twenties, Secretary of State Henry Stimson refused to enlarge what was called the Black Chamber, the code-reading activities, because, he said, "Gentlemen do not read each other's mail." There's someone who had a moral sense, even if it was awkward or wrongly placed. But now our government is so concerned with knowing every tiny little thing that they know far too much. They don't have knowledge, they have mere information about what's going on in this little place or that little place.

At the time of the Vietnam War, I interviewed Robert McNamara, and I said, "Well, after all, the French had been in Vietnam for many years, and they were defeated by these fellows in black pajamas who weren't supposed to have any power." And he said, "But we didn't know." It's so revealing because the fact is, it was perfectly easy to know what the situation was in Vietnam, what the people were like. We had foreign service officers writing all kinds of reports all the time, and there were books, and there were studies. In five minutes, you could learn what the nationalism and the sense of the Vietnamese people were.

MOYERS: Then why do governments persist in folly?

TUCHMAN: They persist in folly because they don't want to let go of their position, or their power. They are afraid that if they let go, if they say, we were wrong, or we're doing the wrong thing, they will be booted out, or they will lose their status. It's not wanting to be left out of the next White House luncheon, or to be shoved into the wilderness if you report unpleasing information.

MOYERS: Cyrus Vance is the only official in recent memory who resigned a high post in protest to his President's decisions. Even though Secretary Shultz and Secretary Weinberger said that they opposed the Iran arms sales—

TUCHMAN: —they didn't stand up against it.

MOYERS: I hear you saying this acceptance by the public of the phony image will in time have disastrous effects for society.

TUCHMAN: You can't go on believing in Santa Claus and have the results be positive. We can't go on living on borrowed money forever, for example. We apparently think we can because we've been brought up on advertising from which we learn that everything will turn out right if you use the right toothpaste or shampoo. That has nothing to do with reality.

MOYERS: Does it help in confronting a steady procession of images to read history? One could say: The past is past, let the dead bury the dead, history is behind us. Is there a value to reading history?

TUCHMAN: Oh yes. For one thing, it's frightfully interesting. People say, what's the use of reading history? I say, well, what's the use of Beethoven's sonatas? You don't have to have a tangible use. You have to have something that gives you pleasure, makes you think, makes life more valuable. Reading history does that even though it only shows what is past. I think it was Coleridge who said, "History is only a lantern on the stern." It tells you where you've been. Well, that's worth knowing.

MOYERS: There's an old debate over whether history is a guide to the future, whether we learn from past experience to avoid mistakes. I think that in our collective wisdom the American people did learn from the Vietnam experience not to let another president take us into a war unless he can present overwhelming evidence that our national security is clearly at stake. Don't you find that encouraging?

TUCHMAN: Yes, I think we have learned from that. I think it's also clear that when you try to fight a prolonged war without national support, you lose. You can't do it because the public just won't stand for it. It took a long time for protest on Vietnam to make itself felt, but it did. We see the phrase all the time, "We don't want another Vietnam."

MOYERS: Some people think that's the wrong lesson to learn from Vietnam.

TUCHMAN: The military thinks that we were robbed, so to speak, because they weren't given the proper support to finish off the Vietnamese. But they weren't on the way to finishing them off any more than the French were. I don't think in the end that they could have, no matter how much they bombed, because the bombing didn't have sufficient targets. Heavy bombing in Vietnam didn't destroy the resources of the opposition. It's true that the appropriations were in the end denied, but that isn't what defeated the conduct of the war—it was the fact that the Vietnamese had a stronger motivation than we did.

MOYERS: You described yourself as a storyteller, a narrator of true stories. If you were writing about America today, what do you think would be the chief theme of your book?

TUCHMAN: I'd like it to be the feeling that was felt about America at the time of its beginnings. For example, why did the French nobles go with such élan to fight over here? After all, the nobles were established in a system exactly the reverse of what they were supporting over here. What did they believe in? This is a tremendous puzzle. The description of liberty by Americans was very exciting even though it represented the reverse of what those people lived by. The belief in what America would mean for many people in Europe as well as over here was extraordinary. You know, Lafayette brought back to France a container of enough American soil to be buried in when he died. Isn't that an extraordinary visual sort of image?

MOYERS: You close your book by quoting another Frenchman who came to this country, Crèvecoeur. You say, if Crèvecoeur came again to ask his famous question, "What is this new man—this American?"—what would he find? What's your answer?

TUCHMAN: Crèvecoeur would not find the free and liberated man that he expected, although such men did exist in certain spots. He thought, as many Frenchmen did, that the American Revolution was a great adventure that would create a new man. But revolutions have not succeeded in doing that. The French believed they would create a new man from liberty, equality, and fraternity. They didn't. And the Chinese thought their Communist revolution would create a new man who would serve the people rather than himself.

MOYERS: But the Revolution did create a new country.

TUCHMAN: Yes, it did, and it did create the system which might have produced a new man if the nature of mankind were more flexible or more malleable. But the nature of mankind is permanent. It doesn't change.

MOYERS: You wrote: "Revolutions produce other men, not new men. Halfway between truth and endless error, the mold of the species is permanent. That is earth's burden." We're a country still becoming, a country still in ferment, a country still unsure of itself—like an oversized adolescent.

> *I wonder if we haven't just accepted things as they are without retaining a desire for a better man or for a better society than we have created.*

TUCHMAN: I don't know that we're still in ferment. I wonder if we haven't just accepted things as they are without retaining a desire for a better man or for a better society than we have created. I don't think we have created the society that Crève-coeur or the other foreign-born who came to fight for us hoped for, or even our own patriots, the Minutemen and the people who left their homes and their pastures and their farms to join the Continentals in very rigorous conditions and to fight for independence.

MOYERS: But we've made a lot of progress. You weren't in the Constitution two hundred years ago. Blacks were slaves. Maybe the social progress of the day is what's behind what you call the incoherence of the modern age. There is more freedom.

TUCHMAN: Oh yes, we have gained a lot in social freedom and individual rights, which is the thing that I personally believe in more intensely than anything else—the right of the individual to guide his own life, to think for himself, to live where he wants. We have created a society in which the individual is self-managing and insofar as he can economically manage, he can determine his own fate.

MOYERS: There's the rub, because political freedom doesn't always bring economic choice.

TUCHMAN: No, it doesn't and that's where we're neglecting the freedoms that we created by neglecting the economic level of too much of our population.

Michael Josephson

ETHICIST

Michael Josephson knows the difference between the letter of the law and the spirit of it. After teaching law for twenty years and establishing a successful bar review business, he moved on to found the Josephson Institute for the Advancement of Ethics. Acting ethically, he says, is easier said than done, but it's the only way to make a world fit for our children.

MOYERS: Just about everywhere we turn, people are talking about ethics—especially about the teaching of ethics and values. How do you explain that?

JOSEPHSON: The news has been full of so many instances where people have not acted ethically that it's natural for us to ask what has caused this, and what can we do about it. We want to understand why people behave the way they do, and what we can do differently to influence them to behave differently.

MOYERS: Do you think that America has lost its moral bearings?

JOSEPHSON: No, but I think there's been slippage. We go through pendulum swings from idealistic periods to less idealistic periods. During the last ten years, as a people, we haven't distinguished ourselves for our willingness to be as candid, caring, and honest as we're capable of being. We're no longer the symbol of all the good things we used to be.

MOYERS: Has something happened in particular at this point in time?—because actually, America has never been as good as it wanted to be, or as good as it remembers itself as being.

JOSEPHSON: That's true, but historically there are shifts in the emphasis on ethics. I came out of the sixties, where there was an awful lot of talk about ethics. Sometimes when people got positions of authority or power, they didn't act any more ethically than the people they were protesting against. But at that period there was a concern for ethics. Then, with the assassinations of Jack Kennedy, Martin Luther King, Jr., and Bobby Kennedy, and the whole Vietnam War, an enormous cynicism set in. The next movement was a kind of self-concern, the feeling that you have to take care of yourself first. Then the economy became a huge problem. And when the economy becomes a huge problem, people start thinking of their pocketbook, and of making things better for themselves.

These grand movements focus people's attention on certain ways of evaluating themselves. Recently, people haven't been evaluating themselves as much on how good they are, or whether they're meeting their highest aspirations as people.

MOYERS: They evaluate themselves in terms of success.

JOSEPHSON: That's right. Of course, success can be defined in so many ways. But right now people ask, how high is your position, how many people work for you, how high is your salary? When you get into that kind of yuppie version of success, you're going to sacrifice things along the way. There's not enough commitment to the ground rules of civic virtue.

MOYERS: Yet the people most conspicuous in the news for violating ethical imperatives have not been yuppies. They've been successful Wall Street brokers; career military officers; top middle-aged advisers to President Reagan. These have not been the yuppies.

JOSEPHSON: But they're the creatures of the yuppies. The yuppie is the constituency that makes it okay. They're the people who applaud success, who allow an Ivan Boesky to say, "Greed is good," and not be hooted down from the stage. They're the people who write books on how to win by intimidation and who can get on every TV show to teach people how to do that. Of course, this yuppie mentality is not really people, it's an approach. It's the philosophy of measuring our lives by what we get, what we acquire, who we know. It's a very shallow kind of life. People find that out in time. But during the period when that philosophy flourishes, we sacrifice a lot.

MOYERS: It's certainly true that the rules of American life today are determined not by the church on Main Street, but by the money changers on Wall Street. There used to be a common American ethical vocabulary for both Jews and Christians that grew out of the Bible and out of civic discourse, an idea of the republic that informed our common language.

JOSEPHSON: That's true, but I think we have to be careful about oversimplifying it. Not everybody doing unethical things is motivated by money. I do workshops for senior staff for politicians, mayors, and the like, and I don't find these people largely money motivated. Yet I find the same kind of creeping corruption—and I use corruption in the broad sense of corruption of ideals, not just corruption in connection with money. The corruption I'm talking about is based on a self-righteous notion of the need to win, on our having the right to have what we want, rather than just having the right to have an even playing field. Many politicians, for example, treat getting reelected as if it were a moral imperative. Once you accept that, you will sacrifice other moral values.

So it isn't just money. It's the need to win, to be clever, and to be successful in other people's eyes that sometimes causes people to sacrifice the fundamental ideals that motivated them to the enterprise in the first place. Politics is a very noble enterprise.

MOYERS: Are the people who are teaching us ethics generally more ethical than the rest of us?

JOSEPHSON: First of all, the people who are really teaching us ethics aren't even thinking about ethics. We don't learn ethics from people who sermonize or moralize or try to preach to us about ethics; we learn ethics from the people whom we admire and respect, who have power over us. They're the real teachers of ethics. Those who purport to teach ethics, whether they are in the churches or in higher education, generally are no better people.

MOYERS: You mean, we get our ethics from our examples, from our role models?

JOSEPHSON: It's complex. We certainly get an inculcation from our parents, and that's a very important thing. But all that does is give us an orientation toward ethics. Now some people rebel against that orientation, and some people adopt it and follow it. We're also influenced by our peer groups. Ethics is taught from all sides, by a coach, for example, or a teacher, or a particular person who inspires someone to his highest self. The first political speech I ever remember was the Kennedy speech that said, "Ask not what your country can do for you, but what you can do for your country." Now that meant something to me. That was an inspirational moment. Occasionally, a teacher can do that. But usually, people function as best they can, day by day, solving their little problems as best they can. How they get rewarded, and what impedes them, and what helps them is what teaches them how to act.

MOYERS: How can we instruct people in ethical behavior?

JOSEPHSON: Well, it's important to reinforce ideals, if they're sincere. It is very important for leaders and role models, whether they be sports figures or politicians, to make positive statements of ethics, if they're not hypocritical. But a hypocritical statement is so counterproductive that it teaches the reverse. It not only negates the ethical message that you've articulated, but it teaches people that hypocrisy is the way to succeed. So I'm very nervous about sermonizing or moralizing about ethics. In our own ethics institute, we want to be careful not to do that because we want to help people see the potential of their highest self, without setting ourselves up as being pious or sanctimonious.

MOYERS: Some formal studies have suggested that moral instruction doesn't really have much effect on ethical behavior. Children who are interviewed may say they know what it means not to lie, but nonetheless, they want to lie and do lie.

JOSEPHSON: That's right. I spent a lot of time looking at the literature because when we looked at the studies on ethics, we found that different stages are subject to different approaches. For instance, the most you can do with children is to orient them. They think very, very specifically. They don't think abstractly, they don't think about the future, and they tend to be ethical, if at all, only because it pleases someone they care about. They don't adopt ethics as a real standard.

When they get older, they begin to make decisions for themselves. In fact, the most significant period of ethical development is early adulthood, between the twenties and thirties, because until that time, people don't have to test their ethics, they don't have to put their money where their mouth is. It's when you first have to decide how important it is for you to keep your job that you decide how much the truth means to you. At that point it's decision-making that's critical, not merely character. Almost everyone wants to be ethical. Everyone I know is capable of being ethical. But whether people are willing to be ethical in a particular decision-making situation depends on a lot of things, including their ability to see the ethical issues, to work out the problems, to anticipate correctly the risks and burdens, and to implement their decision in a way that doesn't cause hazardous and dangerous consequences for themselves. For instance, in most cases, whistle blowing results in terribly damaging consequences to the whistle blower. We have to find other ways to be ethical so that we don't always lose.

MOYERS: You're saying that ethical behavior grows out of the crises and challenges of life, not out of some ideological or theoretical or hypothetical situation.

JOSEPHSON: That's true, but clearly we can prepare people to be more ethical.

We should train our children and our students to be aware of the kinds of challenges they're going to face, and we should help them face these challenges from a problem-solving point of view and reinforce their values. But in the last analysis, what they do when they're in the trenches is a question of how they prioritize those values. Now we have a lot to say about that. If I'm an employer, I can create an atmosphere in my company where a person would not lie because lying is so inconsistent with what is approved in that organization that a person can't lie and succeed. We need to do that. Too many companies have measured success without regard to how someone became successful. As a result, deceit, lying, unfairness, and unaccountability have been allowed to succeed.

MOYERS: So that's why we hold our political leaders to such a high standard—not because we expect them to be perfect, but because we know there has to be an image projected, an expectation aroused, a standard raised.

JOSEPHSON: You're absolutely right. Not only politicians, but our athletes, or anyone who has both the fortune and misfortune to be important enough that people care how they behave—they're role models. They have a responsibility. This society has become so rights oriented—

MOYERS: —I have a right to this, I have a right to that—

JOSEPHSON: —Yes. But there are responsibilities, too. Our rights orientation has led to a kind of legal minimalism—as long as it's legal, it's ethical. We look for the lowest common standard of ethics, and approach life and laws as if everything is the Internal Revenue code. Everyone wants to avoid paying taxes, so finding loopholes and evading those taxes is legitimate. Unfortunately, we find this same attitude in business, politics, and journalism. Look at the libel laws and the way some journalists approach those laws.

> *Our rights orientation has led to a kind of legal minimalism—as long as it's legal, it's ethical.*

MOYERS: You're encroaching now.

JOSEPHSON: Good. I hope so. I want to make you uncomfortable, because growth will only come out of a little level of discomfort. Every professional I've dealt with has a sense that his or her profession is better than anybody else's. They see with absolute clarity the shortcomings of the other professions. And yet they justify their own misbehavior as if they're just occasional aberrations, or that everyone else doesn't understand. One of the goals of ethical decision-making is to make people aware of the kinds of insider assumptions that they make, the excuses, the rationalizations.

MOYERS: We're all inside traders.

JOSEPHSON: That's exactly right. In our professions and our own activities, we are all Ivan Boeskys in a way, and we need to wake up and look at what we're doing and measure it against what we say.

MOYERS: What did you learn in law school about ethics?

JOSEPHSON: I didn't learn a thing about ethics. I learned that you don't lie if you're an attorney, but that wasn't because of ethics, it was because that's what a professional does. It reminds me of the notion that "honesty is the best policy" or "good ethics is good business." Both are very negative messages. Honesty may be the best policy, and good ethics may be good business—but then it's business and not ethics. The reason we ought to be ethical is because it's the right thing to do.

MOYERS: Who says?

JOSEPHSON: History, theology, and philosophy will show that every enlightened civilization has had a sense of right and wrong and a need to try to distinguish them. Now we may disagree over time as to what is right and wrong—but there has never been a disagreement in any philosophy about the importance of knowing the difference. The things that are right are the things that help people and society. They are things like compassion, honesty, fairness, accountability. Those are absolute, universal, ethical values.

MOYERS: And they exist apart from divine revelation?

JOSEPHSON: Yes, I think they do. Religion can be an important source of these ethical beliefs, but secular philosophers have come to the same conclusion. The Golden Rule occurred in Greek culture and in the Chinese culture thousands of years before Christ articulated His version.

MOYERS: The essence of ethical behavior is to ask the question, "How would I want to be treated if I were in that situation?"

JOSEPHSON: Yes. You only ask that question because you care about other people. That's why the essence of ethics is some level of caring. That's what distinguishes us as human beings.

MOYERS: But couldn't you also ask that question from self-interest? I don't want my house burglarized, my body violated, my life threatened—so in order to protect my self-interest, I have to respect your self-interest.

JOSEPHSON: You're absolutely right. Ethics has a practical dimension, there's no question about it. But it also has a spiritual dimension. People have an inner and inherent sense of right and wrong. That's why they feel guilt and shame. I'm not enough of a philosopher to know what light we have inside us that tells us it's better to be a good person. I just know that I feel better when I'm doing the right thing. My highest moments are not the moments where I made a great deal of money, or even won a major case. They're moments where I felt important because I did something meaningful that made a difference to other people.

One philosophy says life is like having your hand in a bucket of water—when you remove it, the water settles down within moments, and no one knew you ever lived. Another theory says, you do what you can to make differences in the network of people that you affect. You bring some happiness, you bring some joy, you remove some pain.

I believe there are enough people in this society who believe that, and we should be more effective at mobilizing them, giving them confidence, empowering them to know that it's important to work in their own sphere. We shouldn't just point fingers at the terrible politicians, and the Jim and Tammy Bakkers, and the Ivan Boeskys. That's all fine, but you have a backyard, and I have a backyard, and we all affect hundreds of people in our network—and we don't do as good a job as we should.

MOYERS: Who taught you about ethics? Who made you what you are by giving you examples for ethical choices?

JOSEPHSON: I had a large family, and learned a lot from my parents about love. But some of what I learned I related to in reverse. I didn't like everything my father did. He came from a New York business background that offended me in many regards. So in some cases, I decided not to behave the way my parents behaved. To me the most moving moment was having a child.

MOYERS: You were how old when that happened?

JOSEPHSON: Thirty-three. I was teaching law, and I was assigned to teach the course of ethics for the first time. You see, after Watergate, this became a mandatory course. Before then, it wasn't required in law schools. Like most law professors, I had not studied ethics myself in law, because that wasn't what I specialized in. I taught that ethics course the first year like I would teach a tax code—how to avoid it, how to evade it, how to see the ambiguities. After all, rules are just restrictions, just limitations. We've got to avoid them. Well, that same year, I had my child. And when I compared how I was approaching teaching ethics to the law students with how I wanted to teach my son ethics, and what I wanted him to be, I saw an enormous inconsistency. My teaching of ethics to law students was not a value-based enterprise. But I wanted to teach my son values—the value of caring, the value of being trustworthy, the value of trying hard, the value of accountability.

And so you shift how you approach ethics. You think about it. You read about it. And then you make decisions about how you want to behave as a person. That's what you and everybody can do—make decisions as to how you want to behave.

MOYERS: But couldn't you have taught your son to be a good person while continuing to teach lawyers how to be successful attorneys?

JOSEPHSON: Yes. I do not believe ethics is inconsistent with success in being an attorney. I do believe it is inconsistent with the particular approach I was taking to being a good attorney.

MOYERS: Which was—?

JOSEPHSON: To be competitive, to win. There's a simple story of a lawyer who goes on a camping trip with a nonlawyer. They both have their backpacks on their backs, and suddenly they see a cougar about twenty yards away. The lawyer starts to take off his backpack, and the friend says, "What are you going to do?"
The lawyer says, "I'm going to run for it."
The friend says, "But you can't outrun a cougar."
And the lawyer says, "I don't have to outrun the cougar. I just have to outrun you."
Now you could tell that story in any business.

MOYERS: I'll tell you one about journalism. Do you know why scientists are now using journalists instead of rats in their laboratory experiments? First of all, because there are more journalists than there are rats. Second, you don't get as attached to journalists as you do rats. And third, journalists will do things rats won't do.

JOSEPHSON: That's good.

MOYERS: You can substitute lawyers for journalists.

JOSEPHSON: And politicians ask me, "Do you know what's black and brown and looks good on a journalist?"

MOYERS: What?

JOSEPHSON: A Doberman pinscher.

MOYERS: What gives rise to these stories?

JOSEPHSON: Each group is keenly aware of how the other group offends them.

The politicians feel totally assailed by the journalists. Business people feel assaulted by the lawyers. Each one is articulate in their criticism of the other, but they're unable to see their own actions and activities. In fact, the funny thing is that in all of these jokes, you can substitute one profession for another, and there will be many who nod. Within the professions, we have an enormous capacity to affect thousands, millions of people. If the professionals would be more sensitive and thoughtful about what they're trying to achieve, and would make more refined distinctions, we would change our behavior just one or two degrees, and we could change the impact enormously.

MOYERS: True. Yet you have said that some young professionals will change their ethical behavior after attending a seminar, or receiving an instruction in class, but that others will not. Are those who change their ethical behavior putting themselves at a competitive disadvantage in our society in relation to those who will not change?

JOSEPHSON: Not always, but sometimes. It depends on how you define the game. If I'm willing to cheat, I could have a competitive advantage in playing golf. But it's not the same game. If we define the purpose of living only as the accomplishment of a particular task, accomplishing the task becomes the moral imperative—winning the election, getting the scoop, making a profit. But we know that nobody on a deathbed says, "I wish I had spent more time at the office." People's values begin to change when they reflect upon how futile most of the flurry of activity was. And the fact of the matter is that a good conscience is the best pillow. Living a good life is the most important thing for us.

MOYERS: Yes, but I find that every day is a constant struggle to decide between right and wrong in small ways that nobody ever sees. I win one day, and I lose the next day—so at nights, my pillow is often like a stone.

JOSEPHSON: If you put yourself out, you're vulnerable, and people are quick to point out where you haven't lived up to your ethical standards. But at least you're in the right game, and you're measuring yourself by the right score. I don't expect to make sainthood.

MOYERS: But you began by making a considerable amount of money—so you could afford to be ethical.

JOSEPHSON: Yes, I guess so. But on the other hand, I also was able to see how much the money didn't make a difference.

MOYERS: But only after you had it.

JOSEPHSON: I suppose that's true. But I didn't make money by sacrificing ethical principles. I am not a reborn ethicist. I didn't do anything I was not proud of. In fact, I was never concerned very much with money. I made money while being a law professor and running a publishing company and bar review business that just grew and grew. I think it was because I wasn't concerned with making money that I made so much.

MOYERS: What was it Plato said?—that virtue does not come from money, but money comes from virtue.

JOSEPHSON: I believe that can happen. It isn't, of course, always true, but it can happen. I think it's added to our credibility as an institute that when I talk about ethics, people know I've been in the real world. I understand. Now I don't want to sound like some pious minister on this, I just want to use whatever teaching skills I have and whatever I know to bring another message. Every time I do a workshop, and people tell me what you have to do to win, I say, this is nonsense, it doesn't have to be that way. It's such a shortsighted view, and it's not analytical. All I do is ask them a question, and then say, take that solution you just said you have to do, and now make it impossible, for whatever reason. Do you give up? Do you die? Is the world over? Or do you figure something else out?

We tell people, unless you have three alternatives to every major problem, you haven't thought hard enough. As soon as you have three, you can find one of them that's ethical.

MOYERS: Sometimes those three alternatives involve shades of ethical judgment. They all may be right, but one may be more appropriately right than the other.

JOSEPHSON: Yes. The first thing you've got to do is understand there are two levels in ethical decision-making. The first is to distinguish the clearly unethical decisions from the ethical ones. It's usually unethical to lie, to steal, to injure others. There's a second level of decision where you're choosing between ethical values, truth and fairness, truth and loyalty, where no one answer is absolutely right or absolutely wrong. Here you just have to analyze the situation as clearly as possible and be sensitive to what your values are. And you're right, you're dealing with shades of gray. But what I find is that too many people have adopted a kind of utilitarian view toward ethics where they no longer consider whether they're dealing with an ethical value or a nonethical value.

For example, it's one thing to sacrifice truth for fairness. It's another thing to sacrifice truth for success. You can only sacrifice an ethical principle for another ethical principle.

MOYERS: Let's see if we can get an example of that. You're at home at night. There's a loud knock on your door. You open it to find a young woman who says she's being pursued by a violent man, and she needs a hiding place. You take her in, and in a few minutes, a drunken, enraged man comes to the door and says, "Did you see a young woman come running by here?" It's permissible to say, "No, I didn't."

JOSEPHSON: That's right.

MOYERS: Or if the man at the door says, "Hand over your money," and you lie and say, "I don't have any money," that's permissible, too.

JOSEPHSON: Yes, because in both cases, you have a legitimate ethical value. Lying against injury is an ethical value. You could lie to a terrorist, for example, or to a Nazi. If somebody's trying to rob you or is coercing you against your will, you don't have the same obligation to tell the truth. We use these extreme examples in what we call quandary ethics. You can give us a quandary and say, "Gee, there's no way of winning; therefore, there's no ethics." But you know, that's not what you face most of the time. As a journalist, you don't face these quandaries, and as a businessman, I didn't face them. We face simple decisions of self-interest versus doing the right thing. That's the reality. The question is, do we have the strength to do the right thing? Or do we start a rationalizing process that says, "Well, this is really for my family," or, "This is really for someone else," or, "If I don't make this money, then nobody will have any jobs." We start getting into a whole process of rationalization.

MOYERS: Let me come back to your twelve-year-old son. What are you telling him about how to make the right decisions?

JOSEPHSON: Well, again, I have to tell you, telling is not my particular mode of trying to teach him ethics. The best teaching is when I do something wrong, and I admit it. I'll never forget, when I first taught law and had to admit I was wrong. I was about six years into teaching law before I ever admitted I was wrong. Some student called me on something. My usual mode was to find a way of fast-footing it around, which you can do when you're a law professor with law students. But for some reason, I said, "Well, you know, you're absolutely right." And the earth didn't open. I didn't fall in. I survived. I had admitted I was wrong, and I still had their respect. In fact, I'll never forget because the student came up afterward and said, "That was the most significant thing I've ever seen in my educational career." He had never heard a professor admit being wrong.

I've learned something from that. I got positive reinforcement for doing the right thing, and secondly, I had overestimated the cost of doing the right thing. I thought if I admitted I was wrong, something terrible would happen. People often overestimate the cost of doing the right thing. They say, "I'll get fired," or "I won't get reelected." They underestimate the cost of not doing the right thing.

MOYERS: So you're not teaching your twelve-year-old specifics—

JOSEPHSON: I don't think I'm teaching them, but I think he's learning.

MOYERS: You learn without being taught.

JOSEPHSON: Yes, the less overt the teaching, the more effective it is. My son gets an allowance, for example, and 10 percent of it goes to a charity of his choice at the end of the year. Now I didn't impose that on him. We negotiated, we talked about it, and we talked about the selection of the charity.

MOYERS: What if he comes to you and says, "Dad, if I'm ethical, will I get what I want in life?"

JOSEPHSON: If you want the right things, and if you have a good set of values as to what's important, sure you will. In fact, it's the only way you'll get what you want. That's the ultimate test. What do you finally want? People want happiness, and they look at money, prestige, and power as a way to get happiness. I like money, I like power, I like prestige. But what does it cost me? The ultimate cost is what's critical. When you feel good about yourself, and you make other people feel good, that's just a good way to be.

MOYERS: You have said elsewhere that we tend to decide our ethical behavior on our reading of society and our perception of our stake in society. So if you're a member of one of the gangs that have received so much notoriety in Los Angeles, wouldn't you say, "My stake in society means not playing the game ethically, but going for all I can get, no matter how I have to get it"?

JOSEPHSON: Sure. That's a problem with a subculture that seems to benefit from having an entirely different value system from the culture as a whole.

MOYERS: One lives in a subculture because one can't get into the mainstream culture and play by its rules. The larger culture is not open or accessible to him.

JOSEPHSON: Well, you're right. I don't want to be glib about this. In fact, our magazine is called *Easier Said Than Done*. The implication that you get everything you want when you are ethical is wrong. There's some sacrifice involved in being ethical. Occasionally, if you lied, you wouldn't have to confront a difficult situation, which you would have to confront if you told the truth. The value of being ethical isn't simply that every day you get every single thing you want. But over the long haul, you feel better about yourself, and you've created a better society.

The cumulative impact of individual selfishness is a terribly selfish society, where we don't know what to expect from people any more. If we translate the Golden Rule—"Do unto others as you would have them do unto you"—into "Do unto others as you think they will do unto you," or, "Do unto others as they have done unto you," we have an awful society in which I don't want to raise my child. I've got to do my part to change that.

MOYERS: But for many people—the gangs, the chronically unemployed, the underclass—it's not an ethical society. I don't want to excuse anyone from responsibility, but they find themselves in situations determined by the way society is run, regulated, and ruled.

JOSEPHSON: That's often true. But the question is, does the solution that they have come upon address the problem? Or does it make it worse? Do gangs and drugs really make society any better?

MOYERS: You see them with the large sums of money they could never have earned in regular jobs. And they say, "Look, I've played the game the way society plays it, and I'm winning."

JOSEPHSON: They might be. That's how they define winning. If all you or I wanted in our lives was to get money, we would be doing different things than we're both doing. Why is it that you and I have chosen in our lives to do things that are less profitable than other options that we had? Why do thousands of people do that, millions of people?

MOYERS: I was a beneficiary of the way the game is played. I was a beneficiary of rules that favored a white male growing up in the postwar era, in an economy carrying me buoyantly upward, and of patrons who plucked me out for scholarships and sent me to school and backed me and befriended me.

JOSEPHSON: Then let's look at it from the other side. Maybe we'll have to acknowledge there are some people who, because of the unfortunate circumstances they're in, can't be expected to be as ethical as we'd like them to be. It's our responsibility to fix that. It's our responsibility to make conditions fairer, more open. If there were, in fact, systemic reasons for their lack of ethics, you and I as ethical people would not simply condemn them, but would say, "I'm not treating them the way I want to be treated." I don't want to be totally nonjudgmental, though. Each of us has accountability. The person who sells drugs is accountable.

MOYERS: I agree.

JOSEPHSON: But by the same token, we are responsible for setting up the best society we can. That's the highest aspiration, that's what this country has always meant. We need to make this the land of opportunity. And we haven't always been doing that. Now you don't have to be sick to get better. I'm not trying to emphasize how bad the society is—but we can do a lot better.

MOYERS: It's a cliché, but it seems to me true, that we can't really stand tall without standing together, and that there's something about caring and generosity that is missing in our society at the moment.

JOSEPHSON: Yes. From caring and generosity, fairness and accountability will come, and we will make dozens of decisions differently.

MOYERS: Let's come back to your son, because he figures very, very vividly in your thinking. I read what you wrote about him. Like most of us who are fathers, you probably have less time with your son in the course of the day than our culture has with him. What about the messages that the culture is sending him that make it hard for you to teach him? For example, Billy Martin, the manager of the New York Yankees, gets into a boozy brawl in a topless joint in Texas, and gets thrown out. He lies to the police about it. Then he throws a temper tantrum on the playing field, and hurls dirt at an umpire. Now, what message is that sending your twelve-year-old?

JOSEPHSON: Well, I'm not so much troubled that he sees negative images. I want him to see the real world, and there are people like Billy Martin who misbehave. But I am concerned with how the world responds to it. When people say, "It's really okay, that's the way to behave," they're telling my son, and others like him, that there's a large segment of society which really doesn't care about those values. I need to tell him that. I say, "Justin, it's not going to be easy to act ethically." The best thing you can do is to try to prepare people for challenges to their ethical standards because there are going to be plenty of them.

Now Billy Martin is just one model. There are also models of people who do behave and do the right thing. When Al Campanis of the Dodgers made statements that were totally inappropriate, he was fired. I feel bad for Al Campanis, but it was a reaction that was important and appropriate. When Jimmy the Greek made statements on TV, he was handled differently. So we have good examples as well as bad. Show him both and tell him why you think the good ones are good.

MOYERS: If his team had been in last place, Billy Martin would have been fired. So one message your son gets is that if Martin is winning, his personal behavior, no matter how obnoxious, is not held against him.

JOSEPHSON: By some people—and that's what's important. There are people who admire Ivan Boesky to this day. But you have to present your children or your employees with a different model. And you reward the model that you believe in. We're not going to change the whole world. There will always be villains and rogues. Let's just have some more heroes. And let's try to be a hero just a little bit every day ourselves.

MOYERS: Oliver North was a hero to many people and still is. He's campaigned enthusiastically out here in Los Angeles for conservative Republicans for Congress. North is considered a hero even though he shredded documents, lied to Congress, lied to the press, lied to his peers, and may have lied to the President he served.

JOSEPHSON: That's one of the toughest issues for me to analyze ethically because unlike most of these cases, where people were acting out of self-indulgence or self-protection, which are obvious motives, North appeared to be acting out of a different and nobler kind of motive. People judge him only on his motives. But self-righteousness can be as much a cause of unethical conduct as anything else. In this case, for example, North was so certain he was right that everything he allegedly was fighting for—a democratic society, making the world safe for democracy—he violated. In lying and ignoring the law, he denied me my autonomy.

MOYERS: What do you mean?

JOSEPHSON: I, as a citizen, speak through my Congress. I have a right to express my opinion on whether or not money should or should not go to Nicaragua. North believes that opinion is so worthless that it's to be ignored, and that he must have it his way. Even though he may believe in what he's doing with every fiber of his being, he has denied to me the most fundamental ethical principle, which is my autonomy.

We need to respect each other, and that's why we must be a law-abiding society. I think Oliver North violated the law, and he did so in order to impose his view of the world on everyone else. He denied people their input.

MOYERS: He nullified congressional mandates simply by ignoring them.

JOSEPHSON: That is the mentality of a dictator, whether it be a benevolent dictator or a malevolent dictator. You know, that's one of the worst things about lying. Even little white lies deny people their autonomy, their ability to decide for themselves on the basis of the true facts. Lies are a means of coercion.

MOYERS: That to me is the chief transgression of the Iran-Contra affair. How do we hold people in power accountable unless we know what they do? The more secrecy there is, the less we know what they do.

JOSEPHSON: And the consequences are enormous. They have done more damage to the very institutions they believed they were advancing than the Russians have done in the last forty years, because now we don't know what to believe. People don't believe their own government. When we reach the point where we can't even trust the facts our government gives us, then we have lost something very significant in a democracy.

MOYERS: What ethical examples are our political leaders setting? Take Congress. Congress exempted itself from the government and ethics act of 1978. It said the ethics act applies to everybody else, but it doesn't apply to us.

JOSEPHSON: There are two problems with that. One, they never should have called it the ethics act because it had nothing to do with ethics. The rules are basically extended rules of bribery that establish minimal standards of conduct.

Two, they have been hypocritical. The Congress has been embarrassingly, unjustifiably, and shamelessly hypocritical about applying its own standards to itself.

MOYERS: It doesn't hold itself responsible for the same affirmative action programs it requires of everyone else in society.

JOSEPHSON: That's right. Unfortunately, you find the same in the state legislators. What we're seeing here is a reflection of a kind of me-firstism. It's okay to regulate you, but not me. The worst part is that these people who are acting unethically and the few who even get condemned or censured are not losing their offices. Mario Biaggi was convicted of a felony, and he ran unopposed.

MOYERS: What does that say to you?

JOSEPHSON: It says to me that the people aren't asking enough of their representatives. They're not demanding enough. Also, a lot of people are being alienated. We have the lowest voting rate ever. A lot of people are just saying, "I don't want any part of this." And the people who might be more accountable, the people who are voting, are voting on self-interest. They say, "As long as this guy gets me my piece of the pie, a little bigger than maybe I'm otherwise entitled, I'm putting him back in office."

But we've got to take a broader view. We have to say that as individuals, we can make a difference in this country. We can demand, we can write letters, we can say, "This is not acceptable." Then, whether we win or lose that individual battle, we have sent forth some kind of energy, some kind of pressure that's going to make a difference.

MOYERS: Is there an ethical stake in the large sums of money that are being spent on political campaigns?

JOSEPHSON: Oh, sure. There's no reason to spend it except that people hope they'll distort the process. So you have two very cynical movements going. One involves the politicians who take these huge sums of money on the theory they need it to buy votes because they can't win the elections without a lot of money. The other involves lobbyists who claim that they only want access and are paying huge sums of money to get a competitive edge. It's very cynical. It's not part of the real theme of democracy that we ought to have. We ought to be putting our people in power because we trust their judgment to act on our behalf on some issues, when it's appropriate, and as neutral judges on most other issues, when they're speaking for the nation. It's a pity that we got into this cycle of money driving politics.

MOYERS: The irony is that as we have begun to pay for presidential campaigns with public funds, we haven't increased the number of voters, and we haven't brought more people into the process. We've simply enriched—well, my business, frankly. We've enriched the television stations, the campaign consultants, the advertising agencies, the people who make commercials.

JOSEPHSON: Well, remember, we can't solve every problem with a single reform. That reform solved at least the problem of preventing any particular group or interest from having undue influence. It hasn't solved all the other problems.

We need to look carefully at where the pressure points are in our society that tend to make certain behaviors tempting. For example, I'm on a diet all the time. I learned one thing: try to stay away from the dessert tray. Once that dessert tray is rolled out, I'm hopeless. It's the same for a lot of things that happen in society. We've got to stay away from the dessert tray.

Now all this money in politics is a dessert tray. Some people are going to stuff themselves. We should have provisions that prevent this self-indulgence, but more than that, we need self-restraint. We need the politicians to understand that's not what democracy ought to be about.

MOYERS: But unless everybody plays by the same rules, somebody will always get a competitive edge in our society.

JOSEPHSON: They might—but in fact, we don't really know the impact of this money. Incumbents win anyway. Ninety-eight percent of the incumbents running for Congress won last year. That's the same percentage as in Russia. So we don't have any proof that there really are serious, open elections or that this money makes any difference. Incumbents get money by a fifteen-to-one ratio because money follows incumbency, not ideology.

MOYERS: It's transactional politics. I'll do this for you, you do this for me.

JOSEPHSON: But you can't convince me that it's necessary, because it doesn't appear to be making any difference. People use the money even if they're unopposed.

MOYERS: The rules are important. In baseball, you can steal second base, but you can't doctor the ball. You play by the rules, and the rules let something happen. But there's more to ethics than the rules, is there not?

JOSEPHSON: Absolutely. We need to understand that there are two levels of things. On one level are rules, or laws. The first thing we need to do is to write laws, to try to establish at least minimal consensus standards. The bribery rules, for example, are certainly essential. Nobody ought to take a bribe. As a law professor for almost twenty years, I certainly understand the law and the rules. And one of the things I understand is that you can't write a law that I can't get around. So, in addition to laws, we have to have people who understand that the underlying purpose of this law is a social ideal, that we're trying to accomplish something for society. We have to have people who are willing to help and not undermine the laws by figuring out all the clever ways that they can violate them.

MOYERS: So what's the mandate for an ethical person in this?

JOSEPHSON: The mandate is that an ethical person ought to do more than he's required to do and less than he's allowed to do. He must exercise judgment, self-restraint, and conscience. Otherwise, we have a minimalist society where everybody's lawyering everybody else, pushing the world to the limit, and twisting the rules. We need to tell people we can do better. And if it costs us a little bit, so it costs us. It's worth it.

MOYERS: What's at stake for the America your son Justin will one day be a citizen in?

JOSEPHSON: Well, things have momentum. We must change the momentum, which is, in my view, denigrating ethics. It's almost as if ethics is for wimps, ethics is for losers, ethics is something you can have only if you're rich. If we don't change that momentum, society is going to get a great deal worse. It's going to be a dog-eat-dog society.

If even a small minority of people will speak up and demand more of themselves and others, even if only in their own lives, we'll turn the pendulum around, and we'll begin to swing back to the days when we could be really proud of the kind of people we are because of what we contribute to each other and society. Ethics is a minority movement, and it always will be. But a strong minority can change the tenor of this society in a meaningful way.

MOYERS: Easier said than done.

JOSEPHSON: Much easier said than done—but it's worth doing.

Joseph Heller

N O V E L I S T

GERARD MURRELL

For nearly thirty years Joseph Heller has been tracing the lines between absurdity and politics. In 1961 his comedy about men at war, Catch-22, *made the term a part of our language. He followed with other novels about American culture, including* Something Happened, God Knows, *and* Good As Gold. *His most recent book,* Picture This, *finds a precedent for our times in the Athens of Socrates.*

MOYERS: When I read *Good As Gold* for a second time the other night, it made me laugh out loud at three o'clock in the morning—the White House assistant who runs around saying, "We're going to tell the truth, even if we have to lie to do it"; a President who spends his first year in office doing nothing but writing a book; or the assistant who says, "We don't want yes-men in this Administration, we want men of independent integrity who will then agree with everything we decide to do." Why is politics so funny to you?

HELLER: Politics is funny to me because it *is* funny. We're talking about American politics now. You gave three illustrations from the book. I think almost everything in *Good As Gold* about politics that makes a reader laugh is drawn from things that are actually happening on almost a daily basis. American politics is funny. There are many, many things that one could say in criticism of it and a few things one could say in praise. But one of the things you could say in both praise and criticism is that it is ludicrously funny.

MOYERS: We look to politics for so much entertainment. Entertainment now dominates the staging of politics.

HELLER: Politics for me is a spectator sport. But it has become less and less entertaining for me over the years, so I'm less and less interested in it than I have been. I have not voted for the last twenty to twenty-five years. I've come to a rather cynical belief that there are many illusions incorporated in democratic philosophy. They tend to be very pleasing and satisfying, but they are misleading, and they are fantasies. One of them is that the democratic ideal is even possible, that there can be such a thing as participatory democracy. One of our illusions—and it's a very comforting illusion—is that by voting, we are participating in government. Voting is a ritualistic routine. The right to vote is indispensable to our contentment, but in application it's absolutely useless.

MOYERS: Isn't the ritual important to the notion of democracy? Isn't the very act of voting an affirmation of consensus toward the society in which you live?

HELLER: No, that's where the delusion is—that one's vote matters at all. It doesn't. That the election matters. It doesn't. That the victorious party will be responsive to the wishes of those electing it. That is not true.

MOYERS: Did it matter to you that Robert Bork was defeated when he was nominated for the Supreme Court?

HELLER: Of course. But that was not done by election.

MOYERS: But Walter Mondale would probably never have submitted Robert Bork's name to the Senate.

HELLER: I'm not saying that there are not differences between Administrations. There are. Occasionally, there is an election in which there is an issue of tremendous importance, an issue that divides the two parties. That happens very seldom, by the way. Most of the voting and party membership is pretty much based on something that might be called parochial loyalties. That's the reason someone like John Connally could switch from the Democratic Party to the Republican Party so easily.

Part of our fantasy is this: We think that we elect the President and choose the people who will represent us. In actuality, that doesn't happen. What happens is that we are presented with two candidates, and we are confined to picking one or the other to win. It makes no difference how strongly we feel about them. Normally, the candidates are supported by people who are from the same financial and social status. Whether they come from Democrats or Republicans, they are backed by money. Finance is extremely important in American politics. H. L. Mencken says that this is the only society in which virtue has become synonymous with money and that the United States is the only large state ever founded solely on the philosophy of business.

> *The best qualification for a candidate in American politics is the ability to get elected.*

In the course of a campaign, the candidates for both parties will make promises they know they can't keep to the people they think are foolish enough to believe them. What's most important is getting elected. The best qualification for a candidate in American politics is the ability to get elected. Apart from that, everything else becomes secondary.

MOYERS: But, like taxes, isn't politics the price we pay for civilization?

HELLER: We can't eliminate politics. And no one who has enjoyed democracy has knowingly voted for a different system of government. It is congenial, it is entertaining. For you and me, who are among those in this country who are well fed and well housed and who can be reasonably sure that our income will continue and enable us to live as we are living, there's no substitute for democracy. Consider how few the alternatives are.

MOYERS: That's true. But there's a paradox in what you're saying. You talk about our enjoying the system that we live under, and yet it's a little bit like a man who says, "I'm enjoying this train ride, but I'm not going to pay for my ticket." In John Kennedy's election, for example, a change of one vote in every precinct in America would have elected Richard Nixon.

HELLER: That change of one vote in every precinct for the same candidate was unlikely to happen. I'm more cynical than you. You seem to feel that if Richard Nixon had been elected, things would have been much worse.

MOYERS: They would have been different. Who knows what would have happened if JFK had not been assassinated, for example?

HELLER: We can't guess, but I'm inclined to feel that it's something of a sentimental daydream to believe that things would have been significantly different if John Kennedy had not been assassinated.

MOYERS: That's not cynical, it's fatalistic. It's as if our fate is sealed.

HELLER: After studying history for my recent novel *Picture This*, I've come to the conclusion that men don't make history; history makes personalities.

MOYERS: But by refusing to vote you are assaulting a fundamental premise that's been drilled into us in this country—that the individual matters, that the individual counts, that the accumulated effect of our joint expression is to be heard.

HELLER: I do believe the individual is important. But the individual does not count to governments. Governments are not normally concerned with the welfare of the people they govern. Even history is not concerned with them. During Rembrandt's life, the potato was brought over from South America and cultivated successfully in Europe during the Thirty Years' War. The cultivation of the potato was more important to more people than was Rembrandt's painting of Aristotle or William Harvey's discovery of the circulation of blood. The potato gave tens of thousands of people life. You will not read about it.

MOYERS: Good government is that government which not only assures the survival of the republic, but also honors the individual, even when it refuses to flatter him.

HELLER: That would be fine, but then what would its objective be? Would it be to improve the living conditions of the population—or would it be simply to improve the gross national product? We tend to measure progress by profit. That's one way of looking at progress, but it's not the only way. We have more millionaires now than any nation ever had in its history. At the same time, we have more homeless. We have very real problems here, and we don't even seem to agree on what they are.

MOYERS: Why did you go back to ancient Greece for your recent novel?

HELLER: I went back to ancient Greece because I was interested in writing about American life and Western civilization. In ancient Greece I found striking—and grim—parallels.

MOYERS: Grim?

HELLER: Extremely grim. In the war between Sparta and Athens, the Peloponnesian War, I could see a prototype for the Cold War between this country and Russia.

MOYERS: Our popular notion of Greece is of a wise, humane, intelligent, moderate society. Is that what you found?

HELLER: No, I didn't find that at all. In fact, I found that as democracy was instituted, Athens became more chaotic, more corrupt, more warlike. Democracy came to Athens with the rise of Pericles, who favored democracy because he could control it. But commerce was important to Athens, so business leaders then obtained control of the political machinery, and Athens became more and more warlike. No historian blames anyone but Athens for the Peloponnesian War. The government of

Athens was completely chaotic from the time businessmen took over with the death of Pericles. I have part of a chapter in *Picture This* that I like very much, in which I draw on quotations from the plays of Aristophanes. In one play, Aristophanes blames Pericles for starting the war, and blames Athens and Cleon for continuing it. Cleon tried to have Aristophanes jailed for sedition, but he failed. Aristophanes in succeeding years wrote two more antiwar plays. Each one was voted first prize by the population, and each time the population voted to continue the war.

MOYERS: My favorite passage in *Picture This* is a very short one: "The motion in the Athenian assembly to invade Syracuse was deceitful, corrupt, stupid, chauvinistic, irrational and suicidal. It passed by a huge majority." What are you trying to say to us?

HELLER: I'm trying to say that the emotions of people in a democratic society are no more rational than they are in any other type of society. They are manipulated. It is the function of a leader in a democracy, if he wishes to be a leader, to manipulate the emotions and the ideas of the population.

MOYERS: You remind me of the Gulf of Tonkin Resolution passed by Congress in 1964, which in effect gave Lyndon Johnson a blank check to go to war in Vietnam. Congress didn't intend it to be a blank check, but that's how LBJ interpreted it.

HELLER: That's exactly what I'm talking about when I speak of the manipulation of emotions and the engineering of consent. Lyndon Johnson told Congress what had happened at the Gulf of Tonkin. And what he said had happened had not happened. I remember Senator Fulbright saying afterward, "I never believed that the President of the United States would lie to me."

MOYERS: In *Picture This* you say, "There were always factions enraged with each other in Athens, and in all the factions there were men who were just and evil; selfish and generous; vicious and peaceful." What's new?

HELLER: I would not say anything to that. You're getting now to the central theme of *Picture This*. I'm not good at talking about my novels until I've read the reviews, but that's very much what I'm trying to say in it. Things have normally been this bad, and they've never been much better. In what I hope is an amusing way, it's really an extremely pessimistic book. Of course, everybody agrees that the quality of our government is not what it should be. But it's never been much better than it is now, and that could be said of just about every Administration in our history.

MOYERS: Somewhere you say that the history of our country is replete with scandalous government, corrupt government, inefficient government.

HELLER: Yes, I've done some reading on the Constitutional Convention. The bitterness and factionalism there before the Constitution was adopted, the various devices and tricks employed to get Massachusetts to accept the Constitution—that was amusing to me. Within ten years of the adoption of the Constitution, the Alien and Sedition Acts were passed; within less than ten years, the Federalist Party split into the Republican Party of Jefferson and Madison, and the Conservative Party of Alexander Hamilton. Those Virginians and other populists who did not want the Constitution and the Federalists were almost always at each other's throats, and adopted various tricks to win their points. What interested me was that when Alexander Hamilton and others made reference to the democracies of Athens and the popular republics of Italy, it was always in a derogatory way. The word "democracy" does not appear in the Constitution at all. Democracy was always a threat that they wished very much to avoid.

MOYERS: They feared the passions of the mob.

HELLER: They felt that the mob—and that's a word they used—would not know how to vote, would not know where their interests lay. The other fear was that the mob indeed would know where their interests lay, and they would vote for their interests.

One of Plato's severe criticisms of Athenian democracy was that the people would set up a popular leader to champion a popular cause. Now, we would assume this to be the function of a political leader—to give the people what they want. For Plato, that meant a chaotic government. He felt that a government run by the people, responsive to the wishes of the people, would be a government administered by officials who then had no control over public affairs. Give the people what they want, and the leaders will not be controlling government. I think if he were living today, he would see that those fears have been realized. As I said, candidates make promises they know they can't keep to people they feel are gullible enough to believe them, and for the sole purpose of getting elected.

I don't know if things have ever been better, but I do feel that with the advent of television, the nature of politics has changed tremendously. I was young when FDR was running. I had no idea that he was as severely crippled as he was because we never saw him. It probably would have made a difference.

MOYERS: I think the primaries have changed politics more than television. Television is superfluous at the conventions because the primaries have already made the choice.

HELLER: In ancient Athens, every male citizen could attend every meeting of the assembly and did have a direct vote on almost every measure. That was not representative democracy; it was true democracy. It didn't function any more effectively than our own, which has been called representative democracy, but which I don't feel is representative at all. I don't even know who my congressman is, and he doesn't know who I am, and certainly he doesn't care.

One of the themes I had in mind in *Picture This* was that instead of a major person as a character, I would use an idea. The idea was of money and conquest and commerce as being the constants in human history. In *Picture This*, they are always present. When the Dutch were losing to England, they sent their capital and their businessmen to England to organize the Bank of England, Lloyd's of London, the Stock Exchange—demonstrating once again that money follows different laws from the rest of nature. Money goes where it will increase fastest rather than where it's needed, and it has no national loyalties. We've seen that since the end of World War II. It may be that we no longer have to go to war to take possession of a country's resources.

MOYERS: I'm struck by the fact that two men I admire very much as writers— you and I. F. Stone—have both written recently about Socrates.

HELLER: Of course, Stone's picture of Socrates is antithetical to mine.

MOYERS: He pictures Socrates as detesting democracy so much that he refused to defend himself because he would have to appeal to the freedom of speech, which he thought would be vindicating democracy.

HELLER: But Stone goes a little farther in suggesting that Socrates was involved in a plot to overthrow democracy—for which there is no evidence that I could find. The classical scholars who reviewed Stone's book pointed that out as well.

For me, Socrates is appealing in part because he has no reality other than the idealization given him by Plato. Socrates, I was amused to learn, never wrote a word. He was too smart to be a philosopher. He was one of these men that I believe exists in every advanced culture, about whom we never hear, and who are truly the wisest men in the society because they have transcended the human vanity and ambition to be noted for their wisdom. Socrates never wrote a word. Plato's four books dealing with the death of Socrates are famous, particularly the death scene of Socrates and his last words, with which I begin the novel, and with which I end it. I took the portrait of Socrates as presented by Plato, and as he was gossiped about by other writers. Stone took the same material and came up with a different figure. Socrates, like Hamlet, is fascinating because he's so vague, you can see in him whatever you want.

MOYERS: I found what you wrote appealing, that "Socrates would not violate the law to save his life. He did not know if the law was good, but he knew what it was. And he would not flee Athens to avoid his trial or execution."

HELLER: That's why I, too, idealize him, and that's why Plato's *Apology* is one of the imperishable works of Western literature.

MOYERS: When you discover that kind of reverence for the law, it clashes with Richard Nixon and Watergate and Colonel North and John Poindexter and the ethics of Ed Meese.

HELLER: What I say in *Good As Gold* is that politics is important to someone like Bruce Gold, not because of the power so much, but because of the social acceptance, the social prestige of moving with a better class of people. You meet pretty women, you get invited to big parties.

MOYERS: Did you learn anything about our society by looking back at Socrates' time?

HELLER: No, my opinion of this society did not change. But it's not a wholly negative opinion.

MOYERS: It's a paradoxical opinion.

HELLER: Well, if you expect the democratic system of government to provide efficient government, you're going to be disappointed. Again, Hamilton and Jefferson and Carlyle and others assumed that in an industrial society the captains of industry would and should be the political leaders. They assumed that they would be men of intelligence, men of integrity, men of vision, and men who, having achieved wealth, would no longer have the accumulation of wealth as their goal and would be interested in the public good. That has not happened, as we know.

Now if we're going to talk about good government, I will confess that I don't know what good government is or what good government should be, and I don't believe anyone else knows, or that we can reach agreement on it. In a general way, we could say we would prefer a President who does not lie. We would prefer an Administration whose members do not use their position to accumulate more wealth for themselves or their family or friends, and who are not cheats in one way or another. We would like men who are competent, who, having agreed on an objective, are intelligent enough to find new ways to achieve that objective. But beyond that, when we come to what is good government, we have a severe division of opinion that is present in both political parties. One, which we might call the traditional or conservative opinion, believes that the government should do no more than preserve order and defend against foreign attacks and provide every member of our society, now including blacks and women, with an equal opportunity to advance as far as they can, and if they don't succeed, to suffer whatever miseries are inflicted upon them, as happens when we have a recession.

The second view is that the government has an obligation to promote the general welfare and provide for the economic needs of the people to the extent that it can. Those are two different positions, two different philosophies of government. Depending on what the needs are or who's in office, attempts are made to promote the general welfare, but there is always broad disagreement on where the general welfare lies. Now, for example, we are the only Western country that does not have a national health program. At the present time, a large faction of people in the country find it more important to send money to the Contras in Nicaragua than to provide low-cost housing. Concerning New York, I can understand that attitude. Prejudice. The homeless in New York tend to be black and Spanish. But when I was in California a few months ago, the homeless were shown on television. And there they are white, blue-eyed, blond. So homelessness is not just the product of New York City with its masses of people on welfare.

MOYERS: The founders were aware that the highest role of government at times would be to correct excesses and to prevent bad things from happening.

HELLER: Yes, but what would be a bad thing? Forget earthquakes and droughts—what would be a bad thing?

MOYERS: Wars that are fought not in the national interest, but because of some abstraction.

HELLER: What wars have we fought that you and I would agree weren't in the national interest?

MOYERS: I would say that Vietnam was a war that was fought for a marginal—

HELLER: —the only exception that comes to my mind is World War II, and I'm not even sure that the War of Independence was in the national interest. During the Revolutionary War, one third of the people were in favor of the war; one third were against it; and one third didn't care either way.

MOYERS: There's a wonderful passage in *Good As Gold* where Bruce Gold, the professor who's called to Washington, knew that the penultimate stage of a civilization was attained when chaos masqueraded as order. And he knew we were already there. Our political system projects the appearance of order. What do you see behind that mask?

HELLER: I don't see that it projects a system of order.

MOYERS: When you looked at the two conventions this summer, they were organized—

HELLER: Oh, the conventions are organized. Of course. It's like the pregame entertainment to the Super Bowl. The conventions were good. But governing well is an impossible job. Somewhere in *Picture This* I say that Aristotle never conceived that cities would merge into provinces, provinces merge into states, states merge into countries so large as to be ungovernable. New York City is ungovernable by any standard, and I believe the federal government is ungovernable. There are too many factions to please, and self-interest is still, as it almost always has been in history, the most powerful motivation for people.

MOYERS: Do you see no system behind the bureaucratic structures? No governing principle behind government? No organization behind the appearance of things?

HELLER: No.

MOYERS: Is it just chaos?

HELLER: It's not chaos. Thank God for the Bill of Rights, and thank God for the Supreme Court, and thank God for the free press. We are a free people. Most of us are prosperous people. I say most of us, although perhaps close to half the population lives near the poverty level. But that may be better than the situation in most other countries. We do have some wonderful traditions. We don't have a tradition of revolution, and I don't believe we'll ever have another revolution, mainly because revolutions are middle-class phenomena. Revolutions are not conducted by the most underprivileged in a society. They're usually conducted by educated people. When Patrick Henry said, "Give me liberty or give me death," he was living in a part of the world that had more liberty than any other place.

MOYERS: In one sense politics is a substitute for the church. Watch Jesse Jackson's speech at the Democratic Convention or Jerry Falwell's prayer at the Republican Convention. And politics also competes with theater. Politics now provides us with the drama.

HELLER: Isn't it disgusting to realize that there are organizations and specialists who exist in grooming candidates for election to office? They tell candidates what to wear, how to stand, where to sit, what to say. But isn't it equally disgusting that we know about it, and that we're not revolted?

MOYERS: Politics is our national soap opera. We know that we're watching a soap opera, but we watch it and respond to it.

HELLER: Well, you can exclude me. I didn't watch this convention, I didn't watch the last one, and I don't vote because I don't see any point in voting.

MOYERS: Do you give money?

HELLER: Yes, I give money because money may help determine the outcome of the election. But I would never cast a vote. It's useless. It does not accomplish anything. There was a recent editorial in the *New York Times* that talks about the progress of the blacks. It's been almost twenty-five years since the Civil Rights Act was passed, and it quotes figures on how many blacks hold government positions. My response to that: Walk through any big city, or walk through the poorest part of any small town, and then see if the conditions of the blacks have been improved by the fact that they have the right to vote. The exceptional can now get ahead. That's one of the things I love about this country, and I love about democracy. There really are very few official prohibitions on any individual advancing if he's able to do it without violating certain laws. But as a group—maybe close to fifty percent in this country still live near the poverty level.

MOYERS: In *Catch-22* Yossarian decides that the system really is insane, and he becomes a hero by escaping it. He leaves in a rowboat and at the end of the book, is heading for Scandinavia, pulling himself away from the shore. But in *Picture This*, your new book, nobody escapes.

HELLER: In *Catch-22*, Yossarian doesn't escape, he's trying to escape. His choices are: Accept the corruption and benefit by it, join us, become one of the boys, and we'll give you a promotion, we'll send you home a hero; or else, go to prison for refusing to fly more missions; or fly more missions until you're eventually killed. The only way he can assert himself without accepting any of these obnoxious alternatives is through saying no. Now he knows he's not going to get to Sweden. The novel ends with him going out the door.

In *Picture This* the subject is not war so much, although wars are continual in American history and in all Western history. In *Picture This* I say that peace on earth would mean the end of civilization as we know it. There is an element of hope in *Catch-22*, and it ends in a very positive way. *Picture This* doesn't.

MOYERS: Both you and I. F. Stone went back to ancient Greece seeming to look for a simpler golden age, and both of you, after writing your books, appear disillusioned with what you found.

HELLER: Give me more credit. I didn't go back to ancient Athens looking for something better than now. I went back looking for a subject for a good novel. I will say this: To someone who wants to be any kind of artist, but particularly a novelist, there's no better environment in which to work than a democracy. A novel by nature is an adversarial form of expression. It is very critical. It is wonderful to be able to write with complete freedom in this country, to talk to you with absolute freedom and know that each of us could be as insulting to any public official as we wanted to without suffering any official type of punishment.

MOYERS: So the fact that democracy is absurd doesn't make it undesirable.

HELLER: There's no other form of government that we can envision that we would prefer to democracy. We would prefer that we had a better class of public officials than we have, that they were more committed to the responsibilities of their office than to the people who financed their coming to office. Instead, it's as Bruce Gold said in *Good As Gold:* The only responsibility of office is to stay in office.

You know, the ideology of democracy is a perfect ideology. The faults come from the human application. There are parochial loyalties in people—ambition, greed, self-interest. People find loopholes to fight for their own ambitions. We all know that a lie is a vice. We know that greed is a vice. We know that patriotism is a virtue, provided we can define what patriotism is, and provided there's a popular national cause which calls upon it. Let me give you a sentence: "All societies we know of are governed by the selfish interests of the ruling class or classes." Can you think of many countries or societies today to whom that would not apply?

MOYERS: No.

HELLER: That statement was made by Plato in about 380 B.C. in *The Republic.* Can you think of many societies in the interval to whom it would not apply? No to that one also, right? We are living in more dangerous times than the past because our techniques of annihilation have improved. But the nature of society, I'm sorry to say, doesn't seem to have changed much for the better.

MOYERS: In dangerous times many people pray for miracles. And that brings me back to the novel you published in 1979, *God Knows*, the story about David from the Bible. As you yourself have indicated, it's really about the silence of God, the discovery that just when one needs God most, there is no answer. You don't believe in miracles, do you?

HELLER: I don't believe in miracles because it's been a long time since we've had any. I forget who I'm quoting now, maybe Mark Twain, who said, "The longer I live, the longer I begin to doubt the wisdom of God."

MOYERS: But perhaps there's something else behind that silence. Perhaps God is silent because the best way to bring us to our senses, to bring us to accountability and self-deliverance, is to make us see that we have to perform our own miracles. Maybe that's the key to democracy.

HELLER: If that's the best way, by destroying thousands and thousands of human lives, of American, Vietnamese, Nicaraguan—masses, masses, masses of lives—if that's the best way God can find, then I think he'd better resign from office and turn it over to George Bush or Pat Robertson.

No, I can't believe that God would operate like that. I don't think anybody would say that. I think you and I and even professional politicians would agree that an efficient level of government is preferable to an inefficient level. An unselfish Administration is preferable to a selfish Administration. All right-thinking persons would agree on those objectives. The problem we face is how to achieve them.

MOYERS: That's the old dilemma.

HELLER: Well, there's no known way.

MOYERS: You didn't find one in Athens, did you?

HELLER: No, I didn't find one in Athens. At the same time that we are always complaining about the quality of government—and these complaints have existed since government was founded—we delude ourselves and create a kind of pantheon of past presidents. In my own experience, I think that with the exception of FDR in the first four years, we haven't had an exceptional President. Thomas Jefferson and Madison had exceptional minds. Jimmy Carter was outstanding for his good character. But I don't know if the presidential decisions have been that important. I think you would find the same thing if you looked at the history of monarchies. There is no system I can envision that would elevate to public office the kind of people that we would like to see elevated.

MOYERS: Therefore?

HELLER: Therefore, we go on and keep our fingers crossed and hope that things will not get worse than they are. There's almost something contradictory in what I say. I'm one of these people who profit from the profit motive. I deal with money as a phenomenon and an inducement and portray this directly in my books as well. Yet, I'm very conscious of money. I don't sell my books to publishers for a small amount of money. Negotiations are very intense. I know the value. I also know when I have enough. But I also know I'd rather write the books I want to than leave writing and go speculate and double or triple my money.

MOYERS: The theme of *Catch-22* was the perverse nature of human intentions, that the regulations designed to save us wound up strangling us in the end. Yossarian stood up against those. He said his no, as you indicated, and rode out to sea. If he came rowing up out here on the south shore of Long Island this afternoon, what do you think would be the theme of the novel you would now cast about him?

HELLER: If he came rowing up, I would say to him, "Get out of here. Don't destroy a good ending." Probably you would be talking to him now and not to me, wouldn't you?

Noam Chomsky

LINGUIST

Noam Chomsky believes in the blunt scrutiny of national power, arbitrary government, and injustice. He is known around the world for his revolutionary work on the structure of language, studies he has pursued at MIT since 1955. But he is most controversial as a freelance critic of politics and power. He was among the first to protest against the Vietnam war. His most recent book, Manufacturing Consent: The Political Economy of the Mass Media, *discusses the role of propaganda in a democracy.*

MOYERS: You wrote recently that this country is more dissident than you can remember it, more so even than during the Vietnam War. When I read that, my mind went back immediately to that period, to the protests in the streets, the mass demonstrations, the riots on college campuses and in the ghettoes. That period of dissidence is unforgettable. Yet you say we're a more dissident nation now?

CHOMSKY: The dissidence now is much wider and more deeply rooted. It's found in sectors of the population that were excluded from the dissident movements of the 1960s. But to compare the present situation with the late sixties is a little misleading because of the scale of what is being protested. The antiwar movement of the sixties became a significant movement at a time when we had hundreds of thousands of troops attacking South Vietnam and expanding the war to all of Indochina. But until that time the peace movement was very limited. When John F. Kennedy began bombing South Vietnam in 1962, there was no protest. You couldn't get two people in a living room to talk about it. By the time Lyndon Johnson sent an American expeditionary force to—if we were honest with ourselves, we would say to "attack" South Vietnam—we were barely beginning to get protest. As late as mid-1966 here in Boston, which is a pretty liberal city, we had a hard time having public meetings because they'd be broken up, often by students. In fact, it wasn't really until late 1966 and early 1967, when we had about four hundred thousand troops fighting in Vietnam, that we got a large-scale protest movement going.

Now, compare the eighties. When Ronald Reagan came into office, one of the first things he did was lay the basis for direct military intervention in Central America. The white paper of February 1981 was a clear effort to test the waters, to see if you could get the population to support direct dispatch of troops to El Salvador and probable military intervention in Nicaragua. That's roughly comparable to the situation that Kennedy faced in 1961 or even to the late fifties. At that time, intervention could take place without any protest, but as soon as the Reagan people made just the beginnings of an indication that there might be direct military intervention, there were substantial and spontaneous protests from all over the country. There were demonstrations, the churches protested, there were letters to Congress—in fact, the protest was sufficient so that the Administration backed off because they were afraid that it was going to harm the programs that they were really interested in.

MOYERS: And they went underground with it.

CHOMSKY: Yes, in fact, the Reagan Administration was literally driven underground by this population. The scale of clandestine activities is a pretty good measure of domestic dissidence. After all, clandestine activities are a secret from no one except the domestic population.

MOYERS: But it never seemed that as many people were participating in the demonstrations against the Central American policy or that the media were paying as much attention as they did during the Vietnam era.

CHOMSKY: Dissidence does not extend to the media—but of course it didn't in the 1960s, either. The media supported the war enthusiastically. With rare exceptions, the only criticism that you heard of the war in the media was the tactical criticism that it didn't seem to be working. Finally, by 1969 or so, after major sectors of American business had turned against the war and were calling on the Administration to liquidate it as being not worth the cost, you began to get protests in the media. In the case of Central America, media protest has been greater than it was against the Vietnam War at any comparable time, even though the scale of the intervention is far lower. It's true, you don't get huge numbers of people in demonstrations, but that has to be measured against the scale of the atrocities that they're protesting. If you want to compare the sixties and the eighties, you should compare the popular reaction at a time when U.S. intervention was comparable. U.S. intervention in Central America today is comparable to what it was in South Vietnam probably in the late fifties or early sixties, at the latest.

MOYERS: Are you talking only about dissidence toward Central American policies?

CHOMSKY: No, it's much broader. It's a striking fact that on almost every major issue, the population has been quite strongly opposed to the policies of the Reagan Administration. The poll results have been quite consistent about this from the beginning. In fact, apart from a brief period in the very first year of the Administration, when there was support for a military buildup, the population has been basically tending toward classical New Deal positions. It favors social spending over military spending, it favors increased taxes if they are used for improving the environment, education, or social welfare, and it has been quite strongly opposed to direct interventionism. The only exceptions to this are the one-day, quick victories—Grenada and Libya. But anything that has extended even to a limited extent beyond that has encountered public opposition.

MOYERS: Are you saying that a negative poll on an issue constitutes dissidence?

CHOMSKY: No, it only constitutes dissidence if it becomes articulated. On many issues it doesn't become articulated. On Central American policy it did become articulated, and that's what drove the government undergound.

MOYERS: But fifty-five percent of the people in the latest Gallup Poll express approval of President Reagan as he is preparing to leave office, so that you have polls showing opposition to his policies while he himself remains unusually popular in the public standing.

CHOMSKY: If you take a look at comparative poll results, he's not that unusually popular. The popularity of a President is usually predicted quite closely by people's sense of where the economy is going. When people sense that the economy is probably improving, they tend to approve of the President. When they sense that the economy's declining, they tend to disapprove of the President. Reagan himself has been reasonably popular, though not by and large beyond the norm for presidents. On the other hand, his policies have been unpopular, and sometimes this shows up quite dramatically. In the presidential election in 1984, there was a very intriguing exit poll which shows that voters disapproved of Reagan's policies by about three to two. The majority said they hoped his legislative programs would not be enacted. Now these were the people who had just voted for him by two to one. So what's happening?

MOYERS: That's a good question.

CHOMSKY: It's pretty clear what's happening. Look at other studies of public opinion. Every year the Gallup Poll asks people, "Who do you think runs the government?" Consistently, about fifty percent say the government is run by a few big interests looking out for themselves. I suspect that the fifty percent who say that are roughly the fifty percent who don't vote, who tend to be the poor and the dispossessed. They don't participate in the political system.

Reagan is a very interesting political figure, a very natural phenomenon in a capitalist democracy. In a capitalist democracy, you have the problem that the general population participates in the decision-making by participating in politics. The state is not capable of stopping them. You can't shut them out, you can't put them in jail, and you can't keep them away from the polls. It's striking that that has always been perceived as a problem to be overcome. It's called "the crisis of democracy"—too many people organizing themselves to enter the public arena. That's a crisis we have to overcome.

MOYERS: According to a certain view.

CHOMSKY: Well, it's the view of a very wide spectrum. In fact, the crisis of democracy was articulated by the group of people around Jimmy Carter.

MOYERS: The Trilateral Commission—

CHOMSKY: —and the report they put out called "The Crisis of Democracy." That report reflects attitudes that go way back. Even the mainstream democratic theorists have always understood that when the voice of the people is heard, you're in trouble, because these stupid and ignorant masses, as they're called, are going to make the wrong decisions. So, therefore, we have to have what Walter Lippmann, back in 1920 or so, called "manufacture of consent." We have to ensure that actual power is in the hands of what he called a specialized class—us smart guys, who are going to make the right decisions. We've got to keep the general population marginalized because they're always going to make mistakes. The Founding Fathers had very strong feelings in this respect. The Federalists, for example, were very much afraid of popular democracy.

MOYERS: That's why we have a representative form of government.

CHOMSKY: The transition from the confederation to the constitutional system marginalized the public. Shays' Rebellion was probably the last reflection of the popular democracy of the earlier period.

MOYERS: You said Reagan is interesting as a political figure. Why?

CHOMSKY: Because from a point of view which perceives democracy as a problem to be overcome, and sees the right solution as being farsighted leaders with a specialized class of social managers—from that point of view, you must find means of marginalizing the population.

MOYERS: Marginalizing?

CHOMSKY: Reducing them to apathy and obedience, allowing them to participate in the political system, but as consumers, not as true participants. You allow them a method for ratifying decisions that are made by others, but you eliminate the methods by which they might first, inform themselves; second, organize; and third, act in such a way as to really control decision-making. The idea is that our leaders control us, we don't control them. That is a very widespread view, from liberals to conservatives. And how do you achieve this? By turning elected offices into ceremonial positions. If you could get to the point where people would essentially vote for the Queen of England and take it seriously, then you would have gone a long way toward marginalizing the public. We've made a big step in that direction.

MOYERS: The President as ceremonial leader.

CHOMSKY: Yes. That's why Reagan is so interesting. Although a lot of intellectuals put the best face they can on it, most of the population knows that Ronald Reagan had only the foggiest ideas of what the policies of his Administration were. Nobody much cared. The Democrats were always surprised that he could get away with these bloopers and crazy statements and so on. The reason is that much of the population understood very well that they were supporting someone like the Queen of England or the flag. The Queen of England opens Parliament by reading a political program, but nobody asks whether she understands it or believes it.

MOYERS: So many books from within the Reagan Administration—from the Stockman book to the Regan book to the new book that's on the newsstands—say that the President was detached from the decision-making process.

CHOMSKY: More than detached. I think he doesn't know what it is.

MOYERS: He's performing well the ritualistic role.

CHOMSKY: It's the flag. To the extent that you feel good about the way things are going, you'll say, "I like the flag, I like the Queen," and so on. To the extent that you don't like the way things are going, you'll say, "I'm unhappy about it," and so on. But this is quite dissociated from your positions as to what ought to be done.

> This is a very free country. . . . But we don't make use of those freedoms.

We have an interesting political system in the United States, one that's different from those of the other industrial democracies. This is a very free country. By comparative standards, the state is very restricted in its capacity to coerce and control us. The police can't come in and stop us from talking, for example.

MOYERS: You're saying we are free as individuals—we can say anything we want to, for example.

CHOMSKY: But we don't make use of those freedoms. Sophisticated mechanisms have been devised to prevent us from making use of those freedoms. In a society where the state does not have the power to coerce, other mechanisms must be found to ensure that the population doesn't get in the way—indoctrination, for example, or elimination of popular organizations like unions. To have ideas, to interchange those ideas with others, to turn these ideas into possible programs, and to press for those programs—all this takes access to information. It takes an independent media. It requires organizations by which isolated people can group together.

MOYERS: Political parties.

CHOMSKY: Active political parties and political clubs. Unions have often played this role in other countries. The United States is unusual in the extent to which all of these structures are weak. The level of unionization is extremely low and in the Reagan period has declined even further. Furthermore, American unions have always been basically apolitical. We're the only major industrial democracy that doesn't have a labor-based political party—a party based on the poor or the working class. We have only one political party—it's the business party.

> *We're the only major industrial democracy that doesn't have a labor-based political party—a party based on the poor, or the working class.*

We have two factions of the business party called the Democrats and Republicans. In the 1980s, the Democrats have been accused of being a party of the special interests. They say no, they're not the party of the special interests. But who are the special interests? Well, take a look behind the rhetoric, and you find that the special interests are women, labor, youth, the elderly, ethnic minorities, the poor, and farmers. In fact, it's almost the entire population. The one group that's never identified as being among the special interests is corporations. They're the national interest. Both parties are basically beholden to them. The special interests—the people—have to be marginalized. So everyone denies that they represent the special interests—that is, the people.

MOYERS: Corporations? Or the capitalist business system whose first priority is profit-making for the general welfare, as its defenders say?

CHOMSKY: The chairman of the board will always tell you that he spends his every waking hour laboring so that people will get the best possible products at the cheapest possible price and work in the best possible conditions. But it's an institutional fact, independent of who the chairman of the board is, that he'd better be trying to maximize profit and market share, and if he doesn't do that, he's not going to be chairman of the board any more. If he were ever to succumb to the delusions that he expresses, he'd be out. Some in Walter Lippmann's specialized class—the experts—are candid enough to tell you the truth. Henry Kissinger defined an expert as a person who is capable of articulating the consensus of people with power. That's true. If you want to be an expert, you have to be able to serve the interests of objective power. If you want to be a journalist, you have to respond to the needs of the institutions. The major media are—

MOYERS: —they're corporations, too.

CHOMSKY: They're just like any other business. They have a product and a market. The product is audiences, and the market is other businesses. They sell their product to advertisers—that's what keeps them going. Fundamentally, the media are major corporations selling relatively privileged audiences to other businesses, so it's not very surprising to discover that those are the interests they reflect. The managers and editors are very privileged themselves. They share associations and concerns with other privileged people. There's a close interaction and a flow of people between corporate boardrooms, government decision-making centers, and media. Without government coercion, the independent media tend to accept as the framework for discussion the interests, concerns, and perspectives of the privileged sectors of the society.

That's true of the information system, and it's also true of the political system. The distribution of resources alone determines it. As other modes of organization and articulate expression have declined, isolated individuals find themselves marginalized, and they end up by voting for a ceremonial figure, if they bother to vote at all.

MOYERS: Are you suggesting that there's a conspiracy—that there are people who gather and decide we're going to eliminate unions, we're going to eliminate popular participation in political parties, we're going to do this and that?

CHOMSKY: My point is exactly the opposite. For example, there's no conspiracy in a board of managers that it tries to raise profits. In fact, if the managers didn't pursue that program, they wouldn't be in business any longer. It's part of the structure of the social system and the way in which the institutions function within it, that they will be trying to maximize profit, market share, decision-making capacity, and so on.

MOYERS: Doing what comes naturally.

CHOMSKY: You might say it comes naturally because they would never have gotten to that point unless they had internalized those values. But it's also constrained. If they stop doing it, their stock is going to decline.

Now pretty much the same is true of these other institutions. Suppose we had an authentic political party reflecting the needs of the special interests—the population. It would not be supported. It would be denounced by the information system, condemned for being anti-American or subversive. It would not even have the minimal resources to keep functioning. Or suppose that some journal emerged which reflected the concerns of the special interests or seriously challenged the elite consensus on some important issue—let's say the war in Vietnam. Suppose there was some journal that had called that what it was, namely, a U.S. attack against South Vietnam. Or suppose there was some journal in the country that thought that the real Iran-Contra scandal was not these various shenanigans, but the fact that the United States was in blatant violation of international law—as it was, and nobody cared. Or suppose some journal were to focus on the fact we are in a tiny minority, worldwide, in our opposition to arms control. All you have to do is look at the U.N. votes to find that right in the middle of the summit, when everybody's focusing on the INF treaty, the United Nations had a series of resolutions on the militarization of outer space, on the creation of new weapons with mass destructive capabilities, on a comprehensive test ban, and so on. The United States was outvoted by numbers like 154 to 1, or 135 to 2, and so on. Most of this wasn't even reported, incidentally. But suppose that some journal were to focus on these facts and say what they mean. Suppose that some journal were to point out that far from supporting democracy in Central America, we have been creating terror states which have destroyed the possibility of democracy. Suppose that issues of this nature were to be articulated. That journal would not long survive because it would not have the resources to survive. Resources come from the source of real power in the country—from ownership. Those who own the productive assets of the country ultimately have the capacity to determine what else functions. Now such a journal could survive if it had mass popular support and didn't have to rely on advertising and the financial markets.

MOYERS: If each reader subscribed.

CHOMSKY: But we've overcome that possibility by the isolation of individuals and by the elimination of organizations that might bring individuals together. If we want to get more insight into this, it's good to look behind us in this process. This is a perfectly natural process under a capitalist industrial democracy. Take a country like England, which is maybe a generation behind us in this respect. England still has a labor-based party, the Labor Party. It's a mildly reformist party. When it's in office, it doesn't do anything very different. But to some extent, it reflects the interests of the poor and the working class—the majority of the population. But it's declining. Up until the 1960s England had a substantial labor-based press. The *Daily Herald*, for example, was one of the major newspapers in England up until the 1960s. It had more readers than the *Times*, and the *Guardian*, and the *Financial Times* combined. That paper and other social democratic papers gave a different view of the world. They responded to different values, to different concerns—not, for example, to the value of maximizing personal gain, but to values such as solidarity and support for others. They recognized that productive workers had a right to a share of what they produced and of decision-making that they didn't have.

Now those different values are articulated and expressed on a regular basis. That journal and the other social democratic journals disappeared, primarily because of standard market pressures. They couldn't get advertising. Their advertising rates were too low because they had the wrong kind of readers. They couldn't reach the capital markets for support, not because they didn't appeal to people, but because they had the wrong ideas. They disappeared. Now there's no conspiracy in that. Those are the workings of power.

MOYERS: All right, you bring me back to Ronald Reagan. Why do you think President Reagan is foreshadowing what is coming politically? Why do you think he's the beginning of something?

CHOMSKY: He's just one aspect of a much more general process of marginalizing the public and ensuring that the stupid and ignorant masses, as they are called, don't interfere. Harold Lasswell, a major political scientist, in an article in the *International Encyclopedia of the Social Sciences*, back in 1933, said that we should not succumb to democratic dogmatism. We should not believe that men are the best judges of their own interests. People in general are ignorant and stupid, so we have to ensure that leaders make those decisions. Since the state does not have the power to coerce, it needs other means. He recommended propaganda. Those were more naive days.

MOYERS: Sixty years ago, when Walter Lippmann talked about the manufacturing of consent, a title not unlike your new book, he suggested that this could mark a radical change in democracy.

CHOMSKY: He said it's a revolution in the art of democracy.

MOYERS: Do you think that's happened?

CHOMSKY: It's gradually happening. Up until the 1930s there was a lively working-class culture in the United States. That's a thing we tend to forget. The unions had an enormous growth in the 1930s, but since the Second World War, they've been increasingly marginalized.

MOYERS: Isn't that because many times they got what they were after—a higher standard of living for the family?

CHOMSKY: They got that, to an extent, for union workers. But the question is, should that be what they're after? Or should they be after a different kind of a society based on different values, different concerns, and different needs? I think they should. If human civilization is going to survive, the population will have to become organized to support different values.

One part of this general process of marginalization is removing elective office from popular control. If you could achieve that, you'd have achieved a lot. In this respect the creation of the ceremonial President is a big step forward.

Over the years, elections have become public relations operations, largely stage-managed. Candidates decide what to say on the basis of tests that determine what the effect will be across the population. Somehow people don't see how profoundly contemptuous that is of democracy.

> *. . . elections have become public relations operations. . . . Somehow people don't see how profoundly contemptuous that is of democracy.*

MOYERS: Contemptuous?

CHOMSKY: Suppose I'm running for office, and I don't tell people what I think or what I'm going to do, I tell them what the pollsters have told me is going to get me elected. That's expressing utter contempt for the electorate. That's saying, "Okay, you people are going to have the chance to push your buttons, but once you're done, I'll do exactly what I intend, which is not what I'm telling you."

If you express what you believe, you don't have to ask what the polls tell you.

MOYERS: If you conduct polls to tell you what people want, and they tell you, are you not listening to the voice of the people?

CHOMSKY: Only if that changes your mind. But of course the system is based on the assumption that it doesn't change your mind, it changes what you say. In other words, a political figure is not testing the waters and saying, okay, that's what I believe. If we had that kind of a political figure, we wouldn't bother voting for him. The political figure is not a barometer—he represents something, and he's supported by certain interests and has certain commitments. Now the political figure comes before us and tells us things which the pollsters have told him will increase his chances of gaining office. After the election, he will do what is demanded of him by those who provided him with resources. This has always been true, but what is interesting now is the extent to which it is recognized to be the democratic system. It is recognized that we don't care what we say. We don't express interests. What we do is reflect power. And so we have a candidate who's rehearsed in the answers that he's supposed to give. The debates, so-called, are basically stage-managed public relations operations.

We see the effects of this in the remarkable decline of the level of what is said. This jingoist flag-waving has a tinge of 1930s populist fascism about it. We don't like to say it, but Hitler was a very popular leader. If he'd bothered to run an election, he probably would have won it. He used populist techniques—appealing to the population, but on the basis of chauvinistic and racist premises. Now we're beginning to see elements of that in the demeaning of the concept of patriotism by reducing it to coerced pledges of allegiance to the flag. That's astonishing. The fact that a political candidate can stand up in public and call someone a card-carrying member of the ACLU—that means his advisers or the people who write his words for him are telling him support for the Constitution is subversive. The ACLU is an organization which supports constitutional rights. The phrase "card-carrying" is a way of implying, of course, that it's somehow subversive. All of these things reflect the general vacuity of the discussion. They are just parallel modes of marginalizing the public.

MOYERS: Of reducing the importance of the individual and the individual's participation in the political process.

CHOMSKY: We're even proceeding beyond the point where people can ratify decisions made by others. We're simply being asked to elect ceremonial figures who will then be a surface for the interests behind the scenes that are conducting policy.

MOYERS: I once interviewed Edward Bernays, the pioneering figure in American business public relations. He talked about "the engineering of consent."

CHOMSKY: Yes, he thought it was a wonderful thing. In fact, he described it as the essence of democracy.

MOYERS: The effort to persuade people to see things your way.

CHOMSKY: He said the essence of democracy is that we have the freedom to persuade. But who has the freedom to persuade? Well, who runs the public relations industry? It's not the special interests—they're the targets of the public relations industry. The public relations industry is a major industry, closely linked to other corporations. Those are the people who have the power to persuade and who engineer the consent of others.

MOYERS: A vice president at AT&T in 1909 said that he thought the public mind was the chief danger to the company. What did he mean by that?

CHOMSKY: The general public might have funny ideas about corporate control. For example, people who really believe in democracy, people who take eighteenth-century values seriously, people who really might merit the term conservatives are against concentration of power. The Enlightenment held that individuals should be free from the coercion of concentrated power. The kind of concentrated power they were thinking about was the church, the state, the feudal system, and so on. But in the subsequent period, a new form of power developed—namely, corporations—with highly concentrated power over decision-making in economic life. We should not be forced simply to rent ourselves to the people who own the country and its institutions. Rather, we should play a role in determining what those institutions do. That's democracy.

MOYERS: That is the premise of your whole view, is it not? That in democracy the people should initiate—?

CHOMSKY: They should run their own organization, whether it's a community or a union.

MOYERS: Should corporations be run by their shareholders?

CHOMSKY: No, they should be run by the employees. I don't think there should be shareholders. The very idea of shareholders reflects the conception of the wealthy getting more votes than the poor—a lot more votes, in fact. If we were to move toward democracy, even in the eighteenth-century sense, there would be no maldistribution of power in determining what's produced, what's distributed, and what's invested. That's a problem for the entire community. In fact, unless we move in that direction, human society probably isn't going to survive.

MOYERS: Why not?

CHOMSKY: We now face the most awesome problems of human history—nuclear conflict and the destruction of our fragile environment. They're of a level of seriousness that they never were in the past.

MOYERS: But why do you think more democracy is the answer?

CHOMSKY: More democracy is a value in itself. Democracy as a value doesn't have to be defended any more than freedom has to be defended. It's an essential feature of human nature that people should be free, should be able to participate, and should be uncoerced.

> *More democracy is a value in itself.*

MOYERS: But why do you think if we go that route—

CHOMSKY: —that's the only hope that other values will come to the fore. If the society is based on control by private wealth, it will reflect the values that it, in fact, does reflect now—greed and the desire to maximize personal gain at the expense of others. A small society based on that principle is ugly, but it can survive. A global society based on that principle is headed for massive destruction. We have to have a mode of social organization that reflects other values inherent in human nature. It's not the case that in the family every person tries to maximize personal gain at the expense of others. If they do, it's pathological. It's not the case that if you and I are walking down the street, and we see a child eating a piece of candy, and we see that nobody's around, and we happen to be hungry, that we steal the candy. Concern for other people's needs and concern for our fragile environment that must sustain future generations are part of human nature. But these elements are suppressed in a social system which is designed to maximize personal gain. We must try to overcome that suppression. That's, in fact, what democracy could bring about. It could lead to the expression of other human needs and values which tend to be suppressed under the institutional structure of a system of private power and profit.

MOYERS: But by your own analysis, we're moving in the other direction.

CHOMSKY: Certainly the institutions are moving toward more centralization, more marginalization, the elimination of options, and so on. On the other hand, the population itself is increasingly dissident.

MOYERS: What's the evidence for that other than the polls?

CHOMSKY: Something much more striking than the polls are the events of the 1980s. In the 1980s the government was driven underground. It was forced to undertake large-scale clandestine activities because the domestic population would not tolerate those activities overtly. The Reagan Administration is the first Administration to have created anything like the State Department Office of Public Diplomacy.

MOYERS: I have to tell you, the Kennedy Administration, the Johnson Administration, and the Nixon Administration all engaged in domestic propaganda.

CHOMSKY: Yes, but there's a substantial increase in scale under Reagan. The Reagan Administration had a massive enterprise to control the public mind. In fact, when this was partially exposed during the Iran-Contra hearings, one high Administration official described it as the kind of operation that you carry out in enemy territory. That expresses the Administration's attitude toward the population—the population is the enemy. You've got to control enemy territory, and by very extensive public diplomacy—meaning propaganda. Sure, propaganda has always been there, but there's a qualitative change in the resources and intelligence drawn upon to ensure that the enemy territory is controlled. When John F. Kennedy sent the American Air Force to start bombing South Vietnam in 1962, he didn't have to keep it secret. It was on the front page of the *New York Times*, and nobody cared. When Johnson sent twenty thousand Marines to the Dominican Republic to prevent a democratic revival there, it wasn't secret. When Johnson sent hundreds of thousands of troops to invade South Vietnam, it wasn't secret. When we subverted the only free election in Laos in 1959, it wasn't secret. Nobody ever cared about these things. The population was really marginalized. That changed as a result of the popular movements of the sixties, which had a dramatic and lasting effect on the country.

MOYERS: You keep coming back, though, to the opposition to our Central American policies, so I have to keep coming back to asking: What's the evidence of other dissidence?

CHOMSKY: In the early sixties there was nothing like an environmental movement or a feminist movement. There was an antinuclear movement, but it was a few people sitting in a room somewhere. It's now a movement so vast that it got something like seventy-five percent support for a nuclear freeze. It couldn't do anything with that support, but that's because the organizational structure was lacking.

But all of these developments are extremely significant. In the 1960s the churches were either supportive of government military intervention or else quiescent. Now it's very different.

MOYERS: But the Civil Rights movement was driven by religious folk.

CHOMSKY: I don't think that's true. The Civil Rights movement was driven by people like the SNCC organizers.

MOYERS: Martin Luther King was himself a Baptist minister.

CHOMSKY: The Civil Rights movement did have wide-scale support, even business support. But the thrust of the Civil Rights movement was not directed against the interests of centralized power in the United States. The protest against the war, or the environmental movement, and the feminist movement in many respects are directed against power. Those movements didn't exist in the sixties.

MOYERS: You're saying there's more democracy today?

CHOMSKY: On the one hand, there's a lot more popular expression of democracy; on the other hand, it's less and less a part of the actual institutions of the system. I can see it in my own life. Over the last couple of years, the demands on me to speak have escalated beyond anything imaginable. And the audiences are interested and thoughtful, and include parts of the population that you couldn't have talked to years ago. Others who are doing similar things notice it, too.

MOYERS: I don't see you on television, and I don't see your books reviewed.

CHOMSKY: Even in that respect, there's an illusion that years ago things were different. It's not true. There's limited exposure for dissidents, but it's more than it was. It's more than it was in the sixties, for example. I wouldn't have been on a program like this in the late 1960s, that's for certain. And while my books will sometimes be reviewed today, the ones I wrote some years ago almost never were.

MOYERS: Do you think you're more tolerated today?

CHOMSKY: Yes, partly because my positions are less out of the mainstream as the mainstream changes.

MOYERS: But there's a paradox here. You say you're invited to speak constantly and people are listening to you, but at the same time the political process itself is not listening.

CHOMSKY: It's listening, but in its own way. It's not listening by giving us the opportunity to express ourselves and control its policies, it's listening by going underground when it can't convince us. In 1981, when the Reagan Administration flew their trial balloon, they listened and discovered that military intervention was not going to play. We know they listened because they then resorted to secrecy in carrying out clandestine activities so as to prevent the domestic enemy from knowing what they were doing. There's a lot of ferment, and the people who have power have to respond to it. Remember, even a totalitarian state—and we're very far from that— has to pay attention to public opinion. Hitler's main economic adviser, Albert Speer, is very, very interesting on this topic. He says in his memoirs that Nazi Germany was unable to become a real, functioning totalitarian state during the war. He says it was less able to do so than England and the United States, because in England and the United States the government trusted its population, and the population was willing and committed, and accepted what amounted to totalitarian structures to win the war. In Germany the government never trusted their own population, so they had to buy them off. Speer claims that that set back the German war effort by maybe a year or two, which may have made them lose the war.

Now the United States began to face that problem in the sixties. Johnson was unable to declare a national mobilization of the kind that was carried out in the 1940s. The result was that the economic system began to be injured. If they had carried out a true national mobilization of the 1940s type, it probably would have helped the economy, as it did in the 1940s. But this kind of guns-and-butter war, a war fought on deficit financing, buying off the dissident public by making them promises because you can't trust them—that's harmful. It led to stagflation and ultimately to the point where corporate leaders pressured to call off the war because it was harming the U.S. economy vis-à-vis its industrial rivals.

That was a victory for dissidents, for the peace movement. In many ways that's continued into the seventies and eighties. It's led on the one hand to much more sophisticated propaganda and public diplomacy and to intensive efforts by the media to narrow debate and discussion. On the other hand, this ferment from below is always interfering. Take journalism, for example. People have filtered into the system who came out of this dissident culture, and they're hard to control.

MOYERS: A lot of people complain that the media are unpatriotic, disloyal, too liberal.

CHOMSKY: That's an interesting complaint because if you take the actual incidents and cases, what you find is that the media are remarkably subservient to power. There are people for whom subservience isn't enough—you have to actually grovel. They're the ones who call the media unpatriotic.

We go through a lot of such cases of media criticism in our book. The most interesting is the coverage of the Tet Offensive. Freedom House did a big two-volume study accusing the press of virtually losing the war because of its adversarial contempt for power. But if you look through that material carefully, you find quite a different picture. You find that the media kept entirely to the framework of government assumptions. The media reporting of the war at the time of the Tet Offensive was probably a little more accurate than American intelligence, but it was basically the same, except that it was more optimistic for American goals, because it was taking the government's public statements seriously and didn't know what intelligence was saying in the background. We know that, thanks to Ellsberg and others and the *Pentagon Papers*. The basis of the Freedom House critique comes down to the argument that the media should not only accept the whole framework of government falsification and perversion of the facts, and it should not only talk about us as defending the country we're attacking, it should do so with great enthusiasm. If it's not upbeat enough about what's going on, then it's unpatriotic. Now that's demanding a very high standard of subservience to the state.

MOYERS: So you meant it when you said that the state and the media act in cahoots to sustain the interests of the superpower they serve?

CHOMSKY: They don't always act in cahoots, but they reflect the same domestic interests. There is often a tactical debate among elites. Take Nicaragua, for example. There's been a consensus among the power elites about what to do. The consensus is, we have to block the Sandinista programs, not for the reasons that are given, but because they might be successful. The Sandinistas were diverting resources to the poor majority, and that's unacceptable. They were not paying appropriate concern to the needs of investors, including American investors. They were what George Shultz calls a cancer. They were raising the threat of what secret documents call nationalism—the kind of nationalist regime that is responsive to the needs of its own population and that we never tolerate, for obvious reasons. No great power ever tolerates those. So we have to stop it. On that there's a consensus. The only debate is about how to do it. On the one hand, the hawks say we have to stop them by violence. On the other hand, the doves say violence isn't working, so we have to find some other way, as Senator Alan Cranston says, to get them to fester in their own juices or to impose regional standards on them. No one argues that we have to impose regional standards on El Salvador, or Guatemala, or Honduras—states which are under military control, in effect, and which serve the interests of the local oligarchy and business and foreign investors while they are torturing and murdering and suppressing their own population. That's already fine; we don't have to impose any regional standards on them.

But on Nicaragua, we have to impose regional standards—if not by force, then by some other way. They have to conform to the Central American mode, as the *Washington Post* put it. I've done a lot of media studies on this. In the opinion columns and news reports, you find close to a hundred percent agreement that the Sandinista regime is intolerable. There's virtual agreement that they don't have an elected president, whereas El Salvador and Guatemala do have elected presidents. That's remarkable. It requires something like a kind of voluntary totalitarianism to say this, since plainly they had an election which had plenty of flaws but was certainly freer than the ones in El Salvador and Guatemala. There's plenty of international testimony to that effect.

But we have a consensus that they didn't have an election, and they don't have an elected President, so we've got to undermine them. The terror states, on the other hand, are just fine. They're flawed democracies, but democracies, and so on. On that there's a consensus, and you find virtually no deviation from it in the media.

MOYERS: If that's so, why did so many journalists go down there and come back with stories of what the Contras were doing?

CHOMSKY: It's very striking that they didn't.

MOYERS: There were many who did.

CHOMSKY: Again, I've reviewed this in detail. The coverage of Contra atrocities has been extremely low, just as coverage of atrocities in El Salvador and Guatemala has been low. On the other hand, there's been an intense focus on Sandinista repression—which falls far below that of the Contras or of El Salvador or Guatemala.

MOYERS: You're saying that the primary function of the mass media is to mobilize public support for the interests that dominate the government and the private sector. But that's not how the media see it. We claim that our news judgments rest on unbiased, objective criteria.

CHOMSKY: The chairman of the board also sees what he's doing as service to humanity.

MOYERS: You mean like a lobster in the trap, we can't see it close behind us?

CHOMSKY: You don't make it to a high position in the media, whether as columnist or managing editor, unless you've already internalized the required values, unless you already believe that the United States is unique in history in that it acts from benevolent motives. Now benevolent motives are not properties of states, whether it's the United States or any other state. The United States acts because of the interests of groups that have power within it, like any other society—but anyone who believes this truism is already excluded. You have to believe that whatever the United States does is defensive. If we bomb South Vietnam, we're defending South Vietnam. But of course if the Russians invade Afghanistan, that's not defense, although the Politburo would tell you they're defending Afghanistan against terrorists supported from the outside. They'll even tell you they were invited in. There's an element of truth to that, but we naturally dismiss it as nonsense.

On the other hand, when we create a government in South Vietnam to invite us in, and we attack the population of South Vietnam, and we bomb people to drive them into concentration camps so we can separate them from the guerrillas, we're defending South Vietnam. Anyone who doesn't agree with this is not part of the system.

MOYERS: You're equating the Soviet Union and the United States. Jeanne Kirkpatrick and others would say the fundamental fallacy of your approach is that you see a moral equivalency—

CHOMSKY: —I don't say anything of the kind. The Soviet Union and the United States are at opposite poles among contemporary political systems. What I'm saying is that even though they're at opposite poles, in some respects they behave alike, for deep-seated reasons that have to do with the exercise of power and institutions. That has nothing to do with moral equivalence.

MOYERS: You do admit that we are a free society.

CHOMSKY: I not only admit it, I insist upon it. I insist that we are a free society, and that the Soviet Union is a dungeon, and that therefore we have completely different methods of population control. In fact, I've written a lot about this. There's no moral equivalence here. No state is truly totalitarian, but as we move toward the totalitarian end of the spectrum, the technique is roughly that satirized by Orwell. You have a ministry of truth that announces official truths. People can believe it or not. Nobody cares very much. It's sufficient that they obey. Totalitarian states don't really care what people think, because they always have a club at hand to beat them over the head if they do the wrong thing.

MOYERS: They force people to do what they want them to do.

CHOMSKY: People can think what they like in private, but they'd better do what we tell them in public. That's the model toward which totalitarian states tend. As a result, the propaganda may not be too effective. On the other hand, democratic states can't use those mechanisms. Since you can't force people, you have to control what they think. You have to have more sophisticated forms of indoctrination.

MOYERS: That's what you meant when you said, "Propaganda is to democracy what violence is to the totalitarian state." What form does the propaganda take in a democratic society?

CHOMSKY: The basic way it works is by taking certain assumptions, which express the basic ideas of the propaganda system, and then allowing debate, but only within the framework of those assumptions. The debate, therefore, enhances the strength of the assumptions. Take the Vietnam War, for example. In the Vietnam War there was an assumption that was shared among elites, but not by the general population: namely, "We are defending South Vietnam in the interest of democracy and freedom."

MOYERS: I can tell you, that's what Lyndon Johnson honestly thought.

CHOMSKY: I'm sure every editor thought it, too. I have found virtually no exception to this pattern in twenty-five years of study of the media. No one describes the United States' attack against South Vietnam as what it was. We can describe the Russian invasion of Afghanistan as what it was. But the American invasion of South Vietnam was defense. Even when we were wiping the population out, even when we were blocking the political system and so on, it was always defense, and to that, there's no deviation. That's the assumption.

Now, within that assumption, you have a debate between the hawks and the doves. As is the case now in Nicaragua, the hawks said, "Look, if we use enough violence, we'll win." And the doves said, "I hope you're right, but I don't think you are. I think no matter how much violence we use, it's going to cost us too much, or it's going to be too bloody," or something like that. Now the debate is encouraged, and even gives the impression that there's a dispute. There is a sort of a dispute, but it's merely a tactical dispute within shared assumptions.

What was particularly striking about the Vietnam case is that a large majority of the population came to deny the assumption. By around 1970, and even up until today, a substantial majority of the population says that the war was not a mistake, it was fundamentally wrong and immoral. But anyone who accepted that view was not part of the discussion, even though it came to be accepted by two thirds or more of the population. Here is a striking case where the propaganda system and the attitudes among elites became very distinct from those among the general population. The propaganda wasn't working. That's the crisis in democracy, in fact—to overcome the problem that the people are out of control.

MOYERS: If all this ferment is going on, if there is more dissidence now than you can remember, why do you go on to write that the people feel isolated?

CHOMSKY: Much of the general population recognizes that the organized institutions do not reflect their concerns and interests and needs. They do not feel that they participate meaningfully in the political system. They do not feel that the media are telling them the truth or even reflect their concerns. They go outside of the organized institutions to act. So on the one hand you have a lot of popular ferment and a lot of dissidence, sometimes very effective. On the other hand you have a remoteness of the general public from the functioning institutions.

MOYERS: We see more and more of our elected leaders and know less and less of what they're doing.

CHOMSKY: The presidential elections are hardly ever taken seriously as involving a matter of choice. Congress, especially the House, is more responsive to public opinion than higher levels, but even here the rate of electoral victory by incumbents is in the high nineties. That's a way of saying that there aren't any elections.

MOYERS: You get those sorts of election results in Communist and totalitarian states.

CHOMSKY: It means that something else is happening, not choice. Options are not being presented. You have a complex situation in the United States. A cleavage is taking place between a rather substantial part of the population and elite elements.

MOYERS: But those elite elements are supported by a substantial part of the population. There are people who take the debates seriously, who go out and vote, who believe they're participating in a legitimate exercise of democracy.

CHOMSKY: It's not a cleavage at the point of revolution. It's not as if you had an aristocracy facing a mass population. It's not Iran in 1978. It's split and complex and fluid—you can see tendencies toward popular marginalization from functioning institutions, and the abstraction of those institutions from public participation, or even from reflection of the public will.

MOYERS: Now put that in the vernacular. That means what?

CHOMSKY: It means that the political system increasingly functions without public input. It means that to an increasing extent not only do people not participate in decision-making, they don't even take the trouble of ratifying the decisions presented to them. They assume the decisions are going on independently of what they may do in the polling booth.

MOYERS: Ratification means—

CHOMSKY: Ratification would mean a system in which there are two positions presented to me, the voter. I go into the polling booth, and I push one or another button, depending on which of those positions I want. Now, that's a very limited form of democracy. In a really meaningful democracy, I'd play a role in forming those positions. Those positions would reflect my active, creative participation—not just me, but everyone, of course. That would be real democracy. We're very far from that. But now we're even departing from the point where there is ratification. When you have stage-managed elections, with the public relations industry determining what words come out of people's mouths, even the element of ratification is disappearing. You don't expect the candidates to stand for anything, you simply expect them to say what the public relations expert tells them will get them past the next obstacle. The population expects Ronald Reagan to have memorized his lines.

MOYERS: I don't understand why the candidates for President don't take the campaign back from the media. Instead of having questions from journalists, they should want to sit like this and talk about abortion, foreign policy—

CHOMSKY: That would allow the population the option of ratification at least. We could find out what this person really believes and decide whether we want that. These are among the concrete examples of how the institutions are less and less structures in which people meaningfully participate.

MOYERS: They see them like a mountain range they will never climb.

CHOMSKY: However, at the very same time people are complex creatures. If they can't organize and act and express their interests and their needs through formal institutions, they'll do it in other ways. To a large extent they are. So that's why I think you have this complex system. There's an increasing cleavage between articulate intellectual opinion and public opinion. The articulate intelligentsia have taken part in this so-called right turn of the 1970s and '80s. They've articulated and expressed it. But I don't think the population has. In fact, they less and less feel that the organized intellectuals are expressing what's on their minds, or helping them clarify what they think. Now that's hard to prove, but it's a sense I have about what's going on now.

MOYERS: What do we do about it? I don't want to leave people with a wholly negative analysis. You have said that we live entangled in webs of endless deceit, that we live in a highly indoctrinated society where elementary truths are easily buried.

CHOMSKY: I do believe that.

MOYERS: What elementary truths are buried?

CHOMSKY: The fact that we invaded South Vietnam. The fact that we are standing in the way, and have stood in the way for years, of significant moves toward arms negotiation. The fact that the military system is to a substantial extent a mechanism by which the general population is compelled to provide a subsidy to high-technology industry. Since they're not going to do it if you ask them to, you have to deceive them into doing it. There are many truths like that, and we don't face them.

MOYERS: How do we extricate ourselves from this web of endless deceit?

CHOMSKY: An isolated individual can do it. Human beings have tremendous capacities. If they're willing to make the effort, if they're willing to look at themselves in the mirror and to think honestly, they can do it—with hard work.

MOYERS: One would at least have to have money to subscribe to journals and newspapers.

CHOMSKY: Unfortunately, that's true. You need resources. It's easy for me to say, because I've got the resources. But for most people, it's extremely hard. That's why you need organization. If a real democracy is going to thrive, if the real values that are deeply embedded in human nature are going to be able to flourish, groups must form in which people can join together, share their concerns, discover what they think, what they believe, and what their values are. This can't be imposed on you from above. You have to discover it by experiment, effort, trial, application, and so on. And this has to be done with others. Central to human nature is a need to be engaged with others in cooperative efforts of solidarity and concern. That can only happen through group structures. I would like to see a society moving toward voluntary organization and eliminating as much as possible structures of hierarchy and domination, and the basis for them in ownership and control.

MOYERS: Do you think a citizen has to have far-reaching, specialized knowledge to understand the realities of power and what's really going on?

CHOMSKY: It's not absolutely trivial, but as compared to intellectually complex tasks, it's pretty slight. It's not like the sciences, where there are so many things you have to study and know something about. By and large, what happens in political life is relatively accessible. It doesn't take special training or unusual intelligence. What it really takes is honesty. If you're honest, you can see it.

MOYERS: Do you believe in common sense?

CHOMSKY: Absolutely. I believe in Cartesian common sense. People have the capacity to see through the deceit in which they are ensnared, but they've got to make the effort. As you correctly pointed out, for an individual to make the effort is very hard.

MOYERS: Let's grant for a moment that your analysis is correct. You have government with its vast propaganda machinery and billions of dollars being spent on "informing the public." You have the media interlocking with the government, and you have corporations themselves. So you've got the dominant institutions of society—business, government and media—all joined in defining what is happening in the real world. How does a lonely individual counter this official view of reality?

CHOMSKY: You struggle on your own.

The marginalization of the population and its separation from institutions could potentially lead to a mass base for a fascist movement. We've been extremely lucky in the United States that we've never really had a charismatic leader who was capable of organizing people around power and its use. There were people who came close, but most of them didn't make it. Joe McCarthy was too much of a thug, and Richard Nixon nobody could trust, and Ronald Reagan people regard as basically a clown. There has not been a figure who could do that. But it could happen. In a depoliticized society with few mechanisms for people to express their fears and needs and to participate constructively in managing the affairs of life, someone could come along who was interested not in personal gain, but in power. That could be very dangerous.

MOYERS: I think the danger is the opposite of that—just a general passivity on the part of people in which the system continues to function.

CHOMSKY: That's another possibility. But the third and more hopeful one is that out of the growing sense of remoteness from actual power, the sense that the democratic forms are not functioning as they should, the sense that you're being deceived and lied to—out of that can come the recognition that popular organization and popular struggle does have effects. Out of all of that can come the basis for a much more democratic order.

MOYERS: Do you believe that by nature human beings yearn for freedom? Or in the interests of safety, security, and conformity, do we settle for order?

CHOMSKY: These are really matters of faith rather than knowledge. On the one hand, you have the grand inquisitor who tells you that what humans crave is submission, and therefore Christ is a criminal and we have to vanquish freedom. That's one view.

The other view, held by Rousseau, for example, is that people are born to be free and that their basic instinct is the desire to free themselves from coercion, authority, and oppression. Where you stake your hopes depends on what you believe. I'd like to believe that people are born to be free, but if you ask for proof, I couldn't give it to you.

MOYERS: You talk about faith. Do you have faith in freedom?

CHOMSKY: I try not to have irrational faith. We should try to act on the basis of our knowledge and understanding, recognizing that they're limited. But you have to make choices, and those choices have to be determined by matters that go well beyond anything that you can demonstrate or prove. In that sense, I have faith—but I would like to think it's at least the kind of faith which is subject to the test of fact and reason.

MOYERS: This is the first time I've met you. To be honest, I expected to find a man somewhat cynical and disillusioned because you haven't played by the games of the consensus. You have dealt with truth that has not been admissible into the realm of the common political discourse, and as a consequence of that, you have for a time been ostracized by the political community. Why are you not cynical and disillusioned?

CHOMSKY: That's not exactly the way I see what's happened. My own views go back to childhood. But I became really active politically in the early sixties. At the time I thought it was utterly hopeless. I never thought there was the slightest possibility that anything could be done to overcome the jingoist fanaticism that had virtually no break in it at that point. In fact, I was doing what I was doing primarily because I simply couldn't look myself in the mirror and not do it. I was spending my evenings talking in somebody's living room to three neighbors, two of whom wanted to lynch me, and taking part in demonstrations so small that we had to be protected by the police to keep everybody from killing us. This went on for a while. I never thought a serious movement would develop.

MOYERS: You were a scholar living a quiet life in the world of linguistics. What propelled you into activism?

CHOMSKY: I was living a very pleasant life, in fact. I remember thinking very hard about whether to get involved because I knew exactly where it was going to go. It's the kind of involvement which only grows. There are more issues and more problems and more needs, and once you are willing to take what is clearly the step that honesty and integrity requires and become involved in these issues, there's never going to be any end to the demands.

MOYERS: So many people want you to write and speak.

CHOMSKY: And to demonstrate and get arrested.

MOYERS: But what was it? Was it the war?

CHOMSKY: That's what pushed me over the limit. Partly it was the fact that the war was so horrible. It was also partly because I was extremely impressed by the young people involved in the Civil Rights movement. As in most popular movements, the people who actually carried that one through to fruition are unknown to history. Some of them were killed or marginalized or forgotten.

MOYERS: And the movement succeeded.

CHOMSKY: The movement succeeded, but it succeeded out of tremendous courage and dedication. That was impressive. And then, as the war began to escalate, I began to think I had gotten involved much too late. I definitely felt that I should have been deeply engaged years earlier.

When I did become seriously engaged in the early sixties, it was with a sense that this is a real step that's going to change my life. It's going to be a lot of unpleasantness. I expected to spend several years in jail, and if it hadn't been for the Tet Offensive, I probably would have. I was actively involved in open resistance. It was not a secret. I could see where it was going, and it wasn't a pleasant sight.

I don't like public life. I don't like demonstrations. I don't like being maced. I don't like giving a talk to a big crowd. There are all sorts of things I much prefer not to do. You asked about cynicism—I felt it was hopeless, but there was nothing else I could do at that point. Over the years it turned out I was very much wrong, and it was anything but hopeless. The achievements went far beyond anything I could imagine.

MOYERS: Stopping the war.

CHOMSKY: Yes, and creating a big cultural change. Lots and lots of people, of whom I was one tiny example, were doing the same thing. The general effect was to dramatically change the cultural climate in all sorts of respects, in everything from civil rights to the war to feminism to the environment. Take Native Americans, for example. That's something we should have been facing for hundreds of years. But it was literally not until the 1970s that it became possible for American citizens to look at what they had done to the native population. That's a remarkable fact. It's really only in the seventies that we got beyond the cowboy and Indian nonsense. Now we've begun to face the fact that there were lots and lots of people here who aren't here any more. Something happened to them, for which the settlers were responsible.

MOYERS: Now, as a result of that, the upcoming celebration of the five hundredth year of Christopher Columbus's "discovery" of the Americas will also be met by a counter demonstration, by descendants of those millions of people who were wiped out after the Europeans arrived.

CHOMSKY: That's right. I hope that others will join in that. I once wrote that every October we have a day celebrating Columbus, who in fact was a major murderer. Some reviewers were absolutely outraged by that. One described it as bitter and humorless. Frankly, genocide isn't very humorous.

MOYERS: Someone wrote that you have taken on too much of the harshness of the world that you've struggled against—

CHOMSKY: Well, I don't feel it. I think I know the person who wrote that, and I think he's missing the point. This is a reviewer who pointed out that the character of my writing has changed somewhat over the years. The kinds of things that I am now saying about institutional structures I did not say in the late sixties, not because I didn't believe them, but because I felt that audiences wouldn't understand what I was talking about. I would not talk about the nature of capitalism. I would not talk about the fact that if you're forced to rent yourself to an owner of capital, that's better than slavery, but it's very far from being a system that a free human being could accept. I didn't talk very much about these things because they were too remote from consciousness and understanding. Now I talk about anything to any audience in the country. No matter who it is, I say approximately the same thing, and I don't feel any constraints any more. The audiences that you reach today are just a lot more sophisticated.

MOYERS: But you have to reach them practically face-to-face because this mass medium pays little attention to the views of dissenters. Not just Noam Chomsky but most dissenters do not get much of a hearing in this medium.

CHOMSKY: That's completely understandable. The media wouldn't be performing their societal function if they allowed favored truths to be challenged because their very institutional role is to establish certain truths and beliefs and not to allow them to be challenged.

MOYERS: In order to cohere, society needs a consensus, does it not? It needs an agreed-upon set of assumptions.

CHOMSKY: I think we need tentative assumptions in order to continue with our lives, but we also ought to be a healthy society that not only tolerates but encourages challenge.
That's what happens in the sciences. In the sciences, where the world is keeping you honest, not only is challenge tolerated, but it's stimulated. When students come

along with a new idea that threatens established beliefs, you don't kick them out of your office. You pay attention.

MOYERS: But in politics?

CHOMSKY: In political life, the object is to preserve privilege and power. But that's not a value that should be protected, that's a characteristic that should be overcome. I'm not saying you should question everything, always—that's hopeless. I walk out the door, and I don't think the floor is going to collapse. Of course you accept things—you have faith and beliefs, and you operate on the basis of them. But you should recognize that they are subject to challenge and that if the past is any guide, they're probably wrong because beliefs have generally been wrong in the past.

For example, it wasn't very long ago that slavery was considered moral. The slave owners offered a moral basis for slavery. Nobody does that any more. That's an improvement. Or take the issues raised by the feminist movement. These are things many people simply did not see thirty years ago. Now the problems are still there, but we have greater insight into our own nature. We discover forms of repression and authority that we know we do not accept as moral human beings and that we try to overcome. You can sense such progress. At the same time, you also have decline. Nazi Germany and Stalinist Russia—

MOYERS: —the genocide of this century, the holocaust—

CHOMSKY: —it's indescribable. That's why it's hard to look at the twentieth century and say that you're an optimist.

MOYERS: What about the twenty-first century?

CHOMSKY: We're not going to get far into the twenty-first century unless these problems are overcome because the problems are no longer localized. Hitler's genocide was probably the worst moment in human history, but it was still, in a sense, localized. It was a huge massacre, but it was bounded. The problems we are now facing are not going to be bounded. If there is a superpower confrontation or even a confrontation among lesser nuclear powers, that's not going to be bounded in any sense that wars were in the past.

MOYERS: Or if we all unplug the environment.

CHOMSKY: If we continue to act on the assumption that the only thing that matters is personal greed and personal gain, the commons will be destroyed. Other human values have to be expressed if future generations are going to even be able to survive.

MOYERS: It seems a little incongruous to hear a distinguished linguistics scholar from the ivory tower of the Massachusetts Institute of Technology talk about common people with such appreciation and common sense.

CHOMSKY: My own studies of language and human cognition demonstrate to me what remarkable creativity ordinary people have. The very fact that people talk to one another reflects deep-seated features of human creativity which separate human beings from any other biological system we know. When you begin to study the normal capacities of human beings, you get tremendous respect for them.

Tom Wolfe

WRITER

Tom Wolfe helped invent the New Journalism in the 1960s. His beat ever since has been our popular culture and follies. His books and essays have become icons of our times: Radical Chic, "The Me Decade," *and* The Right Stuff. *His most recent book,* The Bonfire of the Vanities, *is about New York City in the Age of Acquisition. It is also his first novel.*

MOYERS: Talk to me a minute about reporting. What do you look for that suggests a trend is coming?

WOLFE: I like to come across things that I haven't read about before, things that I just pick up in conversation that other people aren't looking at. I've done that whether I'm writing fiction or nonfiction.

MOYERS: You recently told a wonderful anecdote about Jessica Hahn out on a media tour. A little girl or prep school girl comes up to her with copies of *Playboy* magazine and asks her to sign her own nude photographs. Then the little girl says she's going to take them back and, with the approval of her school, auction them and give the proceeds to the poor. What does that signify about the times?

WOLFE: I didn't say, "Aha, there's something to look at." To me it just seemed so obvious that we've reached the point where a little girl with a buttercup blouse—you know, those little blouses they wear and the cardigan sweater with the little silk ribbon up the front and the pageboy bob and the school uniform skirt with the safety pin hooking it together at the hip—that this little girl should come up to Jessica Hahn, who's just bared her chest for the world in *Playboy* magazine, and want her to sign copies of *Playboy*, and, with the school's blessing, have an auction to raise money for the poor. This sort of thing couldn't have happened twenty years ago, or even ten years ago, because it's only in the last ten years that pornography—and now I sound rather out of date even to use the term—that pornography has become an everyday affair. That's what these magazines are involved in.

MOYERS: We don't even preach against it any more.

WOLFE: No.

MOYERS: During the last twenty-five years, many of us haven't known what we were seeing until you told us. You caught "Radical Chic" on the fly in the sixties, the "Me Decade" was right on for the seventies, and the eighties have been the "Purple Decade," in the sense of a royal pursuit of ambition. What are you seeing now that makes you think you can give a name in time to the nineties?

WOLFE: A lot of different trends that were so spectacular in the sixties and seventies, are just beginning to run into a stone wall. Just to use the most obvious example, it was in the seventies that you began going to towns of about two hundred thousand and finding fourteen theaters, of which eleven were showing so-called X-rated or pornographic movies. Of those, two would be outdoor drive-ins with screens seven, eight, nine stories high, the better to beam all these moistened folds and stiffened giblets to the countryside. That has actually been a tremendous change in a religious country like this. Now it's run into something I don't have to elaborate on—it's run into AIDS. This is, in effect, a stone wall that stops a very, very wild trend.

MOYERS: Pornography also became quite tedious. It's become very boring, don't you think? I was in a hotel the other day and noticed that you could not only put an order on the door for breakfast the next morning, but you could also put one there and order an X-rated film. When I was checking out the next morning, I asked the fellow downstairs if they had many requests, and he said, "Not as many as we have for breakfast."

You've said that the twenty-first century may well become known as the twentieth century's hangover. In what sense?

WOLFE: This has been an extraordinarily free century, particularly in the United States—free not only in the conventional sense of political freedom, but also free in the economic sense of practically everyone who works having surplus income with which to express oneself, to have some slack in the line, some kind of luxury, some kind of recreation. It has also been extremely free in the sense that people are not bound by the religious standards that were ordinary for centuries, if not millennia. It's been a very exciting time. We're living in the freest time that ever was. But this can lead to certain excesses, to certain experiments that don't work out. What we used to think of as the ordinary people are now taking on the privileges that in the past only aristocrats could help themselves to. For example, divorces. Divorce is an expensive proposition. Until 1970 it was considered an immoral tack to take in most parts of this country. Since then, it has become really second nature, so that just a few years ago we reached a point in which more than fifty percent of American marriages were heading toward divorce. This idea of helping yourself to new lovers has always been the aristocrat's prerogative. Now, if you go down to Puerto Vallarta or St. Kitts or Barbados, you'll run into factory workers, electricians—

. . . ordinary people are now taking on the privileges that in the past only aristocrats could help themselves to.

MOYERS: People we used to think of as working class?

WOLFE: To use another term that's disappeared. You'll find them down there with their third wives or their new girlfriends, wearing their Harry Belafonte cane-cutter shirts to allow the gold chains to twinkle in their chest hair, and living a rather luxurious life. These are two sides of the same coin. On one side, which is quite glorious, is prosperity and almost absolute freedom. On the other side are all the hazards of freedom and sexual activity. Divorce, for example, does have its effect on children. Promiscuity has its price. We're entering into a period in which we're busily relearning things that everybody knew seventy-five years ago. This is also something of a worldwide phenomenon. We've been blessed in a way because this is a very stable country. When Richard Nixon was thrown out of office, not only was there no junta rising from the military to take over, there wasn't even one demonstration by Republicans or anybody else. In fact, as far as I know, there wasn't even a drunk Republican who threw a brick through a saloon window.

MOYERS: Republicans don't drink, and they don't throw bricks?

WOLFE: Well, instead, everybody sat back and watched it on television. They said, "Look, he's crying now, isn't that fascinating? He's leaving the White House now." This is really a stable country.

But in Europe, they've gone through communism—that's an out-of-date term now; you're supposed to say "Marxism." They experienced Marxism, Leninism, or monolithic socialism. What was so radical about communism was not that it swept aside the old order. All revolutions do that. It was the fact that it reinvented morality, as in the Maoist expression "Morality begins at the point of a gun." Now, even the leading circles in the Soviet Union and China are both in a period of relearning. Both, with really very little pressure from below, have begun to say, "It doesn't work. We've got to do something about it. This system doesn't work." That's what glasnost is.

MOYERS: As we're reaching an appreciation of the limits of freedom in this country, in Eastern Europe and across the border of the Soviet Empire there's a surge of people crying out for freedom.

WOLFE: I'm not sure how much of it was started from the bottom. A lot of it simply came from the top. Now that there's a little crack in the door, people feel that maybe they can start yelling out a little bit. But some kind of relearning has taken place. The Chinese are apparently relearning something very obvious about human motivation—that you have to give people the fruits of their own labor. This is pretty obvious stuff, but not if you have reinvented morality.

MOYERS: We're certainly learning, as you said, that promiscuity has its price. What else has its price?

WOLFE: We're relearning the nature of debt. I never will forget, in the 1970s, when people started telling me, "You've got to leverage yourself." I said, "What do you mean?" "You've got to get into debt," they said. I said, "Why?" They said, "Because debt is the lever that moves the world." There was some strange logic to it that worked.

MOYERS: Did you get leveraged?

WOLFE: Oh, I got leveraged out of my mind. One night, I was at dinner with some strangers in Texas, and I was sitting next to a man I'd never met in my life, and he said to me, "Son," and I thanked him for the compliment. "Son," he said, "I went down to the bank today, and borrowed 1.8 million dollars." He said, "It wasn't for my company, it was a personal loan." No security, an unsecured loan, 1.8 million dollars—I found myself in all sincerity almost clapping. "That's great!" If he had told me that he had made 1.8 million that day, I would have probably yawned, because you're always hearing that about people. But golly, to leverage yourself 1.8 million in one day . . .

MOYERS: Never go to dinner in Texas with strangers unless you're prepared to borrow money from them.

WOLFE: Since October 19, 1987, there's been more and more talk about the virtue of liquidity, which means having cash and not being in debt. This is a form of relearning on what is oddly enough an ethical level. It used to be considered unethical to be deeply in debt. It showed a lack of discipline.

MOYERS: But does this suggest that ethics is really just being prudent?

WOLFE: Well, the seven deadly sins are all sins against the self, although this is an idea that has vanished pretty much. For example, the reason that lust was considered a sin was not that some man would be leading some nice girl from Akron into white slavery or the pages of the pornographic magazines, but that he would be hurting himself by wasting his spirit on this shallow and pointless, base passion.

The same is true for anger, which is also one of the seven deadly sins. It was not that your anger might hurt someone, but that getting angry hurts you. Again, it's a waste of your spirit.

That idea has vanished. Today, one of the typical forms of absolution is to say, "Why do you object? It's not hurting anybody but me." It's hard to believe that one hundred years ago people didn't say things like that.

MOYERS: What's the significance of that change in how we think about lust?

WOLFE: It signifies the removal of one of the internal monitors that people in this country have had. It's one thing to say society disapproves, therefore you shouldn't do it. But it's a much better restraint if there's an internal monitor that says, "I'm hurting myself if I do this."

You know, we've actually gone pretty far into this program without mentioning de Tocqueville.

MOYERS: I'm sure we would have gotten to it.

WOLFE: I held off as long as I could, but I can't any longer because, as usual, he said it all. In 1835 de Tocqueville said that people in the United States could afford the extraordinary political and personal freedom that they had only because they were so intensely religious. At that time we certainly were a religious people. It was very hard to rise to the level of feed store assistant or feed store manager in a Midwestern town without belonging to the dominant Protestant church of that community. And there was certainly an internal monitor, in the Calvinist sense, in people throughout this country. Listen, I'm sounding like a theologian, but I'm just the social secretary; I just take notes on what I see going on. I have no spiritual agenda for anyone. This is what I see.

MOYERS: But you did say in your Harvard Class Day speech recently that we were celebrating the age of freedom from religion, the fifth freedom. The implication of that was that there ought to be a restoration of the ethical framework which grows out of religious roots.

WOLFE: Perhaps there should, but I wasn't saying that. The fifth freedom comes after the first four. The first American freedom was like everyone else's, freedom from the tyranny that you perceive you must get out from under—in our case, British rule. So we did that. The second was quite unusual, though. It had never been done anywhere in the world, and that was freedom from the class system that had existed everywhere in Europe. Thomas Jefferson, for example, put round tables in the White House so there would never again be a head of the table. As you know, everyone used to be seated strictly by rank, with the head of state at the top and on down the line. To this day in the White House, people dine on state occasions at round tables.

That was the second freedom, and Jefferson spearheaded that. We got rid of primogeniture so that families could no longer pass along all of their estate to the oldest son.

The third freedom was also very much an American phenomenon, which was freedom from want. Now when Roosevelt annunciated his four freedoms, three were rather obvious. Freedom from fear, freedom of expression, freedom of religion. The fourth was freedom from want, which was an astonishing idea to Europeans. But it was very much an American notion. There was this endless territory in the West that any American could have. Actually people used to get to the starting line and run into Kansas, and if you could get to a plot of ground and stand on it, it was yours. This is an amazing form of freedom—and this was an American form.

Now if you've had every form of freedom that has been known to man and then some, the only freedom left is freedom from the internal monitor, freedom from religion. That to me is the fifth freedom—freedom from religion. This is an extraordinary time in which we've dared to have something approaching ultimate freedoms. This is not, by any means, all bad.

MOYERS: It certainly hasn't been bad for women, who many preachers said were by God determined to be unequal. Certainly it hasn't been bad for blacks, because clergy in the South were sometimes the most ardent defenders of segregation. Taking away religion's power to restrain others has been a fairly positive gain in the last hundred years, don't you think?

WOLFE: It has been an experiment that perhaps at some point many had to make. Ken Kesey once said, in effect, "No one can be Godlike without trying."

MOYERS: Do you think that's what we've done in this century?

WOLFE: For most of our history nobody would dare assume that you could be master of your own fate. That's what the whole concept of God was about. But as Nietzsche pointed out, God died about a hundred years ago. Then people began to see just how far mastery of the world could go. And it's been a marvelous experiment in this country, and one that I've greatly enjoyed writing about. But when you take a headlong leap into the unknown, you can crash as well as find great heights. I think we've done both.

You know, I worry that people will think that I'm painting a gloomy picture and that there's hell to pay. I don't believe that. There has never been a greater moment to be alive and a greater country to be alive in. People are going to look back at America in the second half of the twentieth century for centuries to come.

MOYERS: But don't you think that the religious restraints were thrown off in part because people learned there wasn't hell to pay? Hell disappeared.

WOLFE: I think you're right. At least, it certainly seemed to.

MOYERS: And yet you've been suggesting that there's a different kind of hell to pay, which we are reaching at the limits of our permissive, autonomous, self-exploratory dive.

WOLFE: There may be in certain areas—AIDS is pretty forbidding stuff. It could occur in the economic area, but it hasn't yet. We've now been through a forty-five-year boom. It started in the middle of the Second World War, and it hasn't stopped. It took a terrific jolt on October 19, 1987, but the other shoe has never dropped, and it may never drop.

MOYERS: But something has happened to the old idea of our youth—the notion at the heart of the dream was that we were moving toward a more equitable distribution of goods. Do you think that notion of equality is finished?

WOLFE: Affluence has come down to most parts of the working population of this country on a scale that would have made the Sun King blink. It is extraordinary to see. It started in California, with factory workers buying first a car, and then a home, and then maybe a second car, and then maybe having a weekend place. To this day, the idea of a worker owning his own home is an exciting and unusual notion in large parts of Europe. It's been an extraordinary prosperity, and we shouldn't lose sight of that.

MOYERS: I'm glad to have lived in this century as an American because the majority of us have been brought into the middle class for the first time ever. There's an enormous contradiction as you and I sit here talking about what this century has in fact meant for us and what it has meant to others. Does that contradiction ever trouble you?

WOLFE: No, it doesn't. A lot of working-class people in Europe have begun to share in the American form of working-class wealth. If we talk about the people under Stalin, we're talking about an entirely different proposition—in that case, we're talking about communism.

You mentioned the middle class. I was amused when one of the surveys taken after the Republican National Convention asked respondents to identify themselves by social class, and eighty-five percent said they were middle class. I was only sorry that the news item I read didn't tell how the other fifteen percent characterized themselves.

It's a sign of wealth that the term "working class" can't be used in this country, because working class indicates that somebody is a slave to a job or is defined by a job. That just isn't true in this country any longer. I've talked to one of the heads of a big advertising agency recently, and he told me that it's driving the advertisers crazy. These large blocks that they used to be able to pitch ads to no longer exist. There isn't the factory worker and there isn't the housewife any longer. To reach the factory worker, you may have to isolate his hobby, and his hobby may be anything from hang-gliding to handcrafting Venetian boats. So there's this constant market segmentation to try to reach these little special interests, because here are people who have the free time and the money to cater to very esoteric aesthetic interests.

In so many ways, we are now alive in the period that the utopian socialists of the nineteenth century dreamed about. People like Fourier and Saint-Simon and Owen foresaw that industrialism would give the worker the free time, the personal freedom, the political freedom, and the surplus money to express himself and to live up to his potential as a human being. They thought it was going to take place under socialism, and it didn't. It took place here, under what is now called capitalism.

MOYERS: I recently did an interview with Noam Chomsky, who repeated what he and Herbert Marcuse were espousing in the sixties—that this has been the freest period ever in any society, but that in a political sense this freedom is meaningless. No matter how much personal prosperity this freedom brings, it's politically mean-ingless because private and public power so dominate the landscape that they dictate the options from which people can choose. So that while personal freedom can be spent on trivial things, it is lost on political things. What do you think about that?

WOLFE: I think it's absolute rubbish. Marcuse invented the marvelous term "repressive tolerance." This is what is known as "adjectival repression." His idea was: "These people are so free. It's an instrument that the masters use to repress them." This amounts to adjectival fascism, which in this country is usually concocted by writers and thinkers. I think what happened to Marcuse was this: Here's a guy from Europe who ends up in La Jolla, California—that's where he did his deep thinking. He comes to Wind and Sea Beach, and here are these fabulous-looking young men and women, and they're bursting with vitality and power. They look like the people that Marcuse as a young man saw on the strike posters in Europe—you know, Prometheus breaking the bonds of capitalism. He expects them to be the young rebels, and instead they're surfing. And he says, "They're free, they're strong, but the masters have ruined them. They want to go surfing and smoke a little dope. Repressive tolerance." That's absolute rubbish. This is the old "cabal" theory—that somewhere there's a room with a baize-covered desk where a bunch of capitalists are sitting around, pulling strings. These rooms don't exist! I mean, I hate to tell Mr. Chomsky this.

MOYERS: But he picks up on Walter Lippmann, who talked about "the manufacturing of consent," and Edward Bernays, the father of public relations, who talked about "the engineering of consent." And he says that wealth and power enable these corporate interests—public and private—to dictate the terms of the debate, engineering what we think.

WOLFE: This is the current fashion in the universities. You'll find at places like Harvard the term "the masters." This is another term for "the Establishment," "the cabal,"—which is never located, incidentally, but which controls us not through military power and police power and the obvious means, but by controlling the way we think. Hence the tremendous popularity in academic circles of the theory of deconstruction and of structuralism, which preceded deconstruction. Since the masters control the way we think and the structure of language, it's up to the intellectuals to "deconstruct" the language, to take it away from the masters and give it back to us in a form that the masters can't use. It even gets into architecture today. *The* reigning fashion in architecture right now is called deconstructivism. The idea is that in architecture, the masters give us these forms that we work in and live in. We don't realize it, but the very forms of the architecture are leading us to a passive submission to the aims of the masters. The deconstructivist architect must deconstruct the architecture by doing such things as creating crevices in the floor in the master bedroom, to separate the wife and the husband so that they will not succumb to the American dream of domestic bliss. Instead, have a crevice in the floor you can break an ankle in. It's nonsense—it's a kind of marvelous lunacy. It all exists in a hazy, harmless, "late-Marxist mist," to borrow a phrase from Jean-François Reveile.

MOYERS: But Chomsky didn't use the word "masters," he used the word "system"—"the system is interlocked."

WOLFE: When was the last time you heard an American capitalist—another rather antique phrase, to tell the truth—make a political statement? Now of course one way to answer that is to say, "They don't make statements, they control the way we think." You know, it's patent nonsense. It's nothing but a fashion. It's a way that intellectuals have of feeling like clergy. There has to be something wrong.

MOYERS: One of the things they see wrong is that we don't have two parties, but simply two factions of the business party, and that both parties serve wealth, power, and privilege—although in the course of a campaign they may strike different postures with their rhetoric.

WOLFE: I'd love for them to give an example. I don't think they can. You notice how abstract these people become when they get into this area because it's simply not true.

MOYERS: I'm beginning to wonder if this is the same man who wrote *The Bonfire of the Vanities*. The picture you paint in that book is one of utter depravity. The politicians are helpless, and the clergy are either charlatans or marginal. The police, the judges, and the lawyers are all cynical or sold out, and everyone's isolated from everyone else. There's not a significant likable, sympathetic person in the whole book. You get the picture that this is a society at the end of its life, about to fall, like some giant old building that has long ago lost its foundation.

WOLFE: Well, if I may quote that famous philosopher, Goodman Ace's wife, Jane, "You have to take the bitter with the better." I mentioned that there are two sides to the coin. If the coin glitters, it's prosperity and freedom. In the same moment that it shines this brilliant light, it can lead to tremendous excesses, to extreme forms of individualism—one form being vanity. Now, the book *The Bonfire of the Vanities* is about New York City in the 1980s, a period of money fever. There has *never* been such wealth as that generated in New York, chiefly by the investment banking industry.

MOYERS: " . . . white young men baying at—"

WOLFE: Yes, baying for money on the bond market. Right now, we are in a postal zone in which the annual personal income is four billion dollars.

MOYERS: Four billion?

WOLFE: Four billion. Just think of all the countries in the world that don't have a budget of four billion. There's been tremendous, enormous wealth—that's part of prosperity and freedom. But this leads to extreme forms of—to use an old-fashioned word, which I seem to be doing all the time this afternoon—vanity. In the eighties, I've seen it go all the way from Wall Street to the South Bronx. I'll never forget walking through the South Bronx, doing research for this book, and seeing boys, thirteen or fourteen years old, wearing these necklaces with silvery rings hanging from them. In the rings were upside-down Y's. I thought these were peace symbols. And I said, "Isn't it interesting that these boys here in the poorest part of New York are so civic-minded that they are concerned about the threat of nuclear destruction." Of course, when I looked more closely, I saw they were Mercedes-Benz hood ornaments. These boys knew what a Mercedes-Benz was, and they knew how much it cost because they knew that all the hotshots drive them. The drug dealers drive them. They wanted theirs. And they were taking the only part that they could now get, which was the hood ornament. This was the money fever spreading right down to the bottom rungs of the social ladder. This is New York. And this is vanity, operating on all sides.

MOYERS: But it's more than vanity, it's utter amorality that pervades *that* picture of New York. Is that *truly* the way you see the city?

WOLFE: Sure. But in *The Bonfire of the Vanities* there is no corruption in the bald sense of people being bribed—

MOYERS: —the good old-fashioned kind.

WOLFE: It's corruption from within. You know, Sartre was famous for the statement in *No Exit*, "Hell is other people." To which Claude Levi-Strauss said, "No, hell is ourselves." The inferno that I try to present in *The Bonfire of the Vanities* is internal. Let me just cite one example from the book, probably the key example. I present a young assistant district attorney named Larry Kramer. He has gone into public service on purpose. He wanted to go into public service. He wanted to feel that he was doing something that was both real and important and good for the city he lived in, as opposed to his classmates at Columbia, who were going to go down to Wall Street and make a ton of money shuffling papers and protecting the interests of perfume franchises and leveraged buy-out kings and the rest of them.

And that's exactly the way it has worked out for him. He's a young prosecutor in the Bronx, and his classmates are on Wall Street. And yet one morning, when he sees one of his classmates he hadn't seen in years coming out of a terrific apartment house, heading for a car and driver, beautifully dressed, carrying a five-hundred-dollar attaché case, no doubt heading down to Wall Street—he can't stand it. He can't stand it. The money fever has gotten him. He can't stand the contrast between his shabby getup and his thirty-six thousand dollars a year and what his classmates are doing. That is how the money fever gets to people. But is it bad to have a city or a country in which there is that much money around? I say no. Just look back over the panorama of human history. There are two sides to the same coin.

MOYERS: It's certainly not a city that you'd want to leave your mother alone in.

WOLFE: No, I wouldn't, but I live here, and I intend to continue living here.

MOYERS: With bars on the windows. I had to warn you a minute ago that you had left the key in the back door.

WOLFE: It's quite true. Either you find New York an exciting place to be, and you enjoy the level of ambition that exists here and the kind of people that that attracts, or you leave—because it is not a place that ranks very high on the scales of quality of life.

MOYERS: Why do you stay?

WOLFE: Because I love the city. I love the people it attracts. You know, when I say the people with ambition, I'm not just referring to the perfume franchisers and the leveraged buy-out kings and their lawyers. Think of all the Asians, who are by no means from the top of the heap, who are coming to New York City, and who are taking over the candy stores and the grocery stores. Many of them are making it.

MOYERS: In *Bonfire*, you strike hard at that old American notion that somewhere down there along the line there is a system of justice and a rule of law. The system of justice and the rule of law do not exist in *Bonfire*. They are gone.

WOLFE: Well, there are certain figures in the novel, for example, the head of the Homicide Bureau in the Bronx, Bernie Fitzgibbon—he's the real voice of the law in the book. He keeps saying, "Wait a minute, we have to do this in the right way. We have to have sufficient evidence, we can't cater to the mob," and so on. The district attorney keeps overruling him. He is determined to cater to the mob, because he has an election coming up. Now this is really personal corruption, not the corruption of a system.

MOYERS: But isn't that the worst corruption? A kind of "terminal" corruption?

WOLFE: It may not be terminal, but it is inside the individual, responding to the pressures of the money fever. A lot of people, including some critics, said that *The Bonfire of the Vanities* has no heroes. I hadn't thought about it, but the subtitle of Thackeray's *Vanity Fair* is *A Novel Without a Hero*. He was writing about a similar period—flush times, where there seemed to be no limit to wealth and indulgence.

MOYERS: Do you really believe—as the book portrays—that the rule of law is finished?

WOLFE: No, I didn't intend to make that point. As a matter of fact, I wrote that book with a spirit of wonderment. I was saying, "Look at these people! Look at what they're doing! Look at that one! Look at that one!" It was only after I had finished and read it over that I saw that there was a cumulative effect that leads to the kind of conclusion you mentioned. The rule of law hasn't broken down, but in a borough like the Bronx, it's swamped. There aren't enough courtrooms to deal with the level of crime. This is a problem all over New York City and in a lot of major cities. So it isn't the system of justice, it's the sheer volume of crime, and the vanity of certain figures who are looking out for their own political careers.

MOYERS: You said somewhere else that there are principled people in New York, but they don't dominate.

WOLFE: That's part of the other side of a period of great prosperity. Compared to the history of humanity, our prosperity is great! But there is hell to pay, now and again. If you've got this much ambition geared to financial success, or to fame, it exerts a pressure so intense that the self-abnegating, heroic figures tend to be shoved aside. I think it's a well-known fact in the realm of sociology that levels of street crime, personal crime, muggings, this sort of thing, go down in bad times. The Depression was a rather peaceable time in terms of street crime. It's when times are good, like they are now, that the passion to get more is inflamed. There's a motto among the so-called "wolf packs" who come in from Brooklyn into Manhattan, to prey on pedestrians on the street. The motto is "Manhattan makes and Brooklyn takes." Now that's an awareness of the age we're in. These are mostly youngsters, and they're saying, "Those people in Manhattan are making a lot of money." The times are flush. That's what goes on rather than any breakdown of a system of justice.

> If you've got this much ambition geared to financial success, or to fame, it exerts a pressure so intense that the self-abnegating, heroic figures tend to be shoved aside.

MOYERS: You've been around this city a long time, but there's a sense of wonderment in your reporting, which becomes the fiction of *The Bonfire of the Vanities*. What surprised you most as you roamed the city?

WOLFE: One thing is what I would call "media ricochet," which is the way real life and life as portrayed by television, by journalists like myself and others, begin ricocheting off one another. That's why in *The Bonfire of the Vanities* it was so important to me to show exactly how this occurs, when television and newspaper coverage become a factor in something like racial politics. A good bit of the book has to do with this curious phenomenon of how demonstrations, which are a great part of racial and ethnic politics, exist only for the media. In the last days when I was working on the *New York Herald-Tribune*, I went to a number of demonstrations. I would announce to all the people with the placards, "I'm from the *New York Herald-Tribune*." The attitude was really a yawn, and then a kind of "Get lost." They were waiting for Channel 2, or Channel 4, or Channel 5. Suddenly the truck would appear, and these people would become galvanized. On one occasion I saw a group of demonstrators marching across Union Square. When Channel 2 arrived with a couple of vans, the head of the demonstration walked up to what looked like the head man of the TV crew and said, "What do you want us to do?" He said, "Golly, I don't know! What were you gonna do?" The demonstrator said, "It doesn't matter—you tell us!"

MOYERS: When the Tawana Brawley case broke, I thought, "Wait a minute—they set this up to confirm his book!" It was right out of the book.

WOLFE: I was called prophetic after that—although if you think about it, the real-life story made mine look rather tame by comparison. I didn't dare go that far. But in fact it's not a matter of being prophetic. If you're willing to go out as a reporter, whether you're writing in fiction or in nonfiction, and try to understand the mechanisms of the particular society we are in, and look at them without an ideological hypothesis, you'd see, because the mechanisms are fairly obvious. If there was some way that you could remove ideology from writers for about a five-year period, it would be the best thing that ever happened to writing in our period. If you're willing to look, unclouded by hypotheses, you'll see the mechanisms. One of the mechanisms in place in New York—and a lot of large cities right now—is racial and ethnic politics. If you get the mechanism right, the examples are going to pop up. Not many of them are going to be quite as extraordinary as the Brawley case. But they're going to appear.

MOYERS: Many conservatives have praised your book for speaking frankly about the failure of liberal pieties toward race. I was one of those who argued in the sixties for integration, believing that the *other* side of integration is disintegration. Reading your book confirms me in that. The book is about disintegration. Are we a disintegrating society, racially?

WOLFE: No, but we've reached a particular crossover point, politically, in which finally a lot of the have-nots, the people who are not of white, European background, are coming into their own politically, out of sheer numbers, if nothing else. This inevitably heightens the tensions that have been there all along. You can see it in New York every day. Politicians all over the city think about the "racial component" of anything they say. That's not all bad, but it's a very tense period, because the crossover is beginning.

New York has always had waves of immigration. The most famous waves were white and European—first the Germans and the Irish, then the Italians and Jews—and these groups all came to power. The political leaders in this city today are Italian and Jewish. Now their constituency is leaving them, and the waves that have come in since then—namely, a wave of black immigration from the South and waves of immigration from the Caribbean, South America, Asia, and North Africa—are coming into their own. Does this lead to an absolute disintegration? Not at all. New York has been marvelous in accommodating these shifts. When the shift involves a change in skin color, that makes it tougher. But you'll notice there's no pattern of bloodshed in the streets. It has never come to that, and I don't think it ever will.

MOYERS: Politics *is* the alternative to civil war.

WOLFE: It is. Democracy works. That's why my jaw drops when I listen to people like Chomsky and others talk about the system. Well, let's talk about the system—it works! It's not like the Serbs and Croats in the Second World War, who were literally at each other's throats. That isn't the way it works here.

MOYERS: I think where we went wrong in the sixties was to anticipate that integration would mean social acceptance. Actually, as you say, it's meant political power divided according to blocs. And now, in this city, the largest bloc is becoming predominantly black. It's not social acceptance that they're after but political power.

WOLFE: The poverty program had an interesting thesis, which was that the way to cure poverty was to build political power rather than just giving money. That was the real basis of the poverty program.

MOYERS: We sent community organizers out into the neighborhoods until Mayor Daley stopped us.

WOLFE: Well, a lot of it went bananas, but the premise was an interesting one. These so-called community action programs were the heart of it—not giving money.

MOYERS: That's right.

WOLFE: Perhaps the poverty program didn't work. I don't know. But it was an interesting premise and probably, in the long run, a correct one. Probably coming into power is the real salvation. An interesting city to watch would be Philadelphia. I don't know much about it, but there's a city in which the crossover has occurred. I gather things have settled down after a period of inevitable tension. The activists have receded, and the builders, technocrats, and bureaucrats of a typical American sort have come to the fore. I probably shouldn't go on about Philadelphia, because I don't know it that well.

MOYERS: You'll be reporting on it. Nat Hentoff says, "Reporting is the highest form of journalism," and I think it's become the stuff of fiction as well.

WOLFE: I think it's indispensable now. This is a period of thresholds, of tremendous changes, as we come to the end of certain experiments, and as new people come to this country from all over the place. This is an amazing, wonderful period in which to be a writer. I don't see how a writer can operate without going out as a reporter. I don't care if you're writing plays, movies, or even if you're a poet—I don't see any other way to do it. And yet so many writers are at this moment turning inward. I don't get it! Think of the feast that's out there.

MOYERS: Conservatives claim you because in part you find a lot of liberal pieties insufferable, and in part because your own journey has led you to some political conclusions close to their own. But do you find their conservative pieties as insufferable as you do some liberal pieties?

WOLFE: You know, I haven't been thinking in those terms, I really haven't. I hear myself called a conservative both by conservatives and by liberals. It doesn't bother me. It usually means that I've been unorthodox in some way, that I haven't gone along with the reigning intellectual line. My own politics, incidentally, since you've brought this up, are right here on this block. I happen to be president of my block association. This is not a hotly contested job. Nevertheless, I'm in my second term as president of the block association. And to me this is real politics. I go down to City Hall and testify and meet with city councilmen. I go to community board meetings. That's the politics that really engages me. I'm interested, the way everybody is interested, in national politics. But I don't have any national agenda. I have a terrific agenda about developers coming into the East Sixties—if you want to hear about that, I can go on and on about it.

MOYERS: Could this city be turned around from the blocks up?

WOLFE: Nothing's going to happen soon. We talk about "the system," for example, and "the masters." Block politics *do* work, and I'll give you a gigantic example. I have never seen such a coalition of forces—talk about a system, and masters, and the Establishment—as came together in this city for the Westway Project. Everybody from the revered, much-respected Senator Jacob Javits to all the leading banks in this city to all the leading labor unions, even down to the small ones. Every financial interest you can think of was behind Westway, this colossal project not only to rebuild the West Side Highway, but to build gigantic real estate complexes through half of Manhattan down to the Battery. There were billions—*billions*—of dollars at stake, a lot of it already committed. And it was stopped! It was stopped rather easily by a coalition of neighborhood groups, who are against gigantism—with a little help from the Army Corps of Engineers—

MOYERS: —and the snail darter, or some little fish.

WOLFE: It was stopped absolutely cold. Where was the juggernaut in that case? That was democracy. That was New York City. Unfortunately, I can give you examples of things being stopped, but I can't give you examples of things being led forward.

MOYERS: I'm interested to hear you talking about neighborhood politics because the greatest joy I've had in politics—and I've been in and around it for twenty-five years now—was getting involved on my side of Manhattan, in a quasi-successful effort to slow down the development of Columbus Circle. Testifying at the Board of Estimate and speaking to people in the blocks, taking part in such activities, was a political joy.

WOLFE: I think that's where political ideas should begin. I'm going to say something I shouldn't say. I wish my fellow writers would approach politics that way. I'm tired of hearing from writers whose knowledge of the world—and for that matter, their political world—consists of what they see in their apartments, or in the taxicab that they take to work, and in the magazine office. You know, for God's sake, fellas, let's get out and look at something for a change, and stop breathing the same ideas! Literary politics in this country has the whiff of people who work in these sealed buildings, where on Thursday you breathe the same air that went through all the lungs on Monday. It's really tiresome. That's where you get pernicious diseases, you know? Get out there! Take a look! Get involved in something!

> *Literary politics in this country has the whiff of people who work in these sealed buildings. . . .*

William Julius Wilson

SOCIOLOGIST

DAVID JOEL

Dr. Wilson came to public attention several years ago with The Declining Significance of Race. *He argued that most inner-city blacks stay poor not because they are black, but because they live in the wasteland of the inner city. Dr. Wilson is a professor of sociology at the University of Chicago. His most recent book is* The Truly Disadvantaged.

MOYERS: Imagine that I'm a black teenager in the inner city—Detroit, Chicago, New York, Philadelphia—living with a single mother on welfare, and no father—what can I expect of my future?

WILSON: I would say your chances in life are rather limited. Unfortunately, you will experience persistent poverty; you will have very little chance of getting a higher-paying job; you will very likely end up having a child out of wedlock, because the men in your community are not marriageable—that is, they experience long-term joblessness; your children are likely to be attending schools where they are not being properly educated, schools that are overwhelmingly impoverished. So your long-term prospects are rather dim.

MOYERS: That flies in the face of what we were raised to believe about the American dream—that everything gets better for everybody in every way if we just work hard enough and are lucky.

WILSON: That dream doesn't apply to everyone. I can take you to any inner city hospital and go to a ward where newborn babies are and predict with a high probability where these kids are going to end up in life. Most of them will end up living in poverty, trapped in the inner city. When you can make such predictions, you're talking about a very unfair society.

There's something that's happening to black males in the inner city that I think is rather tragic. The best way to illustrate this is to look at what we call our "male marriageable pool index," that is, the number of employed males per one hundred females of the same age. There is a community, for example, in Chicago, called Oakland, which is probably the most impoverished neighborhood in the city. In 1950, there were about seventy employed males for every one hundred females in that overwhelmingly black community. In 1980, that figure had plummeted to nineteen employed males for every one hundred females aged sixteen and over. Now that's a tragic story.

MOYERS: What does that mean for both the young men and the young women?

WILSON: It means that a lot of the young women are not getting married. It also means an increase in out-of-wedlock births, because women do not follow up pregnancy with marriage. It means that a significant number of children are growing up in single-parent families. Now, I don't attach a moral value to living in a single-parent family or a married-couple family. I recognize that there's a social movement emphasizing greater independence for women, so that's not my concern. My concern is that single, female-headed families are overwhelmingly impoverished families. The chances of moving out of poverty, if you're a female-headed family, are about one third of what they are if you are a married-couple family. So you have to take that into consideration.

You also have to recognize that a growing number of black kids are growing up in poor, female-headed families. Seventy-eight percent of the children in all female-headed black families live in poverty. That's one of the reasons why forty-four percent of all black kids are growing up in poverty—almost one out of every two.

MOYERS: You spoke of the tragic situation of black males in this country. Black men are only six percent of the U.S. population, but they compose half its male prisoners. A black minister said recently that by the year 2000, seven out of ten of all black men will be in jail, dead, on drugs, or drunk. More than forty-five percent of all black men in the United States are now drug or alcohol abusers. More than fifty percent of all black men under the age of twenty-one are unemployed. Forty-six percent of black men between sixteen and sixty-two are not in the labor force. The homicide rate of black men is six times higher than it is for white men.

WILSON: I'm not sure I would endorse all of those statistics—some, I think, are exaggerated. But it is the case that the overall socioeconomic condition of black males in general, and poor black males in particular, has deteriorated significantly. But we must not assume that this is true of all black males. If you look at income figures, what you see is that the number of black males who earn twenty-five thousand dollars and more and the number of those who earn less than five thousand are both growing. So there's a growing gap between the haves and have-nots in the black community. Those black males who are getting a college education and moving into professional and technical positions are doing all right. But other black males are experiencing real problems. Those black males who have been traditionally employed in higher-paying blue-collar positions, who worked in automobile, meat packing, and textile industries were paid a fairly decent wage so that they could support their families. In 1974, forty-six percent of all employed black males, ages twenty to twenty-four, were employed in the higher-paying blue-collar sector. By 1986, that figure had plummeted to twenty-five percent—from forty-six percent to twenty-five percent in just twelve years.

MOYERS: In one sense, that's not hard to understand, because so many of these jobs were shipped overseas. If you buy a Toyota, you're not putting a black or white American to work.

WILSON: What we're finding is that a lot of black males who were employed in higher-paying, smokestack industries are now facing either joblessness or employment in low-paying service jobs that don't provide enough to support their families. Some of them have to hold down two jobs, and, in some cases, believe it or not, three jobs, to make as much as they made when they were working in the steel industry, or the rubber industry, or the automobile industry.

Then you have the hard-core, inner-city, underclass black males, who have been crippled in the educational system, who find few job prospects because of the declining opportunities in the manufacturing blue-collar industries, and whose real option is a low-paying service job. A lot of these people get discouraged. They drop out of the labor force. The number of black males with zero earnings has increased sharply since 1959. In 1959, fourteen percent of all black males reported no earnings. In 1984, that figure was twenty-eight percent.

MOYERS: Charles Murray has written that there's nothing we can do for this generation of young black males. We have to write them off and try to save the next generation.

WILSON: I don't believe that. That assumes that people will not respond to opportunities that are presented to them. There is very little evidence for that. If you look at a lot of the more successful programs around the country, what you find is that people respond to what they perceive to be real opportunities. The Job Corps is a very good example of how kids who have been written off all of a sudden experience, after going through the Job Corps, increased earnings, higher labor force participation rates, lower crime rates, and so on. Inner-city kids often stand in line for summer jobs that they hear about. Unfortunately, there are not enough summer jobs to go around.

MOYERS: I remember when the Carter Administration had a special program for summer jobs. There were far more kids lined up around the block looking for those jobs than could get them.

WILSON: When you have a tight labor market or full employment, as in Boston, for example, you find that it has a very positive effect on the black population, particularly on black males. In the city of Boston, in 1985, the black male unemployment rate was only about five percent—one third the national unemployment rate. The percentage of all black males who were employed in Boston in 1985 was seventy-one and a half percent, slightly higher than the national white male employment rate.

MOYERS: What does that say to you?

WILSON: It says that if we open up the opportunity structure, the overwhelming majority of these black males will respond. Now, there will be a handful that will not respond to opportunities. But we shouldn't overgeneralize and assume that they represent a significant portion of the population. There are some youngsters who say that they would much rather push drugs and fence stolen goods than work in a lower-paying job. But they represent only a minority of all the youngsters.

> . . . if we open up the opportunity structure, the overwhelming majority of these black males will respond.

This is a point that I made to Governor Cuomo, when I served on his task force on poverty and welfare. I said, "Don't overgeneralize. Don't assume that this small population of people who would rather push drugs than hold down a steady job represents the typical youngsters in the ghetto."

MOYERS: Mayor Koch said that for many whites, crime wears a black face. Why do you assume that we're going to create these opportunities when there is so much fear of the young inner-city black male in America today?

WILSON: You know, it's interesting. I've been in contact with senators and members of the House, and they are all very concerned about opportunities for inner city residents. My phone rings off the hook. I'm often invited to give testimony and meet with congressmen to discuss these issues. Many of them have read my book.

That's why I was rather surprised that this private concern has not really been translated into public policy initiatives.

MOYERS: How do you explain it?

WILSON: I think that right now the Democrats in particular are feeling their way. They don't know whether the general public will respond to programs that are targeted at a certain population. They're unwilling to push these issues right now because they feel they're still in a rather insecure spot.

MOYERS: Not long ago, a colleague of mine was talking to a California Democrat who said to him that he feared Jesse Jackson, because Jackson was an extremist and a political liability to the Democrats. The reporter said, "Well, why don't you fear Pat Robertson, who is also an extremist? Why don't you think he's a political liability to the Republicans?" The California Democrat said, "Because nobody in this country is afraid of being mugged by a white, born-again Christian." Now what does that say to you?

WILSON: It says to me that people have been interpreting the increasing problem in the inner city, the crime that has spilled over into other communities, as very, very threatening. The symbols of that crime are the black males. So black males are experiencing problems even in the sense that people are unwilling to talk about programs that would help their plight. What I've been able to determine is that black males in the inner city are also experiencing increasing discrimination. Employers would much rather hire black women, white women, Hispanics, and Asians, than hire the black males. Black males are perceived as threatening, as representing the dangerous inner city.

One of the reasons racial tensions have increased in this country is that many whites who feel threatened by the black males overgeneralize to the entire black population and become hostile toward all blacks. Unfortunately, this type of antagonism will continue until we do something about the plight of black males. One of the reasons there are so many in prison is because they are jobless. When you increase employment rates, crime of all kinds decreases significantly. Just to simply say, "Well, let's throw those people in prison" without dealing with the causes of crime is very unfortunate indeed.

MOYERS: But even in good economic times, the black male has a harder time finding a good job.

WILSON: One reason is the problem of education. A lot of the jobs in the expanding sectors of our economy require training and education. There's also the problem of discrimination. But in a strong economy, and a tight labor market, employers are looking for workers, and they are less likely to discriminate against black males. Black males' employment opportunities would be significantly enhanced, even though they would not be as well off as workers from other ethnic groups. If you could create employment opportunities for significant segments of the inner city black male population, then crime and drug rates would go down.

MOYERS: But who creates these jobs? You have said that one reason for the worsening plight of the black male in the inner city is the flight of good jobs, the movement of industry to other countries. Are you expecting our economy to change in a way that will enable young blacks to find these opportunities?

WILSON: I'm hoping that we can start talking about these issues in the public policy arena. For example, we need WPA-type jobs that would help to rebuild the

American infrastructure—parks, playgrounds, working with the elderly, cleaning graffiti off subway walls, and so on. Income from this type of employment could be augmented with earned income tax credits. These would be temporary or transitional jobs because eventually you want to move people into the private sector. And, therefore, some attention is going to have to be given in future administrations to some sort of coherent macro-economic policy to enhance overall employment opportunities. This would require working in concert with countries in other parts of the world, so that initiatives in country A do not offset domestic policies in country B. You know, François Mitterand embarked on a very ambitious program of economic expansionism in France, only to be undercut by German retrenchment, because they weren't buying the cars that the French were producing. There has to be not just a national economic policy, but an international policy as well.

MOYERS: But it isn't realistic to expect that the Japanese and the Germans are going to give a damn about what happens to black kids in the ghettos of Chicago.

WILSON: You don't want to couch the issues in terms of helping poor inner city blacks. You want to talk about putting Americans back to work. This is what I write about in *The Truly Disadvantaged*. I talk about the need to develop comprehensive programs that would ultimately benefit the underclass or the truly disadvantaged, but that would also capture the imagination of other segments of the population.

MOYERS: But you're calling for these programs at a time when, as everybody knows, the American government is floating in red ink. Our deficits are at such a level that people say there can't be any new programs even for defense.

WILSON: What we need is political leadership, people in key policy positions who will talk about the need to move in a progressive direction and to address some of these concerns. Americans are not as conservative or uncaring as a lot of people think. It's how you discuss the issues. If you say, "We are concerned about joblessness; we are concerned about poverty among children; we are concerned about inadequate education; we want to get America moving again; we need programs that are going to put people back to work," you would get a lot of support.

MOYERS: But one of the problems in public policy now is that the middle class, the majority, expect programs for themselves, irrespective of whether or not enough of it gets down to the truly disadvantaged that you're writing about.

WILSON: That is true. But the public opinion polls also show that Americans would support, overwhelmingly, a guaranteed jobs program. That's why I'm so surprised at how timid some politicians are.

MOYERS: I think they're timid because there is in the country now a different mood from the 1960s. Part of it goes back to this image of the young black we were talking about. In the sixties, when politicians began to talk about the poverty of blacks, the picture in the mind was of young blacks who were at the other end of Bull Connor's clubs and dogs, fighting racial inequality. Now the image of the young black in poverty is the man in my documentary for CBS who boasts that he's had six children by four women and doesn't support any of them.

WILSON: Yes, I'm mindful of that. That's why, when I wrote the section of *The Truly Disadvantaged* that focused on public policy issues, I emphasized the need to underline universal type programs that would help the poor but that would also capture the imagination of other groups. And what am I talking about? A job creation program; child care—you're going to get a lot of middle class women supporting that;

child support assurance programs—people will support that. They will also support earned income tax credits, if they're associated with the working poor. These are the types of programs I'm talking about.

MOYERS: In other words, we can't do anything for the truly disadvantaged unless somehow we fake it?

WILSON: Not necessarily. What I'm saying is that it's important how you describe policies if you want the American people to support them. If you just throw up the red flag and say, "We've got to do something about the underclass," they're not even going to listen to the opening sentence, because there is an element of racial hostility that will surface and get in the way of rational thinking about ways to improve our society. All I'm saying is that the rhetoric and the way you define the terms are very, very important in initially getting people to listen. Then you need political leadership to rally support for these programs.

> *. . . it's important how you describe policies if you want the American people to support them.*

MOYERS: I hear you saying that race is not, as you said ten years ago, a declining influence in American life, but rather, it's an increasing influence in American life again.

WILSON: The title of that book can be somewhat misleading. The declining significance of race meant that there was a growing gap between the haves and have-nots in the black community and that economic class had become more important than race in predicting one's life chances. I never said anywhere in *The Declining Significance of Race* that racism was declining in significance.

Racism is a product of historical, economic, and political situations. When you have a slack economy or economic stagnation, you're much more likely to get a manifestation of racial hostilities than when you have a tight labor market where everyone has a job and no one is fearful that some minorities are going to move in and take that job. You have to recognize the situations that enhance racism, and work to create situations that will impede or slow down racism.

MOYERS: Both left and right have been saying that poor blacks must change their ways if they're going to win the support of the white majority. Even Christopher Jencks writing in *The New Republic* implies that like other ethnic groups, inner city blacks must adopt more mainstream ways of thinking, acting, and feeling.

WILSON: Inner city poor blacks do endorse mainstream values. They believe in the value of work. They are critical of welfare. They are as mainstream in their support of traditional values as any middle class white American. But many are unable to live up to these values because of the constraints and limited opportunities in their community. In previous years, the inner city was characterized by an integration of different income groups. You had the working class, the lower class and the middle class, all living more or less in the same areas, sending their kids to the same schools, availing themselves of the same recreational facilities, and so on. There was even high employment, so that a poor black at least had the possibility of experiencing some social mobility and had different role models to look up to that reinforced the association between work and education.

But that has changed because of the population and class changes in the inner city. The inner city is much more vulnerable now to a downturn in the economy. Joblessness has a much greater effect on the institutions in the inner city because you don't have the higher income groups there to cushion the effect of unemployment. All of these things, combined with a deterioration of the schools, make it awfully difficult for people to live up to the norms and values that they believe in.

MOYERS: But aren't individuals still ultimately accountable? When I was growing up in a conservative town in East Texas, mainstream values meant no sex without responsibility, no children without marriage, no love without commitment.

WILSON: People who see some prospect for advancement postpone gratification. People who think that their situation is going to change will conform to certain norms. But people who feel defeated and who don't see any prospects for improvement eventually throw up their hands in despair and say, "I know this is wrong, but there's nothing else I can do." If you want to see people in the inner city change certain types of behavior patterns, open up the opportunity structure. Give people some hope, and you will see changes.

MOYERS: Are you saying that hopelessness, despair, and the lack of opportunity account for the fact that whereas in 1960, twenty percent of all black children were living in homes without fathers, now it's fifty-one percent?

WILSON: I think that's very definitely the case. Let me just take, for example, teenage pregnancy, which is emphasized as a major problem in the inner city. Do you know that the number of live births per one thousand women is down significantly from previous years? What is up is the ratio of births out of wedlock. Fewer black teenagers are getting pregnant and having children, but significantly more are giving birth to children out of wedlock. In other words, they're not following up pregnancy with marriage because the black males are not marriageable. They're unemployed. Their prospects for employment are very dim. Pretty soon, the girls say, to hell with them.

MOYERS: How do we encourage young men not to have children they will not be responsible for?

WILSON: If you talk to a lot of the inner city males, you realize that there is a kind of informal sex code where some of them gain prestige by the number of girlfriends they have and the number of children they've fathered. When you have blocked opportunities, you create deviant behavior. So I don't think we're going to get very far if we just try to sit these young males down and say, "Look, you should be more responsible. You should not have children out of wedlock," without, at the same time, saying, "Look, we're going to provide you with some manpower training and education, so you can get a decent job. We're going to create jobs in either the private sector or the public sector, so that you can make a decent income and can go on to support your family." Unless we do those kinds of things, these young males, many of whom have reached the conclusion that social advancement in mainstream society is not possible for them, are not going to change their behavior.

A few years ago, when I taught at the University of Massachusetts, I went to the inner city in Springfield to talk to youngsters about going to college. They said, "What are you talking about?" They had no idea that there was a possibility of higher education for them. Then the University of Massachusetts created a program for the collegiate education of black students. We had a pipeline into the inner city schools in Springfield, and it changed the outlook of these youngsters. Many of them started thinking about going on to college. Some of them, who are now quite successful, relate stories to me about how this changed their views and opened up an entirely new horizon for them. That's the kind of thing that we have to do in the inner city.

MOYERS: But you're up against some very stiff attitudes from people who differ with you. Here's the headline in *The National Review*, on a review of your book: instead of calling it *The Truly Disadvantaged*, the headline says, "The Truly Decadent." It's referring to the sexual promiscuity, criminal tendencies, and alcoholism that prevail among young blacks in the ghetto.

WILSON: I have been sharply criticized in some liberal circles because of my willingness to discuss these problems. One of the reasons that conservatives have captured center stage in pushing this view is that until recently, liberals have been unwilling to describe and analyze behavior construed as unflattering to inner city residents. That's not the way to go. What you have to do is candidly describe the murder rates and the violent crime and all the other problems in the inner city, and then attempt to explain it. Don't hold your head in the sand and assume somehow that if you don't discuss these issues, people won't talk about them. They're going to talk about them, and they're going to attach a racist connotation to them if knowledgeable people fail to explain what is really happening, what really caused these problems.

MOYERS: Liberals got scared off when Patrick Moynihan wrote his famous, or infamous, report on the black family, and said it was disintegrating. The black community rose up in such opposition to that being said that we retreated.

WILSON: A lot of Moynihan's arguments were distorted. But he recognized that there was a connection between the broader economy and the black family. It is true that this discouraged liberals from writing about these problems. I'm also encountering people who say, "There's no such thing as an underclass. You're stigmatizing a population by using such a term. You shouldn't be describing behavior that's unflattering." That's playing right into the hands of the conservatives because conservatives will attach their own peculiar explanation to these problems. They'll say the problems are due to personal inadequacies, lack of talent, lack of ability, and laziness. They will reinforce the dominant American ideology that poverty, in the final analysis, is due to individual inadequacies. This ideology is emphasized in the United States and the United Kingdom. It is not widely supported in countries such as France, or the Federal Republic of Germany, or the Netherlands, or Switzerland, or Sweden, where people tend to associate poverty with problems in the larger society.

If we have a situation like you have in Sweden, where there is a commitment to ending poverty, and the poverty rate of the female-headed household is no higher than the poverty rate of the married-couple household, then there would be no need to talk about the increasing number of single-parent families.

MOYERS: Let me ask you a personal question. You are a distinguished teacher at one of America's great universities. What drove you as a kid? What made you what you are today?

WILSON: I grew up in a poor family. I'm very, very careful about how I describe this experience, because some people will say, "Well, Wilson pulled himself up by his own bootstraps—why can't others?" My father was relatively uneducated. He only went to the ninth grade. He worked in the coal mines and the steel mines in Pittsburgh and died at age thirty-nine of lung disease. My mother only completed the tenth grade. I had five brothers and sisters. I was the oldest, age twelve, when my father died. We went on relief for a brief period of time. But I was able to get out of that situation because first of all, I always had a role model out there, my aunt Janice, who was the first person in our family to get a college education. My father helped pay her college tuition, so she said she was going to help me in return. My mother always reinforced the idea that eventually I would go on and get a college education, even though we had no resources. But my aunt Janice served as a role model. She used to take me to New York and take me to museums and give me books to read and so on. And then I served as a role model for my other brothers and sisters. My wonderful mother reinforced a lot of the things that we were struggling to accomplish.

MOYERS: Were you raised in a ghetto?

WILSON: No, I was born in rural Pennsylvania.

MOYERS: We used to say, "It's better to be poor in the South than to be poor in the city."

WILSON: That's right. In rural Pennsylvania, you don't have the crowded conditions, the crime, the drugs, the sense of being imprisoned. You get an entirely different outlook on things.

MOYERS: If you were a seventeen-year-old in that ghetto across from the University of Chicago, do you think the gap between where you are now and that seventeen-year-old would be bridgeable?

> *They see that other people are making it, and they come to resent it.*

WILSON: You bring out a very important point. We should not lose sight of the importance of perceived relative deprivation, that is, your situation in comparison with somebody else's. That exacerbates conditions for a lot of these inner city residents. They see that other people are making it, and they come to resent it.

MOYERS: You can't escape that message. From morning till night on television, culture teaches these kids there's a better life out there.

WILSON: That's right. But they know that that life is not for them, so they construct their alternative lifestyles and develop their alternative, ghetto-specific activities—fencing stolen goods, having a lot of girlfriends, and taking some pride in having children out of wedlock.

MOYERS: How do you reach those kids?

WILSON: You reach them by providing an alternative avenue for success, by saying, "Look, how would you like to have a really good job making some fairly decent money? How would you like to get a good education? How would you like to be like that person over there at the University of Chicago carrying books and going to class?"

MOYERS: It's what appealed to me growing up.

WILSON: And it will appeal to these youngsters. I earlier talked about my experiences with inner city students enrolled at the University of Massachusetts. Most certainly it did appeal to those youngsters, once they saw that there was a chance that they could improve their lives.

MOYERS: Did you go to school with financial help?

WILSON: Yes, I had a church scholarship.

MOYERS: So somewhere along the way, everybody's touched by somebody else. Who touches these kids today in Detroit, in Chicago, in Philadelphia?

WILSON: Unfortunately, they're not being touched, so many of them are not being reached. We're going to have to look at things a little differently. We're going to have to have much more compassion and a greater understanding of the dynamics of poverty. We're going to have to challenge the dominant American belief system that these kids are in the situation they're in because of their own fault, or the fault of their families. And we're going to have to look at the broader conditions in society that reinforce and perpetuate poverty.

MOYERS: You say "we"—and yet, the black middle class has understandably left the ghetto. Who is "we"?

WILSON: "We," I would hope, would be not only the people like myself, and not only politicians, but black leaders and progressive people in American society.

MOYERS: But most Americans say that we've already done enough. We've spent all this money over the last twenty years, and look at the results we've gotten—negative results.

WILSON: But there have also been a lot of positive results. I fault some of us for not emphasizing the positive results. The Civil Rights movement was not a failure. There have been significant gains in the black community. The number of blacks in educational and government institutions has increased significantly. The number of black home owners has increased. There has been a substantial increase in black managers and professional workers. When I look at the accomplishments that a certain segment of the black community has made over the last twenty years or so, I'm amazed. But what we have to recognize is that not all blacks are experiencing this kind of economic advancement. So we have to say, "Let's approach the problem of black poverty with the same commitment to alleviate inequality that we had in the Civil Rights movement." If you talk about it in that way, then people will say, "Yeah, okay, I can understand that there was some progress from all the effort that we made, and I can relate to what you're saying, that we can't just emphasize antidiscrimination programs, but we're also going to have to talk about full employment, manpower training, and so on."

MOYERS: Isn't it true that two thirds of the poor people in this country are white?

WILSON: Yes, and I don't think we should lose sight of that. We should also not lose sight of the fact that many whites have been hard hit by deindustrialization, and that we need to talk in more universal terms when we introduce programs to deal with the plight of a lot of American citizens. We need to start talking about programs to help the working poor, programs to help the working class, programs to help all Americans get jobs.

MOYERS: What is the moral ground on which we should be debating and discussing poverty in America in 1989?

. . . no American citizen in this affluent country should be living in poverty.

WILSON: Well, it seems to me that we should be saying that no American citizen in this affluent country should be living in poverty. We should commit ourselves to eliminating poverty in American society in the remainder of the twentieth century.

MOYERS: One journal on the right says that Wilson wants to tax the hell out of the middle class for the sake of the inner city. What you want to accomplish will require ultimately a welfare state like that in Europe. And that's heavy taxation.

WILSON: You may be creating more taxes for these programs, but you get people working, you get them functioning as citizens, and ultimately they will contribute to the revenue and to economic growth. But consider what will happen with a do-nothing policy. In the last recession, for example, we lost an estimated three hundred billion dollars in income and production. Thirty billion dollars in a single year was needed for unemployment compensation. We have to consider these things.

MOYERS: The argument that if we don't do something now, we'll pay for it later is ultimately a cost-benefit argument. What's the moral case? Isn't there a moral value to these lives that are being sacrificed, even as we wait for the political climate to change, or public opinion to rally to the argument that you're making?

WILSON: We should all be outraged at the fact that so many people in this affluent society are living in impoverished conditions and are experiencing hunger and no hope for the future. We should be outraged about this. And this should be the driving force behind any program to improve their lives.

E.L. Doctorow

NOVELIST

*E. L. Doctorow thinks the best
writers are a nuisance to authority
because they prefer the
uncomfortable truth to the
comfortable lie. Never reluctant to
address the controversial issues, he
has searched for meaning in modern
American history. In such novels as*
Ragtime *and* Book of Daniel, *reality
and myth mingle to reveal hidden
corners of American history. His
most recent novel is* Billy Bathgate.

MOYERS: Do you still think, as you did a couple of years ago,
that our literary life is quiet compared to earlier periods in our
history?

DOCTOROW: That's my impression. I don't believe we're
doing work equivalent to our nineteenth-century novelists or even
to some of our early twentieth-century novelists. Beyond that,
several things have happened that have constricted us as a group or
"trade." One of them is the movement of the social sciences into
the realm of fiction. Anthropology, psychology, and sociology are
now using many of fiction's devices and forcing us to become more
and more private and interior. We have given up the realm of public
discourse and the political and social novel to an extent that we
may not have realized. We tend to be miniaturists more than we
used to be.

MOYERS: Miniaturists writing in small strokes.

DOCTOROW: We look for the major statement that comes
from the metaphor rather than trying to put together the sloppy,
all-encompassing novel of a Dreiser, for example. We do less
reportage than we used to do in terms of the great social issues.
Fortunately, there are exceptions. Novelists are writing about
Vietnam. Black women novelists have been writing very social and
political material. But, as a generalization, I think it's true that
we've constricted our field of vision. We have come into the house,
closed the door, and pulled the shade. We're reporting on what's
going on in the bedroom and in the kitchen, but forgetting the
street outside and the town and the highway.

MOYERS: The big story. You once said our writers are less and
less inclined to take on the big story. What is the big story?

DOCTOROW: The big story is always the national soul—who
are we, what are we trying to be, what is our fate, where will we
stand in the moral universe when these things are reckoned?
That's always the big story. But all this is not to say that we're
doing bad work. As a matter of fact, writers today are technically

more expert than fiction writers have ever been in this country. The average first novel is far more accomplished today than it was forty or fifty years ago.

Young writers today know a lot more, too. They have a degree of self-consciousness that perhaps comes of the fact that you can now study the craft of writing in college graduate writing programs all over the country. This is a great thing, but it has its drawbacks. The technical proficiency is an obvious advantage, but the fact is that too often the young writer goes through school, gets a degree in writing, and then stays in school to teach writing to other people who are going to get degrees in writing. There's a tendency to make the writing profession academic. It gets very guarded, and the sensibility becomes a little precious. You're with other writers all the time, and you're working out this little space for yourself and this little voice for yourself, and all the possibilities become smaller.

MOYERS: What do you miss when you're focusing so narrowly?

DOCTOROW: There's something to be said for a writer being out somewhere. Now I don't subscribe to the idea that writers should go out and seek experience. We're all given more experience than we can handle. As a matter of fact, that's why we write. Most experience is probably bad anyway. But, nevertheless, I think of the novelists of the past who came out of journalism, who worked in newspapers. Dreiser was a newspaperman, and he wrote knowledgeably about every element in the society, from the bottom to the top. And Hemingway, of course, worked for the *Toronto Star*. He got to see an awful lot of what was going on.

MOYERS: Of course, a lot was going on then. The novelists I read as a young man wrote in the early part of this century. Faulkner, Hemingway, Dreiser, Algren—they were engaged with the great issues of the times, when society was literally falling apart, and it seemed that America was no longer nourishing life.

DOCTOROW: That's the other thing—the passion they had. Things seemed to be falling apart—rising tyrannies in Europe, the collapse of the American economy, the immense poverty of the Depression. Writers connected with this and began to talk about it. They wanted to report on the misery around them, on what they saw. And they had this passionate involvement with their lives. The critic Malcolm Cowley has pointed this out: Whether they were on the right or the left, whether they were Marxist or Southern agrarians, whether they believed in the past or the future, they were all vitally connected to the crisis, which everyone recognized. I'm not so sure that our crisis today is something that we writers recognize or that we have any particular passion for.

MOYERS: The political passion in fiction today is coming from abroad, from people like Nadine Gordimer in South Africa, Günter Grass in Europe, Gabriel Marquez in Latin America. Why is that?

DOCTOROW: As a practicing writer, I am, of course, happy to put some of the blame on the critics. There's no critical fraternity today that has that much regard for the political novel in America. But when political novelists come along from other countries, the value of their work is recognized. It's almost as if we're too good to need political novels in this country. It's like President Reagan's feeling about trade unions. He likes them as long as they're in Poland. We like our political novels as long as they don't come out of this country. We think if you write from a political awareness, you're bound to preach. We've always had a bias against preaching in our art. We like Tolstoy, but we don't like his moralizing, his essays on history. We like the individual witness. We have a feeling that to the extent politics or political passion or social or religious passion gets into a novel, that it's an impurity.

MOYERS: Aesthetic malpractice.

DOCTOROW: Yes, that's our propriety as practitioners, that any of that stuff that gets in is ruining the work. I subscribe to the idea that you want your convictions to come up out of the work, not be impressed upon it. That you have to trust the act of writing to scan your brain and to represent whatever beliefs you have, but you cannot impose those beliefs on the work, you cannot twist it and bang it and torment it into shape, because if you do, you become a propagandist, a hack, an entertainer, or a shill. All that is true. It's a valid point of view, but as a piety, it restricts us.

MOYERS: I think it has some validity. Are writers the best ones to deal with the great political themes? Shouldn't they stick with what you once so elegantly described as the moral immensity of the single soul?

DOCTOROW: Ah, well, you can do that any which way you want to. You can do that as Jane Austen did, who ignored what was going on around her politically and socially, just to report on the lives of this family of sisters in an English village. Or you can do it on a large social canvas, as Dickens did. That is what we always want to do. I get a little worried talking about this too much because I never want to be in the position of telling any writer what to write. There are no rules, there's no one way to write a novel. As a form it has room for everybody and for every vision. But I can wonder why our work has gone in the direction it has. The artist isn't immune to his life and times. To a certain extent he is conditioned by them and has to overcome them. Ireland was always in Joyce even though he left and wandered around. You see that when you read his work.

> We're living a national ideology that's invisible to us because we're inside it.

What I mean to say is that it's not just the writers today, although you would expect more of them if you were an artist: It's everybody. We seem to be living in a state of mind that's controlling us as a nation but that we haven't quite defined yet. We're living a national ideology that's invisible to us because we're inside it.

MOYERS: Like a fish in the ocean cannot analyze the ocean. But what is this general climate that we don't quite seem to be aware of?

DOCTOROW: Well, I would rephrase that to say we've been living according to premises that we haven't examined for a long time, premises that seemed to be valid and workable for us right after World War II, but which now, forty or forty-five years later, continue to go unexamined, even though they direct our national life. Our unexamined premises cause even artists to reflect the conformity of our thinking. For example, many young artists want to get rich painting. They have no passion for painting, just for the painting game. We have young writers who take up the craft to become famous, so that the doing of it is not what they love, it's the being of someone doing it. Another example is the level of political discourse in this country as it's existed in the past eight or ten years—the pieties, the simplistic reliance on the worst impulses we have to make us fearful or easily patriotic, to make us stop thinking.

MOYERS: In fact, one critic criticized your novel *The Book of Daniel* and Joseph Heller's *Catch-22* because he said they were flawed by an adversarial spirit toward the republic.

DOCTOROW: I found that appalling. The most active and vocal literary and intellectual personages today have been people we call "neoconservative." They've been very shrill advocates of very nonintellectual ideas—like the idea that if you speak out or take a critical position, you're somehow giving aid and comfort to the enemy. Well, who is the enemy? The enemy is clearly Russia, the enemy is communism, the enemy is totalitarianism, the enemy is the enemy. There is that enemy out there, and anything you do to shake things up, to rock the boat, gives aid and comfort to "the enemy."

MOYERS: So if you criticize the United States policy toward Nicaragua, you're encouraging Moscow.

DOCTOROW: Exactly. Dissent is seen as a form of betrayal. Free speech is seen as being most appropriately exercised when it is not exercised at all. Democracy is maintained by not thinking democratically.

MOYERS: And fiction is judged by an ideological standard, not by the measure of truth.

DOCTOROW: Yes, to a certain extent it sometimes is. But the whole idea of dissent has been discounted. The average American no longer sees the value of dissent. People who say things you don't want to hear, people who point out things you'd rather not have pointed out, people who nag and say, "This isn't good enough, that's not good enough—try this, try that"—this kind of discourse is not valued today.

MOYERS: You're not talking about the writer as a critic of this or that program, you're talking about the writer whose works challenge the underlying belief system of the rulers or the prevailing mythology of society.

DOCTOROW: Yes, the key thing is mythology. When ideas go unexamined and unchallenged for a long enough time, they become mythological and very, very powerful. They create conformity. They intimidate. They coerce. The person who says, "Wait just a minute," is going to find himself in a very uncomfortable position. I can't remember who said it—probably a French writer—but there's a line that goes: "My job is to comfort the afflicted and afflict the comfortable."

MOYERS: This is an important point. The novelist of the thirties wrote about the failure of America to nourish life. But today that's considered in many quarters an unpatriotic theme.

DOCTOROW: Or more likely, too tiresome to be borne. There is a definite disinclination to accept writers who take on these big social, political ideas. It's the "Who do they think they are?" sort of criticism. We seem to prefer the perfection of the miniaturist. That may be a reflection of the orthodoxy we live in today.

MOYERS: Orthodoxy?

DOCTOROW: Yes, a cultural orthodoxy has ruled us for some time. There's no more avant-garde, for example. It just doesn't exist. If you were to consider the proposition that culture is something generated to express society's values, then it is the culture that compliments the society that is encouraged and developed by the various commercial establishments of art and criticism.

MOYERS: So the writers are being created by culture instead of creating culture.

DOCTOROW: Exactly. We're not making it as much as we're in it. We're reflecting it. And that's wrong.

MOYERS: Alfred Kazin has a notion that the thirties, instead of being a revolutionary period, was a counterrevolutionary period and that instead of extolling the autonomy of the individual and the freedom of the soul, there grew up in the thirties a relish for the power of the state. He says the thirties produced an orthodoxy, not a revolutionary ideology.

DOCTOROW: I think he's probably right. All I'm speaking of is the great activity, the ferment in culture as it attempted to figure out what was going on in those days. All I'm really saying is that the social impulse, that connection with the larger world, doesn't seem to be characteristic of many of our writers, or more generally, our intellectuals.

MOYERS: How do you explain that so many intellectuals today are in service to orthodoxy?

DOCTOROW: It depends on the generation. Of those notable members of the intellectual class who are on the extreme right today, one generation of them is simply terribly bitter—they're leftists who felt abandoned and betrayed by Stalin and who turned in exactly the opposite direction. But there's a younger generation who simply were absolutely traumatized by the war in Vietnam and the cultural agitation in this country of the 1960s, especially by the antiwar movement, and it's anti-intellectual manifestations—students, for example, would stand up in class and shout at their professors and call them tools of the imperialists and that kind of thing. That coarseness, that abuse of the intellectual dignity of the teacher, was unforgivable. The young people were seen as thankless and angry and anarchistic and nihilistic. Very many of them were in school and didn't appreciate that they were in school rather than out fighting. So lines hardened, and polarization set in. That was another component of the growth of the right-wing intellectual community.

The third element is very interesting, and I think it's been under-reported—and that is the immense influence of the emigré, Eastern European intellectuals who've come over here in the past fifteen or twenty years. Many of them are quite brilliant writers and professors of different disciplines. They have tended to see American life in terms of their own background and suffering, which has been considerable, as people in exile from regimes who have done terrible things to them and their families. They come of the terrible European legacy of monarchism and the reaction to it. So every attempt we make to legislate some advance in our American society, some social enlightenment, they see as a dangerous left-wing weakness leading toward totalitarianism. They've had enormous influence in the American intellectual community. They tend to see things as either/or and feel that you must be rigidly against any idea of improvement because the idea of perfection is what kills society and creates totalitarianism. The utopian ideal leads to revolution. They seem to forget we had our revolution two hundred years ago. Our history is not theirs.

We've always gone out into the barn of the Constitution and tinkered. That's our very pragmatic history. I don't think these people understand that. So any time we tune something up and fix something and make it more just, make it work a little better, they become alarmed.

MOYERS: Or anytime the writer champions change or the belief that while we may not be perfectible creatures, society can be a little better than it is.

DOCTOROW: Exactly. All these things contribute to the state of mind of the union in this particular decade. At this point in our history, anticommunism is a degenerative force in American life. It is doing terrible things to us. It encourages the creation of secret government, it fosters scorn among our public officials for public accountability, it contributes to our loss of sensitivity to civil rights and civil liberties and the loss of honor, and it encourages the self-righteousness in lying, and doing things against the law even though you're in office to uphold the law because you see yourself above the law. All these things come of the state of mind where national security is the shibboleth, and everything else must conform to it.

MOYERS: The justification for this behavior comes from the notion that if we live in a lawless world, we cannot ourselves always act lawfully. Defeating the Communists justifies any effort to beat them at their own game. The Cold War has been the canopy for the last forty years, under which writers have had to write.

DOCTOROW: I'm a Cold War writer. I published my first book in 1960. My whole life as an adult writer has occurred during the conditions and terms of Cold War. It's been a very peculiar experience for all of us. Part of it, of course, is the bomb and the rise of a militaristic culture that must be fed with money, money, money to keep it going. This has eroded our national identity terribly. It's certainly one of the things I've tried to talk about as a writer one way or another, metaphorically or explicitly.

MOYERS: You must be somewhat encouraged by the recent scenes of Ronald Reagan embracing Gorbachev.

DOCTOROW: If Mr. Gorbachev continues and succeeds, and is what he seems to be, he could be seen eventually as one of the major statesmen of the twentieth century. The murderous Soviet state paranoia itself seems to be relaxing a bit. It would be nice to see our own national self-righteousness relax to the extent where we could begin to admit our mistakes and our errors.

MOYERS: Do you think that is happening?

DOCTOROW: You and I are now talking during an election campaign. It's a shame that the political discourse so far is at a very, very low level—who recites the Pledge of Allegiance and who doesn't. This simplistic kind of name-calling, clutching the flag, not dealing with problems or issues, but waving symbols about, is disheartening.

MOYERS: In the sixties and the seventies the intellectuals, to a considerable degree, were opposed to the policies of the state. Now many of the intellectuals support the policies of the state and the ideology of the Reagan years. Is it the duty of the intellectual always to be only against, or does the intellectual also have the privilege of serving the people in power?

DOCTOROW: I think the ultimate responsibility of the writer, for instance, is to the idea of witness: This is what I see, this is what I feel, this is the way I think things are. Writers have the responsibility not to corrupt that point of view and not to be fearful of it, not to self-censor it. There's a certain dogged and sometimes foolish connection to the ideal of just telling the truth—seeing into the delusions, the self-deceptions, the lies, the pipe dreams, including his own. Now, if you do that, you're going to get in trouble both ways. You're going to get in trouble both by being against something and by being for something. Finally, when all of the dust settles, the writer who emerges will be recognized as the one whose work is closest to the reality of the truth. Reality is our ultimate concern. The writer can stake out a very remote place for himself where he doesn't see anybody or do anything, but just sits in the woods and is a recluse. And that can be seen as aesthetically pure. But it can be a very self-satisfying and essentially corrupting position to assume, as dangerous as its opposite—being too attached to power, loving it and admiring it and looking to be patted on the head by it. Any position the writer assumes may be dangerous to him or her. It's a very difficult profession, it really is.

> . . . the ultimate responsibility of the writer . . . is to the idea of witness. . . .

MOYERS: You say it's not the role of the writer to save society.

DOCTOROW: No, you can't have that kind of self-aggrandizing view of yourself. You like to feel that somehow, you might inch things along a little bit in a good way toward civility, toward enlightenment, and toward diminishing the suffering. But you don't want to get too pompous about that. Really what you do is distribute the suffering so it can be borne. That's what artists do.

MOYERS: How does a writer do that?

DOCTOROW: If you or I read a book, and we learn about someone else's life and torment, to the extent that that book is effective and good, we will be participating in that character's suffering. Presumably, when we close the book, it will give us an enlarged understanding of people we don't usually think of looking at. We are at the level, the depth, of the universal. In others we see ourself. So fiction really enlarges our humanity. Poetry, too, shares its perception of what life is, and raises to illumination our awareness of its profundity. That's why political diction and aesthetic diction are always antithetical. Because to get elected or to do what he wants to do, the politician has to appeal to prejudices, symbols, biases, fears—all the ways we have of not thinking. But the artist is always saying, "Wait, this is too simple, this is a lie, this is an untruth, this is a fraud." His diction is more like the texture of real life. Politics scants reality. It diminishes it and makes it small. That's the problem with political discourse.

MOYERS: I watched both conventions, and listened to both candidates, and I haven't heard any description of the reality I know as a journalist in the world. It seems to me the rhetoric has been distancing us from the reality of life.

The grammar of politics today is a visual grammar. Videos introduce the candidates, the political commerical says, "This little seven-year-old girl has known nothing but peace and prosperity for seven years." But if they put a different child in there—a poor white child in West Virginia or an inner-city kid—they couldn't make that claim. The video grammar of politics today manipulates our emotions.

DOCTOROW: Yes, and look at the structures from which they give their speeches—those huge, high podia over a great assembly of cheering people. That's begun to look a little ominous to me lately. When you get everyone feeling the same emotions at the same time, and thinking the same way at the same time, you're in trouble. This is when the myths go unexamined, and the coercion sets in. The rise of religious terminology on television is unfortunate.

The prominence of religious terminology today in the media, the televangelists, and the coercion of fundamentalist religious thinking as it effects its will in various kinds of censorship and as it expresses itself in political terms, seems alarming. Regardless of this or that particular scandal of this or that preacher, I think as a discourse, it violates my sense of what religious thinking should be.

Religion is a private matter. Religious thought, to have any kind of integrity at all, must be the most private, tremblingly sacred kind of awareness we have. When religious terminology is bandied about, it loses its religious character and becomes entirely political and coercive.

This has happened during the growth of civilization over and over again, to the detriment of countries and nations. In fact, it accounts, at least partly, for the founding of this country. Our forefathers ran from this sort of thing. The terrible destructiveness of religious orthodoxy as it infects and comes into the political realm is an indisputable historical lesson that we're perhaps forgetting.

MOYERS: Religious dogma is at odds with democracy because democracy invites and tolerates the clash of opinions. It can't choose one dogma over another. You once said that the mind of the writer has to be a democratic mind. What did you mean by that?

DOCTOROW: Partly this: When I was younger and would see some production of a play by George Bernard Shaw, or I'd read Shaw, I was always very impressed by how he gave the best lines to the people he disagreed with. That touches on the idea. To do justice to all your characters and all their points of view, to give them all honor—that requires a rather democratic mind.

MOYERS: Every truth has an answering truth?

DOCTOROW: Exactly. You have to allow the ambiguity. You have to allow for something to be itself and its opposite at the same time—which political discourse cannot.

MOYERS: The religious mind, seized by the conviction that this is God's truth, cannot tolerate an answering truth.

DOCTOROW: That's right. Faith is closure. It's very hard to discuss faith with militantly faithful people.

But the democratic mind of the writer is also a sign of great chaos. The openness of it will only find order in the work that's created. Out of the chaos of that mind somehow will come an orderly vision. If the writer knows what he feels before he writes and knows indubitably what's right and what's wrong and who's good and who's bad, and that this politics is the only politics, and this religion is the only religion, he's going to write worthless prose.

MOYERS: So that's what you meant when you said that at its worst, the writer's mind can be the tyranny of one argument.

DOCTOROW: The minute you find yourself too convinced of an all-encompassing "Idea" as a writer, then you're in trouble.

MOYERS: The writer is so often at odds with the political order because the tendency of the political order and the need of society is for orthodoxy, for a center that holds, stability. The writer's mind challenges or questions orthodoxy, right?

DOCTOROW: The writer relies on his own witness. And truth can be very, very uncomfortable and inconvenient—it's sometimes perceived as dangerous. I think it was Gorky, the writer-hero of the Russian Revolution, who was dispatched in the 1920s by Stalin's secret police because he couldn't be relied upon to say what they wanted him to say. He'd say, "Isn't our great, grand revolution wonderful? Then why are our glorious Red Army troops on such-and-such street looting that shop?" He got into greater and greater trouble doing that sort of thing. Of course, in this country, we don't erase our writers that way, which is a good thing.

MOYERS: No, but the mind closes very quickly in response to a parochial loyalty. Whatever the record, immediately after Senator Quayle was selected, Republicans said, "He's our man," no questions asked. The National Guard said, "He's one of us, so don't bother to raise those difficult questions." Parochial loyalty brings the mind to heel behind it. The writer has to assault parochial loyalty.

DOCTOROW: Yes, we tend to be wary of orderly rows of marching people, all going along at the same beat, to the same drum.

MOYERS: A couple of years ago, you said that in their nonpolitical, pragmatic vision, artists may be expressing the general crisis of the age. What do you take that crisis to be?

DOCTOROW: The loss of our identity as a democratic nation with constitutional ideals. I seem to be sensitive to that as a crisis—not as a sudden thunderclap kind of loss, but as a slow, almost invisible transformation of ourselves under the pressures of our history and our time and our ideologies. I'm reminded of de Tocqueville's remarks that when tyranny comes to the United States, it will be very, very quiet. It will be the somnolence that comes over quiet and pacific industrial animals. He compared us to sheep. I think that's true. We'll just forget who we are and what a raucous bunch we used to be, so outspoken, so aware of the dangers to our freedom. I don't know if we're that aware of them these days.

MOYERS: Do you think we are becoming a passive society?

DOCTOROW: It seems to be so easy to intimidate and coerce people. For instance, look at the vulnerability of people to television. We see in polls that favor or disfavor expressed toward politicians is directly connected to the amount of exposure the politicians have on the air. That's frightening. It means something is happening to our thinking, and something is happening to the debate we should be conducting at the most serious levels.

MOYERS: It's very easy to turn an opinion without presenting a reasoned case. The right commerical will do it, the right sound bite will do it, the right emotional manipulation will do it.

DOCTOROW: It's theatricalism. I wrote a play once, and while we were rehearsing it, the director—a man I respect—said he hated audiences. I thought that was an odd thing to hear from a director. Then when we started performing the play in front of audiences, I understood immediately what he meant. They were so easy to sucker, so easy to turn, so easy to manipulate and twist. To the extent that that kind of theatrical cynicism enters the political dialogue, as it has been doing lately, we're in danger. Anything that substitutes for thought—that seems to be thought but is not thought—is dangerous. I may be a bit of an alarmist about this sort of thing. I remember someone sent me an old copy of *Time* magazine for the week I was born, and in it some Swedish Air Force general was rightly predicting the coming World War in Europe. This was in 1931. *Time* magazine's reaction was to call him a Cassandra, an alarmist.

MOYERS: A bringer of bad tidings.

DOCTOROW: So it may be that is the sign I was born under. But I do worry about this kind of thing—Wilhelm Reich said that the average man's mind is structured for fascism—for authoritarianism, for dominance, for power. The mind attaches itself to power, it respects power, it defers to power greater than its own, it uses power on individuals' minds that are weaker than its own. If that's true, then it's very much easier for the right to win an election in this country than it is for the left, because it has such a little way to go to tap into the worst instincts of all of us. The true democrat who wants to enjoin us as a society to be better than we are has to go a long way to find some sort of connection with the voter.

MOYERS: The instinct to order in a chaotic world is not to be denied. The need for stability at a time when, as Gabriel said in *Green Pastures*, everything that's tied down is coming loose, is real. This has been a violent century, a genocidal century, a century of enormous evils. Don't you have some feeling for those people who have an impulse toward orthodoxy and conformity?

DOCTOROW: The violence and evil came out of order. Fascism was order. Communism was order. The Holocaust was performed in a monstrously orderly way. There's a difference between the social order that creates civility and certain shared values of decency and understanding and the order that convicts people who think a little differently or wear their hair a little differently or worship God a little differently. The order that wants everything to be the same everywhere and all people to think the same way and look the same way and speak the same way and come from the same background—that is the kind of order that we have to resist.

MOYERS: Do you see a tendency toward that kind of order in America?

DOCTOROW: Perhaps in the stimulus of this conversation I'm overemphasizing this—but I'm certainly aware that the power of government has increased in a malign way in this country in the past forty years. The greatest problem any nation ever has is to deal with its enemies without becoming its enemies. I'm not so sure that we're managing to do that.

MOYERS: In the competition of the Cold War, we take the techniques of the Communists to defeat the Communists, and that changes us?

DOCTOROW: We begin to scant on our own strengths, to cut into our democratic sense of ourselves, to condone secrecy and deception and assassination and all sorts of un-American things. We condone defending democracy by preventing people from having their own. There's a contradiction there. You can't maintain yourself as a power for any length of time without corrupting yourself. After all, the bomb first was our weapon. Then it became our diplomacy. Then it became our economy. Now, if some of the things we've been saying about American culture have any validity, it's become our culture, too. We're becoming the people of the bomb, even though we have evidence everywhere that we're going to go down this way. The Japanese are now the prime economic power in the world, and the European nations are economically powerful and threatening to us. While we've been wielding this bomb, life has been going on all around us in ways that we haven't been perceptive to. Presumably that kind of understanding will help change us a bit and relax our ideological self-satisfaction.

MOYERS: Something also happened to the intellectual under that canopy of the Cold War. He began to be a servant of the very state he once warned us was getting out of hand. I found it an interesting sign recently when Irving Kristol, the so-called "godfather" of the neoconservative movement, moved from New York to Washington, putting him nearer the scepter of power, for which he has become a very able spokesman—the intellectual at the service of the state.

DOCTOROW: That change is reflected in the behavior of two writers, both of whom I've regarded highly. In the sixties, Robert Lowell refused an invitation from the White House because he was opposed to the war in Vietnam. Yet, at the PEN Congress a couple of years ago, the president of the American PEN Center, Norman Mailer, invited George Shultz to come speak, presumably because it would lend a certain dignity or panache to the proceedings. Those two events reflect on some of the things we've been talking about and on the writer's changing view of himself.

MOYERS: The poet Joseph Brodsky said that you can tell a great deal more about a candidate for the presidency from the last book he read than the last speech he gave. Do you think there's any truth to that?

DOCTOROW: I'm sure it's a partial truth. If he does his own reading and doesn't write his own speeches, certainly that's true. But I should imagine a President would be under such enormous pressure on a day-to-day basis that his reading would reflect his need to get out of the Oval Office, and even out of himself. But maybe not. Apparently, Mr. Reagan likes the work of Louis L'Amour, a mythologist of the West who uses a classic good guy/bad guy formula—which does reflect Reagan's own approach to political discourse.

MOYERS: John F. Kennedy liked spy novels.

DOCTOROW: John F. Kennedy liked Ian Fleming's spy novels—and did give the okay for the Bay of Pigs Invasion. So I imagine there's some quick and insubstantial truth to that idea. Maybe it's a half-truth. Mr. Kennedy also liked the poetry of Robert Frost.

MOYERS: Are you ever tempted to follow the example of Tolstoy? At the age of fifty, Tolstoy abandoned the writing of novels. He said he was tired of pandering only to people who had time to read novels, and he became a prophet for justice. He began to preach Christian nonviolence, and he began to teach the peasants how to write. He decided to do something about the condition of the world instead of simply describe it. Were you ever tempted to follow that example?

DOCTOROW: I have talked almost jokingly with my friends about finding the opportunity, sometime in the future, to just see what would happen if I announced my candidacy for the House of Representatives of some district. That's hardly the degree or the magnitude of Tolstoy in torment. But I can't imagine not writing. I'm too weak to abandon it. I love language. I love to be in-it. I love to have my mind flowing its way through sentences and making discoveries that I hadn't anticipated. I need that. If my mind has any distinction at all, it comes of that process, or the commitment to trust the act of writing and see what it will deliver me into.

MOYERS: But you also have a passion to change the wrongs you see. You have a streak of the prophet in you.

DOCTOROW: I'll accept that if you define a prophet as a not necessarily perfect person, who tells people not what's going to happen but what's happening. Very often, everyone knows it anyway, which is what makes prophets so tiresome. No, I don't want that job.

I don't know anything that anybody else doesn't know. But the act of writing conveys some degree of heightened awareness. It's not a function of the ego, it's the opposite. When you write, you're less the person than you usually are.

MOYERS: Why?

DOCTOROW: Because of that democracy we were talking about, that opening of yourself to all the discomforts of contrary perceptions and feelings and guilts and improprieties of thought, and working through them somehow with a story and language to find some sort of truth. I can't imagine giving that up. I may have to. It may be that, like ballplayers, our legs go eventually. But until that happens, I wouldn't imagine myself voluntarily stopping.

MOYERS: I've always envied the writer because you can make happen what you imagine. Journalism can't do that.

DOCTOROW: We all do that to a certain extent. I've written about historical subjects and have caused some people to wonder if I've been quite fair to my subjects.

I think I have. I think I've been honest. But I haven't only stuck to the facts. The facts are not the sole source of truth.

MOYERS: But we journalists are supposed to stick to facts. You can create a Moyers, but I cannot contrive a Doctorow.

DOCTOROW: No, I don't think I could create a Moyers. Journalists are very creative. Journalists cover "stories," a word from fiction. What they decide is a story is important. That's very creative. Assertion is a strong part of creativity. There's great creative power in journalism.

MOYERS: I like what I do, it's just that writers make a world. They don't just report on it.

DOCTOROW: We do try to make people feel whatever the experience is that we're describing. Flaubert had an interesting observation. He said something exists in fiction if it's worked upon by something else. The window exists because the sun comes through it, and the street exists because the wheels of the cart go over it. That's the way you make fiction. You make things in relation to other things. His fiction is so unsurpassingly great because he invokes all the senses all the time. He'll tell you how things smell and not just how they look. And he'll give you ideas of temperatures, and of the air that someone is walking through. He is constantly invoking the sensate responses of his reader.

MOYERS: Do you remember the first time a word on the page became a sensuous creature to you, when you really discovered there was life and power and joy there?

DOCTOROW: I don't remember the first time, but I remember as a blur my addiction to reading as a child. I loved reading and was indiscriminately absorbed in whatever I read, whether it was trash or great. I would go down the shelves of the public library and pick up stuff that looked interesting, not knowing what it was. I read *Don Quixote* just because I found it. I didn't know who he was or what that book was. I read detective stories and Westerns and everything I could get my hands on. Somewhere along the line I began to identify with the people who were doing this sort of work. I read, not just to find out what was going to happen next, but with a degree of consciousness that someone had composed this material that I was reading. I looked at how it had been done. So I made that identification with the author as some sort of older colleague. And when I concluded the book, I felt that somehow the author and I had written it together. I don't remember the moment when I realized that was for me. It may not have been a moment, it may have been a gradually creeping addiction. When I tried it myself, fortunately, there were always some teachers around, and people in the family, to say, "This isn't bad, keep at it, you're good at this." I was very, very lucky as a kid to have that kind of help. And then, of course, I thought of myself as a writer for years before I ever wrote anything.

MOYERS: Why?

DOCTOROW: It was just some sort of declaration to myself. That's not a bad way to begin as a writer.

MOYERS: To think you're a writer.

DOCTOROW: Yes, to think you're a writer, and not to feel any necessity to write anything to prove it.

MOYERS: Thinking about it is a joy, doing it is something else.

DOCTOROW: The fantasy is like someone who wants to be a ballplayer. The kid who goes out in the schoolyard and puts a Mets cap on and plays with a ball and a bat all by himself, and announces the game, and plays all positions, including the umpire—that's the same kind of thing. I just happened to fix on writing.

MOYERS: Do you think writing changes anything? Has literature changed that observable world out there?

DOCTOROW: Well, it's very inefficient. The poet W. H. Auden said that none of the anti-fascist poems of the 1930s stopped Hitler. That's undeniable—but maybe the poems weren't good enough. Sometimes works are written that serve no apparent social utility, but which are predictive and become recognized later on. There are all sorts of weird ways consciousness is changed by literature. Certainly, I can't imagine my mind, or the mind of any of us, without Chekhov, or Joyce, or Mark Twain. All the writers I've ever read or admired constitute my brain, in part, or deliver me to some point in civilization that I wouldn't have reached otherwise. I have to assume that this is true of most people.

MOYERS: This is unprovable, but there was a time when those images resonated throughout society, even among people who had not read the literature. Memories of Shakespeare, fragments of Shakespeare, and others, had come down to us from the general culture. We had a sense of a common heritage even though we might not, ourselves, have read the literature. I wonder if that's as true today, given the dispersing power of television in sending so many disparate images. Is the loss of a common body of literature a danger to us?

DOCTOROW: That's undeniable. One of the reasons writers are let alone to the extent we are is that we're not perceived to have the same distribution for our ideas that people in television have. It's become quite standard for presidents to be very sensitive to the evening news reports. The basic network newscasts are very orderly, moderate, and basically uncritical. They are barely curious, let alone adversarial. But presidents are always saying, "Why did so-and-so say that?"—and they get on the phone. They don't feel that way about book writers, whose depth of discourse is naturally heretical, because we're not seen to have much distribution for our work.

MOYERS: It's intriguing to me that Lyndon Johnson wasn't embarrassed by anything Robert Lowell wrote, but he was embarrassed when Lowell refused to come to that White House reception, because television would cover it.

Trying to change things is a slow process. If you're never really sure you do change anything, why write?

DOCTOROW: I've never had a rational or thoughtful answer to that question. It's a kind of faith. Basically, you want to make something that stands. It's really very selfish. You want to make something that's good and true and something that didn't exist before. You hope it will last. That's all. That's all, but it's everything. It's a monumentally arrogant wish and desire, but it's also very simple. Just out of your own inadequate mind, to make something that stands and holds and becomes something that someone else will use to walk us another bit further toward whatever it is our destiny might be. Enlightenment, one hopes. Salvation. Redemption. All those things.

Sheldon Wolin

POLITICAL PHILOSOPHER

Sheldon Wolin has spent a long career as a scholar searching for the meaning of democracy, the nature of power, and the role of the state. As a teacher at Berkeley in the 1960s, he drew his political insights not from scholarship alone but from the noisy streets where theory confronts the realities of American life. Later he taught at Princeton and founded a journal called democracy. *His book* Politics and Vision: Continuity and Innovation in Western Political Thought *influenced a generation of students in the 1960s.*

MOYERS: You were at Berkeley during the demonstrations of the sixties. What can we learn today, good or bad, from the sixties?

WOLIN: It's easy both to romanticize and denigrate the sixties. But the one essential thing I come away with is the idea of a participatory understanding of politics. The wide range of groups and people who are now involved in politics in America would otherwise have never reached that level of political consciousness—that's the legacy of the sixties.

MOYERS: Power to the people?

WOLIN: —Yes, and the decentralization of power, the notion of power as shared and of political activity as collaborative, and also a kind of antihero understanding of politics. People in the sixties, particularly in the student movements, were very reluctant to repeat the old notion of politics as requiring a strong, single leader. Even though the student movements produced their particular leaders, there was always a reluctance to see them as anything more than temporarily useful.

I suppose the other legacy, for better or for worse, has been a more critical view of the universities and of education generally. The sixties was a moment of educational ferment and agitation for reform.

MOYERS: Do you see any signs of political creativity today at the grass roots level?

WOLIN: I do, much more than really gets through to television or newspapers. There are occasional mentions of a grass roots activist here or a movement there, but they all understate the pervasiveness of the phenomenon. People do take matters into their own hands through innovative, creative ways of developing institutions or practices that will meet a particular concrete need, whether it's public utility rates, or schools, or drug problems, or law enforcement. Those things are going on all over the country, all of the time.

MOYERS: But nothing you just mentioned seems to have much of an ideological purpose or passion.

WOLIN: No, it hasn't, and that has been something of a weakness. People involved in grass roots activities tend to be concerned with a specific concrete problem, with the result that there's always a fragmentation of these groups, each pursuing a particular agenda and each having a particular purpose. It often becomes very difficult for people to unite on a larger scale to meet problems and attack power structures that are more formidable than strictly local ones.

MOYERS: Do you think that the expectations raised by the sixties, of democratic participation and power to the people, have been largely frustrated?

WOLIN: To some degree they have been. One thing that has caused frustration, because it doesn't receive the press it needs to, is the continuous, consistent growth of centralized power in our society. People think of Ronald Reagan as an opponent of state power, as someone who wanted to get government off our backs, and the rest of the campaign rhetoric, but actually one of the legacies of the Reagan era is a stronger state. The state doesn't do as much in terms of regulation of the economy, but in terms of defense, of the protection of American interests abroad, of its role in the advancement of technology, or of law and order—all of those involve extensions of national power. The Reagan era has brought a slimming down of the state so that in some ways it's more effective and less overextended than it had been in the grand days of Lyndon Johnson and in the New Deal period.

MOYERS: Is this for better or worse?

WOLIN: It's for worse because it's been accompanied by an incredible apathy on the part of the American electorate, even in terms of the simple fact of voting. It is a less alert, less involved electorate at the national level.

MOYERS: So the national government becomes stronger, but the participation, knowledge, and involvement of the people diminish.

WOLIN: Absolutely. At the same time, it's becoming much more of a surveillance and control state in the way that it pries into individual lives. I don't mean to imply a sinister conspiracy theory. The most spectacular example of what I'm talking about in recent years has been the AIDS problem, where the dimensions of the problem have evoked a great amount of information gathering, administering, calls for testing, and an attempt to identify a particular population, to extend government investigations into private lives and sexual conduct. The attempt to handle, even if in a benevolent way, a clearly difficult problem means, inevitably, an extension and expansion of state control and state power.

MOYERS: But aren't the conservatives trying to assert a classic principle of the public health, even though it may impinge upon the rights of the individual?

WOLIN: One might want to draw a clear line and say, "We'll confine state control to the question of AIDS." But clearly you can't. As you can see, for example, the question of testing for AIDS has also been accompanied by the exertion of pressure for drug testing, not only for government employees but also for private employees, and the extension of the state into the private lives of students in high schools and grammar schools. Local educational authorities are clearly playing fast and loose with the rights of young people. The cause may appear to be a benevolent and generally praiseworthy one of public health, or drugs, or whatever the case may be, but it's often the good causes that bring the expansion of power. It's all accompanied by a decline of civic culture.

MOYERS: I grew up in East Texas, where conservatism used to be defined by a fear, if not a loathing, of government. Now conservatives pay deference to the state, and talk at times of President Reagan almost as if he were a sovereign, in the same way that Tories used to talk about George III.

WOLIN: It's unfortunately not just conservatives. The so-called neo-liberals also have an expanded view of the state. The questions of state power, accountability, and responsiveness are very important questions that unfortunately don't get the amount of attention they should get because they're very difficult to translate into concrete questions. We fight over deregulation or regulation, or this policy or that policy, but we don't talk about the question of state power itself.

MOYERS: When you talk about the decline of civic culture, what do you mean?

WOLIN: I certainly don't mean highbrow culture. I don't mean opera and art galleries. Culture has to do with taking care of things, that's really what its etymology is. It's the root from which agriculture comes.

MOYERS: Nurturing the public life.

WOLIN: It's more concretely the nurturing of people, places, things, and even institutions. We understand that physical environments have to be taken care of. We've also come to understand that cities have to be taken care of. But what we haven't understood quite so readily is that institutions require taking care of. They are practices and represent skills. Skills not only have to be honed, they have to be transmitted, they have to be looked after—even things as dry as procedures or institutional processes all represent in important ways part of a culture, a way of handling things—especially of handling power.

> ... what we haven't understood ... is that institutions require taking care of.

MOYERS: Are you seeing these practices threatened today?

WOLIN: Very much so. There's a disconnection between the practices of political institutions and the tempos they require for handling affairs of the public, and the tempos we associate with scientific, technological, and entrepreneurial innovation. The world of technology is fast tempo, changing rapidly, with an emphasis on the innovative and the novel. What's going to happen tomorrow becomes very important. But political processes, like marriage and education, really depend upon a rhythm that's less frenetic, less innovative, and that demands some kind of respect for how you've been carrying on something. Clearly, there's a danger that these things can ossify and become rigid, but I don't think that's the issue at this point. The problem is preserving them.

MOYERS: It took a long time to create a Constitution, and it took a long time to amend that Constitution. It took time to nurture the change promoted by the political process. You're saying that now the time it takes politics to transform society is far longer than the time it takes for radical technological and scientific change.

WOLIN: It's the difference between deliberation and decision-making. Deliberation, which is fundamental to politics, takes time. But decision-making often calls for rapidity of judgement, meeting a particular problem promptly and efficiently. Deliberation is slow-moving because you have to consider different points of view, different interests, et cetera, et cetera. That's why legislatures have been at the heart of what we've understood politics to be. We used to call them "deliberative assemblies." Now there's a problem. Every proposal for constitutional reform invariably makes an attack upon legislative power. It's seen as anachronistic in terms of what's required for a high tech, fast-moving, competitive, volatile, international situation.

MOYERS: What are the consequences?

WOLIN: The consequences are twofold. One is that people are always off-balance. The other thing is a paradox—change has a rigidity about it, because you're moving so quickly that the area in which you can see things is limited. You're like a man trying to dance on a log in a stream. You're so preoccupied with dancing on the log that you don't see the waterfall ahead. The result is, you keep doing that same thing more frenetically, which is to say, you're in a groove. It's that particular aspect of high-tech societies that isn't so well understood—that they are rigid, and that change itself, if pursued systematically, becomes a conservative phenomenon.

MOYERS: The New England town hall of two hundred years ago is a far cry from Wall Street with its junk bonds and golden parachutes, and from Silicon Valley out here in California with its freeways and technologies that are changing the landscape almost overnight. That kind of democracy is really anachronistic, is it not?

WOLIN: In one sense it is. The New England town meeting suggests something permanent and unchanging, something that has taken place in the town hall for three hundred years. That's one version of participatory democracy. Another version involves developing institutions and practices to meet changing problems. The question then becomes not how can we use an existing institution to meet this problem, but how can we innovate? Maybe we have to develop new kinds of mechanisms for cooperation and collaboration. You have to ask what kind of commitment you're going to make to democratic participation, which doesn't come cheaply. Democratic practices do demand some measure of time, some measure of commitment, and some measure of seeking common kinds of goals rather than personal or private goals.

But the shoe's on the other foot as well. There's a utopianism that goes with the faith that we have in corporate or large-scale solutions that I find more myopic than the emphasis upon local participation, decentralization of power, and smaller-scale activities. The biggest illusion of those who favor organizational or administrative solutions to problems, and who say, "Let's bring resources and skills to bear on this problem, and let's throw everything we need at it" is that their thinking masks a certain reality. Anyone who has ever had any experience with large-scale organizations, whether they're armies, universities, or corporations, knows that they're inevitably chaotic, and that at their center they do not reflect that nice organizational chart with its hierarchical structure where everybody's got his locus of responsibility. You soon discover that it's a jungle of infighting, with lack of communication, snarled lines of responsibility and all the rest. So it's unfair to posit an immaculate conception of an organization and say that this is really what the future is about—rational forms of organization that won't worry about participation, the involvement of individuals, and equality, but will worry about getting the job done.

MOYERS: Do we have a democracy now?

WOLIN: I think we don't. The idea of democracy and the idea of a strong, centralized state, inherently bureaucratic and administrative in its structure and orientation, are not compatible notions. Democracy implies involvement, shared power, and, above all, a significant equality. State power means the opposite of those

Democracy clearly is at odds with corporate structures and power that are unaccountable and unresponsive.

things. Democracy clearly is at odds with corporate structures and power that are unaccountable and unresponsive.

MOYERS: We have a rather thinly concealed power structure of large public institutions and private corporations.

WOLIN: The most important development in the last twenty-five years has been the closer intertwining of economic and political power structures. The difference in the type of person who sits in one and sits in the other is not what it used to be. The kinds of skills needed in both domains are also increasingly the same.

MOYERS: What do you mean? Give me an example.

WOLIN: Managerial skills, managerial attitudes, managerial ideology, are fundamental to both sets of institutions.

MOYERS: So that the interest of the manager and the institution becomes paramount over the people to whom the institution is ultimately responsible.

WOLIN: I don't think managerialism thinks in terms of that kind of responsibility. Managers may talk rhetorically about shareholders and stockholders, but while bureaucrats do worry about the reaction of legislators, the average citizen is not a significant category for them.

The collapse of the distinction between public and private is a very important development in the last century. One of the interesting aspects is this push toward so-called privatization of public functions, where private corporations are now encouraged to take over what used to be regarded as public functions—education, medical care, hospital care, prisons.

MOYERS: What does that say to you?

WOLIN: Most people think privatization means a decentralization of government power—that you're dismantling the state. That's absolutely wrong. What it means is an extension of power, which now is not coming from the state, but from a combination of public and private powers. The best recent example is drug testing, where you begin to talk about public employees in sensitive positions, and before long, private industry is into the same game, talking about drug testing its employees. The result is a common network of control and surveillance pressing into the private lives of people.

MOYERS: A structure of government and private institutions that is interlocking, intertwining, and self-reinforcing.

WOLIN: It becomes more difficult to bring legal actions against invasions of private lives. It's one thing to challenge the government on the basis of the Bill of Rights, but it's much more difficult to deal with private forms of power. In terms of the extension of control over individual lives, private concentrations of power are as much of a problem now as governmental agencies.

MOYERS: Is this what you meant when you wrote that every one of this country's primary institutions is antidemocratic in spirit, design, and operation?

WOLIN: It is.

MOYERS: That's a strong statement.

WOLIN: Government institutions, educational institutions, communications institutions—they're all hierarchical structures, and hierarchy means inequality of power. Secondly, I think they're fundamentally elitist in character, which is to say that each of them involves a definition of who should lead or control that institution, based upon criteria which can only be met by a relative few. So it becomes a way of excluding.

MOYERS: Yet as you talk, I recall the criticisms of the last ten or fifteen years that there's been an excess of democracy. We have too much democracy, too much participation, growing in part out of the 1960s—that's a criticism from some sources.

WOLIN: The notion of there being too much democracy is hogwash. Most of these are self-serving statements that signify the discomfort of decision-makers. Many of these policy-oriented heads of institutions see democracy as some of the founders saw it, as an impediment to rational decision-making. Democracy involves listening to a lot of discordant voices and disparate interests and conflicting points of view. It's very tough to make a decision in that context. Consultation drags on, and you feel like nothing's being done. That's the complaint. There's a real conflict between an efficiency orientation, which is one understanding of rationality, and a democratic orientation, which is a deliberative understanding of rationality as something that's composed of a lot of different contributions.

MOYERS: A prominent writer said last week that with a little less democracy, we could have won the war in Vietnam, and the whole history of the period since would have been different.

WOLIN: Yes—a little less democracy, and I shudder to think of what winning the war in Vietnam would have meant in terms of executive power, if nothing else. Watergate and Vietnam are inseparable. I would find it hard to see a successful effort in Vietnam that wouldn't also have managed to cover up Watergate. By the end of the sixties, the Vietnam War had become preeminently an executive war. Congress was a critical voice. A triumph would have meant a further consolidation of executive power, not to mention a vindication of military power. The last thing American power needs at this point in our history is many more heady conquests, because everything that's happened since Vietnam, as well as Vietnam itself, indicates a realization, slow and difficult, of the limitations upon power.

MOYERS: But these critics are saying that the United States has become a pitiful, helpless giant in the world. We can't accomplish what we want to because of an excess of democracy and too little executive power. You obviously disagree with that.

WOLIN: I disagree profoundly with the sense in which they understand power. They think of successful American power as broadly coterminous with the globe itself, if not with interstellar space. In this vision of power, which John Kennedy, among others, enunciated in the early sixties and Lyndon Johnson not long thereafter, power is seen as infinitely expandable. There is a heady, technological understanding of power as infinitely reproducible in ways that allow you to surpass all sorts of barriers that hitherto a power had to recognize and stay within. But the world is too small for that understanding of power. It's impossible for fallible, frail human beings to handle those magnitudes of power.

The question of limitations on American power has to do with what kind of society we really have in mind and what kind of collective identity we want as a people. In the first half of the twentieth century through the Vietnam War, our identity as a people lay with the expansion of power, world supremacy, and primacy among nations. That vision has been very difficult to surrender.

MOYERS: But President Kennedy and President Johnson both thought that they were engaged in a moral enterprise in Vietnam, in the shouldering of a great burden for the freedom and well-being of other nations and peoples, not as just an expansion of military or technological power.

WOLIN: A lot of crimes have been committed in the name of morality.

MOYERS: —the "seven deadly virtues."

WOLIN: Yes indeed. American statesmen have combined deep moral convictions and aggressive expansion of power—they've seen those not as incompatible, but as mutually reinforcing.

MOYERS: Certainly one consequence of it was this long train of executive abuses that you talk about—from Vietnam, to Watergate, which was really Richard Nixon's effort to silence the critics of the war in Vietnam, to the Iran-Contra expansion of White House National Security power. There does seem to be an unsavory creature that grows deep beneath the rock of power.

WOLIN: I don't think it's connected to this other problem we were talking about—the problem of the future of democracy. The commitment to power that has characterized America since World War II has been very popular with ordinary citizens. Vietnam was clearly a turning point, but Grenada showed us that you could also still get vast outpourings of popular enthusiasm for that display of American power. In some ways, extension of American power was a compensation for the growing sense of futility and helplessness ordinary people feel in relation to their own lives. The powers that confront us in ordinary life, powers of business corporations, or government agencies, for example, have made it very difficult for people to believe that they could control their own destinies—but lo and behold, here they were, the citizens of what everybody told them was the greatest power that had ever existed in the history of mankind, now controlling an entire globe. So what gets denied in one quarter can find a certain kind of satisfaction or sense of fulfillment in this other area.

MOYERS: I never met a president who didn't mean well.

WOLIN: No, I suppose that's true.

MOYERS: I remember Lyndon Johnson looking out the window after seeing demonstrators on television, and saying, "Why are they doing this to me? I'm the Commander in Chief." Our presidents begin to confuse the state with the self.

WOLIN: In Lyndon Johnson's case, elitism confounded itself with populism, seeing itself not just as itself but as a grander ego, as representing the whole collectivity. That somehow adds a justification that wouldn't be there if it were merely personal self-seeking or personal aggrandizement.

MOYERS: This is why the founders put checks on power. They did not believe that one man alone should presume to speak for the state or that he should have untrammeled license to accomplish his purpose. Do you think the checks on executive power are breaking down?

WOLIN: Well, I wouldn't want to put myself in the position of suggesting that it was all better once upon a time. I don't think it was. Even the founders are equivocal. If we consider the founders as including not just Madison, who probably believed what you said, but also Hamilton, who really didn't, but who thought in much more grandiose terms about the expansion of strong executive power and an affirmative foreign policy and a strong defense establishment, we see that same ambiguity running through American history, from the founders' days to our own. We want power to be restrained, but we also think in terms of glory and have patriotic notions of a strong America, an America that is fully the equal, if not the superior, of any country in the world. It's an old American ambiguity.

MOYERS: You quote Madison, who said that if every Athenian were Socrates, the Athenian Assembly would still be a mob.

WOLIN: I think it's saying that no matter how wise your deliberative assembly might appear, because it is an assemblage of human beings, it is still subject to all the frailties of human nature.

MOYERS: Do you agree with that?

WOLIN: Not really. The founders, in their own secular way, were much more Calvinistic about human nature, which they distrusted. That's one of the reasons that they believed in checks and balances. Commitments to democracy involve a much more positive, optimistic view of human beings. The founders' distrust of human nature is bound up, to a certain extent, with majority rule in legislative assemblies that were doing things that the founders disapproved of—interfering with business contracts and currency, for example.

MOYERS: Irving Kristol says that we are all democrats, but we have a fear of democracy that goes back to the beginning. Do you think that's so?

WOLIN: No, I think that one of the most important developments in this country in the last thirty years has been the steady erosion of faith in democratic values. I've always drawn a distinction between liberal values and democratic values. Liberal values are values that are basically suspicious of democracy. Liberal values stress the importance of constitutional guarantees, bills of rights, legal procedures, due process, and so on, as protections against democratic legislatures of popular movements. Liberalism has become the home base in which you can agree that you have to have a certain amount of legitimacy to government that can only come from popular elections—but that's the end of a serious commitment to equal rights and sharing. The movement away from democratic values toward liberal values is very pronounced. We talk about it in terms of meritocracy, rewarding those who deserve more because of their skills. But this is ultimately a way of hollowing out the content of democracy. It's not that we're really all democrats today who distrust democracy. I think we distrust it, and that therefore we aren't democrats.

MOYERS: How does your idea of democracy differ from those liberal values?

WOLIN: Democracy does include a strong emphasis upon rights. But that orientation isn't really enough. Democracy really does come down to people trying to cooperate, to make common decisions in contexts where there's great diversity and strong conflict. The problem is not to come to the most rationally justifiable decision as an economist might make it. It's a problem of trying to come to a decision in which there are conflicting legitimate claims. Democracy involves a capacity to deal with differences, and to respect them—and this is a different understanding of what power is about, and what the ends of power are.

MOYERS: Explain that to me, because I hear you saying that we've got to learn how to get along well together, even though we differ ethnically, culturally, religiously, historically, geographically, psychologically, politically, and ideologically.

WOLIN: That's really, fundamentally, what a political culture is about. The differences are becoming more pronounced, not less pronounced. Twenty-five years ago we used to worry about mass conformity and the homogeneity of American life.

MOYERS: The Organization Man.

WOLIN: Yes. But the influx of such different ethnic and cultural groups into our society over the last fifteen years has obviously injected cultures, languages, religions and outlooks, not to mention skin colors, that are so at variance with what we thought was an American society that the categories we've used to think about ourselves politically are really anachronistic now. The strength of democracy has been its capacity to confront difference and to cherish it, not just to think about it as an impediment to rational decision-making. The problem of handling diversity is really what makes democracy not just a choice but almost an urgency in the coming future.

MOYERS: How do we do it, then?

WOLIN: We do it by doing. That is to say, we do it by communities, groupings, associations, and structures that enable people to come together to handle problems.

MOYERS: That's what de Tocqueville saw. He wrote about the volunteer associations of life he saw here.

WOLIN: Yes he did. But De Tocqueville's other work on French society before the French Revolution is in some ways much more revealing of what that means, because what he talked about there was practical, concrete activity—buildings, schools, churches, the whole range of things that occupy people in ordinary life. What happened was the development of a modernizing state, an attempt at a rational bureaucracy, using experts with scientific skills, and resulting in the gradual intrusion of that bureaucratic structure into the functions that had been handled prior to that time by local councils, provincial estates—our equivalent of state legislatures. What caused the disintegration of that participatory culture was the gradual creation of a vacuum in which the local committees, local structures, and local practices began to dissolve and be taken over by central powers. What's crucial in all this is the transference of functions from the locality to a centralized power. That's what really destroyed French political culture before the revolution destroyed the old regime.

MOYERS: You seem to be calling for a much more intensive participation at the local level by citizens, in all forms of political decision-making at the very time, to take your own diagnosis, that the impetus of society is toward larger, more hierarchical, more remote, and more powerful organizations. Aren't those two fundamentally at odds with each other?

WOLIN: Absolutely. There's a growing realization of the frailties, inadequacies, dangers, and inefficiencies of that centralized, hierarchical, meritocratic structure.

MOYERS: So what happens then?

WOLIN: We have to think in more complicated terms. I don't think it's a question of going back to small-scale structures. It involves rethinking the scales of central structures. Clearly, there are some things one needs central structures for. You can't run foreign policy on a model of the Articles of Confederation, and you can't run a whole range of other things except by centralized institutions. But the question becomes not whether we have central institutions, but what kinds of gradations we have in between.

In saying that, I'm simply recapitulating the fundamental schema from which the Americans began themselves. We did have a federal system, which meant something very important. It was an attempt, for the first time, to create a complicated political system—not just a national government or a central government, but a structure of independent autonomous states which would be viable centers of political life, and which would handle a great many functions.

The American political system is the most complicated system in the world, but it's complicated in the right way. It's a complication of centralization, in terms of decentralizing things, and it's a complication of decentralization, in realizing the centralized things that have to be done, whether it's foreign policy or military policy or trade policy. Clearly, you need both. The problem is the movement away from a federal, decentralized system to an increasingly, almost hopelessly, overcentralized system, so that the whole emphasis has fallen in the one direction.

MOYERS: You sound like Reagan.

WOLIN: I know. I've been accused of that several times. The difference is that Reaganism stands for the revitalization of power on another level. Reagan talks about voluntary associations and voluntary citizen efforts, but that's a soft solution, because it implies that it's ad hoc. I'm talking about much more serious structures of cooperation and collaboration, much more serious attacks upon centralized state systems. Paradoxically, one of the unintended legacies of Reagan has been to make respectable, at least at a rhetorical level, the vitality of localism. I don't think he's meant it—but the rhetoric has served that end.

MOYERS: Why do you think he doesn't mean it?

WOLIN: Reaganism has been a combination of two elements, one of which is window dressing—

MOYERS: —myth-making.

WOLIN: Yes, right. And the other is not. Reaganism is a combination of a very strong push toward high technology and a strong state—aggressive foreign policy, strong defense, and the rest of it. But it's also been nostalgic in terms of nineteenth-century, or even eighteenth-century, values about home, church, family, and that sort of thing. It's that peculiar combination of technological progressivism, in terms of the political state, and a regressive view toward ethics, morality, piety, and family. It's that American proclivity toward wanting to find yourself sanctified by some set of values that you know very well cannot come from what you're actually into. In other words, defense, high tech, and a strong corporate system can't generate the kinds of values that really make us comfortable and that really suggest that the power we have is good and that we deserve it.

But if, on the other hand, we say we're the most moral people on earth, we have more churches, we have stronger family values, and we have more simple virtues than anybody who has ever lived, then the power that we've accumulated in this other area suddenly appears to be legitimate. The guilty conscience exits, and in its place comes now the sense that we have a mission and that our power is sanctified.

MOYERS: How do you explain this longing of Americans for the past?

WOLIN: I think about it mostly as the paradoxical counterpoint to a people who also believe in the importance of constant change and to a society in which mobility is possible. America is the land where anything's possible. New frontiers are always there. So Americans find security in appealing to biblical myths or myths of the founding or myths about American virtue, of our cities on the hill or whatever the metaphor might be. The progressivism to which the society is committed doesn't generate values that make people feel good about what they've done. They've got to find other modes of justification.

MOYERS: Even as we leave the garden, we want to go home. It's the mobility of American society that is destructive of many of the things that conservatives honor. Family life, community stability, neighborhood—all of those human relations that require time are rent asunder by the rapid change that is remaking our society.

WOLIN: American conservatives don't seem to realize that the corporate board-room, where change is a constant feature of conversation, goes along with this nostalgia for religious values that don't make any sense in terms of what they're doing six days a week.

MOYERS: I think I have an understanding of it. This year President Reagan vetoed the bill providing for sixty days' notice to workers who are laid off. That to me was a conservative bill. Sixty days' notice is a fair requirement if you want to give families time to prepare, if you want to give schools time to get ready for shock, and if you want to give men and women who are breadwinners a chance to relocate. That is a conservative measure, not a liberal measure. But the freedom of capital, the freedom of property, took precedence over the moral requirements of traditional relationships.

WOLIN: I think that's right.

MOYERS: Conservatives always seem to opt for the freedom of capital over the freedom of individuals.

WOLIN: I don't want to discount their good faith, but there is a very tortured relation between the progressive, technologically innovative side of conservatism and its commitment to values that its own efforts are undercutting. All you need to do is look at the society, and you'll see casualties of all kinds. You'll see cities that are unlivable, in which the cultural life is on the edge of extinction, in which there's class conflict, sharp cleavages, and distinctions of rich and poor which are beginning to become mind-boggling. There isn't much to compensate for that kind of destructiveness, except the promise of rising standards of living—which isn't insubstantial, of course. But that doesn't really go very far, because this innovative society we're committed to has clearly developed a superfluous population for whom there may be no work, or for whom, if there is work, it isn't terribly meaningful, and it doesn't have much of a future to it. As a society, we don't really know what to do with that surplus population. It's a surplus more than in the sense of people huddling in ghettos or being on welfare. It's got to do with the substantial number of people who may very well be employed, but who are so marginal and whose fate is so insecure that it becomes very difficult to develop life plans and life projects with any assurance that there's a point to sacrificing for the morrow.

MOYERS: What happens to a society when it has people who are so easily wasted?

WOLIN: It leads ultimately to cynicism because there's a progressive realization that you can't do anything about it, that fundamentally, the poor are with us forever.

MOYERS: Something happens to your own myth when that occurs.

WOLIN: And your own moral justifications become very insecure at that point.

MOYERS: I drove around Los Angeles last night, in the sections where the gangs have been much in the news and in the affluent sections, places like Beverly Hills. Going through these affluent neighborhoods, I was struck with the signs, one after another, that said, "security system," "armed response security system," "armed weapons security system," "armed guards." More and more people are retreating behind armed walls.

WOLIN: I think it's symptomatic of a very difficult situation, not only here, but elsewhere. You see it represented even in the high-rise, expensive apartment. The higher the floor you live on, the greater the chances for clean air. It's clear that the society has problems even assuring the sort of ordinary access to air and water that we used to take for granted not so long ago. The politics of survival is becoming much more intense and much more bitter, in significant ways.

MOYERS: Do we need a revolution?

WOLIN: We need a radical reconsideration of some fundamental assumptions—but violent revolution is as anachronistic as New England town meetings, maybe more so. Modern societies are so fragile that the notion of overthrow makes no sense except if one has an unlimited appetite for barbarism. Ultimately, I'm driven back to the possibilities of education to help ease our way into a better kind of world.

MOYERS: You speak of education. What are the skills of citizenship and how do we gain them? How do we teach them?

WOLIN: I don't think we approach them the way they're currently being approached. The famous Bell Report of a few years ago, which talks about education for excellence, is really based on a regressive understanding of education, in which the question is primarily, "How can we keep America competitive in an international political economy?"—which translates into, "How can we create an educational system in which students are prepared for jobs after they graduate?" The report is concerned with primary and secondary education, but more basically, it is concerned with technological competition. Secondly, it's very much concerned with discipline and control in the classrooms. There are a great many measures for tightening up the screws on students, tightening up teacher evaluation, and centralizing questions of teacher accountability and teacher performance. There's a vast centralization control ethic inside that report.

But above all, the report thinks of a student primarily as a potential producer. It's a producer's understanding of education. I'm a little suspicious of contemporary educational reform proposals, because the business community is so enthusiastic about them. They can see, of course, a way in which public funds get used to create job training for private industry.

MOYERS: But if you want to empower people to function in an economic order, don't you give them a vocational skill that they can use to their advantage?

WOLIN: To a degree. I wouldn't undersell it. But the point is, what are you doing? You're piling the question of job training onto the whole educational structure, and something's got to be excluded. There's only so much time in a school day and only so many subjects you can teach. The more you usurp that time by a practically oriented curriculum, the more you squeeze things out. The first things that tend to go are art and music, then literature courses. The question of what it means to be empowered is at the heart of the whole issue of educational reform. But it's being faced only as a job issue, not as a question of what it means for students to be systematically deprived of the kind of knowledge, sensibility, and understanding that can come from so-called soft subjects like literature, philosophy, history, and some of the softer social sciences. Those subjects teach people not job skills, but how to interpret their experience. They give you an understanding of how power relates to personal hopes and fears and vulnerabilities. People without that understanding are powerless to understand what's happening to them, powerless to relate to people, powerless to understand the true dimensions of what it means to be without power, or what it means to be dependent, or in some kind of nonautonomous relationship. The history of American education over the last twenty-five years has been a history of the steadily increasing deprivation of students of that form of sensibility and understanding, which, because it doesn't translate directly into job skills, appears to be ornamental or impotent.

MOYERS: Does this place you squarely on the side of Secretary Bennett, who's arguing for values of Western civilization being at the core of everyone's education?

WOLIN: It does to the degree that I think humanities are important. But Secretary Bennett is hopelessly parochial in his understanding of what the origin and source of values are. Secretary Bennett believes that Greek and biblical ideas are important to the Western tradition, but we know that those ideas are importantly derived from Near Eastern and Egyptian and other sources. The myth of "Western" values preserves a particular understanding of values that simply isn't true even to the origins of those values. What's important in values are values themselves, not so much the sources of them. So I'm on the side of those who say that you really have to enlarge students' understanding of different cultures and of different ranges of values—for example, values that are more sensitive to the concerns of women and minorities. You don't depreciate the value of cultural norms by admitting values that don't seem to belong to the Greek or Roman or even the biblical tradition, understood in a certain way.

MOYERS: What philosophical principle leads you to that conclusion?

WOLIN: It's the absolutely fundamental value and richness of diversity as a source of the expansion of the human imagination and the human sensibility and the capacity to sympathize and empathize with others.

MOYERS: But we know we're different. Isn't the great task, as we move to the twenty-first century, to find ways that, being different, we can nonetheless collaborate in the building of a society that has room for everybody?

WOLIN: We can't take that step until we honestly acknowledge how deep-seated the differences are. I don't mean to suggest by "deep-seated" that our differences necessarily separate us, but that these diversities are utterly serious and have to do with the various ways cultures understand the world, and what it means to be civil and moral and decent and pious and whatever the value may be. Until we make that first strong commitment to understanding the primal significance of diversity, we can't really move to the level of trying to find areas of commonality.

MOYERS: And that's a political art?

WOLIN: Absolutely a political art—the political art is about commonness and difference.

MOYERS: —how to actively collaborate, not just isolate yourself from people who are different economically, ethnically, and religiously.

WOLIN: America has had a problem with how it handles difference. We treat difference as if it arose from interest groups. That implies that if you can simply let people into the economic mainstream, or allow them to get their slice of the pie, the problem is solved. But that's such a superficial way of exploiting the enormous vitalities that are locked up inside difference. It's also a way of denying oneself the kind of self-criticism that's only possible once you recognize how really limited your own range of values is. Bennett and others simply cannot conceive of Western values as parochial. They simply don't understand that possibility.

MOYERS: I hear so little talk of civic virtue. What's happened to political language in our time?

WOLIN: Political language has become increasingly technocratic, dominated by economic modes of understanding. The cost-benefit analysis approach to public policy issues has become endemic, because it's a handy, easy way of seeming to deal with our problems. The trouble is that you can't reduce lots of important things to those kinds of categories.

MOYERS: You're saying we talk about money and economics.

WOLIN: We talk about money and scarce resources and having to make choices in balancing pollution costs as against production costs. That way of thinking, which is very seductive and compelling, leaves no way of talking about what is fundamental to a civic language, which is, why should I contribute, sacrifice, and cooperate in a particular way that's not going to advance my interests and may even ask me to sacrifice some of those interests?

MOYERS: —for the common good.

WOLIN: Well, for the common good or for others whom I may not know personally or who may be an abstract category to me.

MOYERS: So for all the talk about morality today, we're really getting more economic talk than genuine moral discourse?

WOLIN: There's not much doubt about it. Economic talk is powerful and becomes more powerful when people are economically insecure, because then, economic talk is talk of salvation in a way that people are really concerned about. They're concerned about jobs, about futures, about their families, and about their life plans. A language which seems to be able to make promises about the alleviation of those anxieties then becomes tremendously magnetic and fascinating. People are ready to go along with those who can manipulate that language.

MOYERS: The inscription above the main entrance of the University of Texas, my alma mater, says, "Ye shall know the truth and the truth shall make you free." A few years ago a student ran for the student body presidency on the one single platform of changing "Ye shall know the truth and the truth shall make you free," to "Money talks." It's the idiom of our time.

Here in Los Angeles, there's concern about the loss of the language of print, the language of time and history—which it's said is being replaced by a video language. Do you see evidence that that's happening, and is it having an effect on the moral discourse of politics?

WOLIN: Los Angeles is special, although I don't know that it's unrepresentative. What's special about it is the concentration of cinematic language and culture. The political consequences have been devastating. I don't find a civic culture in Los Angeles. I find a very uneasy kind of politics, which subsists because there has been thus far a quite brilliant state economy, and seemingly room enough for all. Because of the economy, the highly fragmented character of this area with its really diverse ethnic groups and social groupings has been blurred to a large degree. But the cost of this is an inability to deal with problems that require long-run solutions. Those problems are clearly pressing in on this area.

MOYERS: It seems to me you've really put your finger on it here. How do we as a society, given our talk about economics and our self-interest, solve the problems that otherwise will make our planet uninhabitable?

WOLIN: Inherent in the American scheme of things are tendencies which make it very, very difficult to mount long-run solutions. Interest group politics is clearly one way of undercutting that possibility, because you always have to compromise policies. Think of the difficulty we've had in finding an acid rain policy, even though the information suggests that the problem is urgent.

There are other things involved, too. The power of corporations to block long-run solutions to environmental concerns is also accompanied by the fact that the same corporations are paradoxically engaged in the kind of technological innovations that create a large number of the problems—so they've got the combination of political clout sufficient to block long-run action at the same time that they're generating the very difficulties that those long-run solutions are trying to deal with. I'm not simply trying to lay blame at the corporate door, but to say that their structural difficulties are really very profound at this point.

One could also talk about the difficulties of a political party system that's unable to generate policies that are much more than ad hoc solutions to ad hoc problems, so that problems calling for a coherent political will are beyond the capacity of our system at this point. Without radical reconstitution of a civil culture that understands and is willing to commit itself to such solutions, I don't see any way that we're going to deal with those problems, except in ways that are more authoritarian than we really would want to countenance.

MOYERS: Don't we need to begin by developing a political language that we can share? Language sets the limit of what we talk about and think about.

WOLIN: We do have some beginnings along those lines. We really have made some progress in environmental concerns and with certain kinds of health problems. Those areas involve a language of taking care of things, a language of concern, a language of thinking in terms of long-run preoccupations, and so the beginnings of a civic discourse are there in embryo, in those areas and in many others, including education.

MOYERS: What are the questions we must ask as we move toward the year 2000?

WOLIN: The central question to me is the question of collective identity. What do we think we want to stand for, as a people? That's what the preoccupation with a democratic culture is all about. What I think we want to stand for is not expansion of American power and not the endless economic and technological innovation that I think we're committed to whether we want to be or not. Do we want to see ourselves identified with notions of cooperation, diversity, respect and encouragement, and of different kinds of sensibilities and cultures? Or do we want to see ourselves instead as the technological power of the world?

Collective identity is something that the founders tried to deal with in the Preamble to the Constitution.

MOYERS: "We, the People of the United States, in order to—"

WOLIN: "—in order to," yes. Justice is part of it, and so is defense, of course. It's a first stab at an understanding of ourselves and how we wanted to present ourselves to the world.

MOYERS: Is it romantic to think that each of us, high and low, black and white, male and female, has an opportunity to contribute to the answer to that question?

WOLIN: Oh, I think we do, because fundamentally, a democratic culture comes down not to big, highfalutin' institutions or policies, but, ultimately, to how we treat each other in our ordinary range of relationships and conversations.

Forrest McDonald

HISTORIAN

CHIP COOPER

Forrest McDonald believes in pomp and circumstance. The ceremonial function of the presidency, he says, has become as important as the earthy practicalities of governing the country. Now a professor of history at the University of Alabama at Tuscaloosa, he has spent his career plumbing the intellectual origins of the American Constitution. His book on the subject, Novus Ordo Seclorum, *was published in 1987, the same year in which he delivered the Jefferson Lecture for the National Endowment for the Humanities.*

MOYERS: You have said that the presidency requires two functions so different from one another that the ability to perform them both is rarely to be found in a single person. What are those two functions?

McDONALD: One is the function of the king, the head of state, the father of his people, which involves ceremony and ritual. The other is the chief executive officer. The one requires presence and bearing—it's show biz. The other requires attention to detail, hard-nosed practical sense, and the twisting of arms.

MOYERS: One is ruling, and one is governing.

McDONALD: Yes, and there's an irony here. The British had worked out their system of handling the executive in the eighteenth century by dividing the functions. The crown became a symbolic office. They were able to do this because they imported German kings who didn't speak the language and were not much interested in governing as long as they got the goodies. The actual governing part, the executive part, was handled by a prime ministership and a ministerial system. Ironically, just as the British were opting to have a viable kind of executive, we opted to go the historical way, demanding that the two be the same person. Now Washington could do both, and Jefferson could do both. But the number of people who could do both has been extremely rare. For example, Jack Kennedy did the first magnificently.

MOYERS: He performed the ceremony and was the showman.

McDONALD: Camelot and all that kind of stuff. But he didn't get diddley done in Washington in the two and a half years he was there. Johnson was more able at running the government of the United States probably than anybody who ever held the office. But he was a turkey when it came to the monarchical aspect of the presidency.

MOYERS: I was surprised to read your claim that the ceremonial function of the presidency has often been more important than the actual responsibility of governing the country.

McDONALD: Let me give a couple of examples, one contemporary, one historical. When Jimmy Carter was President, whatever Jimmy Carter's virtues or lack thereof, he came across as a wimp, and the country was ashamed of itself. We felt weak. Ronald Reagan came in and made the country feel good about itself. We were no longer ashamed of ourselves, no longer afraid to take chances.

But to go back historically, Washington really embodied the power of the ceremonial function of the presidency. Everybody compared him to a king—"He moves with more dignity and grace than royal George," and so on. Abigail Adams just gushed moon-eyed when she saw him and said, "I was not told the half."

Washington worked very hard to strike a balance between dignified aloofness and excessive accessibility to the people. As for his predecessors, the presidents of the Continental Congress, people regarded the President's house as open at all times, and they just wandered in off the streets and expected to be fed. They tried to mob Washington at first. And Washington was greatly concerned. He sought very learned opinions from Hamilton and Madison and John Jay and various other people—"How do I strike the appropriate balance? What is suitable for a republic?" And he hit it. He understood that it was important.

MOYERS: You think he was doing this by design and that it wasn't just the extension of his character, his nature?

McDONALD: It's both. By this time he was so accustomed to playing the role of father of his country—

MOYERS:—even before he was President?

McDONALD: Oh yes. Bill, you wouldn't believe. I sometimes send graduate students to wallow in the newspapers of the 1780s. The one thing they're overwhelmed by is the adulation for George Washington. He knew he had to live up to his role. That made it doubly important, once he became President, to play the part and to be the appropriate kind of ruler for a republic.

MOYERS: You've gone on to say, though, that no small number of gifted men have failed as president because they ignored or misunderstood the purely ceremonial part of the office.

McDONALD: I submit—William Howard Taft. A disaster. I submit Richard Milhous Nixon. An extremely able man, but a disaster. I submit Lyndon Johnson. What was it like at the end? For all of Johnson's abilities, it was calamity.

MOYERS: But in the case both of Johnson and Nixon, wouldn't you say that it was their policies that proved to be their undoing, not their failure at ceremony and ritual?

McDONALD: It was absolutely not their policies. In the 1968 New Hampshire primary, Johnson was shocked that he was being rejected. Somebody did the 1968 equivalent of exit polls and asked, "Is it because of this policy or this policy or this policy?" and so on. Three quarters of the New Hampshire people polled couldn't even name a policy of Lyndon Johnson's. They just didn't like the man. You may remember an article about Johnson that Richard Rovere wrote for *The New Yorker*. He compared Johnson with Kennedy, and the bottom line was that Johnson got things done that Kennedy dreamed about getting done, but never could have. "The man is infinitely more able than Kennedy," he said. "But why don't I like him? I don't like him because he's a cornball. I don't like his style."

MOYERS: I remember the story of the time Lyndon Johnson was very morose. The polls had shown him down. He looked across the table to his unofficial adviser, Dean

Acheson, and said, "Dean, I just don't understand why people don't like me." And Dean Acheson, who had the courage of candor, or the candor of courage, said, "Well, Mr. President, it may be because you're not a very likable man." Doesn't that mean that people of a certain kind will not be able to perform the ceremonial office of the presidency, no matter what their gifts are?

MCDONALD: Absolutely. It goes back to Washington and Jefferson. Look at the difference between those two giants and the pip-squeak in between, John Adams—who wasn't a pip-squeak, but an enormously fat man. He was an intellectual giant, but still, as President, he was zilch, because he didn't have any kind of presence.

MOYERS: Why is it important for a country to have a ceremonial leader who can perform this role?

MCDONALD: I think it's programmed into human character. It's a basic, deep-seated, genetically rooted human craving to have a leader with whom one can identify and for whom one is willing to fight and die, to have a leader who symbolizes and personifies the aspirations, hopes, and values of the country.

MOYERS: Of course, George Washington set the precedent. As the first President, he became the symbol of the country.

MCDONALD: When Jefferson came in, he objected to the nature of the presidency as it had been established under Washington, where something resembling a ministerial system had been worked out. Now you look at the Constitution, and it looks as if you can't get there from here. But Alexander Hamilton was doing the executive part. He thought of himself as the prime minister. And Washington was head of state, although Washington did take an active hand in administration as well. But it really was a dividing of the functions.

The Jeffersonians attacked this as imitation monarchy and vowed to restore the Constitution. So when Jefferson became President, he delivered his inaugural address to Congress, but he never appeared before Congress again. That established a precedent which was not broken until Woodrow Wilson, by the way. Presidents never entered the Congress because that was a monarchical thing to do. It was a ritual that had been worked out in Great Britain. Jefferson and the Jeffersonians insisted on the separation of powers.

Jefferson was also a man of infinite personal charm. He was shy of large groups, but around a dinner table, he was magnificent. He gave dinner parties, and when the Congress was in session, he routinely invited everybody to dinner. Magnificent wines, great conversation, great food—he had a French chef. He affected homespun simplicity. He wore frayed slippers and jackets like a country squire at home. But Gouverneur Morris said of him that he was a concealed voluptuary. Now at these dinners, they talked about everything—art, architecture, Greek poetry, and so on. But they never talked politics, they never talked policy. Somehow, though, when the people went away, they knew they were going to vote for whatever it was the President was for. Jefferson manipulated them. He ran Congress more effectively than anybody until Lyndon Johnson. But he continued to maintain the principle of the separation of powers.

MOYERS: But he more or less disdained the ceremonial function, didn't he?

MCDONALD: He democratized this monarchical function. He was a man of great intellect and indescribable learning, but nonetheless, he was the man of the people, and he made the office be an office of the people. He entertained the British minister in the same way he entertained the senators and the congressmen.

MOYERS: He kept his office open to all people at almost all times, he held no court for foreign visitors, and he told people not to celebrate his birthday, whereas Washington's birthday was a national holiday even then. Was this deliberate on his part?

McDONALD: Oh yes, quite deliberate. It wasn't simple affectation of simplicity. It came easily to him. It was a public character that he could play. But he really did deliberately set out to humanize and democratize the office of President. A generation later, it got thoroughly democratized with Andrew Jackson. He was truly the man of the people. Gar, blimey, the inaugural! There was such a mob in the White House, they broke all the china, they stole all the silver, and they got so drunk, they began tearing up the building. Jackson had to be carried out to avoid being crushed to death.

MOYERS: What does it say to you that this office is so elastic, so malleable that any incumbent can make it over in his image?

McDONALD: No, it is not that at all. Every presidency is different from every other presidency, this is true. But it takes a genuine master to be able to make it something substantively different. I see a downhill pattern from Washington to Jefferson and Jackson and beyond.

MOYERS: In what sense?

McDONALD: Let me explain it this way: Washington's favorite play was Joseph Addison's *Cato*. In that, there's a fellow named Juba, who's a Numidian and therefore not a Roman. But he seeks the approval of Cato because, he says, he would rather have the approval of that man than riches or anything else. One of the things you did in the eighteenth century to make yourself better than you were was to cultivate the approval of the wise and the just. This is the very opposite of Polonius' advice to Laertes in *Hamlet*. Remember, Polonius is a fool, and it's foolish advice: "To thine own self be true." No, be true to others, and most particularly to the wise and the just among others. Now that was the guiding criterion in Washington's public conduct and in Jefferson's conduct. But by the time of Jackson, the President was seeking the approval of the rabble.

Our founding fathers, believe me, thought of the *demos*, the people, as a great beast. They believed in "the public"—but the public is a very limited concept. We would call it an elite. Who was a member of the public? White, free, adult males who had shown that they could bear the responsibilities of citizenship, which meant they had character and information as well. "The people" included everybody. "The public" only included the group defined. This is the group to whom early presidents appealed. When you start appealing to everybody, you get the kind of presidents we've had lately.

> *Our Founding Fathers . . . thought of the demos, the people, as a great beast.*

MOYERS: But it was inevitable, wasn't it, that we had to enlarge the meaning of "the public" to include those who had been excluded, the slaves and women? We can't begin by saying, "All men are created equal," and speak about virtue and justice without eventually changing our definition of "men" to include women and non-whites.

McDONALD: Oh, it's true. It's a Pandora's box. Once it starts, there's no logical stopping place. But as a Scottish philosopher in the eighteenth century said, "Democracy cannot last long. It's not a durable form of government. It can last only until the people discover that they can reward themselves from the public treasury. And then they become dependents of the public treasury, and they're tyrannized over."

MOYERS: So those first presidents sought the advice and approval of men acknowledged to be wise and just, but later, presidents began to respond to whatever the people wanted at a particular moment, requiring the talents of a flatterer.

McDONALD: Essentially. Of course, today the government is a hopeless mess. Now I don't want to give a false impression here. This is still the freest country in the history of the world, and it is a marvelous privilege to be a citizen of this country. I count my blessings all the time. But that doesn't mean I can't back off and be critical of it in an abstract historical way.

MOYERS: But as with presidents today, something happened to both Jefferson and Washington in their second term.

McDONALD: Yes, the lame duck syndrome. You're a lame duck from the moment that you're reelected for your second term. You're a lame duck because of the structure of American politics and government. In his first term in office, the President deals with domestic affairs because he can work with Congress. They need him to carry them when he's up for reelection. In his second term in office, they don't need him any more, and he doesn't need them.

MOYERS: Because he's finishing, and they've got to be reelected.

McDONALD: Right, so he's a lame duck from the word go in his second term. What that means is that presidents begin to move in the territory of foreign affairs, because there they have a much more nearly unobstructed hand. They always get reelected by a bigger majority than the first time, and they count that as a great popular approval of everything they've done. It's now debasing to have to deal with these congressmen. It's much more fun to go adventuring overseas. Almost every two-term President has done so. That's when you get wars and international troubles.

Another thing that happens is that around the sixth or seventh year, Congress turns the dogs on you. They go after you, yapping at your heels. A lot of them are running again, either for reelection or for the presidency, and you become fair game. At this point, the President tends to turn inside and whimper. Washington's cabinet meetings in the last year were painful because he would come in and swear for an hour at the accusations that had been made in the public press about him. The first draft of Washington's Farewell Address began, "Fellow citizens, you may have read of some horrible things that have been said about me, the calumnies and lies, and I could answer these, but it becomes my dignity just to pay no attention to them." The rest of the draft was a defense of himself against the charges. He sent it to Hamilton to be polished, and Hamilton fixed it into the classic it became.

Jefferson used to say, if you had to abolish either government or the press, we'd be a lot better off abolishing government. You've got to have a free press. He felt this way until he got into his second term, by which time he was ready to institute what he called "a few wholesome prosecutions"—to revitalize the doctrine of seditious libel, for example, because the press was attacking him the same way it had attacked Washington. Jefferson had migraine headaches. He would get so depressed at the viciousness of the attacks on him that he would literally lock himself up in a darkened room for days on end and not see anybody.

MOYERS: When I read that description in your book, I thought about Lyndon Johnson suffering after his reelection from the same syndrome, lying in bed early in the morning in the darkened room with the covers pulled almost up to his chin, and the window shades pulled down, reluctant to get out of bed. He would say, "I can't read the *Washington Post* this morning," or "I read the bulldog edition last night, and it kept me awake all night." He suffered deep depression because of what was written about him.

McDONALD: It began at the beginning, with Washington.

MOYERS: We don't have this picture of Washington today. We think of him as the father of the nation, not as a man vilified by the popular press of the day. But you have said that both Washington and Jefferson could regard opposition and criticism as treason.

McDONALD: That's another thing that happens in a second term. Watergate and the Iran-Contra scandal are nothing new—it happens again and again and again. You begin to think of yourself as above the law because you know that what you're doing is in the public interest, don't you? And the people know it, don't they, because they reelected you by a huge margin, didn't they? And these scumbags in Congress, why should you pay any attention to them? It's not something new that happened with Nixon or Johnson or Reagan. It's been programmed into the presidency from the start.

MOYERS: What did you mean when you said, "The burden of presidential power over a period of two terms has a psychic cost to the office holder greater than any reasonable man can be expected to bear"?

McDONALD: The psychic cost wouldn't be nearly so high if the prospect of reelection were there. Being brought into a war against the press and against the Congress, which is almost inevitable under the present two-term arrangement, wouldn't happen if the President were eligible for reelection. Just the possibility that you could would keep you responsible, and it would also keep them off your back.

MOYERS: So are you advocating that we should have an open-ended presidency?

McDONALD: Yes. We really ought to understand this second-term lame duck syndrome and what it creates. A lot of people have looked upon Ronald Reagan's troubles over the last eighteen months as unique to Ronald Reagan. But it is not unique to Ronald Reagan, it is inherent in the office.

MOYERS: Should we elect two presidents—one to be the national toastmaster and the other to be the prime minister, the man who runs the affairs of state?

McDONALD: It would be wonderful if you could figure out a way to package it to make it seem American and attractive, the way De Gaulle overhauled the French Constitution.

MOYERS: But we're not that kind of people. We're not going to make that radical a change in our Constitution.

McDONALD: That's right. We're going to go right on insisting that presidents play impossible roles, and we're going to go right on having a replay of 1987 and 1988 and Watergate and Iran-Contra again and again and again.

MOYERS: We've been muddling through the presidency for two hundred years now. Haven't we always been ambivalent about it? Even the Constitutional Convention finally gave up. They couldn't arrive at a neat definition of the office, so they left it to posterity to fill out.

McDONALD: Yes, but the reason they could leave it to posterity with some confidence is that posterity was sitting right there in the chair in Philadelphia with them.

MOYERS: George Washington.

McDONALD: They knew he would be the President, and they knew he could be trusted. Knowing that, they could leave it as a blank check, to be worked out with the precedence of the early presidents.

MOYERS: What did they fear in the presidency then?

McDONALD: Tyranny. The Continental Congress had no executive arm, and they went along for a dozen years or so, convinced that executive power is the root of all evil. By '87, the farsighted among them began to realize you can't run a government without an executive arm. But they were scared of it. At least a quarter of the delegates to the convention wanted a two-, three-, four-, or five-man executive because they were afraid. There was more time spent on the construction of the executive branch than upon the other two branches combined. The only reason they were willing to have a one-man executive was because George Washington was there. They all knew it. The whole country knew it. The only reason the country was willing to ratify a constitution with a President in it was because they knew Washington would be the first President.

> The only reason the country was willing to ratify a Constitution with a President in it was because they knew Washington would be the first President.

MOYERS: Do you think they would be surprised today at what's happened to the office?

McDONALD: Horrified. They wouldn't be surprised though. They would say, "Yep."

MOYERS: Let me give you Cassandra's lament, a summary of what one can hear around the country today. There is a widespread sense that our system is overloaded and spinning out of control, riddled with corruption, and gridlocked between a swollen bureaucracy and rampant individualism, as we descend into the permanent status of a second-rate economic power. We're living beyond our means. Congress is for sale to the highest bidder from one election to the next, the Pentagon belongs to the fixers, the President's out to lunch, and the media are drowning us in violence, nonsense, and trivia. Now from the long perspective of the historian, how does that state of affairs strike you?

McDONALD: My first reaction would be to break it into three components. One is the social or public component. We tend to conflate government and society in this country, but they're two different things. Two, on the economic side, living beyond our means, except in government, doesn't bother me in the slightest. If we buy fifty billion dollars more of Japanese goods than they buy from us, we benefit, and they're the ones in trouble. They get pieces of paper, and we get Toyotas. So that part doesn't bother me. But the third component, the government, is in bad shape—not simply because of a decline in moral fiber or the incompetence of particular politicians. It's not a personal thing; it's institutional. The government of the United States was designed to be incompetent because the founding fathers didn't trust power. The way they rigged the institutions to express this distrust of power is based upon the assumption that men in public life are ruled by their passions, their love of power and money. So what you do, in the words of James Madison, is to make ambition check ambition and interest check interest. You rig the government in such a way that all parts of it are working at cross-purposes. Hopefully, on the average, it won't be able to do very much, and therefore, it won't cause much mischief.

MOYERS: But there's also a paralysis that comes from the people themselves, isn't there? People distrust power in this country and always have. You've described the American people then and now as materialistic, worldly, and vulgar. Those are your terms. So you've got a conflict in that people don't trust power, but do want what a responsive government provides.

McDONALD: Yes, but a great majority of the American people are decent, law-abiding, reasonably intelligent, reasonably hardworking, honorable, and interested in public affairs. They have what used to be called public virtue. But they're frustrated because, as the old saying goes, the wheel that squeaks gets the grease. And there are organized special-interest groups who scream loudly, and they are the ones who are getting the real goodies from government.

MOYERS: You've said through the years that the life-giving principle, not just of our republic but of any republic, is the idea of public virtue. What do you mean by that?

McDONALD: I mean what was historically meant, and it goes way back to ancient Greece and Rome. It means simply a devotion to the well-being of the public.

MOYERS: —the public interest, over and above individualism. Didn't it also involve the idea that the highest self-realization came through participation in the public enterprise?

McDONALD: Yes, man attains his greatest fulfillment through participation in the republic.

MOYERS: What does it say to you that the most quoted source by the founders was the Bible, and not only the Bible, but the Book of Deuteronomy?

McDONALD: The Book of Deuteronomy is a lawgiver. There's where the Mosaic Code is set forth. The founders believed in the rule of law, and they understood that you can't have freedom without law.

MOYERS: So they wrote the Constitution to put everyone under the law, including the government.

McDONALD: To put the government, particularly, under the law. There's a lovely quotation from a great patriot named John Dickinson to this effect—that the Constitution is written in simple language so that as long as the people have wisdom, they can understand it, and as long as they have virtue, they will insist that it be obeyed.

Willard Gaylin

BIOETHICIST

Dr. Gaylin has spent his life exploring the emotions and dilemmas that bless and bedevil us all. He is a practicing psychiatrist and president of the Hastings Center, an institute devoted to studying the relationships between biology and ethics. His books include The Killing of Bonnie Garland: A Question of Justice, The Rage Within: Anger in Modern Life, *and* Rediscovering Love.

MOYERS: Here we are, just twelve years away from the twenty-first century. What do you think is the most pressing ethical issue we have to face between now and then?

GAYLIN: The most important thing we face is a rediscovery of community. We're a very individually oriented country, and I love that. I'd rather be more individually oriented than community oriented like the Soviets or the Chinese. But somewhere along the line we've gotten a peculiar idea of what an individual is, what individual pleasure is, what individual purpose is. We see everything in terms of personal autonomy—in terms not only of my rights under law, but also in terms of pleasure, in terms of privilege. I think we have trained a whole generation of people to think in terms of an isolated "I." But anyone like myself, trained in biology, knows that the human being is not like an amoeba, it's not a thing. We're much more like coral, we're interconnected. We cannot survive without each other. But now, communities have broken down. Most people don't really take religious community that seriously any more. It's very tough to identify with something called New York City. In the pursuit of individual liberties we have allowed a corruption of the public space, so that there are areas that are not safe, and where that happens, there is no individual liberty. The people who are living in Harlem, who cannot go out to shop at night because of the crack addicts, are in a prison, and we've helped create the prison by ignoring what community means in this country.

MOYERS: And since blocks and neighborhoods don't exist the way they used to, and institutions are frayed, we have to redefine what we mean by a community. We have to re-create communities, we can't just resurrect what was.

GAYLIN: Yes, we have to work to find community. The issue comes up in a number of ways. For instance, there's a shibboleth against institutions and for home care. Do you know what home care is for most people? It's solitary confinement! We have to rediscover institutions. I would rather be among seven other older and helpless people with one nurse and a housekeeper than confined in solitary confinement even as a wealthy man who could afford around-the-clock nursing. We have to rediscover community.

MOYERS: It strikes me that no one ever prays the Lord's prayer in the first person singular: "Give *me* this day *my* daily bread." It is a collective, a community petition: "Give *us* this day *our* daily bread." I'm dependent for my daily bread on hundreds of strangers I will never meet. I'm in their hands, literally, for that bread. I can't grow wheat, I can't package it, deliver it to myself. There's a cycle of which I'm a part. I have to give back something in exchange for that. If we let each other down, I don't eat, and they don't eat.

GAYLIN: Somehow or other we've developed a concept of personal pleasure, of personal fulfillment—let it hang out, do your own thing—so that all of pleasure is seen as a quick fix, as an isolated experience. The concept of attachment, the concept of service, the concept that somehow pleasure can involve pain or sacrifice—those ideas have simply been dissipated in our culture.

One of the most incredible things to me really is to see the typical middle class kid who's given everything he wants except the privilege of service, the privilege of self-sacrifice, and the joy of being a giver. We've become a passive society that sees everything in terms of our open mouth—fill it with something! The idea that we can actually do things for something broader—a community—is lost.

I happen to know that service is empowering. It's great. It's terrific! Given the opportunity for training toward community and service, people love it and want it. I don't find I'm happy with the kind of narcissistic quick-fix life that this society offers most people.

MOYERS: The other day my wife and I were watching television, and we saw a beautifully crafted commercial for a high-powered, fast, expensive car. It was zooming along a highway with no other automobiles, with no impediments whatsoever, as if that's the way we all drive. But coming up here to see you today, I was bumper to bumper with growling brakes and screeching horns and shouting drivers. And I thought, we keep promoting this fantasy of the Lone Ranger, the American in his expensive car able to gun it and go anywhere he wants. We keep the romance of the individual alive that way.

GAYLIN: There is a concept that somehow or other everything is done by you, with you. And yet if you think of the true pleasures of life, very few involve the isolated individual. Even reading is a shared activity—you are sharing with an author who has the capacity for getting into you and grabbing you.

It's interesting to see how our culture has changed in its approach to the isolated individual. Take masturbation, for example. A hundred years ago it was a sin against God. Then with Freud it became simply immature and neurotic. Then it became healthy, a sign of freedom. And then, if you believe some of the radical feminists, it's the only way to have sex without being exploited.

MOYERS: You once wrote, "An individual human being is only a useful social myth." Do you still believe that?

GAYLIN: Absolutely. Human beings require food, water, protection from the elements, heat, and other human beings. If a child is deprived of contact with human beings, even if you give him perfect nourishment, he becomes an incomplete adult. He loses those qualities that are most identified with being human: the capacity to form attachments, the capacity to have guilt, the capacity to see the future—in other words, the capacity to have conscience and love.

MOYERS: Do you believe that we are biologically endowed with a faculty for caring?

GAYLIN: Absolutely.

MOYERS: Is there any evidence for that?

GAYLIN: There's plenty of evidence. A baby can neither run from danger nor fight it off. It's totally helpless. We have the most prolonged dependency period possible. We had to exist before culture and not gobble up little babies during periods of hunger. No organism so constructed could survive without built-in loving, and not just maternal love.

MOYERS: If there is a caring faculty in us, why is there so much child abuse, so much family violence?

GAYLIN: Because this extraordinary, wonderful, terrifying creature, *Homo sapiens*—with which I've had a lifelong love affair—is unique among all creatures.

There's a wonderful Talmudic quotation that says if God had intended man to be circumcised, why didn't he make him that way in the first place? And the answer, with the wisdom of the sages, is that man alone among creatures is created incomplete with the privilege of sharing with his maker in his own design. And that is true. Of all the animals, we are the one least dictated to by genetics or by nature. We have the capacity to shape ourselves for good or for evil. So that while we are endowed with certain caring features, we can create a corrupt race of human beings and eventually destroy ourselves.

MOYERS: The particle physicists tell us that forces are inextricably bound together, that life is multivalent, and that all of these energies and powers link together in a basic, fundamental, dynamic web. Is that true in your own experience as a scientist?

GAYLIN: Absolutely. We talk about civil liberties, certainly something I agree with. But if you dare mention the concept of responsibilities, duties, or obligations along with these liberties, you can get into trouble.

For example, there was an article in the *New York Times* saying that individuals in the high-risk categories for AIDS should not be coerced into being tested, that they have a right not to know. I answered in an op-ed piece and said, I accept that you have a right not to know, but if you choose not to be tested, you have a moral responsibility to act as though you had been tested and had been tested positively. And while I expressed compassion for the victim groups, I said that even being a victim does not allow you the privilege of being a victimizer. The amount of hate mail I received was incredible.

MOYERS: So, Americans have to begin to accept some limits on their personal, individual autonomy.

GAYLIN: We are capable of doing it in crisis. Certainly we did it during the Great War, when people were mobilized. The fact is that epidemics and crises force us to think collectively, so that New York, for example, is really at its pleasantest during a blackout or a snowstorm, because you have to think about each other.

MOYERS: The danger of community, of course, is conformity. Conformity can lead to coercion, and coercion can lead to denigration of the individual.

GAYLIN: Yes, but I think we're all sophisticated about Marxist utopias. I don't think this country's going to be driven to a totalitarian regime. I think there's more danger if we don't solve the problems of community, if people begin to be frightened, and if there's a sense that things aren't fair. I'll bet you the first ethical statement your kids said was, "It's not fair." It was usually because you did something for the siblings that you didn't do for them. If it's not safe to walk in the streets, if inflation's going to wipe out the savings of the middle class, if illness isn't going to be protected, if we're not going to be able to take care of our indigent and helplessly ill, if we're not going to have housing, eventually there's going to be a feeling that things aren't working. When people feel that this society isn't working and isn't fair, you run the danger of having a collective fascist state.

MOYERS: There's an old idea of transactional ethics where I do something for you if you do something for me. But there is also the idea of a transformational ethic, an ethic that changes our attitude so we all become cooperative and caring people and not merely competitive rivals. Is this just a romantic notion?

GAYLIN: I believe that service involves pain, but once experienced, will never be traded. The most pleasurable thing I ever did in my life was raise my kids. It's also the most painful thing I ever did in my life. It was agonizing! So I am optimistic that if we begin to introduce people to service, we will see that they are hungry for it, hungry for a cause. And I'll tell you something—if we don't give them a good cause, they'll find a bad one. People want someone to show them a better way.

> . . . we have generations of children being born without the capacity for caring, without figures to identify with.

It worries me that we have generations of children being born without the capacity for caring, without figures to identify with. This is a ticking time bomb. And it worries me that our culture continues to glorify a guy out on his own, doing his own thing—and usually it's a very macho thing.

MOYERS: Where do we interrupt that route to isolation? If a child is born to a single mother who must work, what do we do with that child?

GAYLIN: You know, there are community ways of raising children. Studies of the early Israeli kibbutz showed that you could maintain mother-child and father-child ties, even when the child was in a community, if the family slept together at night, and had meals together. Those kibbutzim that totally broke down the family produced much more disturbed and selfish children.

Whatever we do, we're not going to go backward on the feminist revolution. The revolution has worked to a certain extent—for women. A woman can say to a law firm, "I'm only going to work forty hours a week. I'm not going to give you eighty. I want my kids." Interestingly, a man can't say that yet.

We've got to get out of this idea of the eighty- or ninety-hour week as the mark of a successful person.

MOYERS: You have written that this success drive is killing us because no matter where you are on the rung of success, there's always a rung above you—so you're a failure no matter where you stand.

GAYLIN: Yes, in many ways a closed society was easier. If you were a baker's son in small-town France, the most you could ever hope to be was a baker. You were never considered quite as good as your father was, but all you had to do to be a success was to bake good bread. However, now if you're a baker's son, you can own a bakery, you can then own General Foods, et cetera, so wherever you are, someone's ahead of you. The upwardly mobile society is a terrible trap. Worse, it does something else: it means that while the father used to be the symbol of success, now the father is the symbol of failure. The fathers themselves feel that way. They say, "Do you think I want you to end up the way I am? I want you to do better."

Success is measured in such strange things. It's in little pieces of green paper which then you take into a mercantile scene in which you get a big piece of paper called a picture or a piece of cloth that—if it's got the right label on it—says "I am important, I have money."

So we're constantly involved in narcissistic pleasure. It's not true pleasure, but the kind of pleasure that comes when you turn the cold water off, or get the hot water back on the tap—it's a relief of our insecurity. We're driving people to narcissistic pleasures. There are people who have no money, who live a sort of a poor, struggling existence—and I'm not talking about grinding poverty, but about average working people—who are sure that somewhere up there, in the penthouses of New York, in the villas of the Riviera, are wealthy people who love life. You know what? The frustrations in the villas of the Riviera are just as great. The sense of impotence, the sense of anxiety, and the unsureness about whether you're on the top rung of the ladder exist all the way up the line.

I worry that with the high expectations raised by advertisements, there will be a bitter sense of betrayal. During the Depression there was hunger, but there wasn't the sense of paranoid rage that exists now. When the difference between promise and delivery is great, people feel outrage. The underclasses have felt betrayed. Now the middle classes are beginning to feel betrayed, because what's produced? A kind of joyless existence. And when it gets to such things as rationing health care, it's just going to be monstrous!

MOYERS: What does this mean in terms of hard choices? For example, are we going to be able to help everybody who wants to stay alive?

GAYLIN: No. This is the next crisis. We are now on the threshold of a giant success in medicine. And while most people may not realize it, it's always our successes that get us in trouble, because successes give us choices. At one time medicine couldn't do anything except give you comfort. It sure couldn't save lives. My professor of physiology once said medical intervention probably took more lives than it saved. And he was right. But now that we're getting into genetic engineering and molecular medicine, where we actually are down to the level of the cell, we are going to be able to do extraordinary things.

With these new choices—and all of them are expensive choices—Americans are going to have to face a dreadful thing. We are not going to be able to afford the most important thing there is—life. That's the irony—that we'll be forced to think collectively because we will run out of lifesaving devices. They are simply too expensive.

MOYERS: In other words, we can't afford a kidney dialysis machine or an artificial heart for everybody.

GAYLIN: People say, well, we're spending 11 percent of the gross national product on medicine—perhaps we should be spending 15 percent. But if we keep raising this figure, it's soon going to be medicine versus education, medicine versus public safety, medicine versus defense.

We are going to have to limit medical costs. It's hard for people to realize that the costs of medicine are not due simply to greedy physicians and sloppy techniques. Now we do have some greedy physicians, we do have sloppy techniques, but that there is a lot of fat in the system?—that's hogwash. That is not what causes expensive medicine. What causes expensive medicine is our successes. Good medicine increases morbidity. There are more diabetics alive in the United States than there are in Libya. Our successes keep sick people alive.

Some people say we should do preventive medicine. There is no such thing as preventive medicine ultimately, in that we're all going to die. It means that you prevent a child from dying of a childhood disease, which has a humanitarian purpose, but not an economic purpose because he will then live to be a very expensive old man.

We're being faced with a terrible irony—now that medicine can really deliver, can really prolong life, we can't afford to do it.

MOYERS: You are implying that we will have to decide that some lives have a greater claim on us than other lives. The eighty-five-year-old man versus the sixteen-year-old youth.

GAYLIN: I'm glad you said that and not myself, because you'll get the letters from the Gray Panthers. But somewhere along the line we are going to have to decide. Those choices used to be made by physicians because they occurred in the house of medicine, with the language of medicine, and using the metaphors of medicine. But they are not medical decisions. Those decisions are human decisions, philosophical point-of-view decisions.

MOYERS: I've actually heard suggestions that we hold a lottery to decide whose life will be saved.

GAYLIN: What if I were ninety-six, dying of terminal cancer, praying to God that I don't wake up in the morning, and there was a child with an acute intoxication, having swallowed a bottle of aspirins, and we were both in an emergency status, and our names were put into a hat. We can't do it that way.

MOYERS: But as long as you have the power of choice, you could say, I don't want my name in the hat.

GAYLIN: Yes, you could. But what I'm saying is that after we've made certain broad decisions, we may get down to a kind of lottery system. I certainly don't want to sell those lifesaving opportunities, as we do now.

MOYERS: In the marketplace?

GAYLIN: Absolutely. I remember talking to a distinguished transplant surgeon who didn't know I was a bioethicist. He said, "What's all this baloney"—baloney was not his word—"about 'bioethics'?" Now I wasn't going to answer a big, tough-looking guy like that, so I asked him about his work. When he talked about it, he became gentle and tender. He described what it is like to put a liver into a child, and see all systems light up—it was like genesis, it was poetry, it was so touching. And then I asked him, "How much does it cost?"
He said, "Two hundred thousand dollars."
And I said, "How do these kids pay for it?"
It was the shortest, briefest answer I ever got: "Up front." I gave him a look, and he said, "Well, you don't expect the University of X to subsidize this! We couldn't afford it!"
I said, "Does that bother you?"
He said, "Well, what do you think I am? I'm a human being."
I said, "That's maybe what we mean by bioethics."

MOYERS: He was saying the market determines it. Those parents could pay, but if the parents of a child down the block or up the street couldn't pay, that child dies.

GAYLIN: Yes. And even if it isn't pay, it's often something like getting on television. There has to be a better system.

MOYERS: How do we devise such a system?

GAYLIN: I think it's collective wisdom again. I'll give you some extremes, and then you can fill in the tough cases. If I were to name a three-day-old zygote, a three-month-old fetus, a nine-month-old fetus, a one-second-old child, a nine-year-old child, and an eighty-year-old man, we would have a massive consensus. Some might say "I refuse to judge," but most of us would say that the nine-month fetus is a different thing from a three-day-old zygote, and has a different claim on life. Most of us would say that even a nine-month-old fetus is not to be put in a lottery with our nine-year-old child. And most of us would say that the nine-year-old child has a greater claim than the eighty-year-old man. Now as we squeeze down, from the eighty-year-old and up from the nine-year-old, we may go to some kind of lottery system. But first we must make moral judgments.

MOYERS: Doesn't fate run the biggest lottery of all?

GAYLIN: I suppose so, in the sense that my children were lucky to be born in Hastings-on-Hudson and not in Calcutta. But that raises other questions. Is medical humanism something like an export-import product which you reserve for your own country? If we spent piddling amounts of money on tropical diseases, which kill millions, we could have a cure for malaria, for schistosomiasis—all these horrible parasitic diseases. But that isn't a terribly important area of the globe to us.

MOYERS: But the other side of it is that if the children who otherwise would have died, grow up to become childbearing parents, you get a situation like India, whose population is increasing sharply again.

GAYLIN: Population control is one of the major ethical questions, and those who are opposed to population control have to then face up to the problem of how they're going to allocate the limited resources we have.

MOYERS: What is our obligation to people who make claims on society as a result of their own willful behavior? For example, what about the motorcycle rider who refuses to wear a helmet; the mountain climber who against common sense puts himself at peril, suffers an accident, and requires prolonged years of treatment; or smokers—what is our obligation collectively to people who will themselves into bad health?

GAYLIN: You could say, what the hell, if you can't take care of yourself, why should we take care of you? There is a reasonable argument for that perspective, but I'm a little reluctant to adopt it. What about a person who is forty pounds overweight? That isn't exactly a volitional thing. I know how hard it is for a person to lose weight or to give up an addictive habit.

The hard choices are going to be in valuing life. People will say, well, you're on a slippery slope, you're going to say yes here and not there. And they're right, we are going to have to be on a slippery slope. We're going to draw lines, and when we do that, someone will say, "Hey, wait a second. You mean that the person this side of the line is that different from that side?" And they make you look like a fool.

Now of course a person who is seventeen years old, eleven months and twenty-nine days and can't vote isn't much different from a person who's eighteen years old, but we draw a line—or else we go through life taking a passive approach, slopping through real problems and making no decisions.

MOYERS: But don't Americans prefer sloppiness in their moral and ethical situations?

GAYLIN: What we really prefer is optimism and denial. We don't want to believe there's a problem. For example, no one believes we're running out of anything. I think we're running out of everything. We're running out of "out." "Out" is where my parents threw their garbage. They threw the garbage out. You can't throw the garbage out any more. "Out" is where your children are going to live, where your grandchildren are going to live. But Americans can't face it.

Europeans can face limitations and shortages. A friend of mine said that Europeans are raised with boundaries, with frontiers. You can drive your motorcycle only up to the frontier, and then you stop. You cut timber only to the frontier. But even though most of us weren't pioneers, we were raised in tradition shaped by an open frontier.

MOYERS: You can always run somewhere.

GAYLIN: And there's always more. Americans deny there's a problem, they can't accept the concept of limits. There has been simply too much emphasis on the individual rather than the group and the community. When I said that we've lost the sense of community, let me start from what I consider the most fundamental community, the one from which all other communities have come—the family. It's intriguing to me how people will get all exercised about high-tech things when it's low-tech things that really should concern us.

> *It's intriguing to me how people will get all exercised about high-tech things when it's low-tech things that really should concern us.*

MOYERS: What do you mean?

GAYLIN: For example, the surrogate mother issue is interesting, but it's no threat to our society. The illegitimate teenage mother is a threat to our society. We are well on our way to destroying that last nuclear element of the community, the family. The fact that illegitimate children are being born to teenagers, the fact that there's only one parent in the household, the fact that even in the middle class, divorce rates are so high—if we destroy the nuclear family, we are really in trouble.

MOYERS: But the idea of family has changed. I don't think society will go back to the idea of family that existed when you and I were growing up.

GAYLIN: I don't mean we have to have the old kind of family, but that when we talk about priorities and allocation of scarce resources, we take family into account—for example, respecting the time that a parent spends with a child, allowing some funding from the government for that.

MOYERS: You're saying we need to find ways as a society to nurture the nurturers.

GAYLIN: Absolutely—and to give them respect. Look, most jobs that men and women do are disgusting. If—and these are big ifs—I had the same money, the same prestige, the same power, I'd rather be a mother than a pediatrician.

MOYERS: But society rewards the pediatrician and does not reward the mother.

GAYLIN: But why shouldn't society, if it's going to say that being a mother is good or say that being a father is good? We're going to have to find some way of identifying collective units and taking care of them. We have to do it with the elderly, we have to do it with children, and we have to see this as a very high-priority task.

MOYERS: You're saying that our society's going to change; that in order to grapple with and sort out these very tough choices, we have to act more as a community.

GAYLIN: Absolutely. It's intriguing to think that just as ethics got a rebirth with technology, all these high-tech things, which scare us, are forcing us to reexamine things that slid by. You know, science was going to kill God, but it turned out that science rediscovered Him because of all these questions. I think that when we begin to look at the fact of our limited resources, we're going to begin to have to look at all of our institutions because the choices are so massive. We'll have to look at some of the things we've lost and maybe not replicate them the way they were in the past, but find some creative alternatives.

MOYERS: "No man is an island."

GAYLIN: That is a biological as well as poetic truth.

Anne Wortham

SOCIOLOGIST

THOMAS SOWELL

Her peers pressured her, but Anne Wortham could not bring herself to join the Civil Rights movement. It violated her own story, her particular individuality. As a black, she stands apart in criticizing the rights movement for promoting reverse racism and the welfare state. She is a sociologist at Washington and Lee University and a continuing visiting scholar at the Hoover Institution.

MOYERS: Your writings have made you a controversial figure, one who criticizes the Civil Rights movement and its leaders for promoting reverse racism and the welfare state. How would you describe yourself to a stranger who genuinely wanted to know what you stand for?

WORTHAM: I like to say that I'm an individualist. I believe that life is a very important adventure that has to be carried out by individuals—in cooperation with other individuals, yes, but always lived by individuals. I take full responsibility for myself and for the kind of life I create and the relationships I have with other people. I believe very strongly in individual freedom, both internal freedom and external freedom.

MOYERS: Internal freedom being the power to make choices and external freedom being freedom from the restraint of society, of others.

WORTHAM: Freedom from the restraint of society and within that context, therefore, freedom to realize my highest potential but to take responsibility for any failures or lack of knowledge that I have.

MOYERS: Well, that doesn't sound very controversial.

WORTHAM: I think most people would say that they do.

MOYERS: Why, then, are you so controversial?

WORTHAM: The controversy emerges when we begin to ask the question, "But what do you mean by being an individualist? What do you mean by freedom? What do you mean by liberty?"

I read a series of articles recently on the effect of television on the American family and the American character. Throughout these articles there is a bashing of individualism on the grounds that individualism is irresponsible, narcissistic, self-centered. It is, in fact, self-centeredness that is being criticized as "individualism." But this is an incorrect understanding of individualism. The kind of individualism that I espouse is self-responsible. Self-responsibility can never be transformed into self-centeredness.

MOYERS:: You said one of the reasons you looked forward to teaching at Washington and Lee is that they still practice good manners there—good manners is not a self-centered characteristic, it is an expression of living in society.

WORTHAM: Yes, and it is a statement of self-respect and respect for other human beings. It is a device for maintaining civility in human relations. The reason one would have allegiance to good manners and etiquette is because one values being human. And because one values being human, one values oneself and others. You would not want to give to another person more or less respect than you would yourself as a human being.

> The reason one would have allegiance to good manners and etiquette is because one values being human.

MOYERS: So individualism does not mean, "I have the right to do whatever I want to do, whenever I want to do it"?

WORTHAM: One has only the right to be oneself—within the boundaries of respect for others. There is a boundary between you and others. That's why we have etiquette. Behind the walls of etiquette and decorum is the autonomy of the individual. The reason etiquette was developed in the first place was to maintain individual freedom.

MOYERS: Here we sit under a sign that says "No Smoking"—and you don't because—

WORTHAM: —because there is a sign which is a statement addressed to me and to everyone else which says that we, the administrators of the institution, prefer not to have smoking in this setting.

MOYERS: And you go along with that even though, individually, you believe you have the right to smoke.

WORTHAM: Yes, but I don't have the right to abuse an institutional rule, and by doing so, to contradict my unsigned, tacit agreement with the institution that by being a part of it, by accepting its invitation to work here, I shall honor certain rules. One doesn't sign anything—it is just understood in a civilized society.

MOYERS: "Civilized society"—what do you mean by that?

WORTHAM: A civilized society is one whose members expect that each will address at all times, as far as possible, the rational in man; that even when I may want to bash you over the head, I will be checked by my awareness of you as a rational entity, and I will not resort to force as an expression of my disagreement with you or even my feeling that you have been unjust to me; that in my disagreements with you, I will rely on the power of persuasion.

MOYERS: So that even if I act irrationally toward you, you're going to treat me as a rational person.

WORTHAM: I remind myself that this is an irrational person who is betraying rationality and therefore himself.

MOYERS: So what happens inside when we all betray rationality?

WORTHAM: Well, we are very clever beings, you see. Rationality has the capacity for betraying itself. Rational men have the capacity to be irrational and to institutionalize irrationality. We've seen that in Nazi Germany.

MOYERS: It's what Joseph Heller wrote about in *Catch-22*. Irrationality becomes a bureaucratic process.

WORTHAM: Yes, and the unfortunate thing is that it becomes so absurd that it's funny. Literary critics and analysts have always commented on absurdity being comical, but in real life, it's another cup of tea altogether! There you get bureaucracy gone mad. Max Weber was very much aware of this. He worried that the very thing that made freedom, enlightenment, and civilization possible also had the capacity to turn on itself.

MOYERS: You once said, "By most standards, I'm not supposed to exist." What did you mean?

WORTHAM: There are theories of social determinism which view people as being not a product of their thinking, or of their interpretations of the world around them, but as being solely a product of their environment—as being social products.

In the sixties, in undergraduate school, I would meet people who were surprised by me. At first I was baffled by their surprise. Then I understood the reason for their surprise, and I was not only baffled but angry and hurt that Northerners I met had a vision of life among blacks in the South which did not match my own experience. Both black and white Northerners approached me as a caricature, as their version of what a black growing up in the South in the fifties should be. They thought I should be someone who was scarred by racism, who had certain pathologies, who was very race-conscious, who was suspicious of whites. They had a script. They were prepared to love me unconditionally just because I was a socially defined historical victim. So you see, when I say I'm not supposed to exist, I'm saying that the history written recently of blacks and women in America does not count on people like me.

MOYERS: How did the reality of Anne Wortham challenge their image of you?

WORTHAM: Well, for one thing, I was innocent. At first, I didn't even understand their script. They thought that as a victim I should have understood what my saviors were after—and I didn't. Then when I did understand, I just reacted naturally, which was to refuse their offer of liberation, and their interpretation of me as someone who hated all whites. Their mission was to convince me that they were among the good whites.

Behind those walls of segregation, my father was a Christian. To the extent that he ever talked about whites—and we rarely talked about whites in our house—but whenever he did, he said to forget about the Constitution and our neighbors and everybody else, because God said you should love everybody. Growing up, I had this drummed into my head, so it was very difficult when the late sixties came along for me to reconcile the idea that I should love everyone until they show you that they shouldn't be loved with the idea that I should hate all whites because they are whites. I just didn't have it in me, and that upset some people. They wanted me to be their Martin Luther King, and I didn't even like Martin Luther King. I was scared of him. I was utterly afraid of that man.

MOYERS: Of Martin Luther King? Why?

WORTHAM: Because something told me he was saying things that were not right for me. His vision made me as a black person morally superior to whites. Whites would be redeemed by their acknowledging me as an equal. The kid in me said, "I don't want to do all of this. I don't like this."

MOYERS: But hadn't you been discriminated against when you were growing up in the fifties?

WORTHAM: But you see, these are two different things. I'm telling you now—having understood in retrospect—why I was so miserable in the early sixties. I was going through absolute hell because I had peer pressure from everywhere. If you were a student, you had to go and march and do this and that. Certainly, I wanted civil rights. But I thought that something else was being asked of me in addition—and of everybody else, for that matter. We were demanding civil rights, but I felt that we were also asking our country to give us some kind of special recognition that required a diminution of other Americans.

MOYERS: But all that was being asked was that everybody stop discriminating against you.

WORTHAM: That's not what I heard when I was twenty years old. I heard something else from the Civil Rights movement. Now, here I was, a twenty-year-old black kid who had grown up in a relatively sheltered environment in Jackson, Tennessee, whose sense of morality had been very straightforward. When I was in high school, I worked as a maid for whites, so that I knew whites intimately—though most Southern blacks do. The relationship of whites and blacks in the South is a very complex one. Now, in 1962, all of the students were participating in the movement. To be a good citizen as a student, you had to be an activist student.

MOYERS: And you refused.

WORTHAM: I refused. My problem was, "How do I refuse without incurring the wrath of my peers?" I just sort of snuck into the background. I didn't like myself for doing that.

I'll tell you a story. One day in 1961 or '62, we were out on the campus green at Tuskegee. A student was urging us to go down to the town of Tuskegee and show our solidarity with all the student marchers. The tension in the air was thick, electrifying. You felt as though everything you stood for was on the line, that you now had to do something. I was standing there, and one of the students came over to me and asked, "What are you going to do? Are you going downtown?" Now, here's one of these moments of your life, and a choice has to be made. She said, "I don't know what to do."

I said, "Look, I think we should both go up to our dorm rooms and let down the shades and keep the lights off, and we should think and be quiet and we should decide up there. I don't think we should decide out here."

Now, at that time, I had no grand theory about the mechanics of being an individual, and of maintaining the truth of one's identity within a larger society. I didn't have any theory or even any great understanding. I was just going on gut reactions about what you do. And the thing you do is that you don't give up your own story. You don't give up the authenticity of yourself.

MOYERS: What's sacred to you?

WORTHAM: It's the authenticity that is sacred. It is the one thing that is yours.

MOYERS: Your story.

WORTHAM: Your story, your life. It is the thing that you die for, ultimately, if you have to. It is the only thing that you die for.

MOYERS: If you had gone out and marched on the streets and protested, would you have been giving up your story? Would you have been giving up what's sacred to you?

WORTHAM: Yes, I would have. Now, perhaps someone else wouldn't have. What I wanted was an understanding from those other persons, who might have thought their story was to be a civil rights activist. I wanted them to understand that I had for myself a different life vocation, that my story was to be written differently. That doesn't deny the validity of some of the things that were being done in the Civil Rights movement. But one doesn't always have to be an activist to contribute to society or to have a good life.

MOYERS: Did you want the freedom to vote?

WORTHAM: I wanted the freedom to vote, but you see, I wanted to vote to encourage the development of institutions that will see to it that my neighbor will not impinge on the free and fruitful writing of my own story, and of his. I want that vote to make sure that he and I can disagree in peace, that we can go our separate ways without interfering with each other in harmful and malicious ways.

MOYERS: What was it that caused you not to join the Civil Rights movement? What did you think they were asking of you that you didn't want to give?

WORTHAM: They were asking me to condemn all white Americans. That's what I felt at the time. And I couldn't do it.

MOYERS: But what about those who had kept your father from being a first-class citizen and would have kept you from being a first-class citizen if they could have—those who discriminated, who persecuted, who broke the law to keep you an outsider?

WORTHAM: They were wrong, absolutely wrong. You see, it depends on your definition of your situation. Actually, everything I say begins with this. When I left home to go to Tuskegee, I met black students from the deep South, whose relationships with whites were totally different from ours. A lot of Northern whites don't know this, but we down South know this—the intensity of anger and outrage is colored by these personal experiences.

In our household, whites were simply people, some of whom were very bad and did horrible things. My father didn't hate all whites, he hated "the government," which was known as "Uncle Sam" in our house. The government was the one who gave whites the power to do all these horrible things. And the government was not only doing those sorts of things, but the government was a chronic thief, who took your money. My father would say, "Watch out for Uncle Sam. He'll get in your back pocket any minute." If there was any sort of down-home animus, it was toward the government. The strategy was to rely on yourself, to be as creative as possible to get around segregation and discrimination. The attitude was "Discrimination is terrible, but you've got to live, you've got to put your kids

You can't waste psychological energy on feeling downtrodden.

through school. You can't waste psychological energy on feeling downtrodden. Man, you've got to get up in the morning." And he would always tell us, "You know, you've got to get up and get out there."

MOYERS: That was pure Booker T. Washington, you know.

WORTHAM: Of course it was.

MOYERS: He said, "If you learn to do something better than someone else, you'll make your way in the world."

WORTHAM: I was taught this. In fact, my father used to say to us, not knowing that it was Booker T. Washington who spoke these words, "Cast your bucket down." He also used to say, "Knowledge is power," not knowing from where that expression came.

So my view of whites was not that they were so all-powerful as individual people. They never become a stereotype in my mind. I never gave them the power that it seemed the civil rights message had to impute to them in order to make its redress. And I felt that I was being asked somehow to diminish myself by attributing to just another human being who was doing horrible things, that he was somehow much more powerful and a different kind of human being. I was not going to make whites that important. They aren't that important. They never were that important.

MOYERS: They were important enough to exercise state power over you.

WORTHAM: They were that important—but they were not important enough to define who I am.

MOYERS: How did you react when Rosa Parks sat on the bus, and the movement began to swell in the streets, and Martin Luther King emerged, and suddenly there was finally a movement of black Americans to protest this power of coercion?

WORTHAM: Well, I must tell you, I was like a lot of black kids. History doesn't say this, especially history as told on TV, but I had lessons to get. Mrs. Johnson in my English class said, "You must have those papers in by Friday, and if you don't get an A, that's it!" The ethos in our segregated black school was: "Without your high school diploma—forget everything."

When the Civil Rights movement came along, we felt it was wonderful that this thing was happening. It seemed there was this event that was going on that was related to our everyday life but was not central to the business of everyday life.

Now there are a lot of people who would be very upset by my disclosing this very mundane aspect of getting on in the world—but this is what was going on. We were not all running out into the street joining movements. I knew very little about the details of the early Civil Rights movement. Most of it I learned after I had got to college. Some of it was imparted to us in classes—not very much, mind you. In fact, the most I learned was when I actually began the formal study of race and ethnic relations.

MOYERS: But you were bent on getting up and out.

WORTHAM: I had lessons to get. My mother died when I was nine. I had a house to clean. My father had to get up in the morning and go to work. He was breaking into the business of being an independent salesman. He had to deal with the segregation and prejudice of the day. So the Civil Rights movement was a current event, and not just for my family. It was that way for a lot of families.

MOYERS: If everybody had been like you and your father, do you think the change would have come that finally liberated blacks?

WORTHAM: Oh no, no, you must have activists. No, I'm not setting up a kind of model. This is why part of the history that I am now imparting isn't told. There is a mistaken belief that you must make a choice between public activism and private striving, that you must put a very sterile, very politicized face on black history.

There were activists in our community who were marching. There were some, like my father, who didn't and who didn't like the marchers, either. He didn't like the NAACP in our town. The NAACP people were all those doctors and teachers that he wanted us to grow up to be like. He was striving by proxy to outdo them. He didn't like them. He also thought that they were very unrealistic. In fact, at one point, he actually wrote a letter to them and said, "Look, you people want us to boycott the supermarkets. We should be trying to figure out how we can have our own market."

MOYERS: When you finally encountered these Northern Yankees, what actually happened? What convinced you that they saw you as a stereotype?

WORTHAM: They wanted me to give them a story, and the story they wanted was that I wasn't getting my essays written for Mrs. Johnson, and that my segregated high school was terrible, and that I was getting an inferior education. Actually, we now know that my education behind those walls of segregation was far better than the integrated education of the kids in the urban swamps today. This is not a justification of segregation—I'm applauding Mrs. Johnson here. But they wanted the story, and I didn't have it to give them.

They also wanted me to be angry. Later, as I moved into the professional world, the Black Power movement was at its height. I worked at NBC and ABC and the people I met wanted a Black Power pose, and I didn't have it. Not only did I disagree with the Black Power ideology, but I just don't have it in my personality. So, in the most subtle relations, where certain tacit understandings are at work, the typical Northern Yankee wanted to be seen as being more understanding toward me than I required of him. All I required of him was his respect. I didn't require his compassion. The Republicans haven't understood that, you see—

MOYERS: What do you mean?

WORTHAM: Conservative Republicans have thought that they had to show that they were as compassionate as liberals, Democrats, and other people on the left when they should have challenged the nature of the compassion. I've often found, having worked among Northern liberals a great deal, that their compassion lacks respect. An analogy is that abolitionist who really, deep down in his heart, thought that blacks were inferior, though he wanted them freed. He really thought that they were inferior to him.

MOYERS: And respect means?

WORTHAM: Respect means that you leave me alone, that you don't build up in your own mind scenarios for my salvation and that you respect me enough to trust me, even when I'm an idiot, even when I'm wrong.

MOYERS: And to say so if you are an idiot.

WORTHAM: Absolutely. If I am an idiot, tell me, disagree with me. Harold Cruse has written a book in which he touches on this very thing. The history of the Civil Rights movement began with this misunderstanding among its white participants: that they would not demand of blacks what they demanded in their own self-help organizations.

> The history of the Civil Rights movement began with this misunderstanding among its white participants: that they would not demand of blacks what they demanded in their own self-help organizations.

MOYERS: Did you find these Northerners who wanted to love you were asking more than you could give them?

WORTHAM: Yes. They were asking for my sanction. I was the altar before which they stood, and they were asking me to redeem them, which is what Martin Luther King promised them that I would give them.

MOYERS: And you didn't want to give it to them.

WORTHAM: I can't. Nobody can. We cannot give this to each other. I cannot give you a sense of the importance of your life. I can confirm it. I can nod my head and say yes, but I cannot make it so for you. That you must do for yourself. I can't do it for you.

MOYERS: You're saying, "I can't do it at the expense of not being what I am—"

WORTHAM: —Yes—

MOYERS: "—and if I played it your way, if I'd been the beaten-down, put-upon little person that you thought I should be, I would have been betraying myself because I wasn't that person."

WORTHAM: I would have been betraying myself. They would have had a fine old time of loving me and being compassionate and so forth, but they would have nullified that by disrespecting me. If we have to ask of any other human being that for us to love him, he must be something that is closer to our view of him or of our grand scheme of how human beings ought to be, then our own obligation to him is simply not to love him. That is the way to respect him. If he doesn't earn our love, then just don't love him. Don't harm him, don't force him to do anything—just walk away.

But there are some people who can't keep their hands off other people. They just won't. It takes a lot of courage to leave other people alone, you see.

MOYERS: Was slavery an evil?

WORTHAM: Oh, absolutely. It always is.

MOYERS: Is racism an evil?

WORTHAM: Absolutely. Racism is evil in whatever form it takes. However, it is not something that whites have a monopoly on. Blacks are also racist. My grandmother was on certain days.

MOYERS: In what way?

WORTHAM: I remember sitting on her front porch. She would sometimes go on about those "crackers."

MOYERS: A cracker, we should say, for people who don't know—

WORTHAM: A cracker in the South is a lower-class white—sometimes called "white trash," sometimes called "redneck." It's really sort of funny, because you could have the white gentry demeaning white crackers just as spiritedly as you could have any black demeaning them. Blacks look down on white crackers, too.

MOYERS: You have yourself acknowledged that with the exception of the American Indian, no ethnic group has suffered more injustices at the hands of government or its fellow citizens than black Americans.

WORTHAM: Yes.

MOYERS: But you also say the debt's been paid, the protection and preservation of the human rights and liberty of Negroes, as you wrote, is no longer a dream deferred. Do you really believe that's so?

WORTHAM: Yes, insofar as the relationship of blacks to the state is concerned.

MOYERS: You mean the state no longer says, "You cannot vote, you cannot eat here, you cannot go to school."

WORTHAM: In fact, the state has gone beyond that to oppressing us in different ways. It has given us all that any just and moral government or liberal state can give to its citizens, and that is equal rights before the law. One of the paradoxes of democracy and one of the gambles that we make is that citizens have the freedom to redefine their situation. The situation has been defined so that blacks are historical victims and that the state owes them more than just simply what it gives—not gives, actually, but acknowledges. I don't hold to the view that the state gives rights. It simply acknowledges rights that already exist, and institutionalizes those. If rights are thought of as being given, then rights become privileges, things that the state doles out to people. Then blacks can claim, "Look, we are in need of these most, we are behind the most," et cetera. And to make that claim against fellow citizens who have their own list of claims, the life of the black community has to become almost totally politicized, and the individual life of a black has to become politicized.

MOYERS: So you are opposed to affirmative action?

WORTHAM: Yes.

MOYERS: Busing?

WORTHAM: Yes.

MOYERS: Employment quotas?

WORTHAM: Yes.

MOYERS: On the principle that—

WORTHAM: —on the principle that first of all, to institute such policies requires that the state violate the rights of all of its citizens, including those who advocate those policies. And secondly, that even if one disagreed on philosophical grounds, such things don't work. They obscure or ignore the fact that blacks and other minorities make choices that are not always consistent with the statistics. In certain situations, there are not always enough blacks in the population to meet a quota, say, in a given police department or a given sociology department or a given university.

MOYERS: But that hasn't been the problem, of course. The problem has been that the police departments and universities wouldn't open the doors.

WORTHAM: My opposition to affirmative action quotas is the imposition of them on the private sector. So far as the public sector is concerned, the government should make sure that it has equal opportunity operating. If the only way to have opportunities available for blacks in all levels of government is to make sure that you recruit people in black communities who are interested in such occupations, then in fact you give some preferential attention to blacks in the recruitment realm, but only at this level.

MOYERS: Why do you rule out affirmative action in the private sector?

WORTHAM: When I talk about affirmative action for government, I'm talking about recruiting job applicants within particular fields within the government. I don't say that the government should make sure that it hires these people, or that it is unjust if government doesn't. It is unjust only if it refuses to let these people in, or doesn't make an extra effort to make sure that those who want to be policemen or firemen can be.

The private sector can't afford to do this. It is a misuse of its funds to do so. The private sector ends up looking for people who don't want to be in these positions or who sometimes are not qualified to be in these positions. We're finding this in academia with people who want to take positions for the income, but who have no sense of commitment to these jobs, and who would rather be doing something else.

MOYERS: That's a harsh judgment.

WORTHAM: It is a very harsh judgment. But there are backstair horror stories, especially in academia, of some of the effects of affirmative action, and there's a lot of mismatching going on because of the pressure to find a career, and the pressure of the university to have an affirmative action program. Why? Because it needs to show the government it is not discriminating, and because if it does not have such a program, it is thereby considered to be discriminating. Many times, this is not necessarily the case.

This relationship of university to government I would see abolished totally, and the relationship also with business and government I would see abolished. I can't be for affirmative action. It simply cements that relationship, and it makes minorities pawns in this game.

MOYERS: If we say to a young black in the ghetto, "You're free to get a job," and there are no jobs, or if we say to a single-parent family in the ghetto, "You're free to get a house," but there's no affordable housing, are we not perpetrating a cruel hoax on them?

WORTHAM: No, we are being realistic. If we want to be a goal-directed government rather than a government that is based on the rule of law, then fine. But the ideal is that we are a government that wants to respect the rule of law, and if that is the case, then we cannot—at any point ever—justify violating the rights of members of the majority for the sake of the well-being of members of minority groups.

MOYERS: So what if the majority wants to say that because Anne Wortham is black, she won't be allowed to vote?

WORTHAM: Yes, but that's on a different level, you see. Once, I, a black, have the right to vote, I have the freedom to try to persuade my government that my fellow citizens who are white should not have the freedom to deny me entry into their restaurant.

MOYERS: Do you have the freedom to try to persuade your government to set up an economic program that will give advantages to young black kids in the ghetto who need help?

WORTHAM: I have the freedom to do it, which is not to say I approve of the freedom to do it. I do not approve of that particular strategy.

MOYERS: Why?

WORTHAM: I think that one of the unfortunate consequences of the Civil Rights movement was that the economic advancement of the black community and other minorities was defined as being outside the national economy. It pained me so much one day to hear President Reagan trying so hard to make this point. He never did. I read not long ago that Reagan had a message that he could have taken to the minorities and to blacks, which would have been a direct extension of his own basic philosophy—which he's betrayed all over the board, but that's another story. But he never was able to make the point. The point is this: You cannot save the minority community by destroying America. You cannot do it. You cannot save those young black kids in the ghetto who don't have jobs by destroying the American economy.

MOYERS: Job programs for ghetto kids are destroying America?

WORTHAM: That's not the connection I'm making. I'm not saying that by doing so, you destroy America. I am saying that you should not see their fate as being outside the larger problem of what we do about our budget deficits, our overspending, and so forth. We won't look at how we can help them in the correct light. A lot of the programs of the sixties not only did no good, but also they cost us a lot of money.

MOYERS: You've said that minorities could change the direction of American politics for the better by breaking their alliance with the government.

WORTHAM: Yes. You would think, with a history such as ours, that we would have understood two things: first, that the government, while we need it, ultimately cannot be our friend, and also that we don't need it to be our friend, really. It is just an instrument. If minorities broke their alliance with the government, they would depend more on themselves. We would acknowledge the legacy of Booker T. Washington, which is slowly coming back to legitimacy now. We should have kept that side of our story, which some today will call the conservative side of black history and black culture. You see, we would not be here were it not for our own efforts. Most of our history has been in relationship to a government that has not been very kind. Government is not a savior—the American federal government has not acted as a liberator. Civil rights for minorities was no great favor, for Christ's sake! This is what they should have done two hundred years ago. We should have retained a kind of skepticism of the state that my father had, and that in fact, a lot of Southern blacks always had. Our view of the state was always skeptical as opposed to Northern blacks, who tended to be more trusting. Ironically, although the Civil Rights movement came out of the South, it began to take on the Northern view of the state as being a benevolent institution. It isn't. It can't be, ultimately.

> . . . the government . . . cannot be our friend. . . . It is just an instrument.

MOYERS: But it's all right in your scheme of things for blacks to organize to achieve social equality.

WORTHAM: No, that's not what I said. I don't believe in social equality. I believe in equality under the law.

MOYERS: Is it acceptable to organize politically to gain social advantage?

WORTHAM: It's acceptable—but I would not think that political organization would be the way to go at this point. What we need is economic advancement, and economic advancement can't be very substantial if it is done through politics.

MOYERS: You say in your book that blacks and whites should "simply exist as traders, exchanging material and intellectual values for their mutual benefit."

WORTHAM: Yes.

MOYERS: Does that mean the only bond between us is cash and materials—is economic?

WORTHAM: The trading metaphor is meant to convey more than economics. The economic trading relationship is one which Booker T. Washington understood—that if I have something to offer, and if it is good enough, you will buy it. And if you don't buy it, it's because it wasn't as good as this guy's over here. It shouldn't be because this fellow over here was able to use politics to prevent me from even competing with him, or, if once I'm at the door, make it so that in order to compete with him I must have special government contracts and engage in what we now call sleaze politics in order to have an advantage. The advantage should always be merely on the basis of what you offer in the particular situation.

MOYERS: You're obviously aware that you're criticized by many blacks for making what they call the worn-out arguments on behalf of racism that whites used to make.

WORTHAM: Yes. Because of my views, I have difficulties finding a job. Fortunately, I will go to Washington and Lee in January, and I hope that phase of my career is now over. But prior to now, it's been rather difficult. In one of my job interviews two years ago, it was asked of me, very seriously, by the faculty of a Northern urban university, whether I would encourage my students to employ the bootstrap method of mobility. They were concerned that I would, not that I wouldn't.

MOYERS: And your answer?

WORTHAM: Of course I would. I said that I don't teach any particular ideology, that I would come there to teach my subject, but that in talking with students about their careers, I will always tell them, "Look at your assets, look at what you have, and try to do with what you have. Don't first begin thinking of what you can take from the other fellow. That's not a way to go, because in the end, you will lose, especially if what the other fellow has got is a great deal of power." These faculty members were Northern white liberals who would say that I'm advocating benign neglect. But they would want me to neglect black students by encouraging them *not* to pull themselves up by their bootstraps—which is the very thing that white Americans have done.

> The black community doesn't need friends like these, who tell us to deny the self-help element of our heritage.

You know, I don't understand this. What kind of friend is this? I'm merely advocating for blacks what the whites do for themselves. But if I say it, I am encouraging something that is against my race, and so forth and so on. I don't need friends like these. The black community doesn't need friends like these, who tell us to deny the self-help element of our heritage. My father feels that he has been totally ignored in all of this. He's very angry because no one gives him credit for having raised his five children on his own and put all of them through college without any help from Uncle Sam. It's not in the history books. He's very bitter.

MOYERS: Are you bitter?

WORTHAM: No, I'm not bitter. I understand it. But my father is bitter that people say we don't do anything on our own. They say that we always need the government to come in and help us do things. He wants to be known as the man who raised five kids and sent them through college.

MOYERS: You wrote an essay once called "Silence," in which you said, "But all these people have identity. They have a place. They know of fear, anger, anxiety, sadness, graft, hate, inferiority, superiority. I know only of contempt for them, and loneliness for myself, because I could not belong. I could never belong."

WORTHAM: Where did you find that? That essay was written the summer of 1963, when I was twenty. There is something wrong with that statement. I felt that I didn't belong. I was in Washington preparing for my Peace Corps orientation training, and everyone was gearing up for the March on Washington. Everyone knew what they were supposed to be doing that summer. And there I was, feeling that I couldn't do what they were doing and that I was very much alone. I don't feel that now. I didn't know at that time that the ideas I had, which were snatches of thought and floating abstractions, had been thought by people long ago, that I could find them in the Founding Fathers, and in the Greeks, and in literature.

I didn't know where to go. I now know, and I don't feel alone at all. I also don't have contempt. I was then someone who knew that she disagreed but who didn't want to pay the price of disagreement. It wasn't until I was much older that I understood that if I was going to disagree, there was a price to pay. I don't like it, but I'll pay it.

MOYERS: Why do you quote Shakespeare in your book? "Things without remedy should be without regard. What is done is done."

WORTHAM: What I mean by that is that one reaches a point at which you understand that history was here before you, and will go on after you, and that if you tie your own personal destiny, the vocation of your life, to public events, then you ultimately end up burning yourself out in activism—or you get out of the picture altogether, you commit suicide, or you go and sit in a corner somewhere and suck your thumb. So you have to reach a point at which you can say, "I am rational enough, I understand enough of life, and of myself as an individual human being, to know that I am limited in what I can do, and I am limited in what I know. My number one obligation is to fulfill my life's purpose. I cannot save the world. Even if I wanted to, I can't." This is a very realistic statement, not a statement of defeat, or retreat. It is a reorientation.

MOYERS: Do you get tired of being asked questions about race?

WORTHAM: Yes, I do, sometimes. It gets weary. But I have the most interesting conversations and all sorts of opportunities to discuss issues. Sometimes I realize that I allow people to say things they would never say to someone else who is black and female. And so I do.

MOYERS: If legal racism is not a problem any more, why are blacks poorer than whites on the whole? Why do they have less political power? Why do they have fewer job opportunities?

WORTHAM: There are no easy answers. Any way I respond will be inadequate. The coming of political rights and economic opportunities that flow from political rights occurred at a point when the American economy was changing.

MOYERS: Blacks are getting free just as the economy is fundamentally changing?

WORTHAM: Yes. So we have a huge labor force of unskilled and skilled laborers for whom there are just no jobs. That's one layer of analysis at which you can stop, but that does not make the story human, that is not the same as talking about a particular man who's willing to work, but who cannot work, not simply because of prejudice, although that's a factor, but far more importantly because the job does not exist. You see, my father had a high school education and built every house we lived in because the national economy, even under segregation, was different. In a way, my father was economically freer. Although he couldn't vote, he sent me to college. I can vote, but I can't send any kid to college, and I certainly can't buy a house, as my father did. I make enough to just keep going. And I have all the things that he thought he was giving me to prevent just the sort of bind that I'm in. It says nothing about prejudice and racism; it is a reflection of how much the national economy has declined. I don't mean to say that those things don't exist, but that it's just more complicated. I think if we allow that, then we truly appreciate and understand the plight of the black poor—and all poor. But if we keep simply labeling the problem as racism, all we do is put up a screen between ourselves and those we say we care about. We don't really understand their lives at all.

T. Berry Brazelton

By his own count, Dr. Brazelton has helped to raise more than twenty-five thousand babies in his forty years of practice; the title "Dean of American Pediatricians" is his by acclaim. He is chief of the Child Development Unit at Boston Children's Hospital and a professor of pediatrics at Harvard University. The Brazelton Behavioral Scale, a test for newborn babies, is used by hospitals around the world. His books, including Infants and Mothers, Working and Caring, and What Every Baby Knows, bring advice and comfort to thousands of anxious young parents.

MOYERS: You started your career caring for babies as individuals, but in the last couple of years you've been concerned with the families in which babies live. Why have you changed your emphasis?

BRAZELTON: Families are really suffering, and with the increasing divorce rate and the breakdown of the extended family, very few young people can turn back to their own families for support. That is very tragic because we're not handing anything on from one generation to another. Everything that we've got in the way of statistics—increasing teen pregnancy, drugs, suicide—shows that we're in deep, deep trouble in this country. The family is where we've got to turn to try to give kids a different future than the one we've provided in the past generation.

MOYERS: When you and I were growing up in Texas, the typical family was the father who went out every day and worked, and the mother who stayed home as the housewife. Now that family is a minority.

BRAZELTON: It's practically nonexistent. It may exist in twenty percent of families. But we all still have that myth in the back of our minds. We all think, "Oh, if we could only get back to that." We have a very strong bias in this country that families ought to be self-sufficient, and if they're not, they ought to be punished for it. All of our legislation for families comes with a negative base. You have to be poor or unwed or incompetent, and then you get a handout from the government. Otherwise, you get nothing. To me, that carries with it a kind of Rosenthal effect. Rosenthal is the expectancy guy, the Pygmalion guy. He says that if you label somebody, and they know the label—and people always do—then they live up to that label. He did it with rats. He labeled a bunch of rats "dumb rats" and "smart rats," and then he got his graduate students to put them through a maze. None of the "dumb rats" got through the maze, and all of the "smart rats" did. But what he found, when he filmed his graduate students, is that they picked up "smart rats" in one way, and they'd run right through, and they would pick up "dumb rats" differently, and the "dumb rats" couldn't get through. This is what our government is doing to people. We're treating families that are not able to make it on their own as if they were "dumb rats." And, of course, they fall apart.

MOYERS: And the old myth of the rugged individual, the self-sufficient family, is just that: myth.

BRAZELTON: We have a very seriously stressed society in this country. We no longer have a set of values that people can really believe in. Look at what's happening in the campaign right now. Nobody has any real values, except that we have to protect ourselves from somebody else, like Russia. Those aren't real values. What we need are real belief systems. We have diluted the ones we had so much that families don't know what they're raising their kids for any more. A mother will say, "Should I discipline him? Should I not? Should I teach him to help me in the kitchen? Should I not?" It's easy for me to answer these things, but it isn't easy for a mother.

MOYERS: Where are those values? What's happened to them?

BRAZELTON: Young people are very conflicted. They went through such a terrible time in the sixties, and families went through such a terrible time, that I don't believe parents know any longer what they're raising their children to become. They're afraid they'll go through the same kind of drug acting out and all the other acting out that went on in the sixties. So they don't know which way to go. Should I just nurture my children and give them positive reinforcement? Or should I put some limits on them? If I put limits on, they might rebel, and I might lose control. That's not a way to raise a child. You can't constantly be wondering: Am I in control? You've got to give kids a sense of themselves and a sense of yourself as strong and understanding what you're up to. Then you can expect them to have a sense of competence, a sense of importance, and they can face whatever they have to. This is where we're really in danger right now—we're not doing that in any class, but certainly not in the middle class.

MOYERS: But a society can't simply declare by fiat that values shall exist, and presto—they exist. How do we bring these values back into the public place?

BRAZELTON: I would like each child to be seen as a very precious individual, right across the board, in every class. If they're black, if they're Hispanic, value them for that—don't see it as a second-class status. But you have to start with the adults. You have to value them, and you have to value their struggles and say, "Hey, those are really important struggles you're up to, and you're doing a damned good job."

MOYERS: What's a good job?

BRAZELTON: Right now we know some things pretty clearly. Women are in the midst of a real, tearing struggle, which is: "Should I be at home? Or should I not be at home? Should I work? What am I not giving my children if I have to be away from them?" Women's roles right now are very much on the mat. Most women are torn in two, whether they're staying at home or whether they're working.

MOYERS: They feel guilty either way.

BRAZELTON: We've got to back women up. Men are going to be in that same role in a very few years, as they take more and more interest in their families and are more and more involved. Young people are involved in a personality struggle of trying to find identity. I would like to back them up for whatever decision they make and be sure that they can do a good job by themselves. Then they'll bring that sense of power home to their kids, and their kids will do well. As women get into the work force and find they're competent, they come home feeling great, and they can pick that baby up and say, "Ah, hi, I missed you all day long," and sit there and rock these kids and get close to them. If they come home feeling, "Oh, I shouldn't have been away from him all day, I missed him so much," then they're going to pick him up, and he'll scream, and they'll feel, "Oh my gosh," put him down, and walk away. And we've lost them—lost the mother and the baby.

MOYERS: You used to believe that mothers should be there, at least for the first year, with the newborn. Have you changed all that?

BRAZELTON: No, have you?

MOYERS: No, except that as a father I missed a great deal because I felt inadequate when my children were young, and left that to my wife, who seemed instinctively to know what to do. I would like to do it over again and be home more, particularly that first year or two.

BRAZELTON: Good for you. You should. Why don't you try again?

MOYERS: I think that I gave all I have to give.

BRAZELTON: The only reason I asked that is that you would get so much out of it this time. What we're missing is that people who aren't participating in the marvelous miracle of having a baby and raising that baby in the first few months and feeling that baby look back at them and saying, "Hey, she's looking at me, she's smiling at me," don't ever reach another level of development themselves. So I really believe both parents ought to be very involved with their babies and their small children. I hope any mother realizes that staying home the first year is like giving a big gift to your child. But I don't think the first year is even a possibility in this country any longer, because, financially, we've stressed people beyond that. Psychologically, women are really too torn right now to feel comfortable or happy about staying at home for the first year. And most people don't have that choice.

MOYERS: I read the other day that it now takes two full-time wage earners to buy essentially what one check would buy up until the early 1970's. This is not altogether just a matter of choice, is it? There is an economic imperative that drives both parents out into the market now.

BRAZELTON: I think fifty percent of the women in this country don't have a choice. They have to work. Another twenty to thirty percent might have a choice, but there's a very subtle thing going on right now, in my practice, at least, where young women say, "But someday I might be a single parent. Fifty percent of families are breaking down. I might be one of that fifty percent."

MOYERS: "I might have to make it on my own"?

BRAZELTON: "For my children's sake, I've got to keep my career going." That's so subtle that I think there may be other things like that going on in women's minds right now—that if they get out of the work force, they've lost something they can't repair. And I think rather than ignoring it or getting mad at it, we'd better think what it is and help them see what it is so they can make appropriate choices.

MOYERS: But let's look at the contradiction. You still believe that women should be with their newborns for at least the first year. Yet you've said that for economic reasons they have to get out into the marketplace. That seems to be an irreconcilable contradiction.

BRAZELTON: It is at this point. But it wouldn't be if national government, state government, individual businesses, and individual families were willing to share the cost of making it possible for women at least to stay home long enough to know, "That baby is my baby, and I'm that baby's mother"—and for fathers to stay home long enough to feel that, too.

MOYERS: Why are those first few months so important?

BRAZELTON: First of all, they're terribly important to adults. Adults who are about to have a baby go through a real kind of inner turmoil: "Will I ever get to be a parent? What kind of parent am I going to be? I sure don't want to be like my parents." And then, of course, they always are.

The other things that go on in pregnancy include certain fears: "If I don't have a perfect baby, can I really love that baby? How will I ever make it with that baby?" They get a baby who cries at them every night for the first three months with colic, and they think, "I'm not making it." If they cut themselves off right there, they'll never feel like parents. Young people have got to let themselves become parents.

MOYERS: You've seen parents who never bonded with their children in those first few months?

BRAZELTON: Never dared.

MOYERS: And what happened?

BRAZELTON: A lot of young women today will say they don't want to breast-feed because they have to go back to work too early. You'll say, "Yeah, but you can do it and go back to work, and it's so neat to come home and put the baby to breast at the end of the day." And they'll say, "I can't do it." "Why not?" "Well, I can't stand to see him in somebody else's arms." And their eyes fill up with tears, and they'll say, "I don't want to breast-feed, it's too painful." What they're talking about is how painful it is to separate if you're that close and leave the baby with somebody else. Now, we could take care of that, if we thought about it. We could provide decent daycare where they felt safe about leaving their babies, where they felt the daycare person or the supplementary mother was going to back them up to still be the mother. And then, when they came home, we could provide them with enough information about how to get close again—how to dare separate and come back and make it again.

MOYERS: There are countries that permit mothers to take leaves twice a day to go breast-feed, but we haven't come close to that yet.

BRAZELTON: Certain businesses do have on-site daycare for this, and it's working very well.

MOYERS: But out of forty-four thousand corporations in this country with over one hundred employees, only thirty-five hundred of them have anything resembling an adequate child care facility or service.

BRAZELTON: It's true. But, you know, with the threat of this Better Child Care Bill that we're going to put on the floor this fall, many businesses are rethinking that. I get calls every day from businesses who want to do this before the government tells them to. So that's a good sign.

MOYERS: Have you actually seen some successful models for this approach?

BRAZELTON: Sure, lots of them. The first one was here at Stride Rite shoe corporation. They had on-site daycare ten or fifteen years ago. They tell me that the workplace has changed. They have forty percent women with allegiance to this company, and their burnout rate has gone down to zilch. They don't have turnover. Women really feel committed to this company because the company is committed to them. They go and breast-feed all through the day. In fact, the daycare person calls them up and says, "It's time to come." They stop their work and go breast-feed and then return to work.

MOYERS: Isn't that where this should begin? There's a limit to what we can expect a national government to accomplish over a sprawling continental area like the United States. If the institutions or the companies where these women work took the initiative, that would be meeting the need at the most immediate level.

BRAZELTON: Big business is conscious enough now to be ready for that if we gave them just a little bit more of a shove. Small businesses are going to need more help than that. But that ought to be our job. We should find out how to help them do it. We've got to empower young people to say, "We have got to have this." In a country this size, with these kinds of resources, once the public feels empowered enough to get up and say, "We aren't going to put up with this any longer," we'll get action.

MOYERS: What are the main features you would like to see Congress consider?

BRAZELTON: There are two things that are really important. One is that we ask states to match funds, so no state is going to match government funds without looking at what's going on. Once they look around their state, they'll see just what we did—that we're not doing what we should be doing in daycare. The other thing is that we set a base level for quality, which means we're going to have to be responsive to people's needs. We've got to train child care workers, we've got to supervise them, and we've got to pay them. That is going to demand a look at what's going on for kids. Once we look, I think this country will have to respond.

> We've got to train child care workers, we've got to supervise them, and we've got to pay them.

MOYERS: If the four-month parental leave is available, without income, it's still very difficult for a lot of parents to take four months off.

BRAZELTON: That's right, and most people aren't going to be able to—but at least they'll have the choice. Just giving people a choice gives them a sense of power. When we gave women in labor a choice about whether they could stay awake or go to sleep, you could see them take on a whole different attitude toward their labor and delivery. Giving people a choice in this country is a big step.

MOYERS: I like the subtle change in the definition of the word "power" that you have made throughout this interview. By "power" you mean "choice." You don't mean the ability to lord it over anyone, you mean the power to choose directions for one's life.

BRAZELTON: And to feel, "God, that was my choice—now, how do I live up to it?" People pass this attitude on to their kids. A child who is feisty in the second year, where you have to stomp on them, and get angry with them, is a very different kind of kid from one that's cowering in the corner, where you don't dare sit on them. I think we want feisty kids.

MOYERS: When I first read about the Rosenthal effect, I thought, "Well, we're all dumb rats and smart rats, and what we become depends upon what cheese we're fed and when."

BRAZELTON: Yes, it has a lot to do with "cheese"—whether you're on drugs in pregnancy, for example, or whether you're paying attention to what you're doing to that fetus in utero. It's a bigger issue than we're facing.

MOYERS: What about bonding for those children who are borne in the womb of an addict and are, by the time of birth, themselves addicted? Is there any hope for that ten percent?

BRAZELTON: Maybe. But we don't know that yet. I think so. But it's higher than ten percent. It's ten percent in the boondocks, but it's twenty-five percent in every city that we know of now. Twenty-five percent of women who come into a city hospital, or even a private hospital, have positive urine for drugs.

MOYERS: What does this mean to the baby?

BRAZELTON: Cocaine is a bad actor. It causes big holes in the baby's brain, and at least one kidney is always damaged at birth. Some of them are born with amputations of their fingers and toes—things like that. So we know cocaine is really terrible for fetuses, because every time the mother has enough for a rush, her baby gets that rush through the placenta, and he can't excrete the same cocaine back to her. It gets caught in his system, and he may get twenty rushes out of every hit she gets. What goes with a rush is that your blood pressure goes up, and there's a spasm that can cut off circulation to the brain, to the kidneys, and to the limbs. These babies are born with defective systems.

MOYERS: Can even a caring surrogate parent bond with a child like that?

BRAZELTON: It's very tough. I have a newborn baby assessment that people are using all over the country, which shows that for the first month, if you even look at these babies, or talk to them, or touch them, they get overwhelmed and stop breathing. They're very prone to SIDS, sudden infant death syndrome, so they're very high-risk babies. If you wait a month, they get to the point where you can look at them, touch them, talk to them, and begin to reorganize them. The marvelous thing about the human brain is that it's very plastic. There's a lot of redundancy in the immature nervous system pathways that aren't captured yet that can be captured and put to use, even with impairment. We've learned this just recently. This is all brand-new stuff. Then if you start with those babies when they're finally getting rehabilitated, you can look or talk or touch—but only one of these. You can't do two, because they arch or turn away—you'll get negative responses. If you just look, then they'll arch and look at you and finally soften. Then you can say, "Hi," and they'll arch, turn away, and soften. You can finally get those babies going. We think that we can reorganize a lot of them. Still, a lot of them are going to have learning disabilities and hyperactivity and so forth.

MOYERS: Is the family that bonds early more likely, as the years come and go, to function together?

BRAZELTON: I would think so, wouldn't you? What I'm saying, though, is more subtle than that. Bonding is falling in love, but attachment is hard work. It's rare that you ever have that much energy ready to give to somebody else. If you learn to bond to a new baby, you stay attached. If you learn that you can get through those first three months, and that baby still looks at you and smiles and vocalizes and says, "Oooo," and you say, "Oooo," back and then he says, "Oooo," a second time and then you say, "Yeah," and you see that baby, coming right in every time to just grab you with his eyes or his mouth or everything else, you know what it's like to be attached, and you don't want to give that up so much when the stresses come in a marriage or come later. This is an opportunity for young people to learn what the work of attachment's all about—and the rewards of attachment. There aren't many chances like that in life, to really feel that kind of depth of attachment.

MOYERS: You make an interesting distinction. You say that bonding is falling in love, and attachment is a commitment, an act of will, responsibility.

BRAZELTON: It's a learning process. You learn what that person needs to give back to you and what you have to give to get that person to give back to you. When a baby looks at you and says "Oooo," you have to imitate everything that baby's doing. When the baby goes "Oooo," you go "Oooo" with him, then you let down, then you go with him. We know from our work that a mother and a baby get locked into this in-out, in-out, four times a minute. I call it "prostitute's eyes"—they're saying, "Come on in" and "You are important. You are important."

MOYERS: What happens to mothers who don't bond in this early time?

BRAZELTON: I think they always feel as if they've missed something. Fathers do, too. Fathers who went off to the Korean War, for instance, while their wives had a baby—I could see when they got back, they never quite understood that first child. It wasn't until the second child came along, and they watched that baby come through everything, that you could see them say, "Hey, that's what this kid's all about, too." And then they could make it with the first baby. So missing out on that for either parent is like missing a whole part of your life.

MOYERS: In 1960 I was deeply involved in the Kennedy-Johnson campaign and on the road a lot. Our oldest son was just six months old. He thought for a long time David Brinkley was his father because he saw David Brinkley on television—

BRAZELTON: —every day.

MOYERS: I'm not sure he missed as much as I missed. I would like to have that year back. The other side of it, though, is that I never really felt adequate for nurturing. Is that common? Do men generally feel inadequate?

BRAZELTON: They sure do. They need nurturing through that period, too. It's a little bit chauvinistic to say that, but I think a man—well, do you know the concept of gate-keeping?

MOYERS: No.

BRAZELTON: Gate-keeping means that everybody who cares about a small baby is going to try to get to that baby. There's a natural competition for a small baby, so you shove everybody else out of the way to get to that baby. A mother, who's developing this marvelous sense of herself and of the baby, gate-keeps. She does this unconsciously when her husband first picks the baby up to diaper him. She says, "Darling, that's not the way you diaper a baby." Or when he picks the baby up to hold it, or to feed it, she says, "You hold it this way, not that." She's gate-keeping. Men are so vulnerable in that early period that they let themselves get shoved out. And if they do, then it gets that much harder to come in and say, "I know what to do with this baby."

MOYERS: You're saying that nurturing can be taught and can be learned.

BRAZELTON: Oh, no question. We're working on it. You're teaching something that's already there in most people. What you're doing is peeling off onion skins and letting them get to that core of what it's like to care about somebody else. In this rather defended generation, I find you have to peel off those onion skins.

MOYERS: Are you convinced that a father's involvement makes a difference?

BRAZELTON: Every bit of research we have shows that. By seven days of age, a newborn will know its mother's voice from another woman's voice and will choose it every time. He'll choose the mother's smell from another woman's smell, if you give him breast pads to choose. By ten days he'll choose his mother's silent face from another woman's face. So visually and auditorily, he's learning very rapidly. By fourteen days, if the father's involved, that baby will choose his father's voice and face from another male voice and face. So in fourteen days he's learned what his father's all about. Now, by four weeks of age, if you put a baby in a baby chair, and the mother comes in to talk to him, the baby needs either to see her face or to hear her voice, and his fingers and toes and eyes get ready to talk to his mother. If his father looms into sight, or if he hears his father's voice behind him, he'll get ready to play with the father. All fathers come in and pounce. They say, "How are you doin', kid?" They start at the bottom and poke to the top and then when they get a "Woo!" out of the four-week-old baby, they start again. By four weeks of age the baby's learned the modes of each parent and gives back the fact that he knows them. What father doesn't recognize that? When he goes in, and the baby responds, he immediately says, "Hey, you know me." So he starts in to poke. To me this is so important. Every adult is ready for this kind of involvement.

MOYERS: What do you see happen to fathers who never had this experience when they were young men?

BRAZELTON: They have a longing, an unfulfilled longing.

MOYERS: There's a blank place down there that's never been nurtured. Nothing's ever grown there.

BRAZELTON: There's an anger that goes with it. This is what frightens me about young people who are having to leave their babies right now. There's an anger about being torn away from that experience—an unconscious anger, for the most part, but a kind of grieving that goes with it, too. The grief work that I see takes the form of feeling guilty, feeling as if everything that happens bad is my fault. Even twelve years later, if something goes wrong, it's my fault because I wasn't there those first few months.

Then they defend themselves with three defenses, and these are universal, they're right across the board. One is denial, denying that it matters, denying that anybody's suffering. It distorts your point of view. The second is projection—projecting onto other people all the good things and you taking the bad, or vice versa. It's what makes people accuse daycare people of hurting their child or molesting their child. The third is detachment—detaching from the baby, not because you don't care, but because it hurts so much to care. So you pull away. This is what's scary. This is what happens to fathers, and it happened in our generation.

MOYERS: Yet the bias in our generation, for young men, was to get out there, succeed, compete, win. Look at the ads today, look at the television commercials, look at the sporting events, look at the message that comes through the candidates to compete, win, be first.

BRAZELTON: All of our national values reflect that, too. We've got to have enough money, we've got to be on top. What we're missing is the core in all of these people that we're demanding this of. We're missing the real soft part inside of each of these people and what we demand of them becomes defenses. That's what they show.

MOYERS: Are there studies that also show that women take some hope and strength from a husband who is involved as a father in those first few months, and that women begin to feel more confident, less depressed, and less isolated because the father is there taking part?

BRAZELTON: No question. All of the studies that we've got in this country so far about involving fathers show that they're ready to be involved. We can show the newborn to the father on the third day, and we know that he'll be significantly more sensitive to his baby at a month and significantly more involved in a year, with both the baby and his spouse. And also, at a year, the baby will have a higher IQ. But at seven the studies show that if the father's been involved in the first year, the baby will not only have a higher IQ and perform better in school, but have a better sense of humor. To me that's worth fighting for.

MOYERS: What does it do to a baby not to have a father?

BRAZELTON: It's very tough. It's tough on the single mother, too, not to have a father for her child. What I see in older kids, three and four—I call them older—if they don't have a father, they'll come and just climb up in my lap, and they'll fawn and want to feel my face and touch me, as if they just couldn't get enough of what a man is like. I think in a single-parent family this is one of the hardest things, that you can never quite feel enough for that child. And the child shows you you're not enough. This must be very tough.

MOYERS: The burden is really on single parents, is it not? Not only do they have to provide that nurturing, and take bonding to its natural depth in those first few months, but they have to get out in that world and earn the only income that will feed, clothe, and shelter that child. How many mothers today are single parents?

BRAZELTON: Twenty percent, I think.

MOYERS: And this is a problem made more difficult for poor people.

BRAZELTON: Oh, of course. What we all do unconsciously is say something like, "Oh, the poor don't care this much," or "The poor don't make this kind of relationship, this is a middle-class concept." Crap. Poor people are suffering just as much and setting up just as strong defenses because they want so much to have this experience. And our society's not giving them a chance at it. We're demanding too much of people.

MOYERS: Can a teenager who has a child be helped to become a good mother?

BRAZELTON: There are many studies showing that teenagers do very well through the first year, particularly with a little bit of nurturing. The times that they need help are in the second year, when the child gets negative and has temper tantrums, and somebody needs to be there to give an understanding of why the child's pulling away. But the studies that are the most critical show that if their own mothers accept them back into the family, those kids will do very well. If a mother rejects her teenage daughter for her pregnancy, the baby is likely to fail.

> *If a mother rejects her teenage daughter for her pregnancy, the baby is likely to fail.*

MOYERS: So the extended family becomes critical. The grandmother plays a very important role.

BRAZELTON: Or if the teenage woman has a spouse or somebody who cares about her, she'll do well. But she's got to have some supplement herself. We could do that as a society. We could back up young women.

MOYERS: We know what a mother misses if she doesn't bond, and we know what a father misses. What does the child miss if he or she doesn't bond with the mother and father?

BRAZELTON: What a child needs is this: Every time they do something, somebody should be there to say, "Hey, that was great." This helps a child to have an inner sense of having achieved something, like learning to walk. You watch a child trying to learn to walk. When he finally gets on his feet, he walks, walks, walks in a way which says, "Wow, isn't this exciting? I just got where I always wanted to be." And you can see on his face that he gets an inner sense of himself. But if somebody's there to say, "You are great!" then he gets a double-barreled shot of, "Wow, I am important." Now you see that all the way through. When he looks at the mother and says "Oooo," and she says "Oooo" back, he's getting a sense of "I can 'Oooo,' and then I get a response." All of that contributes to a sense of competence in the child. He feels good about himself, and he knows he can conquer the world.

If he doesn't have that through infancy, he never gets that later on, and he grows up with a sense of, "Aw, it doesn't matter what I do." These kids that never get it will run into furniture, they'll trip, they'll make you so angry you want to strangle them. They're showing you they expect to fail. We can see a sense of failure in kids as early as nine months of age. Those kids, we can predict, will become difficult in school; they'll never succeed in school; they'll make everybody angry; they'll become delinquents later; and eventually they'll be terrorists.

MOYERS: Terrorists?

BRAZELTON: That's what I'm afraid of. I think we're creating a generation of kids that are wide open for terrorism.

MOYERS: And you think that goes back to the sense of failure, the sense of unworthiness that happens in this bonding period—or doesn't happen?

BRAZELTON: I saw it in Cambodia when I went over there. Children who have been through that holocaust as adolescents sit there with vacant eyes. If you hand them a gun and say, "Shoot there," they'll shoot there, there, there. They don't have any past, they don't have any future. Why should they care?

MOYERS: Isn't there also a danger on the other side, the danger of saying to children, "You are important," so early that they become another "me first" generation?

BRAZELTON: Yes, there is. That's what we did in the last generation, so we don't need to repeat it. We didn't say to them, at a certain point, "That's enough. You stop right there and now you help me, you come back to the kitchen." I'm telling young parents now who come home from work that they've got to cheat on the work force first and save up enough energy so when they get home, they walk in the door, they pick up all the kids, sit down in a rocking chair, and rock. And everybody gets close again and at some point or other the kids squirm and want to get away. At that point the mother says to them, "Okay, we've had our time together, now come on and help me in the kitchen." And they come to help. They aren't going to do it without yanking them or whatever you have to do, but they will come. You pass on that sense that you're wonderful, and because you're wonderful, you can help.

MOYERS: Do you see a lot of anguish among young parents today?

BRAZELTON: Oh, tremendous. A lot of this is the wish to be perfect—perfect mother, perfect father, perfect child. They're pushing themselves so hard that they don't really learn the subtlety of parenting or the excitement of watching a child make a mistake, bringing it back, helping it try again, giving the child and themselves some leeway. The anguish is the pressure everybody feels under. What we need right now is some space.

MOYERS: So they grieve a lot, don't they?

BRAZELTON: Yes, they do, instead of saying, "Well, I did the best I could, this is what I can do, and I'm going to live with it," and then saying, "But let's have some fun together," or "Let's do something together." I think they get caught.

Learning to parent is learning from mistakes, not from success. You don't learn much when you're successful, but you sure learn when you're wrong. If you start out, ready to make mistakes but learning from them, kids can learn with you. They learn from your mistakes, too. So, really, parenting is made up of many, many failures—but you learn from each one of them.

MOYERS: The messages from society are very conflicting. There are really two women's movements. One women's movement says, "Your place is in the home. Be a mother. Stay in the home and raise that child." The other women's movement says, "You've got to get out into the world for survival reasons and compete and make it." These young women are getting conflicting advice from their own peers.

BRAZELTON: They are. It's got to be a very individual decision. What I'd like to create right now are some choices for people so they can understand what each choice means and then make their own choice—and be prepared to live with their choice.

MOYERS: As it is, a lot of younger people are simply saying, "We're not going to have children." Or they're deciding, as recent polls have suggested, that the ideal family size is one or two children. What do you think this means for the future?

BRAZELTON: I don't think it's bad to have one or two children, if you make that choice. You can do a good job by them. It's hard to have one. It's easier to have two, and even easier to have three. But I think people need to make that choice. But if they choose for the wrong reasons—financial or upward mobility—they don't feel good about those choices later on.

MOYERS: So there are values at work even when we don't recognize them?

BRAZELTON: This is what I mean about young people not knowing what the value system is right now.

MOYERS: But there's another side of it, too. The baby boom has come and gone, and the twenty-to-thirty-year-old population cohort is diminishing twenty percent over the next seven to eight years. Who's going to buy the cars and homes and pay the Social Security?

BRAZELTON: The baby boom hasn't stopped. It's on its way back up again. The more you and I talk about this kind of nurturing and loving, the more babies are going to get born next year, I can promise you. I go out and talk to parents all over the country these days to raise money for my unit at Harvard. I talk to fifteen hundred parents every time, and these young parents sit there. A lot of them are just pregnant, and haven't had a baby yet. But they sit there for two and a half hours asking questions, getting involved. At the end of that two and a half hours, if I don't get out of that hall quick, they come and grab me by the tie, by the belt, by the trousers, and they say, "I'm not letting you go till you answer *my* question." And you think, "Wow, this is really kooky, isn't it?" And then you realize this is power—these kids feel some power when they're pregnant and when they have a new baby. They're not going to give that up easily. I see it as a very positive sign that young people are now sensing the power of attachment, of family. If my generation can back them up, we can have a country that'll pull itself together and get off the ground again.

MOYERS: Let's talk about what you mean by backing them up. What are some specific things society, the community, the country have to do?

BRAZELTON: I have very strong biases, so I can list mine. We've got to give parental leave around a new baby.

MOYERS: To both father and mother.

BRAZELTON: Absolutely. What we're fighting for this year in Congress is four months' protected leave for both parents—the father can take what he wants of it, and the mother can take what she wants. I don't have any illusions that fathers will take a lot, but I think they'll take two to four weeks.

MOYERS: There are countries that give eighty percent of the income to the mother or father on parental leave who stays home with that baby.

BRAZELTON: Those countries are very committed to families and children. We are not as a country.

MOYERS: But we see children everywhere on the television commercials. You would think from watching television this is a child-centered society.

BRAZELTON: What kind of children are you seeing? Little prissy ones with pretty dresses and pretty clothes who sit there and act like models. We're not looking at real people or at the struggles people go through to take care of that kid, to stop him when he goes too far—things like that. That isn't the kind of caring we are up to in this country yet.

MOYERS: If we were caring, we would see that some kind of parental leave is available to a new mother and a new father.

BRAZELTON: Right. Then we'd also be sure that when we have to leave those kids, we're leaving them in decent care. That means we've got to spend some money. We've got to train people to take care of small children, and we haven't done that yet. Otherwise, a mother or a father goes off, and they grieve, and they burn out at work, and they're absent, and they do all the things we know they do. If we provided them with really nurturing daycare, or nurturing substitute care, they'd feel good about what they were doing.

MOYERS: Yes, but child care of that kind is expensive. It's hard to acquire, and it's the most difficult to evaluate. It's very hard for a mother or father to know whom to trust with their child.

BRAZELTON: Sure, that's a learning process, too. But we can do all that. We have plenty of information about how to do it. We just don't have the commitment yet.

MOYERS: But hasn't there also been research suggesting that putting babies under one year of age into full-time child care can be harmful to that child many years later?

BRAZELTON: Sure, yes. I would expect that, wouldn't you? If we don't provide them with top-notch daycare, and aren't sure that they have somebody who pays attention to them, the kids will suffer for it. The thing that hasn't been shown by the kind of studies we've done so far is what it means to the parent to have to leave that child. I think what we're seeing is that not only will kids suffer if they're in less than optimal care, but parents will grieve and detach. So the studies that we've seen so far show that the quality of daycare and the mother's own adjustment to her work and to leaving the child become just as critical to that child's outcome as any of the other factors, such as whether she works or not.

MOYERS: I see that. But given the inadequacy of so many of our schools today, what gives you hope that we can actually put into practice proper daycare facilities?

BRAZELTON: I wouldn't have any hope if I were depending on the way we've approached education. I wouldn't have any at all. I just have hope that because these are young families, there's enough energy in them to demand what they need and enough energy in a whole culture like ours to respond to that demand. I would hope that it won't be treated as schools have been, that we wouldn't let it get into the kind of not-caring attitude we've had toward education. It means we've all got to band together and fight for it.

MOYERS: We care about what kind of education our own child is getting, but not a great deal about what kind of education other people's children are getting. That same fallacy is operable in the daycare system.

BRAZELTON: Sure. You know, we're really making a two-class system very rapidly with the kind of daycare we have—the ones who have good daycare and the ones who don't. Those who don't are going to be the poor and unsuccessful of the future. Unconsciously, in this country, we like to keep people on the bottom. We like to be on top. And unless we recognize that it costs us a hell of a lot more than we can afford to have those kids on the bottom, we aren't going to be responsive.

MOYERS: In what sense?

BRAZELTON: Oh, terrorism, crime, acting out, drugs. You know, all the things that we're running into.

MOYERS: Wouldn't it be a better policy to find some way to reward parents for staying home with their children? Wouldn't that be a better alternative than some vast system of government?

BRAZELTON: Yes, it might. I don't think it would work, but I think it would be a very important thing to do, because it would give women choices, and it would give men choices. Somebody can stay at home and be rewarded for it. I'd love to do that. I think that would be very important. I don't think it would still settle the issues that women are going through right now and that men are going to go through.

MOYERS: I think you're right, by the way. I hope our two sons are better fathers than I, and that our daughter is as good a mother as her mother was.

BRAZELTON: They will be. You know, we're backing up young men these days to really get in there and pitch. When the wife is having a contraction in delivery, they groan with her. When they get that baby, they look at that baby like, "Oh my God, this is what I've always wanted." So they're ready. We just have to back them up for that. I think we're at a time when, if we support these important human values, we can do it. Now you say, "But, gosh, it's going to cost a lot of money." Sure, it does. One missile would pay for this whole damned thing. But are we going to give up one missile? You know we won't be the big shot on the block if we give up our missile.

MOYERS: Do you think that market forces can create the kind of daycare we're talking about?

BRAZELTON: Yeah, sure. But young people can't afford the kind of daycare I'm talking about by themselves.

MOYERS: What does it cost here in New England, for example?

BRAZELTON: Well, for a baby it's between $7,500 and $9,000 a year. For a toddler it's something like $5,000 to $6,000 a year. This is in private daycare. That means the mother who has two children has to make $13,000 to $15,000 a year just to pay for her two children's care. Now, you'd say, "Gosh, why doesn't she stay home? She could do better staying at home." That's true. I guess it brings up the whole issue of why women feel committed to work.

MOYERS: So you don't think we can depend on market forces alone to provide enough affordable daycare?

BRAZELTON: Not without a lot of pressure, no. But with enough pressure we can let business see that unless they do this, they're going to not be able to hire women, and they're going to miss out on nurturant men. I don't think that we're going to get them to give up many of their resources to families and to small children. But I think we can push people right now. Business is getting very sensitive to this as women are more and more necessary in the work force. It's a matter of these young people saying, "Look, unless you care about me as a person, and my family as a family, you're not going to get me. And you're going to have burnout, and you're going to have costly changes"—things like that, which we know happen.

MOYERS: What advice can you give young parents about how to select child care while they're working?

BRAZELTON: There's plenty in the literature for that. I could refer them to many books—my own *Working and Caring*, for example. There are lists of what to look for. You look to see whether the plugs are covered, you look to see whether it's safe, you look to see whether somebody pays attention to a child who's getting into trouble, you look to see if the ratio is okay, if there's one adult to every three or four infants, and one adult to every four or five toddlers. Unless there's that kind of ratio, you can't be sure it's safe. But then you look for one other thing: You look to see how much that nurturant person responds to each individual baby. And what I'd look for is just what I've already shown you. If you see a daycare person that's going to take care of your baby pick up your baby, and the baby gives them that look, and then the daycare person looks back and says, "Thank you," you know you're in good hands. If she's that sensitive to your baby, you can't miss.

MOYERS: Are there that many sensitive surrogate parents around?

BRAZELTON: Not yet. But when we start paying them and training them and giving them enough backup to feel that's important, there will be. There are plenty of people out there ready to do this.

MOYERS: Just like the volunteer army. Once we began to pay young men and women adequately to serve in the armed forces, both the number and quality of recruits went up. You're saying the same principle applies to this other cause.

BRAZELTON: Well, we did it in Massachusetts. We found that we were paying daycare people $8,000 at an average. Well, you can get $9,000 on welfare. Why would anybody do it unless they just were so in love with babies? But being in love with them isn't enough, you've got to know what's making them tick, too. If we wanted them to get trained, we had to raise their base rates. So we did. We raised it to $12,000 in Massachusetts by supplementing it with state funds. Within a year, daycare improved all over Massachusetts. So it can be done.

MOYERS: I find this exciting—to think about the possibility of this country's becoming a really caring society, of making this kind of success the one that is most rewarded by our value system.

BRAZELTON: We can do it. We can really do it if we put our minds to it. This is what's so exciting. These young people all over the country who grab my tie and my belt are saying, "Look, I've got enough energy to go around." So why don't we pick up on that?

MOYERS: We touched on two things—parental leave and childcare facilities. What would be the other features of a Brazelton national policy on child care?

BRAZELTON: Oh gosh, let me dream. Flex-time and even shared job opportunities—two mothers working back to back, or two fathers working back to back. I guarantee that two people doing halftime work are going to give a lot more than halftime each, if they know they're doing it for a cause. The whole workplace becoming sensitive to families and to family issues. Having something provided around sick leave for the kids, and letting people stay home because the child is sick. Don't you remember when you were sick, and your mother would come in and rub your back and put on mustard plaster, and feed you all sorts of—

MOYERS: —I remember enjoying the mumps because I had ice cream every day.

BRAZELTON: It wasn't just the ice cream, either, it was that mother looking at you like that. So, you know, we can't throw things out the window without paying a terrible, terrible price.

MOYERS: And yet we and South Africa are the only two industrialized nations without a real policy toward families.

BRAZELTON: Right.

MOYERS: How do you explain that?

BRAZELTON: I think the same sort of thing goes on in South Africa—that they aren't really committed either to their poor or to their families. In South Africa, it may be the same sort of unconscious thing that we have here—that if we empower the poor people and poor families, we're not going to have the same class system that we've got. We're not going to have the rich and the poor, we're going to have people who feel alike, and that's scary. You know, that's asking for a real revolution in this country. If everybody feels alike, people on top of the heap might not be able to stay up so high.

> *We don't value children, and we certainly don't value their parents, so we're paying a big price right now.*

MOYERS: What happens to a society that doesn't put children in the honored place, that doesn't care, or that allows these fundamental values to come apart?

BRAZELTON: You're seeing a society like that right now. We don't value children, and we certainly don't value their parents, so we're paying a big price right now.

MOYERS: You describe these pregnant women coming to see you, and these eager and grieving fathers who want to know how to nurture. There's something there within us that wants the child. But in society at large, the gap between what we feel and do is so great.

BRAZELTON: I think that gap is really frightening to young people who do care. They say, "Gosh, I don't know what I'm raising these kids for. Here I spent all of my time trying to nurture this kid, and I push him out into a society that doesn't value him." So I think we're into a very serious split.

MOYERS: Don't you think people who talk a great deal about family values fail to see the impact on these values of the unbridled materialism that they also enshrine in their mythology? What would happen to society if Harvard produced parents with the same skill and zeal and financial support with which it produces MBAs?

BRAZELTON: I've been over at the business school for the past two or three years, teaching the second-year class. It's fifty percent women now. So I show them a baby, and I show them this period when the baby and the mother get locked in with each other, and the father gets locked in. At the end of that class, all of these kids are sitting forward, and they're saying, "Oh my God! We're on the fast track. How are we going to do this with our kids?" And I say, "Well, this is the time to make up your mind. You can do it, probably, but you're going to have to figure out how to do it." You see, I think we're in a choice-making period. It's a period of real disorganization before we take a spurt in our society. We're asking enormous questions. We all ought to band together and look for solutions. These young kids, if they really think about it, can figure out how to nurture and still be on the fast track. I don't think we're going to have to give up the fast track, but I think we have to balance it.

MOYERS: But that implies coherence and consensus when, in fact, we're a society where subcultures are warring with each other. The fundamentalists say, "Woman, get back in the home." The feminists say, "Woman, get out there in the marketplace, go for it like everyone else." I've heard both groups damn you.

BRAZELTON: That's right, I have, too. But you realize what you're saying—we're an either/or society, and we don't look for what goes on in the middle. What's the compromise? How do we pay for the compromise? We're an either/or society because we've left everything up to the individual. We've said, "You've got to be competent. You've got to do this, or you've got to do that." But we've come to another era in which we're going to have to look at our governments, state and local, as supplementing families, not pushing them to make either/or choices.

Sara Lawrence Lightfoot
EDUCATOR

Sara Lightfoot, a professor of education at Harvard's Graduate School of Education, sees as much promise as problem in our schools today. In The Good High School, *she tells the stories of real people at six American high schools and describes what makes certain schools good and some teachers memorable. Her most recent book,* Balm in Gilead, *is her account of another remarkable woman—her mother.*

MOYERS: You use an expression I like very much—the "playfulness of learning." You don't mean something frivolous or trivial, do you?

LIGHTFOOT: No, not at all. A lot of learning has lost its play and has become very concrete, very literal, very exacting. It moves towards an end or conclusion rather than turning ideas on their sides and considering them and laughing about them and being whimsical about them. Some of the best teachers are humorous teachers who see the playfulness of language and are quick and intuitive. Learning is at its best when it's deadly serious and very playful at the same time. When I say deadly serious, I mean that learning should be disciplined and that people should find ways of learning how to ask questions, how to think about evidence, and how to find the truths that are out there. That's a very serious pursuit. On the other hand, in every serious thought, there's a line of laughter. In my own teaching, I'm at my best when I have something that I feel passionate about and talk seriously about, but at the same time, that I can find a way of presenting the play in.

MOYERS: Shakespeare's plays pursue a very serious intent but with a lot of witty lines that reveal the relationship between the tragedy and the comedy.

LIGHTFOOT: There is an art—or maybe just a craft—in that interplay of discipline and humor. There is a dynamic, a dialectic.

MOYERS: Do you find this kind of playful learning in schools today?

LIGHTFOOT: Not enough. You can go into a classroom that is an oasis and feel it almost immediately. And you don't hear it everyday in every classroom even when it goes on there. To have this sense of play, you have to be very confident as a thinker and confident in building relationships with students. In most schools today, teachers and students don't feel comfortable enough to be playful. When you're worried about discipline or preoccupied with completing a prescribed curriculum in a particular amount of time, you lose the sense of joy and possibility—the sense of play.

MOYERS: You've got a wonderful example in your book of a teacher who's teaching his class about the impact of Freud on the individual psyche.

LIGHTFOOT: This is a teacher at a very privileged preparatory school in New England working with seniors who have already been accepted to college, and so they are a very relaxed group. They are relatively sophisticated and well schooled. He's teaching them an elective course on Freud at eight o'clock in the morning. He's really trying to guide them through the major themes of Freudian theory, and they're fumbling through these ideas. A number of the students want more certainty, but the teacher really wants them to think, to explore, to weigh the ideas, to consider what might have happened. At one point, a girl comments with cynicism about how old-fashioned and primitive these ideas were. The teacher says, "You know, it takes a very, very long time for ideas to evolve and take shape. It's very hard to challenge authority and change one's view of the world if it's been in place for a long time." This teacher was seeking to give his students a sense of the adventure of learning.

MOYERS: And were they caught up in this?

LIGHTFOOT: Increasingly, as the class went on, they were. Initially, the students were impatient for the answer.

MOYERS: Not the search.

LIGHTFOOT: Exactly. In our schools, students are mostly trained to get to the answer quickly. Part of teaching is helping students learn how to tolerate ambiguity, consider possibilities, and ask questions that are unanswerable. Adolescents have been called "the truth tellers." I don't know that they always tell the truth, but they *do* listen for the truth. They can tell when adults are not authentic—so if you're asking them to take on adventure through a hard set of ideas, and you're not willing to go along, it's unlikely that they will be.

> In our schools, students are mostly trained to get to the answer quickly.

MOYERS: You describe in your book how at the end of one class, the teacher shouts out, "The struggle—I love it! I love it!" If, as you say, "high school is theater," he was having a good play. When did you first learn about the playfulness of education?

LIGHTFOOT: I'm sure I learned it at home and not in school. Our dinner table was always lively with conversation that was both serious and playful. There was never an asymmetry between the adults who had the serious conversation and the kids who watched and listened. All of us were part of the exchange. I learned very early that these two things could go together, so I found the tone of school to be quite monotonous for the most part. There was very little drama, very little play, and very little laughter.

MOYERS: Do you think that's common?

LIGHTFOOT: It's different for different families and subcultural groups. My own parents were very explicit about teaching what I now regard as a counter-curriculum at home. This included reading Frederick Douglass and W. E. B. Du Bois and some of the black poets from our own literary tradition. We also learned how to sing Negro spirituals in what my parents thought was the traditional classic way, which wasn't being taught at all in the schools I went to.

My parents also taught us an ideological counter-curriculum. They were leftists and pacifists. So there was always this contrary conversation going on at home and an attempt to reconcile what we were learning in school with what it was that my parents believed. We became very practiced in the art of negotiating which environment we were in and how to express ourselves in that environment.

MOYERS: So you could change gears from home to school. But what about the child that goes from a difficult home to a bad school? There's almost no hope for that child, is there?

LIGHTFOOT: It's very, very hard because in many families there is not a great conflict between what's taught in school and what's taught at home. The same sort of monotonous values get expressed in both places. It's problematic for a good education because children don't learn to be critical or to ask probing questions. They are just socialized to believe in a set of ideas or ideals that go unchallenged, either at school or at home. I consider myself very privileged to have experienced this dissonance. Most people don't.

The families of poor kids often have no idea what's happening in schools. They send their children off to a setting where they have no participation, no accountability, no voice. There's very little opportunity for them to become critics of that institution.

MOYERS: When did you know you wanted to be a teacher? Was it early?

LIGHTFOOT: No. There were several generations of teachers in my family, so as an adolescent, I wanted to do something different, more exciting. I imagined things like theater and the arts, something more risk-taking and more colorful. My parents had lots of friends in the arts, and I used them as models for what I might become. But I never imagined becoming a professor and doing research and teaching.

Some people regard teaching as a calling; they have wanted it for all of their lives. They may have had wonderful experiences in first grade or in kindergarten, and they say, "That's what I want to be." Then, for the rest of their lives, that's their purpose. Many of them are extraordinary. But teachers can emerge at any time. One of the hopeful signs across the country today is that people are leaving professions like engineering, business, law, and medicine, and becoming what they want to become—teachers. I think that's extraordinary. That's wonderful. Career change of all varieties is invigorating. In careers that are relational, like teaching, it's very important to be able to move out and in because teaching requires such energy and commitment and passion to do well.

MOYERS: I read an essay by your sister, Paula, who is a master teacher and a principal, in which she described the school as "a gathering of gifts." She said, "Everyone—the teacher, the administrator, the principal, the student—brings gifts to that classroom, to that school." Do you see it as a sharing of gifts?

LIGHTFOOT: At its very best. My sister, with her extraordinary talent and commitment, tries very hard to make that kind of environment in her school. She manages, most of the time, to do it. It requires extraordinary courage, nurturance, attention, energy, commitment, empathy, a sense of orchestration—all of that.

MOYERS: The child brings a gift to school and is not simply coming as an empty vessel to receive.

LIGHTFOOT: That's right. The whole experience is negotiated. The child brings himself or herself quite full of history and preoccupations and dreams and hopes and concerns and fears. And the teacher comes with her or his own set of those. That's negotiated every day throughout the year, and it changes over time.

MOYERS: But so much of this individuality gets parked at the door.

LIGHTFOOT: Yes, much of the rich diversity will fade out as school goes on throughout the year. This problem is much broader than school classrooms, however. When we draw people together into a group or a community, we think that's in opposition to individuality—

MOYERS: —that you can't become a member of the community without giving up your own individuality, your own gifts.

LIGHTFOOT: Social scientists often talk about forming the collective as being opposed to individual initiative. But my sense is that it doesn't have to be that way at all. There can be a difficult but harmonious coming together—the building of a rich community *and* individual expression. As a matter of fact, if we would let some of those individual gifts thrive, there would be more possibility for a rich community life.

MOYERS: How do we encourage children to recognize what they have to give in school?

LIGHTFOOT: They need to be praised for individual expression, for the ways in which they are different from others and not always praised for the ways that they are like others. Kids are proud of their gifts. If they do something well when they're little, they announce it. They want praise for it. So it's not so hard to figure out how to get them to feel good about their gifts. But once we've told them that those gifts aren't appropriate or legitimate in the school environment, then it's very hard to rekindle that later on, and they'll stop bringing them there.

MOYERS: Many classrooms are overcrowded. It must be very hard for a teacher to both deal with those thirty children as individuals and at the same time meld them into a community.

LIGHTFOOT: Teachers at their best are wonderful with this process of trying to get kids to recognize what's very special and different about themselves. Good teachers also manage to teach kids about being empathetic and help them recognize that group life in school is different from home life or from "play" life outside. School life is group life, and part of what they're learning in school is how to live effectively in a group.

Good teachers come in all forms and express themselves very differently. Teachers don't always connect successfully with all thirty kids in a classroom. But I think one thing all good teachers have in common is that they regard themselves as thinkers, as existing in the world of ideas. This is true for a nursery teacher and a professor in the most distinguished university. The currency is ideas—but ideas as conveyed through relationships.

MOYERS: I think it was John Henry Newman who said, "We can get information from books, but real knowledge must come from those in whom it lives." The idea has to be incarnate.

LIGHTFOOT: Yes, you not only have to have the knowledge, but you also have to *want* to communicate it. You have to feel deeply about wanting those people to know it. In some sense you have to see yourself reflected in the eyes of those you teach—or at least see your destiny reflected in them.

MOYERS: Your destiny?

LIGHTFOOT: Your future after you're long gone. When teachers can't imagine themselves in their students, when there is no reflection back and forth, then there can be pernicious, discriminatory behavior on the part of the teacher, which is often expressed quite passively. This happens in a lot of schools where kids are very poor or predominantly minority or speak another language.

MOYERS: These are the kids who look around and see devastation and poverty. There are few opportunities and few rewards, so they don't think there's much ahead for them.

LIGHTFOOT: And the teachers don't see the kids' futures as a part of this civilization, or as counting in this world in a significant way.

MOYERS: As you talk, I think about what your book says about how a school takes on the personality of its internal community.

LIGHTFOOT: It's terribly important to recognize that there is a culture alive and throbbing in a school. It takes on the character and color and vitality of those who live inside, the students and teachers. When it doesn't have that kind of reflection of who's inside, then there's something askew.

MOYERS: What does this mean in terms of those schools that are located in the bleak wastelands of the inner city?

LIGHTFOOT: There are all kinds of suggestions for school reform that I absolutely agree with. We need to build schools smaller. We need to give teachers much more of a say in developing curriculum and in seeing themselves as major educational actors in the school and the community. We have to find ways of engaging parents or caretakers in the work of the school and building bridges between families and schools.

But I think what we're talking about here is even more subtle. Somehow we've got to find people to inhabit these schools—adults, teachers—people who see that this work is valuable and valued work and that these children are very much wrapped up in *the teacher's* own future.

MOYERS: The teacher sees her or his destiny in the student, and the student has to see his or her destiny in the teacher.

LIGHTFOOT: It's a very complicated and subtle dynamic, but you can hear it in the voices of teachers when they're talking about their students—you can hear whether they are in fact engaged with people whose lives and futures they care about.

MOYERS: Can you in good conscience urge some of your students to consider going into the inner city of Newark or Philadelphia or Detroit to teach?

LIGHTFOOT: Yes, I can. I think it's imperative that they do.

MOYERS: But how do you teach a teacher to go into a classroom and compensate for broken homes, for alcoholic parents, for a social structure that has collapsed?

LIGHTFOOT: It takes a lot of *chutzpah.* You have to believe that this is possible. I don't think there's any way you could be in this business and not have an optimistic spirit.

Teachers need a very broad outlook on what they're doing. Part of what I try to do with teachers is sketch out the landscape within which they're working. I talk about the origins of some of that deterioration they're experiencing within the school and the community so that they are better able to understand what it is that might motivate their students to tune into school more fully. My whole interest is in trying to get people to understand more comprehensively how to look at communities and school culture so that they can be more effective actors in it.

MOYERS: Do you find a lot of burnout in teachers today? Or is that a cliché?

LIGHTFOOT: It's not a cliché, but it's the wrong word for it. I would call it "boredom"—the need for renewal, change, inspiration, and rewards. When I say rewards, I don't mean only higher salaries, although that's terribly important. It's appreciation, respect, dignity, the recognition that this is a tremendously important role in society and that this is very precious work. The distortions of the negative cultural imagery that is now attached to teaching make it very hard to go in to school every day and work productively.

MOYERS: Do you think there really is a negative image of teaching?

LIGHTFOOT: Oh, absolutely.

MOYERS: But we see movies about teachers changing schools and "60 Minutes" reports on teachers who are dynamically engaging their children.

LIGHTFOOT: This is a new phenomenon—choosing people who are doing extraordinary work in schools and giving them visibility. But for the most part, teachers are demeaned. For example, given a chance, highly educated, high-status, privileged women who now have greater choice are unlikely to go into teaching. They are more likely to choose business, law, medicine, or any of those fields that used to be dominated solely by males.

MOYERS: There's that little saying: "Those who can, do; those who can't, teach."

LIGHTFOOT: There are lots of people who think that and who believe that teaching is a mediocre professional choice. That does a lot of damage to people who have to go in there and work at it every single day.

MOYERS: I cut out from the newspaper this morning a survey by the Carnegie Foundation for the Advancement of Teaching which says that most teachers feel excluded from the most critical decisions on school policy, that they feel like front-row spectators in a reform movement in which the signals are being called by governors, legislators, state education figures—everybody but the teacher on the ground.

LIGHTFOOT: That's a piece of the burnout. When teachers burn out, they aren't saying, "I've worked too hard." They're saying, "I haven't had the opportunity to participate fully in this enterprise." Some teachers are speaking about the politics of teacher's voice. They're saying, "We want more control over our lives in this school." Some of them are making an even more subtle point—they're talking about voice as knowledge. "We know things about this enterprise that researchers and policy makers can never know. We have engaged in this intimate experience, and we have things to tell you if you'd only learn how to ask, and if you'd only learn how to listen." Teachers are talking about their voice as knowledge and insight and control and power.

MOYERS: Why doesn't anybody listen?

LIGHTFOOT: School systems are highly bureaucratized, with people at the top far away from the action, making the decisions about what should go on, and people at the bottom engaged in the enterprise supposedly being the empty vessels through which those decisions get transmitted. When I speak to teachers and talk about this image of teachers as empty vessels, you can just hear moans of recognition and sadness in the room—because that's how they have felt. When you're not participating in making the decisions about what it is you do every day, you feel powerless. It is infantilizing—it makes people feel like children.

> *When you're not participating in making the decisions about what it is you do every day, you feel powerless.*

MOYERS: One of your brightest recent graduates told me yesterday that she was not going into the classroom because she just didn't feel the system gave her the professional autonomy that she wants. She wasn't talking about more money or more time off. She was talking about her professional voice.

LIGHTFOOT: One of the characteristics of the good schools I looked at was that teachers seemed to have more voice in these ways: in decision-making, in being regarded as having special knowledge, and in being given autonomy to express that knowledge. The good schools supported individual teachers in their personal, idiosyncratic expression. They allowed them, as one principal put it, to "disturb the inertia." I like teachers who disturb the inertia and schools that are colorful with diversity among the teachers. Inevitably, that also allows for color and diversity of expression among students.

MOYERS: A school with less fear, a place where the relationship between the characters grows, and where there's a dialogue between the audience and the teacher.

LIGHTFOOT: Right, although, obviously, kids should not be perceived as the audience, but as participants in the drama that unfolds. I think that's terribly important.

MOYERS: You talk about good schools. But every time I mention the word "high school," I can see people's eyes reflecting back to me truancy, dropouts, illiteracy, racial conflict, violence, alcohol, and drug addiction. The image of schools today in the mind of the public is very negative.

LIGHTFOOT: Oh, indeed, I think it is, and some of that imagery is correct. There are too many schools that look like the schools you are describing. But there are many more good schools than we imagine and many more good teachers than we imagine. Part of what I want to do is to describe things that work and not merely things that don't work. I don't want to focus on the pathological or the fragile and weak, but really try to find examples of education at its best and begin to document that in all of its subtlety, complexity, and generosity. I want to convey that portrait so that others might feel inspired to do similar sorts of things. More importantly, others might see themselves in the stories I tell and be able to make up their own story of goodness.

MOYERS: Are there certain things that good schools have in common whether they're in the suburbs, the inner city, or are private academies or church schools?

LIGHTFOOT: Yes, although these may get expressed differently. Good schools have a sense of mission that kids and adults can all articulate. They have an identity. They have a character, a quality that's their own, that feels quite sturdy. They have a set of values. If you walk down the hall, kids will say, in their own language, "This is what this school is about. This is who we are." And adults will echo those same kinds of values. There is a kind of ideological stance that brings coherence to the school.

Also, in a good school, there has to be in the teaching and learning both seriousness and playfulness going on most of the time. Good schools tend to be a chemistry of extraordinary teachers, relatively good teachers, and mediocre teachers. In any professional group we can't expect that we will have goodness throughout. But there has to be this chemistry of wonderful people who are rewarded for being wonderful rather than denigrated for being wonderful, and of good people who continue to be good, and of relatively mediocre folks who are inspired or nudged or supported in becoming better.

Good schools are also disciplined places. I don't mean by that just behavioral discipline, but a place where people set goals and standards and hold each other accountable.

MOYERS: I was struck by the fact that all of the good schools you visited required a lot of the students and expected them to maintain a certain code of behavior. There was a strong respect for law and order and swift punishment for acts of violence.

LIGHTFOOT: That's right, but that requirement is experienced against a backdrop of love and respect. In other words, that respect doesn't come down hard as merely punitive. It's experienced as, "I expect a great deal of you. You are someone." That's a very different message than discipline, which refers to policing schools.

MOYERS: What about the role of the leader—the principal? Do all of these schools have a certain kind of leader?

LIGHTFOOT: The schools had very different leaders. But one quality all of the leaders shared was their focus on nurturance—supporting people and reaching for the best in those who work with them and developing strength rather than expecting blind allegiance and unquestioning loyalty from people. They are people who orchestrate relationships. As one of the principals said to me, "the metaphors are decidedly feminine." In all of these schools, it happened that the six principals were male—but all of them in various ways described the feminine sides of their natures when they talked about leadership in schools. They talked about listening, building a sense of community, sustaining relationships, and supporting people through failure.

MOYERS: Mothering.

LIGHTFOOT: Yes, in the best sense. Interestingly, a few of these principals had stereotypic jock masculine images. A couple of them had been successful coaches in big schools and talked proudly about their athletic heritage and success. But if you watched them in action, they were doing very nonstereotyped things.

MOYERS: Can you teach that to someone, or does that come with the genes?

LIGHTFOOT: It comes with experience, but you can find ways of providing the experience. That can start very young. It has to do with increasing the repertoire of possibilities for male and female children. If we think of leadership as taking the best of the stereotypic characteristics of male and female and deciding when and how to use them, then we recognize that we must offer boys and girls opportunities for developing in myriad ways that most of them haven't been offered before.

MOYERS: If the new President called you and said, "Professor Lightfoot, how should I address the school crisis?"—what would you tell him?

LIGHTFOOT: I would ask him to focus on teaching and learning, on the essence of the enterprise rather than on how to restructure the institution. Somehow the American public has to get back to the great richness and mystery of learning, the playfulness and seriousness of learning, and how that can be nurtured in schools by teachers in classrooms. I would ask him to focus on how to attract good people back into this profession, and how we can continue to support them once they have entered the profession.

MOYERS: There's a general lament in the country that the schools aren't meeting our great expectations of them, that they are not producing civilized and literate populations, that they're not mending inequalities, and that they're not encouraging innovation, creativity, and discovery. Do you share the general view that our schools are in crisis?

LIGHTFOOT: I agree with that lament to a certain extent. But I think we have expected far too much of schools. We have had very high aspirations for schools, asking them to solve all of our cultural, social, and economic crises. This is such an extraordinary set of agendas. Schools have never lived up to our hopes and dreams, even as far back as John Dewey and Horace Mann, who had great hopes for the way schools would reconstruct American society and make it more cohesive and healthy. So this is an old lament.

We must develop a more realistic view of the roles that schools can play.

Part of what we have to do is to look at the broad ecology of education, at the other institutions that educate. We must develop a more realistic view of the roles that schools can play. It isn't only up to schools to undo racism and social privilege and poverty. It is very much a part of their responsibilities, but other institutions have to participate in that process as well.

MOYERS: Teachers can't be parents and preachers and doctors. A lot of teachers say they're expected to play every role.

LIGHTFOOT: In some sense schools have been our most visible and vulnerable institutions. They are the stage on which a lot of cultural crises get played out. We see in schools most vividly the inequities and the hypocrisy. It's right there in front of you, and it's enraging. We tend to blame the teachers, who are the primary adult actors there, or the system, if we don't want to blame individuals. But schools are connected to other institutions of learning and development. This is not a back-to-basics sermon. I'm not saying that schools should omit things like art, theater, or physical education. But we do have to more realistically appraise what it is that schools can do.

MOYERS: For what should schools be held accountable?

LIGHTFOOT: Anyone who graduates from high school should be literate and should be able to reason and think analytically. That's a very basic accountability that we must hold schools to. I don't think we can hold schools accountable for all students feeling good about themselves, for example, or for making sure that kids don't smoke or don't get pregnant. Those responsibilities are broader in scope.

MOYERS: We blame the schools when schools are not the only teachers. Culture teaches all the time. We learn from television, politics, sports, athletes, and business.

LIGHTFOOT: The learning is going on all the time. It's useful to think about the difference between schooling and education. Schooling is what happens inside the walls of the school, some of which is educational. Education happens everywhere, and it happens from the moment a child is born—and some people say before—until a person dies. It's a far more complicated, overarching process than can ever be handled inside the walls of a school. Good teachers know the various ways in which children are educated outside of the school and what their particular responsibilities are inside of the school.

MOYERS: What do we do about bad teachers?

LIGHTFOOT: I am really very disturbed about the processes of tenuring teachers. It takes a very short time for people to be tenured, and the standards tend to be so low that most people, if they are not absolutely pernicious, will get tenure. Once having gotten tenure, many people, particularly poor teachers, relax into getting worse. There is something very wrong with a system that allows that. We need a system to reevaluate teachers and to support them in doing a good job.

MOYERS: That would include a lot of peer judgments.

LIGHTFOOT: Yes. Teaching is a very autonomous experience—but the flip side of autonomy is that teachers experience loneliness and isolation. Teachers tend to miss other adult company, colleagueship, relationship, criticism, camaraderie, support, and intellectual stimulation. There must be time and space in school days for teachers to come together to support one another, to respond critically to one another, and to develop plans together.

MOYERS: Like motherhood, which is the most isolated work in the world.

LIGHTFOOT: Yes, there are very few opportunities for mothers to get together with other mothers and to ask, "Am I going crazy, or does this happen to all mothers of two-year-olds?" That's the real question all the time. Is this just me, or is this quite typical? Do lots of kids do this? Do lots of mothers experience this? The need for company in one's work, for criticism and support, for scrutiny, for someone to tell you you're not crazy, is there in all of us. It's very hard if you are living within the cellular environment of a classroom, and there are no rewards for collegial relationship or discourse.

MOYERS: Do you know what I thought you would have told the new President? Something you have said before: "Tell the country that the way to better schools is to choose better teachers and treat them like chosen people."

LIGHTFOOT: Yes, I think that's right. We need to attract the best people into teaching and then to keep on telling them that they are chosen because they're so good—and to believe that, to be commenting on the reality.

MOYERS: Do you feel like a chosen person?

LIGHTFOOT: I feel privileged to be doing what I'm doing, and I do feel a calling in my work. I feel that my mission is broader than academic inquiry. I want to be part of the world. I want to be part of social change and social transformation. I'm constantly trying to find ways of communicating what I know to broader audiences, and trying to get more people engaged in the conversation that often stops at glib rhetoric about our schools. How can we get teachers involved in thinking about schools, in sharing their knowledge about schools, and in voicing it? Part of it is to write books with which they can identify, not the academic pieces that seem impenetrable and with which they feel no identity.

MOYERS: So it's possible to be within the academy and not be out of touch with the other world out there.

LIGHTFOOT: It's difficult because the rewards of the academy often go with thinking about esoteric abstractions that are difficult for most people in the outer world to penetrate. But there are those of us who see our role as quite different. I am very definitely a boundary sitter, someone who really thinks that knowledge has a great deal to do with how people live and how people think about their living. I want to be able to describe that with a clear enough voice so that people will be able to relate to it, and be identified with it, perhaps even be inspired by it. Communicating what we know is not merely an intellectual, cerebral exercise. We must also try to move people, speak to their head *and* their heart, so that they might do something about it. That's my hope.

August Wilson

PLAYWRIGHT

WILLIAM B. CARTER

Everyone has to find his own song, says August Wilson, and he found his in the blues. From music and literature he has shaped a philosophy of life and some of the country's most compelling drama. Wilson broke onto Broadway in 1984 with Ma Rainey's Black Bottom *and won the Pulitzer Prize in 1987 for* Fences. *He is at work on a cycle of plays that will resurrect black voices from every decade of this century.*

MOYERS: Your plays are set in the past—*Joe Turner* in 1911, *Ma Rainey* in 1927, *Fences* in the 1950s. Do you ever consider writing about what's happening today?

WILSON: I suspect eventually I will get to that. Right now I enjoy the benefit of the historical perspective. You can look back to a character in 1936, for instance, and you can see him going down a particular path that you know did not work out for that character. Part of what I'm trying to do is to see some of the choices that we as blacks in America have made. Maybe we have made some incorrect choices. By writing about that, you can illuminate the choices.

MOYERS: Give me an example of a choice that you think may have been the wrong one.

WILSON: I think we should have stayed in the South. We attempted to transplant what in essence was an emerging culture, a culture that had grown out of our experiences of two hundred years as slaves in the South. The cities of the urban North have not been hospitable. If we had stayed in the South, we could have strengthened the culture.

MOYERS: But wouldn't it have been asking a great deal of people for them to stay where they were the victims of such discrimination and oppression?

WILSON: I'm not sure, because the situation existed very much like that in the North, too. We came to the North, and we're still victims of discrimination and oppression in the North. The real reason that the people left was a search for jobs, because the agriculture, cotton agriculture in particular, could no longer support us. But the move to the cities has not been a good move. Today, in 1988, we still don't have jobs. The last time blacks in America were working was during the Second World War, when there was a need for labor, and it did not matter what color you were.

MOYERS: And now you feel surplus to the economy and to the society.

WILSON: Yes. There's a character in *Ma Rainey's Black Bottom* who says that blacks are left over from history. I think that's true.

MOYERS: What do you see happening today that you might be writing about twenty years from now?

WILSON: Strange as it may seem, I don't look at our society today too much. My focus is still on the past. Part of the reason is because what I do, I get from the blues, so I listen to the music of the particular period that I'm working on. Inside the music are clues to what is happening with the people. I don't know that much about contemporary music, so if I were going to write a play set in 1980, I would go and listen to the music, particularly music that blacks are making, and find out what their ideas and attitudes are about the situation, and about the time in which they live.

MOYERS: If you went to the ghetto in Newark, where I spent time filming a documentary for CBS, you would hear rap.

WILSON: Rap comes straight out of the black tradition. It's an extension of what we used to call the toast. Here's one: "The *Titanic* is sinking, and the banker comes up and says, 'Shine, Shine, save poor me, I'll give you all the money that you can see.' 'Say, there's more money on land than there is on sea,' and Shine swam on." This kind of thing was very common in the forties and the fifties as part of black folklore and culture.

MOYERS: Why were blues so important? Is it Ma Rainey who says that you sing the blues not to feel better but to understand life?

WILSON: The blues are important primarily because they contain the cultural responses of blacks in America to the situation that they find themselves in. Contained in the blues is a philosophical system at work. You get the ideas and attitudes of the people as part of the oral tradition. This is a way of passing along information. If you're going to tell someone a story, and if you want to keep information alive, you have to make it memorable so that the person hearing it will go tell someone else. This is how it stays alive. The music provides you an emotional reference for the information, and it is sanctioned by the community in the sense that if someone sings the song, other people sing the song. They keep it alive because they sanction the information that it contains.

MOYERS: Another variation on the oral tradition, carried from one generation to the other. Do you remember the first time you heard the blues?

WILSON: I do. Very specifically, I remember Bessie Smith. I used to collect 78 records that I would buy at five cents apiece, and I did this indiscriminately. I would just take whatever was there, ten records, and I listened to Patti Page and Walter Huston. I had a large collection of the popular music of the thirties and forties. One day in my stack of records there was a yellow label that was typewritten, which was kind of odd, and I put it on, and it was "Nobody in Town Could Bake a Sweet Jellyroll Like Mine." It was Bessie Smith, of course. I had one of the old 78s where you had to keep putting the needle in, and I recall I listened to the record twenty-two straight times. Just over and over. I had never heard anything like it. I was literally stunned by its beauty. It was very pleasing, but it was very much different than Patti Page singing whatever she was singing. There was an immediate emotional response. It was someone speaking directly to me. I felt this was mine, this was something I could connect with that I instantly emotionally understood, and that all the rest of the music I was listening to did not concern me, was not a part of me. But this spoke to something in myself. It said, this is yours.

MOYERS: You said earlier that music is a way of processing information. What was the information the blues brought to a kid named August Wilson?

WILSON: —That there was a nobility to the lives of blacks in America which I didn't always see. At that time I was living in a rooming house in Pittsburgh. After I discovered the blues, I began to look at the people in the house a little differently than I had before. I began to see a value in their lives that I simply hadn't seen before. I discovered a beauty and a nobility in their struggle to survive. I began to understand the fact that the avenues for participation in society were closed to these people and that their ambitions had been thwarted, whatever they may have been. The mere fact that they were still able to make this music was a testament to the resiliency of their spirit.

MOYERS: Which everyday life squashed.

WILSON: Attempted to squash because the spirit was resilient and strong and still is.

MOYERS: As you talk, I think of those moments in *Joe Turner* when the characters are absolutely struck dumb because, as you wrote, "They ain't got words to tell." And I think of those black teenagers in the ghetto—Newark in particular. Many of them will be dead by the time they're thirty. They don't have words to tell their story. The blues don't speak to them. It's mainly rap. Do you think August Wilson could write a play about those kids?

WILSON: Sure. I'm a part of them in a sense. We come out of the same tradition, the same culture. I haven't actually stopped to look at what is happening with them, their particular life—but there's no question I could, because it's me, also.

MOYERS: Does rap music have anything in common with the blues? I don't think of rap as beautiful, although I do think of the blues as beautiful.

WILSON: Oh, sure, without question. It has something in common with the blues. It's part of the tradition. They're defining the world in which they live, they're working out their ideas and attitudes about the world, they're working out their social manners, their social intercourse—all these things they're working out through the rap. And it's alive and vibrant. You have to listen, and a lot of us are unwilling to stop and listen. In the larger society, we are not listening to our kids, black or white. You have to stop and listen. It may be a world that you have to struggle to understand because it's different from the world that you know. For instance, if I go listen to rap, what these kids are doing these days is different from what I did as a teenager, and the way they're working out their social conduct is different from the way we did. So I simply have to say, okay, I'll buy in on your terms, let me see what you guys are doing, let me understand what's going on with you.

> . . . we are not listening to our kids, black or white.

MOYERS: You were a dropout, like many of them, but you could read at a very early age, couldn't you?

WILSON: Yes, at four years old.

MOYERS: What does it mean to be able to read?

WILSON: To be able to read means you can unlock information. I thought it was absolutely magnificent of the South African kids when they went to war over what language they were going to learn in school, because they understood and recognized the value of language. You cannot liberate yourself by learning the oppressor's language because all the things that oppress you are built into the linguistic environment—and they recognized that. Blacks in America don't have the political sophistication yet to understand the value of language, for instance, or, for that matter, the value of reading.

MOYERS: I can't imagine what it would be not to see words come to life on the printed page. Don't you think not being able to read makes a real difference to these kids?

WILSON: Yes, I agree with you in a sense. I can't imagine what the world would be like if I could see words and not understand what they meant. It's simply the fact that the kids are not being taught to read in school. Everyone says this, everyone knows this, and no one does anything about it.

At one time it was against the law to teach blacks how to read. If you knew how to read, they would pull out your eyes, or if you could write, they would cut off your hands. This is fact. I find it interesting that we're not that many years removed from that. Although it's no longer against the law, someone, somehow, still makes sure that you don't know how to read, because if you can read, you can unlock information, and you're better able to understand the forces that are oppressing you.

MOYERS: Who reached you? Who brought the poet to life in you?

WILSON: I think it was my mother. She's the one who taught me how to read. Reading was very important to her. She stressed the idea that if you can read, you can do anything—you could become a lawyer, you could be a doctor, you could be anything you wanted to be if you knew how to unlock the information. So she took me to the library, and when I was five years old, I had my library card.

MOYERS: What did you read?

WILSON: I started with *Curious George*. I can remember reading *Invisible Man* when I was fourteen years old. In fact, I read all the books in the Negro section of the library. There were only about thirty or forty books there. I read them all. I read Langston Hughes, of course, and *Invisible Man*, and Dunbar—I don't think I ever took that Dunbar book back to the library.

MOYERS: But if you could read, why did you leave high school?

WILSON: I got off on a rocky road in high school. I went to Central Catholic High School in Pittsburgh, where I was the only black. I had a lot of problems in the school. I got in fights a lot. The principal had to send me home in a cab two or three times. After lunch break, we had to walk around the quadrangle. Constantly someone would walk up, step on your shoe, push you—I don't care to recite the litany of all that. It was very difficult. So I left, which was a disappointment to my mother, because she wanted me to go to a nice Catholic college and be a lawyer. She finally said, if you're not going to do that, then go learn how to do something with your hands. So I went to trade school the next year, which would have been my tenth year. She had a brother who was an auto mechanic, so she thought I should be an auto mechanic. But the auto mechanic class was filled, and the auto body class was filled, and so I ended up in a sheet metal shop making a tin cup.

In this trade school, you went to school half a day, but they were basically doing fourth- or fifth-grade work, so I said, "I can't stay here." Then I went to the school that was across the street from where we lived—Gladstone High School. I was bored, I was confused, I was disappointed in myself, and I didn't do any work at the school until my history teacher assigned us to write a paper on a historical personage. I chose Napoleon.

MOYERS: Why Napoleon?

WILSON: Oh, I had always been fascinated with Napoleon because he was a self-made emperor. The title of my paper was "Napoleon's Will to Power." I got the line from Victor Hugo. It was a twenty-page paper. My sister typed it up on a rented typewriter. When I submitted it to my teacher, he didn't think I had written it. He wanted me to explain it to him. I had my bibliography and my footnotes, and I felt that's all the explanation I should give. But he thought one of my older sisters had written it. I told him, "Hey, listen, I write their papers, so I mean, you know, you just have to take my word." Now, in all fairness to him, I hadn't done any work in his class, and all of a sudden, I turn in this paper. Most of the kids would go down and copy right out of the encyclopedia the three or four paragraphs that were in there about whomever. I didn't do that. I threw a little of my ideas in there, and tried to write about Napoleon.

Well, the upshot of that was he gave me a failing grade on the paper. He had written A plus on it or an E, and he said, "I'm going to give you one of these two grades." And when I refused to prove to him that I'd written the paper, other than to say that I had written it, he circled the E and handed it back to me, and I tore the paper up and threw it in his wastebasket and walked out of the school. I was fifteen years old, and I did not go back. However, the next morning I got up and played basketball right underneath the principal's window. As I look back on it, of course, I see that I wanted him to come and say, "Why aren't you in school?" so I could tell someone. And he never came out.

MOYERS: Do you ever go back to where you grew up in Pittsburgh?

WILSON: Oh sure.

MOYERS: What's happened to it?

WILSON: Same thing that's happened to most black communities. Most of it is no longer there. At one time it was a very thriving community, albeit a depressed community. But still there were stores and shops all along the avenue. They are not there any more. It has become even a more depressed area than it was then. When I left my mother's house, I went out into the world, into that community, to learn what it meant to be a man, to learn whatever it is that the community had to teach me. And it was there I met lifelong friends who taught me and raised me, so to speak. I still have family there. So I go back as often as I can. I go and I stand on a corner, and say, "Yeah, this is me."

MOYERS: Have any of those people seen any of your plays? Do they talk to you about them?

WILSON: They do. I go back, and there are some of the guys on the avenue, people just hanging out on the street. They don't know anything—all they know is you did something. They'll walk up and say, "Hey, how you doing, man? We proud of you." It was the fact that someone from that community did something, whatever, that they see you on TV or they hear you wrote a book. Strangers, literally, walk up and say, "I'm real proud of you."

MOYERS: What does that say to you about those folks?

WILSON: It says that it could have been any one of them, that there is a tremendous amount of talent that is wasted; that for every Louis Armstrong there are a hundred people whose talent gets wasted; that there are no avenues open for them to participate in society, where they might prove whatever is inside them. Those same people have vital contributions to make to the society. They could solve some of the problems—transportation, housing, whatever. But no one is asking them. They're not allowed to participate in the society.

MOYERS: One of your characters said, "Everyone has to find his own song." How do these people find their song?

WILSON: They have it. They just have to realize that, and then they have to learn how to sing it. In that particular case, in *Joe Turner*, the song was the African identity. It was connecting yourself to that and understanding that this is who you are. Then you can go out in the world and sing your song as an African.

MOYERS: Do you think those people in Pittsburgh must find the African in them or in their past before they really know who they are?

WILSON: Yes, because it's without question that they are African people. We are Africans who have been in America since the seventeenth century. We are Americans. But first of all, we are Africans. There's no way that you can dispute the fact that we are African people, and we have a culture that's separate and distinct from the mainstream white American culture. We have different philosophical ideas, different ways of responding to the world, different ideas and attitudes, different values, different ideas about style and linguistics, different aesthetics—even the way we bury our dead is different. The way that we participate in life is very much different than white America.

MOYERS: Friends of mine who go back to Africa say that they find themselves thinking and being treated as if they were American tourists. They're Americans.

WILSON: Sure. If you take these people back over to Africa, they'll walk around trying to figure out what the hell's going on. There's no way that they can relate to that. But the sensibilities are African. They are Africans who have been removed from Africa, and they are in America four hundred years later. They're still Africans.

MOYERS: What happens when you get in touch with that sensibility? The Jews in their Passover celebration always end by saying, "Next year in Jerusalem." They have a fixed place. But what does it mean to say, "Next year in Africa"?

WILSON: Part of our problem as blacks in America is that we don't claim that, partly because of the linguistic environment in which we live. I was in Tucson at a writers' conference, and I challenged my host to pull out his dictionary and look up the words "white" and "black." He looked up the word "white," and he came up with things like "unmarked by malignant influence, a desirable condition, a sterling man, upright, fair and honest." And he looked up the word "black," and he got "a villain, marked by malignant influence, unqualified, violator of laws," et cetera. These are actual definitions in Webster's Dictionary.

This is a part of the linguistic environment. So that when white Americans look at a black, they see the opposite of everything that they are. In order for themselves to be good, the black has to be bad. In order for them to be imaginative, the black has to be dull. So you look at Africans, and you say, "Well, he's a violator of laws, he's unqualified, he is affected by an undesirable condition." This is what black means. We are a visible minority in this linguistic environment, and we are victims of that.

MOYERS: What does it mean, then, to go back to Africa?

WILSON: It's not a question of going back to Africa. It's to understand that Africa is in you, that this is who you are, that you can participate, and that there isn't anything wrong with being an African, even though the linguistic environment teaches that black is all these negative things. You understand that there's nothing wrong with the way that you do things, and there's nothing wrong with the way that you respond to the world—it's simply not the way that whites respond to the world.

MOYERS: Some whites are saying today that if blacks in the ghetto are to emerge into the mainstream of American life, they really have to become mainstream Americans.

WILSON: Blacks don't melt in a pot. People hold up the examples of the Irish, of the Germans—these are all Europeans who share the same sensibilities as the mainstream, so it's very easy for them to melt. But we cannot change our names and hide behind the label of being an American, because we're a very visible minority. You can see us coming a block away. When you see us coming, we become a victim of that linguistic environment that says all those things—that we're unqualified, that we're violators of laws, or this, that, and the other. So we have a very difficult time even getting started, and there's no way that we can melt into the pot. We have a culture. Other ethnic groups and other races—the Orientals, for instance—are allowed their cultural differences.

MOYERS: Chinatown in San Francisco is a tourist attraction. Harlem is not.

WILSON: We allow the Chinese to have their cultural differences. Not only do we allow them, we salute them for it. But blacks are expected to become like whites, without really understanding that in order to do that, we have to turn our head around almost three hundred and sixty degrees. Our worldviews are drastically different.

MOYERS: But if blacks keep looking for the African in them, if they keep returning spiritually or emotionally to their roots, can they ever come to terms with living in these two worlds? Aren't they always going to be held by the past in a way that is potentially destructive?

WILSON: It's not potentially destructive at all. To say that I am an African, and I can participate in this society as an African, and I don't have to adopt European values, European aesthetics, and European ways of doing things in order to live in the world—how is that destructive?

MOYERS: But don't you have to adopt American values, American—

Blacks know more about whites . . . and white life than whites know about blacks.

WILSON: —We got the American part together the first hundred years that we were here. We would not be here had we not learned to adapt to American culture. Blacks know more about whites in white culture and white life than whites know about blacks. We have to know because our survival depends on it. White people's survival does not depend on knowing blacks. But we still have our own way of doing things, even though we are Americans.

MOYERS: How does an American black today get in touch with the African that's in him?

WILSON: Simply wake up and look in the mirror—because it's there. You look in the mirror, and you say, "This is who I am." The culture is very much alive. Scholars can go back and trace the Africanisms that are alive in the black American culture of today. The way that blacks participate in the world is fueled by their African sensibilities, so that is alive and vibrant and growing. The culture is organic. We're constantly debating the character of our culture. So it's alive—it didn't disappear, it didn't die.

MOYERS: Did your mother, for example, talk to you about Africa?

WILSON: No.

MOYERS: Did you know anything about Africa?

WILSON: No. What I knew about Africa was that I was a victim, like everyone else. I would go to see Tarzan movies, and I'd root for Tarzan, because this is what we were taught. We certainly didn't want to root for the Africans, because, first of all, they always lost. You know they're always going to lose. And they would do these caricatures of Africans—put bones through their noses and make them look ridiculous. Certainly we didn't want to be associated with that.

MOYERS: So how do these blacks living in Pittsburgh, in Detroit, in Minneapolis, or anywhere, get in touch with the African in them without putting on beads or a dashiki? What do they do?

WILSON: I think they simply look in the mirror and recognize that this is who they are. There's an inner strength that comes with recognizing that this is okay, that there's nothing wrong with being African.

MOYERS: If you look in the mirror, you see black. You say, though, that being black is much more than the color of your skin, it's a condition of the soul.

WILSON: Sure, I'm assuming that this person who looks in the mirror lives in a black cultural environment which is basically an African culture, or it's an amalgamation of African-American culture. It's an adaptation of your African sensibilities to where you find yourself in the world.

MOYERS: You had a white father. And yet you chose the black route, the black culture, the black way. Could you not just as easily have chosen the patriarchal way?

WILSON: Well, no, because the cultural environment of my life was black. As I grew up, I learned black culture at my mother's knee, so to speak.

MOYERS: Even with a white father?

WILSON: He wasn't around very much. There was no question that I was black.

MOYERS: You didn't make a conscious choice, you didn't say, I'm going to choose black.

WILSON: No, that's who I always have been. The cultural environment of my life, the forces that have shaped me, the nurturing, the learning, have all been black ideas about the world that I learned from my mother.

MOYERS: The popular image in our culture today is of the black male who's not there, who's irresponsible, who has several children by several women, and who comes and goes—but it's not just a matter of being black.

WILSON: This is true—which is one of the reasons in *Fences* I wanted to show Troy as very responsible. He did not leave. He held a job. He fathered three kids by three different women, due to the circumstances of his life, and he was responsible toward all of them.

MOYERS: As he brings that little baby home for Rose to take care of, he's not going to abandon her.

WILSON: Because it's his daughter, it's his flesh and blood.

MOYERS: How does it happen that the women in your plays are all so strong, and that they choose to live with these men who are not?

WILSON: The men need support and nourishment, and in the black community, there are always women who can supply that for them. My mother's a very strong, principled woman. My female characters like Rose come in large part from my mother.

MOYERS: You said your mother was principled—in what way?

WILSON: For instance, there was a contest on the radio, where they said, "When it rains, it pours," and if you could name the product, you won a brand-new Speed Queen washer. Well, my mother heard this over the radio, and she called my sister and gave her a dime, because we didn't have a telephone, and she said, "Run out to the store, call this number, and say, 'Morton's Salt.'" My sister did, and she happened to be the first one to call up with the correct answer, "Morton's Salt." And they announced over the radio that my mother was the winner of this brand new Speed Queen washer. But when they found out that she was black, they wanted to give her a certificate to go to the Salvation Army and get a used washing machine. In so many words, she told them what they could do with their certificate. She refused to do that.

MOYERS: They wouldn't give her the one she won.

WILSON: They wouldn't give her the new one, the one she won, because she was black. If you were black, you should be willing to take a secondhand machine.

Now, at that time my mother was washing clothes on a scrub board, where she had to heat up the water, because they didn't have hot water. I can remember her girlfriend saying, "Daisy, go ahead, take the machine. You know, why be foolish, you've got to scrub all those clothes." There was no way my mother would take the machine. So it was many years later before she got a washing machine.

MOYERS: So she wasn't going to play the game by the white man's rules. She was going to live by her own principles, her own code of conduct and honor.

WILSON: Yes. She did that all her life.

MOYERS: One of your characters—was it Toledo in *Ma Rainey*?—hates himself because he has played the game, and has sold out in order to make it in a white man's world.

WILSON: None of my characters hate themselves. Let me say that. Toledo was a forerunner to the African nationalist or black nationalist.

MOYERS: In the sixties, you became temporarily a black nationalist.

WILSON: I still consider myself a black nationalist and a cultural nationalist.

MOYERS: What's that?

WILSON: That's a good question. I simply believe that blacks have a culture, and that we have our own mythology, our own history, our own social organizations, our own creative motif, our own way of doing things. Simply that. That's what I mean when I say cultural nationalist.

MOYERS: What's your opinion, then, of "The Cosby Show"?

WILSON: I watched it maybe once or twice. It does not reflect black America, to my mind. Most of black America is in housing projects, without jobs, living on welfare. This is not the case in "The Cosby Show."

MOYERS: But they are black Americans who have made it. They are successful, their children are going to college, the mother is strong and smart, the father is a professional who is doing very well. They've made it in America.

WILSON: They are black in skin color only. All the values in that household are strictly what I would call white American values. You can search the entire United States, and I think you would be hard-pressed to find that family, despite the fact that there are some blacks who have "made it," who have money and who own their own houses, who are not on welfare, who are educated, and who have jobs that have responsibility to them. We have black doctors, and we have black lawyers. Of the Africans on the planet, we're probably the most educated, but also the most unenlightened, because we don't realize that that's just who we are.

MOYERS: Since Africans don't have a Jerusalem, don't they have to say, "Next year in the American dream"? They say, "I have a dream that I can make it in this country." Isn't that the Jerusalem for blacks?

WILSON: Well, maybe, but see, there's another part of Passover. A friend of mine invited me to Passover once, and I was struck by the very first words. It starts off, "We were slaves in the land of Egypt." That's the first thing. "Next year in Jerusalem" comes at the end. But they were constantly reminding themselves of what their historical situation has been. I find it criminal that after hundreds of years in bondage, we do not celebrate our Emancipation Proclamation, that we do not have a thing like the Passover, where we sit down and remind ourselves that we are African people, that we were slaves. We try to run away, to hide that part of our past. If we did something like that, then we would know who we are, and we wouldn't have the problem that we have. Part of the problem is that we don't know who we are, and we're not willing to recognize the value of claiming that, even if there's a stigma attached to it.

MOYERS: I was brought up in Texas, where blacks celebrated Juneteenth, the day the Proclamation took effect in Texas.

WILSON: I'm aware of the Juneteenth celebration, but that's in certain parts of the country. It should be celebrated like the Jewish Passover wherever blacks find themselves.

MOYERS: What would it say?

WILSON: It would say, this is who we are. We recognize the fact that we are Africans, we recognize the fact that we were slaves, and we recognize that since we have a common past, we have a common present and a common future. There's no progress made in America for blacks unless there's progress for everyone.

MOYERS: Do I hear you arguing for separate but equal cultures?

WILSON: The cultures exist. They are separate cultures, in the sense that they are different cultures. I don't know what equal means. When you say equal, you're talking about equal to what?

MOYERS: —Equally celebrated, equally recognized, equally considered as a legitimate culture. You see, when I went to *Fences*, I wept. I wasn't an outsider, even though it was about the black experience in America. I wept at the relationship between the father and the son, at the mother who was so loyal to a disloyal husband, at the importance of tradition, at the role of the community. I was not an outsider there. I felt a part of that experience you were writing about. But you were writing about black America.

WILSON: I was writing about black America—the specifics of the play are about black America. But there is something larger at work. A painter, when asked to comment on his work, once said, "I try to explore in terms of the life I know best those things which are common to all culture." So while the specifics of the play are black, the commonalities of culture are larger realities in the play. You have father-son conflict, you have husband-wife conflict—all these things are universal.

MOYERS: So you're not unsympathetic to those blacks who look at the Huxtables in "The Cosby Show" and see there something that they want, something to achieve. You're saying that's not the whole story.

WILSON: That's not the whole story. And of course, you can go into the ghetto in Newark, and ask the people what they want—they want decent homes, they want a nice car, they want whatever the society has to offer someone who is willing to work. If you can trade your talent and get something, this is what they want. They want to be the Huxtables. But there are no avenues for them to do that. The social contract that white America has given blacks is that if you want to participate in society, you have to deny who you are. You cannot participate in this society as Africans. Music and sports are the only avenues that are open for full participation of blacks without any further qualifications—you just have to be good.

> *The social contract that white America has given blacks is that if you want to participate in society, you have to deny who you are.*

MOYERS: But the dominant commercial ethos in America is so strong, and there are so many more people who watch television than attend plays, that it seems to me that the Huxtables are winning the battle for the black imagination, and the Ma Raineys and the August Wilsons are losing.

WILSON: Yes, but even blacks who look at "The Cosby Show," and who want to share some of the wealth, say, of the Cosby family, understand that that's foreign to them. That is not the way they live their lives. That is not the way they socialize. They recognize that immediately as the way white people do it. But they would like to have that and still be who they are and do the things they do. They would probably go out and buy a big Cadillac instead of whatever car the Huxtables might drive, because their sense of style is different. It might be a yellow one or a pink one. It's a question of aesthetics, you see. Without question, they would decorate their house differently. Why? Because their ideas are different. Their culture's different. Basically, we do everything differently. But we still would like to have whatever rewards the society has to offer to someone who is willing to work and who has a talent to sell.

MOYERS: You remind me, as you talk, of the fact that both Jews and blacks have been through such great suffering, and yet they kept singing the song of the Lord. And when I think of that, of the faith of both peoples, I think of the character in *Ma Rainey's Black Bottom* who hears that a white mob has forced a black preacher to humiliate himself, and who cries out, "Where the hell was God when all this was going on?" What's August Wilson's answer to that question?

WILSON: It was the wrong God that he was expecting to come and help him, as he later points out. It was the white man's God. He answers the question himself. When the Africans came to America, their religion was stripped from them.

MOYERS: Wasn't it the black church that held together the possibility of hope?

WILSON: The church is probably the most important institution in the black community. There's no question of that. But it's an overlay of African religions onto the Christian religion. The original African religions were stripped away from them. They weren't allowed to practice these religions. Amiri Baraka has said that when you look in the mirror, you should see your God. If you don't, you have somebody else's God. So, in fact, what you do is worship an image of God which is white, which is the image of the very same people who have oppressed you, who have put you on the slave ships, who have beaten you, and who have forced you to work. The image was a white man. And the image that you were given to worship as a God is the image of a white man.

Loomis in *Joe Turner* rejects that image of Christianity. We're talking about image, not the religion—there's nothing wrong with the religion. It has great principles if it's practiced. But Loomis rejects the idea that he needs someone else to bleed for him. Christianity says, "Jesus bled for you." Loomis says, "I don't need anybody to bleed for me. I can bleed for myself." He slashes his chest and demonstrates his willingness to bleed for himself, to be responsible for his own salvation.

MOYERS: So the God of the slaveholder can't be the God of the slaves.

WILSON: Without question, no. It's two different things.

MOYERS: This is why Levy in *Ma Rainey* says that the prayers of the black man should be tossed into the garbage can.

WILSON: That God is tossed into the garbage because you're praying to the wrong God.

MOYERS: You keep writing about each of us finding our own song. How do we know when we've found our song?

WILSON: It comes out. You'll sing it, and you'll go, "There it is." It's just a thing you'll know. It will feel right.

MOYERS: Do the characters in your plays talk to you?

WILSON: They do, yes. They tell me the whole thing. Sometimes I have trouble shutting them up. It's a matter of where you place yourself. I crawl up inside the material, and I get so immersed in it that as I'm inventing this world, I'm also becoming a part of it. You discover that you're walking down this landscape of the self, and you have to be willing to confront whatever it is that you discover there. The idea is to emerge at the end of the landscape with something larger than what you had when you went in—something that is part of the illumination of the truth. If you're willing to wrestle with your demons, you will find that your spirit gets larger. And when your spirit gets larger, your demons get smaller. For me, this is the process of art. The process of writing the plays is a very liberating thing.

MOYERS: Are you able to talk back to these characters?

WILSON: I do, yes, just like I talk to you. They're my partners, my friends. All the characters are part of me. People ask me, "Which one do you identify the most with?" And I say, "Well, I probably make the strongest identification with the male protagonist—but they're all me." Gabriel is me. Rose is a part of myself. Corey, Troy, Loomis, Levy, and Toledo—they're all different aspects of the self. People used to say, "You can only write what you know." I didn't quite understand that. But it's so true. All this is made up out of myself.

MOYERS: But a lot of what these characters told you, they made up, didn't they?

WILSON: They did, sure, yeah. They say them, and I just write them down.

MOYERS: You once said that the most valuable blacks were those in prison, those who had the warrior spirit in the African sense—men who went out and got for their women and children what they needed when all other avenues were closed to them. Who do you think has the warrior spirit in America today? Who's fighting the battle?

WILSON: Those same people are, for the most part. Since the first Africans set foot on the continent, there has been a resistance. The people who look around to see what the society has cut out for them, who see the limits of their participation, and are willing to say, "No, I refuse to accept this limitation that you're imposing on me"—that's the warrior spirit. These are the same people who end up in the penitentiary, because their spirit leads them. I think Levy has a warrior spirit. He does a tremendous disservice to blacks by killing Toledo, because he's killing the only one who can read, he's killing the intellectual in the group. That's a loss we have to make up. We have to raise up another one to take Toledo's place. But I still salute Levy's warrior spirit. It's a progression to the wrong target, but I salute his willingness to battle, even to death. All of the characters demonstrate a willingness to battle. Not all of them are in the penitentiary, but some, because of that spirit, find themselves on the opposite side of the society that is constantly trying to crush their spirit.

MOYERS: I was going to suggest that maybe the black middle class possesses that warrior spirit today in the sense that they're struggling in a white man's world to make it, to provide for their children, to keep that house, to pay that mortgage, to send those kids to school, to live responsibly. There's a struggle going on there in the black middle class.

WILSON: There probably is a struggle. But the real struggle, since an African first set foot on the continent, is the affirmation of the value of oneself. If in order to participate in American society and in order to accomplish some of the things which the black middle class has accomplished, you have had to give up that self, then you are not affirming the value of the African being. You're saying that in order to do that, I must become like someone else.

MOYERS: But it seems a burden to expect middle class blacks to hold on to that mentality where they were put upon and put down, to be thinking all the time about the horrible days, the malignant days.

WILSON: I'm not sure that those were bad days. I guess all I really want to say is that there's nothing wrong with being African, there's nothing wrong with African culture, and there's nothing wrong with the black American culture, which is an African culture. There's nothing wrong with the way that we do things. It's just different. But because it's different, it's frowned upon.

I was in the bus station in St. Paul, and I saw six Japanese-Americans sitting down, having breakfast. I simply sat there and observed them. They chattered among themselves very politely, and they ate their breakfast, got up, paid the bill, and walked out. I sat there and considered, what would have been the difference if six black guys had come in there and sat down? What are the cultural differences? The first thing I discovered is that none of those Japanese guys played the jukebox. It never entered their minds to play the jukebox. The first thing when six black guys walk in there, somebody's going to go over to the jukebox. Somebody's going to come up and say, "Hey, Rodney, man, play this," and he's going to say, "No, man, play your own record. I ain't playin' what you want. I'm playin' my record, man. Put your own quarter in there." And he's going to make his selection. He's going to go back.

The second thing I noticed, no one said anything to the waitress. Now six black guys are going to say, "Hey, mama, what's happenin'? What's your phone number? No, don't talk to him, he can't read. Give your phone number to me." The guy's going to get up to play another record, somebody's going to steal a piece of bacon off his plate, he's going to come back and say, "Man, who been messin' with my food, I ain't playin' with you all, don't be messin' with my food." When the time comes to pay the bill, it's going to be, "Hey, Joe, loan me a dollar, man." Right?

So if you were a white person observing that, you would say, "They don't know how to act, they're too loud, they don't like one another, the guy wouldn't let him play the record, the guy stole food off his plate." But if you go to those six guys and say, "What's the situation here?" you'll find out they're the greatest of friends, and they're just having breakfast, the same way the Japanese guys had breakfast. But they do it a little differently. This is just who they are in the world.

MOYERS: You've answered my question. I was going to ask you, don't you grow weary of thinking black, writing black, being asked questions about blacks?

WILSON: How could one grow weary of that? Whites don't get tired of thinking white or being who they are. I'm just who I am. You never transcend who you are. Black is not limiting. There's no idea in the world that is not contained by black life. I could write forever about the black experience in America.

Vartan Gregorian

EDUCATOR

To Vartan Gregorian, libraries are both the mirror and the memory of society. As president of the New York Public Library, he has been the steward of one of the world's largest collections of memories: forty-four million books, periodicals, and manuscripts. He first gained recognition as a teacher and administrator at the University of Texas and later at the University of Pennsylvania. This spring he became the president of Brown University.

MOYERS: When I walk into this library, I am struck by how calm and serene it is compared to the gridlock, turmoil, and conflict of the street outside. How much does the world of the stacks have in common with the world of the street out there?

GREGORIAN: The contents of the books have everything to do with the street out there. People inside have everything to do with the street out there. But this institution, in a sense, transcends all. It's an oasis in the middle of New York City, and it's supposed to be an oasis—a place for reflection, for contemplation, for privacy, for introspection, and so forth. The library allows one to go five thousand years into the past to try to cope with the present and also to fantasize about the future.

MOYERS: I remember the first time I walked into the small library run by the women's club in Marshall, Texas—a little Georgian building sitting across from the First Baptist Church. I went up and down the small row of stacks, awed by the prospect of visiting the world described in those books. I had the same experience when I walked into the library at the University of Texas for the first time, and when I first came here, and to the British Museum.

GREGORIAN: In the British Museum, sitting there and seeing those millions of books—suddenly you feel humble. The whole of humanity is in front of you. What you are trying to do? Is it worth doing? What are you going to say or add or write that has not been said and written about? It gives you a sense of cosmic relation to the totality of humanity, but at the same time a sense of isolation. You have a sense of both pride and insignificance. Here it is, the human endeavor, human aspiration, human agony, human ecstasy, human bravura, human failures—all before you. You look around and say, "Oh my God! I am not going to be able to know it all." One gets thrilled and frightened at the same time in the presence of a library because it reminds one about one's past, present, and, most, of the possibilities for the future.

MOYERS: You've said libraries are "the most tolerant historical institutions we have." The good and the evil are here. The failures and the successes are here. God and the devil are here. And the library makes no value judgments about them.

GREGORIAN: We're the mirror of humanity, and we're the mirror of our society. We're also the memory of society. As a result, in many ways, we're tolerant, because memory includes both tragedy and happiness. But also, in a library, one sees the relation between the relativistic and absolute elements throughout history. You read about how right people were. And several years later, you know how wrong they have become. So libraries provide the kind of comparison that makes one tolerant. By seeing so many examples, by comparing and knowing about right and wrong, one comes to appreciate shades in history, nuances in history, possibilities, and limitations. As a result, one becomes more willing to accept other people's positions, knowing how arduously they have come to those positions, even though they may be wrong.

MOYERS: But do you see any evidence that we really take away lessons from the library, from the past, that make us different, that cause us to change course before we hit the iceberg?

GREGORIAN: I absolutely do. But whether we're willing to change course or not—that's different. Barbara Tuchman's *March of Folly* indicates that it's not our lack of knowledge that often makes us act wrong, it's our arrogance. We know that we're wrong, but maybe this time one additional factor may be added that may make us right.

Take Vietnam, for example. Nobody put Vietnam in a historical context alone. They kept adding variables. Instead of questioning the major premise, which Eisenhower and others had discussed—not to be involved in a land war in Asia—they kept adding variable after variable after variable, thinking maybe *this* time they could prove history wrong, they could prove Napoleon wrong, they could prove Hitler wrong, that maybe modern technology would bring a new reality.

So it's not lack of knowledge, it's our reluctance to accept our limitations. It's almost Faustian. We do not like to accept either our mortality or our limitations. We would like to be superman. The library—and history—remind us of our limitations. Knowledge, in the abstract, always propels us toward possibilities. There's a great tussle between the two.

MOYERS: I read in a Bell Labs report that in one day's edition of the *New York Times* there is more information than a single man or woman had to process in the whole of his or her life in the sixteenth century. Now, that's intimidating.

GREGORIAN: It's very intimidating. Another point in that report is that all available information doubles every five years.

MOYERS: What does that mean for education and information retrieval?

GREGORIAN: It means two things. One is that no one has any excuse not to be educated in terms of the availability of resources. But at the same time it's very dangerous because we're now able to retrieve less than five percent of the available supply of information. Unfortunately, the explosion of information is not equivalent to the explosion of knowledge. So we are facing a major problem—how to structure information into knowledge. Because otherwise, what is going to happen? There are great possibilities of manipulating our society by inundating us with undigested information. One way of paralyzing people is by inundating them with trivia, giving them so much that they cannot possibly digest it all in order to make choices.

MOYERS: There's another possibility, and that is that each of us is forced further and further into such fragmentary knowledge that we begin to feel utterly isolated from the whole of it.

GREGORIAN: Absolutely. We have two parallel, dangerous things happening. One is this explosion of information and, along with it, an explosion of publication. There are 850,000 new titles around the world every year. The United States has something like 75,000. In the 1950s and '60s you were talking about 10,000 or so. But in addition to this explosion there is fragmentation of knowledge. Specialization is the hallmark of professionalism. We're sub-sub-sub-subspecializing.

MOYERS: We know more and more about less and less.

GREGORIAN: —or more and more about some aspects of less and less. In the early 1930s Ortega y Gasset warned us of the "barbarism of specialization." He was worried that we may be producing one-dimensional people who will be insensitive to the totality of human experience and the human predicament.

The problem is how our educational system is going to provide us with tools. The mind is a formidable machine. I'm told by Jerry Edelman, a Nobel laureate here in the city, that the entire computer system of New York City and New York State can correspond only to five percent of the permutations of the human brain. That means that the human brain is underdeveloped. Education has to allow us to develop a critical mind in order to be able to differentiate between the chaff and the wheat, so that we know what information is truly obsolete, what is only obsolete in appearance, and what is potentially useful in ways that we don't know now. It's very hard.

As a matter of fact, when I came here, I asked that question at the library. We have four thousand telephone directories in this institution from all over the country and all over the world. So, as a facetious remark, I said, "Why do we have to have the 1939 Warsaw, Poland, telephone directory?" I was immediately corrected. That was one of the most heavily used books in this library. Many of the Jewish claims against Nazi Germany had to rely on the 1939 Warsaw telephone directory. It's no longer a source of information only, it's a social history. So we are faced in this institution and in general with the question of what is of potential use. That's why our task as librarians is horrendous.

MOYERS: But the danger is that all these undigested facts lead to mental gridlock.

GREGORIAN: If you have traffic with no traffic policeman, you have gridlock. An education should provide the traffic as well as a way to guide it. It's not only gridlock which is dangerous but also partial information. That creates the fiction that you have a free choice. You want to read about chemistry? There are 800,000 articles—come in and read. But if you don't know where to start, not only will you bring gridlock into your mind, but also you may bring a permanent delusion that you have a free choice. That's another danger. A multiple-choice test lists choices A-B-C-D-E. But there's sometimes another category—"other." Civilization consists, in part, of being able to respond, "Other." You have to know about the range of choices available to you; you have to know the limitations of those choices; and you have to be able to reject all, and seek a new solution. Unfortunately, sometimes a ready-made information supply may suggest that whatever is not in the computer or in the data-base does not exist.

MOYERS: You can't choose what has not been programmed.

GREGORIAN: Yes, unless in school you have learned other forms and sources of

> *Education has to teach us not only what we can know but also what the limitations of our knowledge are—what we* don't *know.*

knowledge and that life did not begin with a computer. Education has to teach us not only what we can know but also what the limitations of our knowledge are—what we *don't* know. It goes way back to the Socratic notion that true knowledge is to know what you know but also, to know what you don't know.

MOYERS: You said you became a teacher because you had great teachers.

GREGORIAN: Yes, we all have been affected by one teacher. Nobody remembers the core curriculum or what course they took. They may remember the major. But you always remember the teacher who said, "Bill, you're a unique moment in history. You are a unique being. The universe is grateful to see somebody like you. What are you going to do to deserve that uniqueness?" Well, that's an awesome thing when a teacher tells you that, and here you are in Tabriz, Iran, and you're nobody, practically, and somebody says, "Not only are you somebody, but you can be what you want to be. But even if you fail, it's all right, because the process of becoming is testing the mantle of our humanity, our worth," and so forth. Teachers like that have been able to influence all of our lives.

I was very moved by Pestalozzi, the Swiss educator, who surrounded himself with people who had been turned out of schools as incorrigibles. He educated them because he appealed to their humanity, not merely their behavior. And when he died, the students surrounded him, crying, because their teacher had died. Education, "*educatio*," means drawing out of you what is already in there, not merely instilling something.

Teaching has two fundamental challenges now. It has to provide a base of knowledge; but it also has to provide connections. T. S. Eliot, in commenting on Dante's *Inferno*, describes hell as someplace "where nothing connects with nothing." The teaching profession has to provide connections between subjects and between disciplines in order to re-create that totality of knowledge. Nationalism used to provide that. Tribalism did. Philosophical views did. Religion did. But as most of these things collapse around us, there's a great burden on the educational establishment to provide some kind of intellectual coherence, some kind of connection with our past, with our current present, and with the future. That's why it's tougher now, not only for the student, but also for the teacher, especially when all of us have become specialists. We frown upon generalists because we think they're cutting corners in coming up with solutions. The result is we have not come up with solutions.

MOYERS: But given what we've just been saying, isn't that an impossible task?

GREGORIAN: We have no choice. If you're in the middle of the ocean, you have to swim—otherwise you drown.

MOYERS: But the ocean of information keeps getting wider and wider and deeper and deeper.

GREGORIAN: That's why education's sole function now is to provide the introduction to learning. We can no longer claim, as we did in the sixteenth century, that in four years we can produce an educated, cultured person, plus give this individual professional training and know-how and a vocation. Life has become more complex. In the Renaissance there were no major environmental problems, there were no mass-destructive possibilities, there was not this complete alienation and fragmentation of individuals, there was not this historical stress, there was not the Holocaust as an example of the inhumanity of man to man. We are kidding ourselves if we think that by providing *Fifty Great Moments in Music* or Hirsch's *Cultural Literacy* we're producing cultured people. We have to tell our students that life is complex. We're living in awesome and exciting times. We're going to provide you with a compass, with a rule, with a Geiger counter, and we're going to give you a critical mind to be able to search throughout your entire life, in order to be an educated and cultured person.

Somehow we are still stuck with the seventeenth-century notion, which Oxford started and Harvard copied, that in four years you are going to be a bachelor of arts and therefore we certify you as an educated person. It's very hard now in view of everything that is to be known. Naisbitt wrote in *Megatrends* that "the world is drowning in detail but starved for knowledge." What we need is meaning now, coherence, unity, connections, but all without trivializing, without giving us a kind of handbook or bulletin that bypasses the process to think critically. Everybody wants ready-made answers so one can follow them without undergoing, as Sheridan said in 1779, "the fatigue of judging for themselves." We are abdicating our right to think and our right to explore. We cannot rely on "credentialing." The school and the university are only means to allow us to rediscover our possibilities and our potentials.

MOYERS: So what does it mean to be intellectually adventuresome today?

GREGORIAN: Oh God, it's the most awesome thing today, because for the first time in history you have no lack of resources.

MOYERS: They're all here.

GREGORIAN: And if we don't have it here, I can get it from the British Library, I can get it from the Moscow Library—I can get it from everywhere.

MOYERS: And I can sit in my apartment and plug in the computer and retrieve it from you right here.

GREGORIAN: Yes, so it's not availability of resources any more, it's what kind of role models we have now, and what kind of teachers we have, and what kind of institutions we have.

MOYERS: What do you mean, "what kind of teachers"?

GREGORIAN: The high school teacher used to be the most exalted profession in the nineteenth century. Unfortunately, we have entered a phase in our society where education is valued for what it will *give* you rather than what it will *make* out of you. The result is that because teachers don't have that which society considers important in terms of wealth and status, the teaching profession is looked down upon in this country. As a matter of fact, the entire public sector is looked down upon. In this city, if you go to the public sector, you're thought to be either an idealist or incompetent—or else you didn't have the stomach to fight in the free-enterprise, entrepreneurial world.

> *Unfortunately, we have entered a phase in our society where education is valued for what it will give you rather than what it will make out of you.*

MOYERS: What's the old saw? "Those that can, do; those that can't, teach." I've always considered that such an insulting—

GREGORIAN: —It is insulting. On the university level, the prestige is still there. But one of the things that we have to do as teachers is to bring some kind of coherence into disciplinary themes. I want to create a course taught by professors from five different disciplines. I want a mathematician, an astrophysicist, a biologist, a geologist, and a philosopher or theologian or anthropologist to teach, for example, "Introduction to the Cosmos." What are theories about the universe? Are we alone in the universe? What happens if humanlike creatures are discovered on Mars? Are they made in the image of God, or are we made in the image of God? Has Christ risen for them, or for us only? What are the theological ramifications of not being unique in the universe? These are awesome questions.

MOYERS: And so these five professors would sit together in this same class every week and converse with these students about the cosmos.

GREGORIAN: Yes—but they would also spend three months in the summer preparing the course. See how idealistic I am?

Another course might be, for example, "Agape and Eros." Why not pick five major texts from Africa, Asia, Europe, and the Americas and study the concepts of "eros and agape"—

MOYERS: —sexual love and filial love.

GREGORIAN: Or take five world religions. We always say "comparative religions"—that's not enough. Why not say, we are going to deal with the issue of mortality and immortality, the issue of free will, the issue of obedience to God and disobedience, the issue of sinning and the possibility of redemption in five different world religions. That way, one would provide a nonparochial view of the human predicament in the universe.

But we're not teaching that way. We're teaching special X, special Y. We're talking about various elements of the elephant, but nobody thinks of themselves as capable of speaking of the total elephant. It's not considered academically sound. But again, I'm talking about introductory-level courses to introduce people to universal themes. Imagine, if a student had four courses during the first year, he or she would know twenty professors intellectually. Suppose we taught the history of World War II not just from an American diplomatic perspective, but also from a European point of view and from Soviet and Asian viewpoints. Suppose they argue about their methodology, archival sources, and so forth. Students would not be brainwashed but would be exposed to various possibilities—not to say that everything is relativistic, but rather that there is a common endeavor honestly to seek the truth and to learn from history. What is missing in our education is integration of knowledge. Somewhere, somehow, we have to provide that.

MOYERS: I can see what this also could do for the teachers themselves. They would be learning from one another, the biologist from the historian, and so on. The teachers themselves would be taking place in a relearning process.

GREGORIAN: It's ironic that in the teaching profession we have not encouraged learning from others outside our individual disciplines. By saying this, I'm not diminishing the importance of the disciplines. Interdisciplinary work is no substitute for strength in one's discipline.

MOYERS: No, it's still the solitary scholar, digging into that field, and then transmitting that information to his or her students, that sends the first current of learning.

GREGORIAN: Absolutely. Let disciplines flourish. But we also need to bring disciplines together.

MOYERS: Aristotle thought that citizens should be taught the shared moral commitments of a society. The question that's been haunting me of late is: Do we any longer have shared moral commitments?

GREGORIAN: We have, but somehow it's not focused. Or let me put it another way—we have, but people have not been able to articulate what it is that they're doing. I'm touched to see so many young men and women dedicated to many social causes. But they have not given it any philosophical, cultural, or historical signifi- cance—any *civic* significance. So it has almost become "situational"—we are doing this because it's the right thing to do. Americans by and large don't like systems. But at the same time we're caught in a difficult dilemma. In the humanities we think we had Golden Ages in the past. In science we consider the Golden Age to be in the future. So we've not been also able to bring the two together so that there is some continuity to our commitment. We are not isolated socioeconomic atoms. We are not here in the universe to be consuming and then, once the consumption ends, to die. There's more to it and to us. Somehow we have not communicated that, or else we have left it to individual inquiry. We say, "Well, here's the library. If they're interested, they can come and seek. If they don't, it's not my obligation to go after them."

I don't agree with that school of thought. I go all the way to St. Augustine, who quotes Jesus, "Compel them to come in." They have to come in. It's your obligation as a teacher and it's my obligation as a librarian to make people know what they are not tapping, what they are missing.

There is yearning to have a worldview. There is yearning to know about the length of one's commitments. But we are put into the position of having to love every good cause. Total commitment to every good cause is equal to total apathy because you cannot act upon all of them. You have to structure your commitments: first commit- ment, second commitment, third commitment, fourth commitment, and so forth. You have to struc- ture a hierarchy of commitments. And that's very hard because it makes you think back to the self, to think, what are your value systems? What are your obligations as a human being? What are your obli- gations as an American?

> Total commitment to every good cause is equal to total apathy because you cannot act upon all of them.

Citizens have to think about what is important for this country's future. We know how to describe individual interests. Then we say nebulous things about "national interests." But we don't discuss what America is. It's a community. It's a people. It's a unity of destiny, a unity of the past. We don't talk about those things. It sounds "corny," or it doesn't sound relevant. But it is relevant, because it makes individuals act as social beings, and makes them develop a social component to their individual- ism. Individualism should not be equated with selfishness. Somehow that's what we have done now. We have said, "Take care of yourself. The universe is too complex and life is too complex to be taken care of, so why don't you retreat into yourself and take care of *only* yourself." That's a kind of moral isolationism that we cannot afford as a nation.

MOYERS: As a teacher, what did you think of our recent election as an instrument of public education?

GREGORIAN: I think it was a complete failure. More than ever this campaign should have dealt with the future of America. By "future of America," I'm not dealing with generalities. All Europe is discussing their future in the twenty-first century.

MOYERS: In 1992 the EEC becomes a single economic—

GREGORIAN: —a unit—a single economic and political unit. They're talking about how to reconcile nationalism and European integrity. They're debating how to cope with American technological supremacy by bypassing America. They're talking about being the intellectual leader of Western civilization again, about bringing the trophy back to Europe. They're talking about how to go from the Atlantic to the Urals by incorporating European Russia, eventually, into their orbit, especially since the Soviet economy is such a disaster. They're talking about how to cope with Japan and the awakening of Asian manpower, now coupled with technological opportunities.

I did not hear a single American presidential candidate discuss the future of America in terms of what will happen in 1992 and what kind of dealings we'll have with Europe. How is America going to be competitive, technologically and scientifically, with Europe? Who is providing the kind of leadership to harness our economic, scientific, and educational effort for the sake of the nation? Eisenhower did it in 1959. To the best of my knowledge, there has not been a major scientific convocation of all the scientific leaders of this country, the presidents of universities, industry, and so forth, saying, "The country wants you to come up with solutions for the twenty-first century." We must be ready to cope with the realities of the twenty-first century, where we're going to be flanked by two major economic powers—and if the Soviet Union under Gorbachev is able to put its house in order, three major industrial blocs. How is the United States going to cope when we have no master economic plan, no master educational plan, no master scientific plan, and no master foreign policy strategy?

MOYERS: If we needed any evidence of the crisis in American education, this campaign was it.

GREGORIAN: There has also been a great deal of anti-intellectualism. Let me mention just a couple of examples. Years ago, Senator Moynihan debated Mr. Buckley, whom he defeated. When James Buckley addressed Moynihan as "Professor Moynihan," Moynihan said, "I knew this campaign would get dirty." People are reluctant to concede the fact that they have Ph.D. degrees because it's considered a liability to be "overeducated." It's all right to have a law degree, and it's all right to have an engineering degree, but somehow higher education is still suspect.

Here's another example. From Woodrow Wilson to Roosevelt to Lyndon Johnson to Carter and others, whenever there was a national crisis, the President conferred with educational leaders along with business leaders. Now education has been shunted aside, not institutionally but intellectually. We have not involved our educational leaders, and we have not galvanized their efforts on behalf of the nation. We're talking about curriculum in isolation. We're talking about literacy in isolation. We're talking about the library in isolation. There is no "ethos," there is no spirit, and there is no moving force.

MOYERS: Where does this ethos come from? You can't order it up the way you do a burger at McDonald's. Where do you get this ethos, this sense of the republic?

GREGORIAN: I would like our elected officials not to apologize for being intelligent and not to appeal to the lowest common denominator of the people. I would like them to say, "You are Americans. This country has had two centuries of greatness. We are appealing to your sense of idealism, your sense of devotion to this country, your sense of patriotism, and your sense of not equating what is merely legal with what is moral." If all of us take as much as possible and give as little as possible to this country, to its people, and to its institutions, somebody is going to pay in the long run. We cannot consider America as a collection of individuals pursuing their narrow self-interests. I hate to paraphrase Kennedy, but we have to ask "what we can do for our country" to contribute to its greatness. After all, this country has allowed people like me—millions of people like me—to become what we are. I have a moral obligation to do *my* share to allow other generations to benefit from what I have received. So I became a teacher because I benefited from my teachers.

MOYERS: Do you think that if you were arriving as a young man now you'd be able to do what you have done? Is American society as open to the outsider, the stranger, the newcomer, as it was thirty years ago?

GREGORIAN: It's not as open as it used to be. There is a certain sense of unease in Texas and California about whether we are having a dual society or a single society. Hispanics are treated as "categories" rather than as individuals who come here. In the case of Soviet Jewry there is a historical anticommunism, and their suffering still allows us to accept them with open arms. But what I find inhospitable is that once you are here, what mechanism do we have to integrate you into American life, to put you on the path of the American dream? When I ride with taxicab drivers who do not speak English, who are doctors or who are engineers, and so forth, there's a certain disillusionment. They have political freedom, but they don't have economic freedom.

MOYERS: When you came here, it was almost a given that next year life would be better than last year.

GREGORIAN: Yes, there was a great deal of optimism. And frankly, I came to the right state, California—where everything was possible. And then I went to Texas, where everything that was not possible had to be made possible. There was that great optimism which is not in Texas any more. Texas was open, firm, vigorous, and so forth. There was nothing you could not do. If you wanted something, you were told, "By God, tell us where it is, why it can't be done, and we'll do it." And then in New York, it's the same way. New York's a powerful city. Everything is possible. Emphasis is put on the individual, which is fine, but all immigrant groups that have succeeded in this country have had support mechanisms. We have downgraded those support mechanisms, such as the local church, the local synagogue, and local communities. Those who don't have these support mechanisms are at a great loss now in this city.

New York has 190 ethnic publications. It's the cultural capital of many, many ethnic groups. One comes to New York because it's the microcosm of humanity, and one is able to cope here. It's very hard in the Midwest and other places without that social mechanism. Somehow we're emphasizing only economic aspects of America now—that you come here to make as much money as possible. All the other values that are very important—freedom of speech, dignity of human beings, religious freedom—have been downplayed. I'm afraid that it has not made life easy for people because they have treated America only as an economic laboratory rather than as one of the best bastions of retaining one's dignity.

MOYERS: You speak about America with such passion.

GREGORIAN: Because America universalized me. I came from Tabriz, Iran, as an Armenian. I'm now a member of one of the greatest nations in the history of mankind. It's almost like a marriage, a historical marriage. Sure, I'm very proud to be Armenian, I love my heritage. But America is now my country. It has provided me with possibilities of reaffirming my dignity and my freedom of speech. It has allowed me to change my jobs. It has allowed me to move into four states without asking permission from anyone. It has allowed me to become part and parcel of larger issues that affect humanity. When I became a citizen, it was a very spiritual moment.

MOYERS: How do we always remain a fresh and new fabric?

GREGORIAN: America's greatness always has been its individuals, its people. We must treat each other and people who come here not as categories but as individuals. We are emancipating the people who come here from historical shackles. That's the important thing. This is not just another place to come and move. This is not Switzerland. We're not saying that for legal reasons, tax reasons, you should come and live here without involving yourself. This organic unit has been able to tolerate all the diversity but with the hope that the diversity will not destroy the unity. Among all Founding Fathers, I found Madison most moving in this respect because in religious toleration he saw the diversity strengthening the foundation of the nation. I'm hoping that people who come here will not be a collection of factions but a collection of individuals who have come to be part of a bigger body politic, not mere economic units. Now, I'm all for success and people being rich. I'm not talking about that. But there's something beyond that. People should come here to create a better society rather than to make a better living. The Founding Fathers did not create a land of opportunists, they created a land of opportunity. We are not going to eliminate selfishness. That's not what I'm advocating. But we must show that in the long run the welfare of America is also their own welfare, and that of their children, and great-grandchildren. Somehow we've failed to convey that, so people talk in terms of merely economic well-being and what threatens it. I'm interested in what threatens our social well-being and historical well-being. We have to give a longer-range perspective to what we are doing, and a larger hope, not merely an instant hope, for our immigrants.

James MacGregor Burns

H I S T O R I A N

James MacGregor Burns has been called a historian's political scientist and a political scientist's historian. A professor of history at Williams College in Massachusetts for over forty years, he has probed the American political system, past and present, to understand its strengths and weaknesses. His books include Roosevelt: The Soldier of Freedom, *which won a Pulitzer Prize,* The American Experiment, *and* The Power to Lead: The Crisis of the American Presidency.

MOYERS: Not long ago you suggested that America might be the worst managed of the great Western countries. What did you mean by that?

BURNS: I mean that we have a constitutional system that so fragments and divides power that it's impossible to give this country effective, long-run leadership. The original framers of our Constitution were so concerned about oppressive government that the way they tamed the beast was to divide power very carefully among the President and the Senate and the House and the judiciary, down to the state level and the local level, very carefully allotting constitutional power to different parts of the government with different constituencies.

We still have that system today. Leaders respond to different constituencies—not just some leaders to a majority party and some to a minority party, as in the parliamentary system, but to a great conglomeration of different interests. That system was built-in through the brilliance of the framers, but it's led today to an inability to plan and get on top of problems ahead of time. Even at best, this country has always been twenty to sixty years behind other industrial democracies in dealing with tough problems.

MOYERS: Look how long it took just to deal with the primitive problem of child labor or the problem of slavery. We tolerated slavery for two hundred years in this country. How long did it take for women to become citizens? We were behind most of the rest of the Western world in responding to social ills.

BURNS: That's an important point. A lot of people say to me, "Jim, don't get so worried. We finally get there." I'd like to say, "Look, there may be a whole lifetime of a child or an industrial worker before workmen's compensation." A whole life and several lifetimes can be spent before we help out. But the point is that when we finally get there, it's usually too little and too late, and then what happens is very interesting in terms of your basic question about fragmentation. We turn to the President. In effect, we say to the President, "You've lived through this, you know the crisis, you do it." Because the government as a whole hasn't worked, the President naturally feels pressured to do it and does it sometimes in ways that we're not very happy about. So in the most curious and unfortunate way, the fragmentation of the system finally results in a concentration of power in the President.

MOYERS: —Seeming power, because we keep electing presidents to accomplish these changes, and yet nothing seems ever to get permanently fixed.

BURNS: You're a little more pessimistic than even I would be. We've fixed some things, but there's so much that remains unfixed, particularly for a nation that ought to be a showcase of achievement.

MOYERS: Are we slow solving these ills because our governmental institutions are fragmented, or because we're philosophically a conservative country where commerce and property take precedence over other imperatives?

BURNS: The latter lies behind and fortifies the constitutionally fragmented system. We have a habit of thought in this country that we call pragmatic. That's become a buzz word—"pragmatic." You hear it applied to someone who really stands for something. In the newspaper there will be a little paragraph saying, "Well, Mr. Jones is okay. He has these great beliefs, but he's a practical man, a pragmatist. He coaches Little League, and he builds cabinets down in the cellar. Don't worry about him, people, he's okay."

But it's precisely the people who are really committed in their beliefs that this nation needs. We have a pragmatic tradition which decrees that people should take one step at a time and be very practical and do anything necessary to win the next election. Never mind about the election after that. Win the next election. As long as we have this tremendous emphasis on the immediate and practical, I think we have a problem. Now, obviously, we do have to be practical. But we seldom combine practicality with principle, and in the long run, that often makes our practicality bankrupt.

> *. . . we seldom combine practicality with principle, and in the long run, that often makes our practicality bankrupt.*

MOYERS: Let me see if I can sum up for a moment. The founders—Madison, Hamilton, Jefferson—feared both the mob, a popular uprising that would overthrow the government, and the monarch, a strong centralized totalitarian power. So they arranged a system that would checkmate power and deadlock it. But the Congress, the courts, and the executive branch have each argued that the national government should do things that the founders would not have wanted the national government to do.

BURNS: As soon as these presidents got into power and had to do things, like buying Louisiana, they forgot some of their grand principles of 1787 and began to do exactly what had to be done—mainly to build a political party that could unite these fragmented parts of government. So for a century and a half we had a party system that made the Constitution system workable by pitting Democrats against Republicans, so you had a real fight for control of the national and state government. The sad thing is that those parties have declined, so that one of the great unifying forces in our system has disappeared.

MOYERS: Have parties declined in part because government has become so pervasive and immediate? Citizens don't need the parties to mediate between them and the bureaucracy of the Social Security system, for example. They can go directly to the Social Security office or speak with their representative.

BURNS: That's part of it. But the main reason for the decline is television and the media generally. The media have given the direct contact to government that the ward boss used to give. The ward boss was a great mediator between the average citizen and the government. He would humanize government for the average citizen. Today there is that kind of access you're talking about, which is quite desirable. We should have bureaucracies that are open and available. In the old days, they knew darned well that Boss Tweed or somebody like him was right there, anxious to help out. But now who even knows who the local party leader is? Whom do you turn to now?

MOYERS: Do you think that television has helped our politicians, particularly our presidential candidates, to run as loners? They don't need to organize a party if they can go directly to the masses. So the party withers because it plays no practical role in the election of a president today.

BURNS: This is very much part of the whole problem. The candidate discovers that the party is not very helpful, so he or she builds a personal constituency. It is that constituency that the candidate, if elected, will be responsive to, not the party. Having been a candidate, I can sympathize with this.

MOYERS: Each candidate wants to be King of the Rock and to have the machinery of power in his hand.

BURNS: And as soon as somebody is King of the Rock, or perhaps Queen of the Rock, everybody else tries to pull him or her down, and you get a kind of guerrilla government instead of the relatively rational government that I look for.

MOYERS: And politics becomes much more of a personal fight, a contest between individuals, than a political or ideological struggle.

BURNS: Who's up on the rock, and who was just pulled down—right.

MOYERS: Most presidential candidates these days are solo acts.

BURNS: But when they get into government, they have to run a huge collective operation, not just at the federal level, but also in working with state governors and legislatures. They discover that power dissipates, and they have to keep re-forming coalitions and alliances. They're playing coalition broker politics all the way through their presidency in a desperate effort to get things done.

MOYERS: There's a story, which may be apocryphal, that when Dwight Eisenhower walked into the White House in January of 1952, he stood behind that huge desk in the Oval Office, looked around, and said, "All right, what do I do now?" This suggests that men arrive at the White House having conquered their main objective, which is the election, without a clear idea of what it is they want to do once they get there.

BURNS: Or they get there with a grab bag of policies that may not really relate to one another and not with a really well-considered program. It's programs and strategies and principles and philosophies that are crucial to successful government. The early leaders were men of committed principle. They were philosophers as well as very practical people. That's why we had that sunburst of leadership two hundred years ago.

MOYERS: But the irony is that while they were leaders in establishing a national government, they set up a machinery that made it hard for the government to act.

BURNS: These great leaders established an anti-leadership system, making it very difficult to govern. But it turned out that it was a particular kind of leadership that they were fostering and a particular kind that they were preventing. They were fostering the kind of broker leadership that, as you know from your days in the White House, is what government mainly has to be in a democracy. There's a tremendous amount of bargaining with members of Congress and the like. But they made it terribly difficult for men to rise to their stature by rising above brokerage, rising above what I call transactional leadership.

MOYERS: They so fragmented the system that it would be very hard for someone once again to be a Jefferson or a Washington or a Madison with an overall large philosophical view. The paradox has been with us since the very beginning.

BURNS: And it's very much with us today as we face another presidential term.

MOYERS: Take the three-trillion-dollar national debt, for example. All the politicians talk about it, or they run from it, knowing that it's a monster. But none of them seems able to solve it or wants to solve it. How does what we're talking about relate to the national debt?

BURNS: First of all, it relates to a lack of committed leadership. The Democratic Party, which I happen to be a member of, has inherited a tax system that Reagan and his fellow conservatives put through. They had every right to put it through. But what bothers me is that neither the Democratic Party candidates nor its program is willing to tackle the problem of taxation, which has to be part of the solution to this deficit problem. They will not even attack a tax system that Reagan put through that did largely benefit the wealthy. They're not willing to tackle that in terms of a very basic principle, equality, which our forefathers talked about—liberty, equality, fraternity.

That indicates two things. One is a feeling on the part of the politicians that, given the system, they simply cannot put through a decent tax revision. Secondly, it indicates a lack of commitment. The great leaders have been strugglers. They have been born in conflict over fundamental principles, like slavery, and they have dealt with conflict, and they have been emboldened by conflict.

MOYERS: You talk about the need for leadership, and you talk about two kinds of leadership. Let's define those. What do you mean by "transactional leaders"?

BURNS: That's the broker type of leader who achieves progress by making a deal here and moving ahead a foot there.

MOYERS: I'll scratch your back if you scratch mine—at which Lyndon Johnson was so great in the Senate. He knew what each senator wanted at the moment, and he was able to trade for it.

BURNS: These are temporary shifting conditions that often get some immediate objectives accomplished. This kind of leadership is about ninety percent of the leadership of the American system. The very fact that we have a fragmented system means that we need lots of people to grease the joints. And that's what these broker politicians do. They're absolutely indispensable. But there comes a time in the history of every nation when a leader has to rise above brokerage. It came in England in the case of Churchill. It comes in our country in the case of a depression and other great crises. The question I raise is whether presidents and governments can rise to the enormity of some of these fundamental problems that cannot be solved through everyday ad hoc brokerage but have to be solved by an enormous effort like the New Deal.

MOYERS: You have to rise above what you call the transactional nature of politics to—

BURNS: —to transforming leadership, which can change the governmental system to make it more effective and can change the party system to bring in tens of millions of people to both parties who are presently unrepresented, and can bring about what I like to call a planning system. Hubert Humphrey used to say that he believed not in a planned society but in a planning society, one that constantly plans ahead.

MOYERS: You've said that great leadership, transforming leadership, comes out of great conflict.

BURNS: I mean the opposite of consensus—I mean a situation where people feel very strongly about issues and divide very strongly, as they did back in the New Deal years, when one can remember the bitter feeling against Roosevelt and the tremendous support for Roosevelt. Great politicians thrive on that. They know how to deal with conflict and to exploit it and to use it for their own purposes, whereas the lesser politician, the transactional type, is more likely to be crushed by conflict.

MOYERS: So without a severe crisis, such as the war or the Depression, you can't really have great conflict unless you have two parties that embody alternative policies and fight over those policies.

BURNS: Exactly. But the problem also is that they may have to wait for the crisis, as in the case of the Depression. The Great Depression, horrible though it was, sent us in a whole new direction, a very constructive direction, and so did war against Nazi Germany. The problem is, I don't want the kind of crisis that will straighten out the system. The next crisis may not be manageable by the system. That's why I'm so concerned that we make moderate changes in the system now in order to be prepared for the next crisis and the endless crises that will come in the next century.

MOYERS: But this is a country deeply resistant to change. We didn't address our economic ills until the Depression struck. We went very late into the Second World War—Hitler had reached the English Channel, and the Japanese had attacked us at Pearl Harbor. We didn't eliminate slavery for two hundred years. We didn't bring women into equality of citizenship until there had been decades of agitation. We still have this persistent presence of an underclass. This is a country far more resistant to change than you seem to think.

BURNS: We have great examples of change in the past—look at Wilson and FDR and Lincoln and earlier in our history. We are a people who are very changeable in every other way except politically.

MOYERS: We change our fashions very fast. We change our taste in movies and television rapidly.

BURNS: Yes. Change calls for a kind of gifted, preaching leadership—leaders who preach, who sermonize, who raise the moral standards, and who hold up our supreme values of liberty, equality, and justice. That's what Roosevelt did so successfully and what Reagan did on the right. There's no reason we can't get back a Roosevelt or a Reagan.

MOYERS: —Someone who sees us not for what we want—give me this, give me that—but for what we want to be?

BURNS: In terms of fundamental American values of liberty and equality. That sounds very trite, but that is what our system is about—to protect individual liberty and to advance political, economic, and social equality.

MOYERS: So a transformational leader not only deals with the immediate problem, but changes the way we think about the problem.

BURNS: Yes, that's even more fundamental. Roosevelt, for example, was a preaching president who taught people you don't need to fear government, but you must use government for your own purposes. You have to change habits of thought about government, and you have to change the nature of parties. A very good, concrete example of a transforming leader would be some Democrat who could realign the party system the way Reagan realigned it on the right. Reagan created a conservative party out of the Republican Party by sloughing off the old Rockefeller wing. We will have a transforming leader on the left the day we get a president who will attract so many tens of millions of Americans into the Democratic Party that he wins elections and has the support of a huge constituency to do what he wants to do.

MOYERS: Has any president ever done this?

BURNS: Yes, Roosevelt created a partial realignment of the party system. He made the Democratic Party into essentially a liberal party although it hung on to its Southern conservatives. But also he brought out liberalism in the South. That was half a realignment. But now we're back to the old system of the Democrats being all things to all men and women. Reagan did his job on the Republican side. Now we're waiting for the kind of transforming leader who has the same impact on the Democratic Party.

MOYERS: Back in 1972 you wrote a book called *Uncommon Sense* in which you identified three main problems we'd have to come to grips with as a nation. One was the pollution of the environment, another was the elimination of poverty, and the third was the defense of civil liberties. How have we done on those three?

BURNS: We're doing relatively well on the environment, but not on the really tough problems like acid rain. The big problems we're not yet dealing with. On poverty we have a glass-half-filled situation. I've been so struck in going to New York by what I call the champagne society. There are thousands of fancy apartment buildings and hotels where people pay five hundred dollars a night or a thousand dollars a night. Then I go up through Harlem, where the glass is half empty. You see new buildings for the homeless and poor, but there are still the shabby old shuttered buildings. So progress on poverty is very mixed.

In civil liberties, we're doing a lot better than the period you and I lived through back in the fifties and sixties. There's a higher degree of tolerance in this country. We're doing better on the race problem to the extent it involves civil liberties. People can speak up. People will listen to a Jesse Jackson. We don't have a Joe McCarthy around. But my worry on this score is what can happen five or ten years from now if there's a new feeling of threat from abroad. We can never feel complacent about how we stand on the Bill of Rights and what we're doing about it.

MOYERS: Someone has said, "Americans never solve their problems, they just amiably bid them farewell." These problems don't just go away.

BURNS: We bid them farewell, and they're back with us on the doorstep the next day.

MOYERS: If you were revising *Uncommon Sense* today and identifying the goals for the year 2000, what would be the comparable problems you'd say our political system must come to terms with?

BURNS: The first problem is the political system itself. We have to put our political system together before we can really tackle these tough, interrelated problems. The other upcoming problems include environment problems and the population migration, people exploding out of their original countries and desperately trying to get into other countries.

MOYERS: Let's come back to the deficit that we talked about earlier. What's wrong with the political system that makes it difficult for politicians to solve the deficit problem?

BURNS: It's a system that does not clearly put responsibility on people in power, so that when the election comes, instead of assuming responsibility for the deficit after eight years of Reaganism, they can evade it through pointing the finger at somebody else. Reagan says, "I tried to save money, I tried to deal with this, and the Democrats wouldn't let me." It's sometimes useful on this score to compare our system with the British. Whatever Margaret Thatcher does in the next election, she cannot evade responsibility. She has had the power, she knows she's had the power, and she cannot go before the British electorate and say, "Oh, I have the most wonderful ideas, but these awful Labourites won't let me do it."

MOYERS: Because her party controls the Parliament as well. You vote for the party, not just for Margaret Thatcher, so when she stands, the whole team stands with her for good or ill.

BURNS: Absolutely. But here you have to do business with the Senate or the House or both. That clouds the issue because voters, unless they're real experts, don't know who did what. It's very hard for the average citizen to figure to what degree Reagan is responsible for this deficit and to what extent the Democrats are.

MOYERS: Ronald Reagan says the Democrats spend too much money on domestic concerns. The Democrats say Ronald Reagan spends too much on defense. The Republicans and the executive branch say, "Yes, but the Democratic Congress voted all that money for these bases and weapons"—so it is very hard to find out who is ultimately accountable.

BURNS: That's what I mean by finger-pointing and buck-passing.

MOYERS: You can't solve a problem like the deficit as a solo act. The deficit is the kind of problem that requires a coordinated, collaborative effort on the part of all of government to solve.

BURNS: The way we get concert in this system is by following a middle way that makes it easier for the different parties and branches of government to cooperate— but the middle way is often not a very effective way. It's not able to deal with something like the deficit, for example. One could mention half a dozen other problems, like the environment and poverty and so on, that the system simply cannot deal with.

MOYERS: The current paralysis over the debt is not new. I remember in 1963, when your book *The Deadlock of Democracy* came out, I gave a copy of it to then-Vice President Johnson, and he said, "Yes, that is exactly right. We are deadlocked up here—no civil rights legislation is passing, the war on poverty is dead, nothing is happening up here." After the tragic assassination of John F. Kennedy, he asked me for that book. He wanted copies of it to ask his aides and others to read. He said, "We have to break this deadlock, we have to get government moving again." Kennedy talked about getting the country moving. Johnson talked about getting the government moving. Circumstances and his own force of will enabled him to do that. But that hasn't happened often. I can think of twice in the last thirty years where this has happened—with Johnson in '64 and '65, and with Ronald Reagan in '81 and '82. They got much of what they wanted. But the rest of the time it's been deadlock.

BURNS: Yes, but the Reagan example is very important because Ronald Reagan showed that if you're really committed to principle—and he was committed to conservatism by the late 1970s—and if you want to work within your party—and he decided to work within the Republican Party—you can at least have a couple of good years in the presidency. What impresses me about the Republican Party is that they got their act together. They made up their mind that they were the conservative party under Reagan's leadership. They dropped the Rockefeller liberal wing that they had fought with over the years. They drew up a conservative platform and then to the amazement of a lot of people, including a lot of Democrats, promptly began to carry out exactly what they had promised to the people. I'm impressed by that even though I might disagree with what they did. I like the idea that a party will go to the people with its own vision and sense of commitment and then carry it out. At that point the system is working. All I ask is that the other party do the same.

MOYERS: You admire the Republican Party because it has decided to be the principled party of conservatism.

BURNS: Yes, but the Democratic Party has not yet decided to be the principled party of liberalism. It's still a great coalition. Tens of millions of people are not voting who would form the solid liberal constituency of the party. The Jackson wing, as I'll call it, feels left out to some degree. And the party simply does not have or has not had the kind of leadership that is willing to make that principled commitment.

MOYERS: But hasn't the Democratic Party lost three of the last four elections because it ran two liberals at the top of the ticket? Is this country as liberal as you think it is?

BURNS: It all depends on your point of view. From the point of view of the Jackson Democratic Party, we have been running moderates except for the McGovern example—Hubert Humphrey, who came across to a lot of people as moderate, particularly on Vietnam, and Carter, who was a lively new face, but did not have a very liberal program, and Mondale. These are all essentially establishment politicians, very good men, but not the kind of people who will attract these tens of millions. The central problem of our democracy today—our democracy, not just our government—is that thirty or forty or fifty million Americans who have a deep stake in what this government does are not showing up at the polls even to vote for President.

MOYERS: If memory serves me, in the national elections of Canada in 1980 seventy percent of the eligible voters turned out. In this country only fifty-three percent of the eligible voters turn out.

BURNS: That's right. We have the worst record of any democracy.

MOYERS: But your assumption is that those lost voters are all liberals.

BURNS: Not all, by any means, but because of their socioeconomic status, most of them with proper leadership would vote liberal and would want a liberal Democratic Party. They're out there. They're just not heard from. They're turned off by the system.

Democracy is never perfect, as Winston Churchill said. But to the extent that democracy can work, I think we've had it working in Massachusetts. We were told when we were trying to make the Democratic Party more of a policy-minded party,

"That's fine in principle, that's a great idea, but you're going to lose every election." Well, to an embarrassing degree, we've won every election since we changed the party in this state. The Democratic Party is enjoying an abundance of victories here.

MOYERS: Because it finally said, "This is what we represent. We are going to be a party of policy, a party of ideology." It clearly defined itself.

BURNS: Partly for that reason and partly because when you do that, you attract talent—as indeed the Republicans did with Reagan. You attract people who are really concerned about what the government does. So you find coming into the party the young lawyers and all the rest who make up a vigorous, youthfully oriented party.

MOYERS: There is such a pronounced tendency in this country toward consensus, toward the center.

BURNS: This is at the heart of the problem of our national mind—the tendency to think that the middle way is the best way. If we can only get everybody around the table, Democrats and Republicans, liberals and conservatives, we'll work out a compromise, and this is the solution. Usually those compromises are exactly that— compromises. They're ineffective. A much better kind of government is one where a majority wins, carries out its mandate, as Reagan did for a year or two, and then gives way to another majority that carries out its left wing or liberal or labor-type mandate. And that's exactly the kind of government we don't have.

MOYERS: I can understand your appetite to see the Democratic Party organize more consistently to the left because the premise of your diagnosis is that there are things government should be doing which it's prevented from doing by this deadlock. Conservatives would argue that the paralysis of government that James MacGregor Burns so deplores might, in fact, be the consequence of efforts by government to do things that government ought not to do.

BURNS: I think you're pointing to the heart of the problem, which is, even if liberal Democrats win, can they put their programs through? However, I would still rather have a party that is struggling to make government serve us than a party that says government really cannot serve us.

MOYERS: But even if a liberal president promising a liberal program wins, he's up against the fragmented, paralyzed system of government that you describe in so many of your books.

BURNS: Yes. Even FDR, the master politician, was finally beaten by the system during his second term. Or take John F. Kennedy—even with LBJ helping him, they couldn't put through his program. It took very special circumstances for that program to go through.

MOYERS: —the trauma of assassination.

BURNS: The history of the last Democratic presidencies that tried to do something is a very sad one.

MOYERS: So you need a party brought to power when the President takes office that is clearly sworn to the President's program.

BURNS: Yes, not just to the President's program but to a program that comes right out of the party. That's why I think these party platforms are rather important. They say that presidential candidates write the platform, and, of course, they do to some extent, but there's a lot of grass-roots participation in those platform hearings.

MOYERS: Ronald Reagan has been in touch with a huge number of the American people out there. That's why, despite the ups and downs of his policies, they continue to say, as the polls report, "We like the man." There's some kind of communication going on there, don't you think?

BURNS: Yes, there's no question that he's a very popular President, and a very likable man. But the tragedy of Ronald Reagan is that of a man who came in with a very definite program, whether we liked it or not, who had some success the first year or two, and then simply lost his way. He seemed to reestablish his program when he ran for reelection, as though more contact with the people brought him back to his basic principles. Then he had another good year, and then just got lost again.

MOYERS: No matter how ideological a President is, once he enters office, doesn't he become a man for all seasons, a President of all the people? Isn't that built into the system?

> *I'm a great believer in that old-fashioned idea of majority rule and minority rights.*

BURNS: You try to be, obviously, in order to get a big election victory, but it doesn't work in the system, because no matter how good you've been, or how much a President of all the people, you're going to have a very strong opponent, and you might just as well go back to your base, the majority that elected you. I'm a great believer in that old-fashioned idea of majority rule and minority rights. I want the man who has won a majority to carry out what that majority wants.

MOYERS: If you could wave a wand and bring about changes in this constitutional and political system, what would some of them be?

BURNS: Change the two-thirds treaty requirement in the Senate so that it's easier to put through treaties.

MOYERS: Right now two thirds of the Senate must ratify a treaty the President has recommended.

BURNS: Yes, but I also would bring in the House of Representatives. I would simply require a majority vote in the Senate and the House.

MOYERS: Why?

BURNS: Because the two-thirds requirement has killed many good treaties and has warned presidents off from doing important treaties. For example, it cost Jimmy Carter enormous support by requiring him to deal with so many people to get through the Panama Canal Treaty. It's a perfect example of how we defeat ourselves by some of these veto traps in our system. The two-thirds Senate requirement is such a veto trap. What happens is that because presidents know they cannot get treaties through the Senate, they do things by fiat through executive agreements. There are hundreds of thousands of executive agreements that the President individually signs with other nations. They are just as important as the treaties. They have the same standing in law. Here's a case where we let the President become much too powerful because we won't bring in the collective government through making it easy to get a majority in the House and Senate.

MOYERS: Presidents have to trade away this and that. They give up a judgeship here, a contract there, to get an important treaty passed.

BURNS: The second change I would suggest would be a very simple one, and that is to give members of the House of Representatives four-year terms coterminous with the presidential term.

MOYERS: So the President, Senate, and House would all run together?

BURNS: That's another change, but the one I'm suggesting is very moderate. The four-year term would simply do away with the mid-term election for members of the House. Eliminate the off-year election, which is one of the most unrepresentative, expensive, and destructive elections in the American system.

MOYERS: What do you think this would change?

BURNS: First of all, it would allow a congressman or -woman to start being a good legislator without immediately having to raise money for the next election. Second, it would give them a chance to be a little bit more forward-looking and even visionary. It also enables more teamwork between the President and House of Representatives in that in every case members of the House would be running on the same ticket as the President.

My third suggested change would be to enable presidents to choose members of their cabinets from Congress without requiring members to give up their seats. This would in a small way bring about more cooperation between the two. I'm thinking of an exceptional case where there might be an outstanding chair or high-ranking member of the Senate Foreign Relations Committee, or even the House Foreign Affairs Committee or one of the joint economic committees, who would be a wonderful Secretary of State, but whose presence you would want to keep on Capitol Hill. So you let him or her keep that Senate seat, and hence you build a little more teamwork between the White House and the Hill.

MOYERS: As it is in the system in Great Britain.

BURNS: Yes. It would be a small adaptation of the parliamentary system.

The other suggestion is my most basic one—that is, to go back to the strong party system we had in the past and try to do away with the mechanisms that have destroyed that system—for example, not have so many so-called party primaries where people seize control of the party who don't necessarily represent the party. We should repeal a lot of the anti-party laws that we have on the books. But above all, we should try to develop among the people a sense that the party has been a great governing, democratizing force, a force for good government. When one party gets control of all branches of government, that party is responsible. That's the party you can happily kick out if they don't do the job.

MOYERS: But we never go back. We can't decree a return to a party system that is gone.

BURNS: If you're saying that you're pessimistic about this, I happen to be, too. I'm just worried that there will be a tremendous crisis sometime in the future—and there will be, we know that—that finds us intellectually unprepared to make the necessary moderate changes in our institutions and parties. I'm worried that we'll become hysterical at that point. We might hold a special Constitutional Convention, and God knows what might happen then. One reason some of us are talking about these moderate changes now is that we want Americans to do their homework, to be thinking about these changes, and to be prepared when the crisis comes to do what we hope would be constructive reform.

MOYERS: I'm pessimistic in the sense that I see the gap growing between the people and their government. So many are not only tuning out but becoming indifferent to the political process in this country. How do people come to a sense of civic self, a sense that "I matter"?

BURNS: That's what the party did when it worked well. That's what the Democratic Party has learned to do in this state, not only through preaching and telling people, "Please come and take part in our party," but by creating a whole level of participation in the Democratic Party that has created for people a new link to the government of Massachusetts.

MOYERS: You ran unsuccessfully for the Congress in 1958. If you had won, would you have had to play the game King of the Rock?

BURNS: That's a very fundamental question I've wrestled with, and the answer is, I'm afraid I would have had to play the game. Let me give you an example. I had some wonderful textile worker unions in this district. Everything's gone now, but these were my troops—the Textile Workers Union. They knocked themselves out for me. The party did its best, but even then the party wasn't very strong. I'd been a party chairman, and I knew it wasn't very strong. So imagine: Burns gets elected to Congress. A tariff bill comes up, and the party, being a low-tariff party historically, would say to me, "Vote for a low-tariff bill." My textile people and their employers are saying, "We're going out of this district, you must protect us." When it came to the crunch, I would think of those textile workers out there on that wet election day working for me, and I would do exactly what I deplore in politicians generally: I would try to work out ways of compromising. But the reason for this would be not just my moral failure, it would be the failure of the system. I would say to myself, "I can do so much good in this job that if I just make a compromise here, I can get reelected, particularly in these tough off-year elections." That's the way the system works. The politicians, more than any of us, are the victims of this system. But I would like a system that lets the politicians rise to the greatness that I think is in them.

John Searle

PHILOSOPHER

John Searle is known as an intellectual prizefighter who leaps into the ring whenever there's a battle of ideas to be waged. A professor of philosophy at the University of California at Berkeley for the past thirty years, he has championed the causes of rationality, intelligence, and the teaching of Western civilization.

MOYERS: When you look back on the student uprisings of the 1960s, do you see them differently from the perspective of twenty years later?

SEARLE: Well, I saw them differently in the course of the sixties. That is, my opinions about what was going on changed during the period of the sixties itself. You won't understand the student revolution unless you see its origin in the Civil Rights movement. But it was transformed by the antiwar protest. The particular genius of that period of student unrest was the ability to focus these larger issues, like the civil rights issue or the protest against the war against university authorities. As long as you're trying to fight the Pentagon, you've got a tough customer. But fighting the dean's office turns out to be a whole lot easier. The way that you fight the dean's office successfully is by getting a whole lot of students to think that the dean is somehow in cahoots with the Pentagon. That was the source of the success of the student movement—the ability to focus large emotions associated with some sacred topic against the authority of the university by identifying the university with the forces of evil on this issue.

MOYERS: Sacred topic?

SEARLE: There were half a dozen or so sacred issues in the 1960s. The first one was free speech. That was where we all got going in Berkeley. The one that had the longest staying power was civil rights, the issue of equality for blacks and for minorities generally. The one that had the biggest éclat in the period was the protest against the Vietnam War. That was so dramatic that after the Cambodian invasion, it virtually shut down the American university system. Those were three. There were others—feminism, or university issues like faculty hiring—but they never really caught on.

MOYERS: It was common in those days to think of this protest as an assault on the authority of the university, but Robert Nisbet says in his new book, *The Present Age*, that it happened in part because the authority of the university was already crumbling.

SEARLE: The way that the authority of the university was undermined was by identifying the university with the sources of authority in the larger society. The structure of power in the United States was thought of as a seamless web going all the way from the Pentagon at the top down to the dean's office. The idea was that by throwing a rock through the window of the dean's office, you were striking a blow against militarism. Now that sounds so stupid, it's hard to imagine anybody believing it. But I can tell you, many thousands of students believed that in the sixties.

MOYERS: Did you believe it?

SEARLE: I never believed that. From the very beginning I thought that was total nonsense. There were problems in universities that needed addressing in university terms. In the early days, I was very active in the FREE SPEECH MOVEMENT because there wasn't any doubt that the University of California was suppressing freedom of speech. They were suppressing my freedom of speech. They forbade me to lecture on the campus about the House Un-American Activities Committee, so I was very bitter about that. But I never for a moment supposed that they were doing this on orders from Washington or that the chancellor's office was doing this because they were in league with some military-industrial complex. I just thought they were being stupid and oppressive.

MOYERS: Was it a revolution then? Or was it a series of expedient protests that found a common target in the university?

SEARLE: That actually is a very deep question. I can only give you a kind of swift answer to it. There were places where it had elements of a revolution. In Berkeley, for example, in 1964 we totally destroyed the established authority of the university administration, and we did something that all revolutionary movements do—we created a wonderful sense of possibility. People thought, "Anything is possible. We can rewrite this university and make it a completely different university."

But nationally it was not a revolution, it was a series of rebellions. The deepest reason for that was these kids never really had any intellectual content. They never had a theory of revolution or of society, and they never had a coherent ideology. It was just one damn enthusiastic moment after another. They lived for these ecstatic moments where there would be ten thousand in the street. But the idea that you need an ongoing organization, some sort of theory of social change, an agenda of social policy—they never had any of those.

MOYERS: They liked to think of themselves as idealists. The report on the student uprisings at Columbia began by saying that these students had come out of the most idealistic generation in the history of American education.

SEARLE: There was a great deal of idealism. The difficulty was that it was a fragile idealism, and it couldn't last through the year-in, year-out contact with reality. It became more and more cynical, and by the late sixties, it had been lost, for the most part, and had also become quite vicious.

MOYERS: Why did it become cynical?

SEARLE: Because part of the idealism was a kind of naïveté. People wanted an instant solution, and when they discovered that they couldn't get an instant solution, they suddenly became disenchanted with the whole of American society. I'll give you one example. I once went on a big march of fourteen thousand people to the Oakland Army Base terminal to protest against the war in Vietnam. A lot of the kids said to me, "When they see this march, they'll have to stop the war." You can guess what I said—"That's idiotic. They're not going to stop the war for one march."

I was brought up in the fifties, and we took it for granted that in the short run, you just get beat. I was secretary of an organization called Students Against McCarthy at the University of Wisconsin. We never for a moment thought we could beat Joe McCarthy, but at least we could protest against him. But these kids thought, "Well, there are so many of us, and we're right, and we have our ideals—we must win." And when they didn't win, when the war went on, and black people didn't have overnight equality, they were quite bitter about this.

So they were idealists, but they were just plain spoiled. When they didn't get their own way, they had a kind of mass temper tantrum.

MOYERS: I remember when I first began to question seriously the idealism was when the chanting came, "What do we want? Everything. When do we want it? Now." And I thought, "Wait a minute. That's not realism."

SEARLE: Well, it's dumb. The idealism very quickly turned into bitterness, and the bitterness turned into cynicism. Now, of course, we're generalizing. But by the late sixties, the student movement in the United States had really become quite vicious.

MOYERS: And yet, the faculties in many cases had buckled. Classes were given with no assignments. Whole classes were given A's. You didn't have to fear any repercussions if you committed an act of violence against a person or property. In fact, faculties often voted amnesties in advance of the violation. Hasn't that permanently damaged the university?

SEARLE: The word "permanent" is a bit strong. It has left long-term damage. But for the most part universities recovered. On the one hand, the university seemed to be the most fragile institution imaginable. I was absolutely amazed how easy it was to overthrow it, or shut the whole place down, or fire the chancellor, or fire the president. But the thing that amazes me in the long haul was how incredibly resilient it is. If you went to the Berkeley campus today, and you hadn't been there since 1959, when I first came, you wouldn't see much difference. The hair is longer, but the university looks an awful lot like it did in 1959. The structure of authority is exactly the same. There's the chancellor and the professors and departments and tenure, and there are freshmen and sophomores and graduate students.

So I am amazed by the sheer resilience. Now a long-term bad effect is that in the face of student demands, we weakened a lot of academic requirements that we shouldn't have weakened. We decided, "Okay, you don't want to take a foreign language, we won't make you do that."

MOYERS: If I went to Berkeley today, would I find any sacred topics?

SEARLE: You would find some sacred topics, but there have been subtle shifts. In the old days, you could easily identify the university with the forces of evil on a sacred topic, but it's very hard to do that now. There was a tremendous effort focused on South Africa and divestment, which got off the ground a little bit, but it never had the kind of sheer punch that we had in the sixties. So South Africa and racism and minority rights and women's rights are still sacred topics, but you can't shut a university down with those any longer.

MOYERS: What's changed?

SEARLE: It's a generational change. It seems old-fashioned to a lot of kids to go sit in the dean's office. That's what their parents did. It just seems like it's oldfogeyism to do that. It's like lying in bed. After a while you get sick of lying in one position, and you lie in another. If somebody said, "Well, what was wrong with that old position?" Who the hell knows? You just feel more comfortable doing it differently. I think these kids just feel uncomfortable doing the kind of stuff that was done in the sixties.

Another change is that students are more concerned about the economic situation than people were in the sixties. They're more worried about getting jobs because the economy seems as if it's more unsettled. They're more career and professionally oriented.

But I have to tell you, at bottom, I don't think those explanations are very deep. Those are sociological, journalistic explanations. The real explanation is they just feel differently about things. It's a different generation.

MOYERS: You say the university is fragile but resilient. What are the threats to the university today?

SEARLE: There is a peculiar intellectual crisis in the sense of our educational mission. We're not quite confident now about what constitutes an educated person. For the generation after the Second World War, there was a certain tacit agreement about what made an educated man or woman in the United States. Of course, in various ways, we failed to realize the ideal, or we didn't always succeed. But at least we were agreed pretty much on what it was. Now it seems like everything's up for grabs. The traditional conception of a liberal education is being challenged from many different directions—from the women's movement, from activist minorities, and even from within the academy—as no longer adequate. The traditional ideal of an educated man or woman in the United States was that you had to have a certain knowledge of Western civilization. You had to know how we got to be what we are, and what were the great intellectual achievements of our civilization, stretching back to the Greeks. Furthermore, you had to be able to cope with the world. You had to know something about science and about social science. You had to be able to speak a foreign language, and to choose a major where you could get some level of mastery so that you could read advanced works in it and maybe even go on to graduate school.

> We're not quite confident now about what constitutes an educated person.

Now that conception of higher education is undergoing a lot of challenges. One challenge comes from those who say, "Well, that's essentially an elitist conception. That conception says Western civilization is superior to other civilizations." One of the sneer words is "DEWMs"—Dead European White Males. According to this challenge, we need to get beyond this idea that everybody has to read dead European white males. We've got to respect the fact that there are all sorts of different cultures in the world, and we've got to get over this cultural chauvinism of supposing that our culture is superior. So it's harder now to get faculties to agree on the traditional definition of a liberal education.

MOYERS: Do you think that what it takes to educate a man or woman is static?

SEARLE: No, of course not. It's constantly changing, because for one thing, what we know is constantly changing. One of the things that makes it fun to be a professor is that knowledge grows. We just know a lot more than we did when I was an undergraduate. So I wouldn't suggest that there is a body of knowledge fixed in stone that we've got to transmit to each and every generation.

Nonetheless, there is one thing we have to get across—a sense of quality. Some books are better than others, and some people are smarter than others, and some ideas are truer than others. It's just not the case in intellectual life that everything is equal, and everything is up for grabs. If we lose sight of that, we're out of business. This is what universities are for—to teach people to make intellectual and moral discriminations, and to be able to say, "This is better than that"; "This is true, and that's false"; "This is rational, and that's irrational."

MOYERS: When you and I were growing up, there was very little awareness of Africa as a culture, or of Asia as a culture, or of women and the life of their minds. My children today need to read African novels and Asian novels and Virginia Woolf. In our day these were not among the sacred texts.

SEARLE: Yes, there was a period when we were wonderfully insular and provincial. But there are two different ways to see the attacks on our insularity. One way is to see that we ought to open up to other forms and varieties of quality, other sorts of experiences. If it's true, as I think it probably is, that a lot of great women writers were neglected just because they were women, then let's start recognizing their quality.

But there's another, more sinister aspect that says the whole idea of this list of great books, the idea that some authors are better than others, that some cultures have made enormous contributions, and others have made lesser contributions is wrong, and that these distinctions are elitist and oppressive and sexist and racist. Now that's where I draw the line. We ought to open the door to all kinds of quality, and we ought to get out of this provincialism of our childhood—but let's not give up the ideal of quality.

MOYERS: Quality, quality, quality. It keeps coming up in what you say. How do you decide what quality is?

SEARLE: That's what we're in the business of trying to teach people how to do. There's no algorithm. I can't hold up a Plato and then hold up some half-witted philosopher, and say, "Look, here are the three rules to apply to see that Plato is smarter than the half-wit." You've got to get these kids to read it, and you have to talk about it—it takes literally years. Many of my colleagues never do figure out how to tell the dross from the gold. But that's what education is supposed to be for. We're supposed to be able to teach people how to think.

MOYERS: Who is going to decide what is true and what is not, what is best and what is worst?

SEARLE: In the end, each person has to make those decisions for himself. But the most tragic thing we could do would be to try to give people the conception that they don't have a responsibility for making those decisions for themselves or that, worse yet, there's nothing to be decided, and that it was all just an elaborate power ploy by the established dead European white males.

MOYERS: But aren't all choices of curriculum in a sense political choices, reflecting the culture, values, ambitions, purposes, and sense of calling of the people who are sitting there saying, "This is a good text, this is the right text, and this is a text for learned people"? Aren't they all political in that sense?

SEARLE: Every decision of a policy nature like this has political consequences. In that sense, it's political. But it doesn't follow from that that the only criteria for making the decisions are political, or even that the primary criteria are political. I'm called on to make decisions all the time about which books do I assign in my courses, and what do I emphasize, and what do I not emphasize, and what do I think is essential for a beginning philosophy student to read and know and think about and write about. All of those will have political consequences in the sense that my students' lives would have been different if I had made them read something else. But I don't make the decision on political grounds. I make the decision on intellectual grounds. I ask, "Does this book articulate general human experiences? Does it deal with central issues? Is it written by a superior intelligence? Does it affect you? Does it change your life? Is it fun to read?" If it's not fun to read, people aren't going to read it, regardless of this other stuff. I would like to convey to my students a sense of the challenge that's involved in reading difficult and important texts.

Anyway, what I'm trying to say is that there isn't an algorithm or a mechanical test. You have to use obvious things, like the ones I've been mentioning, in selecting important books. But don't suppose that any answer you give to this question is absolutely arbitrary and unwarranted and just an expression of your political bias. What we try to do in education is enable people to transcend these biases by getting them to the point where they can be self-aware and can sense their own position as a part of a long historical and cultural development. Of course, you never do transcend it totally. You're always what you are. But that doesn't mean that you're nothing more than the product of a series of political and social forces.

MOYERS: You're talking about learning to think and to discriminate. Can that be taught?

SEARLE: You can teach people to get to the point where they can teach themselves. I don't think I can teach my students how to do philosophy, but I can certainly put their noses in it, and tell them where they're making mistakes, so that eventually they can teach themselves. The distressing thing about that is when they get really good, they start refuting me. This is very annoying, but officially at least, I have to recognize the desirability of that. When they can get to the point where they can respect their teacher, or respect the books I ask them to read, and nonetheless point out what seem to them to be inadequacies, then I know we're on the right track.

MOYERS: Are there certain books that an educated man and woman must have read?

SEARLE: I won't say that there is some list of books that everybody has to read—maybe one or two, like the Bible. But it does seem to me there is a core tradition in our civilization. If that tradition is foreign to you, you will always be an alien to our culture. It's a tradition of rationality and intelligence that goes back to the Greeks, and that survived the Middle Ages and reached a very strong flowering in the Enlightenment. If that tradition is totally unknown to you, you're not fully a citizen of our culture. You really are deprived. It would be a terrible deprivation if we allowed our students to think you can be an educated person without knowing anything about that tradition.

MOYERS: What you say smacks so strongly of common sense that I wonder what the argument is all about—except that I haven't been black, and I haven't been female.

SEARLE: Well, let me give you the argument on the other side: "What Searle has just said has a hidden agenda—that middle-aged white males like him should stay in power and force us to read books by other middle-aged white males, who happen to be dead. Now if that's going to happen, then there's really no place for the rest of us, because the conception of rationality and intelligence and truth that he has is not universal. It's just a product of a certain phase of history. Basically, if you look closely at it, you'll see that it's a device that he and guys like him use to oppress the rest of us."

I don't agree with that. In the old days, people who stood outside this higher culture were invited in by the universities to join this great cultural tradition. Now we've got a sizable number of people, both within and without, who say, "The hell with the tradition. The whole idea of the tradition was that some things are better than others. That's already an oppressive move. What you've got to do is let everybody do their own thing and find their own cultural existence and define it for themselves. Don't worry about the idea that some things are more important than others, or some things are better than others."

There's a deeper threat here that I haven't been able to articulate, but it's this: It's an attack on the idea of rationality and truth as such. This now comes in various different forms in intellectual life. There's a movement in literary theory called deconstruction. There are even philosophers of science who say, "Look, science doesn't tell you the truth about the real world, because there isn't any real world—it's just more texts." There's a certain element in the feminist movement that says the traditional notions of rationality and truth are themselves oppressive devices. That's really what I'm arguing against. As long as you give me the validity of rationality, truth, and intelligence, then I think we could in the end come to an agreement on what higher education is all about. But if you reject those, then it's not all that clear what we should be doing. There is a malady of supposing that somehow or other rationality is over with, and there isn't any such thing as finding out the truth about the world—it was all a massive self-deception to think we could discover the truth about a real world. Rather, there are just texts and power relations. Texts are used as part of power relations. The idea that words stand for things, and that there is such a thing as truth—all of that is a mistake that derives in its present form from the Enlightenment, and the Enlightenment is over. We now live in a posthistorical, postmodern, postcontemporary world. And what we're all post is rationality and intelligence. The idea is that reason subverts itself.

Now this isn't all stupid. If you adopt the critical stance that you and I were taught to adopt in our education, that things have to meet the challenge of criticism, then ultimately, you begin to challenge rational standards of criticism themselves. Religion, history, tradition, and morality have always been subjected to searching criticism in the name of rationality, truth, evidence, reason, and logic. Now reason, truth, rationality, and logic are themselves subject to these criticisms. The tradition of rationality is itself being subverted by people who want to show that you've never really met these rational constraints that you thought you were meeting. You never really did find the truth.

MOYERS: I thought the mark of the liberal mind—"liber," free—was that all things are up for grabs. The mind is free to wander where it will.

SEARLE: That is the valuable element in the traditional conception of the liberal education that you and I both share, namely, the openness, and the willingness to admit anything that meets certain standards of rationality, truth, evidence, reason, and logic. But now what has happened is that those canons of rationality, truth, evidence, reason, and logic are themselves being criticized from within the academy. The idea is that they're as much a part of the dogmatic, superstitious, religious, mystical, power-laden tradition as anything that they were used to attack.

But rationality, truth, and intelligence aren't themselves substantive theses like a particular dogmatic theology. They are standards which any attempt to communicate is forced to meet. The canons of rationality aren't themselves up for grabs. They're built into the nature of what it is to think and speak. If you can think and speak at all, you're already in a situation where the canons of rationality, truth, and intelligence apply.

MOYERS: You've said a lot of people attacked the Western civilization courses because they think you white males want to stay in power. But what about the case that, all right, if you want to learn about the spiritual nature of human beings, you can't stop with just the Hebrew and Christian Bible, you ought to read the Upanishads, because whether or not you find that the Upanishads describe the world to you, they are a way of looking at the world. So the Upanishads ought to be in any course an educated man or woman takes in undergraduate work, just like the Bible.

SEARLE: There aren't enough hours in the day, or enough days in the year for us to teach everything, so we have to make selections. Quality is crucial. Now what you've said is, "You're still leaving out a lot of good quality." But you can't really understand other traditions if you don't understand your own. So the mere fact that we're educating Americans who are brought up in a country which is an offshoot of Europe, and which was founded on a certain eighteenth-century European philosophy, has to constrain what we teach in education. If I were designing a university for people from Mars, then I'd be absolutely neutral between the Judeo-Christian tradition and all sorts of other religious traditions. But given that I'm not teaching people from Mars, it's terribly important that these people know who they are.

> . . . you can't really understand other traditions if you don't understand your own.

MOYERS: I subscribe to that, but let me tell you what happened to me when I came into San Francisco the other night. So help me, of the first ten people I heard when I was waiting for the baggage, not one was speaking English. They were speaking Spanish, Japanese, Chinese, Pakistani, and I don't know what else. I have listened enough to know, they're coming here to live. America is a real place on real ground, occupying a real time in history, and constantly reshaping itself.

SEARLE: We've had immigrants to this country before, and for the most part, we assimilated these immigrants into an existing tradition. They all learned English. They all were educated in the fundamental constitutional structure of the United States, and they became full-fledged citizens in our culture. Now that isn't to say they shouldn't prize the tradition that they came from. But we tried to make each new wave of immigrants into citizens of the United States. But suppose we said, "Look, we'll give you the citizenship papers, but don't think that English has any special status in the United States, or that there's any special importance attaching to American history. You can set up any culture you want in the United States." I think that's a recipe for disaster. We've seen that in Quebec and Belgium. Whenever you get rival cultural and linguistic communities within larger communities, it's very hard to sustain a sense of nationhood.

The single greatest change that has happened in Berkeley in all the years that I've been there is that Asian faces are no longer a minority. When I came here in 1959, it was very unusual to see an Asian face. But now, literally, just about every other face on the Berkeley campus is Asian. And you know what difference it makes to my teaching? None. I teach the courses that I would teach quite oblivious to the racial background of my students. It never occurs to me that I ought to teach Sally Chung differently from Sally Smith. I teach them both the same way.

MOYERS: You want both Sallys to read Tocqueville?

SEARLE: Exactly, Tocqueville in particular, yes.

MOYERS: Mark Twain.

SEARLE: Yes, and Karl Marx. There are a lot of people that Sally Chung and Sally Smith both ought to read.

MOYERS: Do you want the two Sallys to read anything additional because Sally Chung is now here?

SEARLE: If there are enough Sally Chungs, that is, if they form a sense of cultural identity, then there's a case to be made for saying that part of their knowing who they are is an understanding of Confucius. I'm really not competent to teach Confucius. They ought to get somebody who can teach Confucius. But this goes back to what I said earlier, namely, in order to understand other traditions, you've got to know your own.

MOYERS: You do like to teach, don't you?

SEARLE: Oh, I love it, yeah.

MOYERS: Why?

SEARLE: Somebody once said that teaching is a lot like sex—if you don't like it, you won't be good at it. If you do like it, you're certainly likely to be better at it.

Arturo Madrid

EDUCATOR

Arturo Madrid's ancestors made a home on American soil before the Mayflower arrived, but strangers still ask him, "And where are you from?" Weary of always being perceived as "the other," he has devoted himself to challenging the stereotypes that keep Hispanics outside the American mainstream. He lives in Claremont, California, where he is president of the Tomás Rivera Center, an institute focusing on issues and policies affecting the Latino community.

MOYERS: You've said that you've spent most of your adult life trying to explain who you were not. In what sense?

MADRID: When people look at me and find out what my name is and what my profession is—I was trained to be a professor of Spanish—somehow, I am no longer part of their mental set, that is, I'm not part of an American reality that they know. Surely, I must be from somewhere else—Latin America, Spain, wherever. So I have to explain that I'm American, and then I have to explain that my parents aren't first generation, and that my grandparents aren't first generation, and that in fact my ancestors have lived here for a long time. I have to explain that I'm not somebody from some other country who's immigrated to the United States. That's what I mean by explaining who I am not.

MOYERS: This wasn't a problem when you were a child because you grew up in New Mexico, surrounded by people with similar names who looked alike and talked alike.

MADRID: No, it wasn't until I left New Mexico and came in contact with that larger world, particularly with people whose historical experiences have never really connected them to the Mexican origin community, that I began to have to explain who I was and who I wasn't. Los Angeles was very interesting because people in Los Angeles who met me assumed either that I was a recent immigrant or that my parents were immigrants. That then began to involve me in explaining the history of New Mexico and the Southwest.

MOYERS: What did it say to you that so many people perceived of you, a native-born American, as an outsider?

MADRID: It was problematical for me because that had not been part of my experience. My parents were educated folks. My mother was both an appointed and elected public official in New Mexico. People who had names like mine and looked like me held professional and political appointments and were part of the larger world. So I did not suffer the experience that so many other people of Mexican origin or Latinos in general experienced in America of being "defined out." I knew I was part of the fabric of the society. I had come out of a community where we were part of that fabric, and so when this "defining out" began to be a problem for me, I struggled against it and tried to understand where that was coming from and how my experience related to that of Mexicans and other Hispanics in the U.S.

MOYERS: "Defining out"—that's an interesting phrase. What did it mean to you?

MADRID: It meant that by virtue of the fact that my name was not Smith or Jones, my presence had no validity in American life, that what I had experienced and what my family and the people around me had experienced was marginal to what took place in the larger society. We were not seen as part of the American nation but as an accretion to the American nation. We were Mexicans, and, therefore, we had another historical reality, another national process that was not the American process. So in that sense, we were "defined out."

> *. . . by virtue of the fact that my name was not Smith or Jones, my presence had no validity in American life. . . .*

Now, there was another way I was defined out, which was not a cerebral process but a visual process. When I looked at movies and television, I saw that the Latinos in those movies were not Americans, but Mexicans or Latin Americans. So my experiences and the people around me were not to be found in public life, and they were not to be found on TV or in the movies. In that sense, I was defined out of reality.

MOYERS: So the popular culture was not sending back to you reflections of your own experience. When did you begin to feel that you were "the other"?

MADRID: It happened early on in New Mexico, simply because although we were the predominant population, we came in contact with places like Los Alamos. As I grew older, I saw a different life from the life that we were part of, and all of those things and the media, little by little, cumulatively said we were different from the rest of the society. We were the other. That was most acute for me in two places. One was school, where we had a sense of what that larger reality was, and the other one was church, because there were two kinds of churches, the American church and the Spanish church. Even though in some of the communities where my parents lived there was no Spanish church, and we went to the American church, still we knew that our rightful place was in the other church, not in the American church.

MOYERS: Why did you know that?

MADRID: Because there was nobody else like us in that church, and because it was something you felt very much.

MOYERS: What happens to you when you're made to feel like you're the other?

MADRID: Two things happen. One is that you start putting up your defenses very quickly against being made to feel that you're not good enough, that you're different, that you're not part of that larger world. The second thing is, you start working very hard to incorporate yourself into that larger reality, to present yourself as well as you can, and in those areas where you're made to feel that you're not good enough, you make sure that you're not only good enough but even better. So, on the one hand, defensiveness comes into play, and on the other hand, you really work hard to stand out.

MOYERS: Somewhere you said that it makes you feel either like a sore thumb or invisible.

MADRID: Entering a space where you are not wanted or that you haven't occupied before puts you in a very difficult situation. Are you going to be seen and dealt with appropriately, or are you going to be invisible? Are you going to stick out, or are you just simply not going to be noticed, and your interests and your concerns not reflected?

MOYERS: When you read Ralph Ellison's *Invisible Man*, did you say, "That's my experience"?

MADRID: No, it took me a while to come to that position. Rereading it in the mid-seventies, I saw he was talking about me, and I hadn't realized it. I thought this was a novel that had to do with a young man who comes from the South to the North, but no, it has to do with anybody who is an outsider and all of a sudden finds himself or herself outside the environment he or she grew up in. You find that you're not present, that nobody really is attending to your concerns and interests, and that you're not part of the larger reality. All of a sudden, you start doing an analysis of this society, and you say, "Hey, there are places where we aren't. Why is that so?" It doesn't have anything to do with ability, because where I come from, people like me participate at all levels of society. So something else has to be going on here, something very political, something that is not cultural, something that has to do with the history of the society.

In some cases, people fight against being defined out. In some cases, people accept it. In many other cases, people are not even aware of the fact that they're being defined out, and function fairly normally. Once in a while they bump their heads, and they sit up and say, "What was that all about?"

In my case, it just made me more determined not only to do well, but to begin the process of getting more people defined in rather than defined out and to begin to challenge, on a systematic basis, any mental constructs that defined us out. Let me give you an example. In recent years, we've heard much about the lack of political participation on the part of the Latino community. The saw goes that Latinos are not interested in politics and that their culture does not lead them to participate in the electoral process. Yet the community that I came from was deeply steeped in the electoral process. We had ninety-eight percent registration and ninety-six percent turnout for elections, so I knew that old myth couldn't be true. I thought to myself, "Well, maybe it has something to do with the fact that this is an old community." But the fact is that if people have a reason to vote, if their vote is going to make a difference, then they will vote. When Willy Velásquez in the Southwest Voter Registration Project was able to show people that their vote would make a difference when it came down to being able to get the potholes paved on their streets or to get water or sewage lines, then they would register to vote, and not only register to vote, but they would vote. Secondly, if their vote made a difference, in the sense that they could get their people elected, then they would register to vote, and actually vote. In fact, in Puerto Rico, for example, you have extraordinary political participation. People register, campaign, and vote. So the lack of political participation by Latinos had nothing to do with their culture. It had to do with being disenfranchised, with being defined out and not being allowed to participate the way one should.

> . . . if people have a reason to vote, if their vote is going to make a difference, then they will vote.

MOYERS: But, as you said, some people resign themselves to being outsiders. You fought. You got in. You're an insider. How do you explain that?

MADRID: Part of it is a personal history that is connected to a larger history. I have been rather hard on missionaries, but at the same time, missionaries said, "You're part of a larger reality, and part of that larger reality means you participate in the institutions of society, starting with the Church but then continuing with educational institutions." Part of what they brought to my family that I picked up was the necessity to be part of a larger history, to work for the common good, and to put my personal gain second to the public good. So despite the fact that the historical process would have made it possible for me to turn my back on the community that I came from and say, "Gee, anybody can make it. It's very simple. All you have to do is educate yourself and participate," I said, "But there are other folks who, for a multitude of reasons, can't make that move. How do we make it possible for people to feel that the United States is really united, that it's a whole, that it's indivisible, and that there's liberty and justice for all?"

There are two different issues we have to deal with. One of them has to do with the missing persons phenomenon, the fact that there are entire classes of folks in our society who are marginal to the institutional life of the society despite their abilities, interest, and efforts. But a second one is that there are people who, through no fault of their own, do not have the advantages and protections of this society, who are overwhelmingly poor, and who include among their numbers a disproportionate percentage of black people, American Indians, Hispanics, and increasingly, Asians. These are two separate and yet interrelated issues. One of them has to do with empowerment. The other one has to do with social justice and well-being.

MOYERS: Do you think that the perception of Hispanics is changing now that you are becoming the dominant minority in America?

MADRID: I was asked recently by a newspaper reporter about what was called "the decade of the Hispanic." You remember that the decade beginning in 1980 was to be "the decade of the Hispanic." "What are your thoughts on that?" he asked. I said, "Well, if you thought about the decade as being one where Hispanics were somehow going to progress, to get all kinds of support that would resolve all the issues and all the problems that we have as a community, then that clearly didn't happen, and, of course, it was unrealistic to think that would take place. But if you think of this decade as having been one where Hispanics became publicly visible, where what were perceived as private problems began to be dealt with as public issues, and where increasingly the leadership of American society began to be conscious of the fact that this was a reality that needed to be dealt with—in that sense, we made some gains."

But some of the old stereotypes continue today. One stereotype is that this population really is not interested in things that Americans are interested in, namely, good education, political participation, and social and economic well-being, but that we're very much focused only on immediate family, and that our allegiances have to do with a historical culture and with a nation that is outside the United States. Some of the old myths are there—that we're lazy, that we're present-time oriented, and that we're fatalistic.

MOYERS: Some of your studies show that Hispanic kids do not do as well in high school as others, and that their dropout rate is almost fifty percent. There is the stereotype, as you suggest, that the Hispanic community in general doesn't expect very much from its kids or expect their kids to get very much from education. Why is this so?

MADRID: Our studies show that Latino parents have very high aspirations for their children with respect to education, employment, and economic well-being, and that the children share those very high aspirations. But both parental expectations and the expectations of the children are not very high. Somehow a signal is being sent by the larger society and its institutions that they're not expected to do particularly well, and so a dual message is communicated by parents to children—that yes, we'd like you to do very well, but we don't expect you to do very well.

Now what are those signals? Those signals are that you're not wanted in the institutions of the society, that there's room for only so many folks in the society, and that particularly people of a different national and linguistic background don't belong.

The signals become very powerful and self-fulfilling. For example, Latino kids end up in schools that are very large, very crowded, and not very attractive. Very soon they find out that the teachers are not happy about being in those schools and that their materials are not really adequate. That sends a powerful signal to children that we really don't value you, and we don't expect you to do well, and we're not going to ask very much of you. There are schools in this part of the country where the administrators have estimated that between day one and day X of the school year, there will be forty percent attrition in the number of Latino schoolchildren who'll be attending— that many will drop out. So the kids show up for the first day of school, and there are not enough schoolrooms, there are not enough teachers, there are not enough desks, there are not enough schoolbooks to go around. So it becomes a self-fulfilling prophecy.

MOYERS: The kids perceive this?

MADRID: They figure out very soon they're not wanted.

MOYERS: But schools are something we can do something about.

MADRID: That's right. We can have smaller schools, better teacher-to-student ratios, and teachers who really expect that the kids can learn and who demand that they learn. We can make sure that they have all the advantages that other kids in better economic situations have. You can make a difference very fast.

MOYERS: Does the use of the Spanish language within the home make it more difficult for these kids when they get to a school and in a society where English is *the* language?

MADRID: Yes and no. Yes, if the use of languages creates a protective environment, and the child is not disposed to take on the larger world. In that sense, yes, it becomes a problem. But no, if the child learns that there are really two ways of being and two codes at work here, and that he or she can function equally well in both worlds.

When people find out what my name is and what I do, inevitably, I get asked, "Dr. Madrid, what do you think about bilingual education?" My response to that is, "Gee, I don't think you're interested in finding out what I think about bilingual education— I think you're interested in telling me what you think about bilingual education. And I'm not interested in what you think about bilingual education, because that's really not the issue. The real issue is literacy." There are approximately twenty-seven million illiterates in the United States today, and the overwhelming majority of those folks are monolingual English speakers. English is the only language they speak. The issue is not bilingual education, the issue is whether you are a literate person. People who are literate in one language can become literate in another language very fast. The research shows that children learn English very fast. The issue is, do you communicate? Whether you communicate using the language in a variety of ways is much more important than whether you are a monolingual English speaker. It's preferable, in today's world, to be able to speak more than one language and to use language at very different levels.

MOYERS: But what about the burden this puts upon the teachers who have to operate in two learning modes?

MADRID: There are two learning modes, to be sure. But for the most part, schools function with one learning mode—a learning mode in English. If you use bilingual education in America's schools, it's mainly to move children from their home language to English. There is precious little reinforcement of the home language. There are some schools where that in fact does take place. It's very effective where children are beginning to be literate in the home language and are taught to be literate in English at school. But for the most part, kids do not become literate in the language of the home. They become literate in English, if at all.

MOYERS: Hispanics like Richard Rodríguez oppose bilingual education because they say that English is the one public language in this country, and that if kids are going to go out into that world and do what Arturo Madrid did, they've got to function in that public language. It may not be desirable, but it's necessary, because that's the way this country is set up. What's your response to that?

MADRID: Richard Rodríguez is putting up a straw man instead of addressing the real issue—which is to make people literate, to empower people, to give them a public voice. Bilingual education is only a means to an end, it's not an end in itself. The end is literacy, empowerment, and participation in the larger life of the society. If I have a public voice, it's not simply because I'm a literate person, but because I feel that it's important for me to participate in the larger life of the society, and because I've found ways to get the larger society to listen to me. I become stronger, and my voice becomes more compelling, because I can draw on two different experiences, two different cultures, two ways of knowing and being. If I were to be denied one or the other, I do not think my voice would be as strong, and I would not feel as empowered.

MOYERS: No, but the public voice you have used to become a leader is English. You want all those other little Madrids coming along to do the same, don't you?

MADRID: Yes, but I can speak to the two communities, and that's my principal point. My public voice is an English voice, and I want everybody to speak English—that is not the issue. But English alone is not enough. Literacy is important. Empowerment is important—feeling that your vote makes a difference, that you have the same legal protections that everybody else does, that you have similar economic opportunities, and that you can go into a space in America and be treated appropriately. That is as important as speaking English. Speaking English in and by itself is only a first step. I will not back away from the importance of English—but neither will I back away from the larger feeling of empowerment that is necessary for people to be able to get a public voice.

MOYERS: If we accept that the language is something of a challenge and schools are bad, why have so many other immigrant groups in America—notably, Asian-Americans—succeeded in the way that they have succeeded? What makes the Hispanic story different?

MADRID: I don't think the Hispanic story is all that different. We're talking about typical immigrant populations to the United States. However, a population that has been here but has been excluded historically from participation in the larger life of the society creates a dynamic that is very different from the experience of the traditional immigrant. If we're talking about a population that comes across the border to work and returns back to Mexico when work is over, but doesn't come as a typical, traditional immigrant population, then we have a different order of things. They don't expect to incorporate themselves. They learn as much English as they need to in order to do what they need to do. They get as much education as they need to. But if you're talking about a typical immigrant Latino, whether that immigrant comes from Cuba, Mexico, or Latin America, that immigrant is going to participate in the life of the society in the same way that any immigrant does.

MOYERS: You're still fighting a stereotype.

MADRID: Yes, but we're talking about people who've been here a long time, as is the case of my ancestors. The average Mexican-American in society today is either first generation or has parents who are the first generation. For those folks, the message is, "You really are not part of this society. You're a second-class citizen. You do not merit the kind of attention that other folks merit." Those are the folks who get inferior schooling and can't change the conditions. Those are the folks who become marginalized. Those are the folks who internalize the message that this society is not for you.

MOYERS: What do we do? You have said that if we're going to settle some of these issues, we're going to have to change the way we talk about them. What do you mean?

MADRID: Among other things, we have to start thinking and acting like Garrison Keillor in the world of Lake Wobegon, where all the children are above average. We have to start thinking that it's possible for all kids to do very well, and that we could have good housing, good nutrition, and good legal protection for all the citizens in the society. People must feel that it is their society and that it is responsive to them. If you empower people to demand the same benefits and protections that everybody else has, then there's a chance they'll get them. You can do something about your situation as a community. There is the example of COPS, the community organization in San Antonio. They said, "Despite the fact that we're paying taxes, our garbage doesn't get picked up. We don't have a good water system. The potholes in the streets are not fixed." You can organize around those things and make sure that they get addressed.

> *If you empower people to demand the same benefits and protections that everybody else has, then there's a chance they'll get them.*

MOYERS: They organized, and they changed that.

MADRID: You can similarly say, "Schools need to be better for our children. Our children need to feel safe when they go to school. They need to be able to learn. We should have better teachers and better materials. We should demand more of the school." And you can actually go in and do that. You may not be able to do very much about the macro-problems, but you can certainly address the issues within your community.

MOYERS: So we've got to stop saying that Hispanics are noncompetitive, Hispanics are passive, Hispanics are interested in immediate gratification—that's what you mean by "changing the way we talk about problems."

MADRID: Yes. To my Latino community, I say, "You have to develop a public voice, and you have to use it. You have to bring knowledge and information to bear. You can't just complain, you have to act." To the larger community in the United States, I say, "This is part of an American reality. This is part of America's future. You have to make space, and when you do, you'll find a very responsive community, a very creative, dynamic, and hard-working community, ready to participate fully."

MOYERS: You talk about the future—since 1965, seventy-eight percent of all the immigrants coming to this country have come from Latin America, Asia, and the Caribbean. What do you think this says about our future?

MADRID: First of all, what it says about our present is that we have to start dealing with our population in a very different way than we have, historically. We can't write off the human resources any more. You can't just put twenty percent of the population on welfare. You can't put another thirty percent of the population on unemployment. Every person matters. As we get to be an older population, it's important that the younger population be a working population, a healthy population, and a learning population, so that it can sustain this society. If we don't assure that the new immigrants and the people we have historically excluded from the larger life of the society are empowered—become educated, get good jobs, and learn to learn, so that they can be adapting to all the change that's going on—our future is not assured. People are no longer distant or alien from each other. Almost every population group in the world can be found in some part of the United States. So we need to learn to live together and to respect differences.

MOYERS: Does this mean that there's finally a melting pot in our future? Or are we going to remain a boiling caldron in which all of these factions are indissoluble? Or, to change the analogy, will we be like a great quilt of many patches?

MADRID: I like the quilt of many patches. It is not in our interests for it to be a caldron. We need to work together. We need to learn how to deal with that diversity and to understand that the only constant we have today is change. If we understand those two things, we won't have that caldron boiling. Maybe we can get it down to a simmer. But if we really work at it, maybe we can change that metaphor and not talk about a caldron but a "salad bowl," where there are many different ingredients. There are radishes and tomatoes and onions in there—but still and all, they come together, and form a whole, a salad.

MOYERS: The myth is that we have been accepting of immigrants, that we have welcomed them and protected them, and that we tolerate diversity and pluralism. But the reality has not been that benign, has it?

MADRID: It has not, particularly not for the Latino population, which has been denied many of the protections of American society. They've enjoyed some of the advantages and some of the benefits, but been denied some of the protections, especially legal protections. Some of the advantages that have been denied—and they're not so much advantages as rights—are good education, access to good housing, and good medical care. Those things are terribly important. If you are not well rooted in the society, if you always feel that your roots are very, very superficial, then any storm will knock them out. Any storm will make it very difficult for the plant to grow. This has happened time and time again to the Mexican-origin community.

MOYERS: There's a term for that in Spanish—

MADRID: Yes. A *flor de tierra*—that is, a flower that has very shallow roots. We're desert people, and in the desert, that's part of what happens. You have very spare plants with very shallow roots. Sometimes those plants don't last. We have to figure out ways of sending deeper roots into the soil and making it possible for people to function well in this society.

MOYERS: The story of your grandmother illustrates that possibility.

MADRID: Yes, at the beginning of the twentieth century, my grandmother and her family decided to leave their small mountain village in the Sangre de Cristo Mountains in northern New Mexico and move down to the Rio Grande Valley of New Mexico. My grandmother, being a very religious person, went to her pastor to ask his blessing as she moved her family to the valley. Her pastor said, "Well, of course, Doña Trinidad, but I want you to promise something to me before you leave. I want you to promise me that you're going to go to church when you get to the valley." And she said, "Of course I will—but why do you ask?" And he said, "Because in the valley, there is not a Spanish church, there's only an American church." And she said, "But I don't know what difference that would make. I speak English, I write English, I read English, and I would be able to worship there without any problem." And he said, "No, you don't understand. It's not that you couldn't worship there, it's that they might not welcome you into the fellowship, and that's why I want you to promise me that you're going to go to church. And furthermore," he said, "I want you to promise me that if they don't let you in the front door, that you go in the back door. And if you can't go in the back door, that you go in the side door. And if they don't let you in the door, then you come in through the window—but you must go in, and you must worship there."

That's in a sense what has happened to many of us in American society. We were excluded by social, economic, and other types of pressures. And so over the last twenty-five years—and even before then—we were pushing at the doors of the institutions of American society and saying we have to participate in this society. Some of us were able to come in through the front door with all our credentials. But most of us had to come in through back doors and through side doors, and many, many came through windows. What happened in many of those cases is that we ended up in the back rooms or the side rooms or in the lobby or in the niches, and we really didn't get to participate fully in the life of the society. Some have; most have not. So our struggle is to continue working to be accepted in that larger space of American institutions and to participate fully. When that happens, I think we can begin to change some of the other things that happen in society.

Henry Steele Commager

HISTORIAN

Talking with Henry Steele Commager is the closest we can come to interviewing a Founding Father. The patriarch of American historians has been teaching history for over sixty years, the last thirty of them at Amherst College in Massachusetts. Among his scores of books are The American Mind, The Empire of Reason, *and* The Search for a Usable Past. *His honors and awards include a rare gold medal in history from the American Academy.*

MOYERS: You once wrote, "I cheerfully confess an abiding faith in democracy as the best kind of government, and in majority rule. I believe in freedom as a method of arriving at truth and avoiding error, in working out solutions and politics by the pragmatic method of experimentation." Now, you wrote these words a long time ago. Do you still believe them?

COMMAGER: Oh yes. Very early, I instinctively adopted the pragmatic point of view, and I've never seen any reason to abandon it for the subjective point of view. I think we have to have objectivity based on facts, based on what happens, rather than on assumptions about things, like our assumptions about the wickedness of communism or the right of the United States to decide what's going to happen everywhere in the world, or the assumptions that we're God's chosen people, as Mr. Reagan says we are. Whatever we do is all right because we are God's chosen people—but other nations do the same thing, and it's very wicked, because they are clearly not God's people. All of these assumptions confuse our policies very deeply.

MOYERS: You respect the facts. But democracy is actually a very emotional crucible for the playing out of people's passions and their effects on policy.

COMMAGER: Even so, democracy is better than any other method of government that's been tried, as far as I know. There are drawbacks to all forms of government. The miracle is that the democratic system worked. We're the first people really to make it work, and it has taken us a long time to achieve full democracy. We're not quite there yet. I trust we will be in your lifetime. We won't be in my lifetime. But democracy works in an extraordinary fashion in a country as large as ours. You wouldn't expect it to work in a country made up of fifty different states that regard themselves as sovereign in one way or another. It works because the framers were the wisest men politically in recorded history, and they solved some of the great problems that had never before been solved—above all, the problem of federalism.

MOYERS: The capacity of power to be dispersed among many sources, but still retain a cohesive central character.

COMMAGER: Somehow the real problem is to get the cohesion in a country of so many races and so many languages and so many religions and so many backgrounds of one kind or another. It was achieved by the great good luck that anyone who was unhappy in Massachusetts Bay or in Virginia could always go to Ohio or to Kentucky or to Tennessee, and if they were unhappy there, they could go to Iowa and Colorado, and so forth.

MOYERS: There were a lot of misfits in Texas who came pouring across the Red River, including some of my outlaw ancestors.

COMMAGER: I wouldn't be surprised, yes. And they're still coming to Texas in vast numbers, both from the United States and from other parts of the globe.

MOYERS: Having that frontier, of course, was a great cushion against the passions and perils of living closely together—of escaping frustrations before they exploded.

COMMAGER: Quite right. The explosion in our history occurred not because of population density, but over the issue of slavery. Federalism has worked from the beginning. We've had two experiments with federalism. We tend to forget that the Confederate States of America were also a federal union. That broke down, and when it broke down, the Confederacy lost. States' rights killed the Confederacy just as surely as Grant's armies and Sherman's armies did.

But having tried that experiment, we went back to the original federalism, which we alone of modern peoples have been able to make work. It's an enormously complicated thing—it's far and away the most sophisticated of all forms of government, the one that makes the greatest demands on the intelligence, ability and wisdom of men. It distributes power on two different levels between governments and makes it work.

MOYERS: The period of our founding as a nation was such a particular time in the history of the world. Do you think, realistically, we have anything to learn from that era?

COMMAGER: I think we have almost everything to learn from that era. We have, for example, a very elementary thing to learn—what it was like when the generation's leaders believed, above all things, in honor. They believed in the future generations, and in posterity with land enough for our descendants, as Jefferson said in his first inaugural, to the thousandth and thousandth generation.

MOYERS: There was a speech by George Washington in which he used the word "posterity" nine times.

COMMAGER: They all did. They couldn't give a speech or write a letter without talking about posterity. Here is poor old John Adams, the day he signed the Declaration of Independence, writing his wife Abigail. He said, "I do not know what will be the outcome of this. We may pay a very high price. But it is certain that posterity will profit from our sacrifice."

MOYERS: Why did they have that sense of the future, that commitment to generations not yet born?

COMMAGER: I suppose because it was the only place in the Western world then where you could have confidence in posterity. The most elementary fact, perhaps, of American history at that time was that babies didn't die. Fifty percent of the new babies of Warsaw died every year. Fifty percent of the babies in other countries died. Children went to work at the age of six or seven. Even in enlightened England, in the nineteenth century, children worked in the mills ten to twelve hours a day, six days a week. They had half an hour off for two meals. In addition, they went to school one or two hours a day. Many of them were as young as six years old. They worked from six in the morning until midnight.

That wasn't true in America. Infant mortality was very low. It was a healthy place. There was enough food, there was enough milk, there was enough of everything. The mother could stay home and take care of the babies instead of going to work, and children didn't have to go to work. They were healthy. No wonder the population doubled and doubled and redoubled, to the astonishment of every European.

MOYERS: The other thing about the founders' era is that they were starting something brand new. They were inventing the future.

COMMAGER: They knew that. That was one of the mottos—*Novus Ordo Seclorum*—"a new order of the ages." It's on all our bills to this day.

MOYERS: You've written that great things were done by the generation that won independence and wrote the Constitution. Great things were accomplished by the generation that saved the Union and rid it of slavery. Great things were won by the generation that defeated the Fascists in World War II and organized the peace that followed—the Marshall Plan, the United Nations, the planting of democracy in Japan. Perhaps our dilemma is that we don't have a great and compelling cause that summons leaders who will rally us to extraordinary efforts.

COMMAGER: We do, but we have ignored it. We have done far less than we could to save the Third World. If we took one tenth of our military wasting every year, we could take care of these poverty-stricken and desperate areas. We've done nothing to rebuild Vietnam. We dropped eleven million tons of bombs on Vietnam, three times as much as we dropped on the whole of Europe and Japan in World War II. We've given them no compensation at all. We've suddenly become stingy—no Marshall Plan, no great program to help the backward nations of Africa or the backward nations of South America.

> *We have done far less than we could to save the Third World.*

MOYERS: What are some of the issues we can't run from as we approach the twenty-first century?

COMMAGER: Well, there is a throng of them pressing on us. The first and most urgent and universal is the environment. Everybody talks about the environment, but we don't do much about it. We talk about acid rain and signing a treaty with Canada, but we don't enforce the treaty. We're polluting the seas, we're polluting the inland waters, we're polluting the soil, we're destroying the forests. We don't think of our descendants to the thousandth and thousandth generation. They'll be lucky if they have a country in which to live in three or four generations. I think there is a basic failure to think of posterity and to live for posterity the way the Founding Fathers did—to always look a thousand years ahead and see what would be for the benefit of posterity. That has disappeared.

Now I haven't read all Mr. Reagan's addresses—that would be a kind of masochism. But I don't remember that he ever used the word "posterity" in any of his addresses, as you said Washington used it nine times in one of his, and Jefferson used it constantly. If we're thinking of posterity, we must preserve the natural resources and take care of the health of children and end poverty—all of these things. But the commonest attitude now is: "What has posterity ever done for us? Let posterity take care of itself"—which it has to do.

MOYERS: You have lived under fourteen of our forty presidents, from Teddy Roosevelt to Ronald Reagan, and you've studied them all. What's been the biggest change in the presidency since you were born?

COMMAGER: There have been different kinds of changes in different categories. In the political category, for instance, the biggest change is the rise of the imperial presidency, which Arthur Schlesinger has sketched in connection with FDR and Kennedy. Woodrow Wilson fought World War I with eight assistants. Roosevelt fought World War II with about a hundred and ten assistants. Recent presidents have had over five hundred. They lost the Vietnam War with five hundred assistants—but they were proud of conquering Grenada, of course. It didn't take five hundred advisers, it took eighteen thousand Marines. We now have the readiness of the President to take on responsibilities that even Mr. Washington was afraid to take on. He always consulted Madison and Jefferson and others.

MOYERS: The other side of the argument is that presidents don't have enough power. I suspect Ronald Reagan would be surprised to hear you talk about his presidency in terms of an imperial presidency. For eight years he tried to wage a war against Nicaragua, and he couldn't finally persuade the Congress or the country. He's able to invade a small country like Grenada, but he's not able to work his will elsewhere. I think many presidents of late feel that they are hemmed in by the forces of bureaucracy, by the media, by public opinion.

COMMAGER: Well, they were supposed to be hemmed in, the Constitution was designed to hem them in. The Constitution tried to make that clear by the distinction between defensive and offensive action. Presidents were not supposed to declare war or to make war.

One of the interesting episodes in our history was the war with the Barbary pirates. Even though Jefferson, who was then President, was dedicated to peace, he nevertheless sent over warships to deal with the Barbary pirates and prevent their depredations on our ships. But he gave strict orders to the captains: You may use whatever force is necessary to protect your ships, but you may not attack the Barbary ships because to do that is an act of war, and the Constitution assigns that power to the Congress, not to the President.

In a sense, Lincoln took the same position. The Civil War was not a war, it was an insurrection. Lincoln had the extraordinary wisdom to see from the beginning that it must never be recognized as a war. That is why we avoided the constitutional problems of Reconstruction—because suppose it had been a war, and all the soldiers who fought in it were traitors against the United States. Were all these people to be punished? Not at all. This was an act of insurrection. The President has the authority to put down insurrections. He also has the authority to pardon. Lincoln pardoned everybody—

MOYERS: —with malice toward none and charity toward all.

COMMAGER: That's right. He pardoned everybody. He didn't want the awful prospect of trying a million people for treason and punishing them. The only person punished was one who deserved to be punished—the superintendent of Andersonville Prison, who stood by while the Confederates were ordered to shoot some of the prisoners. He's the only one who went to the gallows, not for treason but for murder.

MOYERS: The Founding Fathers had a strong sense that no President should be given the personal prerogative of going to war. The Constitution is so clear on that. "Congress shall declare war." And yet, not since 1941 have we had a declaration of war by Congress although we have fought in Korea and Vietnam, and sponsored low-intensity conflicts all over the globe.

COMMAGER: We fight in Angola, we fight in Lebanon, we fight in the Persian Gulf, we fight in Grenada. All of these are acts of war. If they were against us, we'd regard them as acts of war. If Britain or France should do to us what we do to these peoples, we would consider it an act of war. But I think we probably will never have another declaration of war. You just start a war. You don't declare it any more. We did declare war against Japan, but we didn't need to—the war was under way.

MOYERS: This means an erosion in the balance of powers provided by the Constitution?

COMMAGER: We don't know what it means. It depends on the interpretation of the Supreme Court. The question of the extent to which the operation in Nicaragua was unconstitutional will, of course, come up in some future court. The authority of the Congress versus the authority of the executive branch of the government is going to be a very tough issue for the courts to confront. They will probably try to avoid it as they have tried to avoid it in the past.

MOYERS: Are you not encouraged that the President tried for eight years to rally majority support behind his policy in Central America, and he simply couldn't do it? The American people may in fact have learned the lesson of Vietnam.

COMMAGER: They may have. But eight years is a long time to learn a lesson that should have been learned the first day. I gather from many of the media polls that a great deal of the public opinion supported Oliver North and Secord and others. Gradually, it's come to its senses on these matters. But in any country there's almost always support for the head of the nation in time of war. So if you can create a war where people are getting killed, there will be a rally 'round the flag. That's one of the drawbacks of nationalism. I don't think we've ever sufficiently contemplated the advantages versus the disadvantages of modern nationalism.

> I don't think we've ever sufficiently contemplated the advantages versus the disadvantages of modern nationalism.

MOYERS: It seems to me that the corruption of freedom begins with the corruption of language.

COMMAGER: That's just what Thucydides, the Greek historian, said in his history of the Peloponnesian War. He has a long and very moving passage on the corruption of language.

MOYERS: If we're going to stay free, we have to think clearly and state precisely what the options are from which we have to choose. When we prefer our leaders to comfort us with the rhetoric of reassurance, we're falling victim to the most dangerous of all flattery. When language goes, other things follow quickly. Do you think that's true historically?

COMMAGER: Yes, to a large degree. As I mentioned, Lincoln was very careful about the language he chose, so that he could give pardons after the Civil War. But now there's not the respect for language that there was in the eighteenth or nineteenth century. That's probably inevitable in a democracy where you have universal public education. Of course, we're not alone in failing to use language with care. Think what Hitler did with his language. Think what Stalin did with his language. Tyrants will always resort to language that will support their programs, language designed to inflame the spirits rather than to excite the reason of the people.

MOYERS: The men of the founding era were so precise in their choice of language.

COMMAGER: They were indeed. Not just in public documents but even in their correspondence, they used words with such nice care, such nice distinction. On the whole, the one branch of government that has taken care with the language is the judiciary. It is the one branch of our government which has never come under real disrepute. We have the most distinguished judiciary of any nation in history, and this judiciary has been the great teacher. The Supreme Court, above all, with its four hundred and fifty volumes of reports—well, reading majority and minority opinions with their careful distinctions is one of the exercises that I think all young people should be exposed to.

MOYERS: But there is that gap in the court's interpretation when it came to slavery, that long silence, that great evasion.

COMMAGER: And later the evasion of the obvious meaning of the Fourteenth and Fifteenth Amendments by the courts. After all, as late as 1896, the Court was evading the issue of what equal protection really meant. Only now is it coming around to it. But it is coming around to it.

Both wings of the Court are equally avid for exactitude, for avoiding confusion and distinguishing very nicely and neatly, so far as they can, the meaning of the Constitution and of the laws that come up.

MOYERS: That seems to me a reason to avoid ideology when it comes to putting men and women on the Court. Ideology takes a word and gives the meaning peculiar to the ideologue.

COMMAGER: Yes. Ideology, of course, is what we accuse our opponents of. We are not ideologues, but the other side is—the real ideologies are the Reagan ideologies, not the liberal ideologies. Wasn't it Mr. Bush who attacked Mr. Dukakis as being a liberal? But "liberal" means freedom. We've forgotten, because we don't study languages, that *liber* means "free." Liberalism is the philosophy of a free man, the philosophy which seeks out the truth among free men. I've often wondered why so many conservatives who denounce liberalism nevertheless send their sons and daughters to liberal arts colleges.

MOYERS: Well, many of them do so to their undying regret. The liberal mind, once open, must then follow the scientific method of trial and error to arrive at its ultimate conclusion.

COMMAGER: Must indeed. That is the pragmatic view of history, the pragmatic view of law and so forth. Just as the scientist has his cases in the laboratory, so the lawyer and the politician have their cases in the courts and in the realm of politics. We must learn by those examples as the biologists and the zoologists learn by their examples in the laboratory.

MOYERS: But what happens to language in an era of the visual image? Oliver North said recently that we live in a world of perceptions, not realities. What happens to language in that kind of world?

COMMAGER: I'd say television is what's happened to language. Television has very little respect for language. In a very wicked way, it exploits the public by its gross oversimplification of everything and by, above all, the use of adjectives for everything. It exploits little children by training them to jump up and down with ecstasy when they get a certain kind of breakfast cereal or a certain kind of candy or a certain kind of toy. Children, who don't know what they're doing, are exploited, and their language is exploited, insofar as they have one. I think television has had a very bad effect on language.

MOYERS: In 1960 you were quite critical of the Kennedy-Nixon debates on television because you said they would render considered debate obsolete. Do you think that's happened?

COMMAGER: Yes. We've had no debate so far in this campaign. Everybody's avoiding issues.

MOYERS: What about the corruption of idealism? It seems to me that the true crime of the Iran-Contra scandal was the corruption of idealism, that revolutionary zeal that you've written about from time to time.

COMMAGER: There was idealism, of course, in preserving democracy in Central America. This notion of idealism was emphasized greatly in the Vietnam War, which is much more of an object for contemplation and interpretation than the Caribbean wars. Idealism was always invoked, but there wasn't any at all. We've never made any gesture of idealism toward Vietnam. We've paid no compensation. We've never really apologized for Operation Phoenix, in which some twenty-five thousand people were locked up in cages and allowed to die. No one remembers the My Lai massacre. When we shot down the Iranian passenger plane, Mr. Bush said, "Americans don't kill civilians." And I thought to myself, "Mr. Bush, have you ever heard of the My Lai massacre in which five hundred old men, women, children, and babies were all systematically murdered?"

MOYERS: But it isn't that America is less iniquitous than other nations, it's just that our writers and our artists have expected better of us.

COMMAGER: That's right. And if we go back to our earlier history, they had a right to expect better.

MOYERS: Not if you look at what our ancestors did to the Indians and to the slaves. America has lived in the real world of human depravity and at the same time has expected more of itself.

COMMAGER: The depravity got there before there was a United States. It got there in 1619 with the first boatload of Negroes brought by the Dutch, and it was so established by 1789 that it was very hard to get rid of it. But how fascinating that one man, Judge Cushing of the Superior Court of Massachusetts, in the case of a slave suing for his freedom, got rid of slavery in Massachusetts. He said, "The Constitution of Massachusetts says that all men are born free and equal, and that means there cannot be slavery in the state." And that was the end of it. So it started, again, with the judiciary insisting on the sincerity of the words that were used by Constitution writers. It was John Adams who wrote the Constitution of Massachusetts in 1783.

MOYERS: The philosopher George Santayana said that Americans never solve any of their problems, they just amiably—

COMMAGER: —bid them goodbye. Yes.

MOYERS: Can we keep on doing that with issues like the environment, poverty, and crime?

COMMAGER: We seem to. We seem to think there's always some magic formula that can be achieved by voting some money. But we can't solve our problems of crime or education or environment that way. We have to solve them by laws and by a fundamental change in philosophy. There are eighteen hundred murders a year in New York City, year after year—that's about a hundred times what it is in Sweden, which has the same population as New York City. The Swedes in Sweden don't commit murder. The French, the Germans, the English in their countries don't commit murders. Why do people in this country commit murder? What is there in the American economy or in the American philosophy that takes crime so casually or thinks it can be solved by building more prisons?

MOYERS: What's the answer to that question?

COMMAGER: We've been trying to find out an answer. Tocqueville came over here in 1831 to study American penitentiaries, which were the best and best run in the world. Now people come over here to study our prisons as awful examples. You go to Sweden or to Britain for model penal systems. I suppose the passion for getting ahead and being a success, which requires money, has a great deal to do with our high crime rate. People tend more and more to be willing to take great risks, as we see even among stockbrokers and those who have fiduciary responsibility. They are prepared to take risks in order to satisfy the standards of society, which are the standards of wealth. From the beginning of our history, we've been rather casual about crimes. Just as we're casual about observing speed limits today, we were casual about recognizing the validity of land grants and land titles of one kind or another. We've been casual about a great many things that Europe cannot afford to be casual about since it's too closely knit.

> *From the beginning of our history, we've been rather casual about crimes.*

MOYERS: You said we need a change in our philosophy.

COMMAGER: Yes. For example, we need a change in our penal system. The notion that you can stop crime by just getting tougher on the criminals, that the more criminals you send to jail, the more law-observing citizens you'll have, just isn't true. It doesn't work out that way. Consider capital punishment. Capital punishment doesn't stop crime. The states that have capital punishment have the same rate of homicide as the states that don't have capital punishment—in some cases, a higher rate of homicide.

We've got to find some other way of dealing with crime, which means you've got to find what causes the crime. Why do Europeans, who are law-abiding in Europe, become criminals in the United States? This concerned Tocqueville, even though there wasn't the widespread crime in Tocqueville's day that there is today.

MOYERS: How much of our current situation can be attributed to the fact that we seem to expect less of our leadership today than we did in the founding era? You said the Founding Fathers had an idea of honor.

COMMAGER: Yes. Our leadership today is business leadership. It's financial leadership, not political leadership. Our best people don't go into politics. It's too expensive, for one thing—and we tolerate that. There's no reason why we should tolerate these vast expenses for elections. No one tolerates it in European countries.

You can't spend any money in England on an election. You can't even take a friend to lunch during the election period, which is three weeks, or you'll be disqualified. But Americans think nothing of spending fifty to a hundred million dollars on an election—and therefore buying them.

MOYERS: Much of it goes to television to buy airtime and pay people who create commercials.

COMMAGER: We could get rid of commercials. They've probably done more harm than good. They've inspired greed and jealousy and ambition on the part of a great many people, and children are told to want everything, so they grow up wanting things. We're told all day long on commercials to want something, whether it's a cosmetic, a tennis racket, a new automobile, or a vacation in Florida.

MOYERS: Do you think this has an impact on our political order?

COMMAGER: Not so much on our political order as on our social order and on the questions of crime, dishonesty, and the class system. Those who don't have money and can't afford all this are, in effect, excluded from our society. They don't count.

MOYERS: Are we creating a class society?

COMMAGER: We are indeed, for the first time in our history. Of course, the blacks are emerging from a class society, but a new class society is forming, which is a very dangerous one because it is based almost exclusively on poverty. The situation is illuminated by the curious distinction we make in our unemployment statistics. Government now boasts that unemployment is down to five percent—that's the lowest for many years. But that figure is achieved by ignoring all those who are so desperate that they've given up looking for any employment. Our unemployment rate is probably ten percent, if our statistics were honest. But that kind of dishonesty is accepted by the government because it lets government off the hook and gives us a pretty picture.

MOYERS: What does history have to say about a society that accepts this fundamental division in classes?

COMMAGER: I don't know whether we can gain a great deal from looking at the history of other countries in other times. We can look at our own history, however. In the early years of our nation our history was one of decency and honor and propriety. Hardly anybody cheated anybody. There were very few cases of impeachments for real crimes of any kind. Men took for granted that serving their country was enough of a reward. Jefferson was a bankrupt. His house, Monticello, was sold over his head before he died. Washington came back from the presidency practically bankrupt. John Adams had to go back and get in the hay, as it were, to keep his farm going. People didn't expect to make a lot of money in politics. Now they do, and they're willing to spend a hundred or two hundred or a million dollars to get there.

MOYERS: The fundamental insult of a class society in America is that it defiles the dream. The dream has always been—

COMMAGER: —equality.

MOYERS: "If I can't have a better life, my children will have a better life."

COMMAGER: This was the great thesis. For the early Fathers, "equality" was a great word. Tocqueville's book about democracy in America really was about equality in America. We were the only country in the world that had equality. He thought

France would have it in time. But he also saw the danger in the manufacturing aristocracy—which was his phrase for a wealthy upper class that made a great deal of money. He said that if the manufacturing aristocracy ever gets control, democracy may be the most tyrannical form of government ever known by man. He'd seen this in Engand and was afraid of it, and he thought it might destroy American democracy.

MOYERS: But capitalism here has driven the economy that has enabled the boats to rise.

COMMAGER: Yes, it worked when we had enough land for the thousandth and thousandth generation. It worked when everybody had an opportunity. But it doesn't seem to be working now.

MOYERS: Not for the underclass.

COMMAGER: It can. It worked under FDR. But nothing's happened much since FDR. And the recent administrations have not taken on that responsibility. It's interesting that no one has proposed the revival of the Civilian Conservation Corps to save the environment and to give jobs to young men and women.

MOYERS: But we had the Job Corps in the sixties and seventies. Some of these problems seem intransigent. American society may have bumped up against intransigent problems for the first time. It took a long time to get rid of slavery, but finally we did. It took a long time to bring the majority of people into the class of "haves."

COMMAGER: Yes. And it's taking a long time to give complete equality to women and to blacks. We haven't gotten there yet.

MOYERS: America is not as generous a society as we like to tell ourselves. The generosity comes only under tremendous demand on the part of the disaffected group. You have to fight for liberty and equality in this country. It doesn't come naturally.

COMMAGER: As the British had to. But when the British fought for it, or the Scandinavians, they really got rid of all the excess baggage of the nineteenth century. There is still a class system, but it's meaningless in England. And there's a class system, after a fashion, in Scandinavia. But nobody's poor.

MOYERS: They have a welfare state much different from ours.

COMMAGER: We don't extend a helping hand to what we consider the negligible parts of our society. In Sweden, every pregnant woman gets complete care during the whole of pregnancy. If she is a working woman, she gets seven months' paid vacation so she'll be with the baby. And of course, all medical expenses are taken care of.
But in this country, infant mortality for babies born to black mothers under twenty is twenty percent. Among white mothers, it's nine or ten percent.

MOYERS: Why the paradox, then, in a society whose founding document says, "All men—

COMMAGER: —are created equal." Jefferson was a scientist. What he meant was, of course, accurate. In the moment of creation, all men are, in fact, ninety-nine-point-ninety-nine percent equal—the same eyes, the same ears, the same lungs, the same everything. Most inequalities are imposed by society. As far as creation goes or God goes, all men are equal. Our society was created to enable them to be more equal than in the Old World—but not any more.
Why have we abandoned the zeal for equality? That was our special intention and our special contribution. That is what attracted the attention of every philosopher in

the Western world. Why have the European countries and many other countries outpaced us?

MOYERS: One argument is that, deep down, Americans are too individualistic to want to consider themselves equal to someone else.

COMMAGER: Yes. Tocqueville thought individualism was a great danger to the United States. He used "individualism" as a pejorative term. It was originally a pejorative term in French, when we took it over. It meant that you put your selfish interests ahead of the interests of your society. There was very little individualism in the eighteenth century or in much of the nineteenth century, because everybody depended on everybody else. If you were going out to Iowa, you had to work with your neighbors, or you wouldn't get your fences built, and you wouldn't get your land plowed. You wouldn't get the local school built—and you wouldn't get anything.

MOYERS: Do you think America is a better country today than it was when you were born in 1902?

COMMAGER: You can't generalize. It's better for blacks. It's better for Orientals. After all, think what we did to the Chinese working on the railroads out in the West. It's probably better for children. Child labor is disallowed. It took until 1938 to get rid of child labor. Imagine, that late. But at least we got rid of it.

So, in many fundamental respects, it's much better. But, shall I say, philosophically—or that's such a big word, maybe just socially—in ordinary life, I don't think it is better. There's more crime, more dishonesty, greater inequality. There's a greater readiness to go to war, and a greater acceptance of the military as having the proper priority over civilian interests. We can always find money for anything the military wants, even if there's no money for schools or no money for nursing.

MOYERS: On that point I might challenge you because when you were born in 1902, we had just completed a bloody conquest and occupation of the Philippines—

COMMAGER: And we were so ashamed of it.

MOYERS: Well, some were.

COMMAGER: A great many Americans were.

MOYERS: Earlier in this century, the Marines were occupying Central America, often in behalf of corporate interests.

COMMAGER: Go back a little further! Yes, we got rid of slavery, and we're gradually achieving political and social equality. But our problem is an economic problem, the problem of gross economic inequalities, of desperate poverty side by side with almost outrageous wealth. No other country has this. Nobody is outrageously rich in Britain or Scandinavia or Germany. It's taxed away. There's enough to live comfortably. But as far as I know, the gap between the poor and the rich is far greater here than anywhere else in the civilized world.

MOYERS: Thirty years ago I was a senior at the University of Texas, and my history professor, Dr. Cotner, asked us to read *The American Mind* by Henry Steele Commager—a book you wrote in the early forties. You summed up American civilization at the mid-part of the twentieth century with this sentence: "The shift in the material circumstances of the American people from the 1890s to the mid-twentieth century was all but convulsive. Yet it is by no means clear that this material change precipitated or even embraced a comparable change in the intellectual outlook or in the national character." Forty years ago, in this book, you asked some questions.

I'd like to see if you've had any second thoughts about these questions. You said, "Americans were wonderfully inventive in the physical and technological realm. Would they prove equally resourceful in the realms of social institutions and of morals?"

COMMAGER: I think that was inspired by a very obvious fact of our history, that in the eighteenth century we were incomparably the most inventive people in the world in the realm of politics and society. We invented practically every major political institution which we have, and we have invented none since. We invented the political party and democracy and representative government. We invented the first independent judiciary in history. Montesquieu says in *The Spirit of the Laws*, that judicial power is negligible in England. Ours took a stand at once in relation to the other two branches. We invented judicial review. We invented the superiority of the civil over the military power. We invented freedom of religion, freedom of speech, the Bill of Rights—well, we could go on and on.

MOYERS: Quite a heritage.

COMMAGER: Yes, quite a heritage. But what have we invented since of comparable importance?

MOYERS: You said forty years ago that American society had changed from rural to urban. "Would they learn to master the city as their forefathers had mastered the country?"

COMMAGER: They obviously haven't. We haven't even mastered the city as well as European countries have. Practically all large European cities today build their skyscrapers on the outskirts of the city, not in the interior of the city. But we clutter ours up and create an architecture, as Louis Mumford said, for aviators and angels. We haven't managed the cities, and we can't govern them any more. They're out of hand.

MOYERS: You asked, "What would be the final product of the interracial melting pot? Fifteen million Negroes confronted one hundred and thirty million whites. Would racial conflicts continue to frustrate democracy? Or would Americans find a solution to the racial problem through ultimate amalgamation or through the establishment of such economic and social security as would permit a useful tolerance?"

COMMAGER: Now, of course, you would add the Oriental immigration and the Hispanic immigration. These things have in many ways eased and simplified the racial problem. The four different groups—the whites, the blacks, the Orientals, and the Hispanics—have had to be dealt with on an equal basis. And while we haven't come to equality yet, economically and socially, we have come to it legally and politically. That's a great stride. The blacks and the Hispanics have in their hands the control of their own future to a large degree.

Now we still haven't given equality to women as fully as European nations have. We haven't gone backward, but we haven't made the progress that we might have expected.

MOYERS: You said, "Americans were using up their natural resources more rapidly than they were replacing them. Would science reverse the process, or would Americans be forced to a lower standard of living, or to economic imperialism?"

COMMAGER: I think the second of those alternatives is the one we now face very clearly. We're even cutting down our forests and destroying them. We want to go into the Alaska area and use it for getting more gallons of oil rather than preserving the environment. The struggle for the environment really began in the 1880s and '90s.

We have made enormous strides, but not nearly as many strides as the struggle for the environment of Western Europe.

MOYERS: This summer the planet struck back. It began to send us some very ominous messages.

COMMAGER: Very ominous, yes. And Europeans know all of this because they're older. For example, you can't cut down a tree in England or Germany or Denmark without permission from the government.

MOYERS: You said, "Their society had been almost wholly classless. Would inequalities of wealth create and divide classes?"

COMMAGER: They have divided classes. In the past, Americans avoided the impact of classes by being a land of opportunity. You could work your way out of a lower class. Your children could make good. Mr. Carnegie's little son Andy could make good.

But nowadays it's very hard to make good. You have to go to college and university and law school and medical school and all the other things, at enormous cost, and circumstances are making classes rigid once more, rather than looser, as in the past. The new classes will be largely Hispanics and blacks and Asians.

MOYERS: You wrote, "In a general way it could be said that the two generations after 1890 witnessed a transition from certainty to uncertainty, from faith to doubt, from security to insecurity, from seeming order to ostentatious disorder. By the 1950s Americans had all but banished God from their affairs. Who or what would they put in His place?"

COMMAGER: The last phrase needs lots more elaboration and perhaps modification. Heaven knows God hasn't been banished. He's been welcomed into politics—although He was not degraded by being left out of politics earlier. Now religion is allowed to meddle in politics in a way it never did in the past, except sporadically. Introducing divisions based on religious commitments of one kind or another is one of the most dangerous of all threats to a society. So far we've avoided any serious crisis, just as we somehow managed to avoid a real crisis over the Mormons earlier in our history. But the potential is there in the evangelicals, or in what Mencken called "the total immersion belt." What is dangerous is not religion itself, but religious animosities, and religious attempts to take over the schools and medical ethics, and things of that kind.

MOYERS: But weren't most of the schools Christian?

COMMAGER: Yes, most of them were. They took for granted that Christianity would get into their *McGuffey Readers* and didn't make any fuss about it.

MOYERS: Some people say that because Christianity has been removed from the *McGuffey Reader*—because there is no longer a *McGuffey Reader*!—Americans have indeed, as you said in this book, "relaxed their moral standards and habits. Would Americans preserve themselves from corruption and decadence?"

COMMAGER: I'm not sure we've relaxed our moral standards. However, we've relaxed our moral conduct very seriously.

MOYERS: You said, "The emancipation of women, birth control, labor-saving devices, prosperity, and education should have made for a happier and healthy family life. But one marriage out of four"—I now think it's one marriage out of two—"ended in divorce, and nervous breakdowns became so common as to be almost unfashionable."

COMMAGER: Yes. That is still true. But our government has not acted as governments in northern Europe, especially Scandinavia, have acted to take care of children. The children do not present problems for working parents in these nations as they do in the United States. The flats where people live have nurseries in them with paid nurses to take care of children. There's no reason we shouldn't do that in our country. But we don't get around to these things, and the result is bad both for marriage and for childhood.

MOYERS: You gave us a mixed report card forty years ago. Would you give us a mixed report card today?

COMMAGER: I think I would give a less optimistic report card today, especially because of the militarism. We're seeking wars all over the globe and thinking it's our God-appointed duty to straighten out Vietnam and straighten out Lebanon and straighten out Angola, and so forth and so forth. We never had this particular form of insanity before.

MOYERS: One could say we never had a global rival the equal of the Soviet Union before.

COMMAGER: We created the rivalry. We're the ones who created it, not the Soviet Union. They had no designs on us. The poor devils lost twenty-five million people in the war, and what they needed was peace to rebuild. We're the ones that created the whole psychosis of the Bolshevik menace. We created it partly out of religious fear and partly out of economic selfishness and ambitions. It's been very good for the arms manufacturers.

MOYERS: You quote that famous statement by Ralph Waldo Emerson in 1847: "If there is one test of national genius universally accepted, it is success." Have we really changed?

COMMAGER: I don't think we're the successful nation to which the rest of the world looks today. Japan is successful, Scandinavia is successful, smaller countries are the successful nations. We're successful if you mean by success that we have more weapons than other countries, or more money. But I question the appropriateness of that term "success."

MOYERS: If what you say is true, then the rest of the world doesn't look to us the way it did when Longfellow wrote these lines, which you quote:

Humanity with all its fears
With all its hopes of future years
Is hanging breathless on thy fate.

COMMAGER: Yes.

MOYERS: You don't think that's true?

COMMAGER: Not any longer. They've taken charge of their own affairs and developed their own societies.

MOYERS: Maybe it's good that we don't have that burden.

COMMAGER: We have lost that inventiveness, that resourcefulness we had beyond any other people in the beginning of our history. Every major political institution we have was invented before the year 1800.

MOYERS: Are we finished as a pioneering country?

COMMAGER: Oh no, countries don't get finished. Greece isn't finished. It's still there, but it isn't fifth-century B.C. Greece. Italy isn't Leonardo's Italy, or Titian's. They're not finished, they go right on. And we're not finished. We'll have a revival one of these years, one of these centuries—not in my day, but maybe in your son's day, or your grandchildren's day.

MOYERS: So one doesn't give up on this country.

COMMAGER: How can you give up? The phrase is misleading. The fact that you're critical of it or fearful of it doesn't mean you stop voting or being engaged in what we're engaged in right now.

MOYERS: Or don't love it.

COMMAGER: Well, of course. You take that for granted. You love children, even if they are erring children. Of course you love it. What else have you got? But we're going through a bad period. Maybe we're going through our adolescence.

MOYERS: We are a young country.

COMMAGER: As countries go, we are.

MOYERS: You once quoted a poem by Stephen Vincent Benét in which he talks about liberty and equality:

> They were bought with belief and passion, at great cost.
> They were bought with the bitter and anonymous blood
> Of farmers, teachers, shoemakers and fools
> Who broke the old rule, and the pride of kings . . .
>
> It took a long time to buy these words
> It took a long time to buy them, and much pain.

COMMAGER: Yes, and maybe much forgetfulness. Who knows? All the furor over teaching—the one thing they don't teach are these words. They teach other words. They boast about America rather than contribute to what our forebears did.

MOYERS: And Benét asks, "What if these words pass?" What if they pass and are blotted out of the world?

COMMAGER: They cannot now be blotted out of the world.

Sissela Bok

ETHICIST

As a philosopher, Sissela Bok grapples with hard truths—and with hard untruths, as well. Her writings explore the psychology of lying, the consequences of deception, and the perils of keeping secrets. With advanced degrees in both psychology and philosophy, she has taught ethics at Harvard's Medical School and the Kennedy School of Government. She now teaches philosophy at Brandeis University. Her books include Lying: Moral Choice in Public and Private Life *and, most recently,* A Strategy for Peace.

MOYERS: Your writings explore the psychology of lying, the consequences of deception, and the perils of keeping secrets. Why do these subjects interest you?

BOK: The subject of lying connects for me with all of communication and with the amazing fact that we human beings quite often do communicate with one another rather well. But lying is a way of gaining power over other people through manipulating them in various ways. This is something that children learn. They also learn to keep secrets. Sometimes secrets are deceptive, and sometimes they are not. If we are to mature, we have to unlearn any enjoyment of that power.

MOYERS: —Any enjoyment of deception and the power that deception allows you to have over someone else? Why do you have to unlearn that?

BOK: You have to know that the power is there, and then you have to see if you can possibly live without it. That doesn't mean you never get into a situation where lying might be necessary, but on the whole, you try to lead your life so that you communicate with other people without trying to manipulate them.

MOYERS: When I was White House press secretary, I thought often of the line, "I am not a professional liar, and I'm surprised at the extent to which in my infirmity I'm an amateur one." I kept being surprised at the extent to which I could be an amateur liar. But you're right. It's a question of having to unlearn that it was okay to deceive, okay to dissemble, to evade.

BOK: Yes, especially because lying can happen so easily. Sometimes people just slip into it without even stopping to think. That's another thing I wanted to do with both books: to see if people who read the books might say, "All right, I am going to stop to think: Why am I doing this now? Do I really need to do this now? Are there other ways, perhaps, of communicating with people, of achieving my goals without going this way?"

MOYERS: Do you find people actually going through that process of thinking?

BOK: Yes, I do, quite a lot. Sometimes, for instance, people go through that process who have had problems with addiction, where lying and secrecy are very much part of keeping up a mask. And we face these questions when we are involved in some professional undertaking, or in government, or in sales, or sometimes as parents, or with friends. People tell me, "You know, I am trying to change, and I am realizing that in fact it's more possible than I thought." And then some of them say, "I also find that now I respect myself a little more because I know that other people can trust me, which I was pretty sure they couldn't do before."

MOYERS: Someone said to me recently that he thought all of American life was built upon deception. Given the pervasive influence of advertising, which is usually deceiving; given what's happened to political rhetoric; given the ambitions of each interest group to advance its interests, and each individual to advance his or her interests at the expense of someone else, deception has now become the household furniture of American life. Do you think that's a fair assessment?

BOK: No, I don't think so. If that were true, then I don't think our society could function at all, and after all, it does function reasonably well much of the time. I don't think that human relationships could function if everything were deceptive. Very often, in fact, advertising is not deceptive. You know, there is much factual, informative advertising. We learn to look at certain activities like advertising in a very different way and to listen to what it says in a very different way, so that we develop certain kinds of protections.

In politics and business, there are quite a few honorable, upright individuals around. The sad thing is that whenever somebody comes into the news who has done a lot of deceiving, then it casts suspicion on all the others. You hear that quite a lot from the people who tell you why they're not going to vote. They simply have no confidence any more in public officials. That is terribly wrongheaded, because most public officials are trustworthy. But when somebody comes to public light who is not, that sets an example. Somebody said that examples of this kind are very contagious—and I think that's true.

MOYERS: There is a general lament in the country that we're slipping, that our ethics are going downhill, that this generation isn't as good as the previous generation, that moral standards are deteriorating—well, you mention this in your book when you quote somebody else saying that civilization is on the decline. What's your own appraisal?

BOK: First of all, that's something people have said since the beginning of time, and it seems to happen particularly when they reach middle age. All of a sudden they begin to think that when they were children, everything was much better, or maybe they look back one hundred or two hundred years and say, "When our country was young, everything was so much better." But then when you ask them, "When was this golden age? Was it, for instance, in this country during our period of slavery? Was that so great? Was it so wonderful for women? Who, exactly, was benefiting from these high moral standards?"—then they became more hesitant. I don't think we can show that as a general rule, everything is slipping. Certainly, there are problems that are getting worse—for instance, drug addiction. That's obvious. One hundred years ago, that wasn't the same at all.

MOYERS: But alcoholism was rampant in colonial days.

BOK: Yes, so that I'm not sure we can say that things are getting so much worse.

On the other hand, I would say that we face more difficult problems than any society ever has, if we take society to mean our world at the present time. We are threatened with extinction, either from nuclear weapons or from environmental problems. Nobody else has ever been threatened in that way. Past generations failed to see these problems coming up. We somehow have to do better. So it's not a question of whether we're getting so much worse. I think we could cope if we tried; but the question is whether we're going to try.

MOYERS: So there's not statistical evidence that would suggest we are worse or better in terms of morals, manners, or ethics?

BOK: I don't think I've seen any evidence of a general kind, although certainly, there are groups, communities, even nations, which have deteriorated in that way, and others that have improved. For instance, in Lebanon conditions are much worse than they were fifty years ago, and that's a disaster for the entire society.

MOYERS: The social fabric is gone.

BOK: Yes, and then the country cannot accomplish anything in foreign or domestic affairs. I would say, in the same way, that South Africa, which could otherwise be contributing so much with respect to the environment, to questions of war and peace, is hamstrung because of its brutal apartheid policy.

MOYERS: You suggested in *Lying*, that there was a crisis of trust based upon a proliferation of lies—personal lies, professional lies, political lies. You said then that the social environment is every bit as precarious and threatened as the natural environment. Ten years have passed since you wrote this. What's your assessment today?

> *The social environment is just as important as the natural environment.*

BOK: The social environment is just as important as the natural environment because that's the environment in which we make all the decisions we want to make, in which we communicate, and in which our families and societies exist. It requires a certain amount of trust and, I would say, also, cautious distrust. We obviously have to be careful with respect to potential enemies, for instance.

MOYERS: Skepticism is a form of democratic virtue?

BOK: Yes, I think skepticism is very important. On the other hand, if skepticism veers off into total distrust, so that one decides to have nothing to do with voting or with one's government, then that's very destructive.

MOYERS: People feel cheated by the political rhetoric they hear on television. They feel insulted by the level of discussion that emerges in sound bites and advertising.

BOK: They do. Of course, one also has to say that they don't always make the effort to read the speeches but just sit there and judge the sound bites. If they read the longer speeches that the campaigns produce, they might take a greater interest.

MOYERS: If I were a politician, I'd want to rescue my rhetoric from television. I'd want to find some way to overcome the terrible simplifiers that television makes of all of us.

BOK: I can well see that it would be discouraging for someone in politics to see what happens. Sometimes you make a very good speech that doesn't get on television at all.

MOYERS: Can a republic die of too many lies?

BOK: I think a republic definitely could—especially if the lies are also covered up by various methods of secrecy. If you combine lying and secrecy, and if you also bring in violence so that secrecy covers up for schemes of lying and violence, then I think a republic can die. I don't think it's possible for citizens to have very much of an effect if they literally don't know what's going on.

MOYERS: That's an intriguing point to me, because so many people seem not to grasp the harm of public lies. They don't see that they themselves are the victims of the lying. How do you convince people that lying does undermine a democracy, that we have a stake in the honesty and integrity of government?

BOK: Sometimes you can try to convince them by telling a story. One story that struck me this summer was told by a university president from the Middle West, who was talking about how he was teaching a Sunday school class for adults. In that class there were bankers, business executives, and university professors. This was in the fall of '87, when the Iran-Contra scandal was still unfolding. He posed the following question to his class: "We hear on the news that in the Persian Gulf an Iranian ship has sunk. The Iranian Government explains that this was done by American torpedoes. The United States Government says that the ship hit one of the Iranian mines, or perhaps several. Whom do you believe?" And all of these people, some quite conservative, some less so, thought and thought and thought. And finally, not a single one could answer one way or another. They all said that they wanted to hear more of the facts.

Now, what that means is that not a single one of those people trusted his own government to tell the truth. People in government sometimes think that this little lie and that little lie, told for short-term advantages, will just pass. But this is the kind of damage that is done in the long run.

MOYERS: Excessive secrecy denies people the right to an informed vote. How do we know how to cast our vote if we don't really know what our government has been doing?

BOK: That's right. All one has to do is to look at some very secretive governments—totalitarian governments and others. Nobody knows what's a lie and what's the truth. We certainly don't want to go in that direction. On the other hand, sometimes people in government say, "Well, those totalitarian governments have it rather well, you know. They can really control information. We have to struggle with the media and everything else."

MOYERS: I can tell you from my own experience that there were times when both John Kennedy and Lyndon Johnson wished they had the control over the press that the Kremlin or Mao had. They'd never have to worry about Walter Lippmann or Scotty Reston. They could just do what they wanted, and the results would prove them right—or wrong.

BOK: But then, of course, if you asked them, "Would you really want that? Are you serious about this?" they would probably pull back—or would they?

MOYERS: Well, every President at heart is given to the democratic impulse and understands the strengths of this country. But he is also trying to make things happen, to get policy enacted, to accomplish his goals, and he is sometimes frustrated to the point of paranoia about the opposition.

We've gone through the credibility gap of Vietnam, Watergate, and the Iran-Contra scandal. How would you take our pulse as a political body?

BOK: When I wrote my books, *Lying* and *Secrets*, I could certainly not have foreseen that so many and such far-reaching examples of lying and secrecy would come to light as those in the Iran-Contra scandal. What facilitated the spread of the schemes of bribery, money laundering, arms smuggling, and falsification of documents was the growth of methods of secrecy in our government. When *Secrets* came out in '83, I had a feeling that the growth of secrecy was itself shrouded in silence. People did not care at the time that we were witnessing inroads on the Freedom of Information Act, that there were beginnings of new kinds of censorship, that it was increasingly difficult for people to travel into this country if they had unpopular political opinions, and that many other efforts were under way to establish greater government control over secrecy. Many came to care afterward, especially when there was a real effort to impose secrecy through prepublication review over large numbers of government officials. There is a great deal of concern now in the press and in Congress; but whether the American public realizes the relationship between secrecy, the deceit that it makes possible, the arms transfers, and the violence that it can cover up, I'm not sure.

MOYERS: I don't see evidence of great concern out there. In many respects, it appears to me that the Iran-Contra scandal has dropped into a black hole of public indifference.

> *. . . these issues of lying and secrecy have to do with the essence of democracy. . . .*

BOK: I'm very interested to hear you say that, because certainly the people I talk to still seem to be quite concerned, and members of the press and of Congress do care. We have books coming out about it. I would hope very much that the country at large would also care, because these issues of lying and secrecy have to do with the essence of democracy and of this republic in particular.

MOYERS: What's happening in our government that has given us the deception of Watergate, the deception of the Iran-Contra scandal?

BOK: There is to some extent a desire on the part of every government to have greater control over information. Many members of government feel that with secrecy, they can get more things done. If only they didn't have to worry about what was lawful, if only they didn't have to worry about elected representatives of the people, they could get a lot more done.

So there's always that. But in this country there have also always been limits to secrecy imposed from the outside. Danger would definitely come if, for instance, the government succeeded in permanently cutting back on the Freedom of Information Act.

MOYERS: Now private citizens can sue the government, if necessary, to get information from within the government out of the hands of the bureaucracy.

BOK: The Freedom of Information Act provided that all information should be free with certain exceptions, such as those having to do with national security and personnel documents. The burden of proof is then on the government to show why something should remain secret. That's the way it's been.

MOYERS: But this Administration has tried very hard to limit the Freedom of Information—

BOK: —Yes, exactly, to make it very much more difficult for people to acquire the information. It takes longer and you can get less information. So restricting freedom of information is one method to try to expand secrecy.

Then there is the emphasis on trying to get lie detector tests to be performed on public officials as a deterrent to leaks and whistle blowing. That's another way. There are various avenues, and a government intent on trying all the avenues will often succeed to some extent, especially when people are not looking out for the danger to the country.

MOYERS: It has not escaped me as a journalist that it was not the American press that broke the story of Iran-Contra, but a small, obscure newspaper in Beirut, Lebanon. We're not as vigilant as the circumstances require.

BOK: Members of the press no longer seem to be doing the kind of digging that would be necessary to find out the information. If they simply wait for press releases, it's not clear that they're always to get what they want.

MOYERS: Well, they're certainly not going to get a press release saying that we've agreed to sell arms to Iran in release for the hostages or that we are diverting those funds to the Contras in Nicaragua.

BOK: On the other hand, we do have the countervailing influence that it's getting harder and harder to keep these secrets for very long. You can keep the secrets long enough to do a terrible amount of harm to your nation, but in the long run they will surface. The Iran-Iraq War involved a number of governments in arms trades and other activities that were secret but that have since come to light. With the world press and the kind of information that now travels across all boundaries, it's going to be harder to keep that kind of secret for very long.

MOYERS: And yet there is still so much that never gets out. The public still doesn't fully know what happened in the Gulf of Tonkin in 1964 or what the Navy was doing there. So much that happens never gets known.

BOK: Well, we can't have adequate research about how much never gets known because by definition that's hidden from us. But in the long run, a great deal will surface. And the wise thing for public officials to do is to ask themselves, "What's going to happen if this particular action surfaces? How can I be so sure I've really managed to clamp down on this?" I'm convinced that in the Iran-Contra affair, for instance, if some of the people who were making the decisions had asked that question, they would have said, "Well, you know, for the short-term benefit that we're seeking here, it's not clear that we want to risk the reputation of our government or our country." They didn't stop to think that, in part, because of the atmosphere of secrecy, which lures people into the belief that the secret will be kept for a long time.

MOYERS: The great advantage of opening the debate within the Administration to more and more people is that you get more and more minds that say, "Well, just a minute. Here's the trap in that."

BOK: Yes, you always need to have critics within the government who are ready to stand up and ask those questions. But as within any team or organization, it's very easy to exclude the critic, to try to push that person out, to get that person to leave.

MOYERS: What does it say to you that Oliver North, a man who admitted deceiving Congress, lying to the press, and lying to the public, became a hero to many people, including a national hero to his own President?

BOK: I was thinking about that quite a lot, because I wondered why people seemed to be identifying with him, and not with the people who had been deceived. Now, usually when we get worried about a lie, we worry because we think, "How would it feel for me to be in this situation—for instance, to be the patient who has been deceived about cancer, or a spouse who has been deceived about fidelity?" Why did so many people identify with North? Maybe they didn't care if he lied to foreigners, particularly to the Iranians. Or maybe they didn't care if he lied to members of Congress, because Congress has been on the receiving end of a lot of criticism these last few years. But still, the curious thing was that so many people identified with the person who was telling the lie. That meant they were not asking the question, what happens to the people being lied to? What happens to the country? What happens if more lies are told—perhaps to us, next time? They simply didn't stop to ask those questions, at least not for a while.

MOYERS: I was encouraged that after the initial flush of television coverage, and the profile of patriotism that Oliver North presented on the tube, there was a second thought. The American people issued a second opinion.

BOK: Yes, some of them began to think that patriotism has very much to do with respecting the integrity of the government itself. That's something that all public servants have to take very seriously.

MOYERS: You said, "some of them." But it's been quite intriguing to me that Colonel North is out raising money and making speeches as a hero to right-wing groups. They still look upon him as a true patriot, irrespective of the deception, the lies, the cover-up.

BOK: To some extent these groups are not entering into debate with other people about what patriotism really means. What does it mean to love your country and to honor your country? Does it mean that you lie on behalf of your country? Does it mean that you risk drawing your government into difficulties like the Iran-Contra scandal?

MOYERS: They say it does. They say that we live in a lawless world and that it's naive to expect the United States Government to act lawfully in a world that doesn't respect the rule of law.

BOK: Then I think they should look back at some of the people we respect most in the history of this country who would say, among other things, that we will gain more respect if we respect the law ourselves.

It's true, there are parts of the world that are quite lawless. There are also, in fact, quite a few parts of the world that are not. The question is: How do we expand the number of nations and societies that do respect the law? We don't necessarily want to say that because some don't, we're going to classify our government in that group.

MOYERS: —Because we are working toward a lawful world, not a lawless one.

BOK: Yes, very much. The question has to come up: What are we doing? What am I doing as an individual? What is somebody doing as a public official? What is an entire government doing to make sure that it moves in that direction, to make the world a little more law-abiding?

MOYERS: How do you convince someone that if it's all right for conservatives to lie, it's all right for liberals to lie when they're in office? And that ultimately it is the citizen—conservative or liberal, political or apolitical—who loses the right to cast that informed vote if he doesn't really know that his government has been selling arms to Iran, contrary to its stated policy.

BOK: It's so important for us to be able to shift perspectives and to say, "Okay, here I'm on the side of the people who are telling the lies, and I think it's all right for the moment because it's my side. But how would I feel if I were on that other side? Next time I may be on the other side. In fact, these very same people who say they're my friends now may need for their particular purposes to lie to me next time. And then I would feel very much more troubled than I did when they lied to some foreigners that I didn't care about."

MOYERS: Rereading your book on secrets, I was struck once again by your point that partisanship causes people to condone abuses for their particular ideal that they would never condone in their adversary. It's that parochial loyalty that can corrupt one's own judgment and standards.

BOK: When it goes too far, it does that corrupting. Of course, any community needs the cohesiveness of some loyalty. But when the partisanship goes so far as to say that in order to preserve loyalty within our small group, we can do anything to those other people—we can send terrorists into their country, we can spew forth disinformation, we can do anything—then it has become pathological. And then people don't, once again, stop to ask questions. They have simply blinded themselves to the kind of harm they're doing to the outside.

MOYERS: During the Johnson era, Democrats who had doubts about the Vietnam War nonetheless supported the President because he was their partisan. People remained loyal to Richard Nixon despite the smoking gun because he was a Republican President. And when George Bush announced that the most qualified man in the country to be Vice President was Dan Quayle, I saw some otherwise moderate Republicans swallow, click their heels, and step in line. Partisanship was the ultimate claim on their loyalty, not judgment and rational analysis.

BOK: The word "partisan" can mean two things. On the one hand, it can mean a very brave person who undertakes the struggle against, for instance, the Nazis. On the other hand, it can mean a person who abandons judgment. Unfortunately, very often, the first can turn into the second, unless one is very careful to think about certain moral values that one will uphold whether or not one is going to act in a partisan way.

MOYERS: It's hardest to uphold these standards in a time of crisis.

BOK: Yes, definitely—that's when it becomes very tempting to say, "Well, I'm going to let go of my principles now. For instance, I have the principle that I shouldn't take innocent life. But now, with all these threats, I'm going to let go of that principle and maybe a couple of others as well." That's how we descend into a kind of inhumanity that we see, for instance, in Lebanon.

MOYERS: Speaking of crisis, your new book, *A Strategy for Peace*, talks about "our present predicament." How do you define our present predicament?

BOK: The predicament we're in now and that we have been in for some time is the threat of extinction from nuclear weapons, and the threat of extinction from environmental sources. It has simply never been the case before in human history that all of life—not just human life but really all of life—could be wiped out. That has made an enormous change for us. At the same time, this is also an extraordinary opportunity. People are to some extent making greater efforts. Governments are trying harder. We've had the INF Treaty. Some people say that right now there's an epidemic of peace. Now that may be going a little far, but the fact is that we're bringing certain wars to an end, and there seems to be greater hope for the moment than there has been for quite a long time. It comes, in part, from the awareness of this predicament.

MOYERS: You take seriously all the present talk about governments slowing the momentum of the arms race?

BOK: Yes, I do. I think that there is understanding on the part of governments that we simply can't continue to exist the way we are. That is too dangerous. Even if a nuclear exchange were to begin by accident or miscalculation, that's something we can't risk.

MOYERS: You say, in *A Strategy for Peace*, that our problems are so severe that unless we can marshal a principled, collective response, all the worst predictions of social collapse may finally be coming true. That's a hope I share—but history argues otherwise. Previous generations didn't take principled and collective action in time to stave off the threats they faced in their own day. What makes you think we can do it better or differently?

BOK: It's true that a number of societies have collapsed because they didn't take issues of survival seriously enough. On the other hand, they have never been in the predicament that we are in now. We're all in it together. That may force us, for the first time, to take the common interest into consideration.

Now I'm not at all wanting to say that everything is rosy. I think, on the contrary, that it's a very serious situation—but there are reasons for hope. Our century has been unbelievably violent and brutal and filled with tyranny, but it has also brought forth countervailing powers. We've had popular movements seeking change nonviolently and, in fact, succeeding more and more often. It began, in some ways, with Gandhi in India. We've had the American civil rights struggle. Since then we've had the Philippines, where Corazon Aquino specifically referred to Martin Luther King and to Mohandas Gandhi. Now we have Burma weighing in the balance. We've had Argentina undergoing a peaceful change, and Spain, much earlier.

That's one development. Another is that we have research that people didn't have in past generations about how to solve conflicts nonviolently. We have better history. We know much more about how wars start and how they can get out of hand. Look at all the research, for instance, that's been done on the First World War. So I think that we are in a better position to seize this opportunity.

MOYERS: I want to believe you, but when I look at our century, from Stalin's genocide against his own people to Hitler's genocide against millions, to Idi Amin in Africa, to the racism of South Africa, to the Khmer Rouge in Cambodia, to the warlords of Japan, to what's happening in Beirut and Northern Ireland and Afghanistan, I say that hope is a fragile, fragile bark on which to sail into the twenty-first century.

BOK: Yes, and I certainly don't think we should sail on hope alone. There's only so much that individuals can do. But I think they do need to have some hope. It's much too early to give up hope.

MOYERS: What was it your mother said? "It's not worthy of human beings to give up."

BOK: She felt very strongly about that, no matter what the battle that one might be fighting. It's not worthy of us, as human beings, with all that we've been given in this extraordinary creation, to simply give up and say, "Well, looking back at history, I'm now going to declare that there's no hope."

MOYERS: Do we need a new ethic for this predicament?

BOK: I don't think we need a new ethic at all. Some people insist that nothing will change until our human consciousness changes, or we develop some new way of thinking—even Einstein said that—or we become much more altruistic and charitable. But I think, in a way, it's a little too late to hope for that. I'm not at all sure that the human race can change in that way, or that, if there were some cataclysmic change of consciousness, it would be for the better. It could very easily be for the worse, as happened in Nazi Germany and elsewhere. So we don't need a new ethic at all. But we do need to concentrate more than we have before on the moral principles and values that we have in common with people of other religions and other cultures.

The two most important factors are: nonviolence, to the extent possible; and truthfulness, or the avoidance of lying. If violence or deceit gets too powerful in any society, the society becomes oppressive and may break down. Wherever you look—at Buddhist literature, or the Bible, or Hindu scriptures—avoiding violence and deceit are stressed. Every community that has any kind of law, for instance, struggles against violence and fraud.

> Every community that has any kind of law . . . struggles against violence and fraud.

MOYERS: True. But there's so much evidence of Moslem against Jew, Christian against Christian—

BOK: The trouble is that those principles have never been held very high when it's come to outsiders. What we need to do now is to take those same principles and expand the coverage so that it becomes just as awful for us to take an innocent life in some other country as it is in our own. That will take a little rethinking on the part of a lot of people. But it's not a transformation of the human spirit.

Now a third principle is that of the constraint on betrayal, or breaches of law, or breaches of promise. Every single culture has had to develop some notion of promise-keeping or of covenant, and the notion that breaches constitute betrayal. Those are three very, very ancient principles.

In addition to avoiding violence and deceit and betrayal, there is a fourth principle that's very much newer, and that is, a constraint on excessive secrecy. If we don't constrain secrecy, then all the other things can go on, and we won't even know they're going on. There can be violence within communities or on the part of governments, there can be deception, there can be betrayal, and violations of law, and so long as secrecy covers up all of that, then there is not much that we can do about it. The constraint on excessive secrecy is really an eighteenth-century phenomenon. You don't see much criticism of secrecy in the Bible or in Buddhist texts. The greater the stress on constraining secrecy, the greater the stress on publicity or openness.

MOYERS: Do you think that we could begin to shape a minimum moral framework in which the world could cooperate for survival?

BOK: Yes, a number of governments are trying to do this. And, of course, international law is based, to some extent, on those four principles.

MOYERS: But every government violates international law when it finds it expedient to do so—we in Nicaragua and the Soviets in Afghanistan.

BOK: —That doesn't mean, by the way, every government, but a number of governments have done so. And I think it has backfired very badly for them—certainly for the Soviets in Afghanistan and for us elsewhere. We see the Soviet Union changing with respect to some of these violations. It will be crucial for our government to abide scrupulously by international law.

MOYERS: But you point out in your book that seventeen million people have died in violent acts and wars around the globe since the end of the Second World War. The tendency seems to be in the opposite direction from the collaboration and cooperation that you're calling for.

BOK: That's where this epidemic of peace may give some hope. The more governments undergo democratic and peaceful change, and the more willing they become to abide by international law and to deal nonviolently with other nations, the fewer there will be of the others. And then, perhaps, the world can focus on the pockets that still remain of war and oppression.

MOYERS: Bring this down to the level of one person out there, one citizen. So many people in this country feel helpless to effect any change. They'll say, "How can I make a difference? What can I do? She's talking about international organizations and governments, beyond my reach. What can I do to make a difference?"

BOK: Well, look at some of the movements of social change that have grown during our century as never before: they started in very piecemeal ways. People began doing something in one community and then expanded. Gandhi started that way. Martin Luther King started that way. And although we often hear that there are no heroes, there are lots of heroes. For instance, in many villages in India individuals and groups are trying to make peace between Sikhs and Hindus. In the Middle East and in South Africa, there are many people who are struggling heroically in their own communities—and they're having an effect. Now you may say, "Maybe they're not going to win out in the end"—but maybe they are. It's worth making the effort.

MOYERS: I cherish the notion in the conclusion of your book about starting personal and piecemeal, about carving out a space in one's own life where one begins to practice personally what one advocates politically and publicly.

BOK: Yes. Let's say that you want to carve out in your own life what Gandhi sometimes called a zone of peace. Just say, "In my family and at work and wherever I have human contacts, I am simply not going to engage in the manipulation of people. I'm not going to be coercive or violent with respect to others." Already that will make a difference. That will have an effect on other people. Then one can say, "In our community we're simply not going to deal with one another this way," or "At our workplace, in our factory, or in our government office, there is going to be another way of operating." It seems that when people begin to do that, it does have an effect. This is a form of maturing, of saying, "All right, I know that I can get my way by manipulating people, but I'm not going to do that. I'm going to see if I can work another way." Simone Weil once said, "I would like to achieve the kind of radiance that can bring about nonviolently what other people might have to do violently." We see teachers like that, or parents like that, who have the kind of radiance so that they don't have to raise their voices or beat their children. They simply make a different atmosphere.

MOYERS: So in this personal zone, I don't act violently against my family. I keep my promises, my vows, my oaths. I don't deceive. I practice in that small circle what I hope my neighbor and my government would practice.

BOK: Yes, but then I don't give up on the government at all. If I'm engaged in this practice, I must make every effort to see to it that the government doesn't slip into further practices of secrecy, that there are protests when misinformation takes place, and that there is concern for innocent civilians who are being killed. That means that the private individual, while working within that personal zone, must also reach outward toward the professions and the government.

MOYERS: But the radiance didn't stop Stalin's KGB. It didn't stop Hitler's storm troopers or the Gestapo. It didn't stop the Japanese militarists.

BOK: That's right. And it certainly also wouldn't stop nuclear weapons, once they have been launched. That's why we need arms agreements and many other forms of cooperation to prevent war and to protect human rights and to use force as a last resort only. When Weil was writing in her diary about radiance, she asked herself, "What would I have answered to the question that was asked of Gandhi—'Wouldn't you use violence to defend your sister?'"

And then she said, "Of course I would have to use violence—unless I could achieve the same by nonviolent means." And then she went on to say there were some people who had that radiance—St. Francis, for example.

So Weil was very practical. She didn't give up violence. I don't think one always can, especially not when there's self-defense at stake.

MOYERS: Most of us don't see ourselves as Gandhi or St. Francis or Martin Luther King. We live realistically in a very circumscribed world, surrounded by people who are always trying to relieve us of our money, our sanity, our hope, or our goods. So the pragmatist says, "Well, the Golden Rule works well when everybody practices it. But when they don't, I can't practice it, either."

BOK: Individuals obviously need methods of self-defense, as do nations. There's no doubt about that. But there are so many circumstances where self-defense is not in fact at stake and where people nevertheless use violence and deceit. Those would be times to begin to cut back.

People often ask the wrong question when they think about violence and deception. They say, "Do you mean that there should never be any lies?" or "You mean I should never defend myself by means of force?" or "I should never keep a secret or break a promise?" Those are the wrong questions. Instead, the question should be: "How can we roll back the amount of violence, the amount of lying, the breaches of promise and of law? How can we roll all that back, so that there's less of it?" Because, if we don't manage to roll that back, then we're not going to manage to cope with our common problems. We won't be able to cope with our social problems, nor, in the long run, with those of survival—the nuclear threat and the environmental threat—if we can't manage to work together. And how can we manage to work together if we're so distrustful of one another, for very good reason, namely, that we're always doing these things to one another?

MOYERS: This sounds so old-fashioned as almost to be a cliché: "Do unto others as you would have them do unto you."

BOK: That Golden Rule exists in every culture. Confucius speaks of it. Buddhists speak of it. The Bhagavad-Gita speaks of it, and, of course, the Bible speaks of it. So it's not at all anything new.

MOYERS: But then why do you think it would be more honored now than it has been in the course of human history?

BOK: To the extent that it's honored even a little more, there is an improvement. To the extent that more people begin to ask, "How am I making things worse, and how am I making things better?"—that will make a difference. Now, for the first time, we don't have a choice about improvement. In the past, people could act the way they acted, and maybe their society collapsed, but another one could rise instead. But now, we can't risk that any more.

MOYERS: You think that it's because we have these new threats of annihilation from nuclear war or environmental catastrophe that people might take out the old moral armor that has been growing rusty in disuse?

BOK: Yes. These threats concentrate the mind wonderfully, as the saying goes. We have to rely on principles in larger societies and between nations that we know are indispensable within small communities if anything is going to get done. Now that may not work out. We may fail, as many societies have in the past. But we have certain advantages. Just as we have new fuels and new technologies in combating environmental deterioration, so we also have new ways of arbitrating disputes and new ways of achieving agreement. We have information that was lacking in the past about how disputes get out of hand, and how wars happen. So we are in a somewhat better position to respond to the threats you mention. That doesn't mean that we shall succeed. But it certainly is not the time to give up.

MOYERS: Your father won the Nobel Prize for economics. Your mother won a Nobel Prize for peace. Your father's great petition was for a just economic order, and your mother's constant message to the world was the danger of the arms race. They both lived through much of the bloodiest, most violent, most tyrannical century ever. Do you think that they argued in vain for these principles which the world has so consistently and brutally dishonored?

BOK: I don't think that they stood for these principles in vain at all. In fact, I think a number of people of their generation had that special understanding that came from having lived through our whole century. Sometimes I worry that later generations have not had that entire experience that my parents' generation had, of all the violence and all the problems in the world, while remaining both hopeful and clearheaded about all the dangers. If the people in their generation can inspire the rest of us to feel that same concern, that same awareness, but without giving up hope, then they will definitely not have lived in vain.

Steven Weinberg

PHYSICIST

Dr. Weinberg's world is as wide as the heavens and as small as subatomic structure. He is a professor of physics and astronomy at the University of Texas and winner of the Nobel Prize for Physics in 1978. His book The First Three Minutes *brought the theory of the Big Bang to a popular audience as he groped with the deepest question of all: Why is there something instead of nothing?*

MOYERS: Why do you study physics? What do you get out of it?

WEINBERG: It's a remarkable exercise of the mind. I still can't get over it that you can sit at your desk and noodle around with equations and try out ideas and put together physical principles that may or may not be right, and every once in a while, you can say something about the real world. You can predict the result of an experiment, or a new particle, or say something about the forces of nature or about the way the universe evolves—and all out of pure thought.

Now, of course, it isn't all out of pure thought. We're always being turned on by new experimental data, and hoping that when we predict something, the experimentalists will go out and test it and find it's right. But still, a lot of it is just pure thought, sitting at your desk. And that it works at all is just amazing.

MOYERS: Most of us don't think of pure thought as synonymous with the real world. We think of the real world as that desk, this chair, that body, not some intangible idea up here in the brain. But it is the real world you're talking about?

WEINBERG: Yes, and one of the ways you know it's the real world is that you're often wrong. If we were just a bunch of mandarins feeding each other's egos and making it up, we would all be able to convince ourselves that everything we did was right— but it isn't. Very often we find that ideas that we believed in are overturned by experiment. That's a great experience that we natural scientists have that is very chastening and humbling.

MOYERS: Isn't it true that you're dealing with structures so small they can only be imagined?

WEINBERG: Not only imagined, but described with mathematics. These things cannot be described in the English language. They have to be described in this artificial language that's evolved over the centuries in the effort to understand nature.

MOYERS: Some of your colleagues say that we probably shouldn't even be talking like this because the language of mathematics is so foreign to everyday experience that it confuses people into substituting the metaphor for the reality.

WEINBERG: There's a danger, but we don't really manage to avoid it ourselves. Right now, for example, there's a tremendous amount of excitement about an idea in physics called "string theory." String theory is very mathematical. If I described the way that physicists working in this field really think of it, I would talk about two-dimensional conformal quantum field theories and so on. It has a very mathematical description, but there's a more physical side in which you say, the basic ingredients of the universe, the basic things the universe is made out of are really little strings, little glitches in space-time that go zipping around and vibrating, and when you say you have an elementary particle, what you really have is a string in a certain mode of vibration.

Now the mathematical description, in a sense, is truer, and it's certainly a lot more reliable. You can fall into terrible traps by using the physical description, but in fact we use it all the time.

MOYERS: When you talk about strings, what comes to mind is a string like one I use in ordinary life. The danger is that a layman can confuse what you really mean.

WEINBERG: Yes, physicists aren't mathematicians. Mathematicians seem to have the ability to get inspiration from mathematics itself. I suppose some physicists operate that way, too, but most of us have more concrete pictures that motivate the mathematics. The mathematics expresses the concrete pictures.

MOYERS: Some mathematicians talk about mathematics as the language of God, in the sense that it's expressing ultimate reality.

WEINBERG: There is a spooky thing about mathematics. Again and again, physicists working on a new theory, like Einstein's general theory of relativity, for example, find the mathematics all there ready for them, having been developed by mathematicians with no idea of that physical application.

There are other examples. Group theory, which turned out to be essential to understanding atomic physics in the twentieth century, was developed in the nineteenth century just because of internal problems in mathematics. The mathematicians have often been there before us in some way that we can't really understand.

There are all kinds of theories about why mathematics is so remarkably effective. My own view is that we're in the grip of an enormous teaching machine—the universe—which operates in an essentially random way. Random processes over billions of years, operating through natural selections, have produced birds and flowers and people. In the same way, there is a natural selection of ideas—which ideas work, which don't, what kind of thing is an appropriate description of nature. This process leads us to develop mathematical ideas, even though we don't have in mind any particular physical application, because we're the kind of people we are, because we've had the experience we've had of centuries of trying to grapple with this universe.

> . . . we're in the grip of an enormous teaching machine—the universe—which operates in an essentially random way.

MOYERS: What is it you want to know about the universe?

WEINBERG: It's very simple. I just want to know one thing, which is why things are the way they are. We've already come a long way, you know. If you ask any ordinary question about everyday things—"Why is the sky blue?" or "Why is water wet?"—we actually know the answer. For example, a question about why the sky is blue would be answered in terms of the properties of dust grains and light and air transmitting light.

And then if you ask, "Why are those things true? Why does light behave the way it does? Why are light waves of one wavelength scattered differently than light waves of a different wavelength?"—you can answer those things, too, in terms of a more fundamental description using atoms and quantum mechanics.

Then we ask, "Why are those the way they are?" We've come a long way here, too. We now have a theory of elementary particles, which is more fundamental than the ordinary quantum mechanics of atoms and radiation. It's sometimes called the standard model, which is a way of saying we all believe it and use it without being absolutely sure of anything. And then you ask, "Why is that true?"

Well, that's what I want to do. I want to help to trace these chains of "why" down to their roots.

MOYERS: Like a five-year-old child who goes around asking his or her parents: "Why? . . . Why is the bird singing?"

WEINBERG: Yes. That's it. We want to be thoroughly unpleasant and keep asking, "Why is that true?" When you get an answer, you say, "Well, why is *that* true?" The amazing thing is that we can go pretty far, but in doing it, we discover some remarkable things about the universe. One of the things we discover is that these chains of explanation seem to converge to a common source, because it doesn't matter whether you ask: "Why is the sky blue?" or "Why is water wet?"—you always get down to the level of elementary particles.

When you talk about biology or astronomy, you have to bring in other elements, like the fact that the universe is billions of years old, and it's had a long time to cook. But as you get toward the roots of the chains of explanation, you find that things get simpler.

MOYERS: What do you mean, they get simpler?

WEINBERG: For example, if you do chemistry, you've got millions of compounds. You can simplify that by understanding all those compounds in terms of ninety-two elements. We have more now, because we've been able to create some artificially. But then you can explain these elements in terms of a much smaller set of particles.

Now it isn't necessarily true that as you go to deeper and deeper levels, the number of entities decreases. Actually, we have an embarrassingly large number of particles right now. What's important here is that the principles get simpler. There are very few principles of elementary particle physics. The deeper you go, the less you have to say because there are fewer and fewer principles. We're beginning to feel that we're really getting rather close to the roots.

MOYERS: Is it possible to carry these whys so far back that you can say what's likely to have happened in the first one hundredth of a second? Or the first three minutes?

WEINBERG: We can certainly use our observations in the same way that a paleontologist looks at fossils or dinosaurs and is able to reconstruct what things must have been like one hundred million years ago here on earth. We can take fossils that we find in the universe now—particles, radiation, the chemical composition of the stars—and use these as clues to trace the history back to the first three minutes or the first one hundredth of a second. Cosmologists generally feel that we understand the history of the universe pretty well from the first one hundredth of a second on.

When you go back earlier than that, you get into problems of physics that are difficult, and we have to be a little bit more modest.

Now, that's really just tracing the history back. It doesn't answer the question why the universe started at all. Why is there something instead of nothing? We don't know whether these kinds of questions are forever going to be separate. It may be that in the end, physics and history will come together, and we will not need special assumptions about the beginning.

In fact, some years ago, there was an attempt to develop a steady state theory of the universe, in which there is no beginning. As I said, one of the nice things about science is that you sometimes find out you're wrong. The steady state theory turned out to be wrong, attractive as the idea might be to some people.

MOYERS: You write, "In the beginning there was an explosion." That's a declarative statement, a very affirmative judgment.

WEINBERG: Well, it should have been qualified, because what I should have said, and probably did say somewhere else, is that in the beginning of the phase of the universe that we now find ourselves in, there was an explosion, and the explosion involved conditions of temperature and density so extreme that we find it impossible to trace the history back before. We don't see any reason to believe that there was a before. But we don't know. There may have been a before; there may not have been a before. We really have to be open-minded about that.

MOYERS: Was it an explosion like a giant firecracker?

WEINBERG: In one sense, yes, and in another sense, no. It was an explosion like a firecracker in the sense that each particle of the firecracker is rushing away from every other particle during the explosion. If you count the amount of firecracker per unit of volume, it decreases, and the firecracker cools off as it expands. But a firecracker that explodes on the Fourth of July explodes in an atmosphere that isn't filled with firecrackers, thank God. It's exploding, going out into the air. You can say there's a surface to the exploding firecracker, and beyond that surface it hasn't yet reached. We don't think of the explosion of the universe that way. When we talk about the universe, we think of space perhaps being finite, perhaps being infinite, but in either case being more or less homogeneously filled with matter. When we talk about an explosion, we simply mean that every particle of matter is rushing away from every other particle, and that the universe is getting cooler and less dense. But its surface isn't expanding. There isn't any surface.

MOYERS: So the cosmic firecracker exploded everywhere at once.

WEINBERG: That's right. Everywhere there was space, there was matter, and matter started exploding away from other matter. But it wasn't matter rushing into empty space. There wasn't any surface, there was no boundary to the universe. We're not at the center, we're not at the edge, it's just everywhere.

MOYERS: And you can be reasonably sure of this?

WEINBERG: Yes, it's a good working hypothesis. The best evidence for it is that when we look out in different directions in the sky, we see pretty much the same thing in all directions. If matter formed a sphere, the only way you could understand that observation would be to suppose that we were at the center. And that's kind of hard to believe. You know, ever since Copernicus, we've been a little leery of assuming that human beings live at the center of the universe. If we lived anywhere away from the center of the universe, we'd see more matter in one direction than in the other direction, unless the sphere were really quite enormous. Of course, we can't rule out the possibility that the universe really looks very, very different if you go hundreds of billions of light-years away. We can only look out about ten billion light-years. But so far, everything we see suggests that the universe is the same in all directions when you take a sufficiently large scale point of view.

MOYERS: If the universe began with a big bang, what difference does it make that everything that exists today was once part of a single force?

WEINBERG: It's hard for a scientist to explain why it's interesting to learn about the universe. It just is. I don't understand how to explain that music is beautiful. It's a taste for wanting to understand why things are the way they are and where they came from. If you don't have the taste, talking about it can't give it to you. I think most people do have that taste. I think most people are fascinated with these questions. Just now the leading book on the nonfiction bestseller list in the *New York Times* is a book by Stephen Hawking about time and the universe. There's a tremendous amount of interest in these questions. It gives us a sense of finding out what kind of drama we're actors in. I don't know how anyone could not want to know that.

MOYERS: If you can be reasonably comfortable about assumptions concerning the first three minutes of the universe, can you then go on to contemplate the last three minutes of the universe?

WEINBERG: We try to—and it's a fascinating scientific question, because it hinges on astronomical observations that are going on right now. It all depends on how much matter there is in the universe. If there's enough matter in the universe, the expansion will stop and then start to be reversed. We'll have a contraction, and all be swallowed up in a big crunch.

MOYERS: Some fifty thousand million years from now?

WEINBERG: Yes, that's a fair estimate. And in fact, when we know better what the density of matter in the universe is, we'll be able to tell how far in the future the big crunch is. On the other hand, we may find that there isn't enough matter to reverse the expansion, and the galaxies will just keep rushing away from each other. Things will get very cold and very dead, forever.

MOYERS: Given that it's fifty thousand million years from now, I'll let you worry about that. I have other problems. Most people would say that.

Do you remember the first time that your curiosity was excited and that you thought of being a scientist?

WEINBERG: More or less. I'm not sure I remember the day and week, but I remember that in high school, after playing around with a chemistry set as a little boy, I began to read books. I found my way into some popular books about physics, and I didn't understand a word. They seemed like black magic—mysterious and amazing. Yet I knew that the scientists who had thought of these things and written papers about them were able to predict things about nature that were then found. They predicted that antimatter existed, and then it was found. They predicted that you should be able to release energy from fission, and then it was done. I knew that they weren't just talking, but that they really knew something. And I thought, "This is amazing." The human mind can master these ideas about space and time being curved and about electrons as waves of probability. It all sounded absurd, and yet if you mastered it, you could say something about the real world. It seemed like opening up a power of the human mind that couldn't be exercised in any other kind of life, and it was just infinitely attractive.

MOYERS: Have you been disappointed in any way about choosing science?

WEINBERG: No, it's a great life. It's harder than I ever imagined, in the sense that you have to get used to wasting an enormous amount of time. You have to get the discipline of sitting at your desk fooling around with ideas that almost never work and living for the rare moment when an idea does work.

MOYERS: What's the most arresting insight you've gained into the universe?

WEINBERG: It has to do with the simplicity of nature. The simplicity of nature is very often expressed in terms of principles of symmetry, the symmetries of the laws of nature. For example, there's nothing in the laws of nature to distinguish north from east. All directions are the same as far as the laws of nature are concerned. Of course we know that here on earth they're not. In this hemisphere, if you go north, it gets colder, and if you go south, it gets warmer. But there's nothing in the underlying laws that distinguishes different directions in space. And there's nothing in the underlying laws of nature that distinguishes neutrinos from electrons. You can perform mathematical transformations in which a state that's a neutrino can be turned into a state that's an electron, or even a state that's a mixture of being a neutrino and an electron. The laws of nature seem the same when you make this change in what you call neutrinos and what you call electrons.

These principles of symmetry have been known for a long time. They're very powerful because they dictate the form of the laws of nature. They're probably the deepest thing we know about in physics.

MOYERS: Deepest? What do you mean?

WEINBERG: In the sense that if you keep asking questions about "why," you'll wind up with principles of symmetry. The thing that I have most enjoyed helping to discover is that there are a lot more symmetries than you would think. There are symmetries that are hidden in everyday life in the laboratory—if you can call that everyday life.

MOYERS: And what do you take away from that?

WEINBERG: What you take away from it is that nature is a lot simpler and more beautiful than you had thought. If you look at a table of elementary particles, you see a lot of weird particles with a lot of different masses and a lot of different properties. It all looks like a great big zoo, and you can't make any sense out of it. Then you find that the underlying principles are extremely simple, and all these particles are just different solutions of some very simple equations.

A friend of mine in physics, John Wheeler, says that when we finally learn the underlying laws of nature, they will be so simple and beautiful that we will wonder why they weren't obvious from the beginning.

MOYERS: Whom would you ask about the complexity of life: Shakespeare or Einstein?

WEINBERG: Oh, for the complexity of life, there's no question—Shakespeare.

MOYERS: And you would go to Einstein for—simplicity?

WEINBERG: Yes, for a sense of why things are the way they are—not why people are the way they are, because that's at the end of such a long chain of inference, but why the physical universe is the way it is.

But you know, it's Einstein and Shakespeare together that do so much to create the meaning of life. Shakespeare, after the assassination of Julius Caesar, puts a question into the mouths of one of the assassins—I forget which one, and I don't remember the precise words—but it's something to the effect that: "In future ages, how many times is this going to be reenacted?" Shakespeare had a sense of life as drama. Characters participating in a great event would see themselves as in a drama, and life would take on extra meaning from that. I think it's wonderful to think of ourselves as playing a part in a drama, and when we do that, we can't look to scientific discoveries for the script that we have to play.

MOYERS: All my life I've heard the term "That's a beautiful theory," but I've never really thought about what makes a theory beautiful.

WEINBERG: "Beautiful theory" is a slightly unfortunate phrase because it suggests that physicists are just aesthetes, that we choose theories because they tickle our fancy. A beautiful theory is beautiful like a horse, rather than a poem. If you look at a racehorse, and you say, "That's a beautiful horse," you mean that you're getting a lot of cues, which you can't express in English or bring up to your conscious mind, that the horse has qualities that win races. And when physical ideas are beautiful, you mean those are the kinds of ideas that turn out to be right.

Of course you can ask, "What kinds of physical properties turn out to be right? What is the kind of beauty we look for?" In a sense it is like the beauty of the sonata. It's the beauty of knowing that everything is the way it had to be, that you could not change a note without marring it. Not every work of art has that quality. Shakespeare's plays, for example, are great complicated things that to some extent mirror the complexity of life. But if you take something a little bit smaller in scale, more spare, more controlled, like a sonata, you have the feeling that nothing could be changed, that it is just perfect the way it is; it cannot be improved. That's what we look for in physical theory. It's the sense that the theory is the way it is because any change would sacrifice something that you couldn't bear to see sacrificed.

MOYERS: You said that it helps to understand that this universe is an expanding universe, that we are caught up in a drama that is evolving, changing constantly, inevitably. There has to be some significance to that for our everyday lives.

WEINBERG: There is. Educators make a mistake when they justify science education in terms of the fact that this is a technological society, and citizens have to be able to understand scientific matters in order to cope with living in the twentieth century. That's true, of course, but that's only part of the story and not the most important part.

I think that science has changed the way that we think about ourselves and our role in the universe. There's a lot of historical evidence for the tremendous change in Western societies caused by the scientific revolution of the sixteenth and seventeenth centuries. We stopped burning witches. In most of Europe, at least, we stopped having wars of religion. The historian Butterfield said that since the beginning of Christianity, there's no event in history that's comparable in importance to the scientific revolution. I think the changes are incalculable. I wish they would go a little further.

MOYERS: In what sense?

WEINBERG: Well, it bothers me terribly, for example, that anyone still takes astrology seriously. Now, it's not because astrology is wrong. There are lots of wrong ideas that are simply wrong because there's evidence that they're wrong; but there are wrong ideas that are wrong because if they were right, you'd have to throw away everything you knew. If astrology were right, if the positions of the planets in the sky affected the personalities of people here on earth, it would mean such a change in the way that things influence each other that none of our existing science could survive. It would all have to be scrapped, and we'd have to start over thinking about everything. There's just no room in the house of science as it's built now for astrology. If you believe in astrology, you have no right to get into elevators or take aspirins or use any of the other advantages of technology because you're turning your back on all of the science that produced the technology.

> *It may be that there's no objective importance that registers in the cosmic equations, but importance is what we give to things.*

MOYERS: But many people need to believe that we have a particular relationship to the universe, that we were scripted from the beginning.

WEINBERG: We are important. I find the people around me in my life are terribly important. It may be that there's no objective importance that registers in the cosmic equations, but importance is what we give to things. I think that's not entirely unsatisfactory.

MOYERS: There's a wonderful passage in Chaim Potok's *The Chosen* where he says that the blink of an eye is nothing, but the eye that blinks is everything.

Why do you think people want to believe in astrology, despite evidence to the contrary?

WEINBERG: I think it's a failure of scientists and educators to explain how much we know about the universe. We really know a lot. I remember when I was in high school, we had a speaker tell us that nobody really understood what electricity is. Well, even then he was wrong. We do understand about electricity. We know more or less why matter behaves the way it does on the scale of everyday life.

MOYERS: Why are we doing so poorly in educating ourselves scientifically? So few kids take math today and so few college students are interested in science.

WEINBERG: Yes, I don't understand it. Students sometimes manage to get straight A's in high school mathematics, and then come to college and can't solve simple word problems. I'm not a professional in the field, and I wouldn't presume to say what they're doing wrong. But I can think of a few things that I'd like to see done. One is to open up high school science teaching—and perhaps teaching in general—to scholars who have decided they're more interested in teaching than in doing research.

MOYERS: Without certification?

WEINBERG: Without teacher's college certification. Break the grip of the teacher's college certification in high school education. I remember that when I was on the faculty at MIT, we had a young theoretical physicist who decided he was more interested in teaching than in doing research. He could not get a job teaching physics in the Boston city public high schools because he didn't have the teacher's certification. But Andover, a private high school, was willing to hire him, so they had a Ph.D. teaching high school physics, and he did a wonderful job. I think there's a great pool of potential high school teachers, but they avoid teaching in the public schools. I would advise the society to make the job of the high school teacher more palatable, not only in terms of salary but in terms of independence. Public school teachers should be given a lot more intellectual independence than they have in choosing their course materials, choosing their textbooks, choosing the syllabus so they can feel the same sense of intellectual creativity in teaching that we at the college level are fortunate to feel. If someone has a missionary spirit and wants to help save America, I think it would be a wonderful thing to go teach in high school. But it's not as satisfying as teaching in college because of the lack of independence.

MOYERS: Unless we can somehow bring a sense of wonder and excitement and passion to science, what's going to happen to us?

WEINBERG: We may wind up making a living by showing the Grand Canyon to tourists from Germany and Japan. And we can always sell soybeans when the drought ends. I think we're in terrible trouble, not only because of science education, but because of the general pattern of spending on scientific research. We now spend less on non-defense research as a fraction of our gross national product than Japan or France or Germany. Roughly seventy-five percent of our federal research money goes to defense research. That's up from about fifty percent about a decade ago.

MOYERS: And the implications of that?

WEINBERG: The research scientists are beginning to compete with each other, like castaways competing for the last few crumbs of food. Very, very important scientific projects are going unfunded, or are being spaced out over such long periods that by the time they're completed, history will have passed them by.

MOYERS: Is this an exciting time to be a physicist?

WEINBERG: Yes, of course, but it's not as exciting for elementary particle physicists as it was fifteen years ago. Then there was a tremendous interaction between theory and experiment. Every day the theorists were predicting something new that the experimentalists might test, or the experimentalists might discover something new that sent the theorists back to their desks. That kind of interaction has died down. We've got a theory which is pretty good at explaining everything that we can see in our laboratories, and we don't have the experimental facilities that will push us beyond what we already know.

MOYERS: You and other physicists are calling for the government to build something called a superconducting supercollider at a cost of four to five billion dollars. What is that?

WEINBERG: It's a fifty-three-mile-long oval tunnel underneath the ground. In the tunnel—the tunnel's about ten feet wide—there are two beams of particles, and they're being accelerated; that's why we call it an accelerator. They're getting faster and faster, more and more energy, and when they get up to an energy of twenty trillion volts, then at certain points in the tunnel, the beams are made to cross each other, the particles collide, and you get new forms of matter.

MOYERS: And that will show you—

WEINBERG: It will increase the energy of the particles that we can study by a factor of ten. Now, every time you do that, you discover new worlds of physical phenomena. It's just like an astronomer looking at the sky in a new wavelength, a new kind of light, or a solid-state physicist decreasing the temperature by a factor of ten. You always discover a whole new world of phenomena when you do that.

The supercollider is a no-lose proposition. There are specific questions that are going to be answered. But the general experience is that the questions that you know are going to be answered never turn out to be the most important ones. The most important ones are things that you haven't thought of. It's opening up a new world. It's not a question of improving the efficiency of our work; it's a question of allowing the work to be done at all. Do you want to know the underlying laws of physics? Well, this is the way you have to go about it. I'm not saying that everything in physics is waiting for the supercollider. There are a lot of things that can be done in physics without the supercollider. But there's a certain kind of question—the question "Why? Why? Why?" getting down to the bottom of the chains of explanation—that can't be answered without this kind of facility. There's no argument at all in the community of American particle physicists that this is the right accelerator to build.

MOYERS: What do you say to the scientist who argues that there are cheaper ways than these big giant projects to arrive at basic discoveries?

WEINBERG: There is one kind of question that can't be answered in any other way. We've tried. You know, I'm perfectly willing to do it all myself. Just give me a couple of number one pencils and a yellow lined pad, and I will go to work for you—and I don't cost much. But I can't do it. I've tried, and my colleagues and I are not able, by pure thought, to take the next step.

MOYERS: What do you say to the fellow who's about to retire after thirty-five years in one job, and is worrying about whether or not his pension will suffice, whether his taxes will be too high? Why do we want to spend billions of dollars to find out what happened in the first hundredth of a second of the universe or whether the universe is enlarging?

There are a lot of things in our society that aren't needed to feed and clothe and house us but that somehow make life worth living. I think finding out about the universe is one of them.

WEINBERG: I suppose we could shut down basic research. We could stop supporting the national parks. We could cut out all support to the arts. We could sell the Washington Monument. There are a lot of things in our society that aren't needed to feed and clothe and house us but that somehow make life worth living. I think finding out about the universe is one of them.

In addition, you can't have a healthy technology without a broad range of science, from the most fundamental to the most applied. Our trading partners and competitors have also come to the same conclusion. The Japanese are spending large sums on their own particle accelerator, which for a while will be the largest of its type in the world. The Russians also have plans in this direction. We think we need basic science to serve as the ground on which the technology is built. It doesn't seem to work without it.

I can point to practical applications of the supercollider. There are spinoffs from the building of the thing. The computing needs of this accelerator are quite remarkable. In the accelerator, millions of collisions a second will be produced. These are all observed automatically. For each collision, a lot of information is taken about how the particles fly out, and the energies and the angles of the different particles. What you have to do is throw away almost all of the information in real time. The computer has to be programmed in such a way that as it observes the collisions, it will decide what's interesting, and throw away ninety-nine-point-nine percent of the "uninteresting" information. That's a tremendous task for computing experts. This is going to stretch the state of the art in on-line computing like nothing else. Also, the supercollider is going to be the largest vacuum chamber in the world. It's going to be the largest liquid helium facility in the world. So we'll get a lot of technological expertise out of building the thing. But I'd hate to rely on that for its justification. I think that doesn't do justice to its spiritual value.

MOYERS: Spiritual value?

WEINBERG: Well, what else is it? We're finding out what kind of world this is and what the rules are. It's deeply satisfying, not only to physicists, who are able to work with it professionally, but to the public in general. I think it's of great value to our society. It's one of the things we're proud of in this country, the same way we're proud of retaining our heritage of wilderness. We're proud of doing this sort of thing. If we don't build the accelerator like this on our soil, then the next generation of graduate students in physics will have to go off to Geneva, or the Soviet Union, or Japan to do their work because that's where the front-line instruments are going to be. Our country will lose a generation of elementary particle physicists. You might say you can face that with equanimity, but in fact, these elementary particle physicists provide a very important cadre of scientific talent. They played an enormous role in the war, in developing radar and the atomic bomb. I don't think we can afford to lose a large fraction of our brightest young physicists. And I think we will if we don't build this.

MOYERS: John Q. Citizen listening to you could say, "I can understand that theories are cheap, and experiments are expensive, and you have to take these theories off the blackboard and try to test them in whatever the way the scientist decides is conclusive, either right or wrong." But what bothers John Q. Citizen is how we sort out all of the demands on scarce dollars—twenty-six billion dollars for a space station, four to six billion dollars for the supercollider, three to nine to twelve billion dollars for Star Wars, three to six billion dollars for the research that the government wants to do in human genetic sequences.

WEINBERG: First of all, let's not compare things that are totally unlike. Star Wars is a military system. It has nothing to do with basic science. My own feeling is that it harms rather than helps our security to pursue this program. What you think about Star Wars depends on your judgments about what you need in order to have a stable world. In a world with tens of thousands of nuclear warheads, what do you do to avoid the ultimate calamity of thermonuclear war? It isn't a question of science policy at all.

It's a harder question when you compare things like the supercollider with, say, mapping the human genome, the great biological project. I think they're both very valuable, and they both should be done. They're not expensive on the scale that the space station is expensive or that Star Wars is expensive. The supercollider cost is four billion dollars, but it's spaced out over some years. Its cost is about five hundred million dollars a year, and that's not comparable to the kind of spending that's going on in the Star Wars program, or that would be going on with the space station.

MOYERS: Of course, some people will say we have to have Star Wars to defend us so that the Steven Weinbergs of this world can continue to do their research into basic reality.

WEINBERG: If I thought that Star Wars would help avoid nuclear war or help defend us if there were a war, then the cost would be a minor factor. It would be so important to have it that we should go ahead and have it. To my mind the thing that's wrong with it is not the cost, it's the fact that it's likely to do more harm than good in the way of protection. Whatever capability it has will appear much greater to the Soviets, who are anxious to maintain their deterrent. If we really could defend ourselves, they would have no deterrent left. They would spend any amount not to be in that position. Star Wars will inevitably produce an all-out arms race in offensive weapons as it becomes more and more real. That's not just a theory. It's happened before. There was a time when we in the United States were terrified about the nascent Soviet ABM system. We went ahead and made a tremendous increase in the number of our warheads at that time. In fact, we developed multiple warhead technology, which is very, very dangerous, because for the first time it gave the side that struck first an advantage. This is the worst possible situation to be in, because in a time of crisis, the one thing you don't want is for either side to have any incentive to strike first. Having multiple warheads means that one missile on one side can destroy many missiles on the other side, but only provided it's used first. And that was a terrible, terrible thing, which occurred without much debate and was triggered in part because of the worry about the Soviet ABM system. We can't imagine what kind of destabilizing horrors are going to be produced by the Soviet reaction to even a largely ineffective American defense system.

MOYERS: You were once very pessimistic about our ability to avoid a serious nuclear war. You even said you feared we were moving toward the kind of world in which such a war would be more inevitable. Since President Reagan and Gorbachev have been to the summit four times, have you changed your opinion?

WEINBERG: I think there's a chance of moving away, but I don't think we've really started to move away. I think the way nuclear forces are arranged now, a crisis that might come at any moment, somewhere on the border between Russia and Iran, or Russia and Turkey, or whatever, could put the United States and the Soviet Union in a position where neither side is willing to back down. Each side would raise the ante until we get to that terrible moment where both sides begin to do the calculation that if they strike first, they'll limit the damage to their home country. And, unfortunately, we have now a military system which puts a premium on striking first. It's a horror. I sometimes think I'm paranoid, that I'm the last person who's worried about thermonuclear war. Other people find all sorts of other things to worry about in our society. But I still feel that that's the greatest worry.

MOYERS: Why?

WEINBERG: We've fallen off the roof of the Empire State Building, and we've fallen seventy stories, and so far nothing has gone wrong, and we're beginning to feel complacent, but it won't be long before we find out that we're really in trouble. I don't have confidence in either side, the Soviet Union or the United States, having the ability to get out of a crisis without having to face the terrible choice between what they will see as national humiliation and taking the world another notch closer to war.

During the Cuban Missile Crisis, the Soviet Union's nuclear forces were very inferior to those of the United States. The Soviets vowed that they'd never be in that position again, and now they're not in that position. Their forces are as strong, roughly speaking, as ours. We don't know how these two sides would behave in the next major crisis. And I don't see any reason for confidence that it would work out. We don't even have control over all our nuclear weapons. A submarine crew that enters into some kind of paranoid conspiracy can launch its missiles. One ballistic missile submarine can destroy over a hundred cities.

MOYERS: How does a scientist advise his government? The new President has to face so many competing claims for money. He's looking at a deficit that's growing, government spending that's out of control, and people out there concerned about the essentials of life. He's got to sort all this out. How does he do it?

WEINBERG: First of all, the science adviser has to be able to find the President. In the present Administration, the science adviser doesn't have direct access to the President. He reports through the White House bureaucracy. That wasn't the case in previous Administrations. I think presidents like Kennedy, Johnson, Carter, and Eisenhower were very well served by their science advisers, who had direct access to them.

MOYERS: But Dr. Teller had direct access. He had a chance visit with President Reagan, and from that we got the Star Wars proposal. He sold President Reagan on it.

WEINBERG: Perhaps if President Reagan had had to work with Dr. Teller day in and day out over a long period, he would have begun to calibrate the kind of advice he was getting from Dr. Teller, and might not have been so quick to take that particular piece of advice. The President has to get to know the science adviser.

I remember that during World War II, General Eisenhower insisted that the meteorologist who was giving the Allies reports on weather in the English Channel report to him directly for months before the invasion of Normandy, because he wanted to be able to judge what kind of confidence he could have in the meteorologist's predictions. He wanted to know that meteorologist well enough so that when the meteorologist said something, he could tell how to take the advice. The President has to have this sort of ongoing relation with the science adviser.

MOYERS: If Christopher Columbus came back today still looking for new worlds to discover, but no longer able to find them with wooden ships, do you think he might be a physicist?

WEINBERG: Christopher Columbus would probably have been an applied physicist because he had very definite economic intentions of finding the Indies to open up a trade route, and to find Christian kings to help Spain in the struggle with the Turks. But I think he would have found the experience of trying to get government support very familiar.

MOYERS: The analogy is that you're on the edge of new worlds of discovery—not of a New World across the Atlantic, but of a new world in the cosmos out there. Isn't that what you're looking for?

WEINBERG: We hope we're learning not so much about a new world as about this world. It really is this world. It's true, we make a world for ourselves in the laboratory. We create particles that never existed anywhere else, at least not since the first millionth of a second of the universe, but we're doing it because we're trying to answer the questions that are at the end of the chain of "whys." "Why is the world the way it is? Why is the sky blue? Why are everyday things the way they are?" It's this world we're trying to explain. We create very artificial conditions in the laboratory, but it's not because we enjoy slamming particles together, it's not because we're trying to win any world records for the heaviest and most exotic weird new particle, it's because we're trying to answer that last why in the chain of "whys."

MOYERS: And the last "why" is—

WEINBERG: Well, we haven't got to the last one yet. I shouldn't have said the *last* "why," I should have said the *latest* "why."

MOYERS: But that's just it. It's a little bit like journalism. Our reports are always interim reports.

WEINBERG: Yes, our reports are always interim reports, too. Maybe that won't always be true. We sometimes wonder what it would be like to come to the end, to really get to the final laws of nature, sometimes called the Theory of Everything. Some people think it's in principle impossible. Other people think that it's in principle possible, but we'll run out of money long before we get there, that we'll never know the answer because we can't afford it. Other people think the species is not smart enough. Just as dogs are not smart enough to understand Newtonian mechanics, perhaps we're not smart enough to make progress beyond a certain point.

Another possibility is the one that I've let serve as the organizing principle of my own life. And that is that we're really going to get there, that we're going to get to the end of the chain of "whys," and we're going to see the few simple principles that govern everything.

Now that won't solve all the problems of science. Science will go on forever. I should emphasize this because I don't want to give the impression that I think that elementary particle physics is all there is to science. At every level of nature, new problems arise simply because new things are interesting at that level. When you deal with human beings, you're interested in questions of biology and personality that simply don't arise when you deal at the level of atoms and molecules. And they can't be dealt with in terms of atoms and molecules. But still the question—"Why do human beings have brains that have this kind of mental activity?"—is one that can be traced down to the level of electricity and chemistry and further down to the level of elementary particle physics.

MOYERS: But in dealing with these particles that can only be imagined, how do you ever know you're right or wrong?

WEINBERG: The stock answer is that you know you're right or wrong according to the verdict of experiment. In the long run, that is the right answer. But very often, in the short run, it doesn't work that way. Very often you know you're right because everything hangs together so beautifully, it's got to be right. Sometimes, as Einstein did with special relativity, you get contrary experimental evidence for a while until the experimentalists get their act together, and the experiments agree with the theory. The British theorist Eddington said about fifty years ago that he would never believe any experiment until it was confirmed by theory. But in the end, no matter how beautiful the theory is, if the experimental results from a lot of different laboratories persistently show it's wrong, you have to give up the theory.

AMERICAN VALUES IN THE NEW GLOBAL SOCIETY

Isaac Asimov

W R I T E R

A reader can hardly miss Isaac Asimov. He's written nearly four hundred books. Science fiction, of course: his Foundation Series is a classic. Science fact: chemistry, astronomy, physics, biology. Children's books. History. Math. One scientist has called him the greatest explainer of the age. The American Humanist Association, of which he recently became president, has honored him as Man of the Year.

MOYERS: You've written three hundred and ninety-one books, you read about everything from supernovas to the invention of hay, you have no researchers or clerical help, you do your own filing, your own phoning. When I called to ask you about this interview, you answered the phone yourself. How do you organize it all? How do you keep up?

ASIMOV: When I started out, I assumed that with luck, I'd sell a few dozen stories in my life, so I wouldn't need a secretary or a very fancy filing system. I just made do with card files and my memory. Things got more and more complicated, but never so rapidly that I felt called upon to change. It's like the ancient story of Milo of Croton, who is supposed to have lifted a calf every day until finally he was lifting a full-grown bull. Here I am with a full-grown bull.

MOYERS: A Bell Labs report said there is more information in a single edition of the *New York Times* than a man or woman in the sixteenth century had to process in the whole of his or her life. You seem to keep up.

ASIMOV: You know how we get away with it? When you read the *New York Times*, you read almost nothing in it. You're looking for things that interest you, so most of the things just pass under your eyes without notice.

MOYERS: Is that what you do when you are researching? Do you learn to discriminate?

ASIMOV: I must, otherwise I could never get through everything. It's impossible for me to go through the *New York Times* and not see an article that in any way reflects on science. But on the other hand, it's impossible for me to go through the *New York Times* and notice anything that reflects on fashion.

MOYERS: Do you think that we can educate ourselves, that any one of us, at any time, can be educated in any subject that strikes our fancy?

ASIMOV: The key words here are "that strikes our fancy." There are some things that simply don't strike my fancy, and I doubt that I can force myself to be educated in them. On the other hand, when there's a subject I'm ferociously interested in, then it is easy for me to learn about it. I take it in gladly and cheerfully. I've written more books on astronomy than on any other science, but I've never taken a course in astronomy. I'm completely self-trained in it. On the other hand, I've written relatively few books on chemistry, which is my field of training. I've got a Ph.D. in chemistry, but I know too much chemistry to get excited over it.

MOYERS: Learning really excites you, doesn't it?

ASIMOV: Just yesterday I read about the invention of hay in Freeman Dyson's new book. The thought that occurred to me was, "Why is it I never thought of this? How is it I never knew about this? What made me think that hay existed from the first day of creation?"

MOYERS: What is exciting about that?

ASIMOV: I think it's the actual process of broadening yourself, of knowing there's now a little extra facet of the universe you know about and can think about and can understand. It seems to me that when it's time to die, there would be a certain pleasure in thinking that you had utilized your life well, learned as much as you could, gathered in as much as possible of the universe, and enjoyed it. There's only this one universe and only this one lifetime to try to grasp it. And while it is inconceivable that anyone can grasp more than a tiny portion of it, at least you can do that much. What a tragedy just to pass through and get nothing out of it.

MOYERS: When I learn something new—and it happens every day—I feel a little more at home in this universe, a little more comfortable in the nest. I'm afraid that by the time I begin to feel really at home, it'll be over.

ASIMOV: I used to worry about that. I said, "I'm gradually managing to cram more and more things into my mind. I've got this beautiful mind, and it's going to die, and it'll all be gone." And then I thought, "No, not in my case. Every idea I've ever had I've written down, and it's all there on paper. I won't be gone. It'll be there."

MOYERS: You realize how depressing this thought is for the rest of us who can't write it down the way you can. One could say, "Since I can't write the way Isaac Asimov does, and know what Isaac Asimov knows, I won't do it at all."

ASIMOV: I wouldn't want people to do that. A little is better than nothing. In fact, you could say that I overdo it. Lately I've been thinking that people must look upon me as some kind of a freak. There was a certain pleasure writing a hundred books—you know, I felt I'd accomplished something. Then two hundred. But now it stands at three hundred and ninety-one. It's liable to be four hundred by the end of the year, and I have every intention of continuing because I enjoy the process. In the end, it might be that nobody will care about what I write—just about the number. Maybe I will have defeated myself in that way.

MOYERS: How do you explain yourself to yourself? What is it that causes a man to know so much that he could write four hundred books?

ASIMOV: I suppose it's sheer hedonism. I just enjoy it so. What made Bing Crosby or Bob Hope play all that golf, you know? They enjoyed it—and that's the way it is with me.

MOYERS: Is it possible that this passion for learning can be spread to ordinary folks out there? Can we have a revolution in learning?

ASIMOV: Yes, I think not only that we can but that we must. As computers take over more and more of the work that human beings shouldn't be doing in the first place—because it doesn't utilize their brains, it stultifies and bores them to death—there's going to be nothing left for human beings to do but the more creative types of endeavor. The only way we can indulge in the more creative types of endeavor is to have brains that aim at that from the start.

> As computers take over more and more of the work that human beings shouldn't be doing in the first place . . . there's going to be nothing left for human beings to do but the more creative types of endeavor.

You can't take a human being and put him to work at a job that underuses the brain and keep him working at it for decades and decades, and then say, "Well, that job isn't there, go do something more creative." You have beaten the creativity out of him. But if from the start children are educated into appreciating their own creativity, then probably almost all of us can be creative. In the old days, very few people could read and write. Literacy was a very novel sort of thing, and it was felt that most people just didn't have it in them. But with mass education, it turned out that most people could be taught to read and write. In the same way, once we have computer outlets in every home, each of them hooked up to enormous libraries, where you can ask any question and be given answers, you can look up something you're interested in knowing, however silly it might seem to someone else.

Today, what people call learning is forced on you. Everyone is forced to learn the same thing on the same day at the same speed in class. But everyone is different. For some, class goes too fast, for some too slow, for some in the wrong direction. But give everyone a chance, in addition to school, to follow up their own bent from the start, to find out about whatever they're interested in by looking it up in their own homes, at their own speed, in their own time, and everyone will enjoy learning.

MOYERS: What about the argument that machines, like computers, dehumanize learning?

ASIMOV: As a matter of fact, it's just the reverse. It's through this machine that for the first time, we'll be able to have a one-to-one relationship between information source and information consumer. In the old days, you used to hire a tutor or pedagogue to teach your children. And if he knew his job, he could adapt his teaching to the tastes and abilities of the students. But how many people could afford to hire a pedagogue? Most children went uneducated. Then we reached the point where it was absolutely necessary to educate everybody. The only way we could do it was to have one teacher for a great many students, and to give the teacher a curriculum to teach from. But how many teachers are good at this? As with everything else, the number of teachers is far greater than the number of good teachers. So we either have a one-to-one relationship for the very few, or a one-to-many for the many. Now, with the computer, it's possible to have a one-to-one relationship for the many. Everyone can have a teacher in the form of access to the gathered knowledge of the human species.

MOYERS: But you know, we have such a miserable record in this country of providing poor children even with good classrooms that I wonder if our society can ever harness itself to provide everyone, including poor children, with good computers.

ASIMOV: Perhaps not at the very start. That's like asking yourself, "Is it possible to supply everybody in the nation with clean water?" In many nations it is impossible to get clean water except under very unusual circumstances. That was one reason why people started drinking beer and wine—the alcohol killed the germs, and if you didn't drink that, you died of cholera. But there are places where you can supply clean water for nearly everyone. The United States probably supplies clean water for a larger percentage of its population than almost any other nation can. So it's not that we would expect everybody to have a perfect computer right away, but we can try for it, and with time, I think more and more will. For goodness' sake, when I was young, very few people had automobiles or telephones, and almost nobody had an air conditioner. Now these things are almost universal. It might be the same way with computers.

MOYERS: What would such a teaching machine look like?

ASIMOV: I find that difficult to imagine. It's easy to be theoretical, but when you really try to think of the nuts and bolts, then it becomes difficult. I could easily have imagined a horseless carriage in the middle of the nineteenth century, but I couldn't have drawn a picture of it. But I suppose that one essential thing would be a screen on which you could display things, and another essential part would be a printing mechanism on which things could be printed for you. And you'll have to have a keyboard on which you ask your questions, although ideally I would like to see one that could be activated by voice. You could actually talk to it, and perhaps it could talk to you too, and say, "I have something here that may interest you. Would you like to have me print it out for you?" And you'd say, "Well, what is it exactly?" And it would tell you, and you might say, "Oh all right, I'll take a look at it."

Anything that would make you feel the teacher was more human would be pleasant for you. And yet, you can never tell. I was once shown a device that had a certain number of set statements like "Yes, sir," "Immediately"—things like that. After you've heard it for the tenth time, it irritates you. So I suppose it's not wise to try to figure out in advance too much what things will look like or be, but let the public demand guide what one produces.

MOYERS: But the machine would have to be connected to books, periodicals, and documents in some vast library, so then when I want to look at Isaac Asimov's new book *Far as Human Eye Could See*, the chapter on geochemistry, I could punch my keys and this chapter would come to me.

ASIMOV: That's right, and then of course you ask—and believe me, I've asked—this question: "How do you arrange to pay the author for the use of the material?" After all, if a person writes something, and this then becomes available to everybody, you deprive him of the economic reason for writing. A person like myself, if he was assured of a livelihood, might write anyway, just because he enjoyed it, but most people would want to do it in return for something. I imagine how they must have felt when free libraries were first instituted. "What? My book in a free library? Anyone can come in and read it for free?" Then you realize that there are some books that wouldn't be sold at all if you didn't have libraries.

MOYERS: With computers, in a sense, every student has his or her own private school.

ASIMOV: Yes, he can be the sole dictator of what he is going to study. Mind you, this is not all he's going to do. He'll still be going to school for some things that he has to know.

MOYERS: Common knowledge, for example.

ASIMOV: Right, and interaction with other students and with teachers. He can't get away from that, but he's got to look forward to the fun in life, which is following his own bent.

MOYERS: Is this revolution in personal learning just for the young?

ASIMOV: No, it's not just for the young. That's another trouble with education as we now have it. People think of education as something that they can finish. And what's more, when they finish, it's a rite of passage. You're finished with school. You're no more a child, and therefore anything that reminds you of school—reading books, having ideas, asking questions—that's kid's stuff. Now you're an adult, you don't do that sort of thing any more.

MOYERS: And in fact, like prison, the reward of school is getting out. Kids say, "When are you getting out?"

ASIMOV: Every kid knows the only reason he's in school is because he's a kid and little and weak, and if he manages to get out early, if he drops out, why he's just a premature man.

MOYERS: I've talked to some of these dropouts, and they think they've become men because they're out of school.

ASIMOV: You have everybody looking forward to no longer learning, and you make them ashamed afterward of going back to learning. If you have a system of education using computers, then anyone, any age, can learn by himself, can continue to be interested. If you enjoy learning, there's no reason why you should stop at a given age. People don't stop things they enjoy doing just because they reach a certain age. They don't stop playing tennis just because they've turned forty. They don't stop with sex just because they've turned forty. They keep it up as long as they can if they enjoy it, and learning will be the same thing. The trouble with learning is that most people don't enjoy it because of the circumstances. Make it possible for them to enjoy learning, and they'll keep it up.

There's the famous story about Oliver Wendell Holmes, who was in the hospital one time, when he was over ninety. President Roosevelt came to see him, and there was Oliver Wendell Holmes reading the Greek grammar. Roosevelt said, "Why are you reading a Greek grammar, Mr. Holmes?" And Holmes said, "To improve my mind, Mr. President."

MOYERS: Are we romanticizing this, or do you think that Saul Bellow's character Herzog was correct when he said that the people who come to evening classes are only ostensibly after culture. What they're really seeking, he said, is clarity, good sense, and truth, even an atom of it. People, he said, are dying for the lack of something real at the end of the day.

ASIMOV: I'd like to think that was so. I'd like to think that people who are given a chance to learn facts and broaden their knowledge of the universe wouldn't seek so avidly after mysticism.

MOYERS: What bothers you about mysticism?

ASIMOV: The same thing bothers me about mysticism that bothers me about con men. It isn't right to sell a person phony stock, and take money for it, and this is what mystics are doing. They're selling people phony knowledge and taking money for it. Even if people feel good about it, I can well imagine that a person who really believes in astrology is going to have a feeling of security because he knows that this is a bad day, so he'll stay at home, just as a guy who's got phony stock may look at it and feel rich. But he still has phony stock, and the person who buys mysticism still has phony knowledge.

MOYERS: What's the real knowledge?

ASIMOV: We can't be absolutely certain. Science doesn't purvey absolute truth. Science is a mechanism, a way of trying to improve your knowledge of nature. It's a system for testing your thoughts against the universe and seeing whether they match. This works not just for the ordinary aspects of science, but for all of life. I should think people would want to know that what they know is truly what the universe is like, or at least as close as they can get to it. We don't pretend that we know everything. In fact, it would be terrible to know everything because there'd be nothing left to learn. But you don't want to be up a blind alley somewhere.

MOYERS: You wrote a few years ago that the decline in America's world power is in part brought about by our diminishing status as a world science leader. Why have we neglected science?

ASIMOV: Partly because of success. The most damaging statement that the United States has ever been subjected to is the phrase "Yankee know-how." You get the feeling somehow that Americans—just by the fact that they're Americans—are somehow smarter and more ingenious than other people, which really is not so. Actually, the phrase was first used in connection with the atomic bomb, which was invented and brought to fruition by a bunch of European refugees. That's "Yankee know-how."

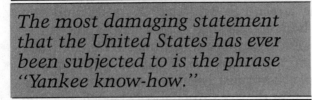

The most damaging statement that the United States has ever been subjected to is the phrase "Yankee know-how."

There's also this feeling that somehow our free enterprise system alone will do it for us. That helps out in some ways, but not if we're lazy about it. It's not going to do it for us if we don't do anything, you see.

MOYERS: It's astonishing how few American students study mathematics or major in science.

ASIMOV: Yes, we are living in a business society.

MOYERS: And yet there's long been a bias in this country against science. When Benjamin Franklin was experimenting with the lightning rod, a lot of good folk said, "You don't need a lightning rod. If you want to prevent lightning from striking, you just have to pray about it."

ASIMOV: The bias against science is part of being a pioneer society. You somehow feel that city life is decadent. American history is full of fables of the noble virtuous farmer and the vicious city slicker. The city slicker is an automatic villain. Unfortunately, such stereotypes can do damage. A noble ignoramus is not necessarily what the country needs. When Andrew Jackson became President, it was felt that any person could fill any federal office. That started the spoils system we have now: when a new guy comes in, everyone is fired, and the new party puts in the people. That works, if in fact any person can run any job. But you and I know that there are such things as experience and education and intelligence. When the Civil War started, the North had no expertise in fighting and no army worth a darn. Most of the officers with any training were Southerners. We had to learn how to fight the war the hard way, and lost a lot of people that way.

MOYERS: In 1980 you were afraid that the fundamentalists who were coming into power with President Reagan were going to turn this country even further against science, especially with their demands that biblical creationism be given an equal footing in the classroom with science. Have they made those inroads that you feared?

ASIMOV: Fortunately, the currents have been against them. But they still put pressure on school boards and parents, and it's become a little more difficult in many parts of the nation to teach evolution.

MOYERS: The fundamentalists see you as the very incarnation of the enemy, the epitome of the secular humanist who opposes God's plan for the universe. In 1984, the American Humanist Society gave you their Humanist of the Year Award, and you're now president of that organization. Are you an enemy of religion?

ASIMOV: No, I'm not. What I'm against is the attempt to place a person's belief system onto the nation or the world generally. We object to the Soviet Union trying to dominate the world, to communize the world. The United States, I hope, is trying to democratize the world. But I certainly would be very much against trying to Christianize the world or to Islamize it or to Judaize it or anything of the sort. My objection to fundamentalism is not that they are fundamentalists but that essentially they want me to be a fundamentalist, too. Now, they may say that I believe evolution is true and I want everyone to believe that evolution is true. But I don't want everyone to believe that evolution is true, I want them to study what we say about evolution and to decide for themselves. Fundamentalists say they want to treat creationism on an equal basis. But they can't. It's not a science. You can teach creationism in churches and in courses on religion. They would be horrified if I were to suggest that in the churches they teach secular humanism as an alternate way of looking at the universe or evolution as an alternate way of considering how life may have started. In the church they teach only what they believe, and rightly so, I suppose. But on the other hand, in schools, in science courses, we've got to teach what scientists think is the way the universe works.

MOYERS: But this is what frightens many believers. They see science as uncertain, always tentative, always subject to revisionism. They see science as presenting a complex, chilling, and enormous universe ruled by chance and impersonal laws. They see science as dangerous.

ASIMOV: That is really the glory of science—that science is tentative, that it is not certain, that it is subject to change. What is really disgraceful is to have a set of beliefs that you think is absolute and has been so from the start and can't change, where you simply won't listen to evidence. You say, "If the evidence agrees with me, it's not necessary, and if it doesn't agree with me, it's false." This is the legendary remark of Omar when they captured Alexandria and asked him what to do with the library. He said, "If the books agree with the Koran, they are not necessary and may be burned. If they disagree with the Koran, they are pernicious and must be burned." Well, there are still these Omar-like thinkers who think all of knowledge will fit into one book called the Bible, and who refuse to allow it is possible ever to conceive of an error there. To my way of thinking, that is much more dangerous than a system of knowledge that is tentative and uncertain.

MOYERS: Do you see any room for reconciling the religious view in which the universe is God's drama, constantly interrupted and rewritten by divine intervention, and the view of the universe as scientists hold it?

ASIMOV: There is if people are reasonable. There are many scientists who are honestly religious. Millikan was a truly religious man. Morley of the Michelson-Morley experiment was truly religious. There were hundreds of others who did great scientific work, good scientific work, and at the same time were religious. But they did not mix their religion and science. In other words, if something they didn't understand took place in science, they didn't dismiss it by saying, "Well, that's what God wants," or "At this point a miracle took place." No, they knew that science is strictly a construct of the human mind working according to the laws of nature, and that religion is something that lies outside and may embrace science. You know, if there were suddenly to arise scientific, confirmable evidence that God exists, then scientists would have no choice but to accept that fact. On the other hand, the fundamentalists don't admit the possibility of evidence that would show, for example, that evolution exists. Any evidence you present they will deny if it conflicts with the word of God as they think it to be. So the chances of compromise are only on one side, and, therefore, I doubt that it will take place.

MOYERS: What frightens them is something that Dostoevski once said—if God is dead, everything is permitted.

ASIMOV: That assumes that human beings have no feeling about what is right and wrong. Is the only reason you are virtuous because virtue is your ticket to heaven? Is the only reason you don't beat your children to death because you don't want to go to hell? It's insulting to imply that only a system of rewards and punishments can keep you a decent human being. Isn't it conceivable a person wants to be a decent human being because that way he feels better?

I don't believe that I'm ever going to heaven or hell. I think that when I die, there will be nothingness. That's what I firmly believe. That's not to mean that I have the impulse to go out and rob and steal and rape and everything else because I don't fear punishment. For one thing, I fear worldly punishment. And for a second thing, I fear the punishment of my own conscience. I have a conscience. It doesn't depend on religion. And I think that's so with other people, too.

Even in societies in which religion is very powerful, there's no shortage of crime and sin and misery and terrible things happening, despite heaven and hell. I imagine if you go down death row, and ask a bunch of murderers who are waiting for execution if they believe in God, they'll tell you yes. I wouldn't be surprised if the number of people in jail for fraud, for violent crimes, for everything, includes a smaller percentage of acknowledged atheists than we have in the general population. So I don't know why one should think that just because you don't want a ticket to heaven, and you don't fear a ticket to hell, you should be a villain.

MOYERS: Is there a morality in science?

ASIMOV: Oh, absolutely. In fact, there is a morality in science that is further advanced than anywhere else. If you find a person in science who has faked his results, who has lied as far as his findings are concerned, who has tried to steal the work of another, who has done something other scientists consider unethical—well, his scientific reputation is ruined, his scientific life is over. There is no forgiveness. The morality of science is that you report the truth, you do your best to disprove your own findings, and you do not utilize someone else's findings and report them as your own. In any other branch of human endeavor—in politics, in economics, in law, in almost anything—people can commit crimes and still be heroes. For instance, Colonel North has done terrible things, yet he's a hero and a patriot to some people. This goes in almost every field. Only science is excepted. You make a misstep in science, and you're through. Really through.

MOYERS: You love the field, don't you? You love science.

ASIMOV: Oh, I'm very fond of it. I think it's amazing how many saints there have been among scientists. I'll give you an example. In 1900, De Vries studied mutations. He found a patch of evening primrose of different types, and he studied how they inherited their characteristics. He worked out the laws of genetics. Two other guys worked out the laws of genetics at the same time, a guy called Karl Correns, who was a German, and Erich Tschermak von Seysenegg, who was an Austrian. All three worked out the laws of genetics in 1900, and having done so, all three looked through the literature, just to see what had been done before. All three discovered that in the 1860s Gregor Mendel had worked out the laws of genetics, and people hadn't paid any attention then. All three reported their findings as confirmation of what Mendel had found. Not one of the three attempted to say that it was original with him. And you know what it meant. It meant that two of them, Correns and Tschermak von Seysenegg, lived in obscurity. De Vries is known only because he was also the first to work out the theory of mutations. But as far as discovering genetics is concerned, Mendel gets all the credit. They knew at the time that this would happen. That's the sort of thing you just don't find outside of science.

MOYERS: If it is truth that excites you, what is the value of science fiction, for which you are justifiably universally known?

ASIMOV: Okay, let's look at fiction as a whole, just any kind of fiction. In serious fiction, fiction where the writer feels he's accomplishing something besides simply amusing people—although there's nothing wrong with simply amusing people—the writer is holding up a mirror to the human species, making it possible for you to understand people better because you've read the novel or story, and maybe making it possible for you to understand yourself better. This is an important thing.

Now science fiction uses a different method. It works up an artificial society, one which doesn't exist, or one that may possibly exist in the future, but not necessarily. And it portrays events against the background of this society in the hope that you will be able to see yourself in relation to the present society. I don't claim that I succeed at this. It seems to me that to do this properly takes a great man, a guy on the level of—well, at least half that of Shakespeare, and I don't come up there. But I try, and who knows? Maybe once in a while I succeed a little bit. And that's why I write science fiction—because it's a way of writing fiction in a style that enables me to make points I can't make otherwise.

MOYERS: Someone once said that one great advantage of science fiction is that it can introduce the reader to changes that may well be inevitable, but that are not now conceivable.

ASIMOV: I've said that myself at different times. The fact is that society is always changing, but the rate of change has been accelerating all through history for a variety of reasons. One, the change is cumulative. The very changes you make now make it easier to make further changes. Until the Industrial Revolution came along, people weren't aware of change or a future. They assumed the future would be exactly like it had always been, just with different people. You know, as things are, so they remain. As Ecclesiastes says, "There is nothing new under the sun." It was only with the coming of the Industrial Revolution that the rate of change became fast enough to be visible in a single lifetime. People were suddenly aware that not only were things changing, but that they would continue to change after they died. That was when science fiction came into being as opposed to fantasy and adventure tales. Because people knew that they would die before they could see the changes that would happen in the next century, they thought it would be nice to imagine what they might be.

As time goes on, and the rate of change still continues to accelerate, it becomes more and more important to adjust what you do today to the fact of change in the future. It's ridiculous to make your plans now on the assumption that things will continue as they are now. You have to assume that if something you're doing is going to reach fruition in ten years, that in those ten years changes will take place, and perhaps what you're doing will have no meaning then. So nowadays futurism has become an important part of thinking in business, economics, politics, and military affairs. Science fiction is important because it fights the natural notion that there's something permanent about things the way they are right now.

> *Science fiction is important because it fights the natural notion that there's something permanent about things the way they are right now.*

MOYERS: You once said that your view of the future changes according to what you read every morning in the daily newspaper. What are you reading in today's newspapers?

ASIMOV: Well, I read that in the Soviet Union, for instance, there are protests here, marches there—that there's a lot of turmoil. It makes me feel that the Soviet Union is gaining strength because when a nation is absolutely quiet, when no one says anything, when you don't hear any controversy going on, that's a kind of death, a death involving fear, a death involving oppression. With turmoil, the Soviet Union is becoming, shall we say, slightly Americanized? I think that's a good thing. I think the fact that Reagan got along so well with Gorbachev, and vice versa, that they were palsy-walsy, with their arms around each other's shoulders, is a great thing. That doesn't mean that tomorrow the Soviet Union is going to be exactly what we want it to be. It doesn't mean that we're going to be exactly what they want us to be. But we're at least moving in the right direction. I hope this means there's just a slightly better chance that we're heading for an era of international cooperation and perhaps the development of a kind of federal world government, which I think is essential.

MOYERS: Use your imagination: If the President asked you to draft his inaugural address and said, "Dr. Asimov, make sure I say the one thing you think I must convince the American people that they should pay attention to," what would it be?

ASIMOV: It would be this: That all the problems that we face now, that are really important, that are life-and-death, are global problems, that they affect all of us alike. The ozone layer, if it disappears, disappears for all of us. Pollution in the ocean, in the atmosphere, in the ground water, is for all of us. The only way we can ameliorate these problems, solve them, prevent them from destroying us, is, again, through a global solution. We can't expect that anything the United States does alone is going to affect the situation the world over. There has to be cooperation among the nations of the world. If we can achieve that in the face of a danger deadlier than has ever faced humanity before, why, one of the advantages we'll have is that automatically we will probably start spending less money on war and preparations for war, which will, in turn, be a beneficial cycle, because we'll have more money for solving these problems we must solve.

MOYERS: You sound more optimistic than you did a few years ago. I read an essay in which you said that we're entering a decade of decision, that we have to make life-and-death decisions about our energy problems, about the fact that we're using up fossil fuel and not developing alternatives, about the population explosion, and about our constant and pernicious tendency to prepare for war. You said we'll know at the end of the 1980s if we made the right decisions. Have we?

ASIMOV: We haven't made irretrievably wrong decisions. I was afraid that with the atmosphere of the 1980s, the Cold War would intensify and become something we couldn't reverse. But quite suddenly it has been reversed, and for reasons of the kind that always upsets me as a futurist—for unpredictable reasons. There's no way you could have predicted that a man like Gorbachev would come to power in the Soviet Union, a man who is young and flexible and post-Revolutionary in his thinking. And there's no way you could have predicted that Reagan would make this Iran-Contra mistake and feel it necessary in his last year to do something that will make him remembered for some other reason.

And so between Reagan, intent on something upbeat, and Gorbachev, intent on somehow ameliorating the Cold War, we had what you might call a meeting of minds, and the beginning of nuclear disarmament, even if only the beginning. So I have felt a little more confidence all this last year.

MOYERS: What about the subject you've written so much about—the population explosion? Right now, the population of the globe is over five billion. You've warned us about what will happen if it continues at its two percent growth rate per year.

ASIMOV: Actually, the growth rate is down to one-point-six percent, but with the higher population, it's the same amount in actual numbers: eighty million a year. By the year 2000, it's going to be perhaps six-point-five billion.

MOYERS: That's just twelve years from now. How many people do you think the earth is able to sustain?

ASIMOV: I don't think it's able to sustain the five billion in the long run. Right now most of the world is living under appalling conditions. We can't possibly improve the conditions of everyone. We can't raise the entire world to the average standard of living in the United States because we don't have the resources and the ability to distribute well enough for that. So right now as it is, we have condemned most of the world to a miserable, starvation level of existence. And it will just get worse as the population continues to go up.

MOYERS: But you can't just say to a woman, "Don't have children."

ASIMOV: That's not the problem; it's that so many people are saying, "Have children." There is such a pro-natalist attitude in the world. We celebrate Mother's Day so enthusiastically, we say, "May all your troubles be little ones," we celebrate additional children. I feel sometimes that if we'd only stop pushing for children, somehow there would be fewer of them.

MOYERS: Why did you say that the price of survival is the equality of women?

ASIMOV: Because if women are allowed to enter into all facets of the human condition, if they can enter business, if they can enter religion, science, government on an equal basis with men, they will be so busy they won't feel it necessary to have a great many children. As long as you have women under conditions where they don't feel any sense of value or self-worth except as mothers, they'll have a lot of children because that's the only way they can prove they're worth something. In general, if you look through the world, the lower the status of women, the higher the birth rate, and the higher the birth rate, the lower the status of women. If you could raise the status of women, I am certain the birth rate would fall drastically through the choice of the women themselves. We're always saying that there's no fulfillment like having children, but I notice mostly it's men who say that. You know, men get along without giving birth to children. They do that by finding other things to do. If women could find other things to do, too, they would have fewer children.

MOYERS: But once again, you are in conflict with a biblical imperative, "Be fruitful and multiply."

ASIMOV: Right. But God said that when Adam and Eve were the only two people in the world. He said, "Be fruitful and multiply and replenish the earth." The earth was replenished long ago. That's one of the problems of fundamentalism. Fundamentalists take a statement that made sense at the time it was made, and because they refuse to consider that the statement may not be an absolute, eternal truth, they continue following it under conditions where to do so is deadly.

MOYERS: What happens to the idea of the dignity of the human species if this population growth continues at its present rate?

ASIMOV: It will be completely destroyed. I like to use what I call my bathroom metaphor: If two people live in an apartment, and there are two bathrooms, then both have freedom of the bathroom. You can go to the bathroom anytime you want to and stay as long as you want to for whatever you need. And everyone believes in the freedom of the bathroom; it should be right there in the Constitution.

But if you have twenty people in the apartment and two bathrooms, no matter how much every person believes in freedom of the bathroom, there is no such thing. You have to set up times for each person, you have to bang at the door: "Aren't you through yet?" and so on. In the same way, democracy cannot survive overpopulation. Human dignity cannot survive it. Convenience and decency cannot survive it. As you put more and more people onto the world, the value of life not only declines, it disappears. It doesn't matter if someone dies. The more people there are, the less one individual matters.

MOYERS: People say the United States is bringing its population under control, that many Americans are not even reproducing themselves, and that what the rest of the world does, we can't control.

ASIMOV: The population of the United States is still going up. The only time it went up really slowly was during the Great Depression, when there were no laws lowering the birth rate, there was just an economic depression, which made people think twice before they had children. But the United States is doing something else—it is absolutely refusing to help nations control population. Our feeling is that it's enough for us to make sure that the United States is in good shape, and what other nations do is their business. It's not just their business—it's our business, too.

MOYERS: Can we exist as a stable economy and a stable society if around us are turmoil and chaos?

ASIMOV: Absolutely not. Right now many nations are destroying the rain forests because they need the firewood, and they need the space for farms.

MOYERS: Why should we care about that?

ASIMOV: Because without the rain forests, we're going to have deserts. The food supply will dwindle. As a matter of fact, there's even the possibility that we're going to lose all kinds of valuable substances we know nothing about. Those rain forests have an incredible number of species of plants and animals that we know very little about. Some of them may produce chemicals of great pharmacological and medical importance. If properly cultivated, some of the plants might be new food sources. In addition to that, nothing produces the oxygen of the atmosphere with the same intensity that a forest does. Anything that substitutes for it will be producing less oxygen. We're going to be destroying our atmosphere, too.

MOYERS: What did you mean when you said once that we have to stop living by the code of the past?

ASIMOV: Times change. For example, in the past we felt motherhood was the most important thing a woman could do, and that to be a good wife and mother was the sum total of a woman's purpose in life. She didn't need an education or interests outside the house. You know, *Kinder, Kirche, Küche*—the children, the church, the kitchen—or in English you say, "Keep 'em barefoot and pregnant." Well, we can't do that any more. We can't raise women to be baby machines. In the old days, we didn't worry about the future. Now we must. Things are changing so fast that we have to worry about the future all the time.

MOYERS: You and I may not be around when it arrives.

ASIMOV: Our children will be, and our grandchildren—and the human race. I don't want to sound like a foolish idealist or as though I just love humanity. But, look, my books are going to survive me—I want to have people alive to read them.

MOYERS: Is it possible that you suffer from an excessive trust in rationality?

ASIMOV: Well, I can't answer that very easily. Perhaps I do, you know. But I can't think of anything else to trust in. If you can't go by reason, what can you go by? One answer is faith. But faith in what? I notice there's no general agreement in the world. These matters of faith, they are not compelling. I have my faith, you have your faith, and there's no way in which I can translate my faith to you or vice versa. At least, as far as reason is concerned, there's a system of transfer, a system of rational argument following the laws of logic that a great many people agree on, so that in reason, there are what we call compelling arguments. If I locate certain kinds of evidence, even people who disagreed with me to begin with, find themselves compelled by the evidence to agree. But whenever we go beyond reason into faith, there's no such thing as compelling evidence. Even if you have a revelation, how can you transfer that revelation to others? By what system?

MOYERS: So you find your hope for the future in the mind.

ASIMOV: Yes, I have to say, I can't wait until everyone in the world is rational, or until just enough are rational to make a difference.

MOYERS: Your latest book—number three hundred and ninety-one—is called *Far as Human Eye Could See*. How far can we see?

ASIMOV: It depends on what we're looking for. If we're looking at human history, we can't see very far because human history is a chaotic thing. Small changes have big results, unpredictable in direction. But if we're looking at something that's essentially simple, such as stars and galaxies and things like that, then it is possible to look far, far ahead. We may be wrong, but it is possible to make a case for something that might happen ten-to-the-hundred years in the future—one with a hundred zeros after it. In fact, that's what I do in the last essay—that's why I call it "Far as Human Eye Could See." It comes from "Locksley Hall," by Tennyson, of course: "For I dipped into the future, far as human eye could see/Saw the Vision of the world, and all the wonder that would be."

MOYERS: You see wonder out there?

ASIMOV: I see a picture of a universe that becomes infinite. It can expand and expand and expand until it is sufficiently thinly spaced to allow another universe to begin. And that perhaps surrounding our universe is the far, faint remnant of another universe; and beyond that, of another one, even fainter, and so on, infinitely. If the universe doesn't expand forever, if it goes into a crunch and disappears, there may be a limitless ocean of vacuum out of which new universes are constantly arising like bubbles in boiling water, some large, some small, some with one set of laws, some with another. We just happen to be living in one that's suitable for life.

And there we get into the Anthropic Principle because we can only exist in one that's suitable for life. The mere fact that we exist makes it suitable for life, you see. There are people who argue that everything in the universe depends upon human observation. Then there are people who say, "Supposing there were no human beings, just frogs. Will the frog observation do the trick?" It's a game for modern scholastics. Instead of how many angels can dance on the point of a pin, we try to argue out quantum weirdness. It's a lot of fun, but it makes you dizzy.

MOYERS: You've lived through much of this century. Have you ever known human beings to think with the perspective you're calling on them to think with now?

ASIMOV: It's perhaps not important that every human being think so. But how about the leaders and opinion-makers thinking so? Ordinary people might follow them. It would help if we didn't have leaders who were thinking in exactly the opposite way, if we didn't have people who were shouting hatred and suspicion of foreigners, if we didn't have people who were shouting that it's more important to be unfriendly than to be friendly, if we didn't have people shouting that the people inside the country who don't look exactly the way the rest of us look have something wrong with them. It's almost not necessary for us to do good; it's only necessary for us to stop doing evil, for goodness' sake.

> *It's almost not necessary for us to do good; it's only necessary for us to stop doing evil, for goodness' sake.*

Robert Bellah

S O C I O L O G I S T

Robert Bellah has long been intrigued by the relationship of religion to politics and society. For five years he and his colleagues listened to Americans talking about the habits of their hearts—about love and marriage, commitment and solitude, private happiness and public good. The result was Habits of the Heart, which asked some provocative questions about the American character. He teaches at the University of California at Berkeley and at the Graduate Theological Union.

MOYERS: With the twenty-first century fast approaching, is there one inescapable question we must face?

BELLAH: Well, I think it's a very exciting prospect to be facing a new millennium. And of course that raises all kinds of fears and hopes. But to me the most critical question is how can we give interdependence—which is so obvious in connection with everything we do—a moral meaning? Interdependence without moral meaning is terrifying. We don't like the fact that we depend on a lot of other people, or that what people do in other parts of the world can have effects on our lives.

MOYERS: If the Japanese sold their securities tomorrow, they might drive the prices of our stocks down?

BELLAH: That's right. We depend on them. Of course, if we can't buy Japanese goods, they're going to have the worst depression in their history, so it works both ways. But the question is, how can we bring that factual interdependence, which is inescapable, into some kind of coherence so that we understand it, and so that it has a positive meaning for us? We need to develop common ways of thinking that could take the fear out of that interdependence, and that would operate to make this new global economy less brutal in its effects on people. I know that's not easy. But I think that's our task.

MOYERS: It isn't easy in part because of what you and your colleagues describe in your book, Habits of the Heart. You paint a fairly bleak picture of American culture—people high on personal gratification, without moderating influences from family, church, or community—people whose only truth is their own feeling about what is true. It doesn't give us much hope for finding moral ground in an international economy when you say that here at home we're not acting as if there is a common good.

BELLAH: I think you're describing the first half of the book more than the second. We do find some wonderful people in the second half of the book who are concerned with the public good. But yes, there is a problem. Americans have come to believe that somehow modern technology will solve all our problems without preventing the individual from doing whatever he or she wants to do. They feel that the combination of private freedom and technological advance is the answer to all our problems. What I think we're seeing is that technological advance is real and has very positive implications, but that without any guidance or any set of priorities, technological advance can create all kinds of severe problems—the greenhouse effect, for example, or the situations where we can't move in traffic in our major cities.

Americans have preferred not to think about the social and political realities that link technology to our individual lives. But that's what we have to work on.

MOYERS: You're saying that most of us want to satisfy our own needs and wants, and we want to do so without considering the rippling impact of our behavior on others. If I want to drive to Mendocino this weekend to see the coastline, fine. But if ten thousand other people want to go at the same time, we have a social problem.

BELLAH: Exactly.

MOYERS: You talk about building a moral frame for interdependence, of making technology socially beneficial, of finding a sense of community in solving these problems. But how do we go about that in practical ways?

BELLAH: First of all, we have to face the reality, and that means we have to talk about it. People who say we talk too much and that we should act are on the wrong track. The first big job is thinking and understanding, and that means talking together.

MOYERS: And this has to be a moral discourse?

BELLAH: Yes. When we do that, we may begin to discover more consensus than we think there is. We may agree on certain priorities. Once we see what those priorities are, then we can realize that if each of us does entirely what he or she pleases at all times, none of us will get those priorities answered. So then we have to figure out what are the social arrangements that will allow as many of us as possible to fulfill those perfectly valid individual wants in a way that's supportive of other people rather than destructive to them.

MOYERS: Who implements what we collectively decide ought to happen?

BELLAH: Well, that is the classic place for the political process. Americans are allergic to politics, because we see it as an area of power and influence that is probably unfairly exercised. But we have to recover a more classical notion of politics as the place where we decide together about the things we need to do.

MOYERS: That's not happening now, is it?

BELLAH: Yes and no. There are people who attempt to get that discourse going, and there are people who simply use easy answers or images that convey fear or hope rather than engaging in serious conversation.

MOYERS: You said some time ago that the campaign of 1988 offered the possibility of opening up the conversation of democracy rather dramatically, and that both parties, Republican and Democratic, could challenge the assumptions they've so long taken for granted. Did that happen?

BELLAH: To some extent. The fact that Jesse Jackson got as far as he did meant that certain things that otherwise wouldn't have been discussed at all at least got into the public forum.

MOYERS: But what I saw was such a growing gap between the rhetoric and the reality. I listened to the candidates, and I didn't hear very realistic descriptions of the world out there.

BELLAH: Part of the problem is television. It has such a powerful way of presenting immediate images that it tempts the politician to go for whatever will have the most impact. That really corrupts the electorate into thinking about voting only in terms of the most short-term interests or fears. The difficulty today is getting the political leadership to think about the larger problems. Even to get to the year 2000 is going to be tough. In a campaign where you're looking at the polls every week to see how you're doing, you're not thinking about educating the public about the next ten to fifteen years, you're just thinking about what will get that poll reaction up tomorrow. It's seductive to both the candidate and the electorate not to think about the hard questions, but to talk only about what's most immediately effective.

MOYERS: But doesn't that say something about the nature of politics and the character of the electorate, something that works against our hopes for reaching consensus on the larger issues?

BELLAH: Well, to take the other side from what I just said, I do think a lot of people are worried about the bigger questions, and they're suspicious of politicians who won't face these. Even though we're in a relatively prosperous period, a lot of Americans know how thin the basis of that prosperity is and how many problems have to be solved to make that prosperity last.

So if you look at it that way, you see that even though we're in a period of peace and prosperity, the fact that anyone is willing to take on the tough problems and talk about them is really quite remarkable. I think that is going on in American discourse today.

MOYERS: Did you hear it in the campaign? I didn't. I didn't hear them reaching for this moral consensus that you talk about.

BELLAH: Well, I have to admit that they did reach for the moral vision mainly at symbolic moments like their acceptance speeches, but I would have liked to have seen them develop some of the ideas they presented there more fully in the campaign itself. We saw the articulation of some of the issues that needed to be discussed— although they did tend to get pushed aside in the day-to-day battle for media space.

MOYERS: You said that democratic politics is always dangerous. What do you mean?

BELLAH: Democratic politics is dangerous precisely because it leaves the decisions to the people. We have to rely on the people to have both common sense and what would have been called in the eighteenth century public virtue. And that's a big risk. If people don't have either common sense or public virtue, then they can easily be seduced into very bad things. After all, in a German democracy in 1932, the Nazis won the biggest vote. That can happen. People have to be educated to be good, and that's a big task. It's a task for a real political leader to engage in that kind of public education for civic virtue.

MOYERS: By being good, do you mean thinking of other people?

BELLAH: Yes, I do. A public official who thinks only about his or her own interests and not about the entity he or she is supposed to serve is a corrupt official. By the same token, a voter who goes to the polls and asks, "Which candidate is best for me? I don't care about which is best for the country, or which is best for other people, just who's best for me?"—that is a corrupt voter, just as corrupt as a corrupt public official.

MOYERS: So democracy has a capacity for a kind of infinite corruption. If politicians can give us what we want in exchange for staying in office, there is a kind of corruption there.

BELLAH: Yes. To some extent, it's the invasion of the market model into the political sphere. The market model is perfectly okay in the economic sphere, but when it invades the political sphere, it is deeply corrupting.

MOYERS: The market model—you give me something, I'll give you something back?

BELLAH: Yes—maximizing self-interest at all times. That makes a certain sense in the economy, but generalizing the economy to all of our lives destroys everything. For instance, you can't have a marriage that works that way. If you're interested only in maximizing your own self-interest, how can you think about the other person to whom you're supposed to be committed?

MOYERS: I did a documentary a few years ago for CBS on no-fault divorce. This was a term that still strikes an odd note in my mind.

BELLAH: It actually is a very unfortunate term that the authors of the California divorce reform bill never used. What they were trying to do was change the notion that one person is wholly at fault to the notion that often both parties are at fault. But we somehow—again through the media—translated that into nobody's fault. And that invalidates the notion of marriage altogether. If marriage is so thin a commitment that the minute either party doesn't like what's going on, he or she can just say good-bye, what do we need marriage for? We can do that without getting married.

MOYERS: Are we approaching a no-fault society, where nobody, politician or voter, is accountable for what happens?

BELLAH: There is a real temptation to move in that direction. My feeling is that that kind of society just doesn't work, and that we will wake up in time to realize that it doesn't work.

MOYERS: But it works in the sense that a lot of people are getting what they want—prosperity and gratification.

BELLAH: Yes, but we have to remember that a very significant number of people are not getting what they want. Take no-fault divorce, for example. The best sociological work on the consequences of no-fault divorce shows that it has been catastrophic for the wives and children, where the wife is the custodial parent. It hasn't worked for everyone. Usually it's worked for the strong, but not for the weak.

MOYERS: Do you think we are becoming increasingly indifferent to cause and effect? You point out that here in California, many people seem surprised that the public school system, which at one time was among the best in the nation, is now below the median level of the states. No one seems to point out that people in the seventies voted for tax cuts with the consequence that now the schools are getting worse. What does that say to you?

BELLAH: It says again that people are seduced into their short-term interests without thinking of all the consequences. Everybody wants to pay less taxes. But you don't necessarily want to lose a first-rate school system. Now I think we're finding a change in public opinion in California. We're quite pro-education. It's kind of foolish that we had to go through that ten-year period of decline, but nonetheless, it shows that the electorate has the capacity to correct itself.

Now while I think there is a lot of selfishness and a lot of self-centeredness, I think we also can find a really remarkable rise in the standards of our moral consensus in some ways. We're more sensitive to things that hurt people than we used to be. I think we're more sensitive to the dangers of nuclear war than we've been any time since 1945. So I'm not entirely pessimistic. I think people do learn, and they do realize that their own good is connected with other people's good. We can overcome this "me first" attitude.

MOYERS: One of my favorite characters in your book is a Californian who says that his ideal home is twenty acres and a moat around it with alligators. What if many Americans don't want a common identity or a community? What if they like being apart, living alone, and gratifying their own desires?

BELLAH: I think reality is going to impinge on those people and show them that they can't have that, that the price is too high even in terms of their private gratification. The only people who can really live like that are the supermillionaires or the billionaires. Most of us simply have to live in a world with other people. We don't have the resources to set up these immense structures that would defend us against what's going on in the society around us. When we realize that, we may realize that doing something about the public good is essential even for maintaining a decent private life.

MOYERS: Walter Lippmann wrote a book on the subject—*The Public Good*. What do you mean by the term?

BELLAH: It is hard to specify it, and nobody has a simple answer. I think that's one of the things that frightens people when they hear about the public good or the common good. They say, "Who are you to talk about that?" The public good is something that we move toward together, in conversation. We define it as we go along. I think it's been very well said that the common good is the good we seek in common. When we come up against these questions of traffic, of pollution, of nuclear war, then we begin to specify what the public good is. The public good is what's good for us as a whole, not just what's good for one or another individual.

MOYERS: But what about the conflict between the public good as defined by the community at Jerry Falwell's church in Lynchburg, Virginia, and the public good as perceived by your church here in Berkeley? These are totally different communities and totally different ideas of the good.

BELLAH: I don't think the ideas are totally different. There are connections. I'm not willing to close the door on anyone. Jerry Falwell is responding to some real problems in this society, and he champions the family. Now he does it in a way I have real problems with, to be sure, but I think he's responding to something that affects all of us. If we could engage in a conversation with people from the so-called Christian right, we might find we had more in common on specifics than we think we do when we're just talking about these ideological clichés. If we don't get a real discussion going, though, we'll never find out.

MOYERS: What do all of us have in common?

BELLAH: Here you may think I'm contradicting myself—but the belief in the inherent dignity and value of the individual person is something we share. I take the position that the dignity and value of the individual person is realized in and through community, not in isolation from community. I know there are those who think the individual and community are in a zero sum game, that the individual has to be totally autonomous to be fully realized in his or her individuality. But if I can at least face that person with the fact that I, too, believe in the dignity and worth of the individual as very, very high, maybe the highest value, then we can talk about how that's to be realized and what kind of society we would have to have that would make that a possibility for more than a very few people.

MOYERS: You write and talk a lot about the meaning of life and the public good. What do you think gives meaning to life that we all have in common?

BELLAH: The things that really give meaning to life are the things that are good in themselves—not the means to something else, but the things that are intrinsically good. Those can be very simple things, like a common meal. We just enjoy being together, we enjoy the food, we enjoy the fellowship. I think the deepest level of the things that are good in themselves inevitably moves in the direction of religion, in the shared fellowship of worship. As you know, I'm a sociologist of religion, and I'm also a religious person. I think that's where we find the deepest meaning of our life— but I'm not saying that's the only place. Wherever we find activities that are really deeply intrinsically valuable, not as a means, not to prove something, not to show that we're better than someone else, but just good in themselves, we're close to that heart of what the meaning of life is all about.

MOYERS: Well, I happen to agree with you, but religion increasingly has become an obstacle to commonality. Religion isn't shared in common.

BELLAH: I think we do share something, however difficult it is. I suspect that when the new President is inaugurated in January, he will use the word "God" in the inaugural address. Every President so far has. Now, that can be considered very shallow, but I think it does mean something. The fact that ninety-six percent of Americans find that the word "God" has some meaning to them is something we share. Also, the fact that the churches are divided, that religious groups are on all sides of the important issues, painful though it is, is nothing new. That has been the case since the year one, certainly in the United States. The best defenders of slavery were the Southern clergy. The strongest proponents of abolition were some of the other clergy.

That's part of our life; we have to deal with that. But the good thing about it, in spite of the controversy, in spite of the brokenness, is that as a religious people, we have been reminded again and again by religion of what the moral problems are. Religion raises the tough issues. The Reverend Martin Luther King, Jr., was the one who made us face the injustice to blacks. The Vietnam War was questioned by people like Reverend William Sloane Coffin. The tough moral issues the society has to face again and again have been raised first of all by the clergy, and by religious people. Then the politicians pick it up.

MOYERS: You're not suggesting, are you, that what we should do is all go back to church? Even if that were the right thing to do, you can't make people do it. And if you make them do it, it isn't religion.

BELLAH: Right. I certainly don't want any coercion whatsoever in the area of religion. I believe strongly in the First Amendment and in freedom of religion. But on the other hand, don't forget that one of the most stable figures in public opinion polls since such polls began is church attendance. The notion that Americans are going to church less today than they used to is simply factually wrong. It's stayed about forty percent for the last fifty years, and church membership has stayed at around sixty to seventy percent. That's one of the most stable things we have. So although many of my colleagues in the university don't like to think about it, the fact of the matter is that we are a religious people.

MOYERS: True, but the people who leave a sermon by William Sloane Coffin are going to meet in the square with a sense of God that is at odds with the people who've just left a sermon by Jerry Falwell. Politically, there are genuine conflicts over theological interpretations. It seems to me religion works against creating this notion of the common good.

BELLAH: Yes, but I think you're working with too narrow a notion of consensus. I don't believe consensus per se is a good. It might be consensus on all the bad things. I don't think controversy, even conflict, is bad. If we can at least go on talking to each other, that's the important thing. We do come to agreement at moments. We decide that keeping black people in the back of the bus is wrong. Almost all Americans agree on that. So we shouldn't forget that we do sometimes come to conclusions that most people share. But the process is one of argument and conflict. We shouldn't be afraid of that. Just the fact that everybody doesn't agree together is not necessarily bad.

MOYERS: We have a lot of conflict and controversy now.

BELLAH: Yes. I hope that it's leading us in the direction of doing something about our real problems.

MOYERS: You talk a lot about communities of celebration. Who do you mean? Are you talking about church services?

BELLAH: In part, yes, although I would include even things like sporting events or rock concerts that bring people together to do something that they enjoy together—

MOYERS: Or political conventions—

BELLAH: Well, if they enjoy them. I guess a lot of the delegates do. That's part of the point I was trying to make about things that are good in themselves. We're not just seeking some special private thing that's going to be good for us, but we are enjoying something together. That's important, I think.

MOYERS: Where do you see that happening in a religious sense today? Or is it confined to our own private worship services?

BELLAH: That certainly is the place it happens most often. I think there are other moments, though. For example, I can remember a CBS documentary on AIDS, which had a very large national audience, that ended with the prayer of a Methodist minister. And I've seen that kind of moment in a series like "Hill Street Blues," where a priest is shown at a moment of great seriousness doing something that was moving. So I think it doesn't mean that we all have to agree with a particular Methodist minister, or a particular Catholic priest, but that somehow religion in our public life is there to remind us of the deepest and most serious things.

MOYERS: And by "religion," you mean—

BELLAH: I mean what I think most Americans mean—belief and practice about those things that are ultimately important. In our culture that's what we mean when we use the word "God."

MOYERS: Are you troubled that politicians, when they bring ultimate things into the public square, often do so in a way that undermines the very values they are invoking? No one has talked more about traditional values than Ronald Reagan. In fact, sometimes he sounds a lot as if he's taken a page out of Robert Bellah's book. But he doesn't live in a small town, he's divorced, he's not close to his kids, he contributes a pittance to charity, and he never goes to church. Now, what does that say about the ability of a politician to invoke the symbols that cause us to respond as a people, and to disregard the practice in real life?

> *... it's better that the politician pretends to virtue and fails than that the politician publicly supports things that are intrinsically bad.*

BELLAH: Well, hypocrisy is again nothing new on this earth. Politicians are often tempted to be hypocritical, to appear to be something they're not. Even there, though, I think it's better that the politician pretends to virtue and fails than that the politician publicly supports things that are intrinsically bad.

MOYERS: Why?

BELLAH: Because, as someone has said, "Hypocrisy is the homage which vice renders to virtue." It at least upholds the standards. We then can criticize the person for not acting on those standards. But if we attack the standards, then we're really lost. We don't know what right and wrong are. That's nihilism—and that's the deepest danger that a society faces.

MOYERS: You're not suggesting that simply being religious will solve these common problems we face. Aren't we going to need grass roots political action, real political debate, and conflict? For example, the socialist Barbara Ehrenreich says that you've got the right emotions, but you don't have the right policies, that the only thing that's really going to create solutions to problems is participatory democracy, people getting out there and talking to each other and arguing with each other and winning each other over to their positions on politics.

BELLAH: I certainly think that we need to reinvigorate our political life together. But I don't think we want to make an absolute dichotomy between religion and politics because the very nature of the way things work in America, as I indicated, is that political initiatives often come from religious communities. But I certainly don't mean to say that going to church is going to solve our problems. We can only solve our problems through the tough process of becoming involved in our neighborhoods, in our local communities, in the larger public issues, and even in the world issues that face us.

MOYERS: But our local communities in many respects don't exist today. Half of the American people move every three or four years.

BELLAH: That's true, but I have to remind you that you're in the city of Berkeley, where we have thirteen very active neighborhood associations who make their voices heard in city hall—and they can scream very loud.

MOYERS: It can still happen, then?

BELLAH: It still happens.

MOYERS: You're not calling for a return to the small towns of America a hundred years ago?

BELLAH: No, I'm not, although many Americans, probably most Americans, are nostalgic for that. But I think our real task is how to re-create some of that sense of moral community that the small town had—only now we have to think about what is our relationship to the people in Africa and India and China, not just in another state in the United States. We live in a world community. One of our biggest problems is to make that come alive, ethically and politically.

MOYERS: Do you think there is a consensus developing in America about the problems we face in the world?

BELLAH: I really think there is. I may be a foolish idealist, or overly optimistic, but I think there is a growing consensus about some of the most important things. For example, the recent treaty between Russia and the U.S. is an extraordinary achievement, particularly coming from an Administration that started its term of office talking about winning a limited nuclear war. But we saw what happened in Europe, and we saw what happened in this country. People really want this nuclear issue resolved. I think there is a will to do that. The Soviet people have that will, too. I think it's a worldwide phenomenon. You might even go so far as to call it a pacifist consensus, not in the principle sense, but in the sense that we can't possibly survive nuclear war, and we simply have to stop it.

There's a growing consensus on other issues, too. On environmental issues, the greenhouse effect—I think everyone realizes that if we cut down forests in Central America, we may create a desert in the Midwest. That requires the world to work together. There is a growing consensus that we need to do that.

Human rights is another area of consensus. I know there's a lot of lip service paid to human rights and a lot of violation of human rights in many societies. But the pressure is on. People like Amnesty International are putting the spotlight on countries, and it's harder to violate human rights than it used to be.

MOYERS: What about the economy? Do you think there is a realization that what happens in Bonn can affect what happens in Berkeley the very next morning?

BELLAH: I think there is a growing understanding that we are all connected, and that the international institutions for regulating the economy that were put in place right after the Second World War are no longer effective. Real leadership is needed there. But again, there is a growing consensus that we have to have a new set of institutions to handle these new tensions.

> *. . . there is a growing understanding that we are all connected.*

MOYERS: What do you think has happened to our language of moral discourse?

BELLAH: Language is very important. Speech is central to what we are as human beings. Our capacity to use language effectively, to think about who we are, both individually and collectively, is critical. We have suffered the loss of some of the richer resources of our language. In *Habits of the Heart*, we find out that a kind of extreme individualism has come to dominate our discourse to the detriment of other forms of language.

MOYERS: You mean the first person "I" as the chief noun in the sentence?

BELLAH: Yes, and always talking about "my needs," or "I don't feel comfortable with that." A lot of people are even afraid to talk about something being right or wrong because they think that might mean I'm trying to force you to agree with me. But when we're talking about our common problems, we have to think about moral issues, and we have to use the resources of the moral language from our philosophical and religious traditions.

MOYERS: But how does one recover that moral language? One can't simply decree its return.

BELLAH: No. We have to use it effectively. You people in television have to use it effectively. We teaching in the universities have to be exemplars of the use of that language in what we teach and the books we write. And our political leaders have to more effectively articulate that moral language. Those are the ways to bring it back.

MOYERS: There is a case to be made, is there not, that for two hundred years Americans have demonstrated an anticommunity, antipolitical bias, that we've been on the run for two hundred years from suffocating family ties, from nagging neighbors, from boring civic rituals, that America as a dynamic, individualistic society is basically anticommunity.

BELLAH: I think that's a half-truth. For one thing, for the people we talk to, including the most individualistic, "community" is still a good word. They want community. Sometimes one feels it's a little bit superficial, a kind of meeting of the feelings on a momentary basis. But even so, there's a great hunger for community. People don't feel entirely thrilled with the idea of being all alone. For example, people are worried about their families. We know, for instance, that something like ninety percent of Americans say they wish they could live their lives with one other person. Then you ask them, do they expect to, and about half of them say no, they don't really expect to. There's a gap between what we wish—which is really not so radically individualistic as you might think, to listen to our talk—and the problems we have with making community come alive today.

MOYERS: When you and I were growing up, one out of four marriages ended in divorce. Today it's one out of two. It seems that the trend is working against your hopes.

BELLAH: It's hard. It's very hard. But my hope is that we can change that statistic with a new understanding of marriage as a more equal relationship. There are still a lot of good marriages out there. Some of the social research, for instance, on long-lasting marriages, shows that the long-lasting marriages that are really happy and satisfying are the egalitarian ones, where both husband and wife share in the major decisions and the daily tasks.

Now the American family used to be structured so that the man was boss. That kind of family is in serious trouble. But the family as a committed relationship I think we can revive on a new basis.

MOYERS: But what about all of those people who, for many reasons, cannot create or share in a traditional definition of family or relationship?

BELLAH: We can still uphold a kind of model of a normative family. The reason I think that's important is because it is through the nuclear family, husband and wife, that children come into the world, at least for most of our population. But I don't think that means we need to put down other kinds of relationships. We can affirm all kinds of relationships where there is a moral commitment to sustain and support each other, whether it's the same sex relationships, or networks of single people, or whatever it is. Where, for whatever reason, there is only one parent in a family, that family needs to be affirmed and supported.

My belief is we can support the traditional family in a nontraditional way, an egalitarian way, and also affirm other kinds of social commitments. I think they go together.

MOYERS: Adherents of Jerry Falwell will separate from you right there.

BELLAH: I know.

MOYERS: Aren't we going to have to live in this country as if we're all riding bumper cars? Somebody who read *Habits of the Heart* said to me, "Wonderful, but what I really need is advice on how to zig when I should zig and zag when I should zag."

BELLAH: Well, if we hope for a situation where there's not going to be any conflict, and we're all going to agree and live happily ever after, we're not going to get that. But I think we can do better than we're doing now. We're not going to agree about the family or anything else in any total way. But, for instance, it's possible in this society to develop a family policy like most societies in the world have that would be more supportive of people sustaining their commitments to each other.

> *...it's possible ... to develop a family policy like most societies in the world have that would be more supportive of people sustaining their commitments to each other.*

Oh, there will be controversy every step of the way, but I think we're actually beginning to move in that direction. So peace and quiet we're not going to get. But a higher level of life together is possible.

MOYERS: Why is family so important to you personally?

BELLAH: I've been married nearly forty years. It's very important to me. That relationship is very much a part of who I am. It's not always easy. Anyone who has brought children into this world and raised them in this crazy society knows it's not easy. But it is, in a certain sense, the core of our common life.

MOYERS: I like the idea somebody put this way: "My children saved me from toxic self-absorption."

BELLAH: That's right. They are also hostages to fortune. You worry about them all the time. But it enriches you to know that you helped bring people into the world, and handed down the traditions, and contributed through them to the ongoing stream of life.

MOYERS: To what extent do you think your own Christian faith has shaped your politics, your view of the world, and your sociology?

BELLAH: Very deeply. When people say to me sometimes, "I don't see how you can be so optimistic," they don't really understand that I'm operating out of what I would call Christian hope—which is not that the odds are in my favor, because if you look at the odds, they don't look too great. But you hope in spite of the odds. That's what religious faith gives you. And then you can go on when you fail. You don't feel it's all your fault. You have a belief that transcends your own weakness and incapacity and that allows you to sustain a commitment to a common moral life.

MOYERS: But it is an act of hope because the evidence is often to the contrary.

BELLAH: Absolutely. I wouldn't say that as a sociologist I can prove to you that any of the things that I'm arguing for are going to happen. But I think they're the right direction. And I think I have good arguments why they're the right direction. In back of that is faith and hope, based on my religious belief, and the fact that every week I participate in the communion and partake of the body and blood of Jesus Christ in common with all the others around the world who are doing that. That tells me who I am in the deepest sense.

MOYERS: It says that you belong to a community, but it also sets you apart from many others.

BELLAH: Well, I don't know if you realize this, but I've also spent half my life studying Japan. I studied Buddhism very deeply, I've served on the board of the San Francisco Zen Center. I don't believe my Christian faith excludes a sensitive understanding and sympathy for all the religions of the world. Ultimately, our religious history on this earth is a common history. So I'm a Christian, but I'm not a Christian in the sense that I will exclude fellowship for those of all faiths.

MOYERS: Do you use the *Book of Common Prayer*?

BELLAH: Yes, a wonderful resource, a language that can get you through a lot of trouble.

MOYERS: But it's not going to help much in the back room of a political convention, when you're trying to cut a deal. And it's not going to help very much when politically we are having to face hard choices of who gets what.

BELLAH: I'm not sure about that. The politician who has character and has committed to an ideal may make a deal that isn't entirely savory. But if there's a faith, a trust in a higher reality, it may help that politician not become completely corrupted because of a momentary lapse.

In working out the solution to our problems a sense that we are all part of a common body is above all what we need to keep in mind. It doesn't overcome the difference in interests, it doesn't mean we won't fight, but it gives us that sense that in the end we are all part of each other. So faith does apply even in the nitty gritty of politics.

Jessica Tuchman Mathews

ENVIRONMENTAL SCIENTIST

For most of her career Dr. Mathews has been a public educator on the health of the planet. Formerly a member of the editorial board of the Washington Post, *where she covered science and technology, she served on the National Security Council in the Carter Administration and advised the White House on international environmental policy. She is currently vice president of the World Resources Institute, which monitors global ecology.*

MOYERS: In the summer of 1988 we heard the earth complain. In the United States forest fires raged across the West. Farmers unable to plow the dust watched crops wither and die. Across the South, rivers dried to a trickle, and barges ran aground in the Mississippi. Fish turned belly-up in lakes and rivers, while poisoned crabs crawled out of the Atlantic. And on Eastern beaches medical waste washed ashore from New York to North Carolina.

Now we are facing the specter of the greenhouse effect, the prospect of overloading the earth's atmosphere with gases released when industrial nations burn fossil fuels like coal and oil, and the Third World strips its forests to farm and burn firewood. These gases trap radiation from the sun, and heat up the atmosphere.

What's going on here? What's happening to this earth, our home?

MATHEWS: What's happening is that twenty years after the phrase "Spaceship Earth" was coined, we're now finally feeling that we have a limited environment with real boundaries. It's happened, perhaps by coincidence, in a lot of different areas at once—the oceans, the atmosphere, the climate.

MOYERS: "Spaceship Earth" may be an analogy more apt than ever, given what happened to spaceship *Challenger*. That's what struck me last summer when I saw the earth's troubles.

MATHEWS: I think there's a really key difference, though, which is that the *Challenger* tragedy was irreversible. What we're seeing now are warning signs of trouble that we can avert. So while it's scary, and it's important that people and governments pay attention at a level that they haven't, it's also not just a time of gloom and doom. There are things we can do about all of it.

MOYERS: Assume we didn't do anything, and that these trends continue. What kind of earth will your three-year-old child inherit?

MATHEWS: If seventy-five years from now things haven't changed, I think he will inherit an unlivable planet. We have to change. But I'm not pessimistic about our ability to take logical action or to see the future and react to it. On the other hand, the greenhouse climate change is already much farther along than we have realized.

MOYERS: Walk me through the greenhouse effect. What is happening?

MATHEWS: Well, it's a natural phenomenon. If we didn't have the greenhouse effect, this would be a lifeless, ice-covered planet. What is new is that through combustion of fossil fuels and the deforestation of tropical forests, we are accelerating this phenomenon so fast that it's throwing the system out of equilibrium. You see, radiation comes from the sun, passes through the atmosphere, and hits the earth. Some of it is absorbed by the earth, and some of it is reradiated back to the atmosphere. These so-called greenhouse gases that we're emitting absorb that radiation. That adds energy to our atmosphere and heats it up.

One of the gases is carbon dioxide. Until a few years ago, we thought carbon dioxide was the whole problem. Then we discovered a number of others: the chlorofluorocarbons, the CFCs, which are also the gases that are depleting the ozone layer in the stratosphere; methane, which is natural gas; nitrous oxide, which also comes from combustion; and ozone down here in the lower atmosphere. And those are just the principal ones.

MOYERS: What difference does it make if the earth warms two or three degrees over the next fifty to seventy-five years?

MATHEWS: Well, remember that figure is centigrade, not Fahrenheit, which we're all used to. So you have to double that number to think about Fahrenheit degrees. But even so, this two- to three-degrees figure is really misleading. For one thing, nobody feels global average temperature. It doesn't exist for anybody. It's a composite of thousands of measurements that are taken on land and sea. But what it will mean is much hotter temperatures in the temperate regions, where we live, and in the Arctic, even hotter temperatures than that. Rainfall patterns will change. Europe's climate may get much colder because the Gulf Stream that warms Europe is expected to shift direction. The monsoons will shift. Sea level will rise, inundating coastal areas where a great part of mankind lives and contaminating water supplies because salt water will intrude on ground water supplies.

The effects on wildlife could be enormous, because nothing that we know about evolution suggests that plants and animals can adapt to such rapid change. There have been big temperature swings before over geological time, but there you're talking millions of years. Now we're talking decades. For example, we know something about how fast trees can move to adjust to different climates, how far the wind blows the seeds in a year, and so how far they can progress. It's a tiny fraction of how far they would have to move in order to keep up with their changing habitat. So you would expect massive extinctions. Senator Bennett Johnson said he was reminded of a Baptist preacher who said that if God meant anything, He meant everything, and that if the greenhouse effect changed anything, it would change everything. In a sense, that's right. It will change everything about modern society as we know it.

MOYERS: These are not isolated phenomena you've described. What seems apparent now is that everything is of a piece, that everything affects everything else.

MATHEWS: We're starting to learn something—very late—about how the planet works, what regulates it, and what makes it the only place in the universe, as far as we know, where life exists. We're starting to study four elements—carbon, nitrogen, phosphorus, and sulfur—and how they circulate and how the atmosphere and the oceans interact. These are systems we've known very little about until the last ten years. We've spent so much money and so much brain power exploring subatomic structure and far outer space, but we've spent very little on the planet and how it works, and this planet's inhabitants and how they behave. We've spent less time in the deep oceans than on the surface of the moon, for example.

MOYERS: Yet we've seen so many documentaries on nature and earth that we have a sense that we know everything. You're saying we don't.

MATHEWS: We know very little. The oceans are really very much of a mystery, especially how the oceans and the atmosphere interact, because circulation in the atmosphere is much faster than circulation in the oceans. So you have these two vast systems that are interacting constantly but on very different time scales. That interaction is what creates our climate. There are great uncertainties about how greenhouse warming will change our regional weather patterns in part because we know so little about that interaction.

MOYERS: But we know enough, don't we, to understand why all of this is happening?

MATHEWS: Yes. There's no question about the phenomenon itself. And we have a pretty good grasp of what gases we're putting into the atmosphere and how fast. We know, for example, the rate of growth of carbon dioxide emissions, which are going up very fast. We know how much CFCs and methane and nitrous oxide are going up. And for many of the gases we know the sources of that growth. For carbon dioxide it's fossil fuel combustion. Everything that modern societies do, after all, is based on energy use, and most of it is fossil fuel use, from coal plants making electricity to automobiles.

MOYERS: When I came to Washington in 1954, I think there were something like fifty-two million cars in the world.

MATHEWS: That's right. Now there are three hundred and fifty million.

MOYERS: Seven times as many in thirty years.

MATHEWS: And it's expected to be half a billion by the year 2000. There's a real question whether the planet can accommodate half a billion automobiles. Not only is there the greenhouse effect, but there are also local air pollution, congestion, and noise. In industrial societies we have to have three parking spaces for every car. We have a parking space at home, a parking space at work, and a parking space at the shopping mall. That raises a question about availability of space. The amount of time spent commuting to work has become a central issue for a great many people in this country. In the next decade, we will be forced to rethink transportation in a very fundamental way.

MOYERS: How? There's no mythological symbol more potent in the American psyche than the open road. You see these commercials with fast, expensive cars zooming along empty roads. How do you change that part of our psyche?

MATHEWS: It will be painful and slow, but it has to happen because of the boundaries that we're bumping up against in so many ways.

MOYERS: "Boundaries" is not a nice word in the American vocabulary.

MATHEWS: No, it isn't. But the optimistic part of this is that people do respond when they see the junk on their beaches, when they see the drought, when they see anomalous, strange weather all around the world. There's pretty good evidence that

1988 will be the hottest year in recorded history. The four warmest years before this were 1980, '81, '83, and '87.

MOYERS: So they're bunching up in this decade.

MATHEWS: That's in one hundred and thirty-five years of records. There's little doubt that people will be forced to think differently about their planet and their daily lives. I may be too optimistic, but it seems as though people do have a sense that we have only one planet, and if we are on a path that leads to irreversible change, we'd better stop, rethink things, and redirect ourselves.

MOYERS: I see some evidence of that. At the same time, as a journalist I also see some contrary things happening. For example, this year the people of Dallas voted to disapprove a mass transit system which they had approved three years ago. Now there are local circumstances behind that, but the significance of it is that many people reject the very notion of mass transit.

MATHEWS: The automobile reaches to the heart of the American self-image in the way the horse once did in the West. It's going to be hard to change. But when the average time it takes to reach work grows from forty-five minutes to an hour and a half to two hours, and the average speed on the Beltway here in Washington is something like eighteen miles per hour, then people start to look for alternatives simply because their own lifestyle has degenerated so much.

MOYERS: Yes, but what does it say to you that France has set a standard of thirty-nine miles per gallon for new cars, and we've just rolled back our standard to twenty-six?

MATHEWS: Our energy future centers around the automobile. We just have a deep emotional attachment to cheap gasoline. The reason that we have such poor performance in Detroit in terms of automobile efficiency is that we're the only country left in the world running on cheap gasoline. It's an anachronism. Nobody else runs on cheap gasoline now. The major reason for that difference between our mileage requirements and those of France is that in France gasoline costs the equivalent of about three dollars a gallon. If you're running, as we are, on eighty-two cents a gallon, then the appetite for an efficient automobile is not there. That's why, when you look around the world, you see Renault with a hundred and twenty-four miles-per-gallon prototype automobile, and Toyota with a ninety-eight miles-per-gallon prototype, and Volvo with a seventy miles-per-gallon commercial model, which they expect to upgrade to ninety—and us with nothing in that category.

MOYERS: Why are we the only industrialized nation, except Canada, that doesn't have a large tax on gasoline?

> . . . having invented the automobile and mass production, our technologies are now really at the bottom.

MATHEWS: Well, partly of course it's because we have such big distances to drive and partly because we pioneered the automobile. In fact, one of the awful ironies is that having invented the automobile and mass production, our technologies are now really at the bottom. If you look at the new technology in automobiles, Japan leads, then come the European producers, and then us.

MOYERS: It's hard to think of the American economy without the automobile.

MATHEWS: We invented the motel and the drive-in, right? And we built more and better highways than just about anybody. The automobile has become a central part of our culture perhaps because of the sense of freedom that it generates. Of course we have to remember that the United States had a wonderful mass transportation system, and it was bought up and dismantled by the automobile manufacturers in the early part of this century. Trolleys and buses were bought and either actively dismantled or allowed to just run down until they folded.

MOYERS: —in order to make room for the automobile.

MATHEWS: To eliminate competition. So now we don't have alternatives in vast parts of the country, and remaking those alternatives is terribly expensive. But we'll be forced to, if only because the quality of our daily lives is getting intolerable.

MOYERS: What do the automobile companies say when you confront them with these facts?

MATHEWS: The automobile companies have made so much money that they can't see the situation as anything other than a great success. They cannot really see the future. They have become innovation-averse. They are allergic to the future in some very profound way. That's why we're so far behind on the new high-efficiency technologies. We simply don't have them. We have the capacity. We spend more money on research in Detroit than anywhere else. But we're not working on the future.

MOYERS: Aren't they playing to the American individualism that wants our own private car, to the ways our highways are built, and to the way our cities are spread out? In a sense, aren't they responding to the market? Or are they creating the market?

MATHEWS: I'm not sure one can separate them. They are both responding to and creating a society that's built around big distances, individual transportation, and people living far apart from where they work. But that's starting to change. People are moving back into central cities and out of suburbs where they sit for hours and hours a day in traffic that doesn't move. People can see what's happening, and things are slowly starting to change.

What isn't changing in Detroit is this aversion to looking ahead. The automobile companies see only quarterly profits, and the quarterly profits are so good that they can't imagine they could be doing anything wrong.

MOYERS: But they, too, are affected by everything you've described earlier that is happening to the earth. Their employees breathe the air we breathe, they swim at the beaches, they vacation in the national parks.

MATHEWS: They do, but I don't think that it reaches corporate decision-making levels. Iacocca is perhaps the only person in that industry who has a kind of a direct policy connection to national issues. But certainly you don't have any sense that the decisions most automobile executives make for their industry are connected in any way to the issues that as individuals they see around them.

MOYERS: Do you think they know the consequences of continuing the course we're on?

MATHEWS: I'm fairly certain that they don't know very much about greenhouse climate change. We're all starting to learn about more familiar kinds of pollution— for example, what's happening to forests. We're beginning to see in this country what has happened in the German and European forests. It's happening now along the Appalachian Mountains, starting in South Carolina and going all the way up through Vermont.

MOYERS: What's happening?

MATHEWS: Tree death. You go along the top of the Appalachian trail, starting down at Mount Mitchell and going all the way up to Camels Hump in Vermont, and you see what looks like the aftermath of a forest fire. Dead forests.

MOYERS: Not of old age.

MATHEWS: No, air pollution is a major factor, especially ozone. We used to think of air pollution as a local problem—it goes up and comes right back down. Now we know it gets changed up in the atmosphere. The atmosphere is not just a passive transport mechanism, it's an active chemical caldron. The pollutants go up, they change, they get transported over long distances, they come down, and now we're starting to see these impacts.

MOYERS: Traces of PCB found in Lake Erie recently are thought to have originated in Latin America.

MATHEWS: Half of the pollution in the Great Lakes comes from pesticides sprayed over crops in Mississippi and Louisiana that blow up north.

MOYERS: So all of the damage is not primarily from automobile exhaust. There are many sources.

MATHEWS: Yes, and there are different kinds of things going on. The automobile industry is paying attention to some of the more familiar kinds of local and regional air pollution—acid rain, for example. The greenhouse effect really is a new one that they haven't thought very much about. Over the long term, we will ultimately be running our automobiles on hydrogen from water made either with nuclear power or from solar energy. But the industry doesn't want to think about that.

MOYERS: A lot of Americans don't want to think about it. We don't want to think about a high tax on gasoline like the taxes Europeans have already accepted. What effect would a high tax on gasoline have on the economy?

MATHEWS: It depends how you do it. If you do it slowly and make a long-term commitment to a gradually rising tax, so that you give the economy time to anticipate and adjust, you can do it with very little pain. With a slowly rising tax, we will create an environment that makes it possible for Detroit to produce high-efficiency cars. If you're paying three times as much for gasoline, but your car gets four times as many miles per gallon, you come out ahead. Right now the average American car gets seventeen miles per gallon. In real terms, gasoline costs half what it did in 1981. Prices have gone way down. But this curve is not going to keep on going down, it's going to turn around and start going up. The challenge is to see if we can respond now when it's relatively painless, instead of waiting for another crisis, where the change becomes quite painful. We're not very good at doing that in this country. One of the unfortunate legacies of the Reagan years is that we're very right-now oriented. We ask, "What's the next quarterly bottom line?" You know, they say, if we think about the future, we make mistakes, so don't let's think about it.

MOYERS: You're saying that technology already exists to increase the mileage-per-gallon of the cars we buy.

MATHEWS: Right. These prototype cars I was talking about are driving the roads in Europe and Japan. Volvo has one that they say they can market at a price that's the same as their existing sedan, but it's a whole new set of technologies—lots of plastic, lots of magnesium, different transmission, different engine. It's a very different car.

But it gets better performance, better handling, and less noise. Some of these cars are going to have solar-powered air conditioners, so that when you park your car in the summer, the car is cooled while you're off doing your shopping, and instead of coming back to a hundred and twenty–degree car, you get in, and it's cool. There's no consumer in the world who wouldn't leap at that.

So these technologies give you a lot of benefits besides high mileage. And they will sell. The only question will be, is American industry going to be ready to market them when we need them?

MOYERS: One could make the case that if we don't act, we will find ourselves economically behind the eight ball.

MATHEWS: There is no question about it. We are not an energy-efficient society, and we're not positioned for what will happen in the nineties, when oil prices go back up.

MOYERS: And you think they will.

MATHEWS: I think they will, unless we act now. We know very well what the U.S. oil base is. Last year production fell ten percent from domestic sources—but it has been falling for eighteen years, despite a tripling of prices. We're reaching the end. We're reaching the expensive oil. So domestic supplies are going down. Worldwide consumption is going up, while prices are low. And so we'll go right back up the curve: as supplies tighten, prices will go up. OPEC, which still has more than two thirds of the reserves, will be back in control. The question will be, when that happens, will we see a repeat of what happened in the seventies, when high-mileage imports came and took thirty percent of our domestic market? Now, I don't happen to believe that we can have a healthy American economy without a healthy automobile industry. I really don't. So I think that somehow we're going to have to thrust Detroit into the next era.

MOYERS: Let's say that we could adopt a higher mileage standard. Can you say for certain that there will be improvements in the environment?

MATHEWS: Yes. There is no question that there will be improvements over what it would otherwise be. But if you're asking will there be improvements felt in the near term, the answer is probably no. For one thing, the automobile isn't the only problem. The scary part of climate change is that a lot of these gases have hundred-year lifetimes in the atmosphere. The chlorofluorocarbons that we put up today are still going to be up there destroying ozone in the stratosphere a hundred years from now. In addition, when you put up these greenhouse gases, they start to trap radiation immediately, but the equilibrium is not reached for several decades. Actually, we don't know exactly how long the lag time is—say thirty years for the atmosphere and the ocean to equilibrate and get readjusted. So we're always thirty years behind the curve. What we're feeling now is the result of emissions from thirty years ago.

MOYERS: And we're pouring more in now than we did thirty years ago.

MATHEWS: Much more. And the rate of growth is accelerating. The situation requires a level of anticipation and an ability to think abstractly about an issue that is rare for governments. In the summer of 1988, in the United States, we paid attention to this issue because of the drought. It's here, we can feel it, there's no question. People see the impacts in a way that three hundred studies would never make clear. And yet, in fact, what we're seeing is not what's happening now, it's the result of what happened in the 1950s. So we have to develop abilities to act in the face of uncertainty and act in anticipation of problems that we don't see yet.

MOYERS: In the 1960s we heard the alarm. There were documentaries on pollution, there were official commissions on the environment, there was the Club of Rome report, there was Earth Day, there were editorials, there was legislation. And yet look what's happening.

MATHEWS: Well, part of this is the difference between a prediction and a projection. A prediction says, this is what's going to happen. But most of those things that you just mentioned were projections that said, *if* current trends continue, this is what's going to happen. Now the purpose of making a projection is to change the trend. So in a way, you're the victim of your own success, because all these things drew attention to real problems and things were changed. We've cut sulfur emissions a lot. We've cut lead to a fraction of what it was. We've improved energy efficiency in the U.S. by thirty-five percent. There have been some big successes. We've changed behavior. Think of everything that is now an accepted part of the political landscape— the clean air act, the clean water act, masses of laws and regulations to protect the environment. All of that has happened since Earth Day.

MOYERS: But our earth pollution levels are almost as high as they were before the clean air act was passed in 1970.

MATHEWS: Some are and some aren't. We've had a lot of economic growth, so they're nothing near what they would have been. In some cases, yes, they're actually higher, and in some cases the absolute levels are about the same. But there's no question that we've made a huge difference. Of course, we've had some real failures, as well. But the world is quite a different place than it would have been had those projections not been made.

MOYERS: Are you optimistic that we will in fact read the signs and act accordingly to change these destructive trends?

MATHEWS: Well, I hope this answer isn't a cop-out. I have moments of optimism and moments of pessimism. There are good grounds for optimism. When I was in the White House in the early part of the Carter administration, I had people coming into my office from the developing countries who treated environmental issues as a form of what they called environmental imperialism. They felt that the developed world, having grown and developed and gotten theirs, so to speak, was now trying to keep the developing world from getting theirs. That's how they saw it. Now you don't hear that attitude anywhere in the developing world. Countries are starting to see that they can't have economic growth without protecting their resource base. The economic growth disappears as the fisheries disappear, as the forest disappears, as soil erosion progresses. They can't have real growth without environmental management.

In the last two or three years, as we've seen these global environmental developments with the stratospheric ozone depletion and the greenhouse effect, I've sensed a new awareness that this is our only planet, and that we are playing a very dangerous game that could be catastrophic—not necessarily, but could be. There does seem to be a different sense of urgency and seriousness than there has been before about, for example, acid rain, where we've sat and done nothing for ten years.

MOYERS: And yet it takes so long to negotiate an international treaty—twelve, thirteen, fourteen years—for nations to act in concert.

MATHEWS: That's right. That's on the negative side. We don't have modes of international cooperation that are up to the task that we're going to face in the next ten to twenty years. It does take ten or fifteen years to negotiate treaties, and then another ten years before the behavior really changes. We're not going to have the luxury of that kind of time.

So we're going to need a new sense of shared destiny, that we're in this together. We, the family of nations, are going to have to develop somehow some shared sense, almost like a joint business venture, that we work together, or we're all going to suffer. I don't see the models out there yet. I don't think anybody knows how to reach that point.

> *. . . we're going to need a new sense of shared destiny, that we're in this together.*

But one sign of optimism, and it's a real one, was the international treaty that was signed about a year and a half ago to protect the stratospheric ozone layer. Here was a case where although there was scientific uncertainty, we knew that we had a problem, that the chlorofluorocarbons were depleting the ozone layer. But nobody had felt the damage yet. You couldn't see it, you couldn't smell it, you couldn't feel it, you weren't tripping over it on the beach. Nobody could feel the impact of this increased ultraviolet radiation. And nevertheless, we negotiated an international treaty.

MOYERS: You've described a global situation. Can any one country protect itself against the pollution from another country?

MATHEWS: No. That's what's new. Before, we worried about pollution at a national level, or we worried about it even just locally. Ohio thought it had one problem, and Vermont was somewhere else. But we've learned that they are connected. Then we started to feel it at a regional level. All of Europe realized that it was interconnected. Now we're starting to see it globally. That's what's really new and different.

MOYERS: You've talked, for example, about environmental refugees.

MATHEWS: Environmental refugees are people who've been forced to leave their home because it has become impossible to grow food. The classic case is Haiti. Haiti was once called the Pearl of the Antilles, because it was so fetile and forested. And then the forests were cut down. Now the soil erosion problem is so bad that there are peasants who believe that stones grow in their fields. In Port-au-Prince, the capital, after it rains, they send out bulldozers to clear the soil out of the street.

Part of the reason that the refugees left was because of the Duvalier regime, but the other reason, and the one that's always overlooked, is because it's impossible to farm bare rock. The policy lesson from all of that is that you can't stop the political convulsions by replacing one regime with another unless you also address the soil erosion problem. Haiti's not the only place. Big swaths of sub-Saharan Africa, parts of Central America, and even parts of Asia, are full of environmental refugees.

MOYERS: I've heard it suggested that we may have our own environmental refugees if the worst-case scenario should prevail, and the heating continues. A lot of Americans could conceivably be moving to Canada.

MATHEWS: There certainly will be people moving from coastal zones if sea level rise happens as it is projected to happen. A one-meter sea level rise by the middle of the next century eliminates an awful lot of people's homes, buildings, and economic wealth in this country, which is clustered, as it is all over the world, on shorelines.

MOYERS: I read recently that seventy percent of the American people live within fifty miles of a coastline.

MATHEWS: That's amazing. I didn't know that.

MOYERS: You often talk about foreign policy, and your field is national security. What does all of this have to do with national security? Most of us think of national security as arms and armies, navies and missiles.

MATHEWS: In the seventies we changed that view. We recognized that economics was a part of the picture. The State Department added a Bureau of Economic Affairs and Business, and the National Security Council added its office of international economic affairs, and gradually during that decade, everybody recognized that a big part of a country's security is its economic strength. We recognized also that our economy was no longer an independent actor, but that it really was a part of a global economy.

I believe what will happen in the nineties is an analogous broadening of the concept of national security to include environmental, population, and resource trends. These trends are already affecting international relations, and will more and more as the decade progresses. In the next eleven years there will be another billion people on this planet. We'll go from five billion to six billion. It took a hundred and thirty years to go from one billion to two billion. We'll add the next billion in eleven. By the end of that time the developed world will be only twenty percent of the world's population. That's about half of what it was at the end of World War II, when our current international system got put in place. Although I can't say how that change will affect international relations, I think it's obvious that a change of that scope and that speed will fundamentally change relations between the developed world and the developing world.

Meanwhile, you have tropical deforestation, which is already affecting the lives of well over a billion people on the planet. Many of those effects—soil erosion, droughts, flooding, local weather—cross borders with impunity. They're not national problems. The loss of genetic diversity, of entire species, which is happening at an extraordinary rate, also affects the whole planet. We have land degradation as a result of population growth and poor resource management—overgrazing, overcultivation. Fifteen percent of the global land area has lost some or all of its agricultural potential. And this is at a time when we need to feed more and more people.

So we have these trends that are affecting countries' ability to feed, clothe, house, and provide jobs for their people. Their economic potential is being dramatically affected in ways that they now see and recognize, and that means it affects their political stability. When economic growth stagnates or slides, as it has all over the continent of Africa, for example, you start having political convulsions and revolutions. That then affects U.S. interests, whether it's in Egypt or the Philippines or Costa Rica or Mexico. We're going to have a foreign policy that will be less dominated by the superpower relationship and the NATO alliance, although those will continue to be central. Our foreign policy will be a global policy. We will have to consider our relations and our interests much more broadly.

Layered on top of all of this is global climate change. That may have the most profound effect of all because that will drive countries together into the sense of a common future that we have not had before.

MOYERS: So if the phone rings in your office, and it's the President, and he says, "All right, Dr. Mathews, you've got us scared, the American people have heard you. How do I both tell them the truth and inspire them to act?"

MATHEWS: I think the truth is, happily, that although the problem is scary and big and potentially awful, there is a great deal we can do about it. We can do everything about it. We can stop using chlorofluorocarbons. We now have a global treaty that says we'll cut back fifty percent. We're going to renegotiate that treaty and phase them out completely.

MOYERS: What does that mean? What do I stop doing as an individual?

MATHEWS: I don't think it will affect your life at all. But your refrigerators will be made with a different chemical, and your air conditioners will have a different chemical circulating in them, and microchips will be cleaned differently. There are substitutes for CFCs.

Next we have to slow and then stop tropical deforestation. We have to do it because it is putting up so much carbon dioxide into the atmosphere.

MOYERS: But those people are cutting trees down for cooking and warmth—essentials of life.

MATHEWS: Yes, but there are ways to meet those needs with new agricultural methods, with what's called agroforestry, where trees and crops are grown together on the same land, which gives you a higher crop yield because the trees are holding the soil and the water. We need to replant trees over the land that has been deforested. What the Chinese are doing in tree planting is really awesome. There is no edge of any road, almost, in China where you don't see newly planted trees lined up two feet apart.

Next—and this is a big one—we have to change our pattern of energy use. The United States is a terribly energy-wasteful economy. But since the first oil crisis in 1973, we have grown by a third, and our energy use has declined by two percent. Now, if we'd been talking fifteen years ago, and I had said that was possible, you would have laughed at me. Every economist would have laughed, because that was a time when we believed that any one percent growth in the economy had to be accompanied by a one percent growth in energy use. Instead we got a thirty-three percent growth with two percent decline in energy use.

But in fact all we've done really is to scratch the surface. We've done the easy things, the simple things. We haven't used technology very much. We have this tremendous horizon of choices of how to improve our energy efficiency. Policy analysts look at something called energy intensity of economies. It measures how much energy you have to use to produce a dollar of GNP. If you rank the countries of the world by their energy intensity, we are in the bottom fifth, down there along with the Soviet Union and the other Eastern European countries, which are terribly energy-wasteful. That's one of the reasons that their economies are in such a mess. Japan is twice as efficient as we are. All of Western Europe is twice as energy-efficient as we are.

So we, along with the other big energy users, the Soviet Union and China, in particular, are going to have to double and then quadruple the efficiency with which we use energy. That doesn't mean freezing in the dark. It will not reduce our quality of life. In fact, it will raise it because there simply are so many options for using energy more efficiently.

MOYERS: To hear you is to be encouraged by the fact that there are alternatives. And the polls show that Americans do care deeply about the environment. Sixty-five percent agree with the statement that protecting the environment is so important that requirements and standards must be exacting. Eighty-one percent are in favor of not allowing toxic waste to be dumped around the country. Seventy-four percent strongly agree that government should be doing more to clean up the environment. There seems to be a body of opinion that says, we want to do something. But then I look at the absence of political will, I look at what we're not doing, and I'm not sure optimism is justified.

MATHEWS: It's valid not to be too optimistic. Over the last eight years energy has disappeared as an issue. Everybody thinks, well, it's over, we worried about energy in the seventies, and that's a past issue. In fact, in the U.S., it's going to be the central issue of the nineties, because we are not going to be able to fix our trade balance and to compete with Europe and Japan unless we improve the energy efficiency of this society, unless we can get more productive use out of every BTU of energy that we burn.

MOYERS: You're saying that the decline of the United States, often seen as a military decline or an economic decline, involves something much more than the military and the economy.

MATHEWS: Our competitiveness problem and our lack of productivity growth relative to other countries are in part a reflection of the fact that we are using energy more wastefully than our major competitors. It's going to get a lot worse when energy prices go up and as the greenhouse issue becomes more and more of a driving concern. Japan recognizes it. They are poised to market more efficient appliances and automobiles than we are. And it's not just the appliances we use, but the amount of energy that's consumed in our manufacturing processes. How much energy does it take to make a ton of steel in this country versus China, versus India, versus Sweden? We ought to be the best, and we're not, by a long shot.

There's no easy fix. It's not like you could say, "Well, we're going to launch a program to build a hundred nuclear power plants," or, "We're going to have the synfuels program." There's no one thing you could do to fix the problem. When I go up to testify in Congress, members say to me all the time, "Okay, what do we do?" And I say, "Well, you've got to give me ten minutes to answer that, because it's not one thing, it's fifteen things across the economy." We know what they are. We can list them. And we have a pretty good grasp of how much energy saving you get from each one of them. For example, there's a kind of light bulb that fits in existing sockets and uses a fraction of the energy that existing light bulbs do.

MOYERS: Which means that less coal has to be burned, less pollutants have to go into the air. Why don't we use that light bulb?

MATHEWS: Because we haven't yet gotten the kind of policy grasp on making energy efficiency a central thrust.

MOYERS: You mean we haven't made it politically popular.

MATHEWS: Right. It's an amorphous kind of thing. In the seventies, when we had the energy crisis, it was easier to say that we were going to have a big synfuels program. You could imagine that happening then. You build these big plants, and you pour all these government subsidies into them, and you make oil shale, and you gasify coal, and so forth. I don't know whether it's typical only of Americans, but we don't think of saving something as a way of producing more. It's true that any barrel of oil that you save is a new barrel of oil produced—it's there to be used tomorrow. But we don't think of it that way. We have to get a new mental picture of what a constructive policy is, and the tricky part is going to be getting it before we have a crisis. Once there is a crisis, then we will be forced to have a new point of view. Then the President could stand up there and say, "We've got this crisis. The OPEC countries are raising prices on us, etc." But we won't have a moment like that with climate change probably. We'll have to act in advance.

MOYERS: A crisis is no less a crisis for being invisible.

MATHEWS: We talked about the ozone treaty, and how that was such a great achievement, a really very encouraging precedent. But I think it probably would not have happened had it not been for the Antarctic ozone hole. Here's a continent-sized hole in the ozone over Antarctica. No scientist had predicted it. Nobody had even imagined such a thing could happen. It just appeared. Well, it didn't just appear, but we hadn't been measuring up there, so we hadn't realized it till it was very well developed. That was a shock to everybody, even though nobody was living underneath it.

Maybe, in a tragic sense, we'll get lucky, and something like that shock will come from greenhouse warming. Some scientists believe that the scariest part of greenhouse change is the possibility of nasty surprises, of things we cannot now predict. We know so little, really, about the planet's mechanisms and physiology. Perhaps there won't be a gradual, smooth change, but some big, quantum change that's really quite expensive, painful, and catastrophic.

MOYERS: You're saying we'll be lucky if we have a crisis.

MATHEWS: It may be a painful prospect, but if it happens early enough, then that probably is really a true statement. Otherwise, it may be that we will wait in our old way of thinking because we don't have a level of scientific certainty or clarity. We can't say, "This is what the weather will look like in Indiana in the year 2010" because we don't have global models that can do that.

So we're going to have to learn to act with less scientific certainty about local impacts, and we're going to have to learn how to act without seeing and feeling and stepping into the crisis, in a way that we haven't very often done before. When we passed the clean water act, all of us could walk out our doors, and see a filthy lake or river or a place we couldn't swim in, or a place that we could no longer sit beside because it smelled so bad. That's not as common now.

MOYERS: You describe a situation that is like another which exists—the deficit. The deficit grows and grows and grows, and because we can't really see it, we say it's not really there, or if it is there, it'll go away.

MATHEWS: I think that's a very apt analogy. The awful thing about 1988 is that we had a chance with the stock market crash. I thought the crash would really shock people into being able to do things that everybody knew we needed to do for economic reasons but couldn't do because they were politically difficult. Then the market rebounded, and the moment was missed. Dan Rostenkowski, the chairman of the House Ways and Means Committee, said some months ago that 1988 was the year of the big wink. Everybody in this town seems to think that next year is going to be a terrible crunch on the budget. No matter who gets elected, it's going to be awful. In some ways, you wonder why anybody would run, with what he's inheriting. But it's there, despite the fact that there's a kind of gentleman's agreement that nobody's to mention it.

MOYERS: And the same is true of the ecological crisis. If we look the other way, there'll be a reckoning.

MATHEWS: Yes. There will be, I think, on climate change. There's a reckoning we are faced with already, because there's a lot of warming in the bank, so to speak. The one thing we can be absolutely sure of is that the sooner we act, the less costly, the less painful it will be. The challenge is to develop a new way of thinking ahead, of being able to take action in anticipation of a crisis, and to avert it.

MOYERS: Your assumptions involve government action, political action. Won't the market take care of our choices?

MATHEWS: The short answer is no. The market functions in a policy context. We may think of it as free, but it's in a policy context. The fact that we're running on cheap gasoline, for example, creates a particular set of conditions for our marketplace. So we are going to have to set new policy conditions in which the market then functions freely. There is no question that the most effective policy arrangement for protecting the environment is when you can make the market go in the direction you want it to go, rather than artificially impose a set of regulations. But to do that you have to set the right policy context. And that means, for example, pricing things so that they reflect something more than just their scarcity cost.

MOYERS: That's why in the campaign we didn't hear much from either candidate about this. You're asking people to pay more now in order to stave off a problem that could develop much later.

MATHEWS: No.

MOYERS: No?

MATHEWS: Many energy efficiency improvements cost less even in the short run. Not all do. I do think we'll have to pay more for gasoline because that is a resource that is running out. We have to use it more efficiently. So we use the price signal as a way to get a whole lot of changes in the marketplace. But we will get all kinds of economic benefit, both domestically and certainly in international trade, by using energy more efficiently.

Energy is a big cost of manufacturing as well. If you can cut the energy you need in half in a given industrial process, then you're a big step ahead. And you can do it.

MOYERS: You make such a persuasive case that I wonder why we keep winking at this crisis.

MATHEWS: Well, we've got three crises on the table. We're winking at the deficit crisis because it's political suicide to talk about anything with the word tax in it in this presidential year. And we're winking at the trade crisis partly for that same reason, and partly because it feels so uncomfortable to think of America now as a debtor nation and supported by foreign investment. But we're not really winking at the greenhouse crisis because we've just waked up to it. It's really only about a four- or five-year-old issue. Scientists have known about the phenomenon for a hundred years and studied it now for about ten or twenty, but it's only been in the last four or five years that we've realized the speed at which things are changing and the urgency with which we must act.

Rather than winking, I'd say we're waking up to it, and the question is, will we wake up fast enough to keep up with the problem? This is an issue where politicians will have to lead public opinion, not follow it. That's hard for elected officials to do. So that probably goes on the pessimistic side of the ledger.

MOYERS: It's hard for politicians to do the right thing now if the benefits don't come for twenty years, when someone else occupies their seat.

MATHEWS: That's true. And that's where an elected official has to rise above self-interest and think about public service. After all, that's what they're elected for. You get that sort of vision and leadership sometimes, but we will have to be lucky to get a big enough dose of it to meet this issue.

MOYERS: No one thanks you now if the rewards come a generation later.

MATHEWS: Your children will thank you. But that's one of the kinds of changes that not only Americans but everybody will have to make in thinking about managing the planet. We are up against a lot of limits that require us to think ahead and to act in advance of damage, rather than going back to clean it up—because there are some things we can't clean up.

We're going to need a new sense of shared destiny. We are the only planet in the universe that we know about where there is life. That is a fact people react to rather strongly and profoundly.

Chen Ning Yang

PHYSICIST

To Dr. Yang, science is as beautiful as poetry and as complex as religion. An American citizen, born and raised in China, "Frank" (after Benjamin Franklin) Yang is the Einstein Professor of Physics and heads the Institute for Theoretical Physics at the State University of New York at Stony Brook. In 1957 he and a colleague, T. D. Lee, won the Nobel Prize for Physics for overturning a long-held theory about symmetry in elementary particles.

MOYERS: A National Report Card was released not long ago by the Educational Testing Service. It said, "American students are remarkably limited in their knowledge of science and their ability to use what they know." And there was also an association that ranked teenagers in seventeen different countries, showing that the United States ranked last in biology, eleventh in chemistry and ninth in physics. What do these reports say to you?

YANG: It's a reflection of the true state of affairs of the American educational system. By that I mean not only the schools, but also the social attitude toward education. This is a big and very complicated issue. But what is very easy to observe is that the kids from the Orient—from Japan, China, Taiwan, Hong Kong, and Korea—are more disciplined. They have a tendency to listen to the advice of their parents and their teachers and learn that one has to work hard before one can get some enjoyment. Here in America, the system is quite different. I noticed when my children were very little, I would say, "Perhaps you should do this." They said, "No, I don't want to do it." "Why not?" "Because it's boring." This concept that something may be boring, so I don't want to do it, does not exist with children in the Orient. There somehow society is structured differently. They hear different things. They, therefore, do not have the idea that they have to find instant gratification before they launch into something. Here the kids all want to see something immediately, to see the point. Often, that's not possible.

MOYERS: If your three kids had been raised in China instead of here on Long Island, how would their education have been different?

YANG: I have speculated on this. I think they would be very different individuals today. They would have learned more things which require steady studying. They would be willing to be drilled. Of course, my wife and I try to say to them, "Look, this doesn't work. You've got to study hard." I think they listen to us, but having grown up in this environment, they have a different set of values. In this respect, the educational system in the Orient has a great advantage. One of the manifestations of that is what you referred to in this report—that if you take high school kids and give them science or mathematics quizzes, American kids on the average don't do as well.

MOYERS: Eleven students from a high school in New York City were named semifinalists in a science awards competition—all eleven of them were Oriental.

YANG: The most important reason for this phenomenon is what we just referred to. Kids from babyhood in the Orient learn to be quiet, sit down, and work before they can get ahead. They take that naturally.

MOYERS: It's just what society expects of them, and they know this?

YANG: Yes. Their parents, their neighbors, their friends—all say the same thing. But don't get me wrong. I'm not saying that that system is absolutely good for everybody. The other side of the coin is that kids trained in the Orient tend to be too timid, tend to say, "My God, there have been all these sages, all these saints, who have done this and that. Who am I?" So there's an attitude that they cannot do anything which would be truly important. This attitude prevents a number of them later from jumping over hurdles to make important contributions. We see this very clearly among our graduate students. The graduate students from the Orient are quieter and more willing to work, and they make very good grades, but they are somewhat restrained from making imaginative leaps.

MOYERS: You mean that if you give them a problem, they can solve it, but if you ask them to find the problem themselves, they have a harder time at it?

YANG: Yes, because there is a tendency for them to automatically, subconsciously say, "I have to follow the rules. The rules have already been given." They don't want to contradict previous authors. They don't want to make jumps.

MOYERS: They're taught very early about the great teachers of Chinese history, philosophy, culture, and religion.

YANG: Yes, everything, and not only Chinese. They are taught that there was Newton, there was Maxwell, there was Einstein—who are you to challenge any of these great people of the past? This produces a quieting influence, but it also produces too timid an attitude. This too timid attitude is a handicap later on in life when they want to be more creative or more imaginative.

MOYERS: So there's a trade-off. They get a more disciplined, determined student, someone who's willing to work hard for the payoff a long time from now. But they don't get the creative daring of the individual spirit that soars beyond the accepted boundary.

YANG: Yes, and in this respect, the Orient is not the only example. If you'll compare the Orient with European cultures and American cultures, Europe is somewhere in between the two, maybe two-thirds of the way closer to the American culture than the Orient in this particular respect. The European students are usually better trained and less daring than American students.

MOYERS: What do you think explains the fundamental difference?

YANG: I'm not a sociologist or a historian, but I like to speculate. I think America is a new country. It is a young culture. The spirit of the opening of the West is still with the Americans. This was even more clear to me when I first came to this country more than forty years ago. I was amazed, for example, when I came here, that some of my fellow American graduate students said that their parents did not approve of their going to graduate school. Why? Because a young man should go out and earn money. It's a very practical and individual-based philosophy that had worked in America for a long time. In the last forty years America has grown older, so the respect for learnedness has increased. My belief is that as cultures age, they gravitate toward a greater respect for learning. You tell kids that you have to sit down and learn all these great things that people have said in the past.

MOYERS: What are the problems you see now in American culture?

The European students are usually better trained and less daring than American students.

YANG: One problem, which we referred to earlier, is that kids are not patient enough to learn. Another phenomenon is that we have drug problems. And then there's theft. For example, libraries keep on losing books. All these phenomena are deeply related to the American concept that the individual is, in the final analysis, supreme. I'm not saying it is a wrong concept. I'm only trying to analyze. In China, you would say that in the final analysis, it is the society that's important, not the individual. This fundamental value judgment trickles down to everything.

MOYERS: Here in this society you are told that what you do is important, that you've got to get out on your own and make it and succeed, and nobody's there to help you. It's just the opposite in China. Your children would not have been told in China, "Well, you've got to make it on your own. Get out and break away and start out on your own."

YANG: No, that is not the system. In fact, you don't even have to be told that. You feel it in your bones. You grow up with that environment.

MOYERS: What happened in your case? You grew up in a poor northern province of China where there wasn't even electricity when you were a boy, and yet you went on to become a Nobel Laureate in Physics. Who told you to matter?

YANG: Well, I was very fortunate. I was born in a backward town. But my father, who came to this country to earn his Ph.D. when I was one year old, went back to China when I was six, and he brought me to various campuses where he taught. And in particular, in Beijing, at that time called Peking, we lived in the Tsing Hwa University campus, which is a beautiful campus with security, with atmosphere. Of the millions and millions of people my age in China, I must be one of the most fortunate, to have had contact with learning in the best way. When the war came in 1937, we moved to southwestern China, and I enrolled in the university where my father taught. I learned the best that the Chinese educational system had to offer. When I came to this country, I was again very fortunate because then I was able to immerse myself in the best of the American system. I went to the University of Chicago and became a graduate student in the beginning of 1946. The great Enrico Fermi was one of the professors. In fact, that's the reason why I went there—because I learned that he was going to teach there. I found that as far as course work was concerned, there was very little that was offered in Chicago that I didn't already know. But I learned a lot there because what was emphasized was not what was in books, but what the physical phenomena were that were newly discovered and how we should understand them. If we don't understand them, could they be understood in terms of known principles or do we have to invent new ideas to understand them? This constant striving to match newly acquired experimental knowledge with the traditions of physics is a kind of learning, or a kind of endeavor, which I did not learn in China. It encouraged me to think about what people had not found before, not just to learn what I was told to learn. So I think I got the best of two systems.

MOYERS: When you won the Nobel Prize in 1957, you were in this country, but China of course was Communist. What did the Chinese Communists think about an American being the first and the only Chinese to win a Nobel Prize?

YANG: In the late 1870s, there were congressional hearings in this country about whether there should be Chinese immigration limitations. There was a famous testimony by a so-called scholar that the Chinese people were undoubtedly inferior. He supplied "scientific evidence." He measured the size of the brain of different racial groups and proved that the Chinese are definitely inferior. That was a manifestation of a feeling at that time among many people that the Chinese could not develop modern science. This was deeply felt by the Chinese people. So I would say that if you want to ask what was the most important reaction in China to the announcement that my friend T. D. Lee and I had won the Nobel Prize, it was tremendous pride.

MOYERS: What do you think we have to learn from the oriental approach to education? And what do they have to learn from us?

YANG: Both questions are important. About the former problem, I don't know what to say. I've thought about it. I think it's a big problem. It's a social problem, not just an educational problem, and I have no wisdom to offer. About the latter question—what could the Chinese system learn from the American?—I have discussed this matter repeatedly with my graduate students here from China, with Chinese leadership, and with Chinese university administrators and professors and students. This is an easier problem. I try to encourage the Chinese students first to broaden their knowledge, not just try to learn what has been written down into books. If you look at the journals, you find newer knowledge which has not yet congealed. The Chinese system has a tendency to channel the students too much. You learn one book, and then another book, and then another book. You have blinders over your eyes. You don't try to look into other things. You're not told to think for yourself. There is the tendency to say that if you do this and that, you'll get the hang of it and the enjoyment of it. That works in a lot of the cases. As a consequence, the students tend to learn this and expect that they will be told what to think next.

MOYERS: What does this do to them psychologically, to always respect authority, to take the teacher's word for it, to follow the given path?

YANG: It has good and bad elements to it. The good element is that compared to their contemporaries in America, they know more because they have studied more, they have been drilled more. But the disadvantage is that when it comes to innovation, they are more handicapped. More than one graduate student from China and Taiwan in Stony Brook has come to me and said, "Professor Yang, I find it very strange that I was the best among my class in examinations, but now here I'm doing research work, and I find that these American students are much more lively, much better than I am." I think that is a true statement for many of them. We see here the two sides of this educational system's results. What I tell them is that you should make an effort to break out of this hold on you, to read more about things which you have not been told to read, to listen to seminars even if you don't understand. There is a very ancient Chinese saying which goes something like this: "If you know what you know, and know what you don't know, that is true knowledge." That philosophy has had a profound effect on the Chinese system and on Chinese society. As a child, you would be scolded if you pretended you knew a little bit more than you actually did. The advantage of this is that you are more solid. You don't open your mouth when you don't really know what's going on. The disadvantage of it is that you become afraid. If there's something which you don't quite know, you have a tendency to externalize it from yourself because you are afraid that if you tangle with it, it gets you into a situation where you are in a semi-knowing state, and that is not comfortable. I told my graduate students from China and Taiwan, "You must overcome this. You go to a seminar, and most of the time you don't quite understand what's going on. You don't have to be afraid. I go there, I also don't understand quite what's going on, but that's not necessarily bad because you go there a second time, and you find that you learn more." I call this learning by osmosis. Learning by osmosis is a process which is frowned upon in China. The reason that the Chinese graduate students are less daring is because they don't want to get mixed up with something they only half know. But in frontiers work, in research, you're always half knowing and half not knowing.

MOYERS: You get right here to the edge, and then you leap.

YANG: Yes, you leap, and you may see only vaguely what is going on, but you should not be afraid of that. That was one of the things I learned after I came to this country, especially from Edward Teller, who was my thesis adviser. Here's a man who has an enormous number of ideas. He probably has ten ideas every day. Nine and a half of them are not right. But if you only have half an idea which is right, that, of course, is a lot every day. Furthermore, he's not afraid to talk about them. This is the opposite to the Chinese attitude that I've been talking about. Teller grabs any person and says, "Look, this is a bright idea, and we'll discuss it." This greatly impressed me. It was a completely new system.

MOYERS: Of course, the whole history of Western science has been to go into the unknown and to challenge all authority and all assumptions and to take everything apart.

YANG: Yes, that's correct. Compared to the West, this spirit is not very much in evidence in the Chinese system.

MOYERS: But given what you say, I would expect the United States to be in a stronger position scientifically. Yet we're told over and over again that we're becoming a nation of scientific ignoramuses, that only ten percent of American high school students ever take a course in physics, and only seven percent of American kids learn enough science to perform well in college-level classes. This daring, this experimentation, this spirit of innovation and adventure does not seem to be taking hold down in the masses of American kids, particularly in regard to science.

YANG: Yes, that's a big problem and it has been discussed from all sides. It's a very tough problem. But in some senses I'm more worried about a related phenomena. You see, the lack of scientific knowledge on the part of the high school students is a dangerous thing, but nevertheless, American science is still extremely good. The cumulative knowledge and drive, the cumulative tradition and buildup of big centers, have made America today still a leader in most areas of scientific research. It's certainly true in mathematics. In physics, Western Europe is vaulting ahead beautifully, but the United States has stayed at least on a par. The point is that the American system is capable of producing enough very good people to sustain this frontiers effort for some time to come. I am not worried that the overwhelming position of the United States in most areas of scientific research will be seriously eroded in the next twenty years. But the general level of education and the general level of scientific knowledge among the general population—that is where there's a great worry.

Look at Japan. Japan today is an important industrial nation. It's a nation with no resources. It's a nation which was very poor immediately after the war. But today they excel in so many things. This does not mean that their science is on top of the world. They are formidable, but the level of basic science research of Japan does not yet rival that of the United States. How then did they achieve the present industrial strength? They achieved it because they have more educated people. They have more people who have real knowledge, not just diplomas. They have more people who have learned science. And, furthermore, there is a different attitude toward life and toward work. I read somewhere that eight percent of the things that come off American assembly lines have to be rejected. The corresponding number is less than half a percent in Japan. If you have these two societies competing with each other, it's obvious which one will win in terms of the volume of sale. That's what we are witnessing today.

MOYERS: Do you think that's because the Japanese are more scientifically educated than we are?

YANG: They are more educated, and in particular they are more scientifically educated. This is very clear. You look at all these tests that you were referring to, and Japanese kids do extremely well because they really learn in schools.

Here the kids don't learn in schools. There are a few very bright ones who somehow learn even in this morass. They are really brilliant, and they are nurtured by the American system of freedom, pushing for the individual achievements. They later rise to the top and either achieve something as a big organizer, or achieve something as a scientist. That's what's still sustaining the United States, and will sustain her for some time to come. But a modern society has to be built also on a general population which is knowledgeable and which has the right attitude. That's where I think the American future has the greatest dangers.

MOYERS: All of the studies show that the trend of general education in science is down. No matter the number of individual bright stars, society as a whole is less and less educated scientifically. So the gap is growing wider between scientists like you and the rest of us.

YANG: I think that the gap cannot continue to widen because there will come a time when reckoning will take place. Look at the national trade deficit. The deficit is a reflection of the fact that American goods can no longer compete with Japanese goods or goods from Taiwan. This just cannot last forever. It will eventually lead to economic disaster. I'm not an economist, but I can read figures. What we're talking about is not just the educational problem, it is the social orientation. You cannot make parents bring up their children in a way so as to make them more willing to sit down and learn. As I said, we tried, and it didn't work. It needs a collective social discussion about the status of American education, not just in the sense of school education, but general education starting from birth.

MOYERS: —what culture teaches us, what the movies teach us, what church teaches us, what neighbors teach us, what the whole society says to us about the values of life and the purpose of learning.

YANG: Of course, if you go to Japan, you would see that they discuss this ad infinitum, too. They say that the kids today are no longer learning as much as they used to in the past. This is probably also true. But I think the relative educational level of American kids and Japanese kids is amazingly different.

MOYERS: The Japanese seem to have mixed the philosophy of the Orient with Western thinking about science in a way that serves their advantage.

YANG: A number of years ago a Harvard social scientist, Vogel, wrote a book analyzing why Japan forged ahead industrially. One of the chief reasons he assigned to this was the Japanese emphasis on education. This is not just a matter of saying, "Let's pour more money into the schools."

MOYERS: What does it say to you that Japan with half our population produces twice as many scientists and engineers every year as we do?

YANG: They're a much more organized society than America is. We know that after the war, when they were very poor, they made a concerted effort—that means government and the population together—to excel in one industry after another. Around the mid fifties, they became number one in shipbuilding. Then they got into electronics. They got into automobiles. Now they've got into computers.

The Chinese and Japanese share a Confucian philosophy which is thousands of years old—but there are tremendous differences. The Japanese are to the Chinese like the Germans are to the French. The Japanese are much better organized, and they know that their first priority is to build their economy—and in a single-minded way, they did that. Now I've heard that they realize that their economy is in good shape, at least as compared to many other societies, and they now want to forge ahead in basic sciences, which they did not pay that much attention to compared to applied areas in the last forty years.

MOYERS: Basic science is where we've been so strong. So now they're coming after us.

YANG: That's formidable. If you have a hundred and twenty million people, there are bound to be a large number of very bright youngsters, and if you have money, and if you know how to organize and how to encourage these kids to get into the fields where they can excel, they will do very well. Japanese basic science is not yet on the same level as U.S. science, but they are coming up very fast.

MOYERS: What does it mean for a society to lose its competitive edge in basic science?

YANG: In the case of the United States, it would be very bad. I think it's correct to say that this century is the American century. America has been richly endowed with natural resources and with a large number of people. There has been an American spirit. Now this American spirit is depreciated because of the industrial competition with the Japanese, but in the sciences, there is still the general belief that America is tops. For America to lose that would be very bad for the morale of the whole country.

Take biotechnology. It's an area of scientific development which is both exciting and most important from the economic viewpoint. Now the United States is tops in this field, but Japan is a very close second, and they are coming up very fast. This science has significant economic connotations. Many people believe that in another twenty years, the economic returns from biotechnology will be equal to that from computers. That's why the Japanese are also pouring their efforts into this area.

MOYERS: Those are the practical aspects of the importance of basic science. What about the spiritual aspects? Are there any of life's answers in your field?

YANG: Of course. In the day-to-day life of a scientist, the greatest attraction is not likely to be the practical usage of what he does. It is that we have penetrated nature in a way which is awe-inspiring.

MOYERS: You get a certain light in your eye when you start talking about this.

YANG: Yes, because what we are doing is reducing the fundamentals of the structure of the universe to a few equations. These equations look very simple, but they contain the basis of most of what we see around us. Everything is made of molecules of atoms. Atoms are made of electrons and nuclei. Now we have succeeded in crushing the nuclei, and we know they are formed of protons and neutrons and so on and so forth. All of these particles interact with each other with forces, and these forces are the basis of all the forces that we see. The forces that we see in nature, including the forces between the male and female, are chemical in origin, and the chemical forces are basically electric and magnetic forces, and we understand those very well. Mr. Maxwell of the last century gave us a few equations. They are just four lines, but they describe electric and magnetic forces comprehensively and with great accuracy. With subsequent developments, we know that these equations are accurate to one part in ten billion at least.

The marvelous thing about it is that if you have an extremely bright graduate student, you can shut him up in a room and say, "Now compute the magnetic moment of the electron," and if he's bright enough, and if you have taught him enough, he should be able to come out after a few months with a number which is eleven decimal points long and agrees exactly with what is measured. Just imagine that. He started with nothing but a few equations. That means that we have penetrated the structure of nature in an unimaginable way. The Greeks thought some general harmony was the basis of the structure of the universe. We now understand partly what this harmony is. They used the word symmetry, and we now understand the word symmetry much better than they did.

MOYERS: What does it mean to you?

YANG: Symmetry means simultaneously two things. One is the common word. When we see a rainbow, we know it's very symmetrical. When we see something that is round, it's symmetrical. When we see a pattern which is repetitive, we say it's very symmetrical. So there's a common, everyday understanding of that word. Miraculously, that understanding is related to the other meaning of symmetry, which is the basis of Maxwell's equations. Maxwell's equations, we now understand, come from symmetry. Now this symmetry shares the same connotation as our everyday understanding of symmetry, but it's in a much more abstract and much more sophisticated mathematical form. This mathematical symmetry explains why atoms behave the way they do, why molecules behave the way they do, why there are these chemical forces—so it's something which is really unbelievable.

MOYERS: What does it say about the underlying structure of the universe?

YANG: It says that the underlying structure is built on some very simple principles which are characterized by a deeper, more sophisticated concept of symmetry.

MOYERS: Why should I care about that? What difference does it make to me as a citizen or as an individual?

YANG: The easiest way to answer that question is to point to the floodlights around us, which are generated by electricity. The reason that we now can maneuver electricity the way we do is because in the last century people like Maxwell and Faraday before him understood the structure of electricity.

MOYERS: So if we understand it, we can control it, direct it, and use it.

YANG: That's right. If there had been no understanding of electricity at the end of the last century, the twentieth century could not look the way it does today. Everything depends on it. Just think about it. If you cannot maneuver electricity, everything collapses. The world would look completely different. When we really understand something in such fundamental detail, I think our experience is that we will be able to use it in a major way.

Now you might ask, "Okay, after Maxwell, what next?" We understand the chemical structures. The chemical structures are outside of the nucleus, and they're very powerful, and our understanding of those dictates most of what we see today. But there are forces which are something like a million times stronger inside of the nucleus that we are beginning to unravel. You might ask, "Are we very close to utilizing the knowledge that we have gained?" I do not know how to answer that question. I only know that when we do understand it, since it's much more powerful, it stands to reason that it would also be harnessed. But I cannot predict when.

MOYERS: You mean the forces within a nucleus that are smaller than the atom—

YANG: Already we have seen the effect of our knowledge because the atomic bomb and the reactors are built on knowledge about the nuclei, which have powerful forces inside. However, that is not enough, because what people in the forties used to release some of this energy was descriptive knowledge. It was not basic knowledge. What we are after is the true fundamental structure. We are after Maxwell's equations for the inside of the nucleus.

MOYERS: Are we going to get there in your lifetime?

YANG: That's a very good question. I don't know. Maybe not, because to do this, we need very high energy accelerators to crack open the smallest domain inside of the nucleus, and that's getting more and more expensive.

MOYERS: After my interview with Dr. Steven Weinberg in which he talked about how you physicists are looking for smaller and smaller particles, I received a letter from a viewer who said, "Particle physics reminds me of a man who throws rocks at a window and then classifies each piece of the broken glass until he finds it necessary to break each fragment into smaller and smaller pieces, all the time looking to discover what is a window." And he said, "Is it possible to find the pieces and miss the meaning?"

YANG: First let me make a comment about the example he gave. The example is totally wrong. It's true that when we strike a nucleus with a fast projectile, it breaks up into many pieces. If physics was interested simply in cataloging these pieces, it would be a useless field and would not attract our interest. Instead, what we find is the patterns of these very complicated phenomena, and these patterns generate laws which are written in the form of equations, and these equations amazingly agree with experiment. So we know that nature has an order, and this order we can aspire to comprehend because past experience has told us that when we did more research, we comprehended large new areas of physics, and they are beautiful, and they are powerful.

> . . . *nature has an order, and this order we can aspire to comprehend. . . .*

MOYERS: Beautiful?

YANG: Yes, because if you can reduce many, many complicated phenomena to a few equations, that's a great beauty.

What is poetry? Poetry is a condensation of thought. You write in a few lines a very complicated thought. And when you do this, it becomes very beautiful poetry. It becomes powerful poetry. The equations we seek are the poetry of nature.

MOYERS: You make me think that maybe the poets anticipated you physicists. It was Blake, after all, who talked about seeing the universe in a grain of sand.

YANG: Yes, yes, that was a beautiful poem. We do have that feeling when we are confronted with something which we know is concentrated structure. When we reflect that this is a secret of nature, there is oftentimes a deep feeling of awe. It's as if we are seeing something that we shouldn't see.

MOYERS: Shouldn't see? Forbidden territory?

YANG: Yes, because it has a certain aura of sacredness, of power. When you are confronted with that, undoubtedly you have a feeling that this shouldn't have been seen by mortal man. I oftentimes describe that as the deepest religious feeling. Of course, this brings us to the question which nobody knows how to answer: Why is nature that way? Why is it possible for these powerful manifestations of forces to be trapped in a very simple, beautiful formula? This has been a question which many people have discussed, but there's no answer. But the fact is, it is possible to do that, and it is possible to do more, and that's, of course, what entices us on. We want to build these machines not because we want to spend four billion dollars of public money, and not because we enjoy cataloging all the particles. Those are not the reasons at all. It is because there is something intrinsically good, intrinsically mysterious, and eventually, presumably, intrinsically powerful about this—and also extremely beautiful.

MOYERS: As you go deeper and deeper, is there any evidence to suggest to you that there is out there somewhere in the universe a complex intelligence that is the shaper of this beauty, that there is an artist or composer of this poetry?

YANG: I wish I knew how to answer that question. It cannot be an accident that things are structured this way. You have simultaneously beautiful things, concentrated things, and yet an infinite complexity of all the manifestations that come out of it. This is just absolutely marvelous. How come? I don't know how to answer that question.

MOYERS: What people grope to understand is whether or not human beings are only a bundle of protons and neurons, a swirling collection of quarks. That's what people don't want to be left with.

YANG: Well, that certainly is partly true. After all, what is a computer? A computer is just a collection of wires. But a computer can do many things. We can do infinitely more. If you ask me the question, "Why is there mankind? Why do we have brains which enable us to make these penetrating studies?"—I don't know how to answer that. These are questions which are deeply religious in flavor.

Now this oftentimes leads to another discussion. We have maybe ten billion neurons. Each neuron has something like ten thousand to one hundred thousand synapses or connections. So this is a very complicated thing—but nevertheless, it's finite. I believe there are limitations of our ability to understand things because we have a finite number of neurons. Therefore, there will be a final limit to the human ability to comprehend the most subtle, the most beautiful, the most complex equations. However, I would say we should not worry about it because that limit is still very far in the future. We don't have to worry about it for many centuries perhaps.

MOYERS: In the meantime, how do we kindle in young people the same passion and enthusiasm to join the search for the mystery that you experienced and that you exhibit here as we talk? How do we get the children as enthusiastic about the voyage?

YANG: This has to be a combined effort. You are clearly doing your bit in this because by interviewing people who are scientists, the fundamental attractiveness of this type of career may be revealed. Of the millions of kids who may watch your program, a small fraction may be inspired and say, "Look, this is something that I would like to do." It doesn't require too many to push the game forward, so I would think that's one aspect. The other aspect is that collectively, parents and society must make an effort to select those children who can do important research and give them the opportunity—collectively again, society and parents—so that they can find what they can really exert themselves doing. Through such efforts, science would continue to make good progress. It has been making amazing progress in the last two hundred years.

> *. . . parents and society must . . . select those children who can do important research and give them the opportunity. . . .*

MOYERS: Well, everybody is turning to science now, even if they don't understand it, for answers to problems, whether it's curing AIDS or putting man on the moon. Has science become the new religion?

YANG: I wouldn't say that. I would say that science has become something that everybody knows he has to pay attention to. But not everybody is a believer. Many people are unhappy about science. We have these periodic cycles in American society during which there'll be an anti-science spirit saying that everything that's wrong with the environment and with this and that is the scientists' doing. So I don't think we should equate science with religion. But science is progressively playing a more and more essential part in the life of every individual. That's obvious. This is likely to increase even further in the future.

David Puttnam

FILMMAKER

David Puttnam believes in the power of film to teach and inspire. An Englishman on intimate terms with America, he sees in our movies the reflection of a nation at odds with itself. Puttnam gained worldwide praise with Chariots of Fire, *which won the Oscar for Best Picture in 1981. His other movies include* The Killing Fields, The Mission, Local Hero, *and* Midnight Express. *He was chairman of Columbia Pictures in 1987 and now heads his own production company in London.*

MOYERS: You've said that the first day you came to this country in 1963 was one of the really exciting days of your life. You felt as if you were coming home. How can someone feel he's coming home to a place he's never been?

PUTTNAM: I think what I was trying to emphasize was the power of American cinema on my imagination. As a child I was brought up on American movies. My dream life and the part of me that I wanted to see develop had been molded by American cinema.

I remember looking out of the plane, flying into what was then Idlewild Airport, and it was so exciting. I thought, "Well, that's the place where all these ideas and images and dreams have been molded."

MOYERS: You were growing up in England in the fifties, watching American movies.

PUTTNAM: Almost exclusively American movies. Funny enough, looking back, I've been a great jingoist in terms of British cinema. I was at the same time a terrible failure as a member of the audience for British cinema. I used to deliberately go for the American film. My first question was "Is it in color?" If it was in color, I'd go and see it. Next I'd ask, "Is it a film with any merit?" and "Is it American?" Then that would be the second film that week. If I had a gap at the end of the week for a third movie, then maybe I'd see a British film.

MOYERS: If you could take only one of those movies from the fifties to a desert island with a VCR, which one would you take?

PUTTNAM: The film that had an enormous impact on me was *Inherit the Wind*—not for its filmic qualities particularly, because it was adapted from a stage play, but because it was the first time that I'd seen debate on screen and found myself moved by it. It was the first time I realized what cinema could do, the way that cinema could move you not just emotionally, in a fairly simple sense, but actually could move you intellectually as well.

MOYERS: Did you think of this as particularly American, or was it universal?

PUTTNAM: Oh, universal. I think the American cinema at that period was universal, absolutely universal. They were taking American experiences, but somehow there was an underlying metaphor that was totally universal.

MOYERS: What values did you learn from those movies?

PUTTNAM: Remember that I came from a lower-middle-class background, from a class-obsessed society of which I was very critical. I was lucky. I was a scholarship kid, and I got a decent education, but I was very aware of the class problems in Britain. My sense of the United States was that it was a place where those problems didn't exist, where there was limitless opportunity, where the notion of what was fair was tremendously important. The notion of what was fair in postwar Britain was fairly tortured. We had the polarization created by the Attlee government, and then the reaction of the old Tories, when they swept back to power in 1951. Americans didn't seem to have that. They seemed to have an accurate vision of what was right for the small man, what was right for the individual.

MOYERS: When I was growing up in the fifties, what I thought of as fair and just came at least as much from the movies—from *High Noon, Inherit the Wind, Twelve Angry Men*—as what I learned from church, school, and other places. Is that what happened to you?

PUTTNAM: Very much so. It's not something I would have stressed when my father was alive, but looking back, I can see that the biggest cultural and intellectual influence on me was cinema. It was the thing that stimulated me, it was the thing that gave me vision, and the thing that broadened my parameters.

MOYERS: The paradox, though, is that in the fifties America was *not* a fair society. We still had entrenched and ugly segregation. No blacks could sit in the front of the bus. They had to have separate segregated water coolers. They had segregated schools. It was a separate and unequal society. So the images you were receiving in London from the movies that we exported to you were at odds with the reality of American life.

PUTTNAM: Yes, there is that paradox. But the cinema itself was pushing at the edge of the envelope of society, and the cinema was perhaps creating an ethos among young people which developed in the sixties to propel the changes that took place. It's the role of the media generally to be pushing for what could be, not merely reflecting what is.

Secondly—and this is where I would appeal, if you like, to self-interest in this country—the image that was being projected overseas was of a society of which I *wanted* to be a member.

Now cut to twenty years later—the image that America began projecting in the 1970s, of a self-loathing, very violent society, antagonistic within itself—that patently isn't a society that any thinking person in the Third World or Western Europe or Eastern Europe would wish to have anything to do with. America has for some years been exporting an extremely negative notion of itself.

So you get into this strange paradox, in which you ask, "Which is more honest?" I've been in this country enough to know that the image that America projects now is not an honest one. This is a really wonderful country to a very great extent. The whole middle of this country is an extraordinarily fair and decent place. It hasn't changed that much from the fifties. I do think that the extremes, the East Coast and the West Coast, have aberrant elements within them which have distorted the image of America.

MOYERS: Give me an example.

PUTTNAM: Oh, I think the totally rampant greed, which somehow the nation seems to have got around to justifying as part and parcel of its heritage, is out of control and is going to do immense damage in the long run.

MOYERS: But the image of greed in some of the movies that we export to the Third World—*Wall Street*, for example—is a reflection of reality. Wall Street is more a casino than it is an investment community. The image that's being exported is a real image.

PUTTNAM: Yes, but I think the notion of the principal financial institution of this country being a casino is a very new one. Frankly, I don't think it's one that's shared by most of the people watching this program. They actually do think that the people who handle their money are responsible and reasonably ethical. Of course, recent events have established that's not necessarily true.

But I'd like to put this to you because it's intrigued me for a long while. In the last few years we've constantly been told about the sanctity of the stockholder and the fact that the corporation's principal responsibility is to stockholders. I challenge that—who are these stockholders? The stockholders, for the most part, are pension funds. Who are the beneficiaries of pension funds? They're the work force. It's a ridiculous situation we've got ourselves into when you can justify the closing down of a factory in which you work in order to secure the pension fund into which you pay.

It's clear to me that there is an element of manipulation here. In the name of the stockholder, in this notional deity, almost like the name of God, all kinds of things are done. If the stockholders themselves, the pension fund beneficiaries, really knew what was being done in their name, really knew what the implications were to their lives, I think you'd have a revolt in this country.

MOYERS: Should movies tell us?

PUTTNAM: Yes, absolutely—movies should tell us, and so should every other form of media.

> *. . . cynicism is a desperately destructive thing within society. And the movies are reflecting cynicism.*

MOYERS: What is your image of America today from the movies you see?

PUTTNAM: A nation at odds with itself. Movies now have an underlying nastiness in them. The thing I loathe more than anything has become fashionable—cynicism. I think cynicism is a desperately destructive thing within society. And the movies are reflecting cynicism.

MOYERS: Where do you see that most significantly? A movie like *Rambo*?

PUTTNAM: Absolutely. The cynicism is in the making of it, in the way the people who make and distribute films like *Rambo* regard their audience. The audience are kind of lumpen proletariat who, as long as they turn up in sufficient numbers and leave their money at the box office, are really, totally ill-considered.

You're creating a society that is a different society from the one I think you want and in the long run you can afford to have. At the sentencing of the Howard Beach trial, when the first defendant was found guilty, he received a standing ovation from over one hundred members of the gallery.

Now, I don't believe this country wants to see itself that way. I don't think this country has deliberately created an ethos where someone found guilty of murder is given a standing ovation. And yet when you look at the movies of the last decade, in a strange way it's the absolute natural conclusion of the underlying ethos of those films.

MOYERS: I had this feeling watching the Iran-Contra hearings. When Colonel North was admitting to Congress that he had lied, that he had withheld information, had deceived the press, the public, and the Congress, he said, "I'm proud of it." The camera cut to a woman looking at Colonel North with deep respect, affection, even adoration. And I thought of the old movie *Mr. Smith Goes to Washington*, where the hero was on the side of truth and decency, openness and fairness. The new Mr. Smith is Oliver North, defending lying, deception, and self-aggrandizement.

PUTTNAM: I guess Oliver North in many ways is a symbol of the times we're living in. And it is a little disturbing.

What I find fascinating is that the colleagues in my industry whom I work with, many of whom are absolutely first-class people, don't want to get into this type of debate. They don't really want to acknowledge the awesome responsibilities that the medium brings. Their position is, "We're in show business, in the entertainment business. Isn't it true that people queue around the block to see well-constructed special-effects movies in which a hundred or fifty or twenty-five people die?"

So I think we've got a kind of conspiracy going between the filmmakers themselves—and I may be part of it—and society, whereby we're all trying to dump responsibility for achieving the type of world we want to live in. Yet we all live in the same world. You can't make a film the net result of which is to create a very violent society or certainly a very irresponsible society—and then merely spend the money you make as a result of the movie building an even higher electric fence around your house and installing a new set of burglar alarms. There's a madness in that. We've all got to start asking, "Well, where are we going to be in the year 2000?" Are we literally going to live in tiny enclaves with individual armed guards, pouring rubbish over the fence in the form of television or films or even journalism at an undereducated and increasingly irresponsible society on the outside?

MOYERS: But I go to the movies to be entertained, not to be lectured. Do I really want David Puttnam sitting there saying, "What kind of moral instruction can I give Bill Moyers?"

PUTTNAM: No, you don't. You have every right not to want that. But I think there's an underlying poverty of ambition. I have never accepted that there's any dichotomy at all between entertaining you, Bill Moyers, and also addressing you with an issue. I don't think there's any dichotomy at all. I think it's the job of the responsible filmmaker—or the *good* filmmaker, forget responsible—to deal in both.

When I'm teaching in England, I have this expression I use all the time, which is: There are "and" movies, and there are "or" movies. The filmmaker's responsibility is to make an "and" movie, to make a film that's entertaining *and* informing *and* has intrinsic values, ongoing values in society, which people can gather around and defend.

The "or" movie is a movie which on day one decides that it merely wishes to exploit whatever aspect of the audience is fashionable at that moment and doesn't wish to bother itself with injecting any other values whatsoever.

MOYERS: Like movies, journalism can either debase or dignify life. But you're not suggesting that we ignore the violence in our society, the greed, the ugliness, the brutality, that part of the human experience, are you?

PUTTNAM: No. What I'm suggesting is that people who communicate, as we do, have an absolute responsibility to decide for themselves what type of society they would enjoy being a part of, and they have a mutual responsibility to promote that form of society and not to take advantage of society's weaknesses.

We're not addressing head-on what society's weaknesses are. They've always existed. What we now think of as the excess of the Roman circuses, where in the end hundreds of thousands of people died, didn't start that way. They started legitimately as circuses, extremely mild entertainment. But the audience demand for more and more resulted over a period of several hundred years in that form of entertainment becoming more and more bloody, more and more grotesque.

What might have been a woman raped publicly by a centurion, a year later was a woman raped publicly by an ass, and ten years later was ten women raped publicly by a hundred asses. The audience's desire for that goes way back, deep into history. Someone has to say, "Enough"—because this is disaster, we are destroying ourselves. Successive societies have destroyed themselves by the failure of their leadership to say, "I know in many respects that's what you'd like to see, but you know what? It's bad for us, we're damaging ourselves. We are untying the fabric of our society."

I see filmmakers, journalists, and people who communicate as having absolute responsibility to say we've got to stop and look. What are we doing to ourselves? Who are we? Where do we want to be? Are we moving in that direction by going down this path?

MOYERS: What did you learn about the weakness of American society from your experience in Hollywood?

PUTTNAM: The most worrying and, in the long term, the most damaging weakness is the fear that goes along with well-paid jobs in industries that offer the opportunity to be enormously successful and to have all the things that society offers. The fear of people losing those jobs and finding themselves on the outside of the small society within which they work or live is very real. That is the most worrying factor because that is likely to only perpetuate the worst of what is. And it will also always delay change.

MOYERS: What did you mean when you said on one occasion that Hollywood is a godless place?

PUTTNAM: I meant that it's a place that has managed to convince itself that the rule of cause and effect doesn't function. Some of the deals that go on, the self-serving quality of many people within that society—there's a notion that somehow or other there isn't a price to pay. Now, interestingly enough, the price that's being paid is in the quality of the movies. I'm not talking about the success of the movies, but about the underlying quality of the movies. As you move around Hollywood in any reasonably sophisticated group, you'll find it quite difficult to come across people who are proud of the movies that are being made. Sometimes they'll say that they're not bad. Other times they'll defend them by saying that the movies are relatively successful. But you'll find very few people who feel that there is a strong vein of first-class movies emerging out of Hollywood.

MOYERS: Are they selling themselves short?

PUTTNAM: Yes, and that's where they're paying the price.

MOYERS: Someone said to me once of a very powerful network executive that he has no Bible in his office—meaning, no guiding ethos. Is that what you're saying?

PUTTNAM: Yes, very much so. Unfortunately, you know, phrases get picked up and rather casually used against you. Maybe I use them too casually. But when I talk about a godless society, what I'm referring to is a society that doesn't believe that at the end of the road there's a price to pay.

MOYERS: And how does this affect movies?

PUTTNAM: I think the movies are by and large trivial. I think that the filmmakers are selling themselves short because there are some very, very fine talents at work who somehow are being convinced that their principal job is to second-guess the audience. I don't think that really good creative work has ever been done in history out of a knack for second-guessing.

MOYERS: But isn't this because they want to sell? It is a business. You keep saying show "business," entertainment "business." In business, the bottom line is the bottom line.

PUTTNAM: Yes, that's an entirely reasonable position for the management or the studios to take. It's not a reasonable position for the creative community to take. The creative community is supposed to be the group who are using their strength, using their power, using their talents to push against what is and to explore what might be. The problem is the poverty of ambition, not the poverty of imagination.

A great number of movies are being made in which before one roll of film has been shot the film has been sold down the river because of the attempt to second-guess what it is the audience is going to want to see. That's why you're not getting great cinema. Great cinema is when you surprise the audience—and maybe sometimes even surprise yourself.

MOYERS: How does that happen? I think it was François Truffaut who said that every filmmaker should say to himself or herself, "I'm going to make a movie that proves my truth is the only truth."

PUTTNAM: I get myself into a lot of trouble because I do sincerely believe in these things that I'm saying, a lot of which may well appear to be nonsense to other people. But I sincerely believe in them. And I'm desperate to get these truths over in cinema. The medium's powerful enough to do it. It isn't the medium letting us down, or the audience letting us down. You make a passionate and committed film, and you do it well, and the audience will always turn up. I've never had the audience let me down. I've never made a fine film as a producer and had the audience not turn up. I've made plenty of films which were inadequate, and the audience has smelled them out immediately. But you make a good film—and I think *The Killing Fields* is a good film—you make a film like *The Killing Fields*, and people will come to see it. They won't say, "Oh, it's about Cambodia," and turn it off. They'll come to see it.

MOYERS: You made *The Killing Fields*, *The Mission*, *Chariots of Fire*, each one of which focuses on some individual who's deeply committed, acting out a principle, whether it's the athletes in *Chariots of Fire* or the environmentalist in *Local Hero* or the Jesuit priests in *The Mission*. Is this the value system that drives you—that the individual is morally accountable and has to act to change the society around him?

PUTTNAM: Yes, I think this is the nub of it. This is why it's exciting. When I sit in a large audience, in Texas, Canada, Hong Kong, Tokyo, wherever, I see the same thing. You give people a character with whom they can identify, and you put that character, man or woman, through a moral crisis, and you allow that character to fight his fights and come out the other end with his dignity intact, true to himself, whether or not he wins, and you watch the faces in that audience anywhere in the world, watch them respond. Why are these battles worth fighting? It's because deep down within us we *are* decent. Go into a group of a thousand people, and you'll have no problem at all finding a commonality in terms of a notion of what's fair and what's just and what kind of life we really want to lead. Somehow what's happened is that the aberrant elements that are in all of us have taken control. Somehow cinema, particularly, has failed to appeal to that deep, decent core in people.

> *Somehow cinema . . . has failed to appeal to that deep, decent core in people.*

I remember seeing *A Man for All Seasons* many, many times, not because of the filmmaking qualities, which were definite, but for what it did to form me. It allowed me the enormous conceit of walking out of the cinema thinking, "Yeah, I think I might have had my head cut off for the sake of a principle." I know absolutely I wouldn't, and I probably never met anyone that would, but the cinema allowed me that conceit. The cinema allowed me for one moment to feel that everything decent in me had come together. And cinema can do that. I think if we can, time and time again, plumb that depth, we'll be doing ourselves and this nation and all of humanity a great service.

MOYERS: I think that *Rambo* appeals to a lot of people for many of the same reasons. Here's an individual on a mission of patriotism for his country, driven by deep abiding affection for his brothers-in-arms, for his country, for his cause, risking his life, going into the dark forest—as the mythologist would say—wrestling with demons, enemies, adversaries, and coming back, having conquered the hordes out there. Now, what's the difference between the Rambo of that image and the Jesuit priests in *The Mission* or the hero in *Local Hero*?

PUTTNAM: I think there are two important differences. One is that it sells us all short because of the simplistic images that it deals in. It doesn't allow us to grapple with the complexities of the real world or the complexities of our society or the infinitely greater complexity of being a human being. There's nothing tougher in the world than being a human being. Rambo tries to give the impression that being a human being isn't very difficult, that it's extremely easy to decide who are the good guys, and who are the bad guys, and to dispatch the bad guys.

It also dangerously reduces the notion of death and violence into an abstraction. Death isn't an abstraction. If you kill someone, if someone dies, there are vast effects. People are left behind, families are left behind. It's a form of devastation. So I think it does a terrible injustice in that it allows us to believe that problems can be solved simply.

The other thing it does is that by dealing in stereotypes it creates chaos. Right now the media in this country and the country itself are going through a fascinating period of having to reappraise our entire attitude toward the Soviet Union. In January I went with a group of Americans to Moscow. I've been twice in the last year. The most exciting thing was seeing my American colleagues, who had never really dealt with Russians before, discovering how wonderful these people are as individuals.

One of the roles of cinema is to strengthen and stimulate the notion that individuals are fine, individuals are decent. Probably within Iran right now ninety-five percent of Iranians are absolutely decent people like us, who want a decent, quiet life, and who want to get on and improve themselves. The leadership may well be aberrant, but the people of Iran are not. There's an American—and maybe British as well—need for enemies, which is basically unhealthy. What I resent in movies like *Rambo* is the exploitation of that need.

MOYERS: When I was growing up, watching the movies about World War II, the Japanese were presented as gooks, the same way the Vietnamese are in *Rambo*. The Germans were presented as amoral, ungodly automatons who deserved the fate visited on them. I remember the Westerns I watched, where the good guy rides into town and kills the bad guy and rides out of town again. Isn't the lesson sort of the same now?

PUTTNAM: No, I don't think so. You're talking about the black hats and the white hats. What was important about those Westerns was that inevitably the black hat was the man who was corrupting the local town newspaper, or the man who essentially was acting in an antisocial way, attempting to distort society. The villain is the person who attempts to distort society. He may be an Iranian, he may be a member of a Western town. It doesn't really matter which. But societies themselves are not aberrant. The Germans, for the most part, weren't aberrant during World War II—they were desperately misled. But it's unhealthy to come down on all Germans or to imagine there's something weird in the German psyche that permanently and forever mustn't be engaged.

MOYERS: You're saying that real people bleed real blood in real life.

PUTTNAM: Yes, and I'm saying more. I'm saying that what's wonderful about cinema is it's a truly international medium. My experience, as I've traveled the world with the films I've produced, is that you get the same echoes. People respond in the same way to the same fine echoes of themselves that they see on the screen.

MOYERS: The first *Rambo* came out three years ago. The *New York Times* carried a story saying that the young men fighting and killing each other in Beirut were lining up at the few movie houses waiting to see *Rambo*. They were going to see a universal image that they had of themselves. They didn't go to see *A Room with a View* because that would have been a lie to them.

PUTTNAM: It comes back to the business of the Roman circuses. I think it was reinforcing the desperately negative aspect that exists within all of this. I don't feel I'm some good guy who's somehow seen the truth and is trying to get a lot of bad guys to come along with him. I'm challenging myself. I've made some desperately bad films. I made some very poor decisions during the time I was at Columbia. I don't think I even turned out to be particularly good at the job I was doing. But what I do know is that I work within a medium which has enormous power and which carries with that power an awesome responsibility. And I'm convinced that it's not a good thing to appeal to the violence of guerrillas by showing them a movie which in one way or another helps to justify that violence. What I think is important is to try to show them a movie—not *A Room with a View*—but a movie which shows them the historical helplessness or hopelessness of the answers that they're being fed. It's much more difficult to make the kind of film that I'm talking about than to make a *Rambo*. And you're *much* more likely to fail. In the next ten years, if I try to pursue the problem I'm giving myself, I'm likely to make some terrible films. Because I have the type of ambition I have, necessarily, time and time again, on the law of averages, I'm likely to fail.

MOYERS: Take *Midnight Express*, which had a lot of violence. It was a bizarre movie in a sense. I shudder at what it reveals of the human being.

PUTTNAM: I think we all go through important cathartic moments in our life. Certainly *Midnight Express* was just that for me. I'm proud of it as a piece of moviemaking. I think it was extraordinarily skilled. Everyone who worked on the film did a marvelous job. But when I traveled with the film and saw the audience reactions, I got the shock of my life. We talked long and hard about the scene where Billy Hayes bites the tongue of one of the other prisoners. The reason we'd done it was to try to give the impression that he'd become demented. We thought the audience would vanish under their seats. But the opposite happened. They got up in their seats, and they were cheering him. That was the shock of my life. That was the moment where I suddenly realized exactly what I'd gotten myself into. It happens to all of us. Where and when do you join the circle? That's when I said to myself, "Never again." I don't ever want to sit in a cinema and look at a film that I've had any responsibility at all for and be stunned and shattered by the reaction it's getting from the audience.

MOYERS: There's a story that after you realized the reaction to *Midnight Express*, you called a priest for some counsel. Is that true?

PUTTNAM: Yes, it is. The means were circuitous, but yes, I ended up, through the confusion I found myself in, spending some time with a quite remarkable Jesuit priest, who is now in fact the professor of theology at London University. I didn't spend a lot of time with him, but during the time I did spend with him, he really came down and said, "Look, you know, it's very much in your hands. Stop being so critical of yourself and do something about it. If you believe the medium that you work in has these qualities and has these opportunities, then it's your job—no one else's job—to steer your own career in that direction."

MOYERS: Were you flagellating yourself because of *Midnight Express*?

PUTTNAM: I think I was stunned by my own arrogance and ignorance. Arrogance because I could see the way in which we had very carefully and very skillfully used the medium and manipulated the audience, and at the same time stunned by ignorance in not fully understanding the manner in which the film would be seen.

MOYERS: But every filmmaker has to be arrogant. You have to say, "I have this truth, you've got to pay attention. You've got to listen." Maybe it was just the wrong truth you had.

PUTTNAM: I think so. Looking back, we did the film because we were bored and fed up with being categorized as art filmmakers, which was what had happened to us in Europe. We wanted to prove that we could make an American film as well as any American filmmakers. I think we got carried away with that notion. Somehow or other, what we were doing, or rather the effect of what we were doing, got lost in the equation. Incidentally, my colleagues on the film don't happen to agree with me about that.

MOYERS: Don't you think that most of your filmmaking colleagues—and not just those who worked with you on *Midnight Express*—would disagree with your position? So in this case, then, don't you have to go on your own? Was it a mistake for you to try to run a major company like Columbia, which wanted pictures that had to represent a larger strategy than your own personal vision as a filmmaker?

PUTTNAM: In hindsight, it was a ridiculous mistake, on several fronts. The biggest single mistake I think was to try and translate an essentially European notion of what cinema is into an American view. The running of an American studio requires a form of discipline and a form of compromise which I'd never been asked to address—and I wasn't able to.

MOYERS: You were so outspoken in your criticism of the big deals, the agents, the high prices, the materialism of Hollywood. You came off like all prophets do—with a hair shirt.

PUTTNAM: Not really, Bill. I painted myself into a corner in that I'd always had those views. Those weren't new views, they were views I'd been espousing for at least a decade. The problem was that if I'd attempted to revise them—and good journalists made sure I wasn't allowed to stay quiet about them—I would have been quite rightly accused of not being true to myself, of being the worst kind of revisionist. I was very concerned about being seen as a character who shifted ground with the shift of a job and a shift of responsibility. That bothered me a great deal. I had painted myself into a very real corner, and I thought I had to continue down the road that I sincerely believed in.

MOYERS: But wouldn't it have been better—and you're not the only one who could say this—wouldn't it have been better to have practiced what you preached and preached less what you practiced?

PUTTNAM: Without doubt. But my father was a journalist, and I was brought up in a household where the worst thing that could happen in any given day, week, or month was for him to come back from a job where he got a no comment, or someone that wouldn't talk. And so I was brought up at a very early age to despise people who weren't prepared to talk about the things they believed in. I can well see that it's more expedient not to talk at times, but it's a difficult thing for me to do.

MOYERS: You've said before that journalists, filmmakers, and architects all have one thing in common—

PUTTNAM: —the need for a patron.

MOYERS: Why do they have to have a patron?

PUTTNAM: Because the *dreams* of all three groupings have no effect—and I guess we're in the business of effect—they have no effect, they don't materialize, without a patron. A filmmaker without a studio to fund his screenplay is just a man sitting in a coffee shop with a hundred and twenty pages of deathless prose. A journalist railing against the inadequacies of the new appointee to the Supreme Court is also sitting in the same coffee shop unless he has someone to print his newspaper column. The most humble people are architects, who have dreams which, without the ability to physically represent them in terms of someone funding their building, have got these large sheets of blue paper which are almost impossible even to file.

MOYERS: This does give filmmakers, architects, and journalists a very precarious existence. One has to have that patron, and at the same time one is trying to express this singular conviction about the truth or the idea or the dream. So there's a conflict. That happened to you, didn't it?

PUTTNAM: Yes, absolutely. And I can't imagine that at certain points in your career, early on, it didn't happen to you. What you have to do is deal with that frustration. Now, I have managed to convince myself that come hell or high water, one way or another, I'll always be able to make films. I may not be able to make big Hollywood movies, but I'll certainly be able to make small films in England. Or, if worse comes to worst, I'll make films for television. So I haven't ever faced the notion that somehow Puttnam and the things that he believes in are to be banned from the screen.

Now, that gives me an even greater responsibility. One of the people I'm flagellating when I'm saying these things is myself. I think I'm punishing myself. And I think I'm urging the studios and other filmmakers to say, "For God's sake, get better. And in getting better, demand more of me. Don't let me do sloppy work. Don't encourage me to assimilate into producing the easy and simpleminded type of movie. Make me do better work. Criticize my work. The only way I can get you to do that is by challenging you."

MOYERS: When you say to Hollywood to do better, you're saying, "Get better, Hollywood, so that you can make me better."

PUTTNAM: Absolutely.

MOYERS: We all have some responsibility for the moral conduct of the organization of which we're a part. But how do you hold on to your own beliefs and values in this chaotic world?

PUTTNAM: I think I touched on that. First of all, I believe passionately in cinema. I love movies, and I believe films are important. That gives me a purpose. If ever I cease to believe that, I would have to quit the business, because there would be no point in doing it.

The other reason is that I come from an extremely stable home life and background. One of the great things about Britain is the sense of continuity, the sense that you're part of a society which is ongoing. I think that helps. You haven't got the sense that you can be swept overboard by a wave.

And the third thing is what I described earlier. I travel with my movies and watch the impact and influence of cinema around the world. This isn't something I hope or I believe, this is what I know, the only thing I think I know. I know that if you make a film which really speaks to audiences, which really has something to say, which really addresses what's best in them, then it doesn't matter what audience in the world that film plays to, it's going to have a terrific resonance. People will walk out of those cinemas in all of those cities, in all of those cultures, all those nations, with better instincts and better able to fight for what's best in the world than they were when they walked in.

MOYERS: That says a great deal about what we have in common as individuals, no matter what our particular culture or religion. I know that sounds banal and trite, but there's something basically true about it.

PUTTNAM: But isn't that the problem? I find that every day. That's why I mentioned that I loathe cynicism. What we're saying is so easy to spite with cynical one-liners. I become crazed. You say something you sincerely believe in, and you know that in part it sounds banal, it sounds obvious, it may even sound simplistic. And then some smartass has a clever one-liner which deflates it. But all that one-liner has done is damage the truth. You see, so often cynicism is used to undermine the truth. The truth *is* frequently banal.

MOYERS: Adlai Stevenson said that clichés mean what they say, and truisms are true. We hear people say, "It's just a movie, it's not real life." You're saying it really matters.

PUTTNAM: I'm saying it really matters.

MOYERS: So people do things differently because of what they see on that screen?

PUTTNAM: I'm glad you asked the question because it's one of the things that's used often to puncture my arguments. No, I don't think any one film is ever going to change anything. I don't think any one newspaper article ever changes anything. But over a period of years, the drip, drip, drip of a lot of good movies, a lot of good articles, the quality of newspapers, the caliber and integrity of newspaper editors—all this is very, very, very important.

The effect of that drip, drip, drip, the daily diet of views and ideas that adhere to and promote what's best in society—that has an effect. Not one movie, not one article, not one building, but just the fact that all of us buckle down and try to do better. And be better.

MOYERS: You said a movie tinkers around inside your brain. It steals up to form or confirm social attitudes. Movies actually can help to create a healthy, informed, concerned, and inquisitive society or a negative, apathetic, and ignorant one.

PUTTNAM: I believe that.

MOYERS: So those young people who go to the movies are, whether they know it or not, taking something out of there.

PUTTNAM: Every single movie has within it an element of propaganda. You walk away with either benign or malign propaganda.

MOYERS: Propaganda—somebody's idea of the way the world ought to be.

PUTTNAM: Yes. And I think it's an important word, a word we shouldn't duck. You and I shouldn't pretend that even in this interview we're not in one respect propagandizing. It's up to the audience at home to decide what we're propagandizing about.

MOYERS: You made a very large claim for movies that I guess I could make for journalism. You said our political and emotional responses rest for their health in the quality and integrity of the present and future generation of television and film creators. That's claiming a lot for this business.

PUTTNAM: Yes, but I think in fairness, even if the claim is only half-justified, what *is* important is that people who come into this business acknowledge the possibility of that truth, and don't merely come in regarding cinema as a frivolous adjunct of show business in which the best thing that could ever happen to them is three pages in *People* magazine and a million dollars in the bank. The business is about more than that.

MOYERS: But most young people who come into it are driven by some artistic vision, some creative command, some ethos, some value system that they believe they can serve. Then they collide with the reality that it is, after all, a business.

PUTTNAM: I think that's absolutely true. They come with those values, and those values are usurped, as it were, by the business. And because the industry's value system is so flexible, they don't have any rocks to hold on to. There is a desperate lack of careers to really look at and say, "Boy, I could really be like him, I could really be like her." I think we suffer from that.

Again, it comes back to responsibility. Unfortunately—and this is certainly true in Britain, as well—the media are obsessed with tearing down rather than building up. Or if they do build up, they build up mainly to tear down.

MOYERS: What kind of men did you find running Hollywood? Was it a place like C. S. Lewis's "warm and well-lighted offices occupied by quiet men with white collars and cut fingernails who never raise their voices"? Bookkeepers, accountants, bottom-liners? You've said that when matters of faith conflicted with matters of finance, finance always won. They do want to sell their product.

PUTTNAM: Yes. I think that is because of the demands of the job for short-term results, which are required of all American executives, not just those in the motion picture industry. They are frequently required to make decisions which I certainly would argue with. But I don't think that it is the role of the businessman or the executive to roll over and capitulate to the artist any more than I think it's the role of the artist or the creator to capitulate to the businessman. We have to find a nexus, we have to find a partnership. The best of those executives running studios *want* better movies. They want to be proud of their movies. They want to be able to turn up at Academy Award night and be proud, and to have a film nominated and to feel the film has a value. I think they want to go back to their families at the end of each week or month and say, "You know, we've got a terrific film we're going to show on Friday. It's come out of our studio." They want all of that.

I sometimes think that they probably get knocked about a bit by the dichotomy involved in getting there. There is a rather helpless sense that somehow they're in an either/or situation: Either they've got to go for the surefire commercial hit, *or* they've got to go for the more complex, thoughtful film. If the creative community would get itself together, people like me would actually do their homework and work harder, be more diligent, be more professional. We *could* actually have our cake and eat it, too. We could make films which had a role to play, which, instead of pandering to what was most negative in society, would actually speak to what's most positive in society. And make—dare I say it?—a great deal of money doing it.

MOYERS: Some of the most decent, religious, affable, well-meaning men I ever met were at the networks, but they thought themselves lashed to this monstrous beast of public taste, and they felt they had to go to where it dragged them. It raises the question of just how much excellence can be tolerated in a democratic culture.

PUTTNAM: It does. I would say that on balance the quality of professionalism and the sheer level of hard work and commitment demonstrated in the executive hallways in Hollywood is probably greater than that which is currently being demonstrated by people like me. The creative community has not really knuckled down. You can't always blame the studios for distrusting the desire for excellence that exists in the creative community. The dream is there, but there is a lack of professionalism. At Columbia I was disappointed many, many times in the commitment that I thought we had received from the people in whom we trusted.

MOYERS: Disappointed? In what sense?

PUTTNAM: I felt that having been given the go-ahead to make a movie, people started cutting corners. Decisions were made that maybe shouldn't have been. There was a sense of second-guessing, a sense of trying to do something which we at the studio would approve of rather than what was necessarily absolutely right for the film. Very, very seldom did I have someone come in and really fight me for what was right for the movie and best for the movie.

In the same way, I had a very healthy relationship for many years at Warner Brothers, and I think it was based on the fact that we told each other the truth. They always knew that if I felt passionately about something, I would come and sit down with them and say so. There wouldn't be any equivocation, I wouldn't be mucking about, as it were, keeping the relationship going, rather than making a film that they could truly be proud of. Strangely enough, over the years, that created an atmosphere of trust between us. That's why I'm very happy to be back at the studio.

Some people at Columbia gave us exactly that. I was amazed by, for example, Jane Fonda and her partners' qualities as producers. Jane Fonda's qualities as an actress are well known, but she's also a very, very fine producer. Her passionate commitment to professionalism, getting it right, getting the script right, getting the cast right, was inspiring. She was marvelous to work with. But I'm afraid, looking back, that there were as many people whom I felt let down by as people who really delivered everything they promised.

MOYERS: What about the people who ran Coca-Cola, which owned Columbia? Did they force you out because of this conflict over art and business?

PUTTNAM: No, I don't think so. I think that probably what happened—and I can only surmise—was that whilst their intentions were absolutely honorable when they first asked me to join the company, they found the pressures and problems and short-term crises that were created by my attitudes weren't justified by the potential long-term benefits that I might have brought to the studio. In a way, I shot myself in the foot by making it clear from day one that I was only going to stay for three years. I think they felt, and maybe rightly, that the changes I wanted to bring about were going to take longer than three years to achieve, and that I might leave a bit of a shambles behind me.

MOYERS: Do you think, when you took the job at Columbia, that in any way you declared war on the prevailing ethic of Hollywood?

PUTTNAM: No, not at all. I feel that in taking me on or encouraging me to join the studio, strangely enough, the Coca-Cola Company declared war on the prevailing attitude. And rightly. They were very disappointed with what they had, and they brought in someone whose views were absolutely declared. Whatever else could be said against me, I was no closet critic. They publicly applauded the stance that I took. I just don't think they were ready for the fallout. I don't think they were ready for the venom that was forthcoming from those people within the Hollywood community who felt themselves threatened by my views, the people who take advantage of the amount of money that washes around within that system and, instead of plowing it back into the business, tend to look after themselves in the first instance.

MOYERS: Why don't they plow it back?

PUTTNAM: Because I don't think they have a belief in the medium. One underlying thing we've been talking about is the fact that I believe that cinema is important. You know, if you needed a title for this talk, the title would be "Is Cinema Important?" If you believe cinema is important, then everything I am saying holds up. If, deep down, we fail to convince the audience that cinema's important, then, really, what I'm saying is nonsense.

The paradox of this is that many, many people who have wonderful careers in the motion picture industry deep down don't believe that cinema's that important. Many of them subscribe to the point of view you raised, which is, you know, it's a lot to ask of the medium. And really, does a film make any difference?

MOYERS: Is it possible that you went to Hollywood having seen too many idealistic movies of the 1950s, where the good guys always won and the endings were always happy?

PUTTNAM: Yes. But on the other hand I defend myself by saying that it's that form of hope that keeps us all going from day to day. I was genuinely encouraged by my family to do it. Their view was that if I didn't take up the cudgel, I could turn into one of those bitter sixty-year-olds who talks about what might have been, and how things could have been different. My experience was a fair price to pay for getting rid of that notion.

MOYERS: You're not very happy with people who say, "Well, this is just the way it is; we can't change it."

PUTTNAM: No, not at all. I think they might as well roll over and give up. The whole point of being here is the battle. I enjoy the battle. I make no pretense about it. I like a fight. It's stimulating and makes me think and makes me question myself, which is important. No, I have no time for people who feel that that's the way it is, and we're just going to have to live with it.

MOYERS: There are some very good movies coming out of Hollywood. I loved *Moonstruck*, and I'll bet you did, too.

PUTTNAM: Yes, I did. I had the miserable misfortune of turning it down as a script, but I certainly liked the result.

MOYERS: Why did you turn it down?

PUTTNAM: I thought it was a film I'd seen before. At that point, it was called *Moonglow*. It wasn't as sharp a screenplay as was later wrought. It was a mistake to turn it down. I made plenty of mistakes. That was one of them.

It occurred to me after *Chariots of Fire* won the Oscar that really and truly, in a healthy movie society, with the movie industry being the movie industry that I would have it be, *Chariots* would be your regular movie, the film you'd expect to see at your local cinema each week. It shouldn't be the Olympian film that at the end of the year climbs a mountain and wins the Oscar. It's a terrible thing to say about your own film, but frankly, it wasn't a good enough film to win what an Oscar *should* represent. When I look back over the years at the films that didn't even get nominated, I can't be anything but a little embarrassed. In fact, the only time I really felt comfortable with *Chariots of Fire* was when *The Killing Fields* didn't win. I somehow felt that the combination of *Chariots of Fire* and *The Killing Fields*, the two of them put together, deserved one Oscar. That was the first time I really felt comfortable.

MOYERS: But you wouldn't turn it down, right?

PUTTNAM: No way. In fact, if anyone, even the "Refrigerator," had tried to tackle me as I went up to collect it, I could have shaken him off.

MOYERS: Do you think the men who started this industry many, many years ago ever realized it would play the role of the modern mythmaker—that movies would become as powerful in our unconscious and conscious psyche as they have?

PUTTNAM: No. But then the people who started the penny sheets that became newspapers, which were, in fact, advertising sheets, never believed that newspapers could form our ideas and influence democracies and voting patterns. In a way, I don't think it's a legitimate question because I think if you start questioning the origins of things, in a strange way, you lead yourself into a negative blind alley. It's what things evolve into that's exciting. I don't know what the next major medium is going to be. I don't think for one moment that when television was first conceived, anyone imagined that it would shape the way this country saw itself. I think the more important thing is the manner in which we, as practitioners, grab hold of these magic media we've been given and run with them. That's what's key.

MOYERS: You said in a recent speech that the United States is in a real danger of becoming a lost land. In what sense?

PUTTNAM: A nation is lost when the soul that it would wish to have becomes more and more removed from the manner in which it sees itself reflected on a day-to-day basis. It comes back to issues like the inside trader. I sincerely think that the ordinary people in this country know that there's something wrong with the underlying financial system. They know that Boesky is not an isolated case. They know there's more to it than that. Somehow there's been a lack of cleansing and a lack of a restart. People know that deep down in this country there's something wrong. At the same time they know that it's a good country and that the instincts of this country are decent. And they know they want to *be* the way they see themselves. Under this present President they were given a benign vision of themselves, but it was a phony vision. Now I think what they would like is for the reality to conform to that excellent feeling.

MOYERS: The reality of America being . . .

> *I don't for one second believe that the people who founded this country wanted to create a nation that was a mirror image of the nations that they had left.*

PUTTNAM: America is the one nation in the world that was conceived and built on the notion of justice and equality. The people who founded this country and the people who created this country ran away from dictatorships, ran away from religious and financial exploitation. I don't for one second believe that the people who founded this country wanted to create a nation that was a mirror image of the nations that they had left. I think history will be very poorly served if America merely turns into a reflection of the evils of the nations its founders fled from.

MOYERS: There's an exiled Russian writer who said that the American dream is really the continual belief that you can change your life, that somewhere in this vast economic phantasmagoria you're going to change the way things are for you, you're going to better yourself, improve yourself, make a different person out of yourself. The movies you and I saw when we were growing up all suggested that we could take charge, we could make a difference, that individuals matter. "Get out there and make it happen." That's the American dream. Do you think that's changed?

PUTTNAM: Yes, I do. I think that what I found most distressing and dispiriting about Hollywood was the sense that only by belonging, only by being *part* of the system, will you elevate yourself. The old dream of the early sixties was that the system was there to be changed, to be adapted, or to be made better. That seems to have vanished. There's a general sense, certainly in Hollywood, that only by being part of the existing system are you going to get anywhere. That's rather sad.

MOYERS: But there is another side of it, too. A story in the *New York Times* quoted a woman, a corporate executive, as saying, "I believe in self-reliance, being aggressive and expressing anger openly—kind of like Rambo." Hollywood is reinforcing individualism—but not quite the individualism you're talking about.

PUTTNAM: It isn't. I can tell you, I don't know who this woman is, but I wouldn't want to meet her. She sounds like someone who will not contribute to any society that I particularly want to be part of.

MOYERS: She might become a very big corporate executive overseeing the David Puttnams of Hollywood.

PUTTNAM: She may, but what I think I'm saying is that there's a need for a different kind of plural society here. Somehow or other, we have to make it together—we can't just make it on our own. And that seems to me what's getting lost in the equation. At the moment, for instance, your school system is creating the work force of the year 2000. What kind of society is that woman going to be running her corporation within? Is she going to employ people who can read and write? Is she going to employ people who won't rip her off for petty cash? My notion of society—even the dictionary definition of society—doesn't allow for mere self-aggrandizement, and devil take the hindmost. It can't. We live in a plural society. There's an absolute obligation to make sure that both we and the people around us and the generation that follows us inherit a better world than the one into which we were brought.

MOYERS: And you really do believe that movies can make a difference?

PUTTNAM: I'm glad you said "make a difference." I believe that movies have a role to play. If movies play their role to the hilt, then they may well embarrass other media, like television and newspapers, into addressing their inadequacies, also, and getting it right together.

MOYERS: But if movies did that, would we still need to go to church?

PUTTNAM: That's an interesting question. I suppose, really, if we reach the apotheosis that I dream of, there would be no need to go to church because church would reside in everyone's home and within each of us. It will never happen in my lifetime, but it's a nice dream.

Chinua Achebe

NIGERIAN NOVELIST

Chinua Achebe is president of the town council in his village in Nigeria, a role that brings him more headaches than honors. He's also a storyteller who hears the music of history, weaves the fabric of memory, and sometimes offends the Emperor as well. His first novel, Things Fall Apart, *sold over three million copies and has been translated into over thirty languages. His latest novel is* Anthills of the Savannah.

MOYERS: There's a proverb in your tradition that says, "Wherever something stands, something else will stand beside it." How do you interpret that?

ACHEBE: It means that there is no one way to anything. The Ibo people who made that proverb are very insistent on this—there is no absolute anything. They are against excess—their world is a world of dualities. It is good to be brave, they say, but also remember that the coward survives.

MOYERS: So if you have your God, that's all right because there must be another God, too.

ACHEBE: Yes, if there is one God, fine. There will be others as well. If there is one point of view, fine. There will be a second point of view.

MOYERS: Has this had any particular meaning for you, living as you do between two worlds?

ACHEBE: Yes, I think it is one of the central themes of my life and work. This is where the first conflict with the missionaries who came to improve us developed. The missionaries came with the idea of one way, one truth, one life. "I am the way, the truth, and the life." My people would consider this so extreme, so fanatical, that they would recoil from it.

MOYERS: And yet your father became a Christian, and you were raised by a Christian family.

ACHEBE: Yes, completely—but there were other ways in which the traditional society failed to satisfy everybody in it. Those people who found themselves out of things embraced the new way, because it promised them an easy escape from whatever constraints they were suffering under.

MOYERS: So one of the reasons missionaries, colonial administrators, and other Westerners seldom penetrated the reality of the African society was that the African could embrace the Christian God while still holding on to the traditional gods.

ACHEBE: Yes. But it was not necessary to throw overboard so much that was thrown overboard in the name of Christianity and civilization. It was not necessary. I think of the damage, not only to the material culture, but to the mind of the people. We were taught our thoughts were evil and our religions were not really religions.

MOYERS: How did you come to grips with this when you arrived in the United States for the first time in 1972?

ACHEBE: Well, I suddenly felt strange in very many ways. America was not unknown to us. While I was growing up, during the period of the nationalist agitation for independence from colonial rule, America stood for something. It stood in our mind for change, for revolution. That image lasted right through the Second World War. When, for instance, Churchill and Roosevelt were talking about the Atlantic Charter, Roosevelt said, "What about the colonial peoples? Would this apply to them?" Of course you would expect Churchill to say, "No," it wouldn't apply to these people. And he did.

Up to that point, America was seen as a friend of struggling peoples, and that was part of the background I brought with me when I came. That kind of image, of course, no longer exists. It is, in my view, one of the tragedies.

MOYERS: What's happened to it?

ACHEBE: Well, I don't want to be overly critical, because as a guest, I should be careful. But it seems to me that something happened in that period between Roosevelt and perhaps the period of McCarthy that made it possible for the South African regime, for example, to say they have a friend in the White House. I think what happened is that America became a power in the world and, after the Second World War, forgot its revolutionary origins.

MOYERS: The dominant ambition became power politics instead of revolutionary fervor.

ACHEBE: Yes, yes.

MOYERS: I remember when I first came to your country, Nigeria, in the sixties, I found three students out at the University of Ibadan who were reading Thomas Paine's *Common Sense*. That was their great revolutionary pamphlet.

ACHEBE: That's right. In addition, two key people in the liberation from colonial rule in West Africa were trained in this country. So, in fact, a lot was expected of America.

MOYERS: What did it mean for African leaders to be trained in this country? What happened to them when they went back? You write about leadership a great deal and about the conflict in leaders between their training in colonial or Western ways of thought and their old traditions.

ACHEBE: Well, I think that the first generation of liberation leaders came back bearing a message of America as a place that would befriend struggling nationalists. That image was possible because America was not in charge of West Africa. America was far away.

MOYERS: Unlike the British.

ACHEBE: Yes, unlike the British. There was a kind of romantic air about America. The newspapers spoke of a land of freedom. Uncle Sam was very popular at that point.

MOYERS: And today in Nigeria?

ACHEBE: Somehow America has found itself mostly on the wrong side of the popular feeling, the popular will. For instance, take Angola. There I think a very, very serious mistake was made from the very beginning. For America to support a government that the whole of Africa—with the exception of South Africa—was against seems to me very, very strange and very, very unfortunate.

MOYERS: Does it seem to you that the United States has allowed the Cold War to determine what it does in Africa—that we embrace the government of South Africa because it's alleged to be a bulwark against communism and the Soviet Union?

ACHEBE: That's the heart of the matter. When America became powerful and found itself in the position of the leader of the free world, its main concern became "Where are the Soviets? What are they doing? And if they're here, then we will be here."

And so it became possible for a regime like that in South Africa—which is in all practical ways very close to the Nazi regime—to get up and say, "We are anti-Communist." Once you say that, you know, you are all right.

MOYERS: All other sins are forgiven.

ACHEBE: Yes, yes, yes.

MOYERS: What has this meant to the American image in Nigeria? Do we appear to be a racist country, even though we have made such strides at home in coping with our own racism?

ACHEBE: Yes. In fact, virtually everything that works against the freedom or the liberation of Africa is blamed on America first of all—even before the Europeans, even before Britain or Germany or France or Portugal—

MOYERS: —the old colonial masters.

ACHEBE: It seems extraordinary, you know, that America would want to take on that kind of burden. But, as you said, I think it is this obsession with the Soviets, with communism.

MOYERS: How would you like for us to see Africa?

ACHEBE: To see Africa as a continent of people—just people, not some strange beings that demand a special kind of treatment. If you accept Africans as people, then you listen to them. They have their preferences. If you took Africa seriously as a continent of people, you would listen. You would not be able to sit back here and suggest that you know, for instance, what should be done in South Africa. When the majority of the people in South Africa are saying, "This is what we think will bring apartheid to an end," somebody sits here and says, "No, no, that will not do it. We know what will work." Margaret Thatcher sits in Britain and says, "Although the whole of Africa may think that this works, I know that what will work is something else."

> *If you took Africa seriously as a continent of people, you would listen.*

That's what I want to see changed. The traditional attitude of Europe or the West is that Africa is a continent of children. A man as powerful and enlightened as Albert Schweitzer was still able to say, "The black people are my brothers—but my junior brothers." We're not anybody's junior brothers.

MOYERS: There is still a lot of Robinson Crusoe. Robinson Crusoe could never accept Friday as anything but a child living in a primitive simplicity.

ACHEBE: That's right. But that's not really true, it's self-serving. What I'm suggesting is we must look at Africans as full-grown people. They may not be as wealthy or advanced in the same ways as you are here, but they're people who, in their history, also have had moments of great success—in social organization, for instance. If you grant that Africans are grown-up, a lot of other things will follow.

MOYERS: You once said that if you're an African, the world is turned upside down. Explain that.

ACHEBE: What I mean is, I look at the world, at the way it is organized, and it is inadequate. Whichever direction I look, I don't see a space I want to stay in. On our own continent, there are all kinds of mistreatment. The most recent, for instance, is the dumping of the toxic wastes from the industrialized world in Africa.

MOYERS: Many American companies and Western countries are dumping their toxic wastes in African countries, and they're often bribing governments to do it.

ACHEBE: Yes. The world is not well arranged, and therefore there's no way we can be happy with it, even as writers. Sometimes our writer colleagues in the West suggest that perhaps we are too activist, we are too earnest. "Why don't you relax?" they say. "This is not really the business of poetry." About a month ago I was at an international conference of writers to celebrate the one thousandth year of Dublin. During the discussion everybody was saying that poetry has nothing to do with society or with history. Poetry is something personal, private, introspective. Now, obviously, poetry can be that.

MOYERS: But a poet is a member of society.

ACHEBE: Yes, yes. When you say poetry is only something personal, you are saying something outrageously wrong. So I took the opportunity to state the other case. I said that poetry can be as activist as it wants, if it has the willingness and the energy. And I gave them two examples.
Toward the end of the colonial period in Angola, there was a doctor practicing his medicine and writing very delicate, very sensitive poetry in his spare time. One day he saw one of the most brutal acts of the colonial regime, and he shut down his surgery, took to the bush, and wrote a poem which had the words "I wait no more. I am the awaited." It is said that the guerrillas who fought with him chanted lines from his poetry. So I'm saying that these things are possible for poetry. Of course, a poet who becomes activist risks certain dangers, such as getting into trouble with those in power.
Here's another example: Some years ago, at a conference in Stockholm, a Swedish writer and journalist said to two or three African writers, "Say, you fellows are very lucky—your governments put you in jail. Here in Sweden nobody pays any attention to us, no matter what we write."
But, you see, the point is this: A poet who sees poetry in the light I'm suggesting is likely to fall out very seriously with the emperor. Whereas the poet in the West might say, "Oh no, we have no business with politics, we have no business with history, we have no business with anything—just what is in our own mind"—well, the emperor would be very, very happy.

MOYERS: So that's what you meant when you said once that storytelling is a threat to anyone in control.

ACHEBE: Yes, because a storyteller has a different agenda from the emperor.

MOYERS: And yet storytelling, poetry, literature didn't stop the brutalities that were visited on your own Ibo people in the Biafran War and didn't stop Idi Amin in Uganda, or Bokassa in the Central African Republic.

ACHEBE: Yes, well, there's a limit to what storytelling can achieve. We're not saying that a poet can stop a battalion with a couple of lines of his poetry. But there are other forms of power. The storyteller appeals to the mind, and appeals ultimately to generations and generations and generations.

MOYERS: I love this line in *A Man of the People*—"The great thing, as the old people have told us, is reminiscence, and only those who survive can have it. Besides, if you survive, who knows? It may be your turn to eat tomorrow. Your son may bring home your share." The power of reminiscing is very important to you.

ACHEBE: If you look at the world in terms of storytelling, you have, first of all, the man who agitates, the man who drums up the people—I call him the drummer. Then you have the warrior, who goes forward and fights. But you also have the storyteller who recounts the event—and this is one who survives, who outlives all the others. It is the storyteller, in fact, who makes us what we are, who creates history. The storyteller creates the memory that the survivors must have—otherwise their surviving would have no meaning.

MOYERS: The knowledge that others have suffered.

ACHEBE: —that others have suffered here, have battled here. That is very, very important, and that is the meaning of *Anthills of the Savannah*, you see. Memory is necessary if surviving is going to be more than just a technical thing.

MOYERS: The anthill survives so that—

ACHEBE: —so that the new grass will have memory of the fire that devastated the savannah in the previous dry season.

MOYERS: So the anthill carries the memory to the new generation, weaving a collective memory.

ACHEBE: Yes. The storyteller, not the emperor, is aware of all this. The emperor may in fact be planning to rewrite the history of the people. Emperors do this all the time. For instance, an emperor who is totally illegitimate, in terms of the dynasty, might decide to rewrite the history a bit to show that power was always in his family. There is an inevitable conflict between him and the genuine poet.

MOYERS: You've certainly done your share of offending the emperor. In fact, you've been unsparing of your own people in these novels you write. You draw a devastating picture of government in Africa—ministers living in princely mansions while the peasants and the workers live in shacks. You write about the corruption of democracy, the bribery, the vulgarity, the violence, the brutality, the rigged elections. Aren't you concerned that in these novels, which are gaining a growing audience in the West, you are reinforcing the stereotypes many Westerners have toward your own people?

ACHEBE: Well, I can see that danger, but that doesn't really bother me because I'm not concerned primarily with Westerners, I'm concerned with the people whose story I am telling. If I'm a bit harsh, that harshness comes from concern. It is not that I hate my people or even that I hate those who rule us. I don't hate them. But when you look at the opportunities that we have squandered in a country like Nigeria, it is really so painful because so much could have been achieved. So much assistance could have been given, not just to the poor in Nigeria but even outside of it, because providence has been so prodigious in its gifts to Nigeria. When you look at the possibility and then at what has been achieved, you can feel very, very bitter indeed.

MOYERS: What happened? There was such great hope back around the early 1960s, such great expectations for Africa as it was moving into the era of independence.

ACHEBE: It's a very complex problem. A whole lot of things played a part. But perhaps the fundamental failure was always there and was built into the independence movements. Independence is not granted. The leader of Nigeria was able to say in 1960 that independence was given to us on a platter of gold. Well, nobody gives independence to anybody. If you don't achieve it, if you don't fight for it, if you don't struggle for it, then perhaps you have not had your revolution. This is basically what is wrong with many countries in Africa.

The withdrawal of the colonial powers was in many ways merely a tactical move to get out of the limelight, but to retain the control in all practical ways. In fact it turned out to have been even a better idea than running these colonies, because now you could get what you were getting before without the responsibility for administering it. You handed responsibility back to the natives, but continued to control the economy in all kinds of ways.

In addition to this, the powerful nations did not leave us alone. If you remember what happened in the Congo, for instance, in 1960, you know the country was not really handed over to the Africans. There were people masterminding what was going on there and determining that some things would never happen and other things would. We saw the same situation with the Biafran experience. Even though Biafra was a self-governing, independent, sovereign nation, Britain was able to say things like, "We will not tolerate the dismemberment of this great market." They always talked in terms of markets, as if people were created for markets. So this is part of the problem—that we were not really left alone. In addition, there were other things—real calamities, like drought.

MOYERS: One theme recurring throughout your novels is of traditional African culture overwhelmed by the forces of a Western civilization that is itself beginning to disintegrate—as if a man had been shanghaied onto a ship that gets out to sea and starts to sink. So Africa's had a double blow. Its own traditional values have been torn asunder by missionaries, colonial administrators, and wealth seekers, and then the civilization which tried to adopt it—

ACHEBE: —was no longer viable—yes.

MOYERS: So you have the sense in Africa of spiritual and political anarchy?

ACHEBE: Yes, I think there is a bit of that, definitely. But I don't allow that to take the upper hand. Artists should not be the ones to offer despair to society. I don't think that is a function of art. There are enough people around doing that.

MOYERS: We journalists will take care of that.

ACHEBE: Yes, there are so many people who can take care of that.

MOYERS: Someone said, "My sense of Achebe is that he is neither yielding to optimism nor falling into pessimism but is carrying on a running campaign against despair."

ACHEBE: That's a good summary. I would agree with that. I'm not an optimist in the sense of saying, "Oh, everything will work out well." We have to work, we have to think, we have to manage a situation to the best of our ability. Success is not guaranteed.

We have to work with some hope that there is a new generation, a group of survivors who have learned something from the disaster. It is very important to carry the message of the disaster to the new dispensation. With luck, they will succeed. But they've got to work at it.

MOYERS: But friends of mine come back from Africa these days saying that life there has taken such a desperate turn that people are talking not about economic recovery but about mere survival. Is it too late for Africa?

ACHEBE: No, it can't be too late. I think we've been through similar periods in the past. The three hundred years of the slave trade must have left that kind of feeling. Africa has been walking around a very, very long time in the world. It has been the home of mankind from the very beginning. So the events of the last four hundred years, which is what the contemporary mind fastens upon, or maybe the last one thousand years or two thousand years, are really nothing compared with the history that has gone before. And there's no reason for us to imagine that in our time Africa will come to the end of the road.

MOYERS: You talk about external contributions to the chaos of Africa. What about Africans' responsibility? You're pretty tough when you write, "We have given ourselves over so completely to selfishness that we hurt not only those around us, but ourselves even more deeply," and that in doing so, "one must assume a blunting of the imagination and a sense of danger of truly psychiatric proportions." That's a harsh judgment.

ACHEBE: You mentioned Idi Amin; you mentioned Bokassa. There are minor examples of the same kind of mindlessness at all levels. You have scores and scores of examples of people who cart away the wealth of their nations to Swiss banks. You have examples of officials who take money so that toxic waste can be dumped in their territory. This is the kind of thing I'm talking about. It's impossible to contemplate that kind of situation without being very, very bitter.

MOYERS: There's a moment in your new novel, *Anthills*, where you seem to say that the ordinary people share responsibility with the politicians for the corruption of Nigeria, that their indifference and cynicism breed cynicism on the part of the leaders. There's a scene where four men are brought before a vast crowd with the television cameras running, and as they're shot, the crowd cheers. You seem to say the people share in this.

ACHEBE: Yes, of course they do. Of course they do. These things would not go on if the people said no. The people are the owners of the land. But they've still got a long way to go because part of the problem is lack of awareness. The weakness of the people, the owners of the land, is that they are uninformed. They do not know. They are not organized. When these things change, when the people become well educated and well organized, then they will be able to say no to this kind of situation.

MOYERS: Yet you talk about a kind of artless integrity at the bruised heart of the people. A kind of powerful, fundamental goodness.

ACHEBE: The writer is aware of that. Now, you'll find many people who'll say, "I'm for the people, I'm a radical, I'm a revolutionary," and so on. But you look closer and find on the whole their attitude to things is selfish, even brutal. I don't believe anybody can work for the people and for the salvation of society without being in some ways a good person. You don't go about making an effort or striving to achieve connection with the people. You instinctively react appro-

> *I don't believe anybody can work for the people and for the salvation of society without being in some ways a good person.*

priately to people and to suffering. The artist may not be a good person, either, but if he's an artist, he's aware of the possibility of this essence and would not obstruct it.

MOYERS: In your third novel, *Arrow of God*, there's a wonderful point when the chief, who's been imposed by the colonial government on his people, goes mad. The people take it as a sign that their god is reinforcing the ancient wisdom of the elders, which is that no man, however great, was greater than his own people, and that no man ever won judgment against his clan. A great leader can't lift a vulgar people. But a vulgar leader can't lift a great people.

ACHEBE: It has to be a combination, a joint effort. I personally place a lot of responsibility on leadership, for practical reasons. If you have a bad people, a bad leader, and a bad system, what do you do? Where do you start? Where can you make the greatest impact if you want to bring about change? In the case of Nigeria, to try to change a hundred million people is a hell of a job. Would you start by trying to create a perfect system? This is not possible, because the perfect system worked by imperfect people will be corrupted.

So I think, in a practical way, it is easiest to address oneself to the leadership, because that's the special group that has had the benefit of a good education, and the investment of all kinds of things in them. They should be enlightened. They are fewer, too. One can address this smaller group more easily than the entire population. But one should also remember that leadership without the people will not really work perfectly.

MOYERS: It was a great gamble that Nigeria and other new nations in Africa took when, leaving colonialism, they embraced democracy. It takes a great deal of discipline, institution building, and tradition to make a democracy. And democracy is corruptible.

ACHEBE: I think you are right. But it goes even beyond that, because, for instance, when people say that we failed to practice democracy in Africa, they assume that we were taught democracy during colonial rule and that we somehow betrayed our education.

That is not true at all. The colonial regime itself was not a democratic system. It was a most extreme form of totalitarianism. The colonial governor was not responsible to anybody in the territory. He was responsible to a minister in Paris or in London, but he was certainly not responsible to the people on the ground. And so there was no model of democracy. We were not practicing the Westminster model in Nigeria under colonial rule. We were practicing colonial dictatorship. So the colonial people really had no experience of this so-called democracy that they were supposed to have inherited. They did not inherit anything of the sort. It is not simply a question of people not living up to expectations. They really were not prepared. They were not trained for democracy.

MOYERS: So candid an admission, once again, can play into the hands of the enemies of black Africa, because so many Westerners argue, "Well, that's right. Nigeria was not ready for democracy. And because Africa can't handle democracy, better we stick with South Africa, because its government knows how to keep order, to prevent Communists from rising to power—whereas the governments of Africa and other black countries have not proven themselves up to the—"

ACHEBE: That is, of course, totally spurious. There's no way you can inculcate democracy through dictatorship. The colonial system in itself was the very antithesis of democracy. So, no matter how long you stayed under it, you would not learn democracy. There was democracy in many parts of Africa before colonial rule came. So to say, "Let's keep ruling them until they learn democracy," is really fraudulent.

MOYERS: But that's what is said in South Africa.

ACHEBE: But of course to say, "Let's support the South Africans, since they're the only ones who understand democracy," comes down to not accepting that Africans are people—because if you accept that Africans are people, you cannot possibly say that a tiny minority of white people should impose their will to the extent of depriving others of even the elementary rights of self-expression. All the rights we know in the so-called democracies are denied, positively denied, in this regime. Now, for anybody to say that's the right thing for Africa shows that that person does not grant full humanity to Africans. We know that there are such people, but we're not really going to listen to them, and they are not ultimately going to determine what happens in Africa.

> . . . if you accept that Africans are people, you cannot possibly say that a tiny minority of white people should impose their will to the extent of depriving others of even the elementary rights of self-expression.

MOYERS: You mentioned Africa before the colonial powers came. There is the opening line of your children's story *The Drum*, which begins: "In the beginning, when the world was young." Does the artist in you ever wish you could start the whole story all over again?

ACHEBE: Yes, that is the strength of stories, and especially of children's stories. I'm happy you raised that, because all of us need to learn to become like children again once in a while. We become so stiff. We are weighed down by so much knowledge, so many possessions, so much special interest, that we lose the flexibility of children. Children can fly. You know, everything is possible to a child. This is something that children's stories can do for us and that we ought to learn again. We ought to keep ourselves young in that particular way.

MOYERS: You took a period of your life away from writing novels and wrote for children. Why?

ACHEBE: Because I felt it was very important. I had some very interesting and very strange experiences bringing up my own children. That really confirmed my fears about the danger of not telling our children stories. You see, our fathers did, and our grandfathers did. But once writing came, we more or less forgot that responsibility to tell children's stories.

MOYERS: So what happened?

ACHEBE: What happened was that all kinds of bad stories, all kinds of junk were being dumped—again, like toxic waste. We were very young parents, so we really had no experience. We used to go into the supermarket in Lagos and pick up a glossy, nice, big-looking, colorful story. We never read children's stories ourselves, so we didn't know what was in them. But then we discovered that our daughter was beginning to have very strange ideas. At that point we began to look carefully into what she was reading. And really, there was a lot of poison there—stories full of racism, full of ideas of Africa as the other place, as the back of the world. I knew then the importance of children's stories. And I knew that we were failing as parents in not bringing down the children after dinner, as our forefathers did, to tell them stories. Then a friend of mine, who was a poet and working for Cambridge University

Press, came to me and said, "Look, we want a children's story from you." I had not written any before, and I didn't know how it was going to work. But I was ready to try.

MOYERS: Did your children read your stories?

ACHEBE: Yes, I read the stories to them before they were published.

MOYERS: Were they pretty good critics?

ACHEBE: Very good. Children are young, but they're not naïve. And they're honest. They're not going to keep awake if the story is boring. When they get excited, you see it in their eyes. That was quite an education for me.

MOYERS: When you were living in the States in the early seventies, were your children with you?

ACHEBE: Yes. The youngest was in nursery school when we were here in '72. She was just two and a half, and it was quite a problem, because I was teaching, and my wife was anxious to do her doctorate in education, so we found her a little nursery school—and she hated it. I don't know why. I had the job of driving her to this school, and it was always such a terrible scene, leaving her there. So, in the end, I promised to tell her a story every morning as we went to school and another story as we came back. She would look forward to this—and this was the way she overcame the trauma of this first alien experience.

MOYERS: Are your children comfortable in this crossroads between Africa and the United States?

ACHEBE: I guess so. There are problems, though. They have to know more than either tradition, you see. This is the problem of being on the crossroads. You have a bit of both, and you really have to know a lot more than either. So their situation is not very easy. But it's very exciting. Those who have the energy and the will to survive at the crossroads become really very exceptional people.

MOYERS: You went home in '76 and came back last year to spend the year at the University of Massachusetts. Has America changed very much in those eleven years?

ACHEBE: Yes. I think there was a loss of the feeling of euphoria. When I was here in 1972, it was pretty close to the sixties, to the era of the Civil Rights movement. There was the feeling that America was on the move. There was a lot of optimism and all kinds of new programs to bring the disadvantaged into the society, for example.

Coming back now, it was quite shocking that within a month or two of my arrival, there were incidents of racism on a level that reminded me of the pre–Civil Rights period. There's a new spirit in the land.

Perhaps it is an inevitable part of the dynamics of society that a period of optimism should be followed by some kind of reaction. Perhaps that's what's happening. But suddenly I have found too many young people saying, "I'm a conservative." Now, I can't imagine a sixteen-year-old conservative. What will he be when he becomes sixty and the president of a bank? Young people at that age are not really conservatives and shouldn't aim to become conservatives. They should be open and free, and they should be flexible. They should be ready to try new things. They should be open to the world.

MOYERS: The title of your novel *No Longer at Ease* is taken, if I remember correctly, from T. S. Eliot's "Journey of the Magi," where the Wise Men leave their own warm and comfortable country to travel through a strange and inhospitable land.

On their way back, they're thinking about this journey and whether they have journeyed toward life or death—the question all of us face. What about Africa? In the last thirty years Africa has been on a journey toward independence, experiencing chaos, anarchy, violence, failure, hope—has it been a journey toward life or death?

ACHEBE: It is difficult to say—and it is too soon, too. If you look at this very small segment of history, then you can talk about it in those terms. If you are frozen in time, you can say yes, it's awful. And it is really awful. But I think if you take the wide view of things, then you begin to see it as history, as human history over a long period of time, and that we are passing through a bad patch. It's not death. We are passing through a bad patch, and if we succeed, then even this experience of the bad patch will turn out to be an enrichment. That's how I prefer to see it. There is no way of saying this is the way it's going to be, because we are not given to know how it's going to be. But I think if we are to keep working, if we are to keep writing books, then for me that's the only way I can look at what's happening. We are going through a very bad patch. We've been through bad patches in the past, and we survived.

MOYERS: And every survivor has an obligation to remember.

ACHEBE: Yes, yes, yes.

MOYERS: What's that old Jewish saying—that in remembrance is the secret of redemption? Is that why you write?

ACHEBE: Well, I didn't put it that way. I write partly because I enjoy it. But also I knew that somebody had to tell my story. We are in a period so different from anything else that has happened that everything that is presented to us has to be looked at twice.

I went to the first university that was built in Nigeria, and I took a course in English. We were taught the same kind of literature that British people were taught in their own university. But then I began to look at these books in a different light. When I had been younger, I had read these adventure books about the good white man, you know, wandering into the jungle or into danger, and the savages were after him. And I would instinctively be on the side of the white man. You see what fiction can do, it can put you on the wrong side if you are not developed enough. In the university I suddenly saw that these books had to be read in a different light. Reading *Heart of Darkness*, for instance, which was a very, very highly praised book and which is still very highly praised, I realized that I was one of those savages jumping up and down on the beach. Once that kind of enlightenment comes to you, you realize that someone has to write a different story. And since I was in any case inclined that way, why not me? What I am saying is there is a certain measure of seriousness in addition to the pleasure of telling stories. There is serious intention. So when somebody gets up and says, "Oh, but the teacher of poetry should have nothing to do with society or with heavy things like politics," I just can't understand.

MOYERS: Earlier, you said that Africans hope the West and America, in particular, will listen. If we listen, what will we hear? What does Africa have to say to the rest of the world?

ACHEBE: First of all, we are people. We are not funny beings. If you took up any newspaper here, you probably won't see Africa mentioned at all for months. Then perhaps one day a year you'll see some strange story. It has to be the kind of story we've come to associate with Africa. I would simply say: Look at Africa as a continent of people. They are not devils, they are not angels, they're just people. And listen to them. We have done a lot of listening ourselves.

This is a situation where you have a strong person and a weak person. The weak person does all the listening, and up to a point the strong person even forgets that the weak person may have something to say. Because he is there, a kind of fixture, you simply talk at him. A British governor of Southern Rhodesia once said the partnership between the whites and the blacks is the partnership of the horse and its rider. He wasn't trying to be funny, he seriously thought so. Now, that's what we want the West to get rid of—thinking of Africa as the horse rather than as the man.

MOYERS: You make me think of that summary passage in *Anthills of the Savannah*—"Whatever you are is never enough. You must find a way to accept something, however small, from the other to make you whole and to save you from the mortal sin of righteousness and extremism." So there is something that the strong can take from the weak.

ACHEBE: Yes, they need to take it. Seeing the world from the position of the weak person is a great education. We lack imagination. If we had enough imagination to put ourselves in the shoes of the person we oppress, things would begin to happen. So it is important that we develop the ability to listen to the weak. Not only in Africa, but even in your own society, the strong must listen to the weak.

Mary Catherine Bateson

ANTHROPOLOGIST

CARL ZITZMANN

Catherine Bateson studies change. She also lives it. A scholar, author, wife, and mother, she has taught anthropology at Amherst, Northeastern, and Harvard and now teaches at George Mason University in Virginia. Her books range from the social consequences of the AIDS epidemic to life with her celebrated parents, anthropologists Margaret Mead and Gregory Bateson. Her new book, Composing a Life, *explores how women create order and sense out of their conflicting commitments.*

MOYERS: You've said that all ethical relationships are expressed in family terms—brotherhood, sisterhood, the fatherhood of God. Is that metaphor still useful in our world when the traditional family is under siege?

BATESON: The family is changing, not disappearing. We have to broaden our understanding of it, look for the new metaphors. When I look at families and relationships in society, I tend to emphasize the importance of growth—continuing growth for every member of the family, and optimal growth for children. Making growth possible is a task of men and women and the political system of the society because the children represent the future.

Now, many family systems depend on putting some members of the family at a great disadvantage. They depend on the subordination of women or on the disowning of youngest sons, who then have to emigrate. I would like to see the family itself not limit people in that sense. I would like to see a society in which all members have the possibility of continuing growth.

MOYERS: Continuing growth—do you mean nurturing in the same sense as when a child is nurtured at home? Once those children have left, do we nurture each other as husband and wife?

BATESON: All human beings need both to nurture and be nurtured throughout their lives. But I'm also including the exploration of new ideas and the discovery of potentials. We live many years after the children are gone, and there is a lot of potential in men and women in their forties and fifties to learn new things. Those opportunities for continuing growth are very important.

MOYERS: You said once that everyone who's concerned about the future ought to have contact with a real flesh and blood child. Why?

BATESON: Because children are the carriers of the future. The most important thing in raising a child is not to try to put the stamp of the past on that child, but to give that child freedom to grow and explore—that's what the future is like. We have to work very hard to ensure that when our grandchildren have grown-up children, this will still be a good country to live in, that it won't be broken by accumulated debt, that our good lives today won't be taken out of the hides of our grandchildren.

MOYERS: But aren't we living at the expense of our children? The debt's one example, the environment's another.

BATESON: Indeed, we are living at the expense of our children, and this is an extraordinary turnabout in the American tradition. We used to be able to contrast the American idea of family with the idea that exists in many traditional societies, where people give birth to a lot of children so that they will be cared for by those children in old age. We haven't done that in the past. Traditionally, we have expected to pay back the debt that we owe our parents not to our parents, but to our children. We inherit so much from the past, and the responsible next step is to ensure a good future. But now, for the first time, this tradition has been reversed, and we are feeding on the future instead of being fed by the past and then in our turn feeding the future and contributing to it.

> *. . . we are living at the expense of our children.*

MOYERS: What's happened? What do you think marked the change?

BATESON: Well, I'm not sure we have fully realized what we're doing. It has been said that the debt is going to be on the backs of our children, but many people don't realize that it means *their* children. This is one reason why I think every adult needs a relationship with a child, a real flesh-and-blood child, so that we can imagine what it will be like as that child's life unfolds into the future.

MOYERS: You're not saying that every couple has to have a child—because some couples, for many reasons, choose not to.

BATESON: No. But it's important that people learn the lessons of caring and then effectively transfer those lessons to the way they care for the city or the landscape they live in, or worry about all the children in the world. There are many expressions of the impulse to care for the future. But the best way to learn it is going back to the elementary school of caring for young children.

MOYERS: Is that what you meant when you said that it's not enough any longer to say that we're brothers and sisters, because that means we have the same parent—but that we need to talk about ourselves as parents, because then we have the same child, and that child is the future?

BATESON: Ethical systems based on family are based on common descent. But in the world today my daughter might marry someone from any country on the planet. There may be no common ancestry that we know of, but common descendents are going to exist for all of us. So, instead of saying we come from the same source, we can say we are going toward the same future—and indeed, giving birth and rearing and nurturing that future together.

My mother used to say that only we can protect the children of the Russians, and only the Russians can protect our children. In that context, she was talking about protection from the dangers of nuclear war. But there are a great many environmental dangers and economic dangers that also call for protection.

You see, if you live in a very short time scale, you can be focused in a very small area. But the further into the future you try to think and plan and project and be responsible, the larger the area you have to take into account, because as you move out in time, the interconnections and interdependencies multiply. When I think about my grandchildren, I have to think in global terms. That's where they'll live—on the planet earth. That's all I know about them. The lesson we have to learn now is how to change our style of thinking and decision-making to deal with a longer time frame and a wider geographical context. We have to get away from the notion that every time we have a problem, we invent a special flyswatter for hitting it away—that flyswatter is usually a government department. We have to see any problem within a wide global context.

MOYERS: But that image from the sixties of "spaceship earth" didn't take hold. By your own admission, we've gone back to thinking "me and mine," to immediate gratification, to our own small circle.

BATESON: "Spaceship earth" was a bad image because it sounded cold and mechanistic. A much more powerful image, which replaced "spaceship earth," was the photograph of earth from the moon. That's not hard and cold and mechanical, that's something living. I can say to people, "We should think of this planet and its future as our child." You wouldn't say that about a spaceship.

MOYERS: What we name something makes a difference. You point out that if you think of a tree more like a woman than as a post, you're going to be thinking differently about how to treat a tree. That applies to what you think about the earth, what you think about family, and what you think about every object and person in your embrace.

> ... there are few things as toxic as a bad metaphor.

BATESON: Indeed it does. You know, there are few things as toxic as a bad metaphor. You can't think without metaphors. Do you think of the ocean as alive, as a cradle of life, or do you think of it as just some gray water sloshing around that you can make grayer by dumping in it? Do you think of rivers, lakes, trees, and forests as alive?

MOYERS: So much of your work suggests that we have to change what we *call* the problems we're facing in this modern world.

BATESON: We've gotten into a habit of separating problems from their context. I can give you an example from the work I've been doing on AIDS. AIDS is a disease which increasingly is going to be affecting people who are already disadvantaged. It's going to be spreading very widely, but we see AIDS increasing fastest in minority communities and in the poorer countries that don't have big budgets for health programs. Now, at a certain level, when you think about trying to address the AIDS epidemic, what you are trying to do is put people in a position where they can do what human beings have done to adapt throughout evolution: They can learn, and they can change their behavior to fit a new fact in the environment. For example, you want people to learn to practice safer sex, to learn to change behavior. That's a form of growth. Well, those people have to have a hope for the future, they have to want to live, they have to be able to look ahead and say, "This is the kind of life I want to have, and therefore I don't want to be cut off early." What's more, they have to trust you. They have to be able to hear what you are saying and be ready to take it on. That's why it's so hard for public health authorities to influence the behavior of drug users—because drug users, with some justice, are not willing to listen to what they're told. It's hard for them to believe it is said with good will.

Now, when you try to create a world where people have positive motivations and trust what they hear from authority, you're talking about democracy—a society in which people have a chance and a future they can look ahead to that they care about, and a government they sense is their government. So these two things—better communication and hope—which are the preconditions of addressing the epidemic and persuading people to change their behavior in ways that make the world safer, are exactly the things that we should be trying to enhance in our country and throughout the world.

MOYERS: An open, trusting society?

BATESON: An open, trusting, and caring society. A society that writes whole groups of people off and leaves them in an underclass and doesn't care should not be surprised when those people make life decisions and take risks that are not based on wanting to live and raise their children.

MOYERS: In dealing with AIDS, we seem to swing from panic to complacency. One month the headlines are bold and black and fearsome, and the next month there's nothing whatsoever said, except in small print on page 74.

BATESON: Fear is not a good teacher. The lessons of fear are quickly forgotten. People get sick of it. That's what's happening with AIDS. They have felt pummeled by the threat and by contact with the very real grief of people who've had loved ones die, and they're happier not thinking about it. They're likely to abandon good resolutions they've made about having safer sex lives.

But there are positive reasons for addressing the epidemic. People can be proud to adjust their behavior, not necessarily in a repressive way, but to get to the point where they're making conscious choices and have some respect and concern for their partners. These are positive goals.

MOYERS: Is there evidence that people are changing their behavior out of a positive, affirmative insight?

BATESON: There's some evidence, but so far, the data that we have concerns whether you can scare people into changing their behavior.

MOYERS: And do you think we can?

BATESON: When people are really scared, then they run in the opposite direction. Still, there is no question that some of the communities most at risk are changing their behavior. This is happening particularly in the gay community. However, AIDS isn't going to go away. There won't be a quick technological fix. We have to regard this virus as also living on our lovely green planet. In fact, we are the environment in which the virus lives. We have no way, and probably won't for a long time to come, of eliminating the virus from the planetary system we live in. What we have to do is what we have always done—learn to live in the environment that we have and to change our behavior.

MOYERS: Since we know how the virus is transmitted, does society not have the right to say to those who are transmitting it, "Cease and desist. You must make some personal sacrifice in order to protect the future of the planet"?

BATESON: There are clearly two ways to go. It would be possible and is likely to be the policy in a number of countries to try to control the epidemic by entirely repressive measures.

MOYERS: Segregate the carriers, forbid sex to them, take all kinds of coercive measures?

BATESON: Not just that. You probably would have to control everybody's sexual behavior because it's not easy to be a hundred percent sure where the virus is. This kind of quarantine has never worked completely and is not a good bet for long-term control. But that's one road.

MOYERS: In fear, many societies may adopt it.

BATESON: That's right. But that's not a road that matches the basic premises of American society. To follow that road would mean becoming a different kind of society over time. We would have to become a repressive, coercive, tightly controlled society in which we don't care about the value of individual lives. We would have to be willing to lock a group of people up, many of whom are entirely innocent.

MOYERS: But wouldn't we in effect be saying that while we care about those individual lives who are carriers of the virus, we are also concerned about the lives of all of the other individuals who run the risk of the virus?

BATESON: The larger claim has to take precedence, if one has tried the alternatives. But I don't think we have tried the alternatives. The alternatives are education toward behavioral change combined with a new commitment to social justice and openness in this society. As a society, we don't live up to the aspirations of giving everybody a chance, of treating people fairly so they can look ahead to their future, of making sure that the government appears beneficent to all, of making sure that everyone can read and has access to information about disease.

MOYERS: What does equal opportunity in a democratic society have to do with the carrier of a virus who, through homosexual activities, transmits the virus to someone else? So many of the carriers are well-educated, knowing, sensitive people, who nonetheless seem to think that their sexual behavior is the first exercise of their freedom.

BATESON: The gay community has taken the exercise of sexual freedom, which was harshly denied for hundreds of years, as the center of their democratic rights. Within less than twenty years they exploded into freedom the way you do when you've been cooped up all day, and you get out and stretch in all directions, jump up and down, or whatever. Now, suddenly, they've been told to get back in the box. There is an equilibrium that could be arrived at, within which the gay community could feel respected and valued and could express themselves responsibly and carefully. You have people who were spat at and called names, and then felt free, and now they're being ganged up on again. This is a very hard situation to adjust to. But we have to remember that many of the heroes of the AIDS epidemic in this country so far, the people who have worked for responsible change, have come from the gay community.

MOYERS: What do you mean by "responsible change," and "responsible behavior"? Safe sex?

BATESON: Always say "safer sex." Nothing in life is a hundred percent safe, and trying to make it a hundred percent safe just creates confusion. Safer sex. By responsible behavior what I mean is people starting new relationships or transient relationships using condoms, and then thinking twice about the transition to not using them if they're going to have essentially monogamous relationships.

MOYERS: So you're saying the individual is responsible for his or her behavior, and the imperative is to persuade individuals to change their behavior without simply using fear.

> *I don't want my safety to be at the cost of someone else's freedom.*

BATESON: Yes. I want to take advantage of positive motivations. I don't want to lose their creativity and willingness to contribute to society in other ways. I don't want to protect myself by persecuting somebody else. I don't want my safety to be at the cost of someone else's freedom.

MOYERS: If their behavior is not threatening, there's no reason for you to have to resort to coercion. So if they change out of their own sense of responsibility, society loses its motivation to act in a coercive way.

BATESON: Well, AIDS is not transmitted by casual contact, but by acts which are essentially voluntary.

MOYERS: But what about the people who come down with AIDS because they've shared drug needles? These people are not noted for exercising concern for their own welfare. Can we trust them to change their behavior voluntarily?

BATESON: You can't trust people to change their behavior when that choice is not free. Part of the problem of IV drug users is they are addicted and are in that very significant sense no longer free. They're constrained by their addiction. Step number one is to do everything we can to make it possible for people to get freedom from that addiction. We're not doing that yet. We're more interested in stopping drug importation than we are in helping people who have been trapped in the prison of addiction. The second thing is that IV drug users, short of recovering from addiction, can take precautions. They can clean needles with household bleach—they can cease sharing needles.

Once they suspect they are infected, they can find that out, and if they have sexual partners that they care about, and if they care about the children that might be born, they can prevent passing the disease on sexually.

In other words, there are a set of behavioral changes that IV drug users can make, short of the difficult achievement of coming off the drug.

MOYERS: But doesn't the compulsion of addiction make it very unlikely that people are going to be thinking about safe needles when they're desperate for the fix?

BATESON: I agree that the drug addiction issue is one of the most critical issues in our society today. But it is disastrous to address it only by police measures, rather than being sure that people have viable and inviting alternatives to living their lives as dealers and users. In that sense, the addiction issue and the AIDS issue are related. They both have to do with what kind of society we have.

MOYERS: That's what you meant when you said that we could win the battle against AIDS but destroy the immune system of society.

BATESON: The body's immune system is a very useful metaphor for thinking about how we sustain our society and make choices within it and for thinking about the health of the body politic.

It's a funny thing that people tend to think they're going to solve the drug question by using the armed forces—the same way that they think they're going to solve problems of discontent in the Third World countries by military dictatorships. People tend to use military metaphors about the immune system. They think of these white cells going around zapping bacteria and so on through the body. But the immune system is really a system of continuous care and maintenance of balance. In the same way that we are concerned for balance throughout the body, we have to be concerned for balance throughout the society.

MOYERS: So the gay person has an obligation to think about his responsibility, and all the rest of us have a responsibility to think about the kind of society which we want to combat this virus or any other threat.

BATESON: Sometimes it's useful to use the old metaphor of the society as a single living organism, just as one can also think of an ecosystem as a single organism.

351 MARY CATHERINE BATESON

Then you suddenly realize that if one part of that organism is being allowed to sicken and die, as in our inner cities, this infection can affect the entire society.

Now surgeons go in and cut things out, but the immune system keeps a continual guard trying to maintain health. We haven't done a good enough job, over the last fifteen years, caring about the overall health of our society and the overall health of the environment we live in, and, increasingly, we're aware that we have to care about the overall health of the planet in order to protect ourselves.

MOYERS: But it's easy to think about the planet and disregard our own immediate opportunities and obligations. Maybe we've climbed aboard that spaceship and floated out beyond the circles of our immediate embrace. It's easy to think globally without acting locally.

BATESON: You've just referred to René Dubos's famous slogan: Think globally and act locally. But you have to add to it: Think globally and act locally, but act locally in a way that will have a global effect. We can't just care for the homeless in our own hometown, even if that hometown is New York. During this period of the AIDS epidemic, it's striking how rarely we have been reminded of the speed with which the AIDS epidemic is spreading in Africa, where it is directly correlated with people who are just scrabbling to get by, and with limitations on medical resources, and with lifestyles that grow out of poverty, and with migrant labor, and with the breakdown of village life and traditional cultures. It's nonsense to think about addressing the epidemic only inside the United States, because the human population really is one organism.

MOYERS: Sometimes you anthropologists wear us out with talk of global obligations. You come up with the artifacts of the immediate and make us think about the necessity of the universal.

BATESON: But to see that as a human being one is involved in a life that embraces the planet, and that one has the opportunity to contribute to the health of that life, is a marvelous vision. Sometimes I think the reason we talk about the loss of values today is because there is really no viable vision that is not inclusive. Either we have to make the leap to a vision that includes all human beings, or we are locked up in tiny, local self-interest and prejudices—and at that point, why not just get rich and enjoy yourself? It's as if the time had come to recognize that we are one. This is foreshadowed in all the world's great religions. The universalistic religions that have spread from place to place all have an inclusive vision that individual human lives are connected to each other as part of a whole.

MOYERS: Why as an anthropologist are you writing a book on AIDS?

BATESON: Anthropology traditionally has been a bridge discipline between biology and culture—those aspects of human behavior that are biologically based and linked with the environment, and those aspects that are learned and that vary from place to place. There is that old question of nature and nurture, and how they fit together. I became interested in the AIDS question because it allows me to take a biological event—the emergence of a new virus—and think about the interface between our capacity to evolve culturally and what's happening in our biological environment.

MOYERS: Our ability to change our behavior by conscious choice, by will?

BATESON: Conscious and unconscious, because much of our behavior we're not working out consciously every minute.

MOYERS: There are little scriptwriters down there.

BATESON: One of the things that you get from being trained as an anthropologist is experience in thinking about the whole. Traditionally, anthropologists thought about very small communities—one relatively isolated village, or one island. Now what we need to do is to apply those ways of seeing to much larger and more complicated communities, so that we understand that family life, and how we make a living, and how our religious beliefs are developing, and how our government institutions function—that all of these things are interconnected, and that we can't really solve major problems without thinking in terms of all these different areas.

I have a fantasy: What if we had a president who said, "I want the members of my cabinet to be committed to actually talking to each other about the problems that they have to face, and to start from the premise that those problems are interconnected, that they're not a group of separate little empires, but that the armed forces are educators, and the schools affect the environment, and even the post office has a fundamental impact on our educational and political institutions." If you had that attitude, you'd save a lot of money, because what we do now is break all the problems up in pieces. Everyone has a totally separate bureaucracy, stepping on each other's toes, and leaving out things that need to be attended to.

MOYERS: But I was in Washington under two presidents, and I've reported on every President since. They all come in saying, "My cabinet is going to function as a body, as an organism. We're going to have meetings and look at the whole picture." Within nine months, cabinet meetings don't take place, members go their own way, the President meets with each cabinet officer, if at all, separately, and pretty soon we're back to the age of specialization.

BATESON: Well, the age of specialization doesn't work very well. One of the problems in this society is that the things that work in the short term don't work in the long term. There's a parable I like to use for this. You've probably heard of the Iditarod, the dog sled race across Alaska—people driving sleds pulled by dogs for more than a thousand miles. It lasts nearly two weeks. It is a long haul as races go, and for the last three years, it's been won by a woman named Susan Butcher. How is it that she has won? She says that her chief competitor starts his dogs early and drives them hard, and they get tired at the end of the day. So every day, he forges ahead of her, and at the end of the day his dogs are getting tired, and she's catching up. She wins the race essentially by not exploiting her dogs, by not exhausting them. Now, if the race only lasted two days, he would always win. If the race lasted a week, he would always win. But the race is long enough so that the caring and protection that she lavishes on her dogs turns into a winning strategy.

Now you see, we have organized our society so that the winning strategies are the short-term ones. We take presidents who care about the future, and we turn them into crisis managers. We lose the possibility of long-term, thoughtful leadership. Whether it's corporations and how they handle their budgets and the fact that their quarterly reports have to please the buyers for big pension funds and so on, or whether it's industry or labor or politics or—

MOYERS: —journalism. You weren't going to say it.

BATESON: We have taught ourselves not to think in terms of the long haul, but the long haul is what lies between now and a decent life for our grandchildren. I've been looking at how women organize their lives and their careers. Sometimes I think that as more women come into full participation at higher policy levels, we may get more of this kind of long-term thinking. This is a moment of opportunity for a change in what we emphasize in our public life.

MOYERS: What makes you think women can bring this sensitivity to our public life?

BATESON: At the moment, every adult woman is marked by child-rearing practices that assume genuinely different roles in society for men and women. We don't know what kind of differences would remain between men and women if this were not true. But, in any case, this is our situation at the moment. We have a population where, even within the same family, individuals have been differently shaped. Nobody, of course, is shaped to express all of his or her potentials. There's evidence that some women are now functioning very much like men, doing what men do, seeking the same kinds of short-term goals that men have been taught to seek. There is also evidence that discussions go differently when there are women involved, that there are changes of tone and attention. Some of the research that's been done on ethical perceptions of women suggests that women attend to a broader context.

We talk now about the conflict that women have between work and the home, and how terrible it is to be torn in two directions. But women have always been torn. We forget that when a woman who's been married for a period of time gives birth to a baby, she has to serve two masters. She has to respond to two different kinds of needs. Then she has a second baby. She's got one baby at the breast and one baby on her knee, and they're quite likely to be quarreling. So the traditional feminine roles as wife and mother of multiple children have involved caring for multiple issues, balancing them off, not neglecting that while you're caring about this, having one rhythm to respond to a husband and another one with an infant and another one with a growing child.

This is what it is to be a woman. And this is what it is to keep a household going, to have multiple skills, to deal with transitions, to deal with the health of the whole. There is a sense in which women have retained the capacity to be generalists, to live in an ecology in which there is more than one life, and you have to balance them off. Now, when you go out of the home and into a corporation or factory, you may spend all day thinking of only one factor in a complex situation. Far too many men have been narrowed to caring for only one thing.

> . . . women have retained the capacity to be generalists, to live in an ecology in which there is more than one life. . . .

Now, when that one thing is the short-term profitability of a chemical company, the men making decisions may not take into consideration the health of the environment in which their factory is, or the lives of their workers, who might come down with cancer in ten years.

You know what people say about women—that they're easily distracted, and that success has to do with focusing on specific goals. But what if the health of the world depends on the same kind of capacity that allows you, while you're feeding one child, to see that the other child is reaching up and about to pull a cooking pot of hot liquid on his head? This capacity to see out of the corner of your eye, and care about the health, not just of one child, but of three or four and a husband and other members of the family—that is the beginning of the capacity to care about the health of a multitude of nations, or an environment of many species.

MOYERS: True, but what happens if the female is rewarded for the next quarter's profit and success? What makes you think she wouldn't start thinking as he does, with that singularity of mission to deliver those profits and make that factory run on time? The reward could change the behavior.

BATESON: It might, and that's why this period is so important. We are in a period that is comparable to the Renaissance. The Renaissance was a moment of cultural creativity produced by the convergence of cultural streams, the introduction of the Greek tradition that was preserved by the Arabs and the encounter of that with the Christian Western European tradition.

Now we are potentially at a moment in which the entry of women into full participation—but still carrying with them the experience of having been socialized for other kinds of roles, such as nurturing and caring—has a potential for changing the tone overall. I can't guarantee that that moment will go on forever, but I am quite sure that we are in deep danger of really wrecking our environment and wrecking the future of this country if we can't learn to think in this more complex way.

I believe that it is exactly those women who are, in a sense, migrating from one role to another—not just women who've been full-time housewives, but women who have included these different ways of seeing in their lives—who provide maybe the best moment of opportunity we'll ever have to find that potential for longer-term thinking that, after all, is there in men, too. Men don't have to go around with blinkers on.

MOYERS: But we're paid well to do so.

BATESON: Well, you are. But then, you pay yourselves to do so, too.

MOYERS: What do you mean?

BATESON: I mean the people making the decisions of who to pay are also men.

MOYERS: Power dictates its own rewards, its own returns, its own behavior, and women are going to be susceptible to the rewards, the power, and, therefore, the behavior, don't you think?

BATESON: It is a matter of shifting gears, and it's going to be hard to do. In the race across Alaska that I talked about, the longer-term strategy wins unless you set the rules in such a way as to make it lose all the time. This is the fundamental problem of our society—to find a way to reverse the process that's taking place at the moment, of narrowing and narrowing and making ourselves more specialized, and to affirm the broader and longer-term way of thinking.

MOYERS: There's another issue here, which is that men are allowed to feel at home when they're at work. We have that office, we're there with our colleagues, we feel at home, in a natural environment—whereas women, even when they're allowed into the workplace, are not yet allowed to feel at home there.

BATESON: Oh, absolutely, and it's one of the great ironies, because the whole rhetoric of home and work was based on the notion that you go to work and work, and you go home and relax, which, of course, women have never been able to do, because they can't relax when they go home. Then they go to the workplace, and they discover the same men that they've been bringing the slippers to are putting their feet up on their desks, and they can't do that either.

It's an uncomfortable transition. Women in the workplace still make men nervous. It's still harder for them to hear what women say. It's a long, slow process, but I think what's important is to understand that this is not simply a matter of fairness to women, which is of course very important. This is a matter of providing the maximum richness of creative input in our society. This is the issue with all immigrant and marginal groups. If we as a society can include everyone living in this country, we will have the benefit of their contribution. We'll have to share some of the benefits, too. We have far more wealth of creativity and vision and productivity in this country than we use, and one of the reasons we don't use it is because of discrimination.

MOYERS: Questions come to mind. One is that so many of the young women I meet and with whom I work have this conflict about having a baby and having a job. They feel a fear, almost, of losing one opportunity when they choose the other. They're torn. So we're not through that transition yet, because there's still something compelling the woman to have it both ways.

The second point is that you're talking about middle class professional women who have freedom of choice to make multiple commitments. You're not talking about the woman who is still dependent, who still lives in poverty, whose opportunities are circumscribed, who has very few choices.

BATESON: The woman in poverty already works. She already has multiple commitments. Don't think of the woman in poverty as staying at home. The woman in poverty is working every day.

MOYERS: What about the women who are poor, who don't have these options?

BATESON: Poor people have fewer options. It has been one of our beliefs as a society that it's important to increase options, so that people can make of themselves whatever they can. At any point where we discover that we are locking people in and denying them options, we should ask whether this is a point for political change, something that has to be worked for.

MOYERS: And the woman who's caught in the midst of this transition, who's been a housewife for twenty-five years? What has twenty-five years of being a housewife prepared a woman to do?

BATESON: The question, basically, is what does the personnel officer she talks to think those years have prepared her to do—because, in fact, she's had a great deal of experience and maturing, and she's juggled a lot of stuff, and she has a lot of potential skills. It's a matter of your classification system.

After World War II, when the GIs came home and went to college on the GI Bill, everybody said what wonderful students they were because of the years they'd spent in the army. Now they didn't say that knowing how to fly an airplane had made this student good at studying philosophy, and they didn't say that driving a truck had made this student wonderful at mathematics. The converse might have been true. They said that dealing with the complexity and the experience and the maturing of those years made them able to learn, right? Now, the group known as displaced homemakers, the middle and upper class housewives who were forced into the labor market at mid-life, are still struggling for the definitions of experience and the acceptance of those definitions that will let them perform at their optimum. Here are these women, who learned that when somebody asked them at a party, "What do you do?" the correct answer was, "Oh, I don't do anything, I'm just a housewife." This is a learned classification system, and it is obviously not true, because they've always worked very hard and done very complex jobs.

MOYERS: You're talking about a new way of seeing what we have taken for granted.

BATESON: I think it's more than one new way, actually. There are a number of pieces that we have to get together, that are hard to change piecemeal. You can't tinker with one part of society, like hiring practices and how people evaluate experience, and then go on telling women they don't have any experience.

MOYERS: What about those people, many of them women, who want to keep the traditional role for females? They really believe that what you're talking about will undermine the very fabric of a caring society.

BATESON: I would not want to coerce or denigrate those women and the choices they make—if their life allows them to make those choices. If we want freedom, the freedom to decide to stay at home as a full-time homemaker and caretaker for children has to exist, also. But many women don't have that alternative, so there is the question of fairness and, indeed, survival for women who must earn a living to support their children. Beyond that, there is the question of freedom and creativity to allow a range of possibilities for the women who are motivated to pursue a different kind of life. I would hope that those who care about the traditional roles would also encourage freedom of choice to women who are exploring new roles.

MOYERS: In many cases they don't. For example, they're lobbying Congress against legislation for equal opportunity and equal pay.

BATESON: I know they are, and I guess it's because they're scared. Anytime there is a transition like this, some people will feel threatened. I lived for a number of years in Iran. When I first went there, Iranian women were gradually increasing their participation in public life. Now women have been forced out of certain kinds of participation in public life, and they're back wearing the veil, very much constrained to a domestic life. It's amazing that change can happen so fast. We used to hold up the resurgence of anti-Semitism in Nazi Germany as an example of the fact that a society could reverse tolerance very rapidly. The situation in Iran is comparable. When I was there, I always had a soft spot for the women of the pivotal generation. What do you do if you're forty-five or fifty, and you've never been outside of your house without a veil, you've never earned an independent income, and, indeed, you've never traveled to another city or stayed in a hotel without someone looking after you? What do you do if all of a sudden you are told that you cannot wear the veil and that you must go out? This is terrifying. It's terrifying to lose one set of privileges and protections and not have the skills and confidence you need to claim the next ones. The women who argue against the ERA in the United States are in the same dilemma of being part in one life and part in the other as the women in Iran who welcomed the Ayatollah so that they could put their veils back on and be locked up again. You sympathize with the dilemma of being caught between the past and the future and wanting the past because it feels safer and more protective and more familiar. But I would always put my efforts on the side of letting people take off the veils and go out the door and live a broader life.

MOYERS: You've done that. You are an anthropologist, professor, scholar, writer, mother, and wife. You've lived abroad. You've composed a fortunate life. What does it take?

BATESON: You used the word "composed," which is part of the title of the book I'm working on at the moment. I'm trying to look at making choices and putting together what comes to hand, as an artistic process. I see other women in my situation. One of the reasons I've had so many careers is because I've adapted to my husband's career changes and often started again when we went to new places.

MOYERS: You went to the Philippines with him, to Iran with him.

BATESON: That's right, and I had to find jobs that made sense. It occurred to me that I could think of having to start again so many times as a terrible burden. Then it occurred to me that the most creative people I know are the people who have done one thing for a while and then shifted gears and done something else. You can look at these discontinuities as a burden, or you can look at them as a stimulus to creativity.

The same thing is true about conflicting commitments. I know what it feels like to be in an office and to be worrying about whether the baby-sitter's going to leave, and what's going to happen to my child, and how do I balance these things. But trying to put these conflicting commitments together to compose a life in which there's room for both of them is an important kind of creativity. So, I'm trying to examine these particular problems and look at the way women solve them, because I think men increasingly face the same problems. Foreclosed farmers who lose their farms are like displaced homemakers. The same kind of thing happens to executives when their company gets bought out and restructured, and they're out on the street, trying to think of what to do next.

This is the century of the refugee. We live longer, and we have more potential discontinuities in our lives, so that the creative life is likely to involve adapting and readapting, maybe several times. It's a burden. It hurts. But you're a different person afterward. You know something you wouldn't have known otherwise. Bill, you must know that from your own experience.

> **This is the century of the refugee.**

Now, I'm not just trying to find a silver lining or to be a Pollyanna about it. But it is possible to look at most problems—whether it is the AIDS epidemic or the conflicts faced by women who work and have children, or the hostage crisis in Iran—and to search for creative solutions. When you do that, you're likely to find that your creative solutions have value outside of the immediate context. They can be transferred or shared or learned from by the society at large. For example, men can learn something from the ways women adapt, and can enrich their lives as a result.

MOYERS: At this moment we're sitting in the bosom of this great cathedral, St. John the Divine, where you often speak. Do the old traditions represented in this cathedral have anything to say about our modern problems of getting from here to the unknown?

BATESON: This cathedral is a very special place, but it's special in a way that could be shared in many other places. The building is designed on a medieval pattern and represents ideas that go back two thousand and, indeed, four thousand years. At the same time, the artists that work here bring in the newest of the avant garde, and contemporary problems are discussed here. The cathedral's very much involved with AIDS, with homelessness, with the problems of the ghetto, which is, after all, just outside.

It's a mistake to shut out the new and just keep things as they are. But is is also a mistake to address the problems of the present and the future without reference to the traditions of the past. What the cathedral does Sunday after Sunday, and day after day, is to juxtapose new social problems and pains with ancient human efforts to understand and find solutions. That juxtaposition is the best stimulus both to responsibility in facing the unknown that lies ahead and to a certain serenity.

One of the things I talk about in the book I'm writing is that composing a life requires improvisation. It's like when, at six o'clock in the evening, four guests turn up, and your husband says, "We can feed them supper, can't we, darling?" You go down to the kitchen, and you start scrambling through the refrigerator and the cupboards, trying to invent some combination that will make sense of the evening. Our past is full of wonderful traditions. The cupboards are full. The refrigerator is full. The situation calls for creative improvisation.

MOYERS: Do you think the day will come when you'll call home and say, "Dear, I'm bringing four guests home. Can you have dinner ready?" And *he* moves into action.

BATESON: I've done it.

MOYERS: He can improvise?

BATESON: We all can improvise—and we're all going to have to.

Leon R. Kass

BIOLOGIST AND PHILOSOPHER

Leon R. Kass joins body and soul uniquely as a physician and philosopher. Trained as a doctor, with a degree in biochemistry, he discovered that the study of science raised questions which science couldn't answer. He wrote Toward a More Natural Science: Biology and Human Affairs *to explore the moral implications of biology in the modern world. Dr. Kass is Luce Professor of the Liberal Arts of Human Biology at the University of Chicago.*

MOYERS: Someone told me that Leon Kass is concerned with the decline of tradition, religion, civility, courtship—and table manners. Why table manners?

KASS: Table manners are an expression of the attempt to humanize and refine our elementary biological functions. It's a way in which we both acknowledge our dependence upon mere nature, and transform it, giving it a certain kind of dignity which it doesn't have to begin with.

MOYERS: Without manners, eating becomes an uncivilized, although necessary, physical act.

KASS: It would be feeding rather than eating. Many languages say, in effect, that animals feed, but human beings eat—and even dine and feast. All kinds of very subtle things take place around the table to distinguish human eating from animal feeding. The meal has an order, it's ritualized, and there is conversation over a meal. The very implements that one uses are a means of distancing oneself from the violence which eating necessarily implies. In fact, there's a very nice remark from the Chinese about the use of chopsticks. It's a Western prejudice to think that chopsticks are rather primitive—but one Chinese remarked that Western man eats with swords.

MOYERS: —with a knife and fork.

KASS: —with the knife, in particular. If you look at the development of table manners, you see the gradual subordination of the place of the knife at the table. The Chinese do all their cutting away from the table, so that there is no evidence at the table of the kind of violence that's necessarily involved in the capturing and preparation of food.

MOYERS: So we eat with the sword, and the Chinese eat with these—

KASS: —these very delicate, selective, and even more distant implements.

MOYERS: Are table manners in decline in this country?

KASS: I haven't made an empirical study, but I do think there's been a general decline of civility and manners. For example, you can notice a certain crudeness of speech and a certain kind of defiance against standing in line.

MOYERS: So many of us eat on the run.

KASS: I generally make it a rule in class that there won't be any eating or drinking on the grounds that one ought not involuntarily be forced to participate in someone else's digestion. The classroom is an occasion, really, for shared speeches. If we were to share a meal together, that would be another thing, but for people to be talking and trying out their best thoughts and have someone crudely eating in their face seems to me to violate the meaning of our coming together there.

MOYERS: And what about courtship?

KASS: That is, in a way, more serious. One of the most important and troubling questions of our time is to understand deeply what it means to be male and female to be man and woman in the present age. The respect and restraint which the old forms insisted upon are gone. The sexual revolution has emancipated sexuality from its most obvious connection with procreation. Partly it's the new emancipation of women, and partly, I suspect, the legacy of the sixties, in which restraint and formality were held to be repressive, and it was thought that one should simply let things "hang out."

The loss of the old forms is, in a way, an enemy of a certain kind of depth and profundity. It feeds the more immediate passions. It gets in the way of a deeper appreciation and even of real love.

MOYERS: It's hard for love to emerge when romance is just, as my late friend Joe Campbell said, "the zeal of the organs for one another."

KASS: Precisely. There's a passage, which I like very much, in Kant's little essay on the "Conjectural Beginning of Human History," commenting on the story of the Garden of Eden and the discovery of nakedness. Kant talks about the importance of the fig leaf as the human response to this first, self-conscious discovery of our nakedness. The fig leaf is an impediment to lust, but it's also an invitation to the imagination to beautify the object. Indeed, to have sensibilities and to have feelings of taste and beauty is to make human love possible.

MOYERS: So romance goes beyond just the emotions one feels for another. It has to do with one's attitude toward the other, one's regard for that other person's being.

KASS: In ways that are probably for most of us most of the time just tacit, there is an expression of a deep aspiration of what it is to be a human being that's connected with our being gendered and engendering beings. With the easy acquiescence in sexual desire and its gratification, we lose sight of this aspiration. It's not unrelated to the matter of manners. There's a difference between copulating and making love. There's a difference between episodic lovemaking and lovemaking in the context of the real intimacy of a shared life, and of a tacit understanding that one is in a way saying yes to future generations and to one's own demise. Sexuality is the one aspect of biological being in which, unbeknownst to ourselves, we are in the grip of a power serving ends beyond ourselves. This is true of the animal kingdom generally speaking. One sees it most dramatically in the notorious case of salmon, who go upstream to spawn, but at the cost of their own lives.

Though nature catches us with the attractiveness of sexual pleasure, we are really in the grip of serving the continuity of the species, of posterity, and of future generations. One of the costs of the technology having to do with reproduction and the sexual revolution is that we have made this too much a matter of simple self-gratification and divorced it from its deeper and even transcendent meaning.

MOYERS: Romance—if I'm courting the one I truly love—means that I impose on my bodily urges a transcendent, higher purpose.

KASS: I think that's right. But I'm not sure I would say "imposing on." It might very well be the discovery of something which is really there. It's a question as to whether romance is a way we pretty up what's ugly and necessary, or whether, in fact, human beings have the opportunity to discover what's latent even in animal life. Even animals are built for the transcendence of their own mortality. Human beings have the opportunity to understand that, and to adapt their conduct accordingly.

MOYERS: So instead of imposing, I am inviting out what is there.

KASS: That would be my hunch. Certainly my aspiration in my studies is to see what pointings if any we can get from our bodily nature, from our special standing and being in the world.

MOYERS: What does that have to do with traditional religion? For a man who's on the frontier of science and biology, you seem to have an unusual respect for traditional religion.

KASS: I do. I've acquired it—I wasn't reared on it. One of the pleasant discoveries of my teaching life has been how much there is to be learned in the Bible. I don't think religion would have exercised its power over the minds and hearts of the West if it was an institution set apart from wisdom or understanding. It's regrettable that today, if things are identified as religious, they are treated as sectarian, or parochial, or prejudicial. It seems to me that there's a very deep anthropological wisdom about the nature of human life, its aspirations, its tendencies to mischief and folly that are contained in biblical stories.

Most of us are probably not able to discover those things for ourselves—though with the help of stories and tales that we couldn't think to tell ourselves, we are brought to a deeper understanding of what our life is like. So I don't really set up a conflict between religion and philosophy. There are issues on which they would diverge. But the thoughtful person tries to find wisdom and understanding wherever he can. It's just foolishness to think that there's none to be had in the religious traditions.

MOYERS: And once again, the will to believe, the necessity of faith and the search come from within our nature as biological creatures.

KASS: The passions of wonder and awe are natural to the human heart. Human beings who come to be thoughtful about themselves and the world soon recognize that they are in the grip of powers and forces not really under their control. That means that certain kinds of sensitivity to nature as a whole and to the power of intelligence trigger certain thoughts about what might be beyond things of our own making. There is a certain kind of natural turn toward cosmological questions, toward questions of the meaning of it all, toward puzzlement that there should be anything at all, or that we should be here. And while this doesn't necessarily lead to one theological view rather than another, one of the things you would say is that by nature, human beings are

> *The passions of wonder and awe are natural to the human heart.*

animals that go in for metaphysical and theological reflection. It's silly to say that because these issues don't have ready answers, or because they're controversial, they should be relegated to second place in our lives.

MOYERS: A striking sentence in your book, *Toward a More Natural Science*, says, "The teachings of science, however gratifying as discoveries of the mind, throw icy waters on the human spirit." When I read that, I thought of Saul Bellow's comment that science today has made a housecleaning of belief.

KASS: Science has raised certain explicit challenges to certain explicit passages of the Bible. The most notorious example, of course, is the challenge to the first chapter of Genesis posed by the teachings of evolution. In fact, I've just finished an essay on evolution and the Bible in which I attempt a very literal reading of the first chapter, trying to show that this challenge is overrated. One can harmonize the teaching of evolution and the teaching of Genesis more than people have thought. But what I meant by that passage about throwing icy waters on the spirit goes much further than the explicit challenge of the teaching of evolution. Science has made great strides by adopting a certain strategy to explain complicated things in terms of simple things and to explain living things in terms of nonliving things, and ultimately in terms of dead matter and its primordial motions.

Also, science has chosen as the paradigm for its knowing a mathematical approach to nature. The great strides made in mathematical physics attest to the genius of the seventeenth century in setting this in motion. On the other hand, biology, especially as it reaches for an account of human biology and of our own life, comes more and more to discover that there's a gap between the world as science understands it mathematically and materialistically, and life as we human beings live it and encounter it. For example, people are at work on the human emotions, studying various chemicals in the hypothalamus part of the brain. One of my colleagues boasts that in a few decades we will be able to provide a biochemical explanation of human love.

Now, while we might be able to find various kinds of chemicals that if injected into the brain, might produce various kinds of feelings, I think one could say, as a matter of principle, that no chemical explanation will rival the experience of human love, or anger, or shame, or any of the things that we, as human beings alive in the world, know best. There are various other examples of science trying to explain us to ourselves, and coming up short. To say that human life is an accident on the stage of evolution, fundamentally no different from not only other animal life, but no different even from inorganic matter in motion, just doesn't square with the phenomena as we experience them.

MOYERS: So that even if we could find the chemical properties behind the emotion of love, or gratitude, or sacrifice, we'd still need to explain it in language beyond the scientific.

KASS: Absolutely. In fact, the scientists themselves must know these passions in a nonscientific way before they can even set about looking for their material substratum. Otherwise, they wouldn't be able to say, these are the molecules related to vision, or these are the molecules that influence anger.

MOYERS: What does that say about us?

KASS: There is a deep mystery about our being. While we can be analyzed and partially made sense of by treating us as inorganic matter having a certain complicated arrangement that can be studied objectively from the outside, it's also the case that with the coming of life, especially of human life, this matter has become self-illuminating. There is an inwardness of awareness and consciousness and aspiration and passion which can only be described in its own terms, and is not reducible to the material conditions or accompaniments of its experience.

MOYERS: Do you think your students think about such things when they cut up a cadaver? There are the remains of an organic life, but nothing remains pointing toward the love, the emotions, the feelings, and the passions.

KASS: It's curious. The science that our medical students study is so powerful in its ability to analyze and predict and control the body, and so impoverished—if I may speak bluntly—in its understanding of the emotional and experiential aspect of human life. The science that the students learn doesn't really adequately prepare them for this first encounter with a dead body. If the living body is supposed to be understood in terms of molecules in motion, then the dead body ought to be no mystery whatsoever. It's just a heap of stuff not doing very much of anything. And yet most of the medical students encounter this with a kind of horror or a recognition that though this is body, it's not body in the sense of the physicists or chemists, but the mortal remains of an individual human being, which in some respects still bears the marks of the life that was lived. One can look at the hands, and just as in life, the hands are expressive of the difference between, let us say, an artist and a construction worker. There are even ways in which the face is marked.

The students are led to wonder: Who was this person? They make distinctions. They show a certain kind of shame with respect to the genitalia. They have great difficulty looking on the face. It really means that these students about to be doctors still have a certain appreciation of the profundity of what's superficial or on the surface of human life that all of their analytic science hasn't as yet washed out of them. Now, whether they lose this appreciation in the process of their technical training is a worrisome question and one that I am very concerned about.

MOYERS: You write about a man you knew, a man with an amazing mind, who dies.

KASS: Yes, this man was extraordinary. In his presence, or in reading his writings, I always had the feeling that his mind was off the scale. I knew him only at the end of his life, when he was a man of failing health and failing powers. One day I went to visit him in the hospital, as I'd done a number of times before. On the way into the room, I asked the nurse, who was coming out, how he was doing. She said, "Didn't you know? He died about an hour ago." I walked into the room, and there he was, lying in bed, very peaceful. Had I not been told by the nurse, I would have assumed he was asleep. I don't really know what happened in the next few moments, but I found myself on my knees at the end of the bed. I was thunderstruck. Here he was, but he wasn't there at all. There was almost a smile on his face. All I could think of was— where is he? Where is this mind? What's happened to it?

This phenomenon of the extinction of a human being is awful whenever you encounter it, and more so under these circumstances because it is so unexpected, and because what was lost was really so great. That gives anybody pause in thinking that one is going to have an adequate physical account of what we mean by the human soul.

MOYERS: You write, "Here there was vastly less than meets the eye. The dead body may be more than what our science teaches, but it is also less than what it appears to be. The body may be more than stuff, but the man seems to be more than his body."

KASS: This is the companion story, really, of the experience in the anatomy laboratory. There the students come upon a body, and they respond to it as if in fact the body is somehow more than the stuff that science has taught them. On the other hand, my encounter with this death makes it perfectly clear that here's a still warm body, which is yet not the man. That's not a problem to be solved as much as it is a deep and profound mystery to be acknowledged. On the one hand we are, in a way, our bodies. Our individuality is written into our fingerprints.

MOYERS: —not like anyone else's.

KASS: Right. And every cell in our body bears the mark of our own unique genetic makeup. That's why it's so difficult to transplant. On the other hand, even as we speak, there's a way in which our bodies are silent, and we are participating in some medium of understanding that is hard to reduce simply to body. At the moment of death one is acutely aware of the fact that however much we are self-identical with our body, there seems to be something about human life not simply reducible to or identifiable with this hulk that we otherwise are.

MOYERS: So, looking at the physical remains of the genius who had just died, one couldn't help but think about the mind and understanding. All that suggests something more than just physical properties.

KASS: I would say so. Of course, one doesn't have access to such things in animals, in whose inner life we really are not privileged to enter. But there is a center of inwardness in all living things, more complex and richer as one goes up the evolutionary scale, and obviously fullest, as far as we know it, in ourselves, where that inwardness can be an object of its own beholding. *We* can become conscious of ourselves as centers of inwardness. One of the interesting and little-remarked-on side products of Darwin's theory of evolution is that, if it's really true that human beings evolved from creatures that were not human, anything present to human beings, however complicated, can't be simply and totally absent from animal life. And that means that whatever we may have lost in dignity as a result of this theory of evolution, the animals and the living world as such have gained. One can no longer simply treat life and the body as worthless stuff and locate our humanity only in this little extra something that's between the ears. One can see through the continuity of man and animals something of the richness of the vitality of life.

MOYERS: Doesn't this also suggest that whatever the history of natural selection, mere survival does not seem to be its only purpose?

KASS: This is a very hard case to make, but I think it's crucial. One of the least appreciated beauties of the evolutionary process is that powers emerge which, to begin with, might be mere means of increasing survival, but which acquire a life of their own, separate from their being merely in the service of survival. They become part of the life of the organism for the sake of which the organism seeks to survive. For example, sensation, the power to see and to perceive the world, is certainly useful for survival, but its meaning to an organism is not exhausted by the contribution it makes to survival. Witness what human beings do in the visual arts and their appreciation of beauty.

Intelligence, which was no doubt selected because of its advantage for our survival, has all kinds of uses which have nothing to do with survival. As we sadly know, some of its uses are even detrimental to survival. So one needs to think not only about survival, but survival of what.

We know in all kinds of ways that it's not mere survival that counts, but the level of vitality and the fullness of vital powers, for the sake of which we ourselves individually and collectively seek to survive.

MOYERS: Do you think these powers within us yearn for something?

KASS: It seems that way. Many philosophers try to say what it is, and I'm enough of an eclectic to be moved by many of them—whether it means yearning to share the soul of another human being that one loves, or craving understanding, or craving some kind of permanent deed in the great cosmic ledger, or craving some kind of participation in the divine. I don't know what it is, but I would have to say I in some way feel it.

MOYERS: What does your soul yearn for? You've got just about everything—you're a successful scientist, physician, philosopher, father, husband, professor.

KASS: I guess I'm in the perpetuation business. I take it as my purpose to try to hand down to my family perhaps fifty percent of what I got in relatively undiluted form. Since children always have to struggle against their parents for their own way, that business is often very, very complicated.

I regard myself in a way as a teacher, keeping alive certain vital questions about what makes a human life worthwhile, what is a good community, what is the human good. These questions should not be submerged in our technical competence or our desire for prosperity.

These are the questions that really bother the young, and if you provide them with the opportunity to think about these things, and if you give them the books that will raise those questions most profoundly, the little candle might stay lit against the barbaric darkness. That's a rather modest ambition, but in helping what I received to survive another generation, I have a feeling that I'm part of something much bigger than myself.

MOYERS: You take a step from reflecting on mortality, on the fact that we will die, to reflecting on morality, on the fact of our conduct. What explains the connection between the two?

KASS: The connection between mortality and morality is very old. The fact that we don't have world enough and time really sets the boundaries within which it is up to us to decide what to make of our limited three score and ten. One response is certainly to say, "We go around only once—we might as well really enjoy it. We're all sitting in the desperation bar together, and we might as well have a good time and go out cheerfully."

But it seems to me that most of the human beings whose lives have stirred us and whom we admire are people who dedicated themselves not to the elementary pleasures, but to something noble, something fine, something that reaches beyond. Some encounter with necessity is the ground of taking one's life seriously. It's the ground of being sensitive to all of the really beautiful things in the world. It's the ground of being open to the call of something higher in which we have a chance to participate, whether it be perpetuation of our young, whether it be the future of our country, whether it be the arts or philosophy or music. And it's the ground, really, of transforming what is otherwise a mere necessity into an occasion of something really splendidly human. The Greek poets made a lot of the difference between the humans and the immortals. The immortals are youthful and ageless but their

> Some encounter with necessity is the ground of taking one's life seriously.

lives are very shallow. One of my very favorite passages occurs in the *Odyssey* where Odysseus is offered immortal life by the goddess Calypso, who's very beautiful. But he turns this down to return home, quite self-consciously, to his mortal wife, Penelope, and to live for friendship, for family, for city, for country. That really is what it means to live humanly in the face of the sentence of death.

MOYERS: Is this because one is aware of the finite nature of our time here? Do you think that moral choices grow out of the knowledge of death?

KASS: Oh, absolutely. The extreme case is courage, where people self-consciously put their lives at risk for the sake of some other cause, or to display their ability to rise above fear and self-concern and all the things connected with survival. But this same kind of rising above the attachment to mere life is found in almost every display of human virtue.

Time is all you have to give, whether you give it all in one moment on the field of battle, or whether, self-consciously, you know that it is that which you are in a way spending and that you have a chance to make something of it. Without the real awareness of time, we couldn't make our days count, and we couldn't make our deeds worth remembering.

MOYERS: You make me think of the Ninetieth Psalm—"Teach us—"

KASS: "—to number our days that we may get us a heart of wisdom." It is Augustine, I think, who says that one should keep one's body as if one were going to live forever, and keep one's soul as if one were going to die tomorrow. Now you could think too much about your death and become morbid. But there is a way in which— well, I'll speak simply for myself—at a certain point, it became very clear to me that time was limited, and it mattered a lot how one looked at things and what one did.

MOYERS: What was that point?

KASS: It was partially the birth of my children. They are daily reminders that one is not a member of the frontier generation any longer. But the point occurred especially at the death of my father. I've always had an image that he stood in front of me before the ditch, so when he died, he was no longer in the way, and the world was a different place. Everything looks different. I'm much more sensitive to all sorts of things.

MOYERS: It seems to me we do good things not just because we're here for a limited period of time, but for other reasons—conscience, altruism, love.

KASS: Yes, certain aspects of morality are not tied to our perception of mortality. The aspect of the moral life that I am speaking about, though, is what the tradition would call the noble. It goes back, in a way, to the issue of table manners. We have this bodily life, and the question is, are we going to turn it into a thing of beauty and a life of meaning, or not? Courage is the virtue that responds to the fear of death. Moderation and refinement are responses to an excessive love of bodily pleasures. Generosity is a virtue connected with the undue attachment to wealth, which is itself connected with survival. Now it seems to me what's left out of this account are certain obligations, let's say, of justice. Certain things having to do with conscience appeal to us as moral beings and might appeal to us even if we were to live forever.

But as I understand the moral life, it's not just a matter of "thou shalt not's," although that's an important part of it. It's a question of how one chooses to live and what one aspires to and what one makes of oneself. And with respect to those things, aspiration depends upon knowing that one doesn't have an eternity to get with it.

MOYERS: Did such thoughts play in your mind when your father died? Did you begin to think more acutely about the choices you had to make as the survivor?

KASS: Very much so. One of my friends, Bill May, works in the field of medical ethics. At a conference a long time ago, he remarked about the presence of death to our consciousness, and he talked about how it hovered over the marriage bed. Since it was a strange thought, and I was a young man, I filed it away. I now understand it. We lost my wife's mother just a year ago. She was a vibrant and beautiful woman, painting and reading novels to the very end. When one understands the fragility of all of these human relations, one treasures them more, and one is inspired to make much more of them.

MOYERS: It's interesting to hear a man contemplate the human body and begin to think about philosophy. Most of us think of philosophy as abstract notions about ethereal concerns.

KASS: The origin of philosophy is in wonder, and there is really no shortage of things about which one can wonder. One of the giants of Western philosophy, Aristotle, began much of his philosophizing by pondering living things and wondering what accounted for their liveliness and what the soul is. So, long ago, the body was a natural place to begin to philosophize, not only because it was mortal, but because it was the bearer of all kinds of vital powers—powers of imagining, of thought, of appetite, of action, of choice. It was only when the body came to be captured by this objectified science of inorganic matter, and humanity receded into some little thing called consciousness behind the eyes, that the body came to be regarded as contemptible and not worthy of our philosophical attention. But it's right there before us, and it's the same body as it was centuries ago.

> The origin of philosophy is in wonder. . . .

MOYERS: When did you begin to contemplate it differently? Was it in medical school?

KASS: I don't think so. I was a rather shallow fellow in medical school, although certain things stuck with me. I knew, for example, that I hated the autopsy room. I couldn't go happily to an autopsy of a patient of mine who had died, partly because I missed the person, but partly because I knew that the explanations of the cause of death—you know, the blockage of this vessel or a hemorrhage from the bowel—was never going to be commensurate with what I wanted an explanation of, which was, where is he, or where is she? So I had those kinds of uneasinesses. But it was really only much, much later and only as a result of the concern for some of the concrete, practical issues of medicine and biology that I was led into a more philosophical study of living nature and of the human body.

MOYERS: Something happened, too, when you were down South working in the Civil Rights movement of the early sixties.

KASS: Right. My wife and I spent a summer in Mississippi working with the Medical Committee for Human Rights in '65. I was already concerned about some of the new developments in biology and medicine. The prospect of genetic manipulation, of organ transplantation, and of new psychoactive drugs raised certain kinds of questions about the uses to which these things were going to be put. But the experience of working with poor black farmers in Mississippi and seeing their quiet dignity and their strength of character despite their lack of education, made me begin to wonder whether it was really true what I had been taught—namely, that enlightenment, schooling, and advantage were really the necessary and sufficient condition of the flowering of character and of the growth of human dignity.

I must say, perhaps with some prejudice to my acquaintances, that when I returned to graduate school, I found these uneducated farmers looking, humanly speaking, their superior. That led me to wonder whether it really was true that morals and progress in knowledge went hand in hand off into the sunset. A friend of mine then gave me a little potboiler of Rousseau's, *The Discourse on the Sciences and Arts*, in which he argues against the Enlightenment. He says wherever the arts and sciences have flourished, they have been the forerunners of moral decline, degeneration, and so on. It was quite a shock. That was the beginning of my serious study.

MOYERS: Did you start thinking there must be something inherent in people that doesn't require education or enlightenment to make them human?

KASS: The farmers were in touch with the necessities of human life—to drag one's own living out of the soil, to have people born or die in the house, to be closer to the vicissitudes of nature, to be steeped in a religious tradition that was the tradition of their ancestors, and would, they hoped, be the tradition of their children. There was an immediacy, a concreteness of their daily life that had a kind of wisdom to it. At least that's the way it seemed to me.

MOYERS: You cause me to think of my father, who has a fourth-grade education, was a workingman all his life, and yet, without benefit of schooling, without traveling a hundred miles beyond his hometown, possesses more dignity than almost anybody I know. I keep thinking, where does that dignity come from? How is it known? Where did it arise?

KASS: I think it has something to do with the encounter with necessity and difficulty, with the richness of family relations, and with the concreteness of daily life. Most of us live richer lives individually. We have many more opportunities and goods, but we are really very much less prepared for the deeply rooted elements of human life—births, marriages, deaths, rites of passage. Families live spread apart, especially amongst those of us who are privileged. You can only get so far with your own children, telling the tales of the hardships that your parents surmounted, when you had no hardships in your own life. I grew up mostly after the Second War, when it seemed the world was waiting for us. I was one of the lucky ones.

MOYERS: Same here. Given the fact that we can't re-create the world that's gone, can we arrive at a consensus about what makes a moral life and about our relations with one another? You're describing circumstances in which the exigencies of living created the moral character and dignity of individuals. Most of us lead secondhand lives now.

KASS: I'm of several minds about it. I like to read the philosophical authors with my students. I find that if you present them not as desiccated texts of the past, but as books to think with and to incorporate into our current lives, they still speak to us in all their diversity and conflict. On the other hand, I don't really think that one can derive a cultural ethos from philosophy. One can't reason one's way into moral sentiments, which are much more crucial to interpersonal contact and conduct and to civic life than are the propositions to which one assents.

When I think this way, I worry about our future. To take the grimmest view, which afflicts me from time to time, it looks as if the great humanitarian project of which all of us are the beneficiaries and about which we can't complain unless we want to be hypocrites, will in fact cure, or at least alleviate most disease, get a handle on poverty, stop war, give us peace of mind—but at the cost of a shrunken humanity. A certain kind of banalization and trivialization of life might be the result.

MOYERS: You once said that we should turn less to science for the answers and should start worrying about leading a moral life. What is your definition of a moral life?

KASS: One of its central features is one's aspiration and concern with one's own character and self-command. It extends to those immediate relations that are ours, either by necessity or by choice, and that have special claims on us—those relations of family, colleagues, and friends. It means being present when there is need. It means not simply giving in to the compassionate impulse, but trying to help people discern what is in fact better for them rather than worse. It means taking a broader interest in the life of one's community, both locally and nationally, and to some extent even globally. It means to deal with many of the external things that have always made life nasty and short and brutal for too many of our fellow human beings—poverty and pestilence, for example. And it also means holding up the possibility of certain high human peaks of noble action, of generosity, of self-sacrifice, of great beautification of the world through music and the arts, and carrying on the familiarity with what the best of the human race has thought and written and sung through the process of education.

MOYERS: I think I know a moral life when I see it, but what's the fundamental philosophical principle of a moral life?

KASS: It's some notion of human excellence or human fulfillment that ties these things together. Too many people would be content to define the moral life in terms of the basic rules that are constitutive for any decent society—taboos about incest and cannibalism and murder and stealing, for example. When my students get into a conversation about ethics, they want to run immediately to those things. If someone is not a thief or a murderer, what else is there to say? The moral life, more broadly understood, has to do with the question of ordering one's aspirations and trying, both in one's individual life and in one's family and communal life, for things that stir the heart and win the admiration of ourselves as human beings.

MOYERS: You use the word fulfillment, but what about the cadaver on the autopsy table—just a pile of motionless molecules now vegetating away. That's not the fulfillment you're talking about.

KASS: If one speaks about human aspiration, one has to confront the fact that we are, if aspiring creatures, only finitely so, and we are born with inevitable tendencies toward decay and finally death. Much in our tradition regards death as a colossal affront to any pretense of human dignity. On this view, only if there is redemption from mortality can one really hold one's human head erect. But like any drama, one has the opening scene and the final scene and, in a good dramatist's hands, five acts in which to have a good show. So fulfillment is not the same thing as the last occasion, although all kinds of people reveal the dignity of their lives to the very end, and have much to teach us about how they have lived by the way in which they die. Even a miserable end that cuts us down may often be the occasion for the display of what's very special about us.

MOYERS: What about the individual who knowingly, consciously, willfully cuts short his or her own play in order to save the life of someone else? Do you think that person is indifferent to the drama? He's denying himself the last two or three acts of his own play.

KASS: I have the highest admiration for these episodes of noble self-sacrifice. Much, of course, will depend upon our judgment of the reason for which the sacrifice is made, but very often, the occasion to do something fine and splendid demands that we wrap it all up in one moment and say, "Here I stand—and I make of my life this occasion." Though the culture doesn't sufficiently appreciate courage, for reasons having to do with modern times and modern war, when one sees episodes of it, where people really give their lives for others, our hearts go out to them precisely because they have paid in coin of their future for something fine, very often for others.

MOYERS: If, as you say, time is all we have, these people have deliberately denied themselves the one gift on which to act out or fulfill their possibilities.

KASS: That's an extreme instance of seeing the meaning of our mortality for how one lives. Much of our culture for the last three hundred and fifty years has tried through science and technology to do battle with mortality and its earlier antecedents, disease and decay, in the hope that maybe eventually we could even hit a home run against it. It is as if somehow our life would be more deeply fulfilled by a continuation of more of the same. But this battle is driven much more by the fear of death than it is by a proper understanding of the gift that mortality really is. To live in fear of death and not to know that that's what's bothering us is very often to scramble frenetically around looking for amusement—whereas the people who really, self-consciously, make a self-sacrificial act very often are, in that one moment, doing what most of us have a lifetime to do, namely, to spend this time knowingly and to good purpose.

MOYERS: Do you think we humans are by nature moral creatures?

KASS: By nature, we are built to have an interest in moral matters. A sign of it is, for example, that human beings blush, and have the psychic experience of shame, very often involuntarily. Now what we blush about may be a product of our rearing, but that we are embarrassed and feel shame means that we have a kind of innate concern with looking good to ourselves. We have intuitive senses of the notion of the fair, of the shameful. To be sure, we need a lot of assistance from culture and from rearing, but we are natured to receive this instruction.

On the other hand, there are very powerful things which lead us always to make exceptions on our own behalf. When push comes to shove, many people put themselves first and the devil take the hindmost. Even people who are rather well off indulge themselves more than is seemly. It's a long question as to whether moral education is really like teaching young birds to fly, which is with the grain, or whether it's really like breaking a wild horse and taming things that otherwise would become unruly.

MOYERS: Does biology tell us anything about this?

KASS: I don't think we know enough yet. Some interesting books by evolutionary biologists indicate that the brain may very well be constructed so as to accept restraint in the early period of infancy. What does it mean, for example, to be built in such a way as to accept something like toilet training, which is, after all, the first kind of instruction of restraint of impulse. Biology also indicates that human beings are born "prematurely," that is to say, we acquire our posture only by effort in the first year of life, and we acquire the natural human gift of speech only in the first or second year of life and then only in a social community with others from whom we learn our language. There are ways in which a richer sociobiology of the future would indicate to us that we are really built not only for reproduction but also with certain kinds of leanings for culture, including certain ethical passions.

MOYERS: You use the word soul more often than I expect from a biologist. Do you believe we have souls?

KASS: If one means by "soul," a center of organized power, of desire, of feeling, of awareness, of freedom, of choice, then certainly we have souls. Whether this is something which survives the body, or whether my soul has my name written on it, or whether when I die, it goes someplace else—about that, I am much less certain and wouldn't pretend to know.

But even to look at other animals and to appreciate their facial expressions and their bodily movements, is immediately to be put in contact with some kind of vital center from which they move and from which they display rudimentary emotions. I would be inclined to attribute soul, in this sense, even to animals.

MOYERS: Soul as an animating power, a consciousness?

KASS: Not only consciousness. I don't want to say it's like a ghost in a machine, but there's something that happens when perfectly ordinary, elementary chemicals are organized in a certain way. That particular organization manifests powers that the parts don't have on their own. Where this came from to begin with, I have no idea. But you could take all the chemicals in the human body, and you could put them together in some certain ways, but they wouldn't add up to the powers that do what living things do—not just cerebration and consciousness, but even these lowly powers of metabolism, excretion, respiration, and digestion, these things which we do automatically. Those are the achievement of a very special organization of very special material. There's no way in the world that you can begin to talk about those powers in terms of objectified body. For that reason, this very classical notion of soul is useful.

MOYERS: You certainly don't find evidence of the soul when you are rummaging around in the ruins of human life, in that cadaver.

KASS: No, but I find every evidence of it I need when I'm sitting here talking to you. I see in your face and in your eyes that there is concentration, that there is a certain desire to understand, that there is a certain generosity of spirit. In some mysterious way, we more or less are understanding one another, and although I'm making my effort to be intelligible, I also have the feeling that something is working through me. I may sound mystical to my scientific colleagues, but it's not just molecules in motion that make up intelligibility. Also, molecules in motion do not explain the experience of grief, or even appetite.

> *Molecules in motion do not explain the experience of grief. . . .*

MOYERS: You bring us to the practical relevance of philosophical consideration for society today. We have some very hard choices ahead of us as a nation, as a culture, as a society. What we believe fundamentally and ultimately will affect those choices we make democratically. These are not just theoretical musings in some book-lined library on Lake Michigan. For example, what would you say to a badly crippled woman in great misery, suffering from terminal cancer in a hospital room as she begged you to help her die?

KASS: There's the short answer and then there's the much longer answer. The short answer, especially if this question is put to me as a physician, is that I couldn't, in conscience and in loyalty to what it means to be a physician, be the administerer of deadly poison. It violates the inner meaning of the art of healing. In fact, it's only because I know that I'll never kill my patients that I'm willing to get in there close to them and struggle with them as they face these agonies of the end of their lives. I'm never going to give up on them and say, "I can't cure you, I might as well kill you." To have that power denied me as a physician is absolutely indispensable to everything I need to do for my patients.

Now on the face of it that might seem insensitive to the real agony of my patients. I don't for a minute deny that there are many people who at the end of life are in not only a painful condition, but also a reduced and degraded and humiliated condition in which they couldn't imagine themselves living. I understand the very powerful pressures for an easy, technical solution.

MOYERS: But what if I say, "The pain is terrible, Dr. Kass. Nothing could be worse than staying alive in the condition I'm in right now."

KASS: Let's speak about the pain for a moment. Friends of mine who work in hospices have provided some rather powerful evidence that the pain aspect of terminal illness is in almost all cases really manageable, if in fact the physicians are willing to take the trouble to do it properly.

MOYERS: The alternatives are not just cure and kill.

KASS: That's right. We are increasingly successful in our ability to relieve bodily, physical suffering. In the vast majority of cases, with the judicious and aggressive use of medications, one can control agonizing pain. Now it's a very different thing if you're talking about dementia or the horror of compelling one's loved ones to see one in this condition.

MOYERS: The long years of a woman suffering Alzheimer's, unable to recognize, respond to, or receive love and affection, lying there, all curled up. Thirty-five, forty, fifty thousand dollars a year being spent on what by some definitions, is a life that's already gone. The soul is gone, by your—

KASS: —the soul is mostly gone. If she's still breathing on her own and still responsive in some way, it's flickering. It's not all out. But let me grant your point. Here we face a very delicate and difficult practical problem, the boundaries of which are easy to describe, but which, in practice, is exceedingly difficult to approach correctly. Precisely because death is not always the enemy, and because the meaning of a life includes a fitting conclusion, I think that physicians, families, and patients ought gracefully to desist from certain kinds of useless efforts to prolong life, efforts that in fact only prolong degradation and suffering.

On the other hand, one still would draw the line at the willful, direct, and deliberate taking of life, especially on the part of physicians. The physician as physician cannot directly and deliberately intend and cause the death of a patient. I think the physician can give adequate pain medication that might run the risk of shortening life. The doses of morphine might, in fact, run the risk of respiratory depression and hastening of death. But here the doctor is not trying to kill the patient but to relieve the patient's suffering. To intend the good of the patients presupposes they will continue to exist in order to experience the good that you're doing for them. Physicians are not terribly good at standing in there those last moments with words of encouragement and gentle speeches. In fact, a very angry society is going to be pushing them by saying, "Look, you guys, you've kept us alive longer than we want. You can't cure us. You've now put us into a mechanized and dehumanized environment. Get rid of us, please." And we know we've got the precedent in Holland, where the physicians have already begun to do this. In California this autumn there was a voter initiative to legalize euthanasia, and it just barely failed. We're going to have a lot of pressure for euthanasia in this country.

We need to find a way to walk the line between standing back to allow death, and deliberate and willful killing, not only because deliberate killing undermines the meaning of what it is to be a physician, but also because we're not going to be able to hold the line between voluntary and involuntary euthanasia. It's just impossible to hold the line there.

MOYERS: You mean, if one can make a case for mercy killings, one can also find people in the name of mercy killings committing murder.

KASS: We've already seen the precedent for this in the withdrawal of treatment. The early cases permitting people to refuse life-sustaining treatment were all people who were conscious and who asked that the doctor leave them alone. The courts upheld their right to refuse treatment.

The next batch of cases involved people who sued in court in the name of the comatose who could not make the request for themselves, saying, "Look, equal protection of the laws. Why should someone be denied a right to refuse treatment just because they're too comatose to claim it for themselves? We will speak in their name."

The courts have already upheld the right of some people to decide for other people that their life is no longer worth living. Now I'm not faulting so much the wish for it, but one sees that the vast majority of cases for which the Euthanasia Society and others want euthanasia are not the small number of voluntary cases whose pain can't be controlled. They own up to this point in print. It's the Alzheimer's cases. It's the people who are in reduced conditions.

MOYERS: So, even though you were contributing to the relief of a dying person seeking escape from his or her agony through euthanasia, you would also be contributing to a change in the attitude of society toward human life itself. And you don't want to have that unintended consequence.

KASS: No, absolutely. There are a number of circumstances in which the power of the plea for some kind of human assistance is very great. But to give in to it for perfectly good reasons would be to embrace consequences for future generations, the cost of which we can't even begin to imagine. If we really made killing patients a "therapeutic option," there would be a considerable weakening of respect for life and a weakening of the hard-won reluctance to take innocent life.

MOYERS: But if I were your patient and had terminal cancer, and I said, "Leon, I know you can't cure me, and you won't kill me. But let me die. Just go away and let me die." Would you be morally offended by that?

KASS: We'd have to talk concretely about it. I would say, "Look, I'm not going to abandon you. You are my patient, a human being I care about until you are no more." If you got an infection, and you said to me, "Is this infection likely to take me?" and I said, "I really think it is," and then you were to say to me, "Look, if you cure this infection, is there any easier and gentler way that I'm liable to get out of this life?" and I said, "No, this is probably the best," and then you said to me, "Look, we've been together for a number of years. If I get this kind of pneumonia, do me a favor and stand aside—no antibiotics," I'd say, "Well, are you sure about this? Can we talk about it with your family?" and so on. But I think, in principle, I'd be willing to do that if I were persuaded that there was a clear understanding, that there wasn't subtle coercion, that you were asking for death because you really wanted to die, and not because you think it's unseemly to stick around when everybody else is choosing death.

MOYERS: But, when you do that, when you're trying to analyze the motives, you're playing God.

KASS: No, but one's got to be very careful. If it becomes fashionable or even permissible for people to plead for death, and the profession is willing to go along with it, we're going to sweep up in this not only people who have deliberately and freely and knowingly chosen that they want no more, but all kinds of other people who are not tired of life, but who think other people are tired of them, or who really would like to live, but think it's cowardly to do so given that choosing death is an option.

One would have to be fairly confident. The attempt to reduce all of this to statements and writing is no substitute for the kind of conversation that you as my patient and I would have over a number of years.

MOYERS: I would plead with you, I think, to let me take the early train.

KASS: If I knew this was you talking and not the despair of a particular episode—

MOYERS: —but despair is a natural part of life, the despair at the end.

KASS: If it were indeed the end, you'd have no trouble from me.

MOYERS: What if the family came to you and said, "Dr. Kass, my mother is eighty-nine years old. She's had Alzheimer's for nine years. There's nothing left there except the biological function. Let her go. Let's don't feed her any more."

KASS: Feeding and hydration is a complicated issue, because it's on the boundary between what's obviously therapy and what is the mere sustenance that is in a way owed to a human being this side of the grave. The AMA has flip-flopped on this and now regards artificially administered food and water as therapy and, therefore, optional. And I suppose there are cases in which I could be persuaded to withhold artificially administered food and water, but I would much rather say, "We'll wait for the infection and then do nothing because it would be useless to do something there." But I wouldn't be saying, "Look, I intend this person's death." I don't see how someone could withhold food and water and pretend that he's doing anything other than intending to kill the patient. I don't think that one can preserve trust in the medical profession once that age-old restraint is lifted.

Now, that means that I am in the awkward position of having to say to certain people, "Look this is not what any of us hoped for," or "This is a terrible situation, it's tragic." But it would be perhaps even more tragic to acquiesce in the request for certain kinds of relief. Certainly no heroic measures—no operations and no antibiotics, and maybe if I know that the patient won't feel the starvation or the process of dehydration, that I won't be inflicting additional suffering, maybe you might persuade me. But I'm very worried about this.

MOYERS: It strikes me that life is not a moral choice for the person who is invested with life. We come into this world without our permission. You're saying that death is not really a moral choice, either.

KASS: That's very nicely put. There is a very popular notion that what counts, humanly speaking, is what's called the person or consciousness, and that when that goes, everything valuable about us goes. And I have seen enough of such instances where you would say, "Grandfather really died five years ago. We're just burying him now, when the rest of him left." But I think the respect for consciousness, for personhood, for everything that we would call the distinctively human in human life, we only find when it's connected with a living, breathing, digesting body. For society to place itself in opposition to life—even to mere circulation and breathing—is to commit an affront against the whole of our being and the whole of our dignity. Except in matters of self-defense or certain extreme cases, we can't humanly put ourselves in opposition to the good which is an individual human life.

MOYERS: All of a sudden, we're confronted by very big, ethical questions, from whether the state should require people to be tested for AIDS before they get married, to whether the cells of a fetus should be used for the study of Alzheimer's disease, from whether the courts can order a woman to have a Caesarean operation in an effort to save the life of a fetus, to whether one Siamese twin should be "sacrificed" in a risky operation that might save the other Siamese twin for a normal life. Who is going to make these decisions?

KASS: Some of these questions are, in fact, social and political questions. It's sometimes said that these are moral and religious questions and, therefore, have no place in our political life. But politics is always about moral questions. We're always trying to figure out what the better or just or right or decent thing to do is. I'm not naive about what kind of results we will achieve through the political process. For better or for worse, in a liberal democracy, those expressions of the beliefs and practices and values of the community are best expressed communally through serious discussion with the populace, in the legislature, in local communities, in hospitals, and so on.

> *. . . politics is always about moral questions.*

Probably only a rather small number of such matters require legislation. Not everything that is of dubious propriety ought to be a matter of illegality. Enforcing certain kinds of laws has its own costs that might be higher than the harm that one is trying to root out. For example, the public health needs of dealing with the AIDS problem and pursuing carriers has to be balanced against the invasion of privacy and the use of the police power in order to get compliance in the tracing of contacts. This is a very delicate subject. But ours is a moral community as well as an economic one, and the media, the schools, and the legislative bodies are the places for the airing of some of these questions.

Individual judgments about when to stand aside from life-prolonging treatment are unlikely to be a matter for legislation. One will never do away with the need for the prudent judgment of decent people on the spot. The attempt to provide rules and institutions to solve these problems—however well intentioned—is finally foolish. One ultimately must have room for judgment and conscientiousness—maybe not a perfect judgment, but the best under the circumstances.

MOYERS: You have said that reproductive technologies are especially dehumanizing. Why?

KASS: Reproductive technologies encourage us to rationalize and make a matter of will and art this deeply ingrained activity whereby we perpetuate ourselves into the next generation. Everybody understands the desirability of family planning. Everyone understands the desire to have a child of one's own or to have a child who is born healthy. But the more one intrudes into this process to produce what one obstetrician has called "the optimum baby," the more one is going to move procreation from the womb and the home into the laboratory and the more a natural and human activity will be transformed into one of production and manufacture. However much we welcome the benefits in terms of "the product," there will be some costs in the dehumanization of the process.

MOYERS: You ask, "What, for example, does the word 'mother' mean if one woman donates the egg, another houses it for insemination, a third hosts the transferred embryo and gives birth to the baby, a fourth nurses it, a fifth rears it, and a sixth has legal custody?" That is an extreme case.

KASS: Yes, but the point is that one of the unexpected consequences of these new technologies to cure infertility is that it's now possible to shuttle eggs and embryos around, introducing a certain kind of confusion about one's biological lineage. The extreme case that we face now is in the surrogate pregnancies. We really ought not to practice this at all. It comes dangerously close to degrading people to allow their bodies to be used merely as incubators for other people's babies.

MOYERS: But the other side of it is that being a mother is not merely—and not always—a biological act. Mothers and fathers are born of love and not just the womb and seed.

KASS: To be sure, and one could cite the case of adopted children, much loved and very well reared. On the other hand, we don't deliberately set out to produce all kinds of babies for the sake of adopting them, and we encourage people eager for such contact to get in touch with their biological parents. All kinds of records, once thought to be confidential, are now being opened up so people can get in touch with their biological ancestry. There's something rather mysterious in the support that biology provides to encourage the sense that this really is one's own flesh to whom one has even extra commitments.

Now I'm not saying knowledge of one's biological lineage is indispensable. But deliberately adding to the confounding of lineage and the confusion of these roles comes close to what is really a kind of marketing of babies, and this risks a degradation of the whole activity of engendering and giving birth, of connecting procreation, marriage, and rearing in a package, which—modern prejudices aside—is perhaps the deepest meaning of this aspect of our humanity.

MOYERS: It could make an economic transaction out of what ultimately is a moral affair.

KASS: Some people criticize this practice of surrogate motherhood, not because they think there's anything intrinsically wrong with it, but because they feel that poor women will be exploited to make money by this use of their bodies. But if there were really nothing wrong with the practice, there would be nothing wrong with making a living at it. You don't object to people working for a living, you object when they're compelled to put their bodies to the use of other people's wills for a living. One could object to prostitution on similar grounds.

MOYERS: We face some hard choices, don't we?

KASS: We certainly do. An old Chinese curse says, "May you live in interesting times." That happens to be our fate. But thanks to these new technologies that cause so many hard choices, it's also an opportunity to rethink the meaning of our own humanity.

Elaine Pagels
HISTORIAN OF RELIGION

JERRY BAUER

Elaine Pagels, a professor of religion at Princeton University, finds in the story of Adam and Eve more than a parable from ancient faiths. In Adam, Eve and the Serpent *she explores what the old story of the Garden of Eden reveals about our attitudes toward sexuality, politics, suffering, and guilt, and the roles of men and women in Western society. Her first book,* The Gnostic Gospels, *won the National Book Award in 1979.*

MOYERS: Why did you get fascinated with the story of Adam and Eve?

PAGELS: I've always been fascinated with it. It's a very provocative story about a man, a woman, a tree, a snake, and a prohibition. They break a prohibition, and then they find out that they're naked. A lot of unanswered, provocative questions come up in that story. But what started me working on this particular book was a conversation I had when I was visiting in Khartoum in the southern Sudan. I was talking with the Foreign Minister of the Sudan, who was from a Dinka tribe, and who had done a book of creation stories about his tribe. We talked about how the creation stories of the Dinka are connected with the social and political structure of the tribe and how tribal attitudes about work, marriage, animals, and death are linked to their creation story. I began to realize it was exactly the same with this story of Adam and Eve. Many of our cultural attitudes about work, animals, death, marriage, sexuality, and suffering are involved with that story.

MOYERS: Was it the realization that there were two parallel stories saying the same thing that compelled you?

PAGELS: Not so much that as the recognition that these creation stories, which looked like very faraway, archaic, funny, old stories, are in fact involved in the way that many of us look at fundamental parts of our experience.

MOYERS: How do you explain that? Here is a story, written by the ancient Hebrews at least three thousand years ago—and they probably told it a long time before they ever wrote it down. Yet it became a dominant force in the self-consciousness of the West.

PAGELS: Well, there are many messages in that story. One of the messages that struck me was that God made Adam in His own image. Adam, in Hebrew, meant "a human being." The statement that every human being is made in God's image proved to be explosively powerful in the Roman Empire because in that world three quarters of the people were either slaves or descended from slaves and so were legally not people, not human. Only one man in the whole society was said to be made in the gods' image—that was the Emperor. Therefore, you must obey him. But to say that every man, every woman, every slave, every child was equally made in the image of God and therefore was of ultimate value was a powerful, radical, dramatic, and extraordinary statement. That's one of the reasons this story caught on.

MOYERS: Not only did it catch on, it held on. Take the Declaration of Independence—"All men are created equal." Few would admit then that slaves were equal, but the idea of universal equality took a powerful and revolutionary hold on the American imagination.

PAGELS: In ancient times, when Jews and Christians used that story, they never imagined that you could make a political or social reality of it. They felt they were equal before God and would be equal in God's Kingdom, in the hereafter.

MOYERS: This tradition gave us a profound sense of our own individual worth, our own dignity, as men and women made in the image of God.

But let's go back to the other aspect of the story. In the time before the Christian era, in ancient Egypt, and Greece, and Rome, sexual love was celebrated as divine. The ancients didn't have the negative, pessimistic view of it that came to us through the Adam and Eve story.

PAGELS: Well, you say "came to us," but who's the "us"? Because if you look at the way many Jews read it—and still do—there's nothing negative about sexuality in the Adam and Eve story. It's a story about blessing and procreation. The first divine commandment is "Be fruitful and multiply." So, really, there's an obligation to procreate, and marriage is seen as a way of fulfilling that obligation. Sexuality in such a tradition is an instrument of blessing.

But when you say "us" and mean the Christian tradition, I think it's very true that for many Christians the story is filtered through two thousand years of interpretation. St. Augustine, especially, read the story with a very negative view of sexuality.

MOYERS: To use the modern cliché of journalism, why did Augustine "spin" the story this way?

PAGELS: It would be unfair to say Augustine was the first to put this negative spin on it. There are strains in Jewish tradition that see the sexual impulse as part of what is called the "evil impulse." And a lot of other people in the ancient world were highly suspicious of these passions that overtake the mind. But even so, one finds a radically different attitude about sexuality in Christian sources. It's surprising that when other Jewish teachers around Jesus' time are interpreting the story, they're usually talking about issues like marriage and sexuality and gender. Jesus was no exception. The only time that the Gospels say He ever referred to that story was when people asked Him what the grounds for divorce were. He said, "Haven't you read that in the beginning, God made the male and female and said for this cause a man shall leave his father and mother, and be joined to his wife?" Then He adds these words: "What God has joined together, let no one separate." That's Matthew 19.

So, in Jesus' "spin" on the story—according to Matthew, at any rate—God had originally intended marriage with no possibility of divorce and no thought of procreation. Then Jesus goes on to say that those who make themselves eunuchs, who, in effect, castrate themselves for the sake of the Kingdom of God, are even more blessed.

So there's an odd, striking, and challenging difference in the way that Jesus is said to have used that story. St. Paul went much further with it.

MOYERS: So many of the Church fathers refer to sexual activity as repugnant, filthy, unseemly. One of them was said not to be at home in his body.

PAGELS: Yes—Origen.

MOYERS: Origen, that's right. This view of sex took over very quickly in the first two or three hundred years after Christ.

PAGELS: Yes. You know, I was struck when I first began studying this because, having been nominally raised in the Protestant tradition and educated in it at Harvard, I was always brought up with the attitude that Christianity affirms the world—that God made the world, and it was good. But when you look at the early Christian movement, it's striking in what negative terms many of the early Christians talk about sexuality.

> . . . it's striking in what negative terms many of the early Christians talk about sexuality.

MOYERS: Why did that happen?

PAGELS: I was curious about that, and also curious about why a movement that negative would be so successful. I think it had to do with another element of the Christian message, which was taken out of that story, too. That's a message about human freedom. God made these humans, in His image—that was taken to mean that they were given more freedom. The capacity to make moral choices was enormously valued.

MOYERS: Even choosing to disobey God is a moral choice.

PAGELS: Yes, and there is also the choice to transcend passion, to say no to natural instincts. In the movement that Jesus and Paul initiated, celibacy was considered to be a preferable life, if not the only life, for many. Celibacy for the sake of the Kingdom of God was a good choice. It wasn't so much that the passions were evil but that other things were more important—human moral freedom, for example, and working for the Kingdom of God. Christianity involved a vision of human nature that was not bound to the old structures of the family or the society. If you were a traditionally-minded Jew, or Roman, or Greek, your moral obligation would be to your family—to marry properly, to bring up a family, to transmit property, to be loyal to the country, and all of that. Jesus' message, in many ways, was radical: "Leave your family."

MOYERS: "Follow me."

PAGELS: "Leave your wife, husband, children, father, and mother, and follow me." It's a very radical message. And it opened up a radical possibility in the ancient world for leaving behind those traditional structures and discovering a new sense of the human self.

MOYERS: And that was found through celibacy, isolation, and denial.

PAGELS: That sounds negative, the way you put it.

MOYERS: That's the way I was taught it.

PAGELS: But celibacy was a means to freedom from the traditional demands of one's family and one's culture.

MOYERS: That radical element became the dominant tendency of the Church after St. Augustine.

PAGELS: We tend to think of the early Christian movement as monolithic, but it was actually very pluralistic.

MOYERS: We think there was a "Golden Age," a time when it was pure and simple.

PAGELS: Right—that there's one grand tradition, and it just keeps growing in strength and depth through the centuries like some grand stream. In fact, there was an enormously complex interplay of different movements within what we call the "Christian movement." Many of them were very affirmative about marriage and family and national stability and all of that. So I was asking myself why this negative view of sexuality that Augustine articulated so brilliantly became dominant. I began to suspect that in the time of Augustine the society, for the first time, was becoming a Christian society. For the first time, the Christian movement was no longer a persecuted sect, no longer a small enclave, which regarded itself as an island of purity against this ocean of corruption which was the Roman Empire. Christians were everywhere. The Emperor was a Christian, and many of his officials were. There were all kinds of corrupt official influences in the churches. Many people became aware that the kind of moral freedom that had been talked about earlier in the Christian movement wasn't as simple as it looked any more. A more pessimistic, darker view of human nature and its possibilities emerged in the fourth century and afterward.

MOYERS: Wasn't it also true that with Augustine, Christians began to believe that because we came into the world poisoned by original sin, we were not capable of self-government, and that therefore we needed the authority both of the Church and the State in order to govern our appetites, to check our instincts, and to regulate our behavior?

PAGELS: What surprised me so much when I was looking at the pre-Augustinian Christian Church is that when they talked about Adam and Eve, they saw it as a story about human freedom in every form—freedom from one's family and obligations, freedom from passions, freedom from the gods, and freedom from the government—in short, freedom to master oneself. With Augustine, it changed completely. He began to talk about a story of moral bondage. Adam may have been free way back in the Garden, but he lost it. He lost it so far back that no human being since Adam or Eve has ever been free morally in the way that he was. We are all tainted by his misuse of freedom. Augustine then developed an ingenious theory that this moral disease that Adam generated was sexually transmitted through semen. Jesus was the only person not "infected" because he was presumably conceived without human semen. But the rest of us, conceived in the usual, depraved way, were infected by Adam's sin. So this moral problem, which he felt was endemic to our condition, is described in sexual terms.

MOYERS: And all of us thereafter were born with fallen natures, because we had been corrupted by the sexual act.

PAGELS: Yes, by the very process through which we're conceived. But this time around, when I looked at the story, I began to see it is more than a psychological or theological statement—it also becomes a political statement. If, for example, you and I are baptized Christians in the second century, and therefore become moral and achieve what God gave in Creation, which is moral capacity to govern ourselves, then you don't really need an external government. Now you could say that everybody's a Christian, what do we need a government for, anyway? Each person can rule himself or herself. We don't need an external government.

But just at this time, there came a new theory of human nature that said, "But you see now, we know that we're so corrupted that we have to be ruled from outside."

That was a useful "strategy" for both the Church and the State to justify the necessity of external control. It has been ever since.

MOYERS: Yes, this union of Church and State was convenient for both. The Church had no sword with which to enforce its orthodoxy. The state had the sword, but needed what the Church could provide as justification. So you had this coupling of power and theology.

PAGELS: That's right, and you still do. If you look at Protestant theology since John Calvin and Martin Luther through the modern theologians like Paul Tillich, they all talk about some deep flaw in human nature. Many of them have held the pessimistic view that because we are so corrupted, we need governmental structures to prevent ourselves from tearing each other apart—"devouring each other like fishes," as one Christian theologian said.

MOYERS: I don't care much for theology. It's one reason I didn't pursue it. But I am fascinated by the story of the Church.

PAGELS: I am, too. I don't get involved in finding the right story because the early history of Christianity is not a single story at all. It's a complex, dynamic, controversial collection of stories about many parties and points of view.

MOYERS: Did your own beliefs as a Christian change during the course of your scholarship?

PAGELS: Yes, but I haven't been looking at it so much for that. I came to realize that my beliefs change as my circumstances change. But what the beliefs are doesn't interest me as much as the kind of issues the beliefs raise. People engage with fundamental questions about how we look at human nature and how we understand our position in the universe.

MOYERS: In the last paragraph of your book you say that one thing you came away with was a new recognition of the spiritual dimension in our human experience.

PAGELS: That is what I couldn't stay away from. That's what fascinates me—how people deal with the spiritual dimension in their lives, how they image it, how they argue about it. What the specific beliefs are doesn't interest me as much.

MOYERS: But do you consider yourself religious?

PAGELS: Yes, incorrigibly, naturally. It's like a taste for music. There are people who can take music or leave it. And there are other people who just love it and can't really live without it. Religion is that way for me, although my background was not particularly religious. But I love to engage the history of religion.

MOYERS: But what about the spiritual dimension that you said you found "inescapable" in your own work? One either honors that and nurtures it, or one puts it on a shelf where it gathers dust.

PAGELS: Yes, there are many ways of exploring it. The way I explore it for myself is in this kind of work.

MOYERS: Does it feed your spirit?

PAGELS: Sure. But it doesn't give me answers. I look at the different doctrines or the different beliefs not so much as something a person looks for to hold on to but as provisional points of view to which people come in different situations.

MOYERS: Have you found out anything about yourself, as a woman, from studying the Adam and Eve story?

PAGELS: Oh, certainly. That was one of the many ways that story engaged me. It expresses many attitudes about women, most of them highly negative attitudes, which I had totally rejected as a 1970s feminist. But I discovered that even though I didn't believe these, they sometimes emerged unexpectedly. When I had children, I would find my attitudes about women negative in a way that troubled me. I found myself thinking about women as gullible or weak—total stereotypes that had nothing to do with my reality or what I thought I believed. These were just cultural stereotypes that I found emerged quite unconsciously. And I discovered they didn't emerge from nowhere. They come out of a culture which tells one that.

MOYERS: They have a history.

PAGELS: They have a history. These myths are the dreams of a whole culture, so they're in the air. And although my family wasn't particularly religious, I heard many of the same stereotypes about women that I found among those second-century Christians. They're part of our cultural attitude.

MOYERS: That Eve had brought sin into the world. That has to influence the way women are perceived.

PAGELS: Some of the letters in the New Testament say that women must not be allowed to teach because they're gullible and irrational and so forth. In fact, one of my tutors from Oxford wrote the same thing in a review of my first book in the *Times Literary Supplement*. He said that women are very susceptible to heresy, and that explained part of my attraction to some of these things. Those attitudes, which look ridiculous and outdated, are far too pervasive a part of our culture. So I started this book partly as an exploration—I was going to say "exorcism"—of some of these attitudes.

MOYERS: Did you succeed?

PAGELS: Yes. When you see how these cultural influences play on us it's easier to bring them to consciousness and to say, "I accept this," or "I reject this." It's when they're unconsciously influencing us that they are most powerful.

MOYERS: Did the historical interpretation of the Bible that put women on the margin of the Church keep you from being more fully committed as a Christian?

PAGELS: Well, I was brought up in a family that was Protestant, but nominally so—and I was brought up to think that religion was for people without an adequate education. You have magic and superstition and then religion and then science. Eventually religion would wither and die out from its own absurdity. But what happened to me was different. I found I was fascinated by religion.

MOYERS: You're one of the most religious people I know. I've sensed it since I first met you, fourteen years ago.

PAGELS: Really? I'm shocked.

MOYERS: Why else would you be drawn to this? Why would you write with such fervor and passion about it if it didn't have something to say, if it were just an intellectual pursuit?

PAGELS: But what is an intellectual pursuit if it doesn't engage one's whole being? It wouldn't be worth doing. I just discovered that these were questions I had to work on. Now, there are many other things that I love that fascinate me, but these issues about human nature, about the way our personal images and dreams are connected with the dreams of our culture, about our religious traditions, about the way that this plays off against Buddhist traditions—these are the issues that I love to explore.

MOYERS: You're saying that the picture of Adam and Eve is not just a picture on a canvas—that it's a picture in the mind, memory, and history of the Judeo-Christian tradition.

PAGELS: It's very deep in our culture and in all of us, although not in all of us to the same extent. I've found to my own shock that my attitudes about being a woman in 1980, when I started this work, had to do with very ancient stereotypes, many of which I totally disagreed with intellectually. I didn't like them, but there they were. Many of our political institutions, and many people who would not consider themselves religious in the least, nevertheless have adopted attitudes which are just there in the culture and which come out of that ancient story.

MOYERS: Tell me: How do you define religion?

PAGELS: That's a hard question to answer. I'm looking at religious traditions, which are relics of certain qualities of experience that people have had in the past and have articulated in stories and songs and dances and in stone. Traditions are the relics of certain kinds of experiences and attitudes about life that people have chosen to take as fundamental.

MOYERS: Religious traditions grow, change, evolve. Some women working in your field of study are trying to create a new canon of spiritual literature. They're using poetry, parables, and ancient hymns to the goddess to try to create a spiritual literature that puts the female back at the center of the religious worldview. Are you attracted to that effort?

PAGELS: I think it's an interesting one, and in some ways I find it attractive. For example, in one of the museums in Luxor, in Upper Egypt, there was an image of Hathor, a goddess who appears in the form of a cow. Now, I had always thought of cows as rather comical characters like something out of Walt Disney. A goddess in the form of a cow didn't sound attractive. But this cow was sculpted in ebony and had gold horns, and the moon disc was in her horns. And she was beautiful, wise, and maternal. An extraordinary being was in that sculpture. I was very moved by the sense of feminine power that came in that sculpture and in some of the Isis figures as well. So I have some sympathy with that point of view. On the other hand, for me, it doesn't work to just make up a canon and exclude a lot of the rest of our cultural tradition. I feel mixed about it.

MOYERS: I think many of us do. Is it possible that feminist theology can become as chauvinistic in its own way as the old Church theology that discriminated so willfully against women?

PAGELS: Well, it might. I haven't thought too much about that because it's very different from the way I approached these materials.

MOYERS: Just recently, the Pope said that women couldn't be ordained as priests because "Our Lord was a man." When I heard that, I wondered why one would not also say that if Christ was a celibate, as is believed by the Church, he couldn't represent those of us who are not celibate?

PAGELS: Absolutely. At the end of one of Mary Gordon's novels, she says, "Christ was a Jew." Now, would they say that one couldn't be a priest if one weren't Jewish? It's of course those attributes the tradition chooses as important.

MOYERS: What "the tradition chooses"—that's an interesting term. Someone, at some time, said, "This is going to be the official view of reality—not that."

PAGELS: Right. And the fact is that when you look at the history of Christianity, you see not a single possibility as *the* Christian view of X, but many, many different points of view and many arguments about points of view. Some of these become dominant. And you can see the historical, political, and social reasons why certain viewpoints, at a certain time, will become the Church's official line.

MOYERS: Those that lost out become the heresy.

PAGELS: Sometimes what was originally fundamental Church teaching becomes heresy later.

MOYERS: Evangelical Christians, of course, still believe that the story of Adam and Eve provides a frame of reference, a setting, a way of making sense of things that inform life. They present this story as if it had universal validity. And they have the comfort of a support system that others who are looking for a new story don't have.

PAGELS: That's true. Many evangelical Christians defend the story as literally true, and there I don't happen to agree with them. But they're also saying that this story is fundamental because it articulates basic values about the nature of human dignity and the nature of human beings. And there I'm convinced they are right. The story is a vehicle of fundamental attitudes about human nature, human value, human work—about so many things.

MOYERS: But fundamentalists go on to say that once we lose that notion of original sin, as interpreted by tradition, we lose the "governor." They say, "Look around at society today. Look at art, look at politics, look at morality, look at culture at large. The restraints have been removed. Anything goes. Society is collapsing." This old story no longer compels the coherence that it once did.

PAGELS: But the old story didn't have one message. If you study how Christians read it, from the time of Jesus for the next four hundred years, you see that it was read many ways. Jesus invoked it for a particular purpose. Paul invoked it for other purposes. Other Christians read it in a whole variety of different ways, with a wide range of possible meanings, some of them totally contradictory. So it becomes very hard to say, "The Bible says this." When you look at the history of Christianity, you see that what the Bible says has been interpreted so many ways that one has to acknowledge that one chooses an interpretation.

> *. . . what the Bible says has been interpreted so many ways that one has to acknowledge that one chooses an interpretation.*

MOYERS: What happens to a society like ours at the moment when, say, half the population still believes the old story and the other half has jettisoned it and is searching for a different story? There is a new movement of people like Thomas Berry, who says, "The old story functioned for a long time. We could wake up in the morning and know where we were in the universe because of this story. We could answer the questions our children asked. We knew our place in the world because the story told us who we were and where we are. But now," he says, "the old story is not functioning properly. We need a new story."

PAGELS: So what do you choose?

MOYERS: What do you choose? That's the question. How do we find a new story?

PAGELS: We can't just choose a culture. It's not like picking a different tie.

MOYERS: But Augustine and the Church fathers chose this story.

PAGELS: It was part of the tradition they had received, and they chose to interpret it in various ways. What happens for many of us is much more powerful when you can change the whole meaning of the story, when you can turn it upside down, when you can invert it completely. Do you know the story of Lilith?

MOYERS: No.

PAGELS: In Chapter 1 of Genesis it says that "God made Adam in His image. And male and female He created them." Then in Chapter 2 it says that Adam was alone. God wanted to make a companion for him, so he made all these animals, but none of them was a suitable companion for him. Finally, almost as an afterthought, God made a woman. Some of the ancient rabbis said, "Now wait a minute! There was a woman in Chapter 1. Why did he make another woman in Chapter 2? Adam was all alone again." So they concluded that Adam's first wife had been created in Chapter 1, and that she had been unfit. They developed a story about Adam's first wife, Lilith, and said that she had been insubordinate to her husband. She said, "After all, You made us both on the same day. Why should I serve him?" The rabbis said that God was so angry at her attitude that He blasted her out of existence and turned her into a great female demon. She became a witch, the inspirer of men's sexual fantasies, and the one who destroys the infants of respectable women in childbirth. In the Middle Ages, Lilith becomes an image of the kind of female that a good Jewish girl does not become—insubordinate, seductive, and so forth. Eve is the good woman.

Now, in the twentieth century, there's a Jewish feminist journal called *Lilith*. Jewish feminists are choosing Lilith as an image, and it's powerful. If you want to reject the old story and the way it's been read, you play off against the story by turning it around.

MOYERS: And the significance of the Lilith story?

PAGELS: There are many ways to deal with different kinds of significance, but one that struck me is that it was socially a very powerful story. It wasn't just a misogynist story, because in the Middle Ages and in the time in which the stories of Lilith were told, infant mortality was approximately fifty percent. Half the children were dying at childbirth or soon after, and people would say, "Why would God let this happen? How could it happen?" The answer was often, "Well, this couple must have opened itself to the evil power of Lilith, either because the man has been unfaithful to his wife, in fact or in fantasy, or because the wife has been insubordinate." It's hard to think of a couple to whom neither applies. So this grief would be interpreted, first, so that there was a moral reason for it, and second, so that the reason would reinforce the society's expectations of proper marital behavior.

MOYERS: And the proper marital behavior was male dominance.

PAGELS: Male dominance and male fidelity, yes.

MOYERS: In fact, you write that "the blight of male domination" has fallen upon the whole structure of sexual relations. Is that because of Adam and Eve?

PAGELS: No, I think that this story is partly effective in the culture because it expressed tendencies that were already there. I don't think this story invented that kind of social structure, but because it explains it in a simple and powerful way, it has been very useful.

MOYERS: Another way to ask the question is this: Could the role of male dominance have survived if the story had not fitted a basic human need for sixteen hundred centuries?

PAGELS: Why that has been the case is an enormous question. I can't think male dominance is there simply because of a story like this. Let's just say that this story plays into a whole complex of social and economic and political factors. Where this is the case, the story functions to show why it ought to be the case, and therefore, it's a story that's adopted and transmitted—

MOYERS: —by a structure, by a hierarchy, by people in authority. So many women in the Church accepted it. They lived by it.

PAGELS: Yes, but there was a lot of diversity in early Christian attitudes about women. It used to be the fashion for historians in my field to say, "Ah well, you know, Christianity made the world so much better for women in so many ways." That's questionable. Some parts of the Christian movement were open in their attitudes about women's roles. For example, if women could be celibate, they could have other roles in the society besides the traditional ones of wife and mother. They could be traveling teachers and evangelists in some parts of the Christian movement. But in others there was a very different attitude.

MOYERS: But on the whole, women have paid a price for the theological pessimism that developed out of the story of Adam and Eve.

PAGELS: I think so, but I wasn't talking only about women. I wasn't trying to write a moral story to say, "Isn't it awful that the story of creation turns from a story of freedom into a story of bondage," but to simply look at how that happened, and what were the social factors involved. One of the reasons I looked at it the way I did is that many Christian groups who are not dominant or in power speak about liberation theology. It's no accident they talk about freedom a great deal. It's no accident they talk about human moral responsibility a great deal. They pick up these elements in Christianity, elements that have been submerged for a long time.

MOYERS: And there are all those people now who are trying to develop an affirmative theology based on human freedom to replace the negative and pessimistic theology that grew out of the old tradition.

PAGELS: But the Adam and Eve story could serve that purpose very well. Some early interpretations offered that affirmative story you were talking about. On the other hand, the story that interests me most is not Adam and Eve but the story of the history of Western religion. That is what interests me—how we have created these cultural traditions, how we relate to them, how we choose them, how they change. That to me is the most fascinating story. Most people, when they think of religion, think of whatever they were brought up with or not brought up with. But the study of religion, whether it's Buddhism, Hinduism, Islam, tribal religions, or whatever, opens up a human range which is far more exciting than any of them taken separately.

MOYERS: What does the story of religion say about us?

PAGELS: It says that there are many different ways that we as human beings can interpret our experience, different ways we can shape and value the world and articulate that value, and we have taken different attitudes toward death and life and sexuality and power.

MOYERS: Does this study give you a sense that the future's going to be difficult because of the conflict of reconciling all of these differences as we learn more about them—or that from the many differences it's possible to construct a worldview that incorporates them more benevolently than we've seen so far in this century?

PAGELS: Many people who are thoughtful in these different traditions are very much concerned with how we live with pluralism. How do Christians, in particular, deal with other religious traditions that they've always treated as inferior? Can Jews and Muslims acknowledge the validity of these other traditions? There's practically no religion that I know of that sees other people in a way that affirms the others' choices. But in our century we're forced to think about a pluralistic world.

MOYERS: What do you see happening in our own culture? We've all heard the voices of conflict within Christianity grow more pronounced in the last several years—in politics, I mean.

PAGELS: When I was working on this book, I realized how deeply these religious traditions are embedded in the very structure of our political life, our institutions, and our attitudes about human nature. For example, a person may think that a woman has a right to make a choice about abortion and will probably make a reasonable, decent, and moral choice. Another person might believe that that decision must be taken out of the hands of the majority of people because they will abuse it. Or take another example: A person may think that countries that have traditionally been our enemies only make decisions in a Machiavellian way in order to trick us into letting down our national defenses. On the other hand, a person may believe that a country like the Soviet Union is indeed changing. In these examples, whether you agree with one side or another depends on your basic attitude about whether human nature is essentially depraved and must be restrained, or whether it can be trusted, which is a liberal, optimistic view institutionalized in some of our governmental structures.

MOYERS: When George Bush and Michael Dukakis talked about abortion during one of the campaign debates, they were expressing two different versions of the Christian-Judeo tradition. Bush was saying that this is a matter on which people can't be trusted, that women can't be trusted to make a moral decision. Dukakis was saying it's a moral choice women must be trusted to make. There's the old conflict in Christianity.

PAGELS: Yes, our traditions are really pluralistic, and they have multiple possibilities within them. It's important to become aware that we are making choices, and that if we're going to take a particular position socially, politically, or religiously, it's not just because it's the only position available but because we have made a conscious choice to take that position.

MOYERS: Where do you come out in the old argument? Are we by nature depraved sinners, immoral and corrupt, or are we fashioned in the image of God and capable of making choices morally and freely?

PAGELS: I'm going to waffle on that because what I find fascinating is the way that issue is polarized, and the way that people keep arguing that question. It's a fundamental question. At certain times each side seems more valid than it does at others. If you ask in a certain situation, like the aftermath of the Second World War, you would say that human nature is essentially corrupt. In another circumstance, one would come up with a very different point of view. I think both are true.

MOYERS: That human beings are both corrupt and moral?

PAGELS: It's not as simple as either view would claim.

MOYERS: One consequence of scholarship is to make one beware the terrible simplifications. When you studied the early history of the Church, you didn't find a Golden Age where Christianity existed pure and simple.

PAGELS: Most people who study the early history of Christianity are doing what I was doing. We say, "Well, Christianity around me is fractured into all these different denominations that say these different things, but back there, at the time of Jesus, it was all very simple and very clear. Let's go back and find out what it was like back then and then try it." Almost every reform movement in Christianity has tried that, from Luther on. So when I went back there, I found a multiplicity of voices in the early Christian movement, just as there is today. In fact, it was very complex and multifaceted. I became fascinated with that.

MOYERS: When you studied the story of Adam and Eve, did you come to any conclusions on suffering? Augustine held that suffering was the consequence of our depravity, that it wasn't just a random event in our lives.

PAGELS: The Genesis story says that, too—that there wouldn't be death or sickness or suffering in the world if it hadn't been for sin. I was intrigued by that and had to struggle with it, as many people do, when it comes close to home. When you go through some difficult or painful experience, you say, "Why me? Why would that happen to me?" Many people instinctively seem to blame themselves for what looks like misfortune that they did not cause. I began to reflect on how our culture has taught us that suffering and death and disease are not natural, are not part of nature, but were brought in because of human guilt and sin. That belief can lead people to blame themselves in ways that are not constructive.

Then I became fascinated by another Christian theologian, Julian, who took a very different point of view. He said that suffering and death are very much part of the mortal condition, and that God offers a means of healing and redemption and perhaps integration of suffering.

MOYERS: Julian's message, then, was that suffering is because life is.

PAGELS: Suffering is part of a natural condition, part of being a mortal creature. It's not because we sinned, but because we're the kind of beings we are. That makes a lot of sense in terms of what we know about biology, for example. And it has psychological implications, too—an acceptance of suffering, not in terms of guilt, but in terms of natural process.

MOYERS: But perhaps the older view of suffering caused by sin also served human need. "I don't understand what's happening to me, but I accept it because I'm fallen, I'm part of the sinful world, and sinners must be punished."

PAGELS: It's reassuring in that sense, and it also says that your action is important. If you are at fault because some catastrophe strikes, then it makes you an important agent in that act.

MOYERS: You have experienced suffering recently. In the last year you lost your husband, and you lost your child.

PAGELS: Yes.

MOYERS: Did you learn from the experience of life something about suffering that you didn't learn in your scholarship?

PAGELS: Scholarship is a way of articulating and working out some of the issues that one confronts, and certainly for me much of what the book articulates on that came out of struggling with the fact that my son, whom I adored, had an illness that was untreatable. I had to struggle with that question and with the question of guilt, which comes up almost like a reflex—"Why is this happening to me?"—as if there were something wrong. In fact, I read an article that indicated that when there's something wrong with a child, the mother—not the father, but the mother—always takes the blame for it. It's like a reflex. So it was illuminating to me to look at the ancient controversies in the history of Christianity and to see that there were people who were saying something very different about the nature of suffering. I found that very useful and much truer to my own experience.

MOYERS: People like Julian.

PAGELS: Yes, people like Julian. I was not expecting or wanting to like another heretic, but I was surprised to see that he was saying something that connected very deeply with my own experience. It was a way of dealing with this almost automatic reflex of "What have I done that this thing happened?"—which I found to be useless, not a helpful response in any way.

MOYERS: There's something Hindu in this feeling that life and death are inseparable, and that one is the half of a parenthesis to which the other is the other half.

PAGELS: That's right, but I also realized at a certain point that I was making myself feel guilty, and that I would rather feel guilty than helpless. The real truth of it was that I was totally helpless as only a parent is when there's something terribly wrong with one's child. The helplessness is awesome, and it's unacceptable, and so it was easier to feel guilty than it was to feel helpless. To say, "I'm powerful," in a situation, even if it means saying, "I'm guilty," is better than not having any input at all. It made me think of the practice of the Hopi, who go out on the mesa every morning and make the sun rise. People say, "Well, what would happen if some morning you just didn't go out there and do that?" And they say, "Well, would you plunge the world into darkness for the sake of your stupid experiment?"

Guilt involves a sense of importance in the drama. To say that one is not guilty is also to acknowledge that one is in fact quite powerless. For me, the only way to stay balanced in the situation was to acknowledge over and over that I was in fact powerless. That was a sane and balancing act. Dealing with that sense of helplessness is very much part of our condition. Religion is often a way of disguising it, a way of avoiding it, a way of pretending that we're not helpless.

MOYERS: So that the image of Adam in the story could represent a defiance of God—"I'm not going to be helpless here in the Garden of Eden."

PAGELS: When people confronted the realities of mortality, of disease, of human vulnerability in the universe, they must have said, "Why do we suffer this way?" To say, "We suffer because Adam sinned," makes a human being much more powerful in the universe. So the story has a very deep psychological appeal.

Of course, there are times when guilt is appropriate. When a person has violated another person or oneself, then guilt is very appropriate. But I'm talking about cases where a disaster happens, like an act of God, and people nevertheless still feel guilty. In those cases, guilt is useless. It vitiates our energy when we may need it. I discovered that there are other interpretations of that story which I found useful and which talk about the human condition as a mortal condition and God as a source of healing and power in the universe. What struck me as interesting and peculiar about Augustine's theory is that he says that neither mortality nor sexual desire is natural. That tells you a lot about the attitude toward sexuality that many people have adopted in Western culture, whether they're Christian or not.

MOYERS: At what price?

PAGELS: Well, who can put a price tag on it? But I don't think it's had a very good influence.

MOYERS: Another advantage of this notion is that guilt can be forgiven, removed, whereas helplessness continues.

PAGELS: It's just part of our nature—that's the notion.

MOYERS: But if you can accept death, you can affirm life.

PAGELS: You know, I wonder how many people today actually believe that mortality is not a natural part of the human condition. That belief doesn't work for me any more.

MOYERS: I still prefer Milton's description of Adam and Eve as the story of man's first disobedience. I don't want to believe that we are by nature corrupt. But I do find there's something about our need to disobey, and our active will that defies God, that is very endemic to being a human being.

PAGELS: Yes. That's why I said I have to take both sides. One side or the other doesn't make up anything like an adequate human psychology. Augustine was an extraordinarily sensitive psychologist. His observations of human nature are powerful and very compelling. They're based on his observations of his own psychology.

MOYERS: Has it occurred to you that so many of the Church fathers who became ascetic in their sexual preachings had lived a licentious life before their conversion, that they had been "men of the world," and then suddenly became something other?

PAGELS: Yes, some of these were the most hostile toward sexuality. But there are others—for example, one, who was a married man, who writes very nostalgically about the great freedom of the celibate from anxiety about family and all of the distress and concern over children. Many of them saw the celibate life as a life of philosophic freedom, of contemplation, of joy, of escape from the troubles of the world—not as a life of deprivation.

MOYERS: A lot of this happened after the belief passed that Christ was about to come again, the Kingdom of God was at hand. When Christians settled in for the long run, they began to think differently about human nature.

PAGELS: Yes, Jesus' preaching looked quite radical. His demands on human beings as reflected in His statements about anger, and lust—well, there is an extraordinary vision of human possibility in some of those statements. One senses a kind of urgency, a conviction that the Kingdom of God is coming, and that one has to radically transform human life. That expectation that the end of time was coming soon receded, and most people in the Christian movement reverted back to normal family life. Others, trying to maintain the challenge and excitement of those austere and powerful sayings, followed a monastic path.

MOYERS: What's interesting to me is that when we hear many Christians today appeal to traditional family values, they're really talking about the tradition espoused by the organized Church and not the teachings and sayings espoused by Christ when He was on earth. Christ said the family came after the Kingdom of God, and that your loyalty to your family was to be set aside in the service of God.

PAGELS: According to Luke, Jesus said, "Whoever does not hate his father and mother and sisters and brothers and wife and children for my sake is not worthy of me." Of course, one can choose the radical statements of Jesus or choose the modified statements. The Church has maintained a wide range of sayings.

MOYERS: Does this have any relevance for us today in our secular age?

> *Precisely at a time when many people are no longer traditionally religious, one can look at these traditions with very new eyes.*

PAGELS: The study of religion is enormously exciting, not only for people who are explicitly religious, but also for people who are not. It's an exploration of how human beings think, how cultures develop, and how societies articulate their values. Precisely at a time when many people are no longer traditionally religious, one can look at these traditions with very new eyes.

MOYERS: And you've done that. Are you going to keep doing it?

PAGELS: I don't know what would be more fascinating than this.

Maxine Singer

GENETICIST

Dr. Singer studies genetics, which many consider the most intimately human of the sciences. Her special concerns are the ethics of science—the dilemmas of choice and consequence that so often accompany scientific progress. Formerly the head of a laboratory for cancer research at the National Institutes of Health, she is now president of the Carnegie Institution, a research center in Washington, D.C.

MOYERS: For years the popular image of the scientist was either Dr. Frankenstein or Dr. Strangelove. You scientists were either creating monsters you couldn't control, or plotting to blow up the world. Do you think that image still prevails?

SINGER: It still prevails in many places. I experience it personally. People meet me casually at dinners or parties and ask what I do. When I say, "I'm a molecular biologist," they go to the far end of the room. I suppose they're puzzled by the fact that I don't look or act like Dr. Frankenstein. But they somehow are frightened and think that I must live in a world apart, without the same kind of human concerns they have.

MOYERS: Perhaps they're ashamed, as I often am, of their ignorance of science, and unable to talk to you about it. So they politely shift the conversation to somebody else who can talk about the weather or politics.

SINGER: That's certainly true, because people do apologize and then, of course, to be polite, I say, oh, don't worry about that, I don't know about whatever it is you know about. But, in fact, I've given up accepting those apologies. I'm much more forthright now. I tell them that I'm sorry for what they don't know, but it's never too late to learn.

MOYERS: What does it say to you that our society has such a negative image of scientists?

SINGER: It says that science was not an integral part of most people's upbringing and education. As they were growing up, they didn't come to understand that science is one of the grand human activities. It uses the same kind of talent and creativity as painting pictures and making sculptures. It's not really very different, except that you do it from a base of technical knowledge.

Science is not an inhuman or superhuman activity. It's something that humans invented, and it speaks to one of our great needs—to understand the world around us. In the end, it makes you wonder whether people have lost their curiosity, because that's all it is.

MOYERS: Given the negative image of scientists, why did you decide to become one?

SINGER: I'll give you the answer that, in fact, many, many scientists give when asked this question. I had one marvelous chemistry teacher in high school. She was an exciting teacher, interested in me because I was interested in what she taught, and very demanding.

MOYERS: That's not a term you hear often these days. In fact, since I called and asked you to do this interview, there was another report saying that kids coming out of high schools are increasingly scientifically illiterate.

SINGER: It would be difficult to give a good scientific education without being demanding. There's a certain amount of hard work, but the payoff is marvelous, because when you do the hard work and come to understand something about the way the world works, then the satisfaction is so enormous that it makes you willing to do more demanding work. But if the hard, intellectual work to understand is not demanded of you, then you can't have the pleasure of it either.

Let me tell you a story that goes back to the days when my now grown-up children went to junior high school. Each of them in turn came into a biology class that was taught by a superb teacher. Within two weeks of the beginning of the school year, on each of those four occasions, I began to get calls from parents of other children in the class asking whether I would join a delegation to the principal, to complain about the amount of work that this biology teacher gave. The parents thought she gave too much homework. They also didn't think biology was that important. They were shocked to learn that I wouldn't join the delegation. Now these parents were highly educated and had great expectations for their children, although none of those expectations included science. They just didn't feel that it was worth the effort that was being demanded of their children.

MOYERS: This happened not just with one child of yours?

SINGER: It happened each time, four times in a row. The parents didn't see the opportunities in being a scientist. They didn't understand the profound importance of scientific discovery and technical competence to the society in which they live. I think their response also indicated that they thought there was a free lunch out there, which there isn't. It was a very depressing experience.

MOYERS: What happens to a society when the curiosity goes, and scientists are seen as marginal at best, wasteful at worst?

SINGER: On any day, if you look at the front page, half the stories usually have a technical or scientific component in them. A society that turns its back on science has to face decay and deterioration.

There are people who romanticize, who say, "Wouldn't it be nice to go back to the lovely old days when we didn't have pollution problems?" In a way it would—but we can't. We have a much larger population on the globe.

Those days weren't so terrific either. Many, many infants died within the first week of birth. Very few people lived the nice long lives that we're living now. Very few people could visit different parts of the globe. Everybody seems to want the fruits of science, and everyone recognizes that those fruits have a cost. But the new problems will not be resolved unless we deal with them in a scientific way. We must advance new knowledge so that we have more ideas about how to deal with the continually new problems that we have.

MOYERS: When you look toward the twenty-first century, which is not that far away now, what are the scientific problems we are going to face?

SINGER: We're going to have to face population problems in our republic and all over the world. And we're going to have to face them as we always face major problems, by a combination of things, including limiting the population and dealing with some of the very difficult issues that arise when we have a large population.

MOYERS: And science is at the heart of that issue?

SINGER: Science is at the heart of how we will continue to grow enough food for all of these people. We're not doing it now. There are people starving all over the world, and the answer is scientific agriculture. A lot of the answers will come from the advances in my own field of genetics and molecular biology. We're coming to a really extraordinarily deep understanding of the way living things work, and of how to manipulate them properly, so that we can improve food production in Africa, for example.

Our environmental problems are to a very large extent derivative of population problems. We're constantly expanding the places that we need to live, so that we're tearing down forests, destroying natural wetlands and savannahs—changing the nature of our planet in order to accommodate this ever-increasing population, which is, at the same time, increasing its expectations for how it's going to live.

Transportation is another problem we must address as we spread populations out. People need to be moved around faster and yet, at the same time, without doing further destruction to the environment.

MOYERS: We think of these as political issues, and of course they are. But you're saying that there's a scientific core that has to be addressed if we're going to resolve them.

SINGER: The political decisions—to the extent that political decisions deal with reality, which they don't always do—will be made on the basis of options that are provided by scientific discoveries and the technological development of those discoveries. One of the things that stems from this is that there is more power in the scientific community than many people realize. Many people default to the scientific community.

MOYERS: What do you mean?

SINGER: They leave the options that will eventually inform the political decisions to the scientists, because people are unwilling to include science as part of their general education.

MOYERS: How do we make an informed choice if we don't know at least the basic vocabulary?

SINGER: The only way we can do it is the way every study of the last dozen years has told us. We insist that our young people learn science. We insist that teachers not turn kids off science. Getting young children interested in science is the easiest thing in the world. You go outside at night and look at the moon, and outside during the day and look at the sun, and then you ask children, "What is our relation to the moon and sun?" You take them down to the Air and Space Museum and show them what the earth looks like if you're up at the moon, which we can do now, because we've been there, and the children begin to generate the same questions that astronomers generate. Then you begin to talk to them about how you learn the answers, and they're engaged. But somewhere between the fourth and fifth grade, something happens. We lose them. We kill that creative curiosity.

There is a fear of science and scientists. It's strange to me that people don't realize that the way to deal with that fear is to learn about it. We scientists are not very fearful people. We look upon the world in a somewhat different way, but we show the same good and bad traits as everyone else. The negative things about scientists are the same as the negative things about anyone else. There's a lesson to be learned there, because if people would talk to us and learn what we're like, they would realize this, and they would then be less afraid of science. But a lot of people don't want to talk about scientific issues. They draw very firm lines.

MOYERS: Don't you think they say, "Let's let Maxine Singer handle it. Let's let the scientists do it."

SINGER: Well, they do and they don't, because eventually it comes knocking on their door. One of the very good examples of this in our society is the constant trouble we have had for forty or fifty years with the notion of evolution. Every couple of years, this becomes an issue in American schools, and we fight this battle all over again. There are people who have a very fundamental belief in the Bible as a description of the world and as essentially a scientific document, but they represent a very small percentage of the population. Yet more than fifty percent of Americans, when asked year after year, say they believe that creationism should be taught along with evolution in the schools. That's an amazing number. It tells us that over fifty percent of Americans, and that includes a lot of very highly educated Americans, are very uneasy about the notion of evolution. I think it's because they think that if we accept the theory of evolution, we somehow leave behind a lot of the premises on which our human interactions are based.

MOYERS: Some religious folks say that the work of people like Maxine Singer establishes the relationship of everything to a common ancestor, that genetics confirms evolutionary biology, and that it leads to a profoundly mechanistic view of the world, in which there is no room for God. That's part of the fear leading to their determination that creationism will be taught in the high schools.

SINGER: It is true that modern genetics has confirmed all of the ideas of evolutionary biology. A very famous geneticist said, many years ago, that there was no way to think about the natural world that made any sense except in terms of evolution. If you try to think about the living world without the concept of evolution, it would be something like teaching lawyers to be lawyers without reference to the United States Constitution. We only think about law in our country in the framework of our Constitution. Biologists can only think about the living world in the framework of evolution. And modern genetics has confirmed that. People fear the challenge of a mechanistic view of life, and that is indeed what modern genetics teaches us—a very mechanistic view of life.

MOYERS: And a mechanistic view means—

SINGER: It means that if you look at a corn plant, you want to explain how the corn plant grows, why it puts out an ear of corn that's yellow, or red, why it grows well with a certain amount of water, what you can do to make it grow better during drought—in other words, you explain the corn plant as you would a machine. We can do that in terms of the molecules that make up the corn plant.

MOYERS: You say it is mechanical, but not like the movement of a clock.

SINGER: No, it's much more flexible than that. A lot of things are changing as part and parcel of the whole system. We know that the simplest organisms on our planet are the same as we are, in terms of being what they are because of DNA molecules that are not very different from our own. We can speak of a common origin someplace at the beginning.

MOYERS: The same thing is in the yeast that is in the human being.

SINGER: In fact, you can take a human gene, and it will correct a mutation in a yeast cell.

MOYERS: And that means?

SINGER: That means that a piece of DNA from human cells, when added to the DNA of the yeast cell—the same yeast that we use to bake our bread and make our wine—can actually be therapeutic for a yeast cell that's sick because of a bad gene. What we're doing is gene therapy on yeast. We have a sick yeast cell because it has a genetic disease. And we can cure the yeast cell's genetic disease with a human gene. That tells us that we have a lot in common with the yeast cell. The same is true for all kinds of organisms. Yeast is the most dramatic example, because it's a simple one-celled organism.

MOYERS: Well, that says to the fundamentalist that what God hath wrought, Maxine Singer can put asunder. It destroys the psalmist's vision—that God has made man "a little lower than the angels."

SINGER: I don't think it destroys the psalmist's vision at all. The psalmist was talking about man, and man remains that way. Our relations with one another and with our society remain quite separate from our ability to understand how we work. Ancient people were just as curious as we were about where the stars came from, and where we came from. They made explanations in terms of what they knew, and they tied their explanations together with expectations about standards of human behavior and notions of human love. We're changing the explanations, but we're not really changing those other things. There are a couple of pieces of evidence for that. There are among scientists deeply religious people in about the same proportion as in the rest of society. There are people who adhere to the highest standards of human conduct, and there are people who are as greedy and money-grubbing as anywhere else, in spite of the fact that we look to natural explanations.

MOYERS: So science doesn't change the essential qualities of human beings, our love for justice, or our passion for greed, or our sense of fairness, or our sense of alienation?

SINGER: What it changes are the old explanations and rationalizations for the way things occurred, but it doesn't change our fundamental human problems or the way we deal with each other. What it does, fundamentally, is give us ways to deal with the difficult things that we find on the planet and ways to enhance our lives. Think of what your life would be without the marvelous ability to have terrific music in your own home. In genetics, we will have ways to deal with diseases which now confound us and cause nothing but misery. We will have ways to deal with diseases that we almost don't recognize yet, including propensities toward certain diseases. We'll be able to deal with those things, because we're beginning to understand the way we work, the way the corn that feeds us works, and the way elements that cause disease work. Remarkably, all these living things work in fundamentally the same way.

MOYERS: What are you working on right now in your research?

SINGER: I'm interested in human genetics, particularly in aspects of the structure of human DNA, what we call the human genome. "Genome" is just a collective word for all the DNA in the human cell. The whole collection of genes and other pieces of DNA that are not genes make up the human genome.

MOYERS: Would it be right to say that the gene is to the human makeup as the thread in my suit is to the suit?

SINGER: No, the best way to look at it is that a gene is like a sentence in an encyclopedia. It's a piece of information buried in the genome, the whole encyclopedia, which is a vast store of information. The gene instructs the cell how to do some one thing. All together, the trillions of cells in your body do all the things that make you who you are, and that make a corn plant what it is, and that make a yeast cell what it is.

MOYERS: So the better analogy would be perhaps that it's like a chip.

SINGER: It's a chip—but I prefer the old-fashioned analogy of a book—like an encyclopedia, or a sentence that gives you a piece of information.

MOYERS: What are you trying to explore about it?

SINGER: Well, in fact, what my colleagues and I in my lab do is not quite looking at what a gene is like. It turns out that a lot of DNA doesn't clearly have any information, at least as far as we know now. It's as though you had an encyclopedia, and on every third page there was a lot of jabberwocky. And then you turned six more pages, and you repeated exactly the same jabberwocky again—and two pages later, there it was again. It doesn't look like a gene—that is to say, it doesn't look like a meaningful sentence. I can't figure out what it is. And I'm certainly confounded by the fact that it occurs so many times. My colleagues and I are looking at a DNA segment in the human genome that occurs probably on the order of one hundred thousand times, and altogether makes up about five percent of the DNA in every cell. Why? We don't know. What is it doing? We don't know. We do know that new copies of it can be made in a human cell and put in a new place in the DNA. And we know, thanks to the work of some human geneticists at Johns Hopkins, that it can cause mutations. That was a very exciting finding in the last year for us, because it says that this piece of genomic jabberwocky can pick itself up from one place in the genome and settle down somewhere else, where it can cause a mutation—in this particular case, two instances of the disease of hemophilia. So, it's very real and very serious.

MOYERS: What is the value of finding this out?

SINGER: The value is severalfold. First of all, if we can understand what makes such a sequence move about, we will have understood the cause of a certain amount of genetic disease. We will be able to understand the role of flexibility in the DNA molecule. The analogy to the encyclopedia falls down once you realize that DNA moves itself about and changes in all of us, all the time. That's one of the things that we'll learn.

MOYERS: There's a lot of talk in this city about the human genome project, which will cost billions of dollars. What is it?

SINGER: To continue the analogy I've been using, it would be equivalent to saying that we could write out the encyclopedia for human DNA, and that we would know all of the information in a human cell. We would know how to find it, as we do when we look in an index of an encyclopedia, or when we look up something alphabetically. We would know how to turn to the gene that causes hemophilia when it's mutated. We would know how to turn to the page that says this gene is going to be important in causing a certain tumor. We would know how to look at that gene in a person, and perhaps make some guesses as to whether that person is likely to develop a certain tumor or not.

MOYERS: So if you knew that, then you could begin to think about altering the gene to prevent the disease.

SINGER: The genome project is defined very grandly. It will do a lot of things along the way. It will tell us a lot about the genomes in other species, because one of the ways we'll do the human genome project is by comparison with plants and yeast cells. One element of science is comparison. You learn a tremendous amount by comparing two things. This is like that, or this is not like that. Why is it not like that? And what can we learn?

MOYERS: But why should the public buy into this project with such vast sums of money? It will cost two or three billion dollars.

SINGER: Those sums of money are going to be spent over a long period of time. But the nice answer to your question, the grand and glorious answer, is because the public is curious about itself, as curious as we are. We scientists will do the work, but we will all share in the understanding that it gives us about ourselves and the world we live in. The public will also be interested because it is with that knowledge that we're going to be better able to deal with starvation, to learn how to grow plants in Africa that can't now be grown there. We're going to learn how to deal with certain diseases. We will improve the lot of all mankind.

MOYERS: New cures for cancer? New vaccines?

SINGER: Eventually new cures for cancer, new vaccines, and things unimaginable to us now, but which we know we will learn by doing this. We can't even describe them. The reason we know that we will discover things that we can't describe now is that this has been the history of science. We do things to learn something we can define, and we wind up knowing things we never imagined even asking about.

MOYERS: A lot of us are nervous about the whole idea of genetic engineering. We're not sure we should be fooling around with our genes.

SINGER: Why aren't you sure? What bothers you?

MOYERS: I'll show you a picture from *The Economist* that illustrates what scares people.

SINGER: Okay.

MOYERS: That's a picture of what's called a geep. A scientist at Cambridge University crossed the embryos of a goat and a sheep and got a three-legged geep. People see this and imagine a future of horrible mutilations, of something beyond human beings. That's one source of fear.

SINGER: The geep is something that someone did in order to learn whether it could be done, but it's not something that people are going to be making, except on an occasional experimental basis. And it is surely not something that will ever be done with human beings in any similar way.

MOYERS: How can you say that with such certainty?

SINGER: Because scientists are human beings, as human as those who are not scientists. They share the same values. The greatest resistance to doing any genetic engineering on human beings has come from the scientific community. There are very strong feelings within the scientific community about doing genetic engineering on human beings. And the evidence for that is the level of review and discussion within the scientific community prior to doing even very small things—nothing that comes even close to a geep. I talked before about correcting a mutation in a yeast cell. We can imagine ways of correcting human mutations, and people are trying to devise ways to do that as therapeutic devices. That's not really very different from therapies that we've used before because they're designed to correct a certain disease. But it's very different in that it will be much more precise and effective, and will be a better cure.

But even before thinking about that, there has been an extraordinary level of conversation in the scientific community as well as in gatherings of people from outside the community to come to some general notion about what we think is useful to do—what is human, and what is humane, and what is something that no one would ever do.

MOYERS: But in the end, the scientific community is not itself responsible for what happens to its discoveries. Your faith in humanity is touching. But when engineers created ovens, I don't think they expected a Christian nation in the heart of Europe to put millions of human beings to death in them.

SINGER: What you're saying is something I would agree with. If the knowledge that is gained is misused, it is not because of science or the scientist, it is because of the same old human problems that have caused evil for eons.

MOYERS: There's a will to use what we know.

> . . . whether evil uses technology that's new or technology that's old, what motivates it are human problems that have nothing to do with developments in technology.

SINGER: And whether evil uses technology that's new or technology that's old, what motivates it are human problems that have nothing to do with the developments in technology. To make technological and scientific development the scapegoat because it gives evil people new tools to do evil seems to be missing the boat. To the extent that the traditional ways of defining moral behavior have failed, the newer ways will fail, too, because human beings will remain the way they are.

MOYERS: Then what do we do about this? There must be standards for the use of that knowledge.

SINGER: Of course there should be standards. Several of my colleagues and I spent the better part of a decade in the seventies working on standards for the very earliest genetic engineering experiments at a time when our concerns were not about misuses of human gene therapy, but about the safety of the things that would be constructed. Scientists now are spending enormous amounts of time trying to inform publicly responsible individuals and groups about the nature of what we're doing so that people can figure out what the standards ought to be. But if we simply say no to everything, then we turn our backs on our abilities to solve the very real problems that we have.

MOYERS: What do you see as the dangers in genetic engineering?

SINGER: I don't actually see dangers in gene therapy for genetic diseases as long as it is carried out under the general kinds of standards that we have come to apply to medical interventions in general—that the research should go on after review by knowledgeable scientists and nonscientists; that things are done with the consent of those on whom new practices are tried; that they are done in the context of institutions which provide guidelines and monitoring of what happens in the hospital and the laboratory.

That's the way we have to do it. It's hard work. It's time-consuming. But it should help us derive the benefits that we want in so many ways, and yet limit the possible dangers.

MOYERS: One poll not long ago showed that forty percent of the people in this country said they thought it was morally wrong to alter the genetic code, but eighty percent of them went on to say that they would be willing to risk it if they thought taking that risk might prevent a disease they had themselves.

SINGER: I find those polls very puzzling. What they tell me is that people lack an understanding of the sciences. The people who say, "I just don't think it's right to meddle with these genes in this way," don't understand enough about what we're doing to be able to sort out for themselves what's right or wrong about it. In my judgment, there's nothing profoundly wrong about it. We're been fooling with genes since the beginning of time by breeding farm animals and plants for better yields. In ancient times, and even now in some cultures, mates are chosen for young people on the basis of what the family thinks the grandchildren will be like. That's breeding human beings, and that's accepted. We're just learning how to do things a little better and in a more humane way.

People used to think that disease was a punishment. Smallpox, for example, was viewed as a punishment for evil deeds that people did.

MOYERS: There was a man named John Woolman—

SINGER: Yes, a famous eighteenth-century member of the Society of Friends, a marvelous man—but he believed that smallpox came from God.

MOYERS: —to instruct humans in virtue. Woolman was also strongly opposed to slavery.

SINGER: Exactly. There are people now who believe that AIDS represents the same kind of punishment. But smallpox didn't come as a punishment to human beings, it evolved on the face of the earth with the rest of us. It evolved, in fact, in conjunction with man. It lived off man. We have killed the smallpox virus. We don't have it any more on the face of the earth.

MOYERS: I wonder, if John Woolman came back today, whether he would think that God had changed His mind.

SINGER: We are much better off for the absence of smallpox, and we have not paid any price for its absence. There are people to this day who look upon AIDS as a punishment. It's not. It's caused by a virus whose structure we can describe in such a way that we can think about it rationally and try to figure out ways to end the scourge that it has brought on our society. These are the kinds of things that come only from science.

MOYERS: I hear you, but there are common concerns out there that people keep expressing about genetic engineering. Now these concerns may come out of a great ignorance, but you hear people saying, "Will it be possible for parents to seek hormones that will produce a seven-foot basketball player so that I can raise my kid to go out there and make money as a professional athlete?"

SINGER: Yes, it is possible to do that. You can do that today without any genetic engineering of humans, because genetic engineering has made growth hormone available cheaply. We need the growth hormone to treat people who are diseased in the sense that they don't make it themselves. It's available, and it's cheap. But people are buying it to give to their children to make them good athletes. That's not a problem of the scientist who cloned the human growth hormone gene in order to help children who suffer from an absence of it and would be dwarves otherwise. The problem is the same old human problem of greedy, thoughtless parents who are using something to achieve an end that the scientists who developed it never dreamed of.

MOYERS: We're back to ethics.

SINGER: We're back to ethics, but not the ethics of scientists, except insofar as they're people like anyone else.

MOYERS: What about the concern that if we start manipulating genes for profit, we will be giving a powerful economic incentive to seeing human nature as essentially a materialistic phenomenon.

SINGER: I must tell you, straight out—I think it's bunk.

MOYERS: Don't mince your words.

SINGER: Let me put it to you this way: It is easily possible—we do it every day in the lab—to synthesize a gene out of chemicals. I can make a human growth hormone gene. There is no way to tell the difference between the gene that I have made in the laboratory and the gene I would isolate from a human cell. Why is this somehow mystical? Why are genes given a quality they don't have simply because they come out of human beings?

MOYERS: Many of us are raised with a sense of reverence for human life. We think of human beings as constituting a special, divine creation, and we're not certain about mucking around with it.

SINGER: We are special. And we are marvelous. There are many living things in the world that are marvelous. How does it diminish our sense of ourselves to understand that we are the product of a lot of molecules coming together in a marvelous way? We are not those molecules, we are all of them together.

One of the things people very often mention in this context is the uniqueness of the individual, that each one of us is marvelously different from every other one. Modern genetics has told us that this is absolutely true. Except for identical twins, no two of us have the same DNA molecules. Biology says that each of us, with our different genetic makeup, is unique. It's the same splendid notion that we came to for a lot of other reasons—and biology underscores it. Knowing how we work in no way diminishes our uniqueness. It in no way changes how we look upon people we love. The physicist, Richard Feynman, asked why poets could write about Jupiter when they thought Jupiter was like a man? What kind of poet can't write about that same Jupiter if he knows that it's a great whirling sphere of methane and ammonia? You look out at the sky, and you look at Jupiter. It brings in all of us the same wonder, the same awe about the universe. I think the astronomer has more awe and wonder because he knows what it is that is up there. His knowledge doesn't diminish his awe; it enhances it.

MOYERS: Do you think a biologist may have more awe and wonder for the human body because he or she knows what's in there?

SINGER: I know that's true. My wonder at the kinds of things that we've learned in molecular biology beats anything that anybody can tell me in grand terms about how extraordinary a human being is. How incredible it is that a few changed genes have given us this tremendous gift of language, of communication, of being able to write down our history, of having culture, of drawing pictures, of making paintings. I think that I appreciate that more, not less, because of what I know.

MOYERS: Some critics of genetic engineering say we are special as humans, but that doesn't give us the right to inflict suffering on the animals we're using for experiments. For example, right over here in Maryland, at the Agriculture Department's experimentation station, they have produced pigs that turn out to be pathetically arthritic and deformed creatures whose offspring are themselves deformed. The animal rights people say we don't have the right to do that to innocent creatures.

SINGER: It's very difficult to argue that we are special as human beings without also arguing that we ought to pay special attention to our own species. Within that special attention is the need to help those of our species who suffer from disease, starvation, and so forth. One of the best ways we have of trying to help that suffering is experimentation, learning new information about how living things work. For many of the questions we ask about living things, the only way that we have to answer them is to do a certain amount of experimentation on animals.

Now, there is no question but that work that has gone on in the past has sometimes misused animals unnecessarily. There is no question but that insufficient attention was paid to the lives and suffering of those animals. And there is no question but that we can still improve the way we deal with experimental animals. But if we were to decide that we did not want to experiment on animals at all, we would not make advances in curing our own ills, or improving our own situation. We do a lot of things nowadays with cells that people used to do with animals. And there are other ways to replace animals for certain kinds of experimentation. But there are many things that we cannot do without animals.

MOYERS: So the animal rights people are not misguided in their concern?

SINGER: The animal rights people are misguided in some of their concerns, and in the extremes to which they go. But they also have a core message which has been important. Many people within the scientific community deal with the same questions that are raised by animal rights people, but approach them in rational, thoughtful ways that are not extreme, and that allow for a balance between our need to help our own special species, and our need to pay some attention to suffering animals.

MOYERS: How would you respond to the more severe critics of genetic engineering, like Jeremy Rifkin, who say we had better be very careful what we release into the environment, because we don't know enough yet about the unintended consequences. Genetic engineering ought to be done under only the most restricted circumstances imaginable.

SINGER: Let me say first of all that Jeremy Rifkin's view of the situation is a very extreme one. Not many people take his view, although we get the impression that they do because he is given a great deal of space on television, and in newspapers and magazines.

The release of organisms, which Rifkin still speaks about, was, of course, the crux of the earliest issue, and that was first raised not by Mr. Rifkin, but by scientists, including myself, in 1973 and 1974. It was the basis of a discussion in the mid-seventies, which engaged the public, and which resulted in the development of very strict guidelines by the National Institutes of Health, guidelines which govern the way my colleagues and I do experiments.

Now, Mr. Rifkin knows that very strict guidelines were put into place and that, as a consequence of a great deal of new scientific information, and consideration by scientists, ecologists, molecular biologists, and physicians, those guidelines have been relaxed. He also knows that there are still strict guidelines in place for those experiments that have the remotest possibility of being dangerous, that there is extensive review of experiments, and that there is extensive monitoring of what goes on. He is still crying about such things even in the face of a history of responsibility on the part of scientists and the government of which we can all really be proud. And one has ultimately to wonder why he is still crying about the safety issue when it has been addressed so extensively by so many people for so long.

MOYERS: I know that many in the scientific community, people like you, have been responsible over the last years in trying to come to grips with whatever possible dangers your experiments might pose. But scientists are always coming up with difficult predicaments for society at large. Knowledge for knowledge's sake I happen to believe in; we have to follow curiosity wherever it leads. But the issues that come out of your research present us with very difficult choices. Example: What happens if businesses insist on screening prospective employees for their genetic code to see if they might be prone to certain diseases? What does this do to liability, to insurance costs, to the cost of doing business? Society has to grapple with the consequences of your research. But, as you said in the beginning of this conversation, we are an illiterate republic when it comes to scientific knowledge. How are we going to cope with the predicaments that you and your colleagues are handing us almost daily?

SINGER: I don't think that we—and now I say "we" because I am part of the public as well as being a scientist—are going to deal with these issues very effectively unless we are willing to learn something about science. Not every person needs to be a scientist. But there are some big ideas about the nature of the world that everyone ought to have as part of his baggage. People ought to know that we all get information in the form of DNA from our parents, and that our competence and our capabilities, both physical and mental, are to some extent dependent upon that. We all ought to know that if you take down a great deal of green stuff from the earth, you put less oxygen into the atmosphere. It's amazing that most people don't know that the oxygen isn't just up there for the taking, it's put there by living things called green plants. People somehow think the oxygen was there from the beginning. It wasn't.

We have to appreciate certain fundamental kinds of things if we're going to deal with these problems. And for the details, we're going to need to bring scientists into the discourse. The President's science adviser must give the President access to the best scientific information in the country, for health purposes, for environmental purposes, for defense, for weapons building—for all these things. Our success as a nation and the success of the planet as a whole depend on scientific discoveries, each of which hands us a new bag of problems. That's not very different from the way the world has always been. There's no free lunch.

. . . the success of the planet as a whole depends on scientific discoveries, each of which hands us a new bag of problems.

MOYERS: Except that we know so much more now than we did, and everything is so interconnected that every advance of knowledge creates a different kind of political and social dilemma.

SINGER: We are very ambivalent about it, aren't we? There's no question that people want the help with disease offered by genetic engineering. There's no question that people in our country will go for the latest device that improves the music they hear on their hi-fi sets. And yet there's the other side of it, the new problems that come from new knowledge. We have this ambivalence. The only way to deal with these problems is the hard way: Look at them seriously, talk about them, and evolve a way to deal with them.

MOYERS: You really do feel that your work is based on human and humane values, don't you?

SINGER: I don't think that there is much happening on our globe that's more humane and more concerned with humanity than science.

MOYERS: Do you get mad at this image of the scientist as Frankenstein and Strangelove?

SINGER: Yes, I get angry with it. It makes me angry with secondary school teachers because it makes me realize that a lot of wonderful, curious, bright young people are never going to have the privilege that I've had—to work for years without a boring day; to think of something new every day; to learn things that no one has ever known before, no matter how small it is. I myself have not learned big things in my own research. I'm not Watson or Crick or Weinberg. I learn small things.

But to learn something one day that nobody ever knew before is something that everyone should have the chance to do. To the extent we're turning off young people in our country from scientific careers—quite apart from the fact that we're turning them off from wonderful careers in terms of good incomes and the availability of great jobs—we're turning them off from the possibility of sharing in this great world of discovery that scientists now have, that explorers no longer have because we've explored every nook and cranny on the planet, and we're not yet able to go to Jupiter or Mars. And if part of what turns them off is that they think that we scientists are somehow not part of the species, it's too bad.

MOYERS: You like your work, don't you, even if it means being ostracized at a cocktail party or a dinner?

SINGER: Oh, that's a fair bargain, as far as I'm concerned. I was a graduate student in 1953, when Jim Watson and Francis Crick announced what a DNA molecule looks like. They started an incredible thirty years for biology. They allowed us to understand things about living organisms that as a graduate student I couldn't imagine. It isn't that the answers were unimaginable—the questions were unimaginable. So I've been part of an extraordinary time in biology. There hasn't been a day when I've wanted to do anything else.

Peter Drucker

MANAGEMENT PROFESSOR

Widely known as the father of modern management, Peter Drucker has advised governments and corporations throughout the world, written twenty-two books that have been translated into twenty languages, and still finds time to write a column for The Wall Street Journal. *The Claremont Graduate School in California, where he has taught management for the past seventeen years, recently named its Management Center after him. His latest book is titled* The New Realities.

MOYERS: You've written so much about leadership and management. Looking at all the men who have come and gone in the White House since you came to this country in the 1930s, what have you learned about presidential leadership?

DRUCKER: That it can be exercised in a great number of ways. FDR and Truman and Eisenhower were very different people. That's the main lesson. The second one is beware charisma, the great delusion of the century. The most charismatic leaders in history were Hitler, Stalin, and Mao. What matters is leadership. Charisma is almost always misleadership, partly because it covers up the lack of substance, partly because it creates arrogance, and partly because it creates paranoia if you're not successful.

MOYERS: Then what are the qualities of leadership that we ought to expect in a president?

DRUCKER: The ones who have been successful thought through what the job was that really had to be done instead of having a program. Lyndon Johnson, who was a great man, destroyed himself because he knew what to do when he became President. He was committed to a domestic program. So was Harry Truman, but Truman took a good look and said, "This is a situation in which nothing really counts except foreign affairs," for which he had no preparedness. He said that before he became President, he had never read the foreign news. But he organized a crash course and got the best teachers. Ike, who had no interest in domestic affairs, looked at the situation and decided it was his job to codify the New Deal, and so he focused on that.

It is the willingness to say, "What is the assignment?"—not "What do I want to do?" but "What has to be done?" It's a certain demanding of oneself and of others a very high standard, and it's a creation of trust. "You mean what you say" may be the wrong way to put it because FDR never meant what he said—but everybody always knew exactly what he meant. You knew you couldn't trust FDR personally. He was as slippery as an eel and treacherous. But you knew what he was going to accomplish, so people trusted him, not personally, but as a leader. Leaders have a goal, and the goal is not what they want to do. They start out with the question, "What is needed?" That makes them more effective. I'm dubious about all this chatter about leadership because what people really want is somebody who substitutes manner for substance.

MOYERS: Ceremony instead of accomplishment. Doesn't the real leader say, "We face some hard choices"?

DRUCKER: Yes, leadership is not personality but performance—what you accomplish and what you enable others to perform. The presidency is very largely an educational job, a value-setting and goal-setting job.

MOYERS: Even presidents who are good at leadership are often bad at management. There's a difference.

DRUCKER: No—they are bad at administration because leadership is part of management.

MOYERS: In your autobiography, you say that politics is America's only genuinely native art form. What did you mean by that?

DRUCKER: Everything else has been imported from Europe one way or another. In the colonial period, it was the only occupation that was open to an educated man who didn't want to become a preacher, whereas in Europe, politics was basically either the privilege of the higher aristocracy, or it didn't exist. Political thinking in the New World began with *The Federalist* papers. Politics is an indigenous art form cultivated primarily by lawyers. Politics is about the only way for lawyers to get a little excitement.

MOYERS: How well do you think we're being served today by our politics?

DRUCKER: I don't think the problem is our politics. The problem is that the two political "integrators" no longer integrate anyplace in the world. We are past the point at which anybody believes, as most of mankind believed for two hundred years, in salvation by society—that if you change society, you will change the human being. For two hundred years, this was the dominant creed, and it enabled the West to conquer the rest of the world. But now at the end of two hundred years of the politics of salvation, nobody believes in it any more, not even Mr. Gorbachev.

In addition, the specific American counterforce, which is a belief in integration through major interest groups, is also gone. Government is no longer the balance wheel of farmer, labor, and business. And our parties make absolutely no sense to any of the younger people because what are they talking about? So, the great task of the politician, which is to integrate diverse interests, is no longer possible. As a result of this, the body politic has splintered into single-cause interests. These tiny interest groups began with the Women's Christian Temperance Union, which imposed Prohibition with a voting strength of probably no more than seven percent. But if you were pro-Prohibition, you got their vote, and if you were even tepid, you didn't. And in almost all elections in this country, seven percent is enough of a margin to decide. Today single-cause interest groups can veto almost everything, and do.

MOYERS: But where does this leave us?

DRUCKER: It leaves us in a turbulent ad hoc situation, one in which every politician very carefully avoids having a program or a profile. At the same time, we have tremendously big tasks ahead. Some of them are not capable of being handled within traditional politics. For example, we have reached the point where armaments have become totally counterproductive worldwide, not just economically, but militarily. Nobody seems to realize that this is the longest period in the history of the world without war between major powers. Not only has no major power fought a major war since the end of World War II, but no major power has won a war. Korea was a stalemate. The French lost in Algiers and Vietnam. We certainly didn't win in Vietnam. The Russians didn't win in Afghanistan. The Chinese didn't win in Vietnam.

MOYERS: You've said that we're back to a period like that before 1700, when the soldier, no matter what his virtue, was a burden on society.

> *. . . one of the major reasons why the Japanese are ahead in civilian technology is that their engineers and scientists work on designing automobile doors, and ours work on missiles.*

DRUCKER: It's very clear that one of the major reasons why the Japanese are ahead in civilian technology is that their engineers and scientists work on designing automobile doors, and ours work on missiles.

MOYERS: So you do believe this enormous spending on armaments is harming civilian economies?

DRUCKER: There's no doubt about that. But it's also harming civilian society. There was that old saying of the French Revolution, "The army is the school of the nation." If you look at what happens in countries that are being run by the military, it's not a school you'd really want for your children, would you? What happened in Brazil or Argentina or Chile or any other place where the army took over? The army can no longer teach civil virtues, or even civil skills. And armaments have become economic liabilities. Don't get me wrong. I used to work—don't ask me for how many years—as an adviser to the Pentagon, and unilateral disarmament is the most dangerous thing we could possibly do. We are in that very critical period where you have to build up military power so that you can "build it down." That was Mr. Reagan's one real success—that he built up military strength with the right hand so that he could then get a real cut in military strength for the left hand. My one criticism is that he got chicken. When he announced that by the end of this century, all nuclear arms should be abolished, everybody said, "He's senile. He doesn't know what he's talking about." I have a suspicion he knew perfectly well what he was talking about. He knew that he needed a very big, utopian goal. He always said he admires FDR. I will never forget when Roosevelt announced that we would build thirty thousand fighter planes. I was on the task force that worked on our economic strength, and we had just reached the conclusion that we could build, at most, four thousand. We thought, "For goodness sake—he's senile!" Two years later, we built fifty thousand. I don't know whether he knew, or whether he just realized that unless you set objectives very high, you don't achieve anything at all. Mr. Reagan made a serious mistake. When everybody ridiculed him, instead of backtracking, he should have said, "Children, you are going to eat your words." We need somebody who says we have reached the point where we have to use military strength to get out of the trap that we have pushed ourselves into. Quite clearly, one of Mr. Gorbachev's main reasons for wanting to cut back armaments is that otherwise, he can never get his economy straightened out—not just because of the money, but because eighty percent of all good engineers and scientists work for the defense effort.

MOYERS: Do you see any real evidence that we are beginning to turn away from our enormous expenditures on armaments?

DRUCKER: Yes. I would say the evidence lies in the fact that when you talk to military people, you find that they are scared silly. Military technology is becoming the master. There is no strategy any more. You are totally determined by technical capacity. Secondly, there is no strategy because you can't define any aims of policy. "Scared" may be the wrong word, but they're very much bothered by the fact that every single military action since World War II has been a disaster. Wars are not winnable any more, partly because the technology is changing so fast that you cannot plan or train. There's the old saying that "war is the continuation of policy by other means." If you have to be prepared for sixty-five different military contingencies, you can't prepare.

MOYERS: Do you think we need to make this step back in order to produce the kind of economy that will carry us into the twenty-first century?

DRUCKER: I don't know whether you should call it a "step back." I think it's a step forward. The only way out is to see that there is a common interest that transcends national boundaries. For the first time, since the seventeenth century—with the exception of extreme pathologies like Germany and Italy in the twenties—we again have private armies. They are now called "terrorists." They cannot be controlled. It doesn't really matter whether Russia or the U.S. cuts back on atomic bombs. One atomic bomb in a post office box in New York City triggered by remote control would be all we need. And biological and chemical weapons are much less controllable and much more dangerous.

MOYERS: Imagine them in the hands of the drug cartel, which also has its own private army.

DRUCKER: Precisely. I think this threat is going to force governments to realize that if they don't work together to control arms, they will lose all control. The last remnant of national sovereignty, which is control of defense, is being undermined by the fact that you can make modern arms on the back of your stove.

MOYERS: Let me ask you about another group that is frightened—workers. As you've pointed out, this century has been a great one for workers in democratic countries. Their real income has increased something like twenty-fold.

DRUCKER: We are in a very funny situation, which, by the way, politicians have a terribly hard time trying to understand. Everybody thinks that American industrial production has done very badly the last fifteen years. It has actually increased steadily and at a pretty fast rate every year except 1981. It's manufacturing blue-collar employment that's going down. There has been no social group in the history of the world that has risen as fast as the blue-collar, mass-production worker—and no group that's coming down as fast. For forty years, the most rational thing to do, economically, was not to finish high school. If you dropped out in your junior year, and the priest gave you a letter to the foreman in the plant, saying, "Joe is a good boy," six months later in the steel plant or the automobile plant, you made more money than you could possibly make getting a college degree. Today that's gone. Today, the only access is through sitting on your rear end in the schools for very long years.

MOYERS: But what's in store for the average worker in this new world?

DRUCKER: You'll see a gentler transition than I expected a few years back. Partly because the average age is so high, there is a lot of early retirement, which, if we have no inflation, is reasonably well cushioned for most of the workers. The real problem is not economics, believe me. The real problem is social status.

MOYERS: What do you mean?

DRUCKER: The easy access to middle class life is gone. The other day I was in a meeting with some of my UAW friends, and we talked about this. One of the very able union men said, "My members are concerned about their recreation vehicles, and their vacation cottages in the north woods," and so on. And another fellow broke in and said, "Joe, I think that's their second worry. Their major worry is that they now see their children cannot make that kind of living becoming a worker. They now have to sit and sit and sit and get that degree in cost accounting," and I chimed in and said, "And never do an honest day's work in their life again!" And Chuck said, "That's exactly the way they feel." The honest work of yesterday has lost its social status, its social esteem.

MOYERS: I read just the other day that it now takes two incomes in a family to equal the purchasing power that one check brought in 1971.

DRUCKER: We have had inflation, and all wages have risen a little lower than inflation. But don't say "purchasing power," say "standard of living," because our expectations have risen incredibly.

MOYERS: You are one of the three foreigners whom the Japanese consider responsible for the recovery of their economy.

DRUCKER: Largely because I knew Japanese art.

MOYERS: How's that—I don't understand.

DRUCKER: Through Japanese art I got a rapport and an empathy with the Japanese people. I understood them. They made sense to me. The most important thing in communication is to hear what isn't being said. When a fellow in my first seminar said something, I could give him an answer. He asked, "How come you understand?" Well, I somehow understood them.

MOYERS: Because of your interest in art?

DRUCKER: I think so. Then I said three things to them. "First, don't do anything that doesn't fit your tradition. It won't work. What are the elements in your tradition that can be building blocks of a modern society?"

The second thing I said was, "You have to learn to treat people as a resource." Japan has the worst history of contempt for people of any society. I said, "You have to change that. From now on, people are a resource, and you have to ask not what do they cost, but what is the yield, what can they produce?"

MOYERS: And the third thing?

DRUCKER: And the third thing I said is that a business exists because the consumer is willing to pay you his money. You run a business to satisfy the consumer. That isn't marketing. That goes way beyond marketing. Also, I helped them with management structures, and technical things—but my important contributions were very simple. I told the Japanese what I'd been saying to my American clients. But there's one difference: My American clients were very happy and didn't do a darned thing. The Japanese did it.

MOYERS: Do the Japanese have better leadership than we do?

DRUCKER: No, in fact, most Japanese management is deplorable. But they don't suffer from certain of our disabilities. For example, they don't have the financial pressures on very short-term results, because the banks have no interest in company profits. That's changing very rapidly now that the Tokyo Stock Exchange has been so successful. The performance of Japanese companies is becoming nearly as short-sighted as ours for the same reasons. Secondly, they spend much more time on people than we do. Lifetime employment, where you can't fire anybody, forces top management to look at people very much more carefully than we do.

MOYERS: And constantly retrain them, too.

DRUCKER: Yes, the top people in any large Japanese company don't do any work. They sit and do two things. They relate to government and to the industry, and they watch the younger people. Here is a twenty-five-year old—by the time he's thirty-two, top management knows all about him. He can be promoted only by seniority till he's forty-five, then suddenly, overnight, the goats and the sheep are separated, and you either stay a middle manager, or you get into top management and stay till you are five hundred and five. The Japanese spend an enormous amount of time and thought on people—which a few American companies do, but not nearly enough.

The third thing is that they have the luxury of a totally protected country, whereas we have to cover the whole waterfront plus defense. It's very hard for us to concentrate. The Japanese have done very well in automobiles, in steel, in consumer electronics, in semiconductors and in microchips. They have done nothing in telecommunications so far. They're barely coming along in pharmaceuticals. In computers, they have laid an egg, because they concentrated on the big main frame, not the PC. But usually they have concentrated on a very small number of areas where markets were already established by the West, so by doing a little better what the West was already doing, they could get ahead.

MOYERS: Should we be afraid of the Japanese? Just this morning there was a big story here in Los Angeles about the Japanese now owning forty percent of downtown Los Angeles.

DRUCKER: Thank goodness, because I'd much rather *they* lose the money. In twenty years the downtown of any city will be a wasteland. But the British are buying up far more American business than the Japanese. So far, do you know who has done best?

MOYERS: Who?

DRUCKER: The Americans in Japan. We now own twenty percent of Japanese manufacturing industry. We used the high dollar of the Reagan years to buy out joint venture partners. Eight percent of all Japanese blue-collar workers work for an American employer now. So we shouldn't be afraid of the Japanese. But we should shift very fast to reciprocity, where we say to the Japanese and the Koreans, "You are no longer undeveloped countries. From now on, it's strictly reciprocal. If you let us in, we'll let you in. If you don't let us in, we won't let you in."

MOYERS: What a world! The national boundaries are no longer sufficient, are they?

DRUCKER: No, there is a transnational world economy in the financial, manufacturing, and service industries.

MOYERS: So do you look forward to the twenty-first century?

DRUCKER: I do look forward to it, but I'm exceedingly happy that I'm not twenty again. It's a very harsh world for young people. There are too many opportunities and too much pressure. Everybody has to be a success. In my time, if you were born a farmer's son, you were a farmer. If you were born a blue-collar worker's son, you were a blue-collar worker. Today, the pressure to be a success is not healthy. We are pushing young people terribly. Sometimes, when I look at my grandchildren and the kinds of choices they have at age seventeen, I think too much of a burden is being put on them. They're not allowed to experiment, to be young, or to make mistakes.

MOYERS: What advice do you give young people who are trying to get ready for the twenty-first century?

DRUCKER: Know your strength. The most important thing is to know what you're good at. Very few people know that. All of us know what we're not good at. But the reason why so few of us know what we're good at is that it comes so easy. You sweat over what's hard to do. So knowing what you're good at is the first thing.

The second thing is to know when to change. There are certain situations in which you don't stay. You don't stay in a situation which corrupts. Better to go off the diving board on your own, even if you're not sure there's water down there. And know when to quit. If you're no longer learning anything, if your work no longer challenges you, if you feel "I've only got twenty years to retirement," then get out. Accept the fact that with modern life expectancy, if you are a knowledge worker, you will have a second career. Yesterday's farmer, with all the heavy physical labor, was an old man at age forty-three. For his great-grandson, who sits behind a desk with a spreadsheet, the greatest occupational hazard is hemorrhoids. Twenty years as a market researcher for the toy company is too long. Then you begin to get the typical degenerative diseases of early middle age—the bottle, the affair with the nineteen-year-old, or the psychoanalyst's couch. Of these, the psychoanalyst's couch costs the most and takes the longest. The results are pretty much the same. But when you reach that point, change careers. You need to be repotted. You need new challenges, even if only new people.

F. Forrester Church

PASTOR

As a college student, Forrest Church was certain about a lot of things, including the fact that his father, the late Senator Frank Church of Idaho, was wrong about everything. Now, as the dynamic pastor of All Souls Unitarian Church, he confronts the ambiguities and contradictions of a ministry in the heart of New York City. He is the author of several books, including The Devil and Dr. Church *and* The Seven Deadly Virtues.

MOYERS: How would you explain religion and politics in America today to strangers who had never been here?

CHURCH: I think I'd go back to my own family. On my father's side, the first member of my family to come here was a man named Richard Church, who came to Boston in 1630, and was a founder of the First Church in Boston, where I served for a couple of years when I was finishing my doctorate. He was a Puritan who came to escape religious persecution in England. Then I'd go to the family on my mother's side and point out one of the first ancestors to go all the way West—a fellow who came from Scotland and went across the country with Brigham Young and became a Mormon bishop in Utah. And another member—my grandfather, actually—was a Quaker, as well as a judge, and he would never sit on a court case where there would be the possibility of capital punishment, because his religion would not allow him to make that sentence. I could also mention my wife's ancestors—Jews from Germany who came over here and intermarried with Catholics and Presbyterians. The whole family is a panoply of faiths, each distinctive. Each person, however, to a certain degree, is guided in his or her life and work by profound religious values. I wouldn't call this chaos, but certainly lots and lots of multiplicity.

MOYERS: A caldron.

CHURCH: Yes, but not a melting pot. Though we may disagree at times with the actions of the President or of a large part of the population, we are a profoundly moral country. We like to think of ourselves in moral terms, and our religion is instrumental in that.

There's another reason why our religion is so strong, and that is the separation of church and state. It's a paradox. We would think that because the church and state are separate, the church would be weaker. But in Europe, for instance, where the church and state are together, the church is compromised by that alliance. It loses its moral authority and its independence.

In this country, where we don't have prayer in the schools and where the state does its best to scrupulously avoid infringing upon religious rights, we let a thousand flowers bloom, and the flowers flourish as a riot of religious color and energy.

MOYERS: But the lament of the day is that we have passed from being a homogeneous country—where the ruling class was white, Protestant, and male, where prayers were said in the schools—into a religious caldron and a moral chaos, where that sense of ultimate allegiance to a Christian God has been lost.

CHURCH: What's happening here is happening all over the world. The world has gotten smaller. Go back into the nineteenth century, and you'll find an enormous variety and religious pluralism. As for moral chaos—in the 1830s and '40s a quarter of the people in this country were alcoholics. We were drinking ten times as much booze as we're doing today. If you want to talk about moral dissolution, you can go to any point in time.

What's happening now is that the world has gotten smaller, and we have a global economy. We saw that with the stock market crash. We have a global nuclear threat where a murder-suicide could take place that would include an enormous number of innocent victims. We have a global communication system, which means that we're much more familiar with the strange customs and ways of people all over the world, and they are familiar with our strange customs and ways.

One result is that people are frightened by the kaleidoscope of ideas, faiths, and ideologies. When we hardly had any commerce with the tribe across the river and knew very little about them, we were secure in our own tribal gods and deities. Now we are confronted with chaos. One way to respond to this fear is to retreat to firmer ground. It's a retrograde response to go back and say, "This is the truth. We have lost it. We must return to it." Another response is to look at all of it, throw up our hands, and become complete relativists.

MOYERS: All truths are the same.

CHURCH: All truths are the same, or there is no truth. The first response, the retreat to firmer ground, is a form of fundamentalism—

MOYERS: —My truth is the only truth.

CHURCH: My truth is the only truth. The opposite of that, which is equally untrue, is the abject relativism we see so often. I use an image of a cathedral, which I call the cathedral of the world. It has many, many windows, and we can't even get close to exploring one apse during our lifetime. But we are born in one part of the cathedral, and our parents and grandparents and neighbors teach us the ways in which to see the light shining through a given window, the one that carries the story of our people, the story of our faith. After a time, we do see the light through that window.

There are people all the way through the rest of the cathedral who are doing exactly the same thing. Some of the windows are abstract, some of them are representational. But there's one light shining through all of the many different windows.

We sometimes confuse the windows with the light. The liberal will say, "All the windows are the same." The fundamentalist will say, "The light shines only through my window." And then the fundamentalist will do one more thing: He or she will exhort his or her followers to go out and throw stones through other people's windows.

Now, of course, we have TV cameras showing people pictures of windows that they never would have seen, and it's a little bit disorienting. It's going to cause us to think in terms of new metaphors for our shared reality.

MOYERS: Between the idea that there's only one truth and I own it, and the idea that all truths are the same, is there a devout middle ground?

CHURCH: There's an ever-shifting and wonderful, ambiguous middle ground. We have to approach that middle ground with humility, knowing that we are limited and that none of us ever finally will be in possession of the Truth with a capital T. But that doesn't mean we should give up the truth with a small t.

I've been playing with an image of a great sphere in which the truth is encompassed by the sphere, but all of us are in the middle from our point of view or perspective. One goes north and says the truth is north, and another goes south and says the truth is south. We do not understand, in effect, that if it's one, it can also be the other, because while these are opposite approaches and opposite directions, it's the distance that people are traveling that is the key. So you have that absolute need for particularity, for tradition, for cultivating the old morals and values, and getting in touch with the old gods. And at the same time, with some humility, you have to recognize that you don't have the whole view, you just have one little vortex that you're following out as best you can.

MOYERS: Two contradictory images come to mind. One is a scene in the final pages of *The Name of the Rose* where William of Baskerville says that we need to save people from the passion for searching for the final truth. The other image is on the tower of the University of Texas, my alma mater, where it says, "You shall know the truth, and the truth shall make you free." Here you have Christ saying that you must find the truth, and you have the world warning that you can go after the truth with too much zeal.

CHURCH: I think what most imperils the planet and all of us are the terrorists for truth and God in every land. But as Thomas Jefferson said, it is in our deeds and not our words that our religion must be read. You cannot judge a person's faith or truth by his or her words. Shakespeare said the devil can quote scripture for his purpose.

We have to look beyond the words. The rhetoric of our time is very difficult to hear through. As it becomes more intense, there's a growing danger that people will not be able to hear, only to shout. If you give those same people weapons, they can become extremely dangerous.

MOYERS: Take one very practical issue. Take abortion. The battle of abortion involves, on the one hand, people who are called "baby killers," and on the other hand, people who are called "right-wing fanatics." Now between these two, is there a moral position to stake out?

CHURCH: These two positions, while they appear to be polar opposites, are very similar in one respect: Each bases its case upon the principle of sovereign individualism.

MOYERS: The right of the individual to do with my body what I wish, or, on the other side, the right of the fetus, the prospective human life—

CHURCH: —to be protected. Now these two positions are mirror images of one another. Even though the two sides think that they're very far apart, they're both founding their argument on this principle of sovereign individualism. When one side or the other becomes completely dominant, everything gets thrown out of balance. Think of Mexico, where the average woman in abject poverty gives birth eight times during her lifetime. Then think of the Soviet Union, where the average woman will have five abortions, and abortion is a kind of cavalier means of birth control.

What we need to do in facing this issue is to recognize that we are not all sovereign individuals. We're much more intimately related than we thought before. The new models for understanding nature, reality, and even God are pointing beyond the individual to a kind of interdependent web of being. The most striking image for that is the earth rising over the moon, blue-green and marbled with clouds.

> The new models for understanding nature, reality, and even God are pointing beyond the individual to a kind of interdependent web of being.

But the body, too, is an image of interdependence. Each of our bodies is made of cells, and each cell has the body's imprint, its individual genetic code.

Lewis Thomas, the scientist, speaks of the earth as an organism. We're not as independent or individual as it might appear. We're interdependent. We depend upon one another. And so, going back to the abortion question, one of the things that we need to do, and that we have to do with fear and trembling, is to recognize that you don't just have a choice between two individuals. You have a question about the larger, interdependent living system, of which all are a part.

You can't take away choice, because otherwise you lose your ethical autonomy. But life has got to be absolute, so you must also be pro-choice to enhance life, and you would recognize that in certain cases killing would be justified in order to enhance life. You can't make these choices easily.

MOYERS: Sometimes life must be taken in order for life to be enhanced.

CHURCH: Yes, and ironically, this argument is very similar to St. Augustine's just war argument, which has been a pillar of the Catholic Church for centuries.

MOYERS: War is wrong—

CHURCH: —but with just means and with just cause, it is sometimes necessary. So the Catholic Church has a model for war that I would also apply to the abortion issue. By the way, the just war theory doesn't work for nuclear war, because you can't have just means or just cause in a nuclear war, when murder/suicide take place. I would consider abortion to be killing, not murder.

MOYERS: You'd say that abortion is wrong, but that sometimes it is necessary to enhance the life of a woman who's been raped, or a woman who has so many children she can't support them.

CHURCH: Yes, certainly in the former case. In the latter case, if the "pro-life" people, who are really pro-birth, not pro-life, were in favor of enhancing, sustaining, and cultivating life, in nuturing it after birth, then abortion would be less an issue because you could say, "This child coming into the world will receive support, nurture, and love, and the commonweal will be enhanced." But that's not the case now. It's a question of choosing between evils. Ideally, we would have a world where abortion was not necessary, even if permitted, because the larger life that we all share would be sustained through our corporate efforts to ensure the greatest quality and the greatest good for the greatest number.

But as we are now, I will come right down between the two sides and say that abortion is killing, and in many cases it is justified.

MOYERS: You're saying that life can be served sometimes by killing.

CHURCH: I think that's right, because we're not talking about murder. Obviously, you cannot serve life by murder, which is one of the reasons, for instance, I would be opposed to capital punishment.

In an area like this, however, there will not be intelligent consistency based upon the old model. There is a Catholic notion of the seamless garment, which would say, "I am opposed to war, opposed to abortion, opposed to capital punishment." There's a kind of surface coherence in that argument, but it falls down when you begin to look at individual cases. It's impossible to have a metaphysical ethics, an absolutist ethics, in this day and age. On the other hand, one cannot have random ethics.

MOYERS: You can't pick and choose where you're going to be moral. What about the single woman of affluence who just doesn't want to have a child?

CHURCH: Ironically enough, what we've done in our laws is suggest that the single woman of affluence can have abortions, but the government won't pay for abortions for poor people. It's exactly the opposite of what it should be.

All we can do here, however, is to do everything we can to educate the individual to be responsible in his or her own actions. In this country, the state is not primarily there in order to make moral decisions for its citizens. Obviously, a person can abuse his or her freedom, and often with tragic consequences.

But once we take away choice, we take away all opportunity for moral action. And if you want to see the results of that, you can go to certain Communist countries where, perhaps not on this issue, but on many other issues, choice is taken away and invested in the government. I think the very people who are most in favor of government interference here would be the first to squeal when they saw the insidious consequences of creeping government control over the moral decision-making of American people's lives.

MOYERS: So I hear you saying that a society may be moral that allows immoral choices.

CHURCH: In this day, particularly, if we don't endure quite a bit of ambiguity, we will become rigid and potentially dangerous and tyrannical. The ambiguity here is that we never can finally know what a right decision is. The people who frighten me the most are the ones who are a hundred percent sure of what's right, and who are hellbent to enforce that on everyone. The people who frighten me almost as much are the people who are sixty percent sure they're right in any given instance, but who can't act because forty percent odds would say that they're wrong. These people are all over the country—they are basically not moral actors, they're reactors, and they're timid and unengaged.

What we need to do, as best we can, is act on our sixty percent convictions with a hundred percent determination, knowing that at least the odds are that we're right. But when we do act, we must remember, as best we can, that there's a forty percent chance we may be wrong. We're not neutralized in our action, but we're humbled by the possibility of our being wrong.

MOYERS: What do we do when we find something, like pornography, to be repugnant? I walk down Times Square and I find the public pornography repugnant to the idea of decency and life, repugnant to the role of women in our society, and repugnant to my family and me as we walk through there. Should I just tolerate that because I'm not really sure?

CHURCH: The word "tolerate" is a great word, but it's become a kind of liberal icon, and that leads to idolatry. Idolatry is worshipping of the part as opposed to the whole.

One of the meanings of the world "tolerate" is "to bear with repugnance." But there are some things so repugnant, we should not bear them. We are too tolerant as a society.

But again, where do you draw the line? I was talking with a fundamentalist talk-show host a while back on this very issue, and at the end, he was celebrating the freedom of speech in this country that would allow the two of us, with such different views, to talk together, and I applauded the country for that as well. Now, on his show, there were advertisements every three or four minutes, saying, "Send money. Stop pornography." One thing that must be said is that there is no pornography in the Soviet Union. So where do you draw the line?

MOYERS: The government can rid the society of pornography.

CHURCH: And does so in the Soviet Union. Is there a middle ground?

MOYERS: On Times Square, there's no middle ground. The pornographers have won.

CHURCH: Well, to a degree. However, one can draw the line and start making basic choices. You should make a choice saying that there can be no telephone porn because a child can get access to it. You should make a choice that there can be no lascivious material on the front of magazines where children can see it. You begin to do things short of censorship, which is the first step down the road to losing our freedoms of speech in this country. But we shouldn't be so pious in our tolerance that we can't act against any of this filth.

MOYERS: You don't think we are discriminating enough as citizens to say, "We want to rid our society of pornography, but we do not want censorship of ideas."

CHURCH: I'm frightened about that. Who is going to define pornography? We've seen it all over this country, in local ordinances and local school systems. They're defining Anne Frank as pornography, they'll soon be defining Snow White and the Seven Dwarfs as pornography.

MOYERS: But it seems to me, the test of common sense needs to be brought back into play in moral choices.

CHURCH: But common sense is still always going to be subject to the sense of the individual.

MOYERS: But we are called upon to be responsible.

CHURCH: I agree with that.

MOYERS: Anne Frank, by any definition, can't be pornography. But a video about Anne Frank being sadistically raped by her SS guards could be pornographic.

CHURCH: Now I agree with that. You're speaking common sense to me. But I'm not quite yet ready to trust the government, and particularly local governments, to make these decisions, because I have seen how arbitrary and capricious such decisions can be.

MOYERS: What if fifty-one percent of the people in the Chelsea area of New York decided to vote the pornographers out?

CHURCH: Well, that would be fine. That could be done. But what we're talking about is the right to publish. There is no law that says this stuff has to be sold. That's another issue entirely.

I just think we have to move with tremendous caution in First Amendment areas, even though my own response is very much like yours.

MOYERS: Driving over here in a cab, crossing Central Park, I looked out and saw in the midst of this beautiful day, right in the middle of the park, a destitute, homeless, almost catatonic individual. Now there flashed into my mind, "I'm going to talk to Forrester Church of All Souls Unitarian Church about moral issues. Wouldn't the moral act be for me to stop the cab, get out, walk over, and take that poor wretched human being to some shelter, to some relief, to someplace where supper can be—"

CHURCH: —the story of the Good Samaritan, of course.

MOYERS: It's the constant story in New York. You must pass many of these people.

CHURCH: Sure.

MOYERS: You must pass panhandlers coming up to you. I do, walking to work every day. What do you do?

CHURCH: Well, again, there is no perfect solution. Late in his life, Tolstoy, the great Russian novelist, was utterly born again in his own sense of illumination with Christ. The first thing he decided was to take all of his royalties, every bit of them, and to give them to the poor. Now this upset his wife and eleven children, because all of a sudden, in Christian Socialism, as he called it, Tolstoy was going to spread everything evenly. The second problem was that when Tolstoy went out and gave this money to the poor in his neighborhood, they all drank themselves into a stupor. He came back and said, "How can I act morally?" He does the right thing, he gets the wrong results.

As long as one recognizes that one can do the right thing and get the wrong results, what one does is give what money is in one's pocket walking down the street. When a person says to me, "I'm gonna use this for food," I don't say to him, "Well, be sure to use it for food." I say, "I don't care what you use it for—here's a little extra."

At the same time, we set up a soup kitchen, and we work to build additional housing, and we're lobbying for a drop-in shelter in this neighborhood, where a person could be taken to get a bath. It's one of the great problems, that these people can't get baths. But there is not going to be a quick fix on this. Some of these people are not going to want to come with you. They're not going to want to go into a shelter, for whatever reason.

MOYERS: I'll tell you what I've done, and you tell me if you think it's a moral choice. I've decided that if I am approached, I will in fact give a buck. And if they go and use it to buy wine, that's their choice.

CHURCH: Yes, that's my approach.

MOYERS: But it's a cheap way to buy grace.

CHURCH: But that's not all you do. One of the great problems, again, with liberals is that they will sit around and say, "Anytime you provide symptomatic relief to an individual or to a group of individuals, you are behaving amorally, if not immorally, because the problem's got to get bad enough that there can be a systemic revolution and a radical change that will transform society. Help to any individual is just a Band-Aid."

Well, you know, morality is a one-on-one operation. Anytime we can provide shelter, anytime we can provide a little food, even perhaps anytime we can provide enough money for a pint of wine to help somebody get through the night, that's okay, as long as we don't just do that, as long as at the same time, the members of this congregation and I get radicalized.

Our children's task force and our young adult group have been working at the Prince George Hotel in this city. Twelve to fourteen hundred children live in this welfare hotel. Now, number one, you go down there and do what you can for those children, but almost immediately, while you don't say that that's nothing, you recognize that you've got to do something more, and that the shelters are not the answer. Next year, we're starting a housing task force.

MOYERS: At the same time we're individual Christians, Jews, or whatever, we're also political creatures. We have to make this web of interdependence, as you call it, work for those who have fallen through the cracks, to create societal support, because no one of us can solve the problem of the homeless across the street from your church. Is that what you're saying?

CHURCH: Yes. If we're going to take this interdependent model seriously, we've got to move beyond solutions that are purely state solutions or individual volunteer solutions.

I was talking to a fellow from India who said, "The crime is not that you have more homelessness than we do. I'm inured to homelessness in my country—people live in the streets all the time. The crime here is that with this incredible wealth and talent, you've not been able to do anything about it."

We've certainly got the people of good heart and good mind to solve it. Government, business, and religious institutions must work in a multiplicity of cooperative endeavors to address the problems of our poor and homeless in the cities. We can do it if we can just get out of our moral superiority, if we can just quit saying that the other guy should do it because we don't have the responsibility or the ability to do it.

MOYERS: It seems to me government finds it much harder to reach down to the neighborhoods in the same way that your church can reach down to them.

CHURCH: So let's use the government in other ways to provide help and services. One of the problems is that we try to get a unified field theory on these things, and we try to get one group to do everything. You know, the Great Society did work tremendously well, it just didn't work completely. And so we swing all the way over to saying, "Government can't handle these things." No, government can handle some of it, and the people in the churches and communities and business can handle some of it. We need cooperation.

> *. . . the Great Society did work tremendously well, it just didn't work completely.*

MOYERS: You said Americans like to think of themselves as a moral society, but something's amiss there, because—

CHURCH: You know, our profound moral nature leads as spontaneously to judgmental behavior as it does to merciful and compassionate behavior.

MOYERS: What do you mean?

CHURCH: We tend to judge another's evil and to think that by virtue of having judged it vigorously that we are therefore good. "Moral" can mean not that the person is moral, but that the person is simply driven by moral concerns. That can lead to judgmental behavior.

The issue is not that the evangelist, for instance, may have sinned. The issue is that this person, who was casting so many stones and was so furiously judgmental about his fellow citizens, may fall to the same thing—and that's not just humbling for him, it's humbling for the entire message. If we're going to work together, if we're going to acknowledge this complex interdependent web of being of which we are a part, we must move from judgmental morality to compassionate, respectful, and cooperative morality.

MOYERS: In *The Seven Deadly Virtues*, you say that the devil almost always appears in drag. In what sense?

CHURCH: The devil is evil in disguise, particularly in the guise of goodness. Angels are goodness disguised, often wrapped in brown paper bags, so to speak—tremendously ordinary. One has to be particularly careful, therefore, in celebrating virtues because virtues, particularly great virtues, can veil great evil. There are terrorists for truth and God and love and faith all over the world today. If a very bright light is shining on you, you can bask in that light and think that you are illuminated by it—but often what you forget is that you're also potentially casting a very great shadow.

In this day, we're much less likely to do harm in the world, either to our loved ones or to our neighbors, because of our sins, which we're often very aware of and quite ashamed of, than we are because of our virtues.

I listened to Oliver North's testimony before the Senate Committee. He was able to justify every one of his acts according to the highest of virtues—faith, love, hope, fortitude, justice. The testimony was so powerful to the American people because rhetorically and superficially, it represented everything we admire. But for that very reason, it's the more dangerous, because the flip side, the dark side, isn't being seen. We can do tremendous evil in this world in the name of good, in the name of God.

MOYERS: There's a line in the tenth chapter of Romans that warns against zeal without understanding.

CHURCH: That's right. When a person wraps him or herself in the American flag and holds the Bible, that person is dangerous, not only to him or herself, but also to us, because we respect the American flag and the Bible, and we are likely to follow a person who is wearing the one and brandishing the other. But that person may be leading us right down the wrong road.

MOYERS: You say we are all inside traders.

CHURCH: Yes, we're all inside traders, each one of us, in his or her own way. We're sinners. I'm one liberal who doesn't have any trouble with the notion of sin. As long as we're open about sins and confess them as well and honestly as we can, and forgive other people for theirs, then we can begin to live together as sinners who are also gifted with a tremendous potential for good in this world. The Kingdom of God is within us. That preposition, *entos*, in the Greek, which we translate as "within," also means "between" and "among."

So the Commonwealth of God is within us and between us and among us, if we will just not block it. One of the ways I think we block it is with judgmental behavior and a celebration of our own virtue. We blame our enemy, whether it be our spouse, our child, our parent, or the Soviets, for being, in effect, evil, where we are good.

MOYERS: Jesus said, "If thine eye offends thee, pluck it out and cast it away."

CHURCH: But you have to act with decisiveness. Let's take a look at the body metaphor, the notion of an organic metaphor for the world, where you have one body and many members—the hands, the eyes, the ears, et cetera.

Now the interdependent notion, and the cooperative virtue notion, would say that the hand has got to respect the foot, and the foot the hand. But it doesn't say that if there's a cancer growing, you can't cut that cancer out. To whatever degree, we must be clear, hardheaded, and realistic, and take what action needs to be taken. But we must not get caught in a situation where all of the parts of the body are at war because they're not all the same.

MOYERS: It takes talent to discriminate—

CHURCH: —Yes, and again, we're going to make errors. You know, Gandhi was not nonviolent because he believed that was the road to purity. He was nonviolent because he knew that he could be wrong, and he didn't want ever to act in such a way that he did harm to another when he was wrong. There's a tremendous humility in that posture. It was not to improve his spirit or soul, it was to acknowledge his own sinfulness and to say that he was going to live in such a way that when he was wrong, he would do the least amount of violence to another.

We need to be at least as discriminating in those ways as we are when we're trying to extirpate the evil that's beyond us. We have a much greater power to cleanse and heal ourselves, and deal with our own evil, than we do to deal with another's evil. We have a much greater opportunity to cleanse and improve this country than we do to cleanse and improve the Soviet Union. But so long as we focus wholly on the other as enemy, whether it be our neighbors in this country, or our neighbors around the world, and don't attend to our own ills and evils, then we're going to be deluding ourselves, and we will be quite dangerous, both to ourselves and others.

MOYERS: I agree with you about Oliver North, but much of the country thought he was a hero. What does that say to you?

CHURCH: I think it says that we're a profoundly moral country, ironically enough, because he was speaking from what he considered to be a moral posture.

MOYERS: A holy crusade against communism.

CHURCH: He'd say those Contras were living and dying young men and women, and everyone would say, "Yes, we have to help them"—forgetting the fact that the Sandinistas were living and dying young men and women. There's a great lesson from history, by the way, which is that we must choose our enemies carefully, because we will become like them. Oliver North would have been much more comfortable in the Soviet Union, where he could have done everything in secrecy, than he was in the United States, which he was trying to protect from the Soviet Union.

MOYERS: Was there a time when you could have been Oliver North?

CHURCH: Oh, I don't know whether I could have been Oliver North, but there was a time in the late sixties when I was very sure I was right. I was on the other side of the issue from Oliver North—

MOYERS: —Anti-war, anti-Vietnam?

CHURCH: That's right. And I was so certain I was right that I was dangerous, there's no question about it. I thought my father, who was a U.S. senator at that time and was leading the battle against the war—I thought he was a corrupt member of the "pig establishment." I was so blinded by my own certitude that I saw no shadings, no nuances.

MOYERS: Did you tell him this?

CHURCH: Oh yeah—as inarticulately as only I could at that time.

MOYERS: Did your certitude estrange you from your father?

CHURCH: Of course it did.

MOYERS: Ironic. You were against the war in Vietnam. And yet, although your father was one of the first and few senators to oppose Lyndon Johnson and the war, you and your father were estranged. I would have thought you would have been soulmates.

CHURCH: I should have been. But I'm talking now in terms of people with extreme opinions. It was almost as if the light were coming through a prism—and I was perhaps on the infrared spectrum. But I looked over and said, "All the other colors are the same, it is only infrared that is true." During that period I was my own kind of fundamentalist of the left. So I certainly recognize the extent to which that kind of passion and assurance can skew one's own thinking and block one from seeing the whole light.

MOYERS: Did you think that even though your father was against the war, he was compromising too much?

CHURCH: Oh yes.

MOYERS: And you didn't like compromise?

CHURCH: Oh, absolutely, no compromise was permitted. We were shutting the university down. And because of Stanford's involvement in the war machinery, we went so far as to turn our American flag upside down. I didn't myself, but it's been a lesson to me. Some people even burned the American flag.

One of the things I've thought about more recently, as a religious liberal dealing with the new religious right, is that when we see irrational, judgmental people banging on their Bibles, we tend to conclude that there's something wrong with the Bible, to say, "The Bible is theirs, not mine." What I would like to do in this case, having learned from that experience, is to say that some of us who were more extreme in our opposition to the war had equal claim to patriotism as those who were so strongly in favor of the war. It's the same way with the Bible. I feel that it is my obligation to do everything I can to preach the good news of Jesus Christ as I understand it, which is to heal the sick and house the homeless and visit those who are in prison. That's the nature of the Gospel. As I see it, the Gospel requires us to do justice, to love mercy, and to walk humbly with our God. Those are my Scriptures now. I read them differently, but my own understanding is part of that spectrum coming through the prism of the Bible. It's part of the truth. It may not be the whole truth.

MOYERS: Did your differences over the war sever the relationship between your father and you?

CHURCH: It didn't sever our relationship because he had an enormous tolerance for my adolescence, and he also embodied my favorite principle in all theology, which is G. K. Chesterton's line that angels can fly because they take themselves so lightly.

MOYERS: He also gave you the book that Thomas Jefferson produced when he was President.

CHURCH: Yes. When Jefferson was in the White House, he put together a Bible for himself by going through the Gospels and cutting out a lot of the miracles and the parts he couldn't understand. Jefferson put together what he believed were the essential teachings of Jesus. It's not unlike what many scholars did later in the nineteenth century, when they tried to determine which of the teachings of Jesus were most likely to be original with him.

Jefferson called his book *The Life and Morals of Jesus of Nazareth*. He did it in four columns—English, French, Latin, and Greek—and had it as his bedside reading. Jaroslav Pelikan of Yale and I are going to be putting out a new edition of the Jefferson

Bible next year. It's a wonderful book. It starts out without any virgin birth, and it ends with the rolling of the stone against the tomb. For me, it was a revelation.

MOYERS: Why?

CHURCH: Because the hero died. I knew how the story was supposed to turn out, but in this, the hero died. It became a kind of touchstone for my own theology, which is not to deny death in order to live forever, but to live in such a way that our lives will prove to be worth dying for. Jesus lived in that way.

MOYERS: And Senator Church, your father, gave you this. What impact did it have on the ultimate reconciliation between you?

CHURCH: Over time, a tremendous one. I was very grateful that I had a chance to go back and campaign for him in his brief attempt at the presidency. He and I quickly became best friends again.

MOYERS: What saved you from your self-righteousness?

CHURCH: Probably my wife. Amy and I got married at that time, and she is much more level-headed about things than I, and helped to keep me from taking myself so very seriously.

MOYERS: What are your own deadly virtues?

CHURCH: Oh, probably self-deprecating humor, which everyone celebrates me for, so that I now use it as a device to gain fans rather than letting it be something that comes spinning out of me. Another deadly virtue might be my own tolerance; probably I'm far too tolerant of things that I shouldn't be, and not nearly as respectful as I should be of things and people I do just tolerate. Freedom, I think, too—I have become such a celebrant of freedom, but I don't practice what I preach nearly as often as I ought to. Reason—I think I am still crippled by a need to know more than can be known, to certify more than can be certified. I need to let myself go into the transrational realm, and enter into the mystery, and just say yes to life. If each one of us would take those things that we're most proud of, I think we could each put together a list of our seven deadly virtues.

MOYERS: And you think they are more dangerous than our sins?

CHURCH: I think so, because we're blinded to them. We don't see them, and others don't see them either. They're beautiful garments. There's no superficial ugliness about them, and therefore, it's a way in which we delude ourselves and others. Our virtues, to the extent that we celebrate them, potentially block us from bonding with others, from establishing the kind of kinship we need. We've got to move from an "I win—you lose" or "I'm right—you're wrong" approach to the world, to some kind of more dynamic interrelationship of mutual respect, of self-acceptance, and forgiveness.

MOYERS: Well, I agree with those pieties, but there is right and wrong in the world, is there not?

CHURCH: Yes.

MOYERS: Have you not seen evil in New York?

CHURCH: Oh goodness knows, there is evil, there is right, there is wrong—but there is also no way, finally, except in the most egregious instances, to instantaneously differentiate between right and wrong. We have to move with tremendous humility and caution in these areas, because throughout history, most of the evil has been done by people who were absolutely sure they were right. Almost all of the massive evil has been perpetrated by people who were cocksure that they were right, so sure that they never stopped to analyze the consequences of their actions. And furthermore, they were so sure they were right, and they were so eloquent in their assuredness, that they gained tremendous followings: great crowds, who bathed in the reflected glory of the virtuous leader. So while yes, there is a need to act as strongly and vigorously as one can against the little and the great evils, one shouldn't assume that evil always comes dressed as evil. It doesn't.

MOYERS: What does this mean for the individual life of a single person? For example, when does charity become a deadly virtue?

CHURCH: Charity can become a deadly virtue when one wholly gives him or herself up to another. We see this in marital relationships. Often a woman will subjugate herself. In every way, she will be kind to her husband and children, and ultimately, she will be diminished, used, and not respected. Charity begins at home in one respect only, and that is, when Jesus said to love your neighbor as yourself. If you hate yourself, you can't really love your neighbor.

MOYERS: What are the danger signs? When do you know that virtue carried to excess is becoming a time bomb that's about to go off?

CHURCH: Oh, I suppose when you get to a point where you are absolutely sure that you are better than somebody else, and therefore, that the ends justify the means. There's always a slipover from deadly virtue to an ends-justify-the-means ethic or approach to action. Oliver North was able to justify what he did because he was so sure his ends were right. But the means themselves may be destructive. Once we start rationalizing and cutting corners, we'd better watch out, because we may be fooling ourselves and others with the nobility of our goals. We may end up trading arms for hostages, we may end up dealing with drug dealers to protect ourselves from communism. In any one of those cases, if you take a look at the goal, it could be said to be noble. But the means themselves not only destroy the integrity of the action, but in many ways make the action much more evil than the enemy that we're seeking to destroy.

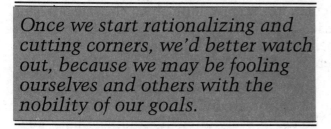

Once we start rationalizing and cutting corners, we'd better watch out, because we may be fooling ourselves and others with the nobility of our goals.

MOYERS: Isn't it possible that liberals in particular can become too accepting of other agendas and just say, in effect, that all value systems are valid? How do you keep yourself from falling into that trap?

CHURCH: Whenever I'm with liberals, I preach against our deadly virtues—tolerance, for example. But when I'm speaking to a group of people for whom those are not their deadly virtues, I'll do whatever I can to alert them to their own.

Lord Acton said that every institution—and I would say, every individual, too—is finally destroyed by an excess of its own first principle. So each of us has to be wary and mindful of our own first principles wherever we're sure we're right. Now this doesn't mean that we can't act. Obviously I, as a liberal religious leader, am far more concerned in my own community about the kind of smug, judgmental, supercilious, arrogant postures of my own people, who yet have nothing to show for their own faith and pieties because they don't ever roll up their sleeves and do anything. They just talk about the President, as if having a couple of drinks and putting the President down will solve all the world's problems.

What makes me so proud of my own church, however, is that people act, they go out and work. They know that they're not saving the world. If they thought they were, they'd probably become as dangerous as any other group. But when they've gone out and worked and come back, then they begin to say, "What more can we do?"

MOYERS: Do you have anything in common with Jerry Falwell?

CHURCH: Oh, I don't know. I've not met Jerry Falwell. He strikes me as being a tremendously good-hearted and sincere man with whom I profoundly disagree. I would love to have an evening with him. Someone once asked me whether I'd rather spend an evening with Albert Schweitzer or Jerry Falwell, and I said, "Well, I guess I'd rather spend it with Jerry Falwell, because I'd probably learn more."

MOYERS: What has been Falwell's influence on America?

CHURCH: Oh, those things only history can judge. The new religious right wreaked quite a bit of havoc, but in doing that, it exposed a fanatical flank that has led the common sense of the American people to be probably less vulnerable to that kind of religious bigotry for the next ten to twenty years. Those people who are the most responsible leaders are becoming broader in their own faith and actions.

There's a natural corrective here. They have probably performed a useful function in reminding us of the importance of putting our faith into action and of witnessing to our values. They learned that, by the way, from the actions of the religious left, in the Civil Rights movement and the Vietnam War protests. They remind those of us in the center—although I'm probably to the left of the center—they remind us that it is our obligation to put our faith into action, to witness to our faith and to the world, and to try to make the world a better place. Clearly, we're going to have to live and work together because we're brothers and sisters.

MOYERS: Yes, but we each are particular. It's hard to think about that ideal when you think of the Amish, who find their identity in their separation, or the Sephardic Jews, who find their own identity in being apart, or the fundamentalists, who find their identity in being separate and different.

CHURCH: It's a great luxury to find one's identity in separation, but it's one we can't afford any longer. The world is too small. We are living cheek by jowl with one another in this world, with neighbors who are of every different color and faith and stripe. Now what do you do with someone who's different from you if you can't retreat to an enclave and protect yourself from them? If you believe that the difference is critical and must be acted on, you try either to convert that person, or to destroy that person—or, perhaps, to ignore that person, to the extent that it's possible for you to do so. Now those three positions aren't really acceptable, because the present day calls for something much more like dynamic pluralism and mutual respect. Yet, at the same time, we must look for some common ground, which I would call the commonweal, because in many of our faiths, there is a basic ethical center that could be stood upon and from which we could work together. We can certainly work together in this country to help fight homelessness and hunger, as Jesus said we should. There's no reason in the world we can't do that. We have to put aside for a time—and perhaps for all time—theological differences when they're as acute as they are, because Jerry Falwell's not going to convince me, and I'm confident I'm not going to convince him.

MOYERS: What's the role of the President in this debate? If the President asked you to write a short note telling him what he should think and do about this issue, what would you say?

CHURCH: It may seem like a non sequitur, but I think what I would say is that there has been a shift in the nature of the world. Of course, every generation has said this—Adam and Eve, leaving the Garden of Eden—

MOYERS: —an age of transition—

CHURCH: —in an age of transition, exactly! But with the global communications, the global nuclear threat, and the global economy, the world has become more one world. It used to be that our security was enhanced by other people's insecurity and that we would build up advantages that would protect us. That goes back to the beginning of time, two little tribes battling with one another. But today, our security is diminished by others' insecurity and enhanced by others' security. That takes a really great conceptual leap to imagine. The Soviet Union will be much less dangerous to us if it is strong than if it is weak because its power in its weakness is sufficient to destroy the entire world.

> *The Soviet Union will be much less dangerous to us if it is strong than if it is weak because its power in its weakness is sufficient to destroy the entire world.*

Also, when you think of what's going on at the other side of the world, we can't just push aside our relationships with others, and build our bunker up, because in this day chaos on the other side of the world is like a great tidal wave that can come all the way over the world and crash down on our own shores. The greatest danger is that as we try to protect ourselves, we make ourselves vulnerable. If we try to protect ourselves in Nicaragua, we make ourselves vulnerable to drugs. So much of what's gone on has this paradox in it. We're apparently acting in our own self-interest by acting against another person's or country's self-interest, but in this day, the individual paradigm or model is inadequate. Our self-interest, at some meta-level, is their self-interest, and theirs is ours. It's going to take an enormous amount of rethinking and retraining, but unless we can begin to see our interrelationships and interdependencies, we won't survive.

MOYERS: Hearing you talk about a new reality reminds me of a paragraph in your book, which I'll read:

> Much of the time, we remain spectators in the great contests. Yet every once in a while, even the most passive among us is cast into the interpretive task. A loved one dies, a marriage collapses, we're given three months to live. Something awakens us, knocking us off our pins, hurling us headlong into a confrontation with reality.

What was the something that happened to Forrester Church that brought you into a confrontation with reality?

CHURCH: Well, it's been a lot of little deaths. I have not had the privilege of a life-changing failure, but my life isn't over yet, so I probably still have that to look forward to. But my own definition of religion is that it's our human response to the dual reality of being alive and having to die. The great privilege of my decade of ministry here in New York is that I've been invited into people's lives at their times of greatest pain as well as greatest joy—and often, most poignantly, at times of death.

When another person is dying, or a loved one has died, it's like a blast of fresh air that blows all the dust off your own desk, and makes all of your own petty grievances and pride and anger and bitterness and envy meaningless. You remember that this is basically the bond, this mortar of mortality that binds us fast to one another. Ultimately, the same sun is going to set over each of our horizons.

MOYERS: And therefore?

CHURCH: And therefore—we are one.

Derek Walcott

POET

NANCY CRAMPTON

Derek Walcott was born a British subject on the Caribbean island of St. Lucia and studied English in school almost as a second language. In the language of great poets and literature, he also discovered the tongue of political mastery—a culture imposed by white foreigners. This contradiction he confronts in both his poetry and his life. His books include Another Life *and* Collected Poems, 1948–1984.

MOYERS: What happens to a culture when its people lose the distinctions of language, when the richness and diversity of language disappear under conformity?

WALCOTT: Without being melodramatic—it dies. It doesn't collapse, but it withers, because the final resort of any intelligence is utterly clear, precise, and honest utterance. A culture also collapses if its words are interchangeable. We all know militaristic euphemisms for destruction. "Taking out" someone is not quite the same thing as "take-out" Chinese food—but if we can accept a language that says "taking out" does not mean death or annihilation, if we accept that as a conventional public metaphor, something happens to morality and to the ethic contained in the word as well.

But we look for the development of languages not in public life or in the media, but in literature. Someone looking at this country is always struck by the analysis of the conscience of the republic which reveals itself in the poets of America. For example, it stayed in Robert Lowell's work continually—the concern for the republic, not on a level of nationalism or jingoism, but as an embodiment of a known thing, a referential thing.

MOYERS: A moral center.

WALCOTT: Something a little more anguished than that. If you're stuck on a moral center, what you want to do is to give lectures and to be ethical and to give sermons—the evangelical equivalent of poetry. As a republic gets older, it gets more challenges to its integrity. In the best American poets, I see a quiet anger and determination that that is not the way things should be, and that I am responsible.

A general criticism I've heard made by European writers about America is that the American writer does not engage himself. The European writer expects the American writer to engage himself or herself on the level of the European writer, in other words, to talk about the particular problem which is relevant to the Eastern European writer—direct repression, barbed wire, police, and so on.

It doesn't exist here, but the American writer must be even more conscientious because it does not exist here, because there's no real need to say that there is any threat. But the threat to the republic because of the threat to the integrity of the mind is a continual theme in the best American language.

MOYERS: Plato banished the poet from his republic—why?

WALCOTT: He was smart. Poets are always making waves. The ideal republic can't tolerate poets. It isn't that they mutter and criticize, it is that the poet does not accept a situation called "the perfect condition of man." In a Communist regime, they say, "What are you complaining about? You're not different from anyone else. You have roads, you have medicine, you have housing—what more do you want?" That's the idea of the state. Everything is working, so who are you to complain? Poets chafe at the arrogance of the idea of an ideal republic because the ideal republic, obviously, would have to be Communist Russia, or a totally functioning, democratized America. Then why should anyone complain? The poet doesn't complain only on the level of sociology. The poet points out the discontent that lies at the heart of man—and how can that be redeemed? It's not redeemed by better medicine, better roads, and better housing.

MOYERS: So what is the "perfection" the poet is seeking?

WALCOTT: That's the point. He does not seek perfection. The poet is saying, there is no such perfection.

MOYERS: Either materialistically or spiritually.

WALCOTT: That's why Plato said, "Get out of here. You guys would spoil things if there were a republic."

MOYERS: But is the worse fate to be banished or to be ignored? We Americans ignore our poets.

WALCOTT: Well, it would be interesting to know how many people actually attended the theater in Sophocles' time—whether they could fill a Broadway house, for instance. I think you've given me an example of the self-flagellating American conscience that says we should do more. Now if one took the average university town, for instance, and thought of the number of people who are in schools or colleges who are writing verse, which is a great occupation for any culture, it's a much happier-looking scene than one says.

MOYERS: Do you find a variety of voices out there? Are poets speaking in their own distinct meter, with their own distinct message and style?

WALCOTT: Yes. It happens regionally. If you are on the Pacific Coast, there is a kind of poetry that comes from there, and in the Midwest there is another kind. Any true poetry is rooted in the parochial, and the sense of place is there.

MOYERS: You once said that the poet is an obsessed person. What's the obsession?

WALCOTT: The obsession is the impossibility of utterly clear utterance. Dante would have been dissatisfied with the *Divina Comedia*. The condition of a writer is a condition of very agonized humility. The masterpieces of the world were never masterpieces to their authors. The writer knows in creating the work that it is not going to be the vision that he had. The poet has divine discontent.

MOYERS: I often envy you poets because you name things. You tell us what things are in language that we can apprehend. That's a moral choice, isn't it? And that's what makes looking for that right word a moral act.

WALCOTT: Yes, it's an enormous responsibility because the responsibility is also to the history of the word. It's not simply getting the right word. The word has a history.

MOYERS: Do you sometimes feel the chaos of so many voices from the past clamoring in your ear?

WALCOTT: No, for a young poet it's exciting to have all these echoes. Critics tend to say, "Oh, you're writing like Dylan Thomas," or, "Oh, you're writing like everybody." Well, actually, the young poet wants to write like everybody.

MOYERS: When you are creating a poem, what are you trying to do?

WALCOTT: Well, I hope this doesn't sound like too simple an answer—you're just trying to find out what the next word is. If you know what you are going to write when you're writing a poem, it's going to be average. Creating a poem is a continual process of recreating your ignorance, in the sense of not knowing what's coming next. A lot of poets historically have described a kind of trance. It's not like a Vedic trance where your eyes cross, and you float. It's a process not of knowing, but of unknowing, of learning again. The next word or phrase that's written has to feel as if it's being written for the first time, that you are discovering the meaning of the word as you put it down. That's the ideal luck of writing a poem.

> *Creating a poem is a continual process of recreating your ignorance, in the sense of not knowing what's coming next.*

MOYERS: Luck?

WALCOTT: You have to connect the practice of writing verse with the sublime accident of poetry. It happens only if the verse is practiced as a craft. You cannot get a phenomenon. There is no such thing as a "prodigy poet."

MOYERS: Unlike a prodigy musician—where the music just comes through him.

WALCOTT: Or even perhaps in painters, and certainly in performers. But not poetry because the language is part of experience. Even Rimbaud, who finished writing at nineteen, had behind him the history of French literature. He was a prodigious reader. That practice of the craft is what induces the sublime accident. But the craft has to be practiced.

MOYERS: Were you a prodigious reader when you were a boy?

WALCOTT: I was lucky, in a sense, that I came from a poor country. Poor countries can't afford trash or mediocrity. Either they have the classics in the library, or they have the comic books. So where I grew up, the access was directly to great writers.

At a very early age I read Dickens and Shakespeare, and because I was taught well, I read them with a lot of delight, not as exercises and not as punishment. People hesitate to give the young books that they can't understand. But the voracious appetite of the young imagination is going to read everything. I used to read Dickens and not understand the whole book. But it used to be a challenge to finish the book because you can say I just read a novel by Dickens. You can go around doing that in yourself.

I hate to sound critical of this country, but everything in America is done in stages. There's a lot of phasing of a career—you start off by doing this, then you become that, then this can happen if you behave yourself and do this. Now that's not true of a lot of talent. I'm not contradicting myself about the need for apprenticeship. I'm just saying that we perhaps are a little too cautious in this country in thinking that the young can't understand a *Moby Dick* or a *War and Peace.*

MOYERS: Do you think the young should be urged to read poetry alone, or is poetry, as Maya Angelou once said to me, "music written for the human ear"?

WALCOTT: I sometimes make my students learn things by heart. They get a great joy in reciting and keeping their private anthology of poems that I have provided for them to remember. The act of memory is a preservation of the language. Sometimes I ask the class to recite a poem. At first you get hesitancy, because in this sort of culture you never part your mouth, whereas in certain other cultures you open your mouth and deliver.

MOYERS: When you are creating a poem, and one word is guiding you to another or creating the energy from which the next word follows, is there a technique you're also dealing with? Are you conscious of that as a skill, in the same way that a carpenter is conscious of the hammer and the plane?

WALCOTT: If you're planing a piece of board, you know that it has an edge and that you can only go as far as the edge of where you are planing. In a sense, as you are writing a poem, you are aware of a coming margin. Metrically, it's going to terminate at some point. So between then and the end of the margin there is a very ecstatic panic. The joy of the construction of a poem lies in the ecstasy of keeping the discipline of the poem. If you amplify these "ethics" of the aesthetics of poetry to the ethics of a society, you see that the responsibility of keeping order—not in some Nixonian sense of "law and order," but in the idea of a created order—is essential to civilization.

MOYERS: Is that what you meant once when you said the poet is trying to "create an order out of chaos"? What's the nature of the chaos?

WALCOTT: The chaos is in the confusion and ambiguity and lies that words can bring. Words by their nature are lies. They're not true until they become what they call themselves. A lamp is not a lamp until it is properly named for what it is. So far, the camera is the finest instrument we have for the representations of reality. But the camera cannot do metaphor—the camera can only do simile. The camera can only do one frame next to another. In other words, you can cut from a lily to a girl, and you're saying this girl has the freshness of a lily. That's one frame juxtaposed to another frame. What you cannot do, in film, is to make the girl alone be there, and the lily alone be there, and to create a metaphor out of that single object. Simile is a secondary condition of metaphor: This is like that. Metaphor is: This *is* that. The two things become one. Whatever people may say about poetry not surviving a media assault, there could never be an instrument that can create a metaphor.

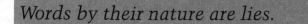

Words by their nature are lies.

MOYERS: The camera does our work for us—it shows us the image, and we accept it for what we see. The poem requires work from us—it requires us to recreate the image in our minds.

WALCOTT: The reader of poetry, as he progresses with the poem, is making the poem along with the poet and is sharing in the creation of the instant of the poem.

The onlooker does not share in the creation of an image but is the recipient of the image.

MOYERS: Television does something to us, but the poem does something with us.

In several of your poems and in at least one of your plays, the story of *Robinson Crusoe* keeps coming up. What is compelling to you about the story of Crusoe?

WALCOTT: A lot of writers are attracted to it in the twentieth century, particularly because Crusoe in relation to Friday is emblematic of Christianizing cannibals and converting people from savagery—that's the dramatic aspect of it. The more involved aspect of it is: How does Crusoe feel? What does he become, isolated from his country and his language? Who is this man who only has himself to perpetuate? What does Friday do for him?

Now another question to ask is what does Friday do for Crusoe? What appears to be Friday's subservience is not a surrender, it is a sharing. Third World writers aren't interested in the dependency of Friday; they are interested in the extension of the idea—"What does a colony do for an empire?" rather than "What does an empire do for a colony?"

MOYERS: We know what empires have done *to* colonies.

WALCOTT: Yes. One of the things that America has to face is the reality that it *is* an empire. It's very difficult for Americans to accept that.

MOYERS: We don't think of ourselves as an empire.

WALCOTT: Our hesitancy to describe this empire as an empire is admirable in some sense because the average democratic citizen says, "I don't want to be an empire." But the inevitability of history has made America an empire, and therefore the responsibility of empire does rest on America's shoulders. Now how could you be a democratic empire? You could have such a thing as a democratic empire, provided the empire realizes that, culturally and spiritually, it could be enriched by other countries. America could be enriched by Nicaragua. Those outer provinces could fertilize and recreate the idea of the republic. That's what I mean by saying that Friday is Nicaragua and Robinson Crusoe is America.

The black man doesn't exist as a problem in the Caribbean. One doesn't get up in the Caribbean saying, "Oh my God, I'm a problem." But if you get up here in this country, you say, "Oh, I'm part of a problem called the black man in America." If Crusoe looks on Friday as a problem, he's going to do a lot of welfare things—you know, give him a hat and so forth. It's the attitude, I think, that one is talking about.

MOYERS: But English words are put in the mouth of Friday. That seems to me the stereotypical image.

WALCOTT: The best poetry in *The Tempest*, apart from Prospero's speech at the end, is spoken by the native Caliban. This is where the greatness of Shakespeare lies. Shakespeare doesn't make Caliban talk like Tarzan or some ape—he gives him the most musical language. Caliban says, "You taught me language, and my profit on't / Is I know how to curse." But he doesn't only curse. He says beautiful things like "Be not afeared; the isle is full of noises." That's his speech. The really great writer is beyond prejudice—but not hatred. Dante was a hater. Prejudice was too little an emotion for Dante. Prejudice is an inferior form of thinking.

MOYERS: So you're saying that because America is an empire, its goods and ideas spread around the globe. If we're smart and open, we'll bring a lot back.

WALCOTT: The other countries of the world know that America is an empire and see how hostile so much of its foreign policy is and how stubborn it can be. But there's another America, which they come to as immigrants, and which they still believe in very firmly. It isn't hard for them to accept the power of America, but when they see an America that pretends not to have power, they get very baffled at the hypocrisy.

I consider myself to have been brought up in a colonial situation that was benign. Someone may say, "How can you talk like that when the background of that is slavery and exploitation?" In my personal experience, I never went through any punishment as a colonial. As a matter of fact, the opposite happened. Politically, I did not feel myself different from a British schoolboy. I was sharing, even more intently, the same education of Latin and classics and feeling completely free because the police in the Caribbean were not armed. The first time I saw armed police was when I went to Martinique, which is a French colony. They were white policemen, and I said, "Is this French law?" It was a shock to me. I was not used to that idea of the law. What I felt as a colonial boy was that I was part of Britain—one seventh of the world. The language that I spoke was a language shared by Shakespeare. I couldn't have an aesthetic hostility to the language of that country—and that's more important in a way than the history. History is looked at by most people—except poets—as a succession of events. But because poetry has no temporality, it does not work in that kind of sequential time. It not only forgives, it absorbs a lot of things, so although the historical experience of slavery is not a very nourishing idea, it is a dramatic idea, and it can certainly be exploited in many ways, either from the oppressor's guilt or from the victim's anger.

It may appear that the Caribbean experience of slavery would be the same as the American experience of slavery. But when I pass the ghettos of 125th Street, I'm appalled at the condition of this colony existing within an empire. Why should America be concerned about Nicaragua when you have 125th Street? Nobody lives like that in Nicaragua. These things seem contradictory to people looking on from the outside. America's hesitancy about taking responsibility is part of the whole problem.

MOYERS: Someone said in a review of one of your books of poetry that miscegenation, a mixture of things, is the key to the modern world—mixed descent, mixed race, mixed English. Do you think that's an apt description?

WALCOTT: The word "miscegenation," if I get it right, means there's something wrong genetically. It's an inhuman concept that any two people of different races are committing miscegenation by joining. Miscegenation is not an idea that we would have in the Caribbean. Anybody could marry anybody. A black and white couple would strike you, but it's not offensive. It's not like something is wrong there. If the critic had said hybridization or Creolization, yes, because in the one city of Port-of-Spain every culture is represented. The day-to-day experience of that has become so habitual that nobody makes distinctions, nobody says, "Oh, this is Chinese." So there's no concept of miscegenation. People can say, "Oh well, Africa has lost its identity because it's all mixed up with China. And China has lost its identity." But what is the identity? The identity is in the criss-crossing of those various cultures within one very compact city. Port-of-Spain is one of the most interesting cities in the world. Someone might ask, "Where's the culture of Port-of-Spain?" The culture of Port-of-Spain lies in the people of Port-of-Spain. It is inevitable that if all these various strains of Asian, African, and Mediterranean people are circulating, something is bound to ferment that is very, very fertile.

MOYERS: Your own story is often held up as a metaphor. You come from African, Dutch, and English descent. You move back and forth between Port-of-Spain in Trinidad and the United States. It's been said that you are from everywhere and nowhere, and you live nowhere and everywhere. Do you sometimes feel that you've become that metaphor and that you belong nowhere?

WALCOTT: No, I know exactly where I want to be and that's in St. Lucia. If there's an idea of dislocation, it's when I identify myself with the rootlessness of the Caribbean people—the reality of discontent about trying to make a living in the Caribbean and the fact that people have to emmigrate. The immigrant dream is inviolable about America, inviolable. What should happen is that the black man's dream there should be equally inviolable. It is not. That's what one feels is unfulfilled.

MOYERS: Is the black man's dream different from the American dream?

WALCOTT: It is made to be different by forces that want to keep him in his place and by limits that are set on his endeavors.

MOYERS: Is racism an attitude or a social structure?

WALCOTT: I came across a shocking passage in Melville the other day about the whiteness of the whale where it is taken for granted that the white race is superior to any of its dusky brothers. It's very hard to read that in Melville. Do you stop and say, "Well, that's racist"? I don't like to use the word "racist" because it's too simple to say racist, and there are deeper things than racism. This is supposed to be a great mind—how could it have such a petty or presumed judgment about the rest of the world or other races? When you say "the dusky tribes," then you reduce Melville to the worst aspect of Kipling and, therefore, he immediately becomes an inferior writer. This is a kind of laziness in a great mind. Now you can also place it and say, "Oh well, he's writing in the nineteenth century." But Shakespeare wasn't writing in the twentieth century either, right?

MOYERS: If blacks from the rest of the world know that here there are two dreams, the American dream and the black man's dream, and the black man's dream is not allowed to become the American dream, why do they keep coming? What draws them to this place of such stark contradiction?

> There's no other country in the history of the world that people want to go to so much in their hearts. . . .

WALCOTT: People come because America is an ideal. There's no other country in the history of the world that people want to go to so much in their hearts, not because of the money, but because of what the ideal says: Everybody is created equal.

MOYERS: They still believe that in places like Port-of-Spain?

WALCOTT: It's tougher to believe it because of your foreign policy, but they still believe it.

MOYERS: Our foreign policy?

WALCOTT: Which is adolescent, immature, irresponsible, impulsive, doesn't listen, and doesn't understand that Latin America is not one country but a complicated minicontinent with all of its own problems. The English language is so authoritative it doesn't listen to Spanish, for instance, or French. There's an inherent superiority in English that says any other language is really not up to it. Most empires have that. But if you have a democratic approach to speech, you don't really listen to other people's languages because you think you're speaking the proper way. If you hear Spanish, you think immediately of saying, "Well, it's an inferior people. They don't really talk English." And so one calls them "Spics," which comes from language. You call a man a Spic because he can't "spic" English. This is an attitude to language: If I am speaking the superior language, and if you want to accommodate yourself, you'd better learn my language.

MOYERS: And yet you say that we speak a democratic language. One doesn't think of anything democratic assuming this superiority.

WALCOTT: Here the man who gets up and says, "We're not gonna take any nonsense" does not speak in the pitch of a dictator, nor does he speak with the polysyllables of a dictator. He speaks with the monosyllables of American averageness. But he's still carrying the same force. So that again is a contradiction. The real language that should be up there on the podium should be a language that contains the polysyllables of power. But it is shielded by the mediocrity of monosyllables that makes it interchangeable. We should be able to characterize a candidate by the vehemence of his rhetoric, not by the accommodations of his rhetoric. That vehemence would have polysyllabic power. It would not be, "I want to do my best for this country" because that says nothing.

MOYERS: What would he be saying?

WALCOTT: "Let's get rid of the Sandinistas" or "Let's get rid of the Contras." A dictator speaks like that. A King speaks like that. But the American candidate can't speak like that because, first of all, that has to be shielded by a kind of universal monosyllabic talk that everybody is supposed to understand, and that appears bland, neutral, and laidback. But the real language back of that is a polysyllabic vehemence. So if Hitler gets up and says, "We are going to exterminate our enemies," these are polysyllabic words. If you're a Nazi, you say, "Heil, Hitler." If you're not, you say, "This man is crazy." But at least what he's doing is talking the truth about how he feels, so you can make a judgment. Here the language is so uniform that everybody seems to be talking the truth. Let's just take Nicaragua, for example.

MOYERS: Ronald Reagan obviously didn't like Nicaragua. He wanted to get rid of the Sandinistas.

WALCOTT: But he didn't say it in that language. He said it in a language that is interchangeable with a McDonald's ad. If at the moments when America appears to be villainous to its allies or its enemies, if its villainy were couched in a language that was equivalent to the passion of the vehemence, it would be more clearly understood. What is bewildering is the fact that the language is ironed out into a uniformity that says nothing on either side.

MOYERS: Maybe English has lost its power.

WALCOTT: No, as I said, it does not lose vehemence in great journalism in this country. That does not happen to the poets in this country. There is a language that can be vehement. The poetry of Ginsberg is very vehement in terms of its abuse of people who he thinks are corrupting the American vision. The prose of Mailer is vehement in terms of its anger, and so on. I'm not saying that the American language is lost and doesn't mean anything any more.

MOYERS: But why has it become in politics such a deceptive and bland language?

WALCOTT: It's a matter of attitude. It's a matter of the empire not growing up. Think of the Victorian rhetoricians. Prime Minister Disraeli spoke like Macauley wrote.

MOYERS: I hear a contradiction in what you're saying about empire. You talked a moment ago about how benign the British Empire was. And yet you have written about and are even now talking about the leprosy of empire. Isn't that a contradiction there?

WALCOTT: No, I was talking about my own experiences. I wasn't aware of anything. That doesn't prevent me from seeing the poverty and knowing that there's an historical guilt at the back of what I saw. Then I suppose as I grew older, the historical responsibility increased in terms of my becoming an older poet.

MOYERS: But historically the leprosy of empires meant that for the whites there was the gain of power, dominance, and wealth, and for the blacks in the Caribbean, poverty, shacks, disease, and death. What's your perception of how Americans see the Caribbean?

WALCOTT: I think they see about ten yards of sand and a margarita. They take a break from the empire's problems and spend fourteen days.

MOYERS: Advertising has fashioned the image of Americans toward the West Indies—the sensuous sunshine, the beaches, the lush palms, the lime-green sea, the innocent souls—Adam in paradise, almost. I sometimes wonder if advertising isn't the modern poetry that has captured the imagination of the average person more so than the poetry of Derek Walcott or any other poet writing.

WALCOTT: Every country sells itself. Greece sells itself. And Shakespeare's a tourist attraction now. So I'm not actually against advertising; I'm against the monotony of advertising about the Caribbean. It's so predictable that you can't tell one island from the other. Somebody leaps out of the water, and it's St. Croix. Leap out of the same water, and it's Trinidad. It's a way of looking.

MOYERS: Do you realize how much you are the language you speak? I've never met you until just now, and yet I see you now in person as I discovered you in the poems. You *are* the language you speak.

WALCOTT: It takes you all your life to write the way you speak without faking it. It's very hard for a poet to hear his own voice without affectation. I couldn't read my poems with a British accent or an American accent. You know, there's an inner thing that makes me speak the way I would write—totally, not just in terms of vocabulary. So if I moved from talking to you now and read something aloud that I wrote, I perhaps would just slide into my own voice. That is what a poet spends his life trying to do.

> It takes you all your life to write the way you speak without faking it.

John Lukacs

HISTORIAN

ALEX GOTFRYD

John Lukacs, an early refugee from communism, fled his home in Hungary in 1946 to come to the United States, where he is a professor of history at Chestnut Hill College in Philadelphia. In The Passing of the Modern Age *and* Outgrowing Democracy, *he explores the destiny and progress of postwar America. His most recent work,* Budapest 1900, *is a portrait of his native city at the turn of the century.*

MOYERS: What brought you to America in 1946?

LUKACS: That's simple. I came shortly before the communization of Hungary. I was very young, but I had no illusions. I thought I knew what was coming. Also, I knew English, and I had some contacts with the American military mission in Hungary. I had a chance to have a priority visa to anywhere in the West. I thought I'd come to America.

MOYERS: What struck you most about America when you arrived?

LUKACS: Let me recall a positive thing and a negative thing. The positive thing was that America was backward. America was like Europe used to be long ago. There was very little government; there was very little police. Philadelphia, where I have elected to live, was a nineteenth-century city in many ways. People let you alone, sometimes to the extent that they were regrettably uninterested in what you were doing. This was, in a way, like a remnant of the old, liberal, nineteenth-century world. That was the positive thing, which far outweighs the negative.

MOYERS: And the negative?

LUKACS: The negative thing was that I was very young, and that I had been a fairly voracious reader. Long before I came to America, I had read a lot about America. When I got here, I found that there were not too many things that were unexpected. This has much to do with the fact that the first nine months I lived in New York. New York was exactly the way I had expected it to be. When you travel, when you go to one country or another, you expect it to be a certain way, and then find that it's different from what you expected. But New York was not.

MOYERS: Did you find America and New York hospitable?

LUKACS: Not at that time, because then a lot of people were accustomed to refugees from Nazism, and I was an early refugee from communism. At that time, many people, especially intellectuals, didn't understand that. Also I was very outspoken, unmannerly, and presumptuous. This wasn't very good, but no great harm was done.

MOYERS: How were you outspoken and presumptuous?

LUKACS: I said, "You're all wrong, the Russians are a great danger, and you really have to do something. You don't understand what's going on." I was twenty-four years old. I said to influential people (although very seldom did I meet influential people), "You're wrong, communism is finished, communism is dead, but it's the Russian armies who matter, you have to do something, you have to engage yourself in Europe."

And of course, with every reason, this set people back. I may have been right, but if I was right, I was right for the wrong reason, and I rubbed people wrong, so this added to my loneliness. But I didn't suffer much.

MOYERS: Did it take you long to become an American?

LUKACS: I do not know whether I am an American. I'm an American citizen. I identify myself with very many things in this country. Where we are talking now— these are my roots in this country. But I still cannot easily use the first-person plural. I find it difficult to say "we."

MOYERS: Why is that? America is full of immigrants like you.

LUKACS: I know. It has to do with my old-fashioned, reactionary sentiments.

MOYERS: Reactionary? You're not a reactionary.

LUKACS: Oh yes, I'm a reactionary rather than a conservative.

MOYERS: What's your definition of a reactionary?

LUKACS: A reactionary is somebody who thinks the clock has to be put back sometimes.

MOYERS: And a conservative?

LUKACS: A conservative doesn't think that. An American conservative now is more enamored with progress than liberals and progressives were two generations ago.

MOYERS: What kind of progress?

LUKACS: This is a very important question because I think that the great task before all of us and our children, not only in the United States, but throughout most of the world, is to rethink the meaning of "progress." Most people think of progress as man's increasing mastery of things. But we have arrived at the point at which man himself becomes a thing. What this world needs is not growth as much as stability. We have to conserve much of the world. We have to conserve much of the past.

MOYERS: If you looked at the definition, you'd find that the traditional meaning of progress is moving toward a goal and constantly improving ourselves as we go there. Are you saying we have to change that idea about progress?

LUKACS: But we're not improving ourselves. Progress now means constantly changing the world outside us without really improving ourselves or our minds. The progressive mind denies the existence of sin, of frailty, of the limitations of human nature. These are very life-giving doctrines because the knowledge of our limitations enriches the human mind.

MOYERS: But the dominant idea of the modern age is the liberal idea that human beings can change the world, that we have mastery over our destiny.

LUKACS: What is taught in our schools and universities all over the world is that we don't have control of our destiny, that we are programmed by genes or hormones or psychology or society or environment. We are more and more destitute of the sense of free will. This is part of technological development and the mind-set of an age at its very end. It is not life-giving. It is really a very despairing view of human nature and of its capacities.

MOYERS: Does it strike you as a paradox that the conservatives now in power grew out of a movement which in the twenties and thirties held tradition to be the enemy of progress?

LUKACS: Yes, but they don't know it. Conservatives now are just extreme progressives. They really are not interested in conserving the country or in conserving old liberties. They are interested in making the world, or actually making the universe, safe for democracy—their brand of democracy. They are interested in development, in Star Wars, computers, high technology. They say they're against big government, but they're very much in favor of big government including the extreme application of the American military presence all around the world. One of the more intelligent women among them, Mrs. Schlafly, said, "God gave America the atom bomb." What's so conservative about that? Not even Coolidge and Hoover were traditionalist conservatives. But in the 1920s, because of the American experience, and the luck, fate, and optimism of this country, Coolidge and Hoover had an excuse to be progressives and not to think historically. The present public people in this country don't have that excuse.

MOYERS: What did it say to you when Ronald Reagan put Calvin Coolidge's picture on the wall?

LUKACS: He should not have put Calvin Coolidge's picture on the wall; he should have put Louis B. Mayer's picture on the wall. It's not only because it was through Hollywood that Ronald Reagan became what he was, but also because what happened in Hollywood in the 1920s changed American life much more profoundly than whatever Coolidge did or did not do.

MOYERS: But it was Coolidge who said that buying, selling, and investing are the moving impulses of our life, that Americans must be stimulated to new wants in all directions.

LUKACS: Yes, this is very telling, because this is not a conservative statement. He does not say, go on and save; he says, consume more. He says, we not only have to consume production, we have to produce consumption. Yet to produce consumption is under no circumstance conservative.

Before the October 1987 stock exchange crisis, my friend Bill Buckley had an editorial in his magazine where he said that some people are worried that the American savings rate has become the lowest among all the advanced countries in the world. He said, "Don't worry about that—it doesn't matter." Now, how can you call this a conservative attitude?

MOYERS: You once said that patriots, especially true conservatives, should be suspicious of ideology. But the Reagan Administration was a very ideological administration.

LUKACS: Very much so. To be a conservative, properly speaking, one should be the very opposite of an idealogue. A conservative is profoundly aware of the sinful essence of human nature, including that of his own country and of its people. Patriotism is essentially defensive. Nationalism is aggressive. Our conservatives are

438 AMERICAN VALUES IN THE NEW GLOBAL SOCIETY

nationalists, not patriots. They believe that it is the destiny and the fate of the United States to extend its interests and to impose its values and standards over vast portions of the world.

MOYERS: When you arrived here in 1946, it was the liberals who were the interventionists, who believed that America had within its power the capacity to make the world over. You're saying that now it's not the liberals but the conservatives who have that ideological sense of mission.

LUKACS: In a way. It was a little more complex than this, because in 1946 the liberals did not want to challenge the Soviet Union. Liberals still believed in another abstraction, that of a world government, getting along with the Soviet Union. They were internationalists but very abstract ones. Now it is the conservatives who are internationalists.

MOYERS: What's wrong with that?

LUKACS: Every nation has a particular destiny that is circumscribed by its history, by its geography, by its interests. This is not a cruelly realistic view. It involves a certain amount of humility, or at least a lack of presumption. As John Quincy Adams said, "We are friends of liberty all over the world, but we are not in search of monsters to destroy."

MOYERS: The conservatives would say the monster we're trying to destroy is the "evil empire," the forces of communism which drove you out of Hungary.

LUKACS: That is true. I may have changed my ideas on this, but not my basic principles. I did not believe even then that the United States should destroy the Soviet Union. I believed that the United States should resist the Soviet Union and somehow correct that very unnatural division of Europe that still exists today, and that, among other things, left my native country on the other side of the Iron Curtain. I believed—but only for a very short time—that the hope for Hungary was a toughening of the American attitude toward the Soviet Union. But very soon after that I realized that the United States will not do anything drastic to correct the division of Europe. So the hope for my native country lay in a betterment of Soviet-American relations, because a worsening would only lead to rhetoric. Also, now that I've lived in this country for forty-two years and have an American wife and American children, my interests in the history of this country have grown, and I look at the world not simply through Hungarian eyes.

MOYERS: You've written that at the end of an era, people lose faith in their ability to reform institutions and change things. Is that happening?

LUKACS: Unfortunately, that's happening in this country on many levels, because a lot of people experience the bureaucratic organization of everyday life—not only of their government, but of their private institutions, their universities, their corporations, their industries, their cities—which is such that it takes immense effort to reform it.

We have reached the stage of bureaucracy where, for example, a letter from your grandmother is not only as much of a historical document as a speech by a President, but it is more authentic, because she wrote it herself. We have presidential speeches, memoranda, and state papers that were not written, not dictated, and sometimes not even seen or signed by a President or by a corporation executive or by a Secretary of Defense. Bureaucracy in this country is a new phenomenon. Today a vast majority of our occupations in this country are bureaucratic. Bureaucracy may not be quite the right word for it, because this is different from the old czarist bureaucracy or the

Roman bureaucracy or the Chinese bureaucracy, where a very small number of bureaucrats, of clerics, of scribes, had an immense power over people. Tocqueville has said that something new is going to come about. In one of his chapters, he predicts something like the welfare state, and then he says, "I don't have the right word for it."

MOYERS: Well, just as fish live in an ocean they cannot name, it seems to me we live in a bureaucracy we cannot identify, which sets certain limits to what each of us can do.

LUKACS: What you say is applicable to the bureaucracies in the past, too. But what's different is that today we have bureaucratic sets of mind. In the little township where I live, I happen to be the chairman of the planning commission. I'm not a bureaucrat. I elected to get involved in politics twenty years ago because of my own vested interests, because the place where I lived was threatened by a big development. The township is very heavily Republican. All of our officials are Republicans; all of them are against big government. But many of them find it very easy and very natural to live with big government, with more and more regulations. In the 1970s, the population of the township grew less than ten percent—but the number of our employees has doubled. The regulations and zoning ordinances we have now are four times as voluminous as they were ten years ago.

MOYERS: But isn't this the consequence of our choices? There are enough of you here in this small little village that if you don't develop some orderly procedure, you'll be stepping on each other's toes and putting your elbows in each other's faces. Isn't what you call the bureaucratic state of mind the consequence of all the free wills being exercised?

LUKACS: No, because this happened at a time when the population had hardly grown. Look, President Reagan said he was against big government, but his staff in the White House was ten times larger than the staff of Franklin Roosevelt at the peak of World War II. In many universities, the enrollment has dropped or remained stationary, and the faculty has not increased, but the administrative offices are twice, three times what they were twenty years ago.

MOYERS: Why? What's at work?

LUKACS: It has something to do with the change in our economy. The vast majority of our people now are employed in no production at all, but in administration and services. The service-sector economy has grown, and the administrative sector of the economy even more so. This is true of many other countries, but it's something relatively new for the United States. When I came here, the United States was a simpler country, and to some extent, a cruder country, a more direct country. It was easier to do some things. There was less bureaucracy in this country than in Europe. There is now in this country as much bureaucracy as there is in Western Europe.

MOYERS: I was going to ask you, what have been the significant changes you've seen in America since you arrived in 1946? I assume you would say one would be the growth of bureaucracy.

LUKACS: Yes. Another change is the growth of a kind of skepticism. Forty years ago, about 1948, I met a Philadelphia lawyer. "Philadelphia lawyer" used to be a term, which is almost extinct now, referring to a particular kind of lawyer, someone at the top of the American legal profession. This lawyer told me that when he paid his income taxes, he took the very minimal deductions or no deductions at all because he knew what he owed his country and his government. This impressed me very much. There was no one in Europe who would have done this. But I also had a sad feeling that this was not going to last. And I'm sure there is no such lawyer in America now. The bureaucratic encumberments on everyday life do leave a sediment, a mark, on people's minds. It's not that people become corrupt—but that they become tired and skeptical.

> The bureaucratic encumberments on everyday life do leave a sediment, a mark, on people's minds.

As we fight mass developments in our township, we have less cooperation now from people whose very interests are involved. Fewer are willing to come to the township meetings, to sign petitions, to do this and that. There are people still willing to do this, of course, and far more than you would find in Europe. It's wonderful how public opinion *can* influence and change things here. But the people who are responsive are seldom the young ones.

MOYERS: Bureaucracies do not summon us to citizenship the way democracy should, so we don't take ourselves seriously, historically.

LUKACS: Precisely. There's a kind of tiredness, a kind of apathy about the system. It's irrelevant whether the system is General Electric, the Pentagon, or the business where you work. It's very odd that this happens, this apathy, which is not yet overwhelming, because the good thing about this country is that in many fields it's unpredictable. People occasionally do take their destiny in their hands. This is good because destiny is not fate. Fate is preordained; destiny is not. But it is more rare than it was in the past. And it's very odd that this should happen at a time when the United States has won the Cold War.

MOYERS: We've won the Cold War?

LUKACS: If you consider the Cold War as the contest between communism, as represented by the Soviet Union, and what people call capitalism, as represented by the United States, there's no question that what the United States seems to represent in the world is far more widespread than what the Russians represent. In this sense, the United States has won the Cold War. But as some great moralist wrote, it takes greater character to carry off good fortune than bad. What are we going to do with it?

MOYERS: You think we are not certain?

LUKACS: We're not certain about it. The splendid thing about a certain kind of American provinciality is that many Americans don't think about this as a great triumph. And that's good. It's much better than when Richard Nixon said that we are number one. That's a very vulgar statement.

MOYERS: Why?

LUKACS: Because when somebody has to say that he's number one, it means that he's not sure of himself. When somebody really knows that he's on the top, whether it's his nation, his profession, his ability, his breeding, or his manners, he does not feel compelled to assert this.

MOYERS: Do you buy into the current argument that America's power is on the decline? If we have just won the Cold War, if capitalism has, in fact, triumphed over communism, our power isn't in decline, is it?

LUKACS: Our prestige is not in decline. Our power is probably in decline. There were two peaks of American power in the twentieth century. Almost everybody regards 1945, the end of the Second World War, as the pinnacle of American power. I am sometimes inclined to think that 1918 was the pinnacle of American power, because in 1918 this country did not have to share the victory with Russia. In 1945 this country had to share the victory with Russia, so some division of Europe was inevitable. But 1945 and 1918 *were* pinnacles of our power. If you look at figures and materials, of course, we have more bombs, we have more missiles, we have more rockets than we had then. But that really does not matter.

MOYERS: The gross national product is larger today than when you came in 1946. In many ways you could say we are stronger today than we were then.

LUKACS: The gross national product is a gross figure. It's an accounting figure, a statistical construction. I think it is much less meaningful than the economists think and probably to a great extent even meaningless.

MOYERS: So we have won the Cold War in the sense that nobody is choosing communism today, and a lot of people are trying to pursue capitalism?

LUKACS: Yes. Even if it's not old-fashioned capitalism, it is the perception of a social and economic order that the United States represents. This is very important because ideas don't exist in the abstract. They have to be incarnated by human beings. In this respect capitalism did not win the Cold War, the United States did. The Second World War involved Nazism or Fascism, but essentially it was Germany. That had to be defeated. Germany incarnated a very strong and in many ways evil historical force, and that historical force had to be defeated on the battlefield. The United States incarnates a lot of ideas about capitalism and free economy that very often do not quite correspond to what is really going on here. But in the short run, no matter. The United States rather than Russia is imitated all over the world, including Teheran.

MOYERS: It's quite a paradox if in fact we've won the Cold War and at the same time are becoming a more ossified, more paralyzed, bureaucratic society.

LUKACS: Of course. But then there is the question of prestige. Prestige is something more profound than image. It is something real, like old-fashioned credit in business. A person who has a reputation will withstand a loss of material power much easier than somebody who doesn't have it. The prestige of the United States exists at all levels. Some of them are very mundane and very shallow, but they still exist, and this perception governs the imagination of very large masses of the world. But such things do not last forever. If at a future time people realize that there are many things in America that are much less free than they had thought, and that don't work as well as they had thought, there will occur an erosion of prestige irrespective of what the material and military power of the United States is at that given point. When that happens, it will be dangerous, because it's much more difficult to recover prestige than it is to recover power. This is as true in the life of individuals as it is in the life of nations.

MOYERS: Do you think our prestige at the moment is at a peak?

LUKACS: No, although it's still very considerable. But we have to do something with it. By this I do not mean to propagandize it. Many things have to be done to reform the functioning of American institutions, the quality of American culture, the actual results of the immense amount of money and trust we pour into education.

MOYERS: You've said that you don't believe Americans are being well served at the moment by their educational or informational bureaucracies.

LUKACS: The trust in education is perhaps the basic American superstition. It goes back to the Puritans. The idea that you can educate people, and not only teach them but improve them, is a belief that is much more widespread and has much deeper roots here than in many European countries. But that idea can be exaggerated and misused by an educational and informational bureaucracy that in the late twentieth century has begun to go contrary to all American tradition. American tradition, to a great extent, depended on an overestimation of the intelligence of the people. This sometimes may be wrong, but not as wrong as to proceed from an underestimation of their intelligence. By now our educational, informational, and entertainment bureaucracies proceed from a fairly cynical underestimation of the intelligence of the common people. Many of our schools are only custodial institutions. We have reached the point where perhaps thirty-five percent of the population spends twenty years in schools, going on to college, and we cannot be sure that they know how to read and write.

MOYERS: What is the evidence that our bureaucracies—the educational bureaucracy, the entertainment bureaucracy, the information bureaucracy—take a cynical view of the intelligence of the common person?

LUKACS: The evidence is all around us. The reason for this cynicism is not some kind of conspiracy or evil. It is laziness. The bureaucratic mind is lazy. It thinks in categories. It wants to follow definitions. It seeks the easy way out. Some people believe that large numbers of us are just too stupid to be able to think. But the problem in a modern mass society, and perhaps a problem since Adam and Eve, is not the inability to think. It's the unwillingness to think. Most people are unwilling to think about certain things, they're unwilling to exercise their minds, and they're unwilling to ask questions.

MOYERS: So should we begin to think differently about thinking itself?

LUKACS: Yes, we have reached a stage in the evolution of consciousness when we have to begin thinking about thinking itself. Not about its motives, the subconscious, the unconscious, psychology and psychologizing—which are often lamentable results of the growing internalization of the mind. We have to think about the conscious level, not the unconscious level. There is a very mundane illustration. In forty-one years of teaching in this country, I may have taught about six thousand students. I don't think that among these six thousand I have ever met more than one tenth of one percent who were really stupid. But I have met many who wanted to be stupid, that is, who did not want to study, who were lazy. This was a question of their will, not of how their minds were wired. Obviously there were some people who found it easier to memorize, learn, and connect than others. But that was a very small fraction. There were many more students who really wanted the easy way out. They could have gotten B's or A's if they had studied, but they didn't want to.

We have public figures like that, too. I have nothing against Gerald Ford. I think he's a decent man. So far as I know he was the first President of the United States who was a graduate of Yale Law School—and his press secretary said he never read a book. It's not because he did not know how to read a book. This was not the result of stupidity. There is such a thing in this world as a kind of willful ignorance.

MOYERS: So how would one apply this idea of thinking about thinking to the problems of democracy at the moment?

LUKACS: We have to face the mental mirror, as an individual or as a nation. We have to ask ourselves: "Why do I think this? Why do I want to think this and not that? Why do I choose this and not that?" We have to be honest. This involves a kind of self-knowledge which is not a question of quantity but of quality. Quality can never be calculated by a computer. Quality too involves a certain amount of courage. The only way you can break a bad habit is by not deceiving yourself and by being conscious about this. The moment you rely on the subconscious, when you say, "I am this way because I have this complex, I have that complex, and so forth," that's an easy way out. You are relieving yourself of your own responsibility. This is as true of a person as it is of a community. Every person, every nation has to reach a certain level of conscious self-knowledge.

> *Every person, every nation has to reach a certain level of conscious self-knowledge.*

MOYERS: I hear you saying that this conscious self-knowledge is the way to attack the problem of bureaucracy, to attack the problem of a nation that no longer has a sense of itself or of its destiny.

LUKACS: The nation with a sense of itself and a sense of destiny may sometimes have an exaggerated sense of itself. That may not be unhealthy. But there comes a point when the slogans, the rhetoric, and the sincere beliefs of this destiny do not correspond either to external reality or to internal reality. The discrepancy between what people believe and what they think they believe is much more complicated than the discrepancy between what people think and how they act. The latter is normal human failure: the spirit is willing, but the flesh is weak. But the confusion of spirit when somebody ascribes to himself, or when a nation ascribes to itself, certain spiritual qualities that either do not exist or are contradicted by other beliefs, leads to self-deception. Self-deception is very dangerous. Moreover, if we deceive ourselves, we also deceive others.

MOYERS: It intrigues me to hear a self-described reactionary old-worlder express a greater faith in democracy than a lot of people who call themselves democrats—because what you're saying is that the common man and woman are far more capable of thought, analysis, and self-willed direction than he and she are given credit for today.

LUKACS: Yes, I have come to believe that, not because of the institutions of this country, but because of what I've experienced in the character of so many Americans in different walks of life. I believe Edmund Burke, who *really* was a conservative, when he said, "The people must never be regarded as incurable."

MOYERS: But they have a harder and harder time knowing who's in charge, who's accountable, who's responsible.

LUKACS: The process through which decisions are made has become very, very slow and very, very cumbrous. This goes against the accepted belief that we live in a revolutionary age, when young people are told in commencement speeches that they will find it difficult to adjust to a world where things change so rapidly.

This is not true. All essential things in our age develop extremely slowly. The movement of ideas is very slow because ideas have become institutionalized. It is much more difficult to change the course of an institution or the giant American ship of state than it was in the past.

This may sound very abstract, but let me illustrate it with another example. Forty-three years ago a world order emerged in which Europe was divided between two great powers, the United States and the Soviet Union. We are now in 1988. This world situation hasn't especially changed. But look what happened forty years after the First World War. The world looked entirely different. Entire empires had disappeared.

The same thing was true forty years after the previous great world war, the Napoleonic Wars. Now things are changing, but very, very slowly.

MOYERS: It's not all bad. After the First World War came a Second World War. So far we've managed to avoid a conflagration since the end of the last great war.

LUKACS: Yes, that's not all to the bad; but there are other things that *are* bad. The intellectual categories of the 1980s, as they are taught in our schools and our universities, are not very different from what they were fifty or sixty years ago. Darwin, Einstein, Marx, Picasso, Stravinsky—these principal figures for the twentieth century are still greatly debated and discussed and are the subject of innumerable disquisitions in the Western world in 1988. They were the same people that were discussed in 1928. Now, if you look at the main ideas, figures, and trends of thought in the so-called staid Victorian century, in 1828 and sixty years later in 1888, you get a totally different list.

On the surface we have different bestsellers, different designers, different rock bands, and things move very, very rapidly. But on the second level, things move agonizingly slowly. They move so slowly that people cannot see some very important changes that do happen on this lower level, but that don't happen on the surface.

MOYERS: If the President before his inaugural speech called you and said, "Dr. Lukacs, I don't want to talk to the American people in my inauguration just about the obvious problems, I want to talk to them about the invisible reality that's going to catch up to us before we know it—what is that invisible reality we're going to have to deal with?" How would you answer?

LUKACS: Allow me to be frivolous. I would say, try to find an astrologer.

MOYERS: But what is at work shaping our future society right now?

LUKACS: I cannot say, because I'm an historian, not a prophet. But I can give you one example of the great mutations of American consciousness that goes contrary to what almost everybody else believes, and yet there's evidence for it. When I said we have to rethink the idea of progress, I was not giving you a recondite conception of an intellectual. Many of my neighbors understand this. They want to protect us against the destruction that goes under the name of progress and development. They are concerned with the environment. They want to ensure a certain permanence of residence: They want to have a certain kind of solidity and stability in their everyday lives. These are not revolutionary ideas. Many people on all social levels act on these ideas. You see, I believe that Darwin was all wrong. The only evolution is the evolution of consciousness; and the material evolution of the world is a consequence of this. To put it another way, mind precedes matter, and is not only morally, but practically, more important than matter. It is on this level of consciousness that there are some very evident changes in America.

> The only evolution is the evolution of consciousness; and the material evolution of the world is a consequence of this.

For example, in American schools, students today are taught less history than before. The standards of history teaching have vastly deteriorated. The actual ignorance of some young people about recent history is appalling. At the same time, the American people are much more history-minded than they were a hundred years ago. In this country today, there are three times as many local historical societies than there were thirty years ago. When the first Centennial took place here in Philadelphia in 1876, except for a few plaster busts, there was no interest in history at all. There was interest in progress, machinery, technology. But the Bicentennial in 1976 was consumed by history—on a junk level very often, but history nonetheless. There is an appetite for history in this country and for a sense of the past that is very often satisfied with junk food, but never mind—the appetite exists.

And now comes my profound illustration, which to me means very much because history consists of words because we think in words. Sixty years ago in this country the word "modern" was a very good word. In 1925, in England, a "modern" woman was a fast woman. In America a "modern" girl was an all-American girl. At the same time, in the 1920s, "old-fashioned" was a more pejorative word in America than in England. "Old-fashioned" meant fussy, stuffy, fuddy-duddy, Victorian. An "old-fashioned" boy was a sissy boy. Today the word "modern" has lost its shine completely, and the word "old-fashioned" is a positive word, an appealing word. Today, if you ask somebody—"Where would you like to live, in a modern house or an old-fashioned house? Where would you like to go for dinner, to a modern restaurant or an old-fashioned restaurant? Whom would you want your little sister to marry, somebody from a modern family or from an old-fashioned family?"—I would say ninety-eight of one hundred people would choose the old-fashioned. This amounts to a mutation of consciousness. This is more than just mere nostalgia. It means that people are beginning to recognize that the past is real, that the past is connected to the present, that the past is solid. It means that the American consciousness is beginning to include a historical element and not merely the so-called progressive element, which very often was an escape from history.

MOYERS: So this new idea of progress we must strive for is not progress as defined merely by material possessions and fortune.

LUKACS: The new idea involves not so much the difference between material and spiritual progress as an understanding of the limitations of what is still called growth, production, progress, advancement, development. A lot of these words have become very fuzzy on their edges. They are losing their meaning, or their meaning has become corrupted.

MOYERS: If you are right, it is a profound change in the American psychology, because for two hundred years this has been the country of the future. It is always the future that beckons, the green light out on the horizon drawing us toward that ever-expanding frontier. Now you're saying that the past must be part of that future.

LUKACS: Yes, to a great extent. That does not mean that people are turning away from the future in fear, though many people are. For the first time in the history of mankind, we have an invention, the atom bomb, that the vast majority of people wish hadn't been invented. But it is not only a question of fear or of middle age or of worry about the future. It is part of what I was talking about earlier—self-knowledge. Self-knowledge means not only "know thyself," but "know thy past."

MOYERS: Being a reactionary, as you say, and looking backward, favoring the past—does this mean the future has no appeal to you, no purpose to you?

LUKACS: No, it probably has something to do with the other human condition that if you're too much afraid of death, you won't enjoy life. About the future—as I said, I'm not a prophet, I'm a historian. There are two things that occur to me. One of them is what a great moralist once said, that things are never as bad or as good as they seem. The second thing is that the knowledge of the past, while a very important thing, can be very badly misused, like all kinds of knowledge. Knowledge, as you know, is a question of quality, not of quantity. A very bad intellectual habit of the twentieth century is to constantly look at the past of people and draw illegitimate conclusions from it. Much of modern biography, philosophy, and psychology consists of attributing motives to people, to their subconscious, and so forth. Now, there's something wrong about this. In Anglo-Saxon law, as Dr. Johnson said, intentions must be judged from acts.

There's a difference between motives and purposes. Motives are the push of the past. Something in the past has happened with our hormones, with our genes, with education. There are complexes that push us. We really know very little about this, and it's very wrong to psychologize about it.

But purposes are something different. We can know something about our purposes, and we can judge the purposes of people because purposes are usually expressed in word or action. Purposes are the mysterious pull of the future that really makes human life function. Human life, in many, many ways, is the desire for more life. When this desire fades or dies, we die. This is one area where we have to do a fair amount of rethinking. We have to think less about motives and more about purposes.

MOYERS: What about national purposes? Can a nation of two hundred and sixty million individuals, cantankerous and idiosyncratic—can a nation have purpose?

LUKACS: In an odd and mysterious way, it can. The definition and functioning of the purpose are very complicated things. But nations have purposes and self-ascribed destinies as have individuals. They work in different ways, because the human soul is immortal and a nation is not immortal. But nations do last a very long time.

MOYERS: Does it occur to you that the United States is not certain at this moment as to its purpose, and that this is behind so much of the self-doubt that one finds?

LUKACS: I cannot answer this. I think to some extent, but I would not choose this as a summary analysis of the problems of the nation at this point, because this is a free country and, as you say, an idiosyncratic country. It is composed of so many individuals, and so many different races and nationalities, and it is becoming more kaleidoscopic every year—so that although it is not impossible, it is extremely difficult to separate the desires of people from the picture they have about their nation at large. This kind of analysis congeals only in retrospect. So you see, the historian is a kind of prophet—but only a prophet of the past.

Martha Nussbaum

CLASSICIST AND PHILOSOPHER

Human goodness is such a fragile achievement, says Martha Nussbaum, that leading a moral life sometimes requires more luck than anything else. A professor of philosophy and classics at Brown University, she finds lessons for modern Americans in what the ancient Greeks thought about virtue and tragedy. Her most recent book is The Fragility of Goodness: Luck and Ethics in Greek Tragedy and Philosophy.

MOYERS: The common perception of a philosopher is of a thinker of abstract thoughts. But stories and myths seem to be important to you as a philosopher.

NUSSBAUM: Very important, because I think that the language of philosophy has to come back from the abstract heights on which it so often lives to the richness of everyday discourse and humanity. It has to listen to the ways that people talk about themselves and what matters to them. One very good way to do this is to listen to stories.

MOYERS: Out of all of this vast array of stories is there one that you find most gripping, that you think speaks to us today?

NUSSBAUM: I wake up at night thinking about Euripides' *Hecuba*, a story that says so much about what it is to be a human being in the middle of a world of unreliable things and people. Hecuba is a great queen who has lost her husband, most of her children, and her political power in the Trojan War. She's been made a slave, but she remains absolutely firm morally, and she even says she believes that good character is stable in adversity and can't be shaken.

But then her one deepest hope is pulled away from her. She had left her youngest child with her best friend, who was supposed to watch over him and his money and then bring him back when the war was over. When she gets to the shore of Thrace, she sees a naked body washed up on the beach. It's been so badly eaten by the fish that she at first doesn't recognize it. She looks at it more closely, and then sees that it's the body of her child, and that the friend has murdered the child for his money and just flung the body heedlessly into the waves. All of a sudden the roots of her moral life are undone. She looks around and says, "Everything that I see is untrustworthy." If this deepest and best friendship proves untrustworthy, then it seems to her that nothing can be trusted, and she has to turn to a life of solitary revenge. We see her end the play by putting out the eyes of her former best friend, and it is predicted that she will turn into a dog. The story of metamorphosis from the human to something less than human has really taken place before our very eyes in the fact that she's become totally unable to form a relationship of trust with anything outside herself.

Now this comes about not because she's a bad person, but in a sense because she's a good person, because she has had deep friendships on which she's staked her moral life. So what this play says that's so disturbing is that a condition of being good is that it should always be possible for you to be morally destroyed by something that you couldn't prevent. To be a good human being is to have a kind of openness to the world, an ability to trust uncertain things beyond your own control, that can lead you to be shattered in very extreme circumstances for which you were not to blame. That says something very important about the condition of the ethical life: that it is based on a trust in the uncertain and on a willingness to be exposed; it's based on being more like a plant than like a jewel, something rather fragile, but whose very particular beauty is inseparable from that fragility.

> *To be a good human being is to have a kind of openness to the world, an ability to trust uncertain things beyond your own control. . . .*

MOYERS: But the other side of it is expressed by Victor Frankl, who survived the death camps. He says, "I'm not responsible for my circumstances; I'm only responsible for my attitude toward those circumstances. I may live in the degradation of the camps, and I may be put at the mercy of beasts, but I will not let them turn me into a beast."

NUSSBAUM: If you can maintain that separation, that's very fortunate. Actually, Aristotle supports this position. "Look," he says, "bad fortune can prevent you from doing good things, but what it can never do is make you do really, really bad things, because it can never erode the foundations of your character once that character has been formed."

Here I think the tragedians see more deeply than Aristotle because they see that character itself, if the circumstances are crushing enough, can be "polluted," as Euripides puts it, by something that you don't control. However much Hecuba tried to live well in the world of uncertain things, she had to be able to trust something. And when this very best friend, the one who was the basis of her connectedness to the world, proved untrustworthy, then it was not her fault that she couldn't sustain the moral life.

MOYERS: Maybe the unintended moral of Hecuba's story was that by transposing herself into a dog, she relieved herself of all emotions, of all necessity to make moral choices. A certain contentment comes from being a dumb beast.

NUSSBAUM: This can happen. Being human means accepting promises from other people and trusting that other people will be good to you. When that is too much to bear, it is always possible to retreat into the thought, "I'll live for my own comfort, for my own revenge, for my own anger, and I just won't be a member of society any more." That really means, "I won't be a human being any more."

You see people doing that today where they feel that society has let them down, and they can't ask anything of it, and they can't put their hopes on anything outside themselves. You see them actually retreating to a life in which they think only of their own satisfaction, and maybe the satisfaction of their revenge against society. But the life that no longer trusts another human being and no longer forms ties to the political community is not a human life any longer.

MOYERS: But what about free will? Hecuba could have chosen to remain an ethical person.

NUSSBAUM: The Greeks don't think of freedom that way, and neither do I. They don't think that there is, on the one hand, the animal body that lives in the world and can be affected by it, and on the other hand, the free will which is in some sense impervious to all that and can will the good in spite of its natural circumstance. For the most part they thought of the human being as a rational animal whose rationality and animality are inseparable, and they thought of choice as having to be brought forward from more rudimentary human abilities by the support of loving parents, society, and education. What can be brought forward in that way can also be destroyed if the society, the family, and the friends prove untrustworthy.

MOYERS: But doesn't that mean that moral values depend upon circumstances?

NUSSBAUM: The Greeks say that if you value the most important things, then on the whole and in most circumstances you're going to be able to live well. The good life does not require unlimited amounts of money. In fact, Aristotle thinks that having more money actually can hurt your life rather than help it. It's a heretical thought in the contemporary political context, but he really thinks that to live well, you don't need exorbitant resources, you just need resources that any pretty good society ought to be able to give people. If you're really attached to virtuous action and friendship rather than to money or reputation, then in most circumstances you should be able to live well. But this does not mean that there won't be extreme circumstances, where choice is not so free. The world hedges you about, and you're not going to be able to choose well, even if you're a good person who has all the right values.

MOYERS: You write about these ancient Greeks—Aristotle, Hecuba, Antigone, Creon—as if they were next-door neighbors. Are they really so vivid to you?

NUSSBAUM: They are. The big problems haven't changed all that much, and the Greek works face these problems head-on, with a courage and eloquence that I don't always find in modern works on moral philosophy.

MOYERS: What kinds of problems?

NUSSBAUM: Take the problem of moral conflict: In Aeschylus' *Agamemnon*, a king is trying to do his best to lead his army off to Troy. Suddenly he finds that his expedition is becalmed, and he's told that the reason is that the gods are demanding a sacrifice. He has to kill his own daughter in order to complete that expedition.

So here we have two deep and entirely legitimate commitments coming into a terrible conflict in which there's not anything the king can do that will be without wrongdoing. On the one hand, if he doesn't sacrifice his daughter, he's disobeying the gods, and his entire expedition is probably going to perish; on the other hand, he's got to kill his own daughter. Thinking about this, as the play says, with tears in his eyes, he says, "A heavy doom is disobedience, but heavy too if I shall rend my own child, the pride of my house, polluting my father's hands with streams of slaughtered maiden's blood close by the altar. Which of these is without evils?"

Often, when you care deeply about more than one thing, the very course of life will bring you round to a situation where you can't honor both of the commitments. It looks like anything you do will be wrong, perhaps even terrible, in some way.

MOYERS: Do you think it's true for the taxi driver out there on the street right now? He doesn't see himself as a King making those horrific choices. Life doesn't present itself to him that way.

NUSSBAUM: Oh, but I think it does, on a smaller basis. Just take a person who has a career and who also has children, and who has to juggle those two responsibilities every day. Nothing will guarantee that in some event you can't prevent from arising, you'll have to neglect one of those commitments and neglect something that's really ethically important because the very course of life has produced a terrible conflict.

I face this every day myself as a mother who has to juggle career and child-raising. So often, just on a very mundane level, you've got a meeting, and your child's acting in a school play, and you can't do both things. Whatever you do, you're going to be neglecting something that's really important.

MOYERS: So that's what you meant when you wrote that daycare is a modern version of an old Greek tragedy.

NUSSBAUM: If you realize that people face these conflicts, there's an awful lot society can do to provide institutions that make those conflicts arise a little less often. But no social situation, however ideal, is going to make those conflicts just go away.

MOYERS: No, but we were taught to rank obligations—you know the old term, choose priorities—and not to make of every conflict of competing goods a great moral drama.

NUSSBAUM: I think that moral philosophy has had a very bad influence here in two areas. One traditional moral view is that there are no conflicts of obligations, that that's an illogical view. Immanuel Kant and Thomas Aquinas said, in different ways, that any conflict of obligation is really only apparent, that it's a violation of logic to think that there could be a genuine conflict of this kind. I think that view is just a misdescription of what actually happens in people's lives. There is nothing illogical about saying, "I am going to care deeply about my work and my writing; I'm also going to care deeply about my family, my child." That's not illogical. That's perfectly coherent. Over the course of a life, not only can you combine these things, but they actually enrich each other and make the life of each of them better. But that doesn't prevent these terrible situations that you can't entirely foresee.

MOYERS: Is this what you meant when you wrote once that "Tragedy is trying to live well"?

NUSSBAUM: Tragedy happens *only* when you are trying to live well, because for a heedless person who doesn't have deep commitments to others, Agamemnon's conflict isn't a tragedy. Somebody who's a bad person could go in and slaughter that child with equanimity or could desert all the men and let them die. But it's when you are trying to live well, and you deeply care about the things you're trying to do, that the world enters in, in a particularly painful way. It's in that struggle with recalcitrant circumstances that a lot of the value of the moral life comes in.

Now the lesson certainly is not to try to maximize conflict or to romanticize struggle and suffering, but it's rather that you should care about things in a way that makes it a possibility that tragedy will happen to you. If you hold your commitments lightly, in such a way that you can always divest yourself from one or the other of them if they conflict, then it doesn't hurt you when things go badly. But you want people to live their lives with a deep seriousness of commitment: not to adjust their desires to the way the world actually goes, but rather to try to wrest from the world the good life that they desire. And sometimes that does lead them into tragedy.

If you really feel what it is to love someone or some commitment and be bound to that, then, when a conflict arises, you will feel deep pain, and you will feel what

Agamemnon felt. Even at a smaller level you will feel, "Which of these is without evils?"

MOYERS: And the good life is the life lived according to your moral values, the life that is trying to find an ethical path through the wilderness.

NUSSBAUM: It's a life that is trying to live well toward friends, toward fellow citizens, and toward one's own capabilities and their development.

MOYERS: There are so many conflicting obligations for an individual today: religion, family, friends, state, country, party, neighborhood.

NUSSBAUM: Sometimes people find this so messy that it can't be tolerated, and they retreat into some simplifying view. Either they say, "We know that obligations have to be consistent, and so if there's an apparent conflict, it's not really conflict, and all I have to do is find out which one takes precedence, and the other one just simply drops away and ceases to exert a claim on me"; or they might say, "Well, yes, it's a sort of conflict, but really we see that all values are commensurable, so that if I measure up the quantities of goodness that are here and the quantities of goodness that are over here, then all I need to do is ask myself, 'Where is there a greater quantity of goodness?' and then I go in that direction, and missing out on the other one is sort of like missing out on fifty dollars when what I'm doing is getting two hundred dollars"—and it doesn't seem very painful any more when you look at it that way.

Very often people take up some such way of looking at things because to see that they are really two altogether different things here, both of them seriously worthwhile, both of them things to which you have made a commitment in your own heart, and you can't follow both in this particular circumstance—that is very painful. What the tragedies show us is that temptation to flee into some sort of simplifying theory is a very old temptation, and it probably is going to be around as long as human beings are faced with these problems.

MOYERS: I asked you about the moral lesson, and you said what the tragedies show us. In one sense there is no lesson and no moral, is there? It's simply the revelation of life as seen through the artist, the philosopher, the sufferer, the pilgrim. There's no effort to instruct.

NUSSBAUM: But you know, sometimes just to see the complexity that's there and see it honestly without flinching and without redescribing it in the terms of some excessively simple theory—that is itself progress. It's progress for public life as well as private life, because it's only when we've done that step that we can then ask ourselves, "How can our institutions make it less likely that those conflicts will happen to people? How can we create schemes of child care, for example, that will make this tragic conflict of obligations less of a daily fact of women's lives and perhaps more of a rare and strange occurrence?"

MOYERS: Do you say, "Well, philosophy has helped me to see that this is a natural part of life, and I'll accept the stress and the strain and the conflict, and I'll walk on the tightrope with the balancing rod and hope to get to the other side"?

NUSSBAUM: Sometimes it's pretty clear which one you ought to choose, but it's very, very important to separate the question, "Which is the better choice?" from the question, "Is there any choice available to me here that's free of wrongdoing?" Agamemnon has to sacrifice his daughter because it's clear the gods are going to kill everyone, including the daughter, if he doesn't. Looked at that way, he had better make that choice. Still, he has not got the right to think that just because he's made the right choice, everything is well. In the play, he says, "May all be for the best," and the chorus says that he's mad. You don't accept an artificial, easy solution to this, but the hope would be that through that kind of pain, you understand better what your commitments are and how deep they are. That's what Aeschylus means when he says that through suffering comes a kind of learning—a grace that comes by violence from the gods.

MOYERS: My favorite Greek tragedy is *Antigone*, which dramatizes the conflict between Antigone's loyalty to her family—"I must bury my dead brother, even though he's been a traitor to the state"—and Creon's loyalty to the state, and to the welfare and protection of the whole society. No one comes to peace with that conflict.

NUSSBAUM: And yet Creon, by the end of the play, has seen something that he hadn't seen before. In Creon you see a particularly fascinating example of how one might try to evade this conflict, because all through the play he thinks of the supreme good as being the good of the state. He refuses to admit as binding or claiming in any way anything that comes into conflict with that, so he defines enemies simply as anyone who opposes the good of the city, even if it happens to be a member of his own family. The claim of the family just doesn't exist for him. But by the end of the play, the fact that his son has died does mean something to him. He says that his deliberation has been very bad. He should not have thought that there's only a single thing in human life. He should have clung to the richer conception of what's valuable.

MOYERS: I saw *Antigone* with a clarity that I had never imagined possible when I watched Lyndon Johnson pursuing the war in Vietnam, which he thought absolutely right to do for the sake of the state. He refused to stop his two sons-in-law from going. I saw the torture of the conflicting loyalties there, and I thought, "Aeschylus was right."

NUSSBAUM: The sad thing is that he didn't learn enough from that, perhaps. He didn't see quickly enough what that meant for families in America generally.

MOYERS: Did Creon do something about what he saw, or was the recognition enough?

NUSSBAUM: Until then, he thinks of the state as though it doesn't consist of families. He keeps talking about "the city," but he forgets that "the city" consists of families who love their children and who are torn apart by civil war and who have relatives on the opposing side.

MOYERS: You just said something that I think is very important: that what these moral conflicts reveal is the truth of personality behind the abstractions. If you think of "the state" without thinking of the family, you're thinking of something abstract that enables you to do what you would never do as a ruler if you thought of the human beings behind those abstractions.

NUSSBAUM: The Greeks were on the right track when they thought that what we're aiming at in political life is to produce a good life that is very complex and that has many different elements. That means also understanding the tensions and conflicts that arise among them. It means looking at the family and seeing how the good of the family might come into conflict with the good of the whole city in times of stress.

MOYERS: But isn't this saying, ultimately, that "Life is life"? We all know such choices are a part of being human.

NUSSBAUM: Yes, in a way. In these tragedies you see rich descriptions of life, and you don't often see any ambitious solution to life's problems. But so many things that parade themselves as solutions are really under-descriptions, excessively abstract descriptions, failed descriptions of those problems. When you say, "Okay, we have here two alternatives, let's see how one can maximize utility in that situation," and you treat the people as productive of quantities of good—that's just a bad description of human life. A lot of moral philosophy as it has an impact on public policy has started from bad description. So if we start with these tragedies, we are at least looking and seeing the way people actually feel about the deepest things in their lives.

> . . . so many things that parade themselves as solutions are really under-descriptions. . . .

It's only when we face this head-on and describe it well, with the richness of language and feeling that these works of literature show us, that we can actually go on to think what we might do about that. The stories that we sometimes tell ourselves, that the free will is free no matter what conditions people are living in, and that these people in misery are really okay because they have free will—those are evasive and pernicious stories, because they prevent us from looking with the best kind of compassion at the lives of other people.

MOYERS: You have written that these ancient Greeks were preoccupied with the notion of "a livable life." What is "a livable life"?

NUSSBAUM: It means, first of all, that they are preoccupied with the idea of a life that is rich and full and involves many different activities. These activities are not entirely under people's control at all times. A lot of them, like the ability to love and care for a family, the ability to get an education, the ability to think well—all of these require support from the surrounding society. So they have the image of the person as like a plant—something that is fairly sturdy, that has a definite structure, but that is always in need of support from the surrounding society. The political leader in that image is like the gardener who has to tend the plant. The role of politics is to provide conditions of support for all the richly diverse elements in the full human life.

MOYERS: What are the essential elements of a good human life?

NUSSBAUM: You want to describe these elements at a pretty high level of generality because within each of these areas you want to allow some latitude for people to adopt their own account of what it is to live a life of personal love in their own way and to live a life of thought in their own way. But one of the essential elements is relationships among people, including both close personal relationships, either in the family or with close personal friends and loved ones, and political relationships. Another essential element is thinking and reasoning on many different levels, including moral reasoning, because one of the most essential things in the Greek view—and in mine, too—is to become capable of making a plan for the good life. Those are just a few. There are many other things one could mention here.

MOYERS: Those you mention start with a certain assumption that one has the means to take care of the physical appetites of life. I wonder how what you've just said would fit in places where they don't have the luxury of asking questions about moral choices but have to worry about where the next meal is coming from.

NUSSBAUM: What this view urges you to do at every level is to look at the totality of the person's life and ask what that person is able to do or be. That is, you look at how people are able to function as human beings. Now that means, for example, that you look at the role food plays in a human being's life. Don't just think of yourself as handing out some things as if they had value in themselves, but try to think, "What is the role that the goods, property, income, and food play in the overall life of a person?" Sometimes when these questions are asked, they're not asked in that way. Often, when people are measuring the quality of life, what they're doing is measuring the opulence of the society.

I've done some work for the last several years at the World Institute for Development Economics Research in Helsinki, and it's been fascinating to see how and why people have been coming around to some of the approaches of the ancient Greeks on these questions, even in the Third World. When you talk about development, you're telling about what progress is being made—so you have to ask yourself, "What direction are we taking? How do we define a 'good life'? What is the quality of life that we're looking for?" The economic tradition has usually looked at that in a very superficial way, defining an improvement in quality of life as an improvement in GNP—more things—not asking about what the things are doing for the people. Aristotle had a lot to say about people who thought of money and goods as ends in themselves. They are making a big mistake, he said, because they don't ask the fundamental question, "How are these things playing a role in making people capable of functioning and of living well by their own choice?"

The slightly more sophisticated approach is the utilitarian approach that asks, "How are preferences being satisfied?" But there again, Aristotle had some very shrewd things to say. He said, "Look, desire is something that's shaped by the conditions you live in." If you live in extremely impoverished conditions, for example, and you don't know the alternative ways of life, you won't form desires for the things that you don't know about. In the development context this comes out very clearly, because, for example, women in many parts of the world don't express the desire for education. If you're taking an approach based on utility, you'll say, "Well, then, so much for them—there's no reason for us to think about educating them." But the Aristotelian approach urges you to ask instead, "Let's look at what they're actually able to do, and let's not be so sure that what they say right now, before they're exposed to all the alternatives, is the thing we want to go by." If we have a reflective conception of what it is to function well as a human being, we might try to do something about that situation, even when the people are too cowed or too convinced by their tradition that it's not good for them to express that desire themselves.

MOYERS: Aristotle thought that the government that did not educate was not performing its role, and that its purpose in educating was not just in relation to the quantity of goods that you could have, but in what you did with the life of the mind that the education made possible.

NUSSBAUM: He thought that to be morally good, to be able to choose, to be free, you had to have an education, and that you weren't born with a pure soul that was capable of willing the good all by itself without any support from the society. First of all, you had to be given food, clean air, and clean water. Aristotle talks about all those things, although people don't read those parts very often. Then, most of all, you had to be given a good education. He was very critical of societies that thought of themselves as progressive because they were equalizing the distribution of property, but who weren't thinking about education. They didn't have a complex enough view of the role that property can play in the whole life of the human being.

Aristotle is not a traditionalist. He says, "All human beings seek not the way of their ancestors, but the good," and what he wants to do is to provide the resources for people everywhere who would like to think about the human good, and to do it by appealing to certain ideas of our common humanity that we share across all the boundaries of tradition that separate us. He does that by appealing to some of the myths and stories we tell when we ask, "What is it to recognize someone as a human being rather than as a beast?"

MOYERS: I hear you saying two things: one, that we need a different measure of well-being than simply the gross national product, the sum of the goods and services that a society creates; and second, that political choice alone is not sufficient for the good life, because economic choice is equally important.

NUSSBAUM: The economic sphere and the political sphere are interrelated. The Aristotelian thinks government ought to look at the totality of life and see how the various institutional conditions impinge on human functioning and human choice, how the educational system is working to create or impede good choice, how the economic system is working, and how political participation itself is a part of the good life. Political planning goes well beyond politics, narrowly understood.

MOYERS: Of course Aristotle lived and wrote in a time when the polis—the city, the state—was a relatively small community. Today we have a continental government with two hundred and sixty million people. Are you suggesting that the same principles that Aristotle embodied and wrote about could apply here?

NUSSBAUM: Aristotle was living in a very small city, but he was also interested in talking about what's good and right for any society whatsoever. He believed that you could take people who agree on nothing but the name, he says, of what they're going after—they all want a good human life, he says, but they don't agree on what it is—and by arguing with them, by getting them to really see what they consider important in each of these areas, you could make progress across cultural differences and across boundaries of tradition. He did this himself. He looked all around the Greek and Mediterranean world and sent his students to gather their histories and their constitutions. It was out of the whole world that he wanted to make his conception of "the good life."

MOYERS: "We can't expect people to be free to choose unless we create the conditions for them to be free." Is that a notion that you find in the ancient Greeks?

NUSSBAUM: Oh yes. The ability to choose is the ability of a natural being who lives in the world and who needs support at every stage from the world in order to do and be all the things that a human being can be. Aristotle thought you had to start with the love and care of the family, and after that, you had to consider other necessary conditions for a good life. He certainly was in favor of public education, since he thought that people should be able to share a debate about the good. That would happen only if the government took it upon itself to devote itself to education. So he wanted a combination of private education in the family and public education in the city, open to all people and comprehensively supported for the citizens so that they didn't have to work at jobs that were, as he put it, "subversive of excellence," while they were being educated. Of course Aristotle didn't face a lot of the problems that we have to face in thinking about that because he always imagined that women were left out of this. You could have comprehensive support for the people who were going to be educated if the women stayed at home and did the housework.

MOYERS: Well, you raise an old question that keeps coming back: How did these profound thoughts arise in a culture based on slavery? Where women were not first-class citizens? How is it these noble ideas rested on such an unjust foundation?

NUSSBAUM: It's particularly surprising in Aristotle because he was a resident alien in Athens who was denied political rights. He lived most of his life without being able to own property or take any part in the political life of the city. It's especially strange that somebody who had that kind of life, and who also was one of the greatest scientists in history, and who had the principle that every part of philosophy had to be based on careful perceiving and recording of what was there, should have made such dumb mistakes where women are concerned—dumb even at the biological level when he says, for example, that they have fewer teeth than men, and that when a menstruating woman looks into a mirror, it turns the surface red. Now these are signs that he just was not following his own philosophical method where women are concerned.

There is no doubt that Aristotle's arguments about the good life lead to the conclusion that the good life ought to be open, as he says, "to anyone who is not maimed with respect to excellence." So any normal human being ought to have a chance to lead a good life. Where slaves are concerned, he is more subtle, because he says that the only beings who are rightly held as slaves are those who are by nature completely unable to plan a life by their own reason, and he argues that anyone who isn't like that, but who has the capability for practical reason, should not be held in slavery. Which people he thought fell into each category is less clear. But the principle is one that shows most of the actual slavery in his time to be completely unjust. Whether he knew that or not is less certain. But where women are concerned, there is a great blindness and a real refusal to look in the eye the daily reality of women's lives and women's reasoning, even though his own political view makes the family a very important part of the city.

Plato, who did defend the equal education of women in the ideal city, was able to do that because he also wanted to abolish the nuclear family. There was no need for the nurturing love of the mother because he had argued that children should all be brought up in common by all the citizens.

Aristotle, on the other hand, does see the tremendous importance of family love in knowing what each particular child is like and in being able to respond to their individual needs. So he has a much harder problem on his hands, socially, one that was almost impossible to face in his day—how could one design a society with families and also with opportunities to get an education in the city?

MOYERS: The very process of critical analysis, which the early philosophers triggered, in time became the undoing of the unequal society that they were a part of. Every time I read, "All men are created equal," I know that while this ideal wasn't practiced as such even in the 1700s, letting it loose on the continent made its fulfillment ultimately possible. In a way, philosophy has done that through the ages.

NUSSBAUM: Aristotle's philosophy hasn't always done that because it was taken up through the Catholic tradition and associated sometimes with conservative views that did not lead to the equal treatment of women. Aristotle was presented as a systematic and hierarchical thinker who believed in fixed first principles for ethics rather than what he was—a very experimental, very tentative, very humble thinker about the variety and the complexity of ethical life.

MOYERS: Were you intimidated as a woman about approaching Aristotle and all of the original Greeks who had particular views about women?

NUSSBAUM: I came to the Greeks first through the tragedians, where there is a rich expression of women's experience. It is a great paradox that these tragedies and comedies like *Lysistrata*, in which women take such an active and intelligent political role, were written by men in a culture that treated women in a particularly repressive way.

MOYERS: How do you explain the paradox?

NUSSBAUM: It's very difficult. I can only say that a profound artist, who sees deeply with a complex imagination, often sees things that the surrounding society doesn't see and puts a record out there for people who could respond to it. It led, ultimately, even in the tradition of Greek philosophy, to changes in women's position.

By the time of the Roman Stoics, the position for women in Rome was much better than in Aristotle's Athens, and the philosophers were arguing in an interesting way for the equal education of women. The Stoic philosopher Musonius Rufus wrote a little treatise in about 60 A.D. called "Should Women, Too, Do Philosophy?" He argues that yes, women were created with exactly the same faculties as men. So using the principle that what education ought to do is to make them capable of using all their faculties, especially their reason, he says, "We ought to teach them philosophy." Then he imagines the person who says, "Ah, but if they get educated, they won't do their housework, and they'll just sit around and talk philosophy with the men." And he says, "Now, wait a minute—you ought to think this as well about yourself. You shouldn't just sit around talking if there are things to be done. You should be thinking about the society, too." So the problem is a perfectly general one. No one should neglect their duties for the sake of talk. But to do their duties well, everyone has to learn to think well.

MOYERS: But what does thinking well involve?

NUSSBAUM: Of course there are a lot of different views on this in the ancient world, but I'm in sympathy with Aristotle's view that it's very important to think of ethical life as involving a rich perception of particular individuals in particular situations. If you go to a situation with some fixed abstract principles, and you think of the situation just as a scene for plugging in the principles, very often you're not going to see the new challenge and the characteristics of the person before you that you might not have noticed.

Aristotle's directive is always to think of yourself as though you're improvising. He compares this idea to what a good navigator will do. The navigator has studied the navigation manual, but when he goes out there in the boat, he's going to look at the scene before him and go not just by the rule book, but by what's actually there at hand. A good ethical judge is like that. You bring to the situation your ability to perceive it for what it is, and to describe it in richly qualitative terms. You also bring your emotional resources, and your ability to respond to human beings in human situations. If you do all that, ethical change takes place more appropriately, because when you see a real live human being, you see the full person, and when you really look at that concrete human life, it's much harder to maintain some of these discriminatory judgments.

MOYERS: But the men in Aristotle's time could see the lives of women and the slaves, whom they kept in subservience. What does it say about philosophy that ultimately power and culture prevail? Well, maybe not ultimately, because you're an equal citizen now.

NUSSBAUM: Actually, I think philosophy was doing a lot better than the surrounding culture. We now know that Plato had women in his school and that he was doing something in education that no one had dreamed of. And we know that the Stoics taught women and slaves. The Stoics felt strongly that we have to overcome cultural narrowness and that the best society would be a fully international society in which every rational being would reach their full potential.

MOYERS: What has long excited me about the ancient Greeks is that they were carrying on a vital discussion about the kind of culture they wanted.

NUSSBAUM: It's extraordinary the way the whole society was involved in this debate. Going to a tragedy was not like going to a Broadway show where you enter a darkened auditorium and see somebody up there on the stage and think, "Well, what has this got to do with me?" The tragedies were a civic festival where citizens came in and looked across the theater at their fellow citizens. They saw this as a scene for feeling and thinking about the life of the city. People were very strongly involved. We know that sometimes they wept and they stood up. It seems strange to imagine somebody caring that much about a Broadway show today. But the whole drama was a way for the community to investigate its own values, to look at the tensions among them, and to show young people what the community stood for and what its problems were.

MOYERS: Politics was really a conversation among the artists, the politicians, the statesmen, and the people in the audience.

NUSSBAUM: The artists saw themselves as speaking for the city, and as being not just providers of an elegant diversion but important teachers of the young. This is an attitude toward literature that we've, to some extent, lost and that it's very important to recover, because these poetic works, with their richness of exploration of emotional experience and of the various ways in which human life is vulnerable to disaster, are doing something in ethics that we need to look at.

MOYERS: You've expressed the wish that politicians were more like poets. Why?

NUSSBAUM: We want people who are capable of describing what's going on correctly, with the qualitative language that more often we associate with literary art, and then who are capable of responding to that emotionally—not simply looking at it with intellectual detachment, but looking at it as a human scene in which that person is emotionally involved.

Walt Whitman calls for a larger role for literature in American public life, and I think he was right. He preferred the poet's language because it was concrete, human, and suffused with feeling. That's the language we need in political life. It's not so silly to think that it might actually work, because in talking with people from many different cultures, I've found that what gets through to them is a story—when you are able to use language in a way that captures vividly and with great particularity the complexity of some human situation.

> Walt Whitman calls for a larger role for literature in American public life, and I think he was right.

That is the way to get a cross-cultural debate going, and not by trying to use language that's so abstract people can't see themselves in it. You have to be a good storyteller. You have to tell what it's like to live that life and be that person, and do it in a way that makes them see the point of view of a woman, for example, who doesn't think she wants an education, but whose life is being circumscribed by a lack of awareness of her possibilities. You have to bring them into the situation of the person who is hungry but who believes that the male in the family ought to have all the food when there's a scarcity. You have to understand what it's like to be that person before you can ask any of the questions that social science asks, like, "How do we promote development here?" If you start by saying, "How do we maximize utility?" then you miss the full understanding of the problem.

MOYERS: What do you think about the level of our public discourse today?

NUSSBAUM: It's very impoverished. It's lost a lot that it had in the time of Walt Whitman, for example, who could speak of Lincoln as "the large sweet soul that has gone." How many people today could you reasonably say that of? We've lost the idea that politics are part of the humanities. We don't expect them to have the contact with literature and the richness of descriptive language that the humanities have always stood for. That's a great loss.

> *We've lost the idea that politics are part of the humanities.*

MOYERS: What's happened?

NUSSBAUM: To some extent it's a gap in the way people are being educated. We do not stress the essential importance of the humanities for public life. Where we do offer the humanities as a central part of the curriculum, very often it's not with the idea that this is going to improve ethical and public discourse. We see works of literature as amusing and diverting, but not as having a bearing on the most important ethical questions.

This has come about, in part, because of disciplinary separations in the university. People are reading literature in the literature department, which is usually understood to be a place where you pursue questions of form and style without asking about the ethical and social content. We pursue the ethical questions in departments of philosophy and political science, which usually don't read works of literature and so miss the approach to ethical questions that I have tried to characterize.

MOYERS: I like the idea of public figures as teachers of the young. But when you listened to the recent campaign, to the public rhetoric, to the debates, and to the news reports, did you get any sense of teaching going on?

NUSSBAUM: No, I think that people are shaping their language to advertising and the media, and they're not willing to just come out with a very rich account of how they feel about the concrete problems of public life.

MOYERS: What is the difference between the language of advertising and the language of politics as you would like to see it articulated? What does advertising do to us?

NUSSBAUM: Advertising simplifies us, when I think what we want to do is to become more aware of complexity, nuance, and the complicated messiness of human situations. Advertising gives us a simple, two-second message in language that has to be grasped right away, whereas the great works of literature draw us into a complex, highly textured language that is much more adequate for a grasp of ethical reality.

MOYERS: What does the quality of our public discourse in America tell you about our understanding of what it takes to be fully human?

NUSSBAUM: There's a real danger that we're becoming a nation of narrowly technical thinkers, and losing the sense of the richness and the multifacetedness of the good life that the heritage from Greece gives us. To lose that is to lose the opportunity to have an effective public culture. If we don't start thinking with imagination about the different parts of the good human life and what it is to make a citizen capable of functioning in all these areas, then we're in danger of losing any chance to make good lives for our people.

Louise Erdrich and Michael Dorris

WRITERS

Michael Dorris and Louise Erdrich collaborate in life, in love, and in art. Husband and wife, they attribute their beliefs in family, community, and place to their Native American heritage: she is half Chippewa, and he is half Modoc. They are currently working together on a novel about Christopher Columbus, whose arrival in 1492 changed forever the destiny of Native Americans. Erdrich's most recent book is Love Medicine; *Dorris's is* A Yellow Raft in Blue Water.

MOYERS: So many of your characters are bonded across time and space by ties of kinship and community. In fact, it's very hard to single them out as separate from their community or from their extended family. What does kinship mean to you and to those characters?

ERDRICH: I think it's being enmeshed and sometimes not being in control. The characters in the books are always trying to take control, and they're never succeeding.

MOYERS: What spins the web of kinship?

ERDRICH: Accident sometimes. Even when you plan to have a family, you never know who the person is going to be that you decide to become a parent to. We're accidentally born to our own parents.

DORRIS: It's one of those things that's larger than the sum of its parts. For us as writers it's interesting because we are discovering stuff about our characters as we go along, and when one or the other of us is writing, we go to the other and say, "You'll never guess what so-and-so just did, or who so-and-so really is." We have the illusion that we know more about these people than they know about themselves. But we're discovering all the time, too.

MOYERS: You said kinship is an accident in the sense that you don't choose the children you have, and that you will your love for them after they come.

ERDRICH: Will? It's helplessness—you're in love.

MOYERS: I've learned as a father that while I might have had certain expectations, they don't matter as long as I learn to love the person who once was my child.

DORRIS: That's the struggle—and it's a struggle for our characters as well. Many of them don't even know who their parents are.

MOYERS: Do you take real-life characters and invest them in the fiction?

ERDRICH: No, they're all inventions. The people are invented between us in conversation. We're out here in the country, and we walk around, and we talk about these people.

MOYERS: You really talk to each other about these people who come alive in your books?

DORRIS: Oh, for months before the first word is written. We'll open a Sears catalog and figure out what they would choose from it, or we will pick out on a menu what they would eat. Once they exist, once they have a voice and a bit of a history, then they're in control more than we are. Our job as a writer is to put them in a situation and portray how they really would react rather than to manipulate them. There's kind of an inner bell that goes off and says, "Tilt" if they're saying or doing something they shouldn't. On the other hand, they've got to surprise us in those situations to be interesting to write about.

ERDRICH: It's not that we go out and say, "We're going to write a book about this kind of person." It's as though the characters choose us. They come to us and present themselves and seem inevitable, as though they're necessities.

DORRIS: We dream about them, you know, and draw their pictures.

MOYERS: Michael said, "Our job as a writer"—singular. Do you realize how incredible that is? "Our job as a writer"—two people writing a novel, not one. We think of the literary act as such a solitary invention.

ERDRICH: I know. I did when I first began. It was this romantic ego versus the world.

DORRIS: You are a romantic ego.

MOYERS: So that changed?

ERDRICH: Before we were married, we began to talk about one particular manuscript, and at first it was very hard for me to be open about it because everything was a secret. I felt if I let anything go, it would never find its way into words. But as time went on, and we began to work together in a closer way, it changed. It's hard to go back and say how something like that could happen. I suppose it's a process of gaining trust and going through the rough times when one of us had to say, "This stinks," and the other person had to take it. It was rotten and rough, but after you let go of the self who has everything invested in that particular character or that piece of language, you realize that what's important is the work. We're not important, it's the work that's important. However we work together on it is not important, it's the work. If that's out there, and if it gets to somebody and makes them respond, I don't care how—even if they throw the book at the wall—then something's happened. So there's often those times of letting go of that pull from the ego.

MOYERS: —The self that says I would like to be the only one in the picture.

ERDRICH: Right.

MOYERS: Do you realize that a lot of people would say that just can't happen? Two people cannot create a sentence because that's a solitary act of a struggling, creative soul. It's impossible to merge those two, no matter how good the marriage is.

ERDRICH: There's more than creating a sentence. We both write in separate places. We've both got an individual relationship with a page. But there's so much more to it than sitting down and writing.

MOYERS: All right, take the book you've just agreed to write on Columbus. Have you talked about how you're going to do it?

ERDRICH: This will be jointly written.

DORRIS: We've talked about it for years and years and years. We've started working on it, and we're greatly relieved that the main character sounds the same whether Louise is writing her voice or I'm writing her voice. She's got her own voice already, and we both hear it the same way.

MOYERS: Why Columbus? He's not been the subject of many novels. History, yes, but novels, no.

ERDRICH: We were inspired by the diary he wrote about his first voyage. We found it a revelation. Here was this truly openhearted man interacting with the natives, who were, of course, what he thought of as the East Indians. Terrible things happened afterward, but the first meeting was genuinely moving, and it intrigued us. Then because our backgrounds are partly Native American, the glorification of Columbus as a person seems so terribly ironic. Columbus only discovered that he was in some new place. He didn't discover America. There were incredibly complex indigenous cultures—

> Columbus only discovered that he was in some new place. He didn't discover America.

DORRIS: —in addition to which, it's anthropologically so interesting what happened, because Europe compared to the rest of the world was a very homogeneous place. Almost everybody spoke Indo-European related languages and shared the same cosmological worldview and even the same general political system. Indians, on the other hand, were used to an enormous plurality—five hundred different cultures, seven different language families, four or five hundred languages spoken, and many different religions. Within a day's walk of any place, you would encounter another group of people who looked differently, spoke differently, and had a different view of men and women. When Europeans came to Indians at first, it was no big deal. You read account after account of Indians saying, "Oh yeah, and they came too—and they don't bathe." That was the other big thing that all the Indian accounts talk about. Whereas for Europeans, it changed everything. Whose child were Indians in the Adam and Eve schema? Were they human beings or not? These questions were argued in Spanish universities for eighty years until the Pope said Indians had souls. It changed the European worldview.

MOYERS: When Columbus arrived, how many Native Americans were there throughout the hemisphere?

DORRIS: Over a hundred million. In the United States in the 1910 census, it was down to two hundred thousand people because of diseases. There were diseases that existed in Europe, Asia, and Africa that had never come to the Americas before. The first time a European, Asian, or African came over here and sneezed, these diseases and bacteria were introduced into the networks of the Americas, and most Indians were gone before the Europeans had any conception they were here.

MOYERS: Entire cultures wiped out?

DORRIS: Yes—a perverted form of germ warfare. In the nineteenth century it became intentional.

ERDRICH: Blankets were traded that were deliberately infected with smallpox because it was obvious that this was a way of clearing the path.

MOYERS: The whites would trade blankets with the Indians after deliberately infecting them with smallpox?

ERDRICH: Oh yes. But what we want to do with the book we're writing now is not to have Americans feel more of that comfortable guilt that is felt over reading *Bury My Heart at Wounded Knee*, where you think about American Indians being treated horribly in past centuries. We would want to transfer that guilt into the present reader and say, "These Americans haven't vanished." The ordained push West was supposed to clear the land of the native inhabitants. They were supposed to vanish before progress. That never happened. There are over three hundred tribes surviving and somehow managing to keep together language, culture, and religion. These are not visible people.

MOYERS: But the picture you draw in your books is of a people serving a life sentence—chronic poverty, chronic alcoholism, isolation. Indians have the highest teenage suicide rate and an enormous infant mortality rate. That is not a pretty picture.

DORRIS: It isn't a pretty picture, but there's a different status for Indians in this country than for any other indigenous group anyplace else in the world, because there is a political status that comes from treaties. The reservations that exist in this country are the remainder of Indian North America. They were never given up, and, consequently, they are defined by the Supreme Court as domestic independent nations within their boundaries. There's a nation-to-nation relationship with the United States.

MOYERS: But they're not treated as independent powers.

DORRIS: That's the point exactly. None of the treaties was kept by the government to the letter of the law. Those treaties provided for a continuing political identity for Indian nations which has not been supported by the kinds of prerogatives that should have come as a result of treaties. So unlike any other ethnic group in the country, when Indians look at the government, they don't say change things. They say, keep the laws that were made in the nineteenth century, which were more advantageous to Indians than laws that you might make now. And consequently, Indians often make poor coalition members for other minority groups because they're not looking for social change. They're looking to uphold the laws that exist. When cases go to the Supreme Court, they are almost always decided in favor of Indians, because the cases are rooted in the Constitution.

MOYERS: Are you saying Indians still have faith, despite the last hundred years, in the law and in the political process?

DORRIS: What's the alternative?

ERDRICH: What else is there?

DORRIS: We're talking about one half of one percent of the American population, and goodwill and following the law are the only options.

MOYERS: But isn't the alternative what you write about—alcoholism, poverty, and chronic despair?

DORRIS: I don't think our characters have despair. I think they have grit. Now,

I'm not defending poverty. Indians should have the ability, through treaties, to be competitive economically in every sphere and have much better educational and health opportunities. During this current administration, funding for Indian health has declined by almost fifty percent and education by more than a third. We're in a dreadful crisis right now, but on the other hand, there is not necessarily a poverty of spirit that follows.

MOYERS: If you go to the reservations, you see American Indians honoring the flag of the white society that has desecrated them. One of your characters advises her brother to go fight in Vietnam. He goes to fight in Vietnam, and he's killed.

DORRIS: But, you see, you have to believe in American ideals if you're an Indian, because those ideals set up treaties that recognized Indian sovereignty, and if ever Americans lived up to those ideals, it would be a good day for Indians.

MOYERS: When you see the flag above the reservations, you're seeing people paying tribute to the ideal, not to the history.

DORRIS: Yes, and to their personal history. A greater percentage of Indians fought in the world wars than almost any other group. They're honoring their own valor and courage and determination to fight for the ideals that other people have fought for.

MOYERS: I can see that on the level of patriotism. Psychologically, it's a different kind of problem. You have a character, Marie, in *Love Medicine* who has a strange relationship with a Catholic nun who has scalded her and scarred her with a poker. "And yet," Marie says, "there are times when I want her heart in love and affection, and there are times when I want her heart on a black stick." Then at the end, Marie comes back as this elderly nun is dying and kneels like a child beside her bed and is drawn in affection toward the one who has been her tormentor. There is a psychological bonding that takes place between the victim and the wrongdoer. Is there something of that in the Native American psyche today?

ERDRICH: There's more of an ironic survival humor between the victim and the oppressor.

DORRIS: —and an understanding. It's much more necessary for the victim to understand the oppressor than for the oppressor to understand the victim. There have been five hundred years of study of European systems by Indian people, but very little reciprocity in that respect.

ERDRICH: Vine Deloria, Jr., said that when Western Europeans came over, they possessed knowledge, while the people of the western hemisphere possessed wisdom.

MOYERS: And they possessed humor, too. Many of your characters have a wry outlook on the world.

ERDRICH: It may be that the one universal thing about Native Americans from tribe to tribe is survival humor—the humor that enables you to live with what you have to live with. You have to be able to poke fun at people who are dominating your life and family—

DORRIS: —and to poke fun at yourself in being dominated.

ERDRICH: We're a mixture of Chippewa and Modoc and German-American and French and Irish. All of these different backgrounds have aspects that are part of us. If we took ourselves too seriously in any way, we'd be overwhelmed.

MOYERS: It'd probably be like sitting in the General Assembly of the UN all day.

ERDRICH: Probably we don't take ourselves seriously enough even as writers, although that's the deepest thing in our lives. But the most serious things have to be jokes. Humor is the way we make our life worth living.

MOYERS: Why did the Native American culture become a dominant one in your writing?

ERDRICH: It's partly that once one is a citizen of both nations, it gives you a look at the world that's different. There is an edge of irony. If you have a Native American background, it's also a non-Western background in terms of religion, culture, and all the things that are important in your childhood. There's a certain amount of commitment because when you grow up and see your people living on a tiny pittance of land or living on the edge, surrounded by enormous wealth, you don't see the world as just.

MOYERS: What are you telling your children about their identity?

ERDRICH: We're doing just what I did when I was a child. I didn't grow up on a reservation but went back and forth. You get a view of what life is like in very different cultures, and, of course, you tell your child, "You should be proud of your tribal background. We are proud of our tribal background. We are proud of our relatives. These are our relatives. These are our people."

MOYERS: There's a character in *A Yellow Raft*, the fifteen-year-old half-breed, who dreams of having a dog named Rascal and of two parents. When I read that, I thought, "Is he trying to say something there about the further subversion of Native American identity with the images that come constantly through television to the young Indian child, or is Rayona just an interesting character?"

DORRIS: Rayona is a contemporary character. Her father is a black mail carrier from Oakland. Her mother is an Indian from eastern Montana. They met in what her mother describes as the wrong bar on the right night in Seattle. They love each other, but they can't live together.

Rayona grows up very much an urban, black, Indian kid in a northwest city. And then, suddenly, through a set of circumstances, she finds herself on a reservation where she's inappropriate in every respect. She's the wrong color, she's the wrong background, she doesn't speak the language well—all these complications. What she's looking for is some stable form of identity. Like all of us, she finds that from the movies and television. That is the media barrage she's been exposed to. Where do people go when they try to imagine Indians? They imagine Jeff Chandler and Sal Mineo. We had one guy come to dinner, and we cleaned our house and made a nice dinner, and he looks and says, kind of depressed, "Do you always eat on the table?" Contemporary people are contemporary people.

MOYERS: You tell the story about the boy scouts going out to be Iroquois.

DORRIS: Yes, our mailman several years ago stopped by and said that he was a Scout leader, and his troop wanted to be absolutely authentic Iroquois, so they were going to go live in the woods for a week. What would I recommend that they take along? I said, "Their mothers"—because Iroquois were matrilineal, and these little fourteen-year-old kids wouldn't know what to do without their mothers telling them what to do. Well, that didn't work. They wanted hatchets or something.

MOYERS: This seems to me to be a critical point with your children and everyone's children. Rayona in *A Yellow Raft* is on a search for her identity. She has to pick here and pluck there and put it together in her own right.

DORRIS: I think that's a plus, though. I worry about people who find themselves and life too uncomplicated and don't have to struggle.

MOYERS: Or the people who are trapped on that reservation, mentally, psychologically, geographically.

ERDRICH: I don't think people who are living on reservations or the half of American Indians who are urban Indians think of reservations as traps. They are homelands. They are places where the culture is strongest, where the family is, where the roots are—

DORRIS: —where the language is spoken—

ERDRICH: —and where the people around you understand you, and you understand them. Even if you are of mixed background, you feel comfortable on a reservation. The best way to celebrate Columbus's quincentennial would be to begin keeping over four hundred treaties that were made and never yet kept. That would mean returning some of the land back to Native American people. Over the years, award moneys have been given to people, since about half of the United States was bought for less than a dollar an acre, and the rest of it simply taken. If some of the treaties were kept, perhaps through returning some of the land from the public domain to Native American communities, that land itself would mean that standards of living would rise. It really comes down to the land. The federal government has refused to return land in almost every case that has come up before the Indian claims commission. And yet there is public-domain land adjacent to almost every reservation that could be returned without causing angst and fear to private landowners.

> The best way to celebrate Columbus's quincentennial would be to begin keeping over four hundred treaties . . . never yet kept.

MOYERS: You once quoted Chief Standing Bear, who says that America can be rejuvenated by recognizing a native school of thought. What do you mean by that?

DORRIS: There is one common experience that Indian people across the hemisphere have and that Europeans, by and large, lack, and that is the experience of pluralism, of cultures that developed in an atmosphere in which they were surrounded by other cultures.

MOYERS: We all are tribes?

DORRIS: We are really like that, you know. There are people whose languages have a whole different set of assumptions. The language that I learned to speak doing field work does not have a singular pronoun—no "I," "my," "me," "mine." Everything is collectively "we" or "you"—the people do this, and the people do that. That gives you a whole different worldview about ownership and about your responsibility to somebody else. If I say, "I punch you in the nose," it is expressed in that language as "I punch myself in the nose." If you say it that way, you don't do it all that often.

MOYERS: But that flies in the face of the dominant American individualism.

DORRIS: Cooperation comes in the most secure cultures. I would hope that we would move toward that kind of security.

MOYERS: A skeptic listening to you might say, "Well, Indian cultures shared those assumptions and honored those values, and look at them."

DORRIS: And I would say, but for the accident of being exposed to European germs, it might be a very different story. To use the accident of biology as a justification for domination is exactly what happened five hundred years ago. Europeans thought, "They must be weaker than we because they're dying off. Our culture must be God-ordained because we're winning." But victory is not the only judge of a culture's viability and wisdom.

MOYERS: What do you think we would hear if we listened to these Indian voices?

ERDRICH: The first thing is that people want to be who they are. People don't want to assume a kind of rippling identity that America thinks makes it the envy of the rest of the world. Even within our own borders there are three hundred different cultures who do not envy Americans so much that they want to give up their tribal status.

MOYERS: But being realistic, can people survive this way in a highly individualistic, competitive—

ERDRICH: —technological—

MOYERS: —era?

ERDRICH: Yes, and it becomes more and more imperative that people do survive that way. Native American people are surviving tribally within the borders of a dominant country. This should cause people to think twice about how they're living, what their assumptions are, and what their view of the world is. When we talk about the wisdom that was here, we're talking about cultures who managed to survive very well on the land without pushing it toward the brink of a serious ecological crisis. We need to look at how people managed to do that.

MOYERS: What happens to a people whose gods have been banished? Because it wasn't until 1934 that the federal government allowed—

DORRIS: —1978—

ERDRICH: Yes, the Indian Religious Freedom Act was passed in 1978.

MOYERS: What happens to a people when for over a hundred years their gods have literally been outlawed?

DORRIS: It's devastating. In the nineteenth century there was something called the Ghost Dance that was practiced in the Plains and in the Northwest. The land had been taken away, the natural subsistence base had been denied, and people were confined to reservations. The Ghost Dance was a desperate belief that this was all a test, that this had not really happened, and that if the people believed strongly enough, if they joined hands and wore Ghost Dance shirts and danced in a circle and denied this reality, that it would all go away. All the animals that had died and the buffalo and the people—everything would be restored the way it was.

This was a response of people who had no other power but faith. What happened was the first Wounded Knee. A group of people, old men and women and children, traveling in the dead of winter from one reservation in South Dakota to another to do a Ghost Dance, were surrounded and obliterated by Gatling guns. The Ghost Dance shirts didn't work—they didn't turn away bullets. It was the low moment.

ERDRICH: It did convince the government that religious beliefs among Native Americans were really dangerous. Some Indian people joke and say, "When missionaries came here, all they had was the book, and we had the land. Now all we've got is the book, and they've got the land." In so many cases the missionaries were the first contact with European society. When the missionaries' religious zeal was followed up by government withholding of food, it was not, in many cases, a gentle kind of conversion. And who shouldn't believe, when people are dying of diseases, and you don't have a cure, that the god of some healthy people isn't a better god? Now people are religious according to what denomination was issued to what reservation.

DORRIS: Under the Grant Administration—

MOYERS: —the government would say, this is a Methodist reservation. The Methodists have the franchise here.

DORRIS: —No competition, right.

ERDRICH: You get this one.

MOYERS: And the Presbyterians have the franchise there.

ERDRICH: But those religions are very strong because in some places the greatest advocates for American Indians—

DORRIS: —and social justice—

ERDRICH: —are within the church. Since the Indian Religious Freedom Act, and during the revival of interest in native cultures in the sixties and seventies, there's been a lot of interest in traditional religion among younger people on reservations. It's a very positive thing. There are revivals of Sun Dances and of communal celebrations. And sometimes these things change with time. Native American people are adaptable within their own culture, too.

DORRIS: And religion is not something that's segmented away from other aspects of the society. In the Northwest cultures in Vancouver Island, British Columbia, and Washington State, there's a revival in the economic system of potlatching, which is a system of exchange in which you have an enormous party. At the end of it, your hosts of the party put all of their worldly possessions down, and the guests carry them away. You've given a successful party if you're impoverished, if you have absolutely nothing left. Then you go all the way up on the status hierarchy and all the way down on the wealth hierarchy. But you know that eventually they're going to have a birth or a death or a marriage or something like that, and the expectation is that you will take away more than you gave, so it's a spur to production. This is a system that worked for a thousand years among Northwest peoples that always keep things going, but with a twist, as it were.

MOYERS: Given what you know from the past, given what you've learned in your research, given what's happened since Columbus came—the treaties, the broken promises, the perfidy, the betrayals—how do you trust people any more?

ERDRICH: Who said that we do? Maybe we don't. Maybe we are somewhat cynical.

MOYERS: I don't get that in your books. I don't get that from talking with you.

DORRIS: It's the same thing we were talking about before. Why do many Indians today have a sense of identification with the American government in spite of the example of its past history? The answer is: Because what choice do you have? What choice do we have as writers? What choice do we have as people who have children and want a future for them? You get angry. You become an activist. You don't just stop. You have to believe that somewhere there is something that can be appealed to that is common to human experience.

MOYERS: What do you think that is?

DORRIS: I think it's empathy. We all share certain experiences, like being a child and a parent and so forth. The prime directive for cultures the world over is to survive. When you look at the greenhouse effect and overpopulation and perfidy and war and nuclear disaster possibilities, unless we've collectively lost our minds, we still have somewhere that determination to survive. It's a matter of making it clear that this is the time to ask that question—that there's no luxury of time.

ERDRICH: I think you're probably right in that if we truly were cynical, we wouldn't be writers. There's a great French writer who said that the purpose of a writer is to try to increase the sum total of freedom and responsibility in the world. We think of ourselves as citizens of two nations, as writers, and as parents, and we just keep trying to do the best we can. But that doesn't mean that we think everything is going to turn out for the best.

Things are more complicated. We'd like to believe, and probably most people would like to believe, that we can keep going the way we are, that things that we hear about in the future don't relate to things in history, that things from day to day won't change for us living in the United States. To me, that doesn't appear to be true. It appears that we're on a course that will cause us to have to reevaluate ourselves in the very near future. We have to start thinking, more than anything else, and trying to learn from whomever we can what our solutions are going to be. They're going to be technological, and they're going to be solutions of the spirit. We've grown technologically, but we haven't progressed as far spiritually. We're talking about knowledge coming from Europe—but we need wisdom about how to deal with so many of the problems that we're going to face. Not having a happy-ending mentality may be something that we need.

Mary Ann Glendon

LAW PROFESSOR

SUSAN GREEN

All laws, says Mary Ann Glendon, tell stories—stories about who we are, where we came from, where we are going, and what we value. As a professor of law at Harvard University, she specializes in comparative and family law. Her book Abortion and Divorce in Western Law *contrasts the legal practices of Europe and America as they bear on the difficult choices of these controversial issues.*

MOYERS: You say that the laws of a given society tell us a story—in what sense?

GLENDON: Laws do a number of things. They adjust and avoid disputes. Some people say they advance or promote interests of various groups in our society. But one of the other things they do is tell us something about the society that produces them. Every society's laws employ certain symbols and project certain visions about the people, about the society's aspirations, about where we came from, where we are now, and where we'd like to go.

MOYERS: Like any good story, they enable you to understand what you can't always see.

GLENDON: Laws are ways that society makes sense of things.

MOYERS: What story are abortion and divorce laws telling us about our society?

GLENDON: They're telling what I believe is an oversimplified story. The abortion decisions of the Supreme Court are telling us that abortion is a matter of individual, private choice, and that a fetus is not a person. Now, of course, when lawyers hear that a fetus is not a person within the meaning of the Constitution, they understand very well that a technical legal definition may not correspond to ordinary usage. A lawyer, for example, will know that a corporation is technically a person within the meaning of the Constitution. But when a layperson reads in the newspaper that the Supreme Court has said that a fetus is not a person, there's a possibility of misunderstanding. When the Supreme Court speaks this way, it communicates a message about the value of human life. I don't think the message that's currently being communicated by the Supreme Court is really the story that most Americans want to tell about the complex issues involved in abortion.

MOYERS: Except that there's this notion in America of the rights of the individual—so when you say that the Supreme Court is telling the story of individual rights, the Court is connecting with something basic in American tradition.

GLENDON: That's right. The story that the Court is telling is related to stories that we Americans like very much. But there are other stories besides those of individualism and self-reliance. They have to do with generosity. The Marshall Plan is an example of a language that's not unfamiliar to us.

MOYERS: So the other side of individualism is society, even though so often in American life it's the individual versus society that informs our mythology.

GLENDON: That's the problem. The mythology as communicated in our legal system isn't as rich as the mythology in our society as a whole. There's more depth and complexity to the way Americans think about such matters as abortion, divorce, and neediness than our legal system communicates through its laws about abortion, divorce, and welfare.

MOYERS: The purpose of law sometimes goes beyond regulation. It not only governs, constrains, and guides us, but also promotes a vision, a way of life that may be desirable even if the law cannot achieve or enforce it.

GLENDON: The law does that whether it is meant to or not. We have no choice, really, about communicating messages through the law. The Supreme Court's decision in *Roe v. Wade* communicated a message about freedom of choice—about the paramount nature of that value. So whether or not the law has that purpose, the law has that effect.

MOYERS: One of the justices told me last year that every time he writes a decision, he feels he's adding one more chapter to the American saga.

GLENDON: It's good for the justices to be attentive to the fact that that is one of the things they are doing. Particularly in American society, it's important to be attentive to that aspect of law because we as a people don't have much in common. We don't have a common religion, or many common traditions, and we don't even have a common history in the sense that so many of our ancestors arrived at different stages in the formation of the republic. A society like that is apt to look more to the law as an expression of its values than people would in a country like Ireland, for example, where there are many common customs and traditions and not too much regard for the laws as a value carrier.

MOYERS: I hadn't thought of it quite that way before—that the law may be the one thing that all of us disparate pilgrims from so many different sources of the globe do have in common when we take that oath and say, spiritually or literally, "I'm an American."

GLENDON: We've put a lot of weight on the law. There's a question of whether law can bear all the weight we've put on it, and whether it's really desirable for the law to be such an important value carrier in society. Montesquieu and Tocqueville, among others, thought that what was really important was what undergirded the law—the manners, customs, and mores. If law wasn't grounded in the mores, the philosophers didn't think there was much hope for it.

MOYERS: Isn't that one reason that the abortion laws were changed? People discovered that the laws which made abortion a criminal act were at odds with the mores of people who were determined to have an abortion anyway, so the law had to be changed to square with reality.

GLENDON: That's a big question: Should law conform to whatever we mean by reality, or should we recognize that law has some modest but nontrivial role in shaping reality? In the 1960s, abortion laws began to change all over the world, generally in the direction of partial decriminalization. Where the process of adaptation to changing behavior and moral notions would have led us in the United States is really hard to tell because it was brought to a halt in 1973 when the Supreme Court took the issue away from the legislature.

MOYERS: How do you explain this worldwide loosening of abortion restrictions over the last twenty years?

GLENDON: There are many causes one could point to, and it would be hard to say which predominated—but one factor was surely that medical science had advanced to the point where very few abortions needed to be done any more to save the life or preserve the health of the mother. So a kind of problem arose for the medical profession. Abortion wasn't necessary under the old legal categories as often as it had been, but abortions were still being done, and their numbers were increasing. The medical profession was the first to see the discrepancy between what the criminal law said about abortion and what was actually happening in practice. The early movements for change in the abortion law were inspired by doctors. This was not originally a woman's issue because it started before the women's movement got up a head of steam. In Canada, the United States, and many other countries, the early liberalization of the abortion laws had to do with protecting doctors from liability. They weren't worried about being sent to jail, they were worried about losing their licenses.

MOYERS: Then the women's movement came along and carried that medical institution into the political realm.

GLENDON: Yes, but we have to remember that other things were happening at that time—the thalidomide scandal, for example. A woman in the United States who had taken thalidomide had extraordinary difficulty finding a court that would permit her to have an abortion or a hospital that would do it. She eventually went to Sweden. So all of these things came together—the women's movement, the concern of doctors, and the increasing discrepancy between law and practice.

MOYERS: Why did you decide to compare the abortion and divorce laws of Europe with our own?

GLENDON: Well, I fell upon this subject by accident. I teach a course in comparative law, and one of the subjects in that course is judicial review. Teachers always look around for interesting cases to use as pedagogical devices. You want to keep the students awake while you're discussing separation of powers and proper relationship between courts and legislatures. It occurred to me that *Roe v. Wade* would be interesting, since it was a highly controversial case in the United States and was not only an abortion case, but also a very important landmark in the history of judicial review. I thought it would be interesting to compare *Roe v. Wade* with the decisions of other high courts in other countries.

Now, when I did that in the classroom, a question occurred to me: What would have happened if *Roe v. Wade* had gone the other way? What if the United States Supreme Court had done what supreme courts or constitutional courts in other countries had done and left the regulation of abortion pretty much to the legislature within certain limits? It seemed to me there would be two avenues to pursue to try to figure out what the United States would look like today, so far as abortion is concerned, if *Roe v. Wade* had gone the other way. One would be to look at what the states were doing until 1973. There I found that between 1967 and 1973, nineteen states had already liberalized their abortion laws, and the solutions that they proposed differed in some details but basically were very similar to the kind of legislation that I found when I looked all over Europe. My second branch of inquiry was to see what European countries had done when they had tried to approach the problem legislatively.

I entered the research believing that American law was probably going to turn out to be similar to the law of a number of other countries. I expected to find that the United States was one of a group of countries that would have a fairly lenient approach toward abortion. The other attitude that I took to the research—and I think this attitude is fairly widely shared by Americans—is that there really isn't any compromise possible on this issue. Either abortion is illegal, or it's pretty freely available. I found that both of those conceptions that I brought to the project were wrong. I was very surprised to find the United States absolutely in a class by itself when compared with other Western countries—or indeed, even when compared with countries in the socialist bloc, except China. You have to go to a country like India or China to find such an extreme approach to the problem.

MOYERS: United States abortion laws are as extreme as those in China?

GLENDON: No, but you have to go to China to find anything that is in that same category. In the United States, no regulation of abortion is permitted in the interest of preserving the life of the fetus until viability, which the Supreme Court estimates at between twenty-four and twenty-eight weeks—six months. In all of the Western countries that I looked at, regulation in the interest of the fetus begins around ten to twelve weeks—the very latest was Sweden, with eighteen weeks. So already there is one big difference.

The other big difference was that in almost all of these European abortion laws there was an affirmation of the sanctity of human life together with the recognition that there may be some circumstances under which the position of the woman involved such hardship that abortion ought to be permitted. So I found not only that compromise was possible on the issue, but that in fact it was the typical solution.

MOYERS: So if you were summing up the difference between the American and European attitudes toward abortion in these laws, what would it be?

GLENDON: The situation in the United States is absolutely unique as compared to the legal approaches taken to abortion in other Western countries. Most dramatically, in the United States there can be no regulation of abortion at all in the view of protecting the fetus until the sixth month. The second interesting thing is this is the only country where the courts have taken the problem so completely away from the legislature. The third interesting thing is that this is a country which does very little to promote alternatives to abortion by supporting maternity, childbirth, and child raising. Finally, our courts now speak of a constitutional right to abortion. The language that we use in talking about abortion is unknown on the European continent. Even in countries which permit abortion rather freely in the first trimester, there is no talk of a right to abortion.

> *The situation in the United States is absolutely unique as compared to the legal approaches taken to abortion in other Western countries.*

MOYERS: European laws generally allow abortion in the first twelve weeks.

GLENDON: The typical European statute would have very little regulation in the first twelve weeks, with regulation increasing as the pregnancy progresses. It would have two other provisions that have been held unconstitutional by our Supreme Court: One is that the typical European statute requires a brief waiting period between the first request for an abortion and the abortion itself. Our Supreme Court has said that even a twenty-four-hour waiting period was an impermissible interference with the woman's freedom of choice. European statutes also typically provide that the woman ought to be informed by a brochure or by counseling about alternatives to abortion. She ought to be told about adoption. She ought to be told what material assistance would be available in carrying the pregnancy to term, which often is quite substantial in European countries. The United States Supreme Court has said that kind of information is an impermissible attempt to wedge the state's message discouraging abortion into the privacy of the woman's decision.

MOYERS: What about the abortion clinics? What did you find in Europe?

GLENDON: Most European countries do not have a large, private, profit-making abortion industry. They regulate fairly carefully where and by whom abortions can be carried out.

MOYERS: Usually in state-sponsored hospitals?

GLENDON: Not necessarily, but a typical provision would be that they should be in a facility where not more than a certain percentage of the business done there is abortion.

MOYERS: So what did you conclude the Europeans are trying to say about abortion?

GLENDON: The statutes often start out with an affirmation of the sanctity of human life. On the other hand, they say abortion is available quite freely in situations of, as the French say, "distress," or as the Germans say, "hardship," in the early part of the pregnancy. But if one tries to read the message that those laws are enunciating, it is that we have several important values in tension with each other. One is respect for developing human life. Another is compassion for women who find themselves in extremely vulnerable circumstances, often a terrible crisis in their lives. Another is the interest of society as a whole in what we are saying about the kind of people we are through our abortion laws.

MOYERS: They're saying that the woman has a tough choice when she's having an abortion, and the state recognizes this and wants to help her. But at the same time the state has doubts about the taking of developing life.

GLENDON: It at least affirms that this is a very serious matter, and that human life is involved.

MOYERS: What is different about the story our Supreme Court decision is communicating?

GLENDON: Our Supreme Court hasn't been willing to talk about the different values that are in tension with each other. It's been throwing its weight behind a fairly straight characterization of the situation as one involving the woman's individual privacy and freedom of choice—which masks the complexity of the situation.

MOYERS: It leaves it wholly to the woman—

GLENDON: —for the first six months. After that—and this is another way in which American abortion law is quite extreme—even after six months have expired, states are permitted to regulate only if their regulation does not interfere with the woman's health, very broadly understood as her well-being.

MOYERS: We come down very hard on the side of individual privacy and the rights of the woman to sovereignty over her body.

GLENDON: That's the way we characterize the situation.

MOYERS: And you were surprised that this is far more liberal than in most of the countries you surveyed?

GLENDON: I was surprised to find that the United States was quite different—in a class by itself. Not only is there disregard for the value of human life in the first six months, but also there is a relative indifference to alternatives to abortion, such as providing maternity benefits, parental leave, child care allowances, and daycare. It's a strange message that involves not only women and children, but also a whole societal attitude toward dependency. It's almost as though there is a disdain for dependency.

In Europe we have well-established, noncontroversial welfare states. It's taken for granted by political parties on both the right and the left in Europe that the state will insure health and employment at more than a minimal level. That has been absolutely noncontroversial—so that, for example, when Helmut Kohl, a conservative European politician, was asked what his government was doing about abortion, he said, "Well, our abortion policy is to increase maternity benefits and child allowances to help people with raising children." We don't hear much of that kind of talk from persons who are opposed to abortion in the United States.

MOYERS: Some of the strongest opponents of abortion are also the strongest opponents of public support for single parents and dependent children. What does that say to you?

GLENDON: There is something puzzling about the message we are communicating through our legal system about children, the future, and attitudes toward neediness and dependency.

MOYERS: In a sense, the Europeans are allowing abortions even as they are subtly encouraging alternatives to it with their social policies.

GLENDON: They are indirectly, but substantially, encouraging alternatives.

MOYERS: A young woman knows that if she carries a pregnancy to term, she's not going to be left out there alone in the wilderness, so to speak.

GLENDON: Let's take Sweden, for example, because by European standards Sweden has a very lenient abortion law, with abortions pretty much on demand for the first eighteen weeks. That's as far as any European country goes with freedom of abortion, although even in Sweden it wouldn't be called a right. Now, a woman who finds herself pregnant and worried about that situation in Sweden knows a number of things. She knows that if she carries the pregnancy to term, she will subsist. Even if she's not employed, she will be able to subsist on an amount of money that is almost the equivalent of what a production worker takes home. It's more than a minimal level of subsistence.

MOYERS: But in this country a young woman who has two children gets only about fifty percent of a production worker's wage from welfare.

GLENDON: That's right.

MOYERS: Of course, Sweden is so much more homogeneous. Our society is riven by different and conflicting religious views. We are a much more varied and combustible society than Sweden.

GLENDON: That's right. One of the problems that a great diversity gives rise to is the problem of devising some legal norms that will be acceptable to a broad range of people in the population. Right now one problem with our abortion law is that the story the legal system tells is not shared by a broad range of people. The support for *Roe v. Wade* has always come from a minority of the population. Polls taken every year since 1973 show that most people feel uncomfortable with abortion, for any or no reason. But they also feel uncomfortable with the idea that abortion should be completely illegal. That suggests to me that Americans would feel more comfortable with a European-style compromise. But most Americans believe what I believed when I started my research—that compromise isn't possible. Either you're for abortion on demand, or abortion has to be completely illegal. That's not what legislatures have done when they've been left to sort out the questions by themselves.

MOYERS: Did you find in Europe that where the policies were liberal, the rate of abortion was high?

GLENDON: No, as a matter of fact, that's one of the most interesting findings. There's very little correlation between strict and lenient abortion law and the abortion rate. The Netherlands, which has one of the most lenient abortion laws, has the lowest rate in Europe. Romania, which has one of the strictest in the world, has an abortion rate even higher than the United States. So what does all this tell us? It tells us that something else besides the criminal law is correlated with abortion rates. We can only guess at what that might be.

MOYERS: What is your guess?

GLENDON: Well, again, I have to speak about Sweden, which, as you've pointed out, is very different from us in many ways. But Sweden did the impossible. In one decade, beginning in the 1970s, Sweden dramatically reduced both its teenage pregnancy rate and its teenage abortion rate. How could they do that? When the Swedish abortion law was passed in 1974, it went into effect as part of a big package of legislation. One part of the package was to make birth control information and devices very readily available. Another part was a program of education for sexual responsibility.

MOYERS: And they took those seriously?

GLENDON: They took those seriously. Of course, one can only speculate about whether that had anything to do with the dramatic reduction in pregnancy and abortion in the ten-year period. The other factor that I've already mentioned is that Sweden has probably the most generous alternative to abortion of any country in the West.

MOYERS: So these countries allow abortion, but they also support alternatives in both sex education, cheap and easily available birth control devices, and, if a pregnancy is carried to birth, liberal social policies that support the young mother and child.

GLENDON: That's right. There are many ways of being pro-life other than through the criminal law.

MOYERS: That's Sweden. What about some of the other countries?

GLENDON: If we tried to arrange the European countries in groups, we could say that there is a Nordic group which is very generous with public aid for child raising. Then, as you move south, there is what I call the Romano-Germanic group, which tends to rely more on the private sector and on the imposition and vigorous enforcement of realistic child support obligations. Then, as you move farther south, Spain is an interesting example because the Spanish Constitutional Court recently agonized over an abortion statute. This is a Catholic country, which has recently become a Socialist country. It agonized over an abortion statute which permitted abortion in the case of fetuses that were likely to be born with serious physical or mental defects. The Constitutional Court thought this was probably a serious infringement of the right to life. On the other hand, they thought that as an emerging social state, they weren't rich enough yet to be able to do all that they ought to be able to do to help parents bear the cost of raising children with severe physical and mental disabilities. So they envisioned a temporary situation in which abortion would be permitted in that instance, but they also articulated a social aspiration that the time would come when society as a whole could help people out with that part of the child-raising task. It's a different way of talking about the issues involved. The Spanish Constitutional Court is speaking out of a Christian Socialist tradition. It means not only that you have rights, but also that along with your rights come responsibilities. It means that you not only have a criminal law which says something about the aspirations, the ideals, and the hopes of a people, but also a social welfare law that ministers to the dependent and the needy.

MOYERS: How do you explain that Europeans hold this attitude that allows abortion, but tries to send a message about life, then provides the services to mothers and children—and we don't?

GLENDON: I'm sure there are many strands in an explanation, but as a lawyer I am interested in one particularly legal strand of it, which is this: In the late nineteenth century, legislatures all over the Western world started passing what we would today call social legislation. It was happening in the United States, as well as in France and Germany and England. That legislative process went forward in Europe, and the foundations of the welfare state were laid then. But in the United States something intervened. The United States Supreme Court and supreme courts of individual states began striking down infant social welfare legislation as a violation of the constitutional rights to property and freedom of contract. Now, there's an example of what bothers lawyers like me, whether we're pro-life or pro-choice, about *Roe v. Wade* and a certain hubris on the part of the United States Supreme Court— the idea that it knows better than the elected branches, as imperfectly representative and fallible as they are, what is good for the people of the United States.

MOYERS: Of course, the Court could be seen as correcting the tendencies of the previous Courts in saying that property is not the final value, that rights of the individual and the personhood of the woman take precedence.

GLENDON: It's a change in the constitutional basis for striking down state legislation. In the nineteenth century the constitutional basis was property. In the abortion cases one really can't find a firm constitutional mooring for these decisions. That's one of the things that makes lawyers uneasy about *Roe v. Wade*. It doesn't have to do with abortion so much as who governs. Who makes these important decisions for us? Is it going to be the Court, or is it going to be the legislature?

MOYERS: Someone said you thought that *Roe v. Wade* was a social disaster. Is that putting it too strongly?

GLENDON: I would feel more comfortable with characterizing it as an unfortunate *legal* event, because the Court did a number of things in that case that are disturbing just from the point of view of how our legal system functions. When the Court declares a statute unconstitutional, it brings the legislative process to a halt. It brings to a halt that process of education and persuasion and bargaining that goes on in and around legislatures. That's one of the ways in which a vital, healthy society has a conversation about the goods that it wishes to pursue. I don't want to get involved in sterile debates about judicial activism or strict construction. I'm saying that there are prudential reasons why the Court should be very, very careful before it shuts down the legislative process.

MOYERS: And as you say, several states were moving politically to liberalize abortion policies before *Roe v. Wade.*

GLENDON: Between 1967 and 1973 nineteen states had already liberalized their abortion laws. These were compromise statutes, very much of the European type. I think it's realistic to expect that if that process had gone forward, the legal map of abortion in the United States would be like the legal map of abortion in Europe. There would be some differences in detail, but basically abortion would be available fairly readily in the first trimester.

MOYERS: What explains the ferocity of the debate still raging here?

GLENDON: The reason it's raging ferociously is that the Supreme Court has ruled one side of the debate completely out of court. One of the aspects of the compromises in Europe that is appealing is that while debate goes on in Europe, it goes on in the form of a conversation, an exchange of views. It's heated, it's intense, and people's feelings about this matter are very strong in Europe. But what the European experience shows is that societies that are just as bitterly and deeply divided as we are made a compromise in such a way that it's still negotiable. Legislation can be changed. There's always another day. The losing side can come back and try again. Our Supreme Court has spoken the language of rights, which is the language of no compromise, and has told one side to go home until there's a constitutional amendment, which is a very cumbersome process, or until the Supreme Court changes its mind.

MOYERS: Now, is this true also in divorce? Why do you link divorce and abortion?

GLENDON: I linked them only because I thought the connection was in what each body of law was saying about dependency. Our divorce law is very similar to European divorce law, in one way, in that marriage has generally become freely terminable all over, in varying degrees. But curiously, in the United States you can not only free yourself of the marriage bond, but also free yourself substantially from economic responsibilities associated with marriage and having children.

MOYERS: Of the countries you surveyed are we the only one that practices no-fault divorce?

GLENDON: We're the only one that calls it no-fault divorce. This is another area where I think language makes a difference. When I began my survey of divorce law, I asked people in countries where divorce is granted at the request of one party whether they called that no-fault divorce. We had discussions about what you would call that in German or Swedish. And people said, "No, we don't use that term. We'd find that kind of shocking."

MOYERS: It comes from the automobile insurance industry here.

GLENDON: It migrated into divorce law by a kind of accident. Actually, it came into tort law, into the automobile insurance picture, because of a headline writer in

Massachusetts who wanted to find a clear, simple way of describing this new insurance plan. He said, "No fault," and it stuck to tort law, and then it migrated into divorce law. The idea that they're trying to capture with that term is that the litigation process is not very well suited to finding out the relative degrees of fault of the parties to a troubled marriage. It's better not to go into that sort of thing in court. But when it migrates into the law in that form, and that term takes hold, it connects with a certain language of psychotherapy and tends to be translated into a notion that the legal system is saying that nobody is ever to blame when a marriage breaks up. Add to that no responsibility, and we have a very unusual treatment of divorce in the United States, as well as an unusual treatment of abortion.

MOYERS: No fault becomes no responsibility?

GLENDON: We glided from no fault to no responsibility because we do not vigorously impose and collect child support.

MOYERS: Do the Europeans?

GLENDON: The Europeans have virtually solved that problem, to the extent that it can be solved, by establishing tables for calculation of realistic child support and by deducting child support from the paycheck. Now we're making great progress in the United States along those lines. It's possible that in a few years we will do as well as the European countries do in that area of child support. But, of course, there will always be situations where child support won't provide for the dependents. Sometimes the former provider is just too poor. Sometimes he or she has formed a new family and has dependents. So the other question is: What about public responsibility?

MOYERS: What do the Europeans do?

GLENDON: In many European countries now, when the child support obligation can't be collected, the state advances up to a certain amount of the child support obligations. And then there is, of course, the generally higher level of welfare in northern European countries.

MOYERS: So, once again, the story in Europe is trying to say something slightly different.

GLENDON: It's trying to say, first of all, marriage involves a lasting commitment, and having children involves undertaking a responsibility. The European story expresses an understanding that there are many situations where things don't work out, but when they don't work out, either there is going to be a vigorous imposition and collection of child support from the former provider, or society is going to step in and help with the problems of dependency created by the breakup of the union, or there will be some combination of the two, which is more typical.

MOYERS: The story is that the individual has a responsibility to society not to take the loss of life lightly. But society also has a responsibility to the individual, to the single mother, and to the child.

GLENDON: I don't want to exaggerate the differences between the United States and European countries because they're very much differences of degree. But the United States is communicating to mothers, especially, that it is a very risky proposition to devote yourself entirely, or primarily, to child raising. Is that really the message that Americans want to communicate through their public and private law? I don't think so. I think we're better than that.

MOYERS: Better than the story we're telling ourselves through the law?

GLENDON: I think so. The legal story doesn't do justice to the richness and complexity of feelings that people in the United States have about tragic situations.

MOYERS: Are women and children better off in Europe than they are in this country?

GLENDON: Children are better off in many European countries than they are here. I have no hesitation in saying they are better off because of the large percentage of children in our population who are poor. Whether women are better off really depends on how we would define better off—whether we see that as being the possessor of a great many individual rights, or whether we see that as having a component of being protected in the areas of procreation and motherhood. Certainly the American woman is very well off as an individual and a possessor of rights. But many European women are better off as mothers and members of interdependent family units. This difference of opinion on what better off means makes it very difficult to say what is a feminist in the United States at the present time.

> *Children are better off in many European countries than they are here.*

MOYERS: Isn't it possible that there's another story to the story, and that this story is one that many women feel they are now finally beginning to tell? That *Roe v. Wade* established that we are our own competent moral agents, that we, as women, have gained equality with men as a group, that we're no longer at a disadvantage, that we are the possessors of our own bodies and can control our destinies, and that we are not to be subject to the whim—or power—of men or the state. Isn't that a legitimate story that women are now beginning to tell?

GLENDON: That's a very powerful statement, but it's not the whole story. Like so many American stories, it leaves something out. What's being left out is that there is a question of life involved here, and that's a value that women have to be interested in—probably even more interested than men are.

MOYERS: Life?

GLENDON: Developing life—what the Supreme Court of the United States has refused to call either human or alive or a person. Somehow the story has got to take account of that. The story has to be one about moral complexity. As it stands right now, it is oversimplified and doesn't do justice to the richness and complexity of American life. It's basically an impoverished moral discourse.

MOYERS: There's an anomaly here. You mentioned earlier that a lot of these European countries are acting out of the Christian background. The conservatives in this country like to say we are a "Judeo-Christian" country, but, by contrast, we're not acting in public policy from that Christian perspective, are we?

GLENDON: There is no political home right now in the United States for what Europeans would call the Christian Socialist position. In most European countries there would be a political party that would be very interested in social values and would, at the same time, be very interested in providing a decent level of subsistence to every single member of society. Now, it's an interesting question why there is no such political party in the United States. It is standard in Europe. I suppose this has something to do with the problem of heterogeneity that we keep coming back to.

MOYERS: The diversity of America?

GLENDON: Apparently we just don't feel that all American children of all colors and social classes are our children, the way I think a Swede quite easily feels that a child up in Lapland is very precious to a worker in Stockholm.

MOYERS: Isn't there something else, too? Isn't it possible that the answer lies partly in the capitalist language that is used to tell the story? You are on your own. If you can make it, fine. If you can't make it, that's reflective of your worth, your merit, your character. You're talking about a capitalist story here, are you not?

GLENDON: Yes, that's very definitely a big part of our story. It's also a part of the European story, but there it's moderated by older classical and Christian notions about having duties along with your opportunities. If you have advantages from the society, you give something back to the society.

MOYERS: It's also moderated there by strong popular movements such as labor unions and social welfare organizations.

GLENDON: This is another problem that intersects with the law in the United States. Our law speaks the language of individualism to such a degree that the decisions of our Supreme Court tend to neglect the protection of those intermediate associations that you referred to—churches, labor unions, families, neighborhoods. We don't really have a good language in our legal system for speaking about anything that exists as a buffer between the individual and the state.

MOYERS: You seem to suggest there could be compromise on abortion in this country. Do you think that's possible, given the passions on both sides?

GLENDON: The passions would be greatly reduced if the discussion could continue to go on in the legislatures the way it went on until 1973. We would see here exactly what we see in Europe—that the discussion goes on, but without the desperate sense of outrage and the sporadic eruptions of violence that characterize the situation when one group has no place to go.

MOYERS: But how do you develop a common story between the pro-lifers, who say there must be no violation of the sanctity of life, and the feminists, who say, "We have struggled so long to win equality with men, to become our own moral agents, and to prove that we're not the property of men or the states." It seems to me there are two irreconcilable extremes there.

GLENDON: Most of us Americans and our political candidates have accepted the idea that there isn't a common story and that you have to make a drastic either/or choice in the area of abortion. In fact, as I said, the polls indicate that the majority of Americans don't feel comfortable with abortion on demand and don't feel comfortable with making abortion completely illegal. If the legislative process were allowed to go forward, we would see here what we saw in Europe and what we saw in the United States until 1973—the production of laws that would vary somewhat in detail from state to state, but which would be conversations about balancing compassion for the pregnant woman who finds herself in a very vulnerable, difficult situation and respect for the developing human life that society in some way has an interest in.

MOYERS: So you would permit abortions without undue harassment of the pregnant woman, but you would encourage the legal alternatives to abortion?

GLENDON: I would let that be worked out by state legislatures under the circumstances that prevailed within each state. I don't think there is a single solution. The legislators will respond, to some degree, to diversity in the population. I can imagine that one story might be told in New York and another story told in California.

MOYERS: But then the citizen of the United States becomes not first and foremost a citizen of the United States, but first of Texas or of New York—and if Texas discriminates in some way, what happens?

GLENDON: I'm not sure that it's an incorrect or unhealthy vision of the United States to see the fifty states as laboratories where different approaches to a variety of very hard social problems can be worked out.

MOYERS: But the feminists are not going to agree to that because they say a woman should have the same right of privacy, the same right of choice, and the same moral agency in one state that she does in another.

GLENDON: I'm not sure that feminists wouldn't agree. The polls show that women, just as much as men, are uncomfortable with the idea of a constitutional right to dispose of developing life. The majority of women would support some kind of compromise. Women understand, I think even better than men, that there are conflicting values here. There's a real tension.

MOYERS: What are the forces that are shaping the story today as we sit here and talk?

GLENDON: I regret to say that I see really a dark side to both the pro-choice and the pro-life movements. Pro-choice has some silent support among men who don't want to take responsibility for fatherhood, among persons involved in a profit-making abortion industry, and, maybe saddest of all, among taxpayers who see abortion as a way of keeping down the size of an underclass. So there's a lot of unspoken support for the status quo. On the other hand, pro-life has this dark side of punitiveness toward women that I find absolutely incomprehensible, but it seems to be there, as well as a certain unwillingness to recognize that if you're going to be pro-life, it shouldn't be with a view that life begins at conception and ends at birth. You have to be pro-life all the way, and that means supporting maternity, childbirth, and child raising, which has become very difficult in our society, where both parents are usually in the labor force.

> . . . if you're going to be pro-life, it shouldn't be with a view that life begins at conception and ends at birth.

MOYERS: Do you think a compromise is emerging in our country?

GLENDON: A compromise can't really emerge until there's some movement on the Supreme Court, and that's very difficult to predict or foresee. I think if the Supreme Court were disposed to make some movement, it would be fairly easy to do in a way that would not involve overruling *Roe v. Wade.*

MOYERS: What would that be?

GLENDON: There's a time-honored technique of cutting decisions back to what we call their narrow holding. *Roe v. Wade* really only held that a Texas statute that made abortion illegal except to save the life of the mother was unconstitutional. Many other constitutional courts, for example, the constitutional court of Italy, have held such statutes unconstitutional because they give insufficient weight to the interest of the pregnant woman.

MOYERS: In Catholic Italy?

GLENDON: In Catholic Italy. The courts returned the question to the Italian Parliament, while saying to them, "You can't go as far as you did before." So *Roe v.*

Wade could be cut back to its narrow holding, which would leave quite a bit of leeway to legislatures to experiment with other approaches.

MOYERS: Do you think we're paying a price for individualism in America?

GLENDON: There is always the danger that if you speak a language that recognizes only individual rights, you will become a people that can think only about individuals. Choices last. Choices that we make as individuals make us into the kinds of people that we are. Choices that we make collectively as a society make us into the kind of society we are. So if you put together a whole lot of legal decisions that give priority to individual rights, and that let them trump everything else, you're contributing in some unquantifiable but nevertheless real way to shaping the society.

MOYERS: How would you rewrite the story?

GLENDON: The only way we can talk about that in modern times, when everybody is worried about imposing one version of morality or one person's values on another person, is to talk about keeping a social conversation going.

MOYERS: When Tocqueville came here one hundred and sixty years ago, he feared that democracy would not be able to address itself to these long-term issues, that all of us would be so caught up in our immediate needs and interests that only the philosophers and sometimes the statesmen could address the horizon out there. Was Tocqueville a prophet?

GLENDON: He certainly was right in saying that democracies would have a terrible time dealing with the long run and with making long-term plans. That problem affects not only the family, but also the environment, the economy, and many other issues that we're struggling with. Tocqueville placed some hope in philosophers and statesmen. The challenge for philosophers and statesmen is still today very much the same challenge that Hamilton identified in the famous first paragraph of *The Federalist*, where he said that it seems to have fallen to one people by their conduct and example to show whether we can have good government by reflection and choice. That question is still open, except that today we have the added complication whether a heterogeneous people in a large commercial republic can establish good government by reflection and choice. As you know, the classical political philosophers were skeptical about that—but that's the challenge.

MOYERS: In Plato's *Laws* the Athenian stranger is going to Crete to study its laws, and he asks, in effect, "Are your laws written by the gods, or are they written by human beings?" In our society laws are not written by gods, they're written by human beings.

GLENDON: They certainly are.

MOYERS: Does that give you much hope that this compromise can happen?

GLENDON: Human beings have the faculty of imagination, of reaching out for the transcendant. I'm still optimistic enough to place a little hope in human laws.

Peter Berger

S O C I O L O G I S T

BOSTON UNIVERSITY PHOTO SERVICES

Peter Berger believes the economic miracle of East Asia tells us something important about the state of our democracy and about the relationship of religion to capitalism. He is a professor of religion and sociology at Boston University and director of the Institute for the Study of Economic Culture. Berger has written about subjects as varied as modern society, the rediscovery of the supernatural, personal ethics, and social change. His most recent book is In Search of an East Asian Development Model.

MOYERS: You're spending a lot of your time these days studying the societies of East Asia. Why are they so important to you?

BERGER: They're not so important to me personally. I find other parts of the world in many ways more congenial. But for most of my professional life I've been concerned with modernization and development, and that's where it's really happening in the most dramatic way.

MOYERS: And by modernization you mean . . . ?

BERGER: The transformation of the world by modern science and technology. Japan, especially, is the most successful case outside the West. It's a mirror for us in many ways. But Japan is no longer alone. There are other successful societies in Eastern Asia. It's terribly important to know what makes them tick, not only to understand them, but also to understand ourselves. Looking at them, we can see much more clearly what our own society is and is not.

MOYERS: You said these societies are a mirror. When you look into that mirror, what do you see about us?

BERGER: We see what is and what is not essential to certain institutions. For example, capitalism has been the dominant economic institution of the West. Many people, whether they advocate capitalism or criticize it, argue that it is inevitably linked to individualism. Some people say this is great; others say capitalism is linked to selfishness. But whether they praise it or criticize it, they agree this is a necessary linkage.

Now look at East Asian capitalism—there's no question it's capitalism. But in Japan, Taiwan, and Singapore it's not linked to individualism, it's linked to a culture which is much more communalistic.

MOYERS: The goal is the welfare of the group as opposed to the profit of the individual.

BERGER: —What the Japanese call groupiness—as opposed to personal self-realization. Apparently capitalism managed to link up with cultures that are much less individualistic than ours. So one important conclusion we get from looking in the East Asian mirror is that the necessary linkage between individualism and capitalism is not as necessary as both advocates and critics of capitalism in the West thought.

MOYERS: Were you surprised to find in Japan a dynamic culture paying more attention to the group than to the individual?

BERGER: Yes, one is always surprised when things go against one's expectations—because I, like almost everyone else in the West, from right to left, believed in this necessary conjunction of capitalism and individualism.

MOYERS: What accounts for the success of capitalism in nonindividualistic cultures?

BERGER: The most popular hypothesis on this has been the so-called post-Confucian hypothesis, which says that it is the modifications of Confucian morality which basically explain the East Asian economic miracle. I think the matter's a little bit more complicated. There are other elements involved.

MOYERS: Do you find that just as Protestantism played a role in this country, religion is playing a role in the capitalist explosion in Asia?

BERGER: Some people argue that Confucianism is not a religion. I would say it is a religion, if one means by a religion a philosophical and moral system.

Last year I was in Singapore, during the Chinese Festival of Hungry Ghosts. A hungry ghost is the ghost of someone who dies without leaving children to perform the necessary sacrifices, and who therefore doesn't get fed in the other world, and comes back and does mischief. At the Festival of Hungry Ghosts, the community feeds the hungry ghosts so that they will go away and not create mischief. Well, I was at dinner with some friends. When I went back to my hotel, there was a little tent next to the hotel. The employees' association of the hotel had a shrine for the hungry ghosts—that in itself was not surprising. Inside was a Chinese man selling paper money, which you burn and which then is transferred to the other world for the use of the hungry ghosts. But back of where he sat he had a big piece of paper on which were entered the exact amounts that each person had given for the hungry ghosts. It was a bookkeeping arrangement. That is East Asian folk religion—a pragmatic, indeed capitalistic, attitude in dealing with the next world. The ghosts can actually go and look at the balance statement. There's a hard-headed practicality in dealing even with ghosts. That has a lot to do with economic culture.

MOYERS: Are these East Asian societies more materialistic than ours?

BERGER: Oh, much more. Compared to East Asians, Americans are mystical dreamers.

MOYERS: I think of the United States as a very materialistic culture.

BERGER: You have to ask, compared to what? Compared to India, the United States is a materialistic culture, although maybe even that isn't true. But we're certainly not materialistic compared to East Asia. They are much more hard-headed. We are very sentimental. It's very easy to sway Americans with appeals to compassion and to all sorts of, let's say, soft values. I'm sure there's a Judeo-Christian religious influence here. Try to raise money for any humanitarian purpose in Hong Kong. It's very, very difficult.

MOYERS: Reading Peter Berger, one has the strong impression that democracy and capitalism are necessary partners in the gathering of wealth. And many of those

Asian societies are authoritarian. Have you also been surprised to discover capitalism taking root in authoritarian societies?

BERGER: No, that does not contradict my view. Capitalism is a necessary, but not adequate, condition for democracy. You need a market economy in order to have a successful democracy, but the other way round is not correct, although I would wish it were, since I very much believe in democracy. We may not like it, but you can have successful capitalism under authoritarian auspices. In fact, this has frequently happened, beginning, incidentally, in Japan at the time of the Meiji restoration, which was the beginning of Japanese capitalism. What you can say to give comfort to us democrats—I mean that with a small *d*—is that a successful capitalism, even if it begins under authoritarian auspices, tends to release democratizing pressures. Well-fed children of peasants tend to become politically uppity. We can see this in Taiwan and South Korea. So some effects of capitalism tend toward democracy, but not in the way that people think who say that you can't have capitalism without democracy. Unfortunately, that is not true.

MOYERS: But if capitalism can prove to work without democracy, authoritarian societies might choose a capitalism that is more controlled in order to protect the ethos of the group.

BERGER: Yes, that is possible. On the other hand, when people are actually given a choice between an authoritarian and a democratic regime, even in East Asia, they almost always choose the democratic direction. Look at what's happening now in South Korea, for example. Korea is very much of a communalistic culture, as much as Japan. Yet it is moving toward democracy by popular will. Japan, by any reasonable criterion, is a democracy like the United States in its formal political structure, but it is linked to a nonindividualistic culture, which makes these democratic institutions actually function in quite a different way. So opting for democracy, as for capitalism, does not necessarily mean opting for our individualistic culture.

MOYERS: But capitalism works to undermine the group ethic. Ultimately it is "my success, my cunning, and my reward" that make capitalism pay off. In time, won't capitalism in these East Asian societies undermine the very culture that has given rise to it there?

BERGER: Mr. Moyers, the reason I'm smiling is because the question you've just asked is the sixty-four-billion-yen question—good money, yen, not our cheap Third World currency. It's one of the most important questions about East Asia. Are they becoming more like us? Are capitalism, democracy, and the Western-dominated culture of the nonsocialist world going to change Japan and the other East Asian societies so that they'll become more like us in such matters as individualism? I don't think at this point we know the answer. The evidence is mixed.

MOYERS: The world will certainly look different if they do, because while modernization has created great affluence in the West, it has also created a kind of anarchy that you can see any given day on our streets, in our cities, and on our highways. If these collective-minded societies go the same direction, then along with greater affluence comes even more anarchy, does it not?

BERGER: I don't want to use the word "collective" because it suggests a socialist society, and these societies are not. So I use the word "communalism." Their community-oriented culture has been what economists call a comparative advantage. The term I use is "economic culture." Their economic culture has obvious traits which are useful to them in international competition—hard work, saving, the famous East Asian work ethic, et cetera. If they become more like us, they're going to lose some of their comparative advantage vis-à-vis us.

Let me illustrate with a story. In the early days of the Roman Republic, when Rome was at war with Greek kingdoms in southern Italy, the Roman envoy, a robust old Roman type, was sent to the court of the Greek King. He was next to an Epicurean philosopher who explained to him the Epicurean philosophy that the purpose of life is happiness. The Roman listened to all of this and then said, "I hope that you continue to hold these beliefs as long as you are at war with Rome." The last time I was in Japan, I said to a group of Japanese that they should say to us, "We hope that you Westerners continue to hold these beliefs as long as you are in competition with us."

> . . . our cult of self-realization and the pursuit of individual happiness, carried to this crazy extreme, is not helping us economically.

MOYERS: Because?

BERGER: Because our cult of self-realization and the pursuit of individual happiness, carried to this crazy extreme, is not helping us economically. Their hard work and their ascetic, self-denying, group-oriented ethos has helped them economically. It would be to our economic advantage if they became more like us.

MOYERS: Now, there's a paradox—this individualism at the heart of our democratic capitalism has in fact been the dynamic behind our affluence. But you say that it's not serving us that well now.

BERGER: I don't think it's a paradox. The older individualism of the West had a different ethos attached to it. It was what Max Weber called the Protestant ethic. Even in non-Protestant countries, which were far more individualistic than East Asia, individualism was coupled with hard work and saving.

MOYERS: There was an ethic of responsibility to the whole.

BERGER: Yes, an ethic of communal responsibility—not like the East Asian one, but certainly not like what is much more common now in the West, an ethos of self-realization and never mind the community. No, I don't think it's a contradiction. We're talking about different phases of Western culture.

MOYERS: Do you think this "celebration of individual cunning in the pursuit of status and wealth," as somebody said, is making us less competitive with these East Asian societies?

BERGER: What is making us less competitive is that common effort for the purpose of a collective goal is much less strong than it was in our own culture a half century ago. By "collective goal," I don't mean the nation as a whole, but loyalty to one's enterprise, to one's company.

MOYERS: The late economist Charles Schultz worried that the market, where everything is reduced to an economic contract, diminishes the need for compassion, brotherly love, patriotism, and civic virtue. Do you think that's so?

BERGER: No, I don't think so, not by itself. It depends on what the market is coupled with, culturally. If you take the old Protestant-inspired culture of America, which was linked to the early days of American capitalism, the market didn't have that effect at all. Human beings play different roles in life. The entrepreneur who pushed his own advantage in the market, which is what the market is all about, wasn't that way at all in his life as a family person, as a citizen, or as a member of his community. The ethos of the culture was very much geared to communal responsibility, citizenship, and concern for those who did not make out well in the market. So the market in itself does not lead to these things.

MOYERS: What's happened, then? There is a loss of the community ethic. "We the People" is much heralded rhetorically, but oft violated in practice. Do you think something fundamental has happened?

BERGER: It's less fundamental than some critics of contemporary America have argued. I don't think we're all engaged in a mindless, greedy pursuit of wealth, although there are sectors of society of whom this is true. But one thing that is striking about America, especially if one goes abroad, is the amount of concern that this country has for every conceivable sort of disadvantaged group. I don't mean the country in the sense of the government, but in the sense of people, churches, associations. So I would not take a generally gloomy position as to how these old, wonderful values have decayed. They have decayed in certain sectors, and these, unfortunately, are strategic sectors.

MOYERS: Where, for example?

BERGER: There is a so-called yuppie sector of the business world in which young people seem to be severed from all moral moorings, and certainly from all religious moorings, and are in there, no matter what, criminally or otherwise, to make money. That's a very unfortunate development, but even more serious is the alienation of important sectors of the cultural elite—the creative people and the knowledge class— from the values that originally shaped the society. For example, the United States is the most religious country in the West. We are like India in terms of how many people go to services, give money to religious institutions, elect to be ministers, et cetera. But the cultural elite is very different. It's the most secularized portion of the population. It's a Sweden superimposed on an India. No wonder these two don't get along very well. I'm not making a political distinction. It so happens that this class tends to be to the left of the main street of Americans—not the far left, but certainly more left of center than people of similar income who are in business or in the old professions. But it isn't the political thing that's crucial, it's the cultural thing that's crucial.

MOYERS: Do I hear you saying that religion is more important as a cultural anchor, as a dynamic in developing a sense of the whole, than freedom?

BERGER: Well, freedom's a fundamental political issue, and democracy is the institution which allows for the expression of freedom. But if you look at freedom a little bit more philosophically, it is essentially an empty thing. It's freedom from certain constraints in order to do certain things. The value of freedom in itself doesn't tell you what to do. It just says you should be free from these constraints. It's the culture, the value system, and especially the religion of a society that make it possible for people to utilize these freedoms in constructive ways.

MOYERS: Do you think this absence of a religious drive in so many people today is costing us coherence, connection, community?

BERGER: There is a correlation in certain groups of the population between their alienation from religion and some of these chaotic moral conditions that you have referred to. Now, I am myself a Christian. I don't think one should be religious because it's socially useful. Even if it were not socially useful, I think one should worship God. And there are other things I believe as a Christian. It so happens that if I looked at the same phenomena as a social scientist, I would reach the same conclusion if I were atheistic or agnostic—that the decline of religion in certain populations has had some social consequences that are unfortunate. Conversely, religion in most of the world, certainly in Asia, is a very potent force.

MOYERS: I agree that religion is an animating force in the civil life of a people, but that raises a couple of questions. First, if religion is diminished among elites, it can't be willed back. Religion is by nature voluntary—so what happens to a society whose intellectual class is no longer paying attention to the transcendent?

BERGER: At worst, what happens to society is increasing social and political conflict, the kind of thing that happened in France at the time of the Third Republic. Another development might be that the secularized group and the rest of the society become more tolerant of each other and make certain compromises. That, I think, is the most likely course in America and is not too bad. It is also, of course, possible that a religious revival might occur in areas of society that used to be secular.

MOYERS: Why do you think tolerance is the most likely course? It seems to me the opposite is happening with the rise of an aggressive religious right that is pressing its claims with a cooperative state power. And those people are not very tolerant.

BERGER: I wouldn't put it that way. I think both sides want to use state power to achieve their purposes. Each group thinks that its position is so self-evidently moral that of course the state should use its power to support the purposes of that group. Take something like various items on the feminist agenda, which are part of the quasi-religious beliefs of the knowledge class. They certainly want to use state power to push them through. The difference is not in the use of state power. Fanaticism is pretty nicely distributed all around the spectrum here.

A greater tolerance comes when people arrive at certain formulas that no one quite agrees with but that everyone is willing to live with. American democracy has been quite ingenious in this. Take the issue of school prayer. I can see such a formula developing—a moment of silence, for example—which no one will be terribly happy with, but which most people will live with. The one issue where it's most difficult to see this compromise happening is abortion. That's a very important issue because it most sharply creates moral polarization.

MOYERS: Given the strong convictions on both sides, is there any room for a moral compromise?

BERGER: I would hope so. I'm not committed to either of the two polarized positions. The answer lies somewhere—not in the middle, but also not in the polarized positions. The population is split pretty much down the middle, by class. For example, the knowledge class is very strongly pro-abortion. When one part of the population thinks that an act is an act of homicide and the other part thinks it's an expression of the personal freedom of a woman and of a basic human right, it's very hard to arrive at a compromise.

MOYERS: What the political culture has done is to leave it to the courts, and the courts in the first major round decided for the right to have an abortion. Now the courts are beginning to swing in the other direction.

BERGER: We have put on the courts of this country an intolerable burden of deciding philosophical and moral issues.

MOYERS: Let me come back to this question of individualism and society. It's not only the loss of a religious dynamic, but the nature of our capitalist economy today that diminishes civic virtue. Among so many young couples today both husband and wife must work. They're having to delay children, and they can't afford a mortgage. They have to borrow more and more and save less and less. They're having such a difficult time that they no longer have the opportunities for the civic life individuals used to express. For example, here in New York, in the villages surrounding Manhattan, we're finding it hard to recruit volunteer firemen. The young men who used to volunteer now have to commute too far, and often have to work multiple jobs. They no longer have time for this civic duty.

The point is, our culture is changing because of the dynamics of our economic situation, which requires more and more from the individual just to stand still.

BERGER: I'm not sure. It depends which group of economists you believe in. Is the middle class better off? My sense is that, on the whole, it is better off. But I'm not sure the situation of firemen out in Long Island has as much to do with capitalism as it has to do with modern technology and modern urbanism. If we had a socialist society in which people lived way out and had to travel an hour to the people's commissariat or wherever they're working, we'd have the same problem. A highly complex, modern, technological society does not as easily encourage the old-fashioned virtues expressed by the voluntary fireman of an older type of society.

But this situation doesn't trouble me all that much. So they're going to have a professional fire department out there—so what? I don't think that's the end of the world.

MOYERS: But if by "capitalism" we mean the enterprising individual in pursuit of his or her profit, and if in order to be a capitalist today one has to run harder and harder, there is less time for other personal, civic, and social pursuits. You can trace it at least to how capitalism is practiced in an economy where rampant individualism pits us all against one another.

BERGER: But there's also a cultural variable here. Forgive me for bringing in economic culture again, but to some extent it's a matter of decision. In other words, what is the standard of living that a particular couple regards as desirable at that stage of their life? It's obviously true that many people couldn't live the way they want to live if both husband and wife didn't work. That creates problems. But they made the decision that at this stage of their life, say in their twenties, they wish to live on that level of material well-being. One could make a decision, as would a Japanese couple of the same age, that we are not going to live that well in our twenties. The woman is going to stay at home, to take care of the children, at least until they go to school, and in the meantime the family income will be less. At a later stage we will make more. Now, that has nothing to do with capitalism or the state of the economy that the two parties are debating about right now. But it has an awful lot to do with cultural expectations and values. I'm not being critical of the young people who say we both have to work because we need the standard of living. I'm simply describing it and saying there's a cultural element here, and a matter of personal decision.

MOYERS: What about the future? Is it going to come down to a competitive race between capitalism combined with something else, and capitalism with democracy?

BERGER: It's very hard to say. A lot will depend on what the socialist world does. If the present developments in China and Russia really lead to a great liberalization of these economies, we'll have a very different ball game. Capitalism, as an economic system, is so successful, and so resilient in its successes, that I do not anticipate a drastic reversal. A much more serious thing to worry about is how different capitalist societies relate to each other. For example, the most important issue right now, in that department, is the competition between East Asia and the West. Very often people act as if the West, or even one's own country, were alone in the world, rather than seeing it as engaged in a contest with other societies.

MOYERS: Is it possible that we will take our survival for granted, that these other dynamic cultures will come sneaking up from behind, and the next thing we'll know, we'll be looking at their bumpers? Maybe we have so taken your message about the moral superiority of democracy and capitalism to heart that we now take for granted this combination will survive without our having to study hard, compete vigorously with other cultures, learn from them, and adjust empirically and rationally.

BERGER: I don't think that's a lesson I wanted to teach. The fact that something is good, alas, does not mean it will necessarily survive. We do have to worry about it. But I'm not so much worried about the survival of capitalism and democracy in general in the world. I'm fairly optimistic about that. I'm worried about how different societies will relate to each other. We cannot afford, politically or culturally, to think of the problems of our own society as if we were alone in the world. We cannot continue to have a greater and greater expansion of the welfare state with no regard to how that affects us vis-à-vis our major international competitors. Now, I'm not speaking for the dismantlement of the welfare state. I'm not a right-wing reactionary. We need the welfare state. The question is, how large is it going to be? What is it going to include?

> We cannot afford . . . to think of the problems of our own society as if we were alone in the world.

MOYERS: But there are countries in the world where the welfare state is much more protective and pervasive than ours, countries that are growing, viable, and prosperous, making their way in the world. One doesn't have to choose a welfare state or no welfare state.

BERGER: No, no. That would be a false dichotomy. It's not that kind of absolute choice. The question is how large the welfare state and what kind of welfare state. One can have, for example, a welfare state that encourages people to get into productive lives. One can have a welfare state that discourages productivity. So it's a much more fine question we have to ask. But we have to become more conscious of our competition with Asia, not in an ethnocentric or hysterical way. I don't think there's a yellow peril. These people aren't out to get us.

MOYERS: Are the East Asian societies more competitive because they place less emphasis on the welfare state?

BERGER: Historically, that has been the case. Japan went through its great period of economic growth with a minimal welfare state and, what was equally important, a virtually nonexistent defense budget, because we took care of their defense.

MOYERS: That seems to me a very important fact.

BERGER: They can continue neither indefinitely, though they are certainly trying to keep the defense budget down. But their welfare state is mushrooming, because they have a rapidly aging population which they'll have to take care of. So they will lose that comparative advantage.

MOYERS: How do these East Asian societies handle their poor as compared to us? For all of our prosperity and affluence, thirty-one million Americans live in poverty. How do they deal with the poor compared to us?

BERGER: Well, traditionally, they dealt with their poor through the families, rather than through the state. I think for a while that worked quite well. There's no principle that says if I'm poor, it's better to be taken care of by a social worker than by my uncle.

MOYERS: We used to take care of our poor through extended families.

BERGER: That's becoming increasingly impossible, and the state has to move in.

MOYERS: Will that happen there?

BERGER: Probably. But you see, I would not like to give the impression of saying that because something is economically successful, therefore we have to do it. That's a very big danger in the comparison with Asia. The assumption is that they are successful, and that therefore we must become like them, and then we'll be just as successful.

First of all, that premise is a little doubtful, because we are not them. We have a different culture. For an American manager to try to imitate a Japanese manager, apart from its being funny, may not work. But more seriously than that, we cannot do it. Maybe we don't want to do it. There are values of our own culture, such as the values of individual liberty, which I would not want to give up, even if they turned out to be economically unsuccessful. I would not want the United States to become like East Asian societies. I wouldn't want us to become as materialistic, or as highly obsessed with hierarchy, or, most of all, as diabolically meritocratic. This inhuman examination system they have where essentially, at age twelve, an individual's life is decided—I wouldn't want us to become like that. If the price for our own values, such as individual liberty, was that we are going to be number two or even number three in the world, in the twenty-first century, so be it. It might even be somewhat of a relief.

MOYERS: A relief?

BERGER: Yes. Let the Japanese worry about the Persian Gulf, for example. I don't think that would be so bad.

MOYERS: They don't seem to want to.

BERGER: No, of course not. It's much more convenient for them that we do the patrolling and the worrying and the paying for all of this.

MOYERS: The smart culture would take the best of both. The East Asian societies would say, "We want a little more individualism because we want that competitive edge that comes from the individual who strives very hard—but we also want to protect our sense of the group, our sense of community, and not go overboard." We would say, "We want a little more of their community ethic, their sense of responsibility, one to another, and a little less of this rampant individualism that gives us Ivan Boesky and other examples."

BERGER: Ideally, you know, we would look at cultures like philosopher kings and take something from here, something from there—which, by the way, the Japanese did in the nineteenth century when they actually sent missions all over the world to see what they would pick and choose. Most of the time that doesn't work. We can't assemble our own culture the way we assemble a Tinkertoy. Sometimes the clashes are unavoidable, and we have to make choices rather than simply combine things. There are choices I would make in favor of our own cultural traditions, even if such a choice should turn out to be an economic disadvantage.

MOYERS: Are you in any way worried about this multicultural future, this clashing, competitive, discordant world that's emerging from so many different sources?

BERGER: Yes, I tend to worry about everything. I'm a worrier by nature. But intellectually I worry much less about this than I do about other things. It's much more of a challenge than a danger, and human beings respond to challenges. The West confronting the Soviet Union is in a different position, because, except for a few marginal types in Western society, the Soviet Union is so unattractive a society, it doesn't really have much seductive power, certainly not to most people.

The East is a different thing. It's so successful. In this cultural contest between Asia and us, we're going to discover more what we are. It's like when you go abroad—you suddenly discover what it means to be an American.

MOYERS: Does it require a change in our collective mentality as Americans? We used to be rather provincial.

BERGER: Americans haven't been that provincial for a while now. Since World War II, America has been a world power, and American civilization has increasingly reflected that fact.

MOYERS: Yes, but we've approached other countries with the sense of the superiority of the American way of life. We haven't gone out to negotiate with, bargain with, respect those other cultures, and to absorb what they have to offer.

BERGER: I think the future will require some changes in attitudes in two different directions. Again, we come back to class. Most Americans who are not terribly well educated still tend to believe in the old "America is superior" ethos—which in many ways is healthy. It's mistaken, but it's also kind of healthy. Then you get the cultural elite—or at least essential elements of it—who have tended to think of America as the worst possible place. "Blame America first" is also a terrible mistake. In looking at Asia, particularly, we have to avoid both extremes. The old sense of "We are superior, and you have to learn everything from us, from democracy to hamburgers," is not very good.

On the other hand, the sense of "How wonderful Asia is, we have to become more like them"—this kind of expatriate romanticism is also terribly wrong. What we have to do, especially if we have some pretension to intellectual sophistication, is to be very conscious of what we are, of what we accept and identify with in our own tradition, but yet be open to what comes from elsewhere.

Apart from these economic things we've been talking about, there are wonderful things to be learned from Asian culture. On the whole, I am quite optimistic about this.

MOYERS: What's one wonderful thing you've learned from Asia?

BERGER: Oh, a greater sense of—how should I put it—the vastness of time and the universe, and of not taking the historical scene on earth as seriously as Westerners tend to do. That, I think, you get in Asia.

Northrop Frye

CANADIAN LITERARY CRITIC

ROY NICHOLLS

Northrop Frye believes that studying literature can produce, out of the society we have to live in, a vision of the society we want to live in. In nearly fifty years of teaching at the University of Toronto, he has gained a reputation as one of the world's foremost literary critics. His books include Anatomy of Criticism *and* The Educated Imagination. *He is currently writing a second volume to* The Great Code, *a study of the language and metaphors of the Bible.*

MOYERS: Does it bother Canadians that the United States pays them so little attention? Or do you just consider yourselves lucky?

FRYE: Well, there is a good deal of resentment about the Americans' ignorance of things Canadian, considering that the first thing the American learns about his own country is that it's bounded on the north by Canada. At the same time, the American policy of taking Canada more or less for granted rather suits the Canadian temperament.

MOYERS: Poor Mexico has to wake up every morning wondering what good deed the United States is going to do to it that day.

FRYE: Exactly, yes. But Mexico has a different language and a radically different culture. It's quite a different situation.

MOYERS: Some stereotypes of Canada appeared recently in an American humor magazine called *Spy*. One was that obedience is in the Canadian blood, that every citizen knows the thrill of being a follower, and that Canadians won't cross against a red light even if there's no traffic coming and a dog is chasing them. Now what do you say about that caricature?

FRYE: Well, it has this much to be said for it: that historically Canada was developed in a very different way from the United States. For example, we don't have the tradition of the bad men, the outlaws in the West. We started out with the British military occupation of Quebec, and then went on to the Northwest Mounted Police. The violence in Canadian history has been mostly repressive violence, mostly from the top down. That has made us, to some extent, a country that puts up with pragmatic compromises. But I don't know that it's any different from the way that Americans follow their donkeys' carrots in elections.

MOYERS: Canada didn't become a nation until 1867. By then the United States was a nation almost a hundred years old.

FRYE: Canada, of course, had spent the eighteenth century with the English and French battering down each other's forts. In other words, we didn't have any eighteenth century, and we have nothing corresponding to culture heroes like Washington or Franklin or Jefferson.

MOYERS: Is there a dominant figure in the Canadian idea similar to Washington or to Lincoln?

FRYE: There really isn't. The closest we have are leaders like Sir John A. Macdonald, who was the architect of confederation, and later on, Sir Wilfrid Laurier. But we don't have a father of the country.

MOYERS: What about the stereotype in the United States that Canadians are so friendly that they even say thank you to the bank machine?

FRYE: Well, that could be true. I remember a Chicago taxi driver who heard me say something like, "Sorry," or "Beg your pardon," to something I didn't hear, and it impressed him for the rest of the morning.

MOYERS: There's also an old saw about a culture that thrives on Valium—that although the United States and Canada share a 3,968-mile border, Canada doesn't keep troops on that border because Canadians know that if the United States invaded, you would win by simply boring us to death in the first three days.

FRYE: Yes, or scaring you to death. After all, we won several battles in the War of 1812 with about thirty Indians scattered through the woods.

MOYERS: What do you think is the dominant image of Canada in the United States?

FRYE: I think it's a bit dim. They regard it as a neighbor they can more or less take for granted, and otherwise don't think too much about it. It's very reassuring to the United States to feel that there's a country in which most people speak the same language they do and have a great deal of their culture in common.

MOYERS: One of your intellectuals, the novelist Mordecai Richler, says that most new ideas and energy come from the States. Canadians find that they're subject to the finest in American culture as well as to the worst. People here are brought up on American literature and American films. When all is said and done, therefore, Canadians and Americans are all North Americans. Do you think that's a fair assessment?

FRYE: Well, I think it's very largely true. It's a trifle oversimplified—there are differences in temperament that he isn't altogether taking account of. But it is true that Canadians are sometimes apt to talk rather glibly about the Americanizing of Canadian culture, forgetting that the features they disapprove of are also at work in America itself, and that the United States has to struggle between its best culture and its worst culture.

MOYERS: What do you see as the best of United States culture?

FRYE: It's the same as the best in any culture, I suppose: the arts themselves, and the respect for freedom and individuality that makes the American ideal something real. There's a Canadian novelist, Frederick Philip Grove, who wrote a book called *Search for America*. Grove says there are two Americas, one connected with Whitman and Lincoln, and the other with selling encyclopedias from door to door, which is the job he had. And he says in a footnote at the end of the book that he thinks that the former way of life has been better preserved in Canada. But that is not a statement I would buy, particularly.

MOYERS: What do you think is the worst aspect of American culture?

FRYE: The worst aspect, I suppose, is what anybody would say was the worst: the violence, the lawlessness, the corruption and greed and so forth—all the human vices.

MOYERS: You don't seem to have the crime here that we do.

FRYE: Well, that's the elementary arithmetic of original sin—twenty million people can't get up to all the hell that two hundred million people can get up to.

MOYERS: But although you don't have this mythological idea of a nation that the United States has, there seems to be more obeisance to the obligations of society, to the sense of community.

FRYE: That's because the sense of community in Canada is more complex than it is in many countries. The oscillation of national feeling and regional feeling makes for rather a quieter setup in general. And that is why, I think, various ethnic groups in a city like Toronto can get along with each other to a degree that doesn't seem possible in a comparable American city.

MOYERS: The homogeneity of Canada is changing, is it not? When I came into the airport last night, I was struck by the number of people arriving, either as visitors or as potentially new citizens, who were of ethnically diverse backgrounds.

FRYE: The Toronto that I'm living in in 1988 is a totally different city from the Toronto I entered in 1929. Then it was still a hog town, and still entirely a WASP city controlled by the Orange Order. There's almost nothing of that left now. There's no room for it.

MOYERS: Is there a sense that Canada is becoming more like the United States, not only in this regard but in others as well?

FRYE: It's bound to become more like the United States for a rather paradoxical reason: that the more diverse it becomes, the more homogeneous the continent becomes. The statement that you quoted from Mordecai Richler is quite right on that point.

MOYERS: Someone said that you gave us Saul Bellow and we gave you the Cosby show. You exchange a great intellectual and novelist for a sitcom mass-produced in Hollywood.

FRYE: But again, that's one of these rather simplistic contrasts, where the side of American culture that you can't praise very highly is something which is just as lethal to American culture as it is to Canadian culture.

MOYERS: Lethal?

FRYE: In the sense that it creates a market, which to some degree curtails the richness and variety and scope of the genuinely creative people in the country.

MOYERS: You once talked about Canada as being an anti-intellectual society. Of course, that's a common lament made in the United States, too. Do you think that's still true?

FRYE: Oh, I think it's true in most countries. Actually, it's less true in Canada than in many other places, and it's becoming less true in proportion as more and more Canadians begin to realize that the creative people in Canada are the people to be prized, the people who are actually defining the country at its best and producing the best image of it.

MOYERS: Eighty-five percent of all Canadians live within a hundred miles of the United States border. That's close enough to hear Ed Koch even when the television set is not on. Is Canada a kind of cultural colony of the United States?

FRYE: Canada may very well be the only genuine colony left in the world. The degree of economic and to some extent political penetration by the United States is of course very great, and the reasons for it are quite obvious.

MOYERS: But does the mindset of the colony exist here—that there is a great paternalistic and pervasive force shaping the culture from the outside?

FRYE: I don't think Canada has ever thought of the United States as in any sense a mother country or a country that would shape its imagination. It has regarded the United States as a friendly ally, but always on equal terms with itself. There's nothing corresponding to the somewhat romantic views that nineteenth century Canadians had about Great Britain or French Canadians about France. The Americans were simply the Whigs who won the revolution, and the Canadians were the Tories who lost it.

MOYERS: And burned the White House in the process of the war that followed the revolution.

FRYE: But you know why they burned the White House—because the Americans burned Toronto a year before. The Americans burned York, as Toronto was called then, in the middle of the winter, and half of York got pneumonia. In reprisal for that, the British shelled Washington the next year.

MOYERS: It's fascinating to me that the United States won its independence from Britain and then fought with Canada, and yet among no nations of the world do more amicable sentiments manifest themselves than between these three societies.

FRYE: That's true. Canada, of course, had its civil war first, with the British and the French. The War of 1812, however stupid a war it was, was something of a war of independence for Canada. It meant that Canada was going to go its own way. At the same time, it never seems to have left any legacy of bitterness behind it, the way the American Civil War did in the South.

MOYERS: Do those wars of Canada's history play the role in the mind of your country that our war of revolution and our Civil War play in our mind?

FRYE: It's not nearly as intense. Canadians really know very little about the War of 1812 and care less. The eighteenth-century struggle for the country is still remembered with a good deal of heart-burning in the French part of Canada. They speak of 1759 as *l'année terrible*—the year of disaster. But that's something they more or less get out of the history books. I'm not sure how much they feel it.

MOYERS: So much of American history has taken on mythological proportions in our society—the city set upon a hill, frontier, the manifest destiny to make the world safe for democracy. Mythology plays a powerful role in the American consciousness.

FRYE: I rather regret that the same mythological patterns are present in Canada and yet are paid so little attention to. We also have our city on the hill, namely Quebec, the fort where the river narrows, a fort that was taken and retaken about five or six times. And we also have our Maccabean victories in the War of 1812 and the Fenian raids later, and so on. We have all that mythology potentially. But because Americans started with a revolution and a Constitution, they brought the myth right into the foreground of their lives in a way that has never happened with Canada.

MOYERS: We talk about the American dream, but I don't hear anyone talking about the Canadian dream. Does mythology play a part in the Canadian's sense of himself or herself?

FRYE: Mythology does play a part, but it's a different kind of mythology. The Americans started with a revolution, and a revolution tends to impose a deductive pattern on a society, so you get phrases like "one hundred percent American." Of course, nobody ever can find out what one hundred percent Canadian is. To start with, you've got the Anglo-French division. Every Canadian feels himself part of a federal unity, but he also feels himself very intensely a part of a more regional unity. Very often in Canadian elections he'll vote one way federally and the opposite way provincially. All of that means that the Canadian dream is very much more complex than the American dream. In American terms, it's much more Jeffersonian.

MOYERS: So it appeals more to the romantic idea of individualism.

FRYE: I don't know that it gets as far as individualism, but it gets as far as regionalism.

MOYERS: What role does the imagination play in the shaping of a nation's sense of itself?

FRYE: It builds up the sense of the empire expanding without limit, the inscriptions from Assyria saying "the king of kings, the king of the world," and so forth. That's an imagination that gets out of touch with reality. Then eventually you begin to see how the historical process works, that there are always other societies in the world. The imagination takes on other constructs, such as the rise and fall idea—Herodotus explaining that the Greek resistance defeated that tremendous Persian machine because the gods don't like big empires.

MOYERS: I've often thought that one of the secrets of Ronald Reagan's appeal was that he was able to make Americans feel as if we were still the mighty giant of the world, still an empire, even as around the world we were having to retreat from the old presumptions that governed us for the last fifty years. Did you see any of that in the Reagan appeal?

FRYE: Oh yes, very much so. It's the only thing that explains the Reagan charisma. In fact, I think that what has been most important about Americans since the war is that they have been saying a lot of foolish things—the Evil Empire, for example—but doing all the right ones. I think nobody but Nixon could have organized a deal with China, for example.

MOYERS: Well now, what does that say about a society, that it says one thing even as it must do another?

FRYE: It means that the mythological imagination functions on two levels. There is the superficial level of the stereotype, and there's another and very much more realistic one, where you actually do the things that promote self-preservation and survival.

MOYERS: Is it really superficial? Isn't the myth a binding power, an integrating force, for people? What people believe becomes what holds them together, even as they're having to operate more realistically?

FRYE: Yes, it's the function of myth to make a binding force in society. But if that other, more realistic level in mythology is not there, then the stereotype runs away with the realism, and you're heading for disaster. That's the Nazi direction.

MOYERS: When we talk about myth this way, what do we mean?

FRYE: We mean a story extrapolated from history which takes the form of an ideology. That is, because of the American Revolution and the American Constitution, there is such a thing as an American way of life. The American myth becomes the American ideology.

MOYERS: So to know the American story is to buy into the American way of life.

FRYE: I think so.

MOYERS: And why is that important? You say you wish Canada had more of the story, more of the myth.

FRYE: Well, I just wish that the imagination in Canada had something more coherent to work on, that's all. We've always got along on an Edmund Burke type of pragmatic compromise. The conquest of Quebec by the British, for example, was not really a conquest, and they had to make compromises as a result. The Quebec Act was a very humane document by eighteenth-century standards, but it meant that every episode of Canadian history is a crisis in which the country seems to be falling apart at the seams. It never quite does. There is always some ad hoc compromise or arrangement. It's an entirely different attitude from the deductive, revolutionary American model.

MOYERS: How do you see our myth?

FRYE: I see it as the myth of a social unification that is geared to the idea of a progress through time. There are passages in Walt Whitman, for example, where he compares American democracy to something very like an express train—he doesn't use that image, but that's what he means. The country's just going ahead. But since Vietnam, the American imagination has become much more like the Canadian imagination in that it realizes that no imperial power, however great or however wealthy, is immortal.

MOYERS: And you see this since Vietnam, the war America lost?

FRYE: It was the beginning of a sense of mortality about a certain part of American history.

MOYERS: I agree with you. Now there are even books being written about "the decline of the United States," and Americans—except for Ronald Reagan—are talking with a fatalism that is new in my country. Does it strike you as ominous or just mature?

> Every empire has to get to the point where it loses its swelled head and begins to get a sense of proportion about its role in the world.

FRYE: To the extent that it's fatalism, it's ominous. But to the extent that it's an acceptance of certain historical processes, it's very healthy and realistic. Every empire has to get to the point where it loses its swelled head and begins to get a sense of proportion about its role in the world. The British Empire began to do that after the Boer War, and the Soviet Union has been doing it in the last twenty to twenty-five years.

MOYERS: Does American society strike you as acting fairly maturely at this moment?

FRYE: It's acting as maturely as it has done in its history. I don't feel uneasy about the climate of opinion in the United States, to the extent that I felt uneasy about it during the Joe McCarthy period, for example, when the stereotype was running away with the reality.

MOYERS: I think that we are showing some signs of maturity at the moment, although the rhetoric sometimes reminds one of the worst excesses of American pretension.

FRYE: Yes, but there's another streak that doesn't take the rhetoric too seriously.

MOYERS: We've been through the season of American politics. How does it strike you?

FRYE: It's a process that has become like a sporting event. That's really what keeps it going and what keeps the public interested in it. I listen to the discussions on American television and notice how they ascribe mental processes to things that don't strike me as mental processes at all. That kind of discussion—building up the speeches of George Bush and others as though they were all part of a great intellectual debate—all that seems to me to be extremely healthy. It's a way of getting people to participate in their own democracy.

MOYERS: But do you see much evidence of a genuine debate about ideas and policies?

FRYE: I see evidence not in the politicians themselves, but in the people who talk about the politicians.

MOYERS: The politicians play the storytelling role, while the real making of the life of the country goes on, including the intellectual life of the country.

FRYE: Yes. If you watch a Japanese puppet play long enough, you start thinking that the puppets are saying the lines themselves.

MOYERS: Is it different here in Canada?

FRYE: It's different to the extent that it's a parliamentary system. It's becoming more and more like the American system, but there is less emphasis on the party convention, and there is still the possibility of the prime minister going down with his party. The operation of the parliamentary system is different enough to make for a slightly different climate of opinion.

MOYERS: Is television here influencing politics the way it is in the United States, making it a sporting event or entertainment?

FRYE: Very much so. I would like it better if I thought we had people who could play up to it. On the other hand, it doesn't matter all that much who's president of the United States. What did it matter in twentieth-century history that George Ford was a President of the United States?

MOYERS: Gerald Ford.

FRYE: Gerald Ford. Sorry.

MOYERS: Are you saying the President is the front man for a system that continues to operate irrespective of his leadership?

FRYE: I'm not sure that the pyramid myth, the notion of the man at the top of society, really conforms to the realities of twentieth-century life. There is a whole machinery that is bound to continue functioning, so that ninety-five percent of what any President can do is already prescribed for him—unless he's a complete lunatic. For that reason, it doesn't seem so profoundly significant who is in the position of leadership.

MOYERS: What does that say about the role of the leader in the modern world?

FRYE: It means that the leader has to be a teammate. The charismatic leader, to the extent that he is that, is a rather dangerous person if he starts taking himself seriously. I'm a little leery about the adulation bestowed on Gorbachev. He has a very complex piece of machinery to try to help operate. The historical process works itself out in ways that really don't allow for the emergence of a specific leader. It's only in the army that you have the specific leader because that's the way the military hierarchy's set up.

> ... *the leader has to be a teammate.*

MOYERS: But historical processes are the accumulated actions of autonomous individuals expressing their wills, appetites, desires, passions in the world out there. Those are subject to being changed by leaders, are they not?

FRYE: People are much more pushed around than that by the cultural conditioning in which they're brought up and the social conditions under which they have to operate. The person who emerges as leader is really the person who is the ultimate product of that social conditioning.

MOYERS: There was an Italian Marxist in the 1920s who said that in the future, all leaders will be corporate. There will not be single leaders. Of course that was before Mussolini and before Hitler.

FRYE: He was right to the extent that the charismatic single leader turned out to be a disaster.

MOYERS: So maybe the corporate leader is not only an historical necessity, but a desirable phenomenon as well.

FRYE: He's desirable because I think he's essential for movement in the direction of peace. When I said that it was only the military that gives you the person on top, the supreme command, you notice that the dictators, the supreme leaders, have always been leaders of an army and have always imposed what is essentially martial law on their communities.

MOYERS: Mao, Mussolini, Hitler—

FRYE: Yes, and some of the African states.

MOYERS: I remember something you said in a sermon delivered on the one hundred and fiftieth anniversary of the founding of Victoria College here. You said, "I seldom hear people talking about systems with any confidence now. The world today is in so deeply revolutionary a state that all systems, whatever they're called, are equally on the defensive, trying to prevent further change." Do you still hold to that?

FRYE: Oh, I think so, yes. Doctrinaire Marxism will not work anywhere in the world—not because it's Marxism, but because it's doctrinaire. I don't think anything doctrinaire will work anywhere.

MOYERS: And by "doctrinaire," you mean—?

FRYE: I mean a simplified deductive pattern that carries out policies from major premises about ideology—

MOYERS: —instead of from the experience of the real world.

FRYE: Yes.

MOYERS: Gorbachev is trying to change his system.

FRYE: He's trying to loosen up his system. It's because he doesn't have the belief in the system that the followers of Lenin did in the 1920s and '30s that his policies take the shape they do. It's the same in China.

MOYERS: You've lived through the revolution of Russia, the Stalinist era, the Holocaust, two world wars, genocide around the world—this has been quite a century.

FRYE: It's led me to the feeling that the historical process is a dissolving phantasmagoria. When I was young, George VI was the Emperor of India, and Hitler ruled an empire from Norway to Baghdad. All that has vanished into nothingness. That says to me that history is a process of continuing dissolution, and that the things that survive are the creative and the imaginative products.

MOYERS: —the mind, the life of the mind.

FRYE: —the arts and the sciences.

MOYERS: Thirty years ago, you wrote that the hope of democracy rests entirely on the earnest student and the dedicated teacher. Do you still believe that?

FRYE: Yes, I do. That is the only stable and permanent thing in human society. I'm not bringing in religious perspectives at this point, but insofar as we're speaking of human beings constituting a human society, that is what stabilizes and makes permanent the whole structure of society.

MOYERS: The "earnest student"—how do you differentiate the earnest student from the student who's not earnest?

FRYE: The student who's not earnest is simply a middle-class product. He's a member of a privileged class who takes his privileges because he thinks it's the thing to do. But his is a career without discovery. And a career without a discovery is going to move within the prison of his social conditioning. He's never going to see a crack in it anywhere.

MOYERS: And what's the dedicated teacher as opposed to the teacher who's not dedicated?

FRYE: The teacher who is not dedicated is a mass man, and he gets a mass product. He teaches largely because he has particular certainties that he wants to implant in the minds of his students. But the dedicated teacher realizes that the end of education is to get yourself detached from society without withdrawing from it. If a man is teaching English literature, for example, he's in contact with the entire verbal experience of his students. Now nine tenths of that verbal experience is picked up from prejudice and cliché and things the student hears on the street corners, on the playgrounds, and from his family and his home, and so forth. The dedicated teacher tries to detach from all that and to look into it as something objective. It's not something he can withdraw from, because it's his own society, but it's something that he can cultivate a free and individual approach to.

MOYERS: Doesn't this lead to a lonely life, the life of a dissenter, the life of someone who's always questioning instead of affirming?

FRYE: Except that the next person who is also doing this can form a very intimate society with you.

MOYERS: You said that "the mind best fitted for survival in any world is the mind that has discovered how knowledge can be joyful, leading to the friendship with wisdom that is pure delight, and is ready to tackle any kind of knowledge with clarity of perception and intentness of will." There's a difference between a trained mind and a dedicated mind.

FRYE: I was suggesting that the trained mind has acquired techniques which, in a world like ours, will probably be out of date in ten or fifteen years. Training is not the important thing, it's the readiness to take on training. That's what I mean by the dedicated mind.

MOYERS: As the world dissolves, you learn to swim to the next ship.

FRYE: That's right.

MOYERS: I noticed that the inscription on Victoria College is the same as the inscription on the main tower of my alma mater, the University of Texas. "You shall know the truth, and the truth shall make you free." What kind of truth?

FRYE: In its original context in the Gospel of John, Jesus says that He is the truth, meaning that the truth is a personality and not a set of propositions, and that the truth about him was the union of divine and human natures. The feeling that the human destiny is inseparably involved with something divine is for Jesus what makes one free.

MOYERS: Is that true for Northrop Frye?

FRYE: Yes.

MOYERS: No separation of the secular and the sacred—even in learning?

FRYE: Oh, there are separations, yes. But the separations are in many contexts much less important than the things they have in common. Everything in religion has a secular aspect. Everything in secular life has a religious aspect.

MOYERS: What do you mean by the divine?

FRYE: That's quite a big question. I think that in human terms it means that there is no limit toward the expansion of the mind or of the freedom and liberty of mankind. Now, of course there are aspects of freedom and liberty, such as wanting to do what you like—which really means being pushed around by your social conditioning.

MOYERS: —your appetites, as well.

FRYE: Yes. But the feeling that the genuine things you want, like freedom, are inexhaustible and that you never come to the end of them—that's the beginning of the experience of the divine, for me.

MOYERS: And you said that the truth that makes one free must be shared. It can't be owned.

FRYE: Truth is not a possession. If it's a possession, it becomes a secret and becomes untrue. If a scientist makes a new discovery, the first thing he wants to do is publish it. If a novelist has a new imaginative model for a story in his mind, the first thing he wants to do is publish it.

MOYERS: As Jesus said to his disciples, "Go publish the good news."

FRYE: Yes. And also, if you invest your talents, you're doing something sensible. If you bury them, you're committing suicide.

MOYERS: You said once that the differences over faith are far less important than the agreement on charity. Is this what you're talking about—this sharing impulse, this sense of solidarity with others, this need to help others?

FRYE: Yes, I think so. The word "faith" is so often associated with assent to propositions, usually without enough evidence, and wherever you have that, of course, you have disagreement.

MOYERS: If I think a statement means one thing, you're going to think it means something else.

FRYE: That's right. And if one person is Christian and the other Jewish, it means they differ on certain doctrines, like incarnation. But when it comes to things that make for the freedom and happiness of mankind, they can be solidly united.

MOYERS: Propositions create holy wars because people differ over them.

FRYE: That's right.

MOYERS: So you're saying we need an agreement on charity.

FRYE: Yes. Charity is not only the greatest of the virtues, but the only virtue there is.

MOYERS: What do you mean by charity?

FRYE: Agape, the New Testament sense of love.

MOYERS: Don't you sometimes feel like Isaac Newton's imagined child playing with pebbles on a beach while there's an undiscovered ocean out there? There's so much to know and so little time.

FRYE: Oh yes. Everyone feels that who has ever collided with any serious subject at all.

MOYERS: Do you still feel that in your own field of literature and culture?

FRYE: I still feel it very strongly, except that I don't think that the ocean has to remain undiscovered. I think one can go on exploring it indefinitely, and that it wants to be explored.

MOYERS: In *The Educated Imagination*, you say that the Bible should be taught so early and so thoroughly that it sinks to the bottom of the mind, where everything that comes along later can settle on it. Why the Bible?

FRYE: Because the Bible is the definitive mythology in the Western world, which the imagination has incorporated into a social life. The Bible to me is not a structure of doctrine, not a structure of propositions, but a collection of stories making up one single story, and that's the interrelationship of God and man. You can understand the importance of that interpenetration without necessarily believing in God.

MOYERS: But in your case, it points toward God, does it not?

FRYE: Oh yes. Yes.

MOYERS: Mankind's creation, mankind's fall, mankind's constant restless search to get back to the paradise lost. Do you think that's the controlling vision in most of our lives?

FRYE: I think it is a very fundamental vision. It may come out in some very queer ways, like the man who just lives to get out of this rat race and go to a summer cottage. But in its way, even that is a kind of paradisal myth.

MOYERS: What does one come to grips with when the Bible has sunk to the bottom of one's mind?

FRYE: One comes to grips with the essential questions of human nature and human destiny. When you develop a knowledge of nature, as science does, you're really looking into a structure of intelligibility that you've constructed yourself. In other words, you're a narcissist, falling in love with your own reflection. That wonderful book of Martin Buber's, *I and Thou*, talks about the feeling of the divine as the "thou" which gets you out of the prison of looking at your own reflection. You're still looking at your own reflection when you're talking to him or her on equal terms.

MOYERS: In the Bible story, you also look at the face of God, which is the least narcissistic glance one can cast.

FRYE: Yes.

MOYERS: Do you think we can find in literature a vision of the society we want to live in?

FRYE: That, to my mind, is what the paradisal vision is. We've been living with this myth, which I think is a sound myth, for thousands of years—that we're living in a world that is not the world either that man wants or that God intended for him, and that there is another world that we can get to, though not necessarily the world we enter at death. It's a different kind of thing altogether.

MOYERS: As I was watching the Democratic and Republican conventions, I thought that politics, too, is trying to create out of the world we live in a world we would like to live in. And while I admire the aspiration, I'm reminded by the Bible that it's an almost hopeless quest.

FRYE: It may be almost hopeless, but we have to keep on doing it. The voter has to say to himself, "Now, which of these visions corresponds more closely to my own paradisal vision?"

MOYERS: —of getting back into paradise, creating heaven on earth.

FRYE: He knows that ninety-nine percent of this is nonsense, and yet, nevertheless, what else keeps him going?

Carlos Fuentes

MEXICAN NOVELIST

DON PERDUE

Carlos Fuentes has created a role for himself as interpreter of North and South America, explaining each to the other, looking at their conflicts from both sides of the border. Raised in Washington, D.C., where his father was a Mexican diplomat, he is a man of and between two worlds. His novels include The Death of Artemio Cruz, A Change of Skin, *and* Distant Relations. *His most recent book is* The Old Gringo, *which is also appearing as a movie.*

MOYERS: Recently, a colleague and I produced a documentary about the Rio Grande border of Texas, between my part of North America and your part of Latin America. We called it *One River, One Country* because we found there a country that is neither Texas nor Mexico. Do you think we're right when we say that there's a new country growing up between the United States and Mexico?

FUENTES: In a way, yes. You have an influence over the culture of Mexico, but we have an influence over the culture of the United States. When you get a proposition in California to vote the English language as the official language of the State of California, this only means one thing—that English is no longer the official language of the State of California.

A long time ago I read an extraordinary book by Garrow called *The Nine Nations of North America*. And I took from him an idea which I incorporated into my latest novel, *Christopher Unborn*. In my novel, Mexico has been dismembered, more or less, in the year 1992. On the frontier there is a new nation one hundred miles north of the present frontier between Mexico and the United States, and one hundred miles south. It's called "Mexamerica," and it goes from "San DyEgo" on the Pacific and "Auntie-Jane" which is Tijuana, to "Kilmoores," which is Matamoros, and "Cafecitoville," which is Brownsville. There's a great mixture of Spanish and English. It's a new nation that protects human rights, lets refugees go by, has its own industries, its own drug smuggling organizations. It thrives on its own.

MOYERS: Yet in your novel *The Old Gringo*, you write that this border is not really a border, it's a deep scar.

FUENTES: This is a border unique in the world. It's the only border between the industrialized world and the emerging, developing, nonindustrialized world. It is the border between the northern, Protestant, capitalistic culture of the United States, and the southern, Mediterranean, Catholic culture of Latin America. We're very conscious in Mexico that Latin America begins with that border—not only Mexico, but the whole of Latin America.

And it's a scar because it's the place where we lost half our territory to you in the wars of 1847 and '48. We don't forget that. And neither do the workers. Robert Kennedy said that the war against Mexico had been an unjust war. I think he was the first politician since Abraham Lincoln who said such a thing. Mexican workers who cross the border are not crossing a frontier, they're crossing a scar into a land that they consider theirs. I'm not an undocumented worker here. The gringos are undocumented. Who documented the people who landed on Plymouth Rock? I was here before they were. This is my land.

MOYERS: Does the presence of this scar, this border, have a practical effect on the psyche of Latin Americans today?

FUENTES: On Mexico it does, but not on all of Latin America. It's a psychological, historical problem, but I think you can overcome it by finding solutions to the real problems we share. You can build bridges. In *The Old Gringo*, the bridge over the Rio Grande suddenly bursts into flames. You can build a bridge; you can also burn it. But I think we are entering an era in which we should be building bridges.

The frontier will show to what degree Mexico and the United States are or can be interdependent. But only independent nations can be interdependent. You can only be a partner if first you have a certain degree of independence. I know there's been a lot of talk about the integration of Canada, the United States, and Mexico. But I think it's unacceptable for both Canadians and Mexicans. On a bilateral footing with the United States, we're very, very weak. The only real possibility of meeting this challenge of interdependence is to join the United States through the Pacific Ring, through a closer association with Japan and China. The Japanese presence in Mexico is absolutely extraordinary. The Japanese are fueling our industrial ports in the Pacific, our resorts in the Pacific, the inland industries in Mexamerica, our debt for equity schemes—it is the Japanese who finance all this. Do you know that the Mexican upper class, which used to send its children to learn English and French in high schools, now sends them to Japanese high schools in Mexico City? There's a realization that through Japan, we can participate in the world of interdependence without having to pay political dues to the United States.

> . . . only independent nations can be interdependent.

MOYERS: So you're not afraid of what my late friend Joseph Campbell called "a mighty multicultural future"?

FUENTES: I'm not at all. I'm convinced that cultures that live in isolation perish, and that only cultures that communicate and give things to one another thrive.

We've been under the influence of so many cultural beacons in the past, starting with the Middle Ages and the European Renaissance, then the French Revolution, the Century of Lights, which was the nineteenth century, and then the American influence in the twentieth century. I'm not afraid of communication with another culture.

I want to be a Greek, not an Aztec. Greeks communicated. They felt the presence of the other, the presence of the foreign, the menace of Persia, of Asia. They had to fight with what negated them. But the Aztecs didn't know the world existed outside the boundaries of the Aztec empire. When the Spaniards arrived, they died of fright. There was another world they had never thought of, and they were paralyzed to death.

Having an identity means that you can accept challenges and influences from everywhere. The great cultures of the world have been formed by this contagion of other cultures and not by their isolation. A culture that is isolated becomes first a provincial culture, then a tribal culture, and then it perishes.

MOYERS: If you were a twenty-year-old novelist, where would you go to find what Hemingway found in his day in Spain, and Steinbeck found in his day in Southern California?

FUENTES: That's a very American question. America is a country of pioneers, of people on the move, of a great trek from the Atlantic to the Pacific, which finally reaches California and goes crazy because there's nothing after California.

But Mexico has always been a country of isolation, of little pockets, valleys, deserts, people closed in. You know that when Charles V asked Hernando Cortés, the conquistador, to describe the country he'd conquered for him, a country nine times the size of Spain, Cortés took up a stiff piece of parchment from the King's table, crumpled it up, put it on the desk and said, "There's Mexico." A country of tremendous isolation.

MOYERS: I would have thought you might have gone to Mexico, to this new frontier down there on the border, this Mexamerica you talk about, because it seems that something very extraordinary is happening there.

FUENTES: Yes, all of Latin America is changing in such an extraordinary fashion. We see the debt, the crisis, but we don't realize that this is part of a huge growth, a very disordered and anarchic growth. The population of Latin America has doubled since the 1950s and will double again to four hundred million by the end of the century. And it is a very young population—half of it is fifteen years old or less. It is an urban population—most Latin Americans today live in cities. It is a population anxious for jobs, for social care, for opportunities. Every single Latin American child born today is born owing one thousand dollars to a foreign bank. And the problem of Latin America is that the political institutions do not coincide with this enormous social change.

MOYERS: When Americans look at this enormous burgeoning population of young people, at the high unemployment and rampant poverty, they grow concerned about their own national security. Do people with whom you deal in Latin America have any understanding of how frightening the scene looks from this side of the border? Let me tell you how Mexico looks to a lot of North Americans: a one-party state. A corrupt party, where union officials, government officials, the police are all imminently available to bribes. A party where journalists are killed for speaking up against the official policies of the state. A country where the rich ruling class looks the other way. A country that hasn't come to grips with its population explosion. A country that isn't facing up to the mature responsibilities of modern nationhood. Now to many North Americans, that's how Mexico looks. Fair appraisal?

FUENTES: Shall I tell you how the United States looks to many Mexicans?

MOYERS: I have a feeling you're going to.

FUENTES: A corrupt country where officials are constantly indicted. Look at all the people indicted in the Reagan Administration, look at Watergate. A country that is indebted, more than Mexico, Brazil, and Argentina, that cannot take care of its trade deficits, that cannot handle its economy seriously, that is incapacitating generations to come in order to get a quick fix and live off credit and borrow, borrow, borrow, with total irresponsibility. A country that cannot take care of its education. A country that cannot sustain its infrastructure. Its bridges are falling down. Its streets are plagued with drugs, it cannot take care of the demand for drugs that creates the drug problem in Latin America. A country that cannot take care of its homeless, of its old people. Wow, when are you going to get your house in order, gringos, huh? We both have problems, you see.

MOYERS: All right. I'll tell you what's good about Mexico, as I see it, and then you tell me what you think is good about the United States. I love the feeling of life in Mexico, the literature, the care that seems to exist among families. I admire the faith that people have in life. I see a country rich in tradition. I find people who are patient and kind. I like the buoyancy of those people. That's what's good about Mexico to me. What's good about this country?

FUENTES: Oh, so many things. The capacity for self-criticism of this country is admirable. The vitality of the civil society in this country, and of its institutions. Its capacity to identify problems and to propose solutions for the problems. The independence of the judiciary, the sense you have that any citizen of the United States can get a fair hearing in court. That is admirable, given the corruption of the judiciary systems throughout Latin America. Its care for the world, when it's authentic, when it means really understanding the point of view of the other, and not trying to impose your own point of view. The sense of informality of the Americans, their lack of stuffiness, their easygoing ways, their amiability in receiving people, in opening their houses, in having confidence in people. Their sense of familiarity, of basic goodness, of basic faith in one's fellow man. Its great literature, its great films, its great art, its extraordinary culture, its extraordinary journals and newspapers, its extraordinary sense of communication, its extraordinary sense of education, its universities. All this I find extremely admirable, and I've been trying to communicate this to my fellow Latin Americans for a long, long time.

MOYERS: In January of 1988 you went to Nicaragua. When I read that you were going to Nicaragua, I was intrigued by what you would find there that would confront your own prejudices. In much of your writing runs the theme of revolution being corrupted, that all revolutions are eventually corrupted, that human beings cannot handle power. It strikes me that the Sandinista revolution has been corrupted, has it not?

FUENTES: I wouldn't say so yet because it's very difficult to speak of the shape, not only of the revolution, but of the state of the society and of the opposition in Nicaragua. It is in such a state of change, such a state of flux. Yes, all history is an act of corruption because it is a separation from nature. The American Revolution, for example, was corrupted by slavery, the worst corruption imaginable. The Civil War was an attempt to cauterize that corruption.

But what is happening in Nicaragua is extraordinary. For the first time in its history, this country—which has always been the object of American dominance, occupied almost constantly since 1909, ruled by American puppets like Somoza since 1934—for the first time, Nicaragua has become a nationalist state. On the one side, Nicaragua is a state bent on achieving national independence, fighting a war against what are perceived as foreign-backed forces.

But on the other side, you have the rise of an internal opposition, which is also a first in Nicaraguan history. There is a spectrum of opposition that goes from conservatives on the right to Marxists and the Communists on the left, who detest the Sandinistas. And in between these two forces, the state and the opposition, you see a society moving, an unleashing of dormant economic, political, and social forces and new instructions being fashioned out of this encounter. You don't know the shape of it yet. The government is not monolithic, the society will not remain frozen, the economy is weak and devastated. The country has to make agreements with its neighbors. It is not Cuba. The Soviet Union will not salvage the Nicaraguan revolution, so the Sandinistas have to make accommodations and arrangements.

MOYERS: What's to prevent the Sandinistas from reimposing that harsh censorship of the press, on which they've yielded a little bit now, or to further restrict the opposition parties? What's to keep them from following that urge you describe in so many of your books, of revolutionaries who take no chances of losing what they've gained?

FUENTES: The force of the society makes that almost impossible, or at least we're in for a very protracted struggle between the state seeing itself as a national state, which wants to create a degree of unity and modernity in Nicaragua, and a society that breaks through these grounds and opposes the state. In the era of glasnost and perestroika, I find it very doubtful that the Sandinista regime will go over to a Stalinist form. They're not going to get help from the Soviet Union, and if they become Stalinist, they're certainly not going to get help from western Europe and Japan, which is where they count on getting help. They depend very much on diplomatic support from other parts of the world. Their economy is really devastated. So they have to recreate an economy with western European and Japanese help, and eventually with the help of the United States. If an enlightened American administration were really to offer help to Central America, to participate in the real problems of Central America, of illiteracy, communications, working conditions, production, health, housing, then Nicaragua would be part of that parcel and would not refuse to make political concessions.

MOYERS: President Reagan tried throughout the eight years of his Administration to carry on a war against Nicaragua, and he was unable to mobilize American public opinion behind him. Every poll showed that he didn't have support. I think that is because so many Americans have actually been to Nicaragua—church people, civic people, scholars, students, ordinary folks. Sister cities and churches in Nicaragua have been adopted by American cities and churches. People's own experience has been more powerful in their lives than the propaganda of their government. That's a different situation from what would have happened twenty years ago.

FUENTES: Yes, when Guatemala occurred in 1954, there wasn't any need to sway public opinion. It was with the United States. Now it isn't. People say it's because of Vietnam. But I always say, "Let's not talk about the Vietnamization of Central America, let's talk about the Central Americanization of Vietnam," because this kind of thing had been going on in Central America before you went into Vietnam.

Our problems must be solved by diplomacy, by negotiations, by political settlements. We've lost a lot of time, and what is worse, a lot of lives, by not understanding this. The Latin American initiatives, the Contadora process and the Arias peace plan were constantly torpedoed by the Reagan Administration. Nevertheless, it's fantastic that the Central American nations were finally able to capture the diplomatic initiative and retain it. After all, it's their land and their problems.

MOYERS: Doesn't the United States have a legitimate national security interest in Central America?

FUENTES: Yes, but that is something that can be arranged. There is a basic quid pro quo in inter-American relations—you give us nonintervention, we give you security guarantees, and we both give each other cooperation. How about that?

MOYERS: There is this fear that the Sandinistas, with their Marxist mentality and their ties to Cuba and the Soviet Union, will give the Soviet Union a beachhead in Central America to go with the one in Cuba, and that suddenly the United States will find the balance between the two superpowers has shifted.

FUENTES: In the first place, that particular issue you're referring to is something that could be negotiated away. The Sandinistas were always willing to sit down and say no Soviet presence in Nicaragua, no Soviet bases, no Soviet aid, and as soon as there is a true semblance of peace, not even any Soviet arms. In the second place, in the Gorbachev era, the Soviet Union is not about to salvage the revolution in Nicaragua or any other place in the world. They have too many problems of their own. Suddenly this paranoid nation, the Soviet Union, finds itself surrounded by challenges of an enormous nature. These challenges are called Japan, they're called China, they're called India. India feeds the Soviet Union. There is Afghanistan and the Islamic revolution and the Fundamentalists and the Ayatollah communicating with the Islamic underbelly of the Soviet Union. There is eastern Europe wishing to get out from under the tutelage of the Soviet Union and join western Europe in freedom and development.

Under its present economic system, the Soviet Union will not be a great power in the twenty-first century. This is something that Gorbachev has understood. So his problem is transforming the Soviet Union into a minimally viable country for the twenty-first century. I don't think he's going to gamble it away on a faraway spot in Central America.

MOYERS: Both the Soviet Union and the United States sometimes appear like two aging, overweight, exhausted prizefighters. They're still in the ring, they're on tour, they're going twenty, thirty rounds, but it's slow motion.

FUENTES: It's like Tony Gallento and Slapsie Maxie Rosenbloom meeting forever, you know, you get bored with it. They're punch-drunk by now. And other centers of power are arising in the world. We're going to a multipolar world. We're leaving behind the age of Yalta—the agreement that was made more or less to say the world will be ruled by two great powers—the Soviet Union and the United States—and the rest of us will play secondary roles, cameo roles in the world, as it were. This is over now. The rise of western Europe as an economic power in itself, the rise of Japan, which is spectacular, the rise of China—all these new centers of power assure that the twenty-first century will be the century of multipolar and not bipolar organization. The Soviet Union and the United States will continue to be great powers, very important influences, but not as much as they have been since 1945. They will have to adjust, and sometimes it's difficult for a great power to adjust to a diminished position in the world.

MOYERS: Most people have been losers, most people have suffered, most other nations have been trod upon by history. The United States has basically escaped unscathed.

FUENTES: It's a success story, and most nations are not success stories. That's one of the reasons that in Latin America, our favorite North American writer is William Faulkner—because he's the one who really deals with defeat. We recognize ourselves in Faulkner. But it's very difficult for people to recognize themselves in the American success story, much as it may be envied or admired or people want to participate in it. It is alien to the experience of most of humanity. So I think with a diminished role the United States will be a more humane society. I certainly hope so.

MOYERS: If you could write a one-paragraph letter to the President of the United States trying to explain what's happening in Latin America, what would you say?

FUENTES: The era of dominance is over; the era of cooperation is opening. It's the only policy that has worked. It's not as though we have to invent a new policy for relations between the United States and Latin America. We had a policy that worked for twenty years under the Roosevelt and Truman Administrations.

MOYERS: But these Administrations were supporting Somoza.

> *The era of dominance is over; the era of cooperation is opening.*

FUENTES: They were also supporting the Mexican Revolution. What I mean is an attitude of saying, "You Latin Americans deal with your Latin American problems. We won't intervene. Whatever kind of government you give yourself, okay. We cooperate with everybody."

MOYERS: Including Pinochet in Chile?

FUENTES: Including everybody on the map. This is the point. The most detestable aspect of the United States is its self-righteous, holier-than-thou aspect. That will have to change. The United States simply will have to deal with any kind of regime in Latin America. Look at Roosevelt. He dealt with Somoza. Cynically, he said, "Somoza is a son of a bitch, but he's our son of a bitch." He dealt with Trujillo. But he also dealt with Mexico under Cardenas—agrarian reform, expropriation of oil, and so forth. Roosevelt resisted urges to boycott Mexico, to apply sanctions, to invade Mexico. His attitude was "Negotiate with the Mexicans, even though we may not agree with what they're doing." He dealt very well with the Estado Novo in Brazil, Getulio Vargas, a fascist cooperative estate, and with the popular front in Chile made of Communists, Socialists, and radicals. He dealt with everybody on the scene. This is the policy I would favor, you see. If problems arise, we negotiate them.

MOYERS: If we see blatant examples of the abuse of human rights, if we see opposition in Nicaragua or Guatemala—

FUENTES: None of your business. Let us deal with our problems. If we see opposition in the United States, if we see abuses of human rights, if we see your prisons, if we see your homeless, do we rush in and invade you and tell you what to do and insult you? No. It's your problem. If we do not define your internal policies, don't try to define ours.

MOYERS: Take Guatemala, which for a number of years was run by a murderous group of military butchers, or Argentina, when the civilians were disappearing. The Argentinians and the Guatemalans say, "Help us, America." Now you're saying that it's all right for Japan to go in there and trade with them and just close their eyes to this butchery, and that the United States should do the same?

FUENTES: It is not the business of the United States to give certificates of good conduct and morality and good behavior in Latin America. And it is not our business to give the same to you. That's all I'm saying. Now the concern of citizens is another matter. You have a very strong civil society, very strong organs of public opinion. Citizens can manifest themselves through writing, through the press, through giving interviews, doing this and doing that. What is not possible is for any government to believe that it has a right to intervene in the internal affairs of another government.

You speak of Guatemala. The genocide that has occurred in Guatemala has its origin in the American intervention of 1954. For ten years the Guatemalan revolution was able to organize itself on a democratic basis to create public corporations, to create workers' rights. And suddenly the CIA marches in, topples the duly elected government, and opens an era of thirty years of repression and of military dictatorship in Guatemala. This is the result of interventionism—exactly what you are denouncing. Or you pour three billion dollars into El Salvador, and what do you get? Death squads and repression. You're not solving anything through intervention.

MOYERS: Is trade all that matters?

FUENTES: No, it's good relations and settling of actual differences through diplomatic means. If not, we get into the same trouble we see in Central America, where you close your eyes to what goes on in El Salvador, and you forget what goes on in Honduras, but you denounce what goes on in Nicaragua. It's a choosy thing. It's difficult for a nation to go on playing goody two-shoes all the time while actually keeping some skeletons hidden in the cellar. No, it's better if you finally act as a responsible nation that is serious in its diplomatic arrangements and doesn't go around as the puritan, moralistic preacher of this world. I have never found the truth, and if I found the truth, and told you, you would have me shot. I believe in people who are looking for the truth, not people who have found the truth. I hope that you and I are looking for the truth. We won't find it. And if we say we have found it, we wouldn't believe each other, would we? If the United States does not understand this principle, there will be trouble in Latin America.

MOYERS: Isn't that denying a substantial sentiment in America, among people who are your friends, who say that if the politically persecuted of Cuba cry out, we cannot turn our backs on them. If the Sandinistas repress, we can't turn our backs on their victims. If Pinochet oppresses, we can't turn our backs upon his victims—that the United States has to respond to the cry of the oppressed, the cry of the prisoner, the cry of the fallen?

FUENTES: Should we do the same in regard to your problems? That's okay as long as the citizens do it. What I don't see is a coalition of Latin American governments creating a Contra force to come into the United States to see that the prisons are humane or that the homeless get a roof. We can cooperate, not intervene. We are not asking the United States to roll over and play dead. What we're asking is that it not go abroad in search of monsters, as John Quincy Adams once warned. Is this so difficult to understand? Simply, let's have a cooperation between our governments. Cooperation is the word. Latin America is not going to be the backyard of the United States any more. It's going to cooperate with Europe, it's going to cooperate with Japan. We're going to sail the world. So are you. You've always done it. And so the sector of our cooperation will perhaps diminish a bit, but I think it has to. American investment in Latin America has gone down from seventy percent in the sixties to barely thirty percent today, and direct aid has diminished to the same extent. Japanese investment and trade has gone up twenty or thirty times. So we are coming into a different sort of world. This kind of crusade to change things in Latin America will simply not play any more. We have a lot of problems to solve from here to the year 2000. We'd better get down to it and stop losing time with stupid wars and Contras and all the things that we've lost time with in the last ten years.

There are different systems in the world. There are different nationalities, different cultures, different personalities. There are many people that are not like me in the streets, but that doesn't mean I can't communicate with them. On the contrary, it's a wonderful challenge to be able to communicate with what is not like you. What is terrible is when a nation with power says that what is not like me should be exterminated—Nazi Germany or Stalinist Russia, for example. But as long as you say, "I am what I am, but that doesn't mean I'm better than anybody else, it means I'm different, and the other one is different too, and we can understand each other, we can talk, we can communicate"—that is the basic attitude that makes life civilized and diplomacy possible. That is the expression of civilized concourse between nations.

Bill Moyers would like to thank the following people for their work on the television series:

EXECUTIVE PRODUCER
Jack Sameth

EXECUTIVES IN CHARGE
Joan Konner
Judith Davidson Moyers

ADMINISTRATIVE DIRECTOR
Judy Doctoroff O'Neill

PRODUCERS
Leslie Clark
Kate Roth Knull
Elena Mannes
Betsy McCarthy
Judy Doctoroff O'Neill
Gail Pellett
Matthew Pook
Catherine Tatge
Andie Tucher

ASSOCIATE PRODUCERS
Rebecca Berman
Lynn Novick
Amy Schatz
Kate Tapley

COORDINATING PRODUCER
Judy Epstein

CAMERA
Charles Barbee
Robert Beyer
Barrin Bonet
Larry Bullard
Joe Cantu, Jr.
Tony Cobbs
Thomas Conner
Jeff Cooke
Thomas Cosgrove
Brian Dowley
Mark Falstad
Herb Forsberg
Phil Gries
Walter James
David W. Jones
Leland C. Kenower
Alan Lebow
Robert Long, Jr.
Rick Malkames
Rob Mulligan
Gregory Pettys
Ralph Schiano
Robert Shepard
Alan Stecker
Jeff Stonehouse
Brian Tyson
Joe Vitagliano
Renner Wunderlich

EDITORS
Girish Bhargava
Michael Collins
Scott P. Doniger
Gregg Featherman
Mark Fish
Alfred Muller
David Pentecost
Rochelle Pinkowitz
Bill Stephan

EDITORIAL ASSOCIATE
Andie Tucher

RESEARCH
Derek Vaillant

PRODUCTION EXECUTIVE
Arthur White

BUSINESS ASSOCIATE
Diana Warner

EXECUTIVE ASSISTANTS
Alex Banker
Doreen Murray

PRODUCTION ASSISTANTS
Deborah J. Kazis
Chuck Smith

INTERNS
Eliza Byard
Eve Grubin
Daniella Malin
Jonathan Nichols
Rebecca Wharton

STAFF SECRETARY
Naomi Golf

PUBLICITY
Susan Dudley-Allen
Michael Shepley

"A World of Ideas with Bill Moyers" was a production of Public Affairs Television, Inc. The series was made possible by a grant from the John D. and Catherine T. MacArthur Foundation.

Special thanks to the Florence and John Schumann Foundation.

BILL MOYERS is an acclaimed television journalist, widely respected for his work at PBS and CBS News. His "A World of Ideas" series, broadcast in the fall of 1988, put outstanding thinkers on the air every night for ten weeks. His conversations with teacher and mythologist Joseph Campbell were the basis for the bestselling book *The Power of Myth*.

BETTY SUE FLOWERS directs the Liberal Arts Honors Program at the University of Texas at Austin. She also teaches classes in poetry and myth, and serves as Associate Dean of the Graduate School. She has written or cowritten several books, including *Four Shields of Power* and *Daughters and Fathers*, and was the editor of *The Power of Myth*.